Abu Dhabi
Residents' Guide

there's more to life...
ask**explorer**.com

نحو مستقبل
مستدام لطائر الحبارى

TOWARDS A SUSTAINABLE
FUTURE FOR THE HOUBARA BUSTARD

INTERNATIONAL FUND FOR
HOUBARA CONSERVATION

www.houbarafund.org

A good move delivers the biggest smile.

When you see their smiles, you'll know you've made a good move. Trust Allied Pickfords to make your home moving simpler, seamless and stress-free for the entire family. Relax, we carry the load.

Call us now
+971.2.677.9765 (Abu Dhabi),
+971.4.818.0400 (Dubai)
www.alliedpickfords.ae

ALLIED PICKFORDS
The Careful Movers

Spinneys Abu Dhabi L.L.C.

HOME OF ABU DHABI'S
FINEST SELECTION OF BEVERAGES
WITH CONVENIENTLY LOCATED SHOPS IN ABU DHABI, AL AIN & RUWAIS

Get your liquor licence
at your nearest Store of GMP

A liquor licence is easy to apply for & allows the holder to legally buy alcohol.
Obtain your licence through GMP & we will give you vouchers worth AED 100
to spend on beverages. (terms and conditions apply)
Apply online at www.auhsl.ae or contact your nearest store.

 Najda Street Branch - 02 671 4400

Located next to Mitsubishi Motors Showroom and the
ADCP building at the junction of Al Falah (9th Street)
and Najda St (6th) Street.

Trading Hours:
Sat - Thur 9:30am - 8:30pm / Friday 4:00pm - 8:30pm

 Mussafah - 02 554 3919

Head to Mussafah E30. Take exit at the interchange
after ADNOC onto road 16. Go straight over 3 round-
abouts. After 3rd roundabout take 1st right turn – 200m
on the right is The Mussafah Branch.

Trading Hours:
Sat - Thur 11:00am - 7:00pm / Friday 4:00pm - 8:30pm

 The Club - 02 643 2899

Located in The Club premises in Mina.

Trading Hours:
Sat - Thur 11:00am - 8:00pm / Friday 11:00am - 6:00pm

 Khalidiya - 02 665 2334

Located behind Khalidiya Mall, next to Khalidiya Village
Compound.

Trading Hours:
Sat - Wed 9:30am - 1:00pm / 4:00pm - 8:30pm
Thursday 9:30am - 8:30pm
Friday 4:00pm - 8:30pm

 Tourist Club Area - 02 676 5954

behide Al Salama Hospital near misterbaker in tourist
club   area opposite of smokers and fresh chicken

Trading Hours:
Sat - Wed 9:30am - 1:00pm / 4:00pm - 8:30pm
Thursday 9:30am - 8:30pm
Friday 4:00pm - 8:30pm

Gray
Mackenzie

f gmp.abudhabi.7
www.graymackenzie.com

Abu Dhabi Explorer 2015/12th Edition
First Published 1999
2nd Edition 2002
3rd Edition 2003
4th Edition 2004
5th Edition 2006
6th Edition 2007
7th Edition 2009
8th Edition 2010
9th Edition 2010
10th Edition 2012
11th Edition 2014
12th Edition 2015   ISBN 978-9948-22-522-5

Front Cover Photograph – Abu Dhabi Corniche – Gary McGovern

Explorer Publishing & Distribution
PO Box 34275, Dubai
United Arab Emirates
Phone   +971 (0)4 340 8805
Fax   +971 (0)4 340 8806
Email   info@askexplorer.com
Web   askexplorer.com

To buy additional copies of this or any other of Explorer's award-winning titles visit askexplorer.com. Special discounts are available for quantity purchases.

Welcome...

...to the Abu Dhabi Residents' Guide. This 12th anniversary edition gets straight to the crucial information you need to know about moving to, living in and enjoying life in this fascinating emirate. From red-tape procedures to schools, restaurants and things to see and do, it's all covered here.

Abu Dhabi is a modern, thriving metropolis – one that is constantly growing and changing. We can only fit so much exhaustive information onto these pages, so to keep abreast of the latest news, as well as reviews on the newest restaurants, information on upcoming events and updates to UAE laws, make askexplorer.com your online companion while in Abu Dhabi.

Finally, don't forget that Explorer publishes hundreds of maps and activity guides that help you to extract the most from life in the UAE. Discover more at askexplorer.com/shop.

In your hands, in the glovebox, in your rucksack; on your laptop, tablet or smartphone. Wherever you're going and whatever you're doing, be sure to take us with you.

There's more to life...
The Explorer Team

We'd love to hear from you, whether you make a great insider discovery or want to share your views about this or any of our products. Get in touch with us at askexplorer.com or through any of our social media channels.

      /ask**explorer**

CONTENTS

CONTENTS

CONTENTS

FOR THE FIRST TIME IN THE UAE, ICE CREAM IS AT YOUR FINGERTIPS

THE UAE

THE UAE

Located in the heart of the Middle East, the United Arab Emirates (UAE) is proud of its own Islamic culture while also being one of the most progressive and open-minded countries in the region.

Abu Dhabi Corniche

The United Arab Emirates (UAE) comprises seven emirates: Abu Dhabi, Ajman, Dubai, Fujairah, Ras Al Khaimah, Sharjah and Umm Al Quwain. Located in the heart of the Middle East, its rise from a quiet strategic trading destination to a regional and global economic powerhouse is nothing short of remarkable – and makes it one of the most exciting places to live.

The UAE Today

While its culture is still rooted in Islamic tradition, the UAE is also one of the most cosmopolitan countries in the Middle East.

The country has a bold vision for its future and is working towards becoming a first-choice destination for tourism, finance, industry and trade. This makes it a vibrant and opportunity-filled place to live in and work. Trade and commerce are still the cornerstones of the economy, with the traditional manufacturing and distribution industries now joined by finance, construction, media, IT and telecom businesses. With so many world-class hotels, and leisure and entertainment options, the UAE is certainly becoming a popular tourist destination too. Similarly, people from over 150 nations now call the UAE home as they bring their skills and manpower to help in the country's plan; and many expats find the country so welcoming that it becomes difficult to leave.

Sunshine and tax-free salaries may be why expats come, but what keeps them here is the ability to mix with other cultures, live in a liberal Middle Eastern country, and enjoy the sort of lifestyle they would be hard-pressed to find at home.

COUNTRY PROFILE

However, aside from the huge number of people from nearby India and Pakistan settling in the UAE, Emirati nationals still make up the largest ethnic group and have considerable influence.

If you're looking to move to the UAE, live here already, or are just visiting, there are a number of things that are useful to know. This section highlights some of those facts and figures that can help you make your way in the UAE, or, at the very least, arm you with some good ammunition for a quiz night.

Capital

The capital city of the United Arab Emirates is Abu Dhabi. The city is part of the largest emirate and is continuing to grow at a significant rate. To the east of the main Abu Dhabi island an area of land between Khalifa City and Shakhbout City had been designated as the Capital District, or Zayed City. While still largely a huge patch of sand, the plan is for Capital District to become the seat of government for the whole of the UAE. It will accommodate federal ministries as well as foreign embassies. More details can be found in the Abu Dhabi Vision 2030 plan, which outlines the city's plans to grow and diversify over the next 15 or so years.

Be Happy

Good news for UAE residents: a recent report by the UN Sustainable Development Solutions Network ranked the country as the 14th happiest country in the world, higher than the USA, UK, Germany and Japan. The latest World Happiness Report also lists the UAE as the happiest Arab country.

Population

The UAE population has grown rapidly in recent years as expat arrivals, robust economic expansion and high birth rates have continued to push up the total number. According to the World Bank, the UAE's population was just 322,439 when the country was formed in 1972. However, by 2002, 30 years later, that had ballooned by 10 times to just over 3.2 million. After more than 40 years, the population has now grown by almost 30 times that 1972 figure, currently recorded at around 9.2 million. Compared to just 10 years previously, that's an increase of 185%.

Unsurprisingly, the vast majority of this population growth has come from foreign workers moving to the UAE from a number of countries across the world.

Area

The total land area of the UAE is approximately 83,600 sq km, with around 1,318 km of coastline. Abu Dhabi accounts for a huge 67,340 sq km of that total. While not particularly mountainous, the highest named point is Jebel Yibir at 1,572m, 'jebel' meaning mountain or hill in Arabic. The UAE's coordinates are 24°00'North 54°00'East.

Flag

The UAE flag incorporates the Pan-Arab colours of red, black, green and white, symbolising Arabian unity. It was adopted on 2 December, 1971 as the official flag of the country. Interestingly, each of the seven emirates aside from Fujairah also has its own flag, all of which use just red and white.

Currency

The monetary unit is the dirham (Dhs.), which is divided into 100 fils. The currency is also referred to as AED (Arab Emirate Dirham). On notes, all denominations are marked in both Arabic and English, although coin values are shown only in Arabic. Notes come in denominations of Dhs.5 (brown), Dhs.10 (green), Dhs.20 (light blue), Dhs.50 (purple), Dhs.100 (pink), Dhs.200 (yellowy-brown), Dhs.500 (blue) and Dhs.1,000 (browny-purple). Watch your Dhs.500 notes though, they can be mistaken for a Dhs.5 note if you're in a hurry.

All coins are silver in colour, with a total of six in circulation, but you typically only come across the three largest denominations: Dhs.1, the largest coin with an Arabic coffee urn image; 50 fils, which is a heptagon in shape; and 25 fils, that is small with a gazelle pictured on one side. The dirham has been pegged to the US dollar since 1980, at a mid rate of $1 to Dhs.3.6725.

Time Zone

The UAE is four hours ahead of the UCT (Universal Coordinated Time, formerly known as GMT). Clocks are not altered for daylight saving in the summer, so when Europe and North America gain an hour in spring, the time in the UAE stays the same resulting in a shorter three hours' time difference to countries like the UK. Time differences between the UAE and some cities around the world (not allowing for any daylight savings in those cities) are: Bangkok +3, Hong Kong +4; London -4; Los Angeles -12; Moscow -1; New York -9; Sydney +6; and Tokyo +5.

Country Code

The international dialling code for the UAE is +971. Each city also has its own dialling code too, which is the first digit (or two digits in some cases) that you dial when calling. These are: 2, Abu Dhabi; 6, Ajman; 3, Al Ain; 9, Dibba; 4, Dubai; 9, Fujairah; 7, Ras Al Khaimah; 6, Sharjah; and also 6, Umm Al Quwain.

Business Hours

The UAE working week is from Sunday to Thursday. Friday is the Islamic holy day and therefore a universal day off for offices and schools, so the two-day weekend spans Friday and Saturday. Some companies still require a six-day working week from their staff, while others operate on a five-and-a-half-day system. Restaurants, cafes, shops and malls are open seven days a week, 356 days a year, although some places will open later on a Friday.

Larger shops and shopping centres are generally open throughout the day and into the evening until around 10pm or midnight. Traditional shops and street retailers often operate under split shift timings, closing for three or four hours in the afternoon. Meanwhile, some food outlets and petrol stations are open for 24 hours a day.

If you're working in the UAE, 8am to 5pm or 9am to 6pm, with an hour for lunch, are normal shifts in the private sector. It is common for working hours in the UAE to be longer than in other countries when working for a private company.

Most government offices are open from 7.30am to 2.30pm, Sunday to Thursday. Embassies and consulates operate similar hours, but may designate specific times and days for certain tasks (such as passport applications), so it's best to call before you go. All will have an emergency number on their answering service, website or on their office door during times they are closed.

Ramadan Hours

According to UAE labour laws, all companies are obliged to shorten the working day by two hours during the holy month of Ramadan. This is to assist Muslim employees who are fasting but the law also technically applies to non-Muslim expats. In reality, many international companies will not follow this

principle, so it's a bonus if an expat is allowed to work Ramadan hours.

Many schools and businesses do change their hours during Ramadan, and shops may open later in the day and stay open until midnight or even 1am. The city's many shisha cafes and some restaurants stay open until the early hours. Alcohol is only served at licensed premises after sunset during this month.

Ramadan Traffic

Abu Dhabi's traffic has a totally different pattern during Ramadan; instead of being gridlocked in the mornings and quiet in the afternoons, the mornings are almost jam-free and you'll sail through all the usual trouble spots, while in the afternoons the roads are totally clogged.

GEOGRAPHY

Located in the heart of the Middle East, the UAE borders Saudi Arabia and the Sultanate of Oman, with coastlines on both the Arabian Gulf and the Gulf of Oman. Of the seven emirates – Abu Dhabi, Ajman, Dubai, Fujairah, Ras Al Khaimah, Sharjah and Umm Al Quwain – Abu Dhabi is by far the largest, occupying over 80% of the country; the emirate of Dubai is the second largest, although Abu Dhabi and Dubai share similar population sizes.

The country is perhaps best known for the modern, rapidly expanding metropolises of Abu Dhabi and Dubai, but visitors may be surprised by the variety of landscapes when they venture beyond the cities. The coast is littered with coral reefs and more than 200 islands, most of which are uninhabited. The interior of the country is characterised by sabkha (salt flats), stretches of gravel plain, and vast areas of sand desert. To the east rise the Hajar Mountains ('hajar' is Arabic for 'rock') which, lying close to the Gulf of Oman, form a backbone through the country, from the Musandam Peninsula in the north into Oman.

Weather

The UAE only really experiences two seasons: hot and hotter. Without a doubt the best time to live in, and visit, the country is from October to April, when it's all blue skies and temperatures of 10°C (50°F) to 24°C (75°F). Everyday in the winter is a sunny reminder of why you chose to live here – tepid sea water to swim in, cloudless skies to sunbathe under, and warm,

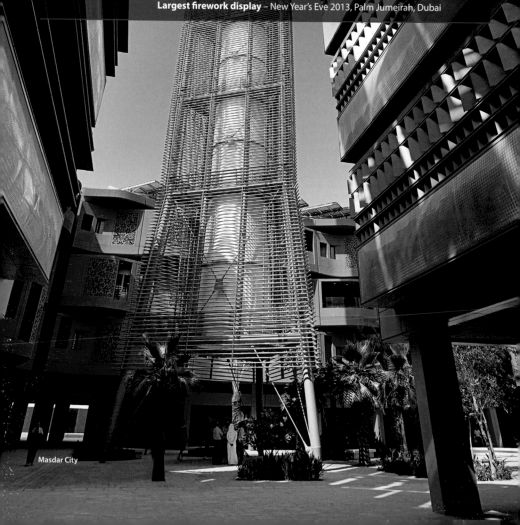

HOME OF WORLD RECORDS

There's barely a week goes by when something from the UAE doesn't claim to be the world's biggest, tallest, fastest or most expensive; and even then you can be sure there are plans to go bigger, taller, faster or even more costly. While it may look like showy extravagance, it's actually a smart way to get this relatively new country on the map and make it a must-visit destination for tourists and a more attractive proposition to foreign companies looking to invest. For residents though, the 100 and more entries by the UAE in the Guinness World Records 2014 mean a seemingly endless list of things to see or do while living in the country.

Fastest rollercoaster made from steel – Formula Rossa, Ferrari World, Abu Dhabi
Most environmentally friendly city – Masdar City, Abu Dhabi
Tallest man-made structure on land – Burj Khalifa, Dubai
Largest shopping centre – The Dubai Mall, Dubai
Longest driverless metro – Dubai Metro, Dubai
Tallest residential building – Princess Tower, Dubai
Furthest leaning man-made tower – Hyatt Capital Gate, Abu Dhabi
Largest automated car park – Emirates Financial Towers, Dubai
Largest firework display – New Year's Eve 2013, Palm Jumeirah, Dubai

Masdar City

comfortable evenings for alfresco dining. In the summer, be prepared for triple-digit temperatures and high humidity, from 41°C (106°F) up to a scorching 48°C (118°) in August. Yes, it's undeniably hot, but the UAE is well and truly geared up for it with AC in every mall, restaurant, office and even bus shelter.

Humidity is usually between 50% and 60%, and, when combined with high summer temperatures, even 60% humidity can make it a little uncomfortable. Many expats escape the suffocating heat during the summer and head home for an extended holiday.

Leave those umbrellas at home, as rainfall is almost non-existent – just 25 days per year. So, there's more than enough about the weather to brag home about.

HISTORY

As a country, the UAE is still relatively young having only formed in 1972, when unifying the seven emirates was seen as a progressive move to enhance security and improve influence in the area. However, the region has a long history before that.

Much of the early existence is closely linked to the arrival and development of Islam in the greater Middle East. Islam developed in modern-day Saudi Arabia at the beginning of the seventh century AD with the revelations of the Quran being received by the Prophet Muhammad. Military conquests of the Middle East and North Africa enabled the Arab empire to spread the teachings of Islam from Mecca and Medina to the local Bedouin tribes.

Periods of dominance from other empires followed over the centuries, with the Turks, the Mongols and the Ottomans all exerting their influences over the region. In the early 19th century the British and Portuguese dipped their oars into Arabian waters, attracted by the area's strategic position between Europe and India and the desire to quash the rise of piracy in the local waters. By 1820, the British had flexed their naval muscle in the region and a general treaty was agreed upon by the local rulers, denouncing piracy. The following years witnessed a series of maritime truces, with the emirates subsequently accepting British protection in 1892. In Europe, the area became known as the Trucial Coast, a name that it retained until the departure of the British in 1971.

British Withdrawal
When Britain announced its withdrawal in 1968, the ruling sheikhs of Bahrain, Qatar and the Trucial Coast realised that they would have a stronger voice in

the Middle East by uniting forces as a single state. Negotiations collapsed when Bahrain and Qatar chose independence; however, in 1971, the federation of the United Arab Emirates was born from the Trucial Coast, Ras Al Khaimah joining in 1972 to establish the UAE we know today.

Under the agreement, the individual emirates retained a certain amount of autonomy, with Abu Dhabi and Dubai providing the most input into the federation. The leaders of the new federation elected the ruler of Abu Dhabi, His Highness Sheikh Zayed bin Sultan Al Nahyan, to be the president of the newly-founded country.

The well-liked and highly respected Sheikh held the position until he passed away on 2 November 2004. The eponymous Sheikh Zayed Grand Mosque in Abu Dhabi was his final place of rest, his mausoleum complete when the mosque opened in 2007. The mosque itself was his great vision and was intended to unite not just the UAE but the wider Arab populace. His eldest son, His Highness Sheikh Khalifa bin Zayed Al Nahyan, was elected to take over the presidency and oversaw the final few years of the mosque's fantastic construction.

The formation of the UAE came after the discovery of huge oil reserves in Abu Dhabi in 1958. The discovery dramatically transformed the emirate. In 1966, oil was also discovered in Dubai, which was already a relatively wealthy trading centre by then.

Heritage Village

UAE TIMELINE

The UAE's history is both rich and colourful, from the arrival and development of Islam in the greater Middle East region to the radical changes resulting from the discovery of oil to the formation of the federation of the United Arab Emirates.

Stone Age	Modern human settlement in the UAE dates back to circa 7,000BC
Bronze Age	Archaeological evidence of human settlements; the domestication of the camel boosts trade
Iron Age	The invention of falaj, an irrigation technology, takes place somewhere between 1,300-300BC
630	Envoys from the Prophet Muhammad arrive, heralding the conversion of local people to Islam
1761	The Baniyas tribe discovers fresh water in Abu Dhabi and settles on the island; leading to the construction of Qasr Al Hosn
1790s	The pearl trade is booming off the coast of Abu Dhabi
1835	Maritime Truce signed between the Trucial States and Britain
1930s	The first oil concession in Abu Dhabi is granted to Trucial Coast Oil Development Company
1950s	Oil is discovered in the UAE, exports begin in 1962
1966	HH Sheikh Zayed bin Sultan Al Nahyan becomes ruler of Abu Dhabi
1971	Britain withdraws from the Gulf and the UAE is established, with HH Sheikh Zayed bin Sultan Al Nahyan of Abu Dhabi as the leader. The UAE joins the Arab League
1972	Ras Al Khaimah joins the UAE
1973	The UAE launches a single currency, the UAE dirham
1981	The Gulf Cooperation Council is formed, with the UAE as a founding member
1985	Emirates Airline is founded
1999	The doors of the Burj Al Arab, the tallest hotel in the world, open for the first time in Dubai
2001	Construction starts on Dubai's Palm Jumeirah
2003	Etihad Airways is founded
2004	Sheikh Zayed bin Sultan Al Nahyan dies and is succeeded as leader of the UAE by his son, Sheikh Khalifa bin Zayed Al Nahyan
2005	Emirates Palace, billed as the world's most expensive hotel, opens to the public
2007	The Sheikh Zayed Mosque, the eighth largest mosque in the world, opens during Ramadan. Work also begins on Yas Island and Saadiyat Island
2008	In the wake of global economic crisis, much of the UAE's property market crashes
2009	Abu Dhabi hosts its inaugural Formula 1 Grand Prix at Yas Marina Circuit; the Sheikh Khalifa Bridge opens, linking the new areas of Abu Dhabi directly to the Corniche; Dubai Metro, the region's first public mass-transit system, is launched
2010	The tallest building in the world, the Burj Khalifa, opens; Ferrari World Abu Dhabi, the world's largest indoor theme park, opens
2011	The first hotels on Saadiyat Island open their doors to the public; Capital Gate, the world's 'most leaning' tower also opens in Abu Dhabi
2012	Yas Waterworld opens in Abu Dhabi
2013	Dubai wins the bid to host the World Expo 2020
2014	Abu Dhabi Ports Company's, Zayed Port, unveils plans for a new cruise terminal which is due to open in 2016; Dubai's Canal project progresses

GOVERNMENT

The United Arab Emirates (UAE) is a federation of seven emirates, each with its own ruler and some degree of autonomy over its own rules and regulations. The Supreme Council of Rulers – made up of the hereditary rulers of the emirates – is the top policy-making body in the UAE, responsible for laws governing education, defence, foreign affairs, communications and development, and for ratifying federal rules.

The current President of the UAE is the ruler of Abu Dhabi, Sheikh Khalifa bin Zayed Al Nahyan, who took over the post in November 2004 from his late father, Sheikh Zayed bin Sultan Al Nahyan. The Vice President and Prime Minister of the UAE is Sheikh Mohammed bin Rashid Al Maktoum, ruler of Dubai. Both members are elected by the Supreme Council for a five-year term, and are often re-elected time after time.

The UAE's Prime Minister, appointed by the President, chairs the Council of Ministers, which meets once a week in Abu Dhabi to oversee the development and implementation of federal policy across all portfolios of government.

The Federal National Council (FNC) is a consultative assembly of 40 representatives, half of whom are elected by the people. The FNC reports to the Supreme Council but has executive authority to initiate and implement laws. It monitors and debates government policy too but has no power of veto. The last election was in 2011, and one-fifth of its members are currently women.

Key Government Figures

Sheikh Khalifa bin Zayed Al Nahyan is the President of the UAE and the 16th ruler of Abu Dhabi. Born in 1948, in the Eastern Region of Abu Dhabi, in Al Muwaiji Fort, Al Ain, Sheikh Khalifa is the eldest son of Sheikh Zayed.

Under Sheikh Khalifa's leadership, the country, and especially Abu Dhabi, has witnessed astonishing growth. With his focus on the continuing development of the country's infrastructure, economic health and cultural contributions, he has laid the foundations for a prosperous UAE.

Sheikh Khalifa has always been generous with Abu Dhabi's oil wealth, ensuring other emirates within the country aren't left behind. In 2009, Abu Dhabi gave a US$10 billion loan to Dubai at the height of the financial crisis. The Burj Khalifa in Dubai, the world's tallest building, is named after Sheikh Khalifa.

The Abu Dhabi ruler is well-known for his philanthropic commitments, particularly through the Khalifa Bin Zayed Al Nahyan Foundation, which focuses on providing support to the health and education sectors on a domestic, regional and global scale. The foundation responds to emergencies around the world, and has, to date, helped more than 35 countries in need. One example is a US$150 million grant given to MD Anderson in Texas, to help advance research into personalised cancer therapies.

Emirs or Sheikhs?

While the term emirate comes from the ruling title of 'emir', the rulers of the UAE are called 'sheikhs'. You may associate terms like 'sultan' with the Middle East; however, this is a title given to rulers of sultanates.

Aldar HQ

Sheikh Mohammed bin Rashid Al Maktoum is the Prime Minister and Vice President of the United Arab Emirates, and ruler of Dubai. He is considered the driving force behind Dubai's exponential growth, pioneering Free Trade Zones (FTZ), such as Dubai Media City, offering tax exemptions which have attracted foreign companies to set up in the emirate, helping Dubai's economy flourish and reducing its reliance on oil-based industries. Sheikh Mohammed bin Rashid Al Maktoum has overseen the development of numerous iconic projects in Dubai including Palm Jumeirah, the seven-star Burj Al Arab hotel and Burj Khalifa. Find Sheikh Mohammed on facebook at facebook.com/HHSheikhMohammed. His brother, Sheikh Hamdan bin Rashid Al Maktoum, is the UAE Minister of Finance and Industry.

Shams Abu Dhabi, Reem Island

ECONOMY

The UAE is considered the second richest Arab country, after Qatar, on a GDP per capita basis. Globally that equates to being the eighth richest country in the world. With just under 10% of the world's proven oil reserves (most of it within Abu Dhabi emirate) and the seventh largest proven natural gas reserves, hydrocarbon exports still play a large part in the country's wealth.

Since the financial crisis of 2009, which hit Dubai particularly hard, the UAE's perceived safe haven status amid regional political and social unrest has supported growing economic confidence. At an estimated $284.4 billion in 2014, the UAE economy is the second largest in the Gulf, after Saudi Arabia, and in the Where-to-be-born Index, 2013 (which highlights the countries where new babies could expect the highest quality of life), the UAE came a respectable 17th; the highest ranking Arab country and just behind the United States and Germany.

While there are still issues such as readdressing the post-financial crisis increase in public spending, reducing energy subsidies and the challenge for Dubai to service its large debts, the outlook remains positive. Successful economic diversification means that the UAE's wealth is no longer solely reliant on oil revenue; just 25% of GDP is based on oil and gas output now. In June 2014, the Samba Economics Group reported that Dubai's win to host the Expo 2020 will boost the UAE's overall economy. It also forecast that growth would increase by 4-5% in 2015. The UAE's non-oil sector is also predicted to accelerate supported by a recovery in construction and real estate, as well as ongoing growth in tourism-orientated sectors.

However, while the UAE GDP per capita income stands at around Dhs.183,000 ($49,800) this figure includes all sections of the community and the average labourer can only expect to earn Dhs.600

($165) per month. Even before the financial crisis hit, the salaries for most job types were dropping too. Aside from highly skilled professionals, the average expat coming to seek employment in the UAE shouldn't expect to automatically be on a huge salary.

While the unemployment level of the national population in the UAE is lower than that of many other Arab states, there are still a significant number of Emiratis out of work (over 20% according to some reports). This is partly due to a preference for public sector work and partly because of qualifications not matching the skills required in the private sector.

Abu Dhabi

Abu Dhabi escaped relatively unscathed from the global economic crisis at the end of the last decade. While the city's GDP slowed temporarily and a number of projects were put on hold, newcomers to the city would be hard pushed to notice any impact now.

During 2013 the government announced that major financial allocations worth around Dhs.330 billion would be pumped into various capital projects across a number of sectors up until 2017. The aim is to increase Abu Dhabi's appeal as one of the top investment-attracting countries in the world.

The free trade zones in the capital are a major attractor, and the first financial free zone, due to open on Al Maryah Island, will help further. Benefits to businesses in free zones include 100% foreign ownership, which negates the usual need for local partner sponsorship where a UAE national or entity owns at least 51%. They also get tax exemptions and 100% repatriation of revenue and profits.

In 2009, the government published the Abu Dhabi Economic Vision 2030 (abudhabi.ae). The 142-page document identifies two key priority areas for economic development in Abu Dhabi: building a sustainable economy, and, ensuring a balanced social and regional economic development approach that brings benefits to all. While there's still some way to go, the fact that, in 2014, Abu Dhabi was seeing year-on-year growth in the non-oil sector, 15% growth in airport traffic, and was also showing an increase in the production capacity of hydrocarbons, suggests the emirate is well on target.

Really Tax Free?

Do taxes exist in the UAE? Yes and no. You don't pay income or sales tax, except when you purchase alcohol from a licensed liquor store – a steep 30%. The main tax is the municipality tax of 5% on rent and 10% on food, beverages and rooms in hotels. The rest are hidden in the form of 'fees', such as your car registration renewal, visa/permit fees and Dubai's Salik (road toll).

Trade

Strategically, the UAE has always been well-placed geographically, but with a trade policy based on economic openness and liberalisation the country continues to flourish. With flexible and investor-friendly laws, tax exemptions, low tariffs and the availability of raw materials and funds, the climate in the UAE is an ideal one for foreign investment. Non-oil exports have grown significantly with a particular emphasis on re-exports. In 2014, new results published by the World Trade Organisation ranked the UAE 17th in its International Trade Statistics 2013 report, an increase of 16% compared to 2011. When it comes to exporting goods, the UAE surpasses India, Sweden and South Africa and claims almost a 2% of the world's total exports.

Roughly 60% of exports are manufactured goods, fuels and mining products; India, Iran, Iraq, Switzerland and the European Union (EU) being the main recipients. Meanwhile over $200 billion of merchandise is imported into the country every year, mainly coming from the EU, India, China, USA and Japan. Main imports include: pearls and other precious metals and stones, machinery, vehicles, base metals and chemicals.

Tourism

The UAE is well ahead of many other countries in the Middle East in terms of travel and tourism. Boosting tourism plays a central part in the government's economic diversification plan and is a major force behind the array of record-breaking infrastructure and hospitality developments of recent times. Dubai is perhaps the most famous tourist destination in the UAE, with over 600 hotels and attractions like the man-made Palm Jumeirah island, the Burj Al Arab hotel and an ever-expanding marina and coastline. Meanwhile, in the Downtown Dubai area records are set: the Burj Khalifa, the world's tallest building and observation deck, towers over the world's largest dancing fountain and nearby is The Dubai Mall, the world's largest mall. Inside, visitors can even visit the world's largest sweet shop and a record-breaking aquarium. And the World Expo 2020, which Dubai is proud to host, is expected to bring an influx of tourists and investors.

Abu Dhabi has become a major tourist destination in its own right, having seen an unprecedented boom in new hotels. In November 2014, the Abu Dhabi Tourism & Culture Authority reported that over 2.8 million tourists visited the capital in the first 10 months of the year, a 25% rise compared to 2013. By the end of 2017, Abu Dhabi expects to welcome 3.7 million; its ultimate aim is for 7.9 million visitors to stay in 80,000 hotel rooms across the capital by 2030.

The official figures do not account for the large numbers of visitors to Abu Dhabi who stay with their expat friends already living there, or those simply travelling or day-tripping from other parts of the country, so it's certainly safe to say that true visitor figures are significantly higher than the official stats.

Major developments have helped to boost visitor numbers to the emirate such as Yas Island's Yas Waterworld and the impressive Yas Mall, which opened in November 2014 becoming the second largest shopping centre in the UAE. Yas Marina Circuit and Ferrari World for Formula 1 fans are popular, and Yas Marina is home to a plethora of popular restaurants, bars, leisure pursuits and excellent fitness clubs. Meanwhile, the famous Louvre Abu Dhabi on Saadiyat Island, Zayed National Museum and the Guggenheim are expected to open in the near future, making Abu Dhabi the region's cultural centre, too.

International Relations

The UAE remains open in its foreign relations and firmly supports Arab unity. HH Sheikh Khalifa bin Zayed Al Nahyan is very generous with the country's wealth when it comes to helping Arab nations and communities that are in need of aid.

The UAE became a member of the United Nations and the Arab League in 1971. It is a member of the International Monetary Fund (IMF), the Organisation of Petroleum Exporting Countries (OPEC), the World Trade Organisation (WTO) and many international Arab organisations. It is also a member of the Arab Gulf Cooperation Council (AGCC, also known as the GCC), whose other members are Bahrain, Kuwait, Oman, Qatar and Saudi Arabia.

All major embassies and consulates are represented either in Abu Dhabi or Dubai, or both.

Yas Viceroy

World Expo 2020 Dubai

In November 2013, Dubai won the bid to host the World Expo 2020. Fireworks erupted from the Burj Khalifa and the ruler of Dubai promised that the city would 'astonish the world.'

What is the Expo?

Every five years and for a period of six months, World Expos attract millions of visitors. Also known as the World's Fair, it is an event that has been around for over 150 years. It is similar to the Olympic Games, except that instead of sports, it's about science, technology, culture and economics. The World Expo is effectively the largest mix of trade exhibitions or world fairs and is not by any means a new concept, with the first noted World Expo being hosted in London in 1851. Indeed, previous Expos have yielded legacies such as the Eiffel Tower, the telephone, ice cream and Heinz tomato ketchup.

Plans and development

While the majority of the design and construction of the Expo site is still in its infancy, organisers have reported that the site for the World Expo 2020 Dubai will be at Dubai Trade Centre – Jebel Ali: a 438 hectare site on the south western edge of Dubai which is set to be one of the largest ever developed for a World Expo. Equidistant from the centres of Abu Dhabi and Dubai, the site is located next to the new Al Maktoum International Airport and also located in close proximity to Jebel Ali Port, the third busiest port in the world.

The theme for World Expo 2020 Dubai is Connecting Minds, Creating the Future – a nod to the importance of fostering partnerships and innovation to build a sustainable world today and in the future.

Designed by architectural firm HOK, the sprawling new district features three main pavilions designed to symbolise opportunity, sustainability and mobility with 'innovation pods' and 'best practice areas' in each thematic zone. Different areas will be linked by walkways that are inspired by the layout of a traditional Arabic souk but their construction is set to be futuristic. A photovoltaic fabric structure is said to cover the walkways acting as a solar-powered sun shade capable of absorbing energy and supplying half the Expo's power requirements. At night, the fabric will act as a canvas for light displays and digital projections. At the core of the site there's said to be an open plaza called Al Wasl which is Arabic for

'the connection' – again in keeping with Dubai's Connecting Minds, Creating the Future theme – that will act as the central souk.

The plan for what to do with the site when the Expo closes is currently a hot topic for discussion. Recent news suggests that the organisers have agreed to combine the three major pavilions – the Welcome Pavilion, the Innovation Pavilion and the UAE's Pavilion – and transform them into one structure – the Museum of the Future.

The region's first

World Expo 2020 Dubai is the first to be held in the MENASA (Middle East, North Africa and South Asia) region. As the global community faces ever more complex and increasingly interconnected challenges, the links between people, societies and ideas have never been more important. The Expo promises to be a platform for connectivity to help pioneer new partnerships for growth and sustainability for the future. It was reported that the last Expo held in Shanghai in 2010 received over 73 million visitors from 250 countries. The site that showcased this phenomenon measured a massive 5.28 sqkm, and a new record attendance for a single day was set with more than 1.03 million people visiting the site. These numbers, by any standard, are hugely impressive, and an indicator of how important for the local economy the winning vote is to Dubai – especially when you consider the reported profits reached in excess of US$157 million for the Expo alone.

It is already predicted that there will be an influx to the region of 25 million visitors going through the turnstiles in Dubai. The knock-on effect is a predicted 277,000 jobs created for both the country and the region and a huge boost not only to the ensuing job market, but for the infrastructure of Dubai. With Al Maktoum International Airport's ambitious plans to overtake the likes of London Heathrow in the coming years, and its central location here in the Middle East, it is easy to see why this is the perfect platform and opportunity in which to raise the bar.

For updated information on news and events for the Expo, check out expo2020dubai.ae.

ENVIRONMENT

The UAE has certain environmental issues that can't be ignored thanks to a hot climate, a scarcity of natural drinking water and a growing population. Being a relatively wealthy country with high demands means that the average person in the UAE is consuming more than the country can produce on its own. The ecological footprint in the UAE, according to the WWF's Living Planet Report 2012, is 8.44 global hectares (gha). Meanwhile the capacity of the land to produce useful biological material and absorb waste created by humans is just 0.64gha. Globally, the UAE has the third largest deficit between these two figures, meaning a continued reliance on imports, which could lead to problems in the future.

Couple that with being one of the largest consumers of water on the planet, with a large population of expats who are less likely to invest time into conservation than locals or long-term residents, and the situation needs addressing. Fortunately the government is conscious of this and has agencies set up across the emirates to help tackle the issues.

Date palm tree

Flora & Fauna

The region has about 3,500 native plants, which is perhaps surprising considering the high salinity of the soil and the harsh environment. The most famous is, of course, the date palm, which is also the most flourishing of the indigenous flora. In mountainous regions, flat-topped acacia trees and wild grasses create scenery similar to that of an African savannah. The deserts are unexpectedly green in places, even during the dry summer months, but it takes an experienced botanist to get the most out of the area.

Indigenous fauna include the Arabian leopard and the Arabian oryx, but sightings are extremely rare. Realistically, the only large animals you will see are camels and goats (often roaming dangerously close to the roads). Other desert life includes sand cats, foxes, desert hares, gerbils, hedgehogs, snakes and geckos. Studies have shown that the number of bird species is rising each year, due in part to concentrated greening efforts. This is most apparent in parks, especially in spring and autumn, as the country is on the migratory route between central Asia and east Africa.

Off the coast of the UAE, the seas contain a rich abundance of marine life, including tropical fish, jellyfish, coral, dugong ('sea cows') and sharks. Eight species of whale and seven species of dolphin have been recorded in UAE waters. Various breeds of turtle, including loggerhead, green and hawksbill, are also indigenous with sightings off the east coast by Snoopy Island and Khor Kalba not uncommon.

Wildlife

A number of indigenous animals have been hunted to the edge of extinction in the past, including the Arabian oryx (a type of antelope) and houbara bustard (a large bird and popular quarry for falconers). Meanwhile, others have found their habitats disappearing. The survival or continued protection of these animals has been mainly thanks to government activities. Even back in 1968, the late Sheikh Zayed ordered the capture of the four remaining Arabian oryx in the wild to initiate a captive breeding programme at Al Ain Zoo. After the development of Sir Bani Yas Island, he also started another captive breeding programme for the oryx, where they are today flourishing in the island's Arabian Wildlife Park. In 2007, a release program began for the Arabian oryx in the emirate of Abu Dhabi, with 100 animals being released into the wild.

Al Ain Zoo continues to be instrumental in conserving species, while the Breeding Centre for Endangered Arabian Wildlife at Sharjah Desert Park, has been particularly successful in breeding the endangered Arabian leopard. The International Fund for Houbara Conservation (IFHC) has also become a world authority on understanding and protecting this large desert bird so integrated in the UAE's cultural traditions.

Similarly, agencies like the Environmental Agency – Abu Dhabi (ead.ae) and Emirates Wildlife Society, a national environmental NGO that operates in association with the WWF, work tirelessly to ensure the conservation of native and migrating animals, as well as their environments. Projects at Saadiyat Island in Abu Dhabi have helped protect nests of rare hawksbill turtles. Meanwhile, tagging of passing dugong have helped to keep their migratory routes safe, and specific protection has been given to breeding colonies of the rare Socotra cormorant on the islands of Marawah and Al Yasat. Internationally, the UAE-based Mohamed bin Zayed Species Conservation Fund has donated over Dhs.33 million to projects dedicated to helping the threatened flora and fauna of the world.

My Environment, My Country

Each year, the UAE hosts the My Environment, My Country initiative in schools. It aims to inspire and educate children to protect the natural world, focusing on the concepts and challenges faced by the UAE. An App 'named 'Beatty', meaning 'My Environment' in Arabic, was launched in 2014 to support the cause.

Sustainability

From the outside, the UAE looks totally unsustainable. Huge petrol use, massive energy consumption (for all that air conditioning) and a seemingly never-ending generation of waste – it all looks like an environmental headache. Rapid growth has necessitated much of this but the UAE government is keen to spread the message of sustainability. In fact, the late president of the UAE, Sheikh Zayed, was a passionate environmentalist and much of what happens is part of his legacy. There's a realisation about energy and water issues in the UAE; generating energy requires water, and producing water (through desalination) requires energy. The government is active in finding ways to use less of both through increased efficiency. In 2014, the International Water Summit took place in Abu Dhabi during the Abu Dhabi Sustainability Week. The annual summit is part of the capital's continuing resolve to address environmental issues. Visit worldfutureenergysummit.com for the 2015 agenda.

Masdar City in Abu Dhabi is a leading light, aiming to become a zero carbon, zero waste city by 2025. Phase one is complete, with eco-friendly buildings using 65% less energy than the average building in the city. Masdar also opened the world's largest solar thermal energy plant in 2013. The project creates 10% of the world's solar thermal energy (where mirrors heat a boiler full of steam which then generates turbines), enough to power 20,000 homes in the UAE.

Heroes Of The UAE

This environmentally-friendly initiative, jointly developed by The Emirates Wildlife Society in association with the Worldwide Fund for Nature (EWS-WWF) and The Environment Agency-Abu Dhabi, provides a go-to resource for individuals, schools and businesses to find out how to save energy and water, and reduce the UAE's carbon footprint – which currently has the highest per capita ecological footprint on earth – with virtual calculators, tips and information. As part of its commitment, Abu Dhabi government recently fitted Watersavers to taps, in homes and offices in the emirate. It also organised its 34th Plantation Week in March 2014 to flag up sustainable farming.

Recycling

Recycling is a relatively new concept in the UAE, with just over 20% of all non-hazardous waste being recycled. While the importance of reducing waste through the three 'R's (reduce, reuse, recycle) is being taught throughout the country, different emirates are taking different initiatives. In Abu Dhabi, the Centre of Waste Management has already taken a lead on things. Just a few years ago around 60% of waste from construction was going to landfill, roughly 3.5 million tonnes. This is now re-used in road construction, footpaths, playgrounds and sports areas.

Domestically, there can be some confusion about recycling. Even amongst expats, what seems obviously recyclable might be quite different in the UAE compared to your home country. The Abu Dhabi government rolled out a scheme that saw villas given two bins; green bin for organic waste and black bin for solid recyclable waste. By 2014, most residences had received the bins and the Centre of Waste Management plans to make recycling mandatory in the UAE capital.

There are recycling points around Abu Dhabi, including sites conveniently located at Spinneys supermarkets. However, while it's not always an easy task, if you don't have access to recycling bins, try to persuade your landlord, community management company or company to implement a recycling scheme. In line with many countries, plastic bags are being phased out across some supermarkets and stores in the UAE. Regular 'Say No To Plastic Bags' campaigns aim to reduce the estimated 11 billion bags used annually. The number is slowly declining.

CULTURE & LIFESTYLE

The UAE manages what some Arab countries fail to achieve; a healthy balance between western influences and eastern traditions. It is still a country very much rooted in Islamic culture; however, the country's effort to become modern and cosmopolitan is highlighted by an open-minded and liberal outlook.

Culture

Islam is an integral part of UAE life and to followers it is more than just a religion; it's a way of life that governs even everyday events, from what to wear to what to eat and drink. However, the UAE is progressively tolerant and welcoming; foreigners are free to practise their own religion, alcohol is served in hotels and the dress code is fairly liberal. Women face little discrimination and, contrary to the policies of neighbouring Saudi Arabia, are able to drive and walk around uncovered and unescorted.

The UAE has changed dramatically over the last 40 years, fuelled by economic prosperity that has made mega malls, towering skyscrapers and expensive 4WDs the norm. Yet the country is also keen to safeguard its heritage, with active promotion of cultural and sporting events that represent their traditions, such as falconry, camel racing and traditional dhow sailing. Arabic culture in poetry, dancing, songs, art and craftsmanship is encouraged too. Traditional virtues of courtesy and hospitality are also highly prized, although you may not always find this extended to the highways.

The Sheikh Mohammed Centre for Cultural Understanding (cultures.ae) near Dubai Creek actively promotes awareness of the local culture through various events and talks. Its motto, Open Doors, Open Minds, signifies a free and safe space to discuss sensitive topics openly and honestly. You can share a traditional meal with the hosts, learn about Muslim culture and ask questions that perhaps you were too nervous to ask before.

Language

Arabic is the official language of the UAE. However, English is so widely used in all areas of life, including in business, that you might live here for years without needing to learn a single word of Arabic. Most road signs, shop signs and restaurant menus display both English and Arabic. That's not to say that learning a few words or phrases isn't a good idea though. Arabic isn't the easiest language to pick up, or to pronounce, but if you can throw in a couple of words here and there, you're more likely to receive a warmer welcome or at least a smile – even if your pronunciation is terrible. Expats make up the vast majority of the UAE (around 85%, with the majority from India, Pakistan and Bangladesh) and you can expect to hear languages like Hindi, Tagalog, Malayalam and Urdu.

Religion

Islam is the official religion of the UAE, and is widely practised throughout the country. The Islamic holy day is Friday. The basis of Islam is the belief that there is only one God and that the Prophet Muhammad is his messenger. The faith shares a common ancestry with Christianity and many of the prophets before Muhammad can be found in Christian as well as Muslim writings. There are five pillars of Islam that all Muslims must follow: the Profession of Faith, Prayer, Charity, Fasting and Pilgrimage. Every Muslim is expected, at least once in his or her lifetime, to make the pilgrimage (Hajj) to the holy city of Mecca (also spelt Makkah) in Saudi Arabia.

Arabic Family Names

Arabic names have a formal structure that traditionally indicates the person's family and tribe. Names are usually taken from an important person in the Quran or from the tribe. This is followed by the word bin (son of) for a boy or bint (daughter of) for a girl, and then the name of the child's father. The last name indicates the person's tribe or family. For prominent families, this has Al, the Arabic word for 'the', immediately before it. For instance, the President of the UAE is His Highness Sheikh Khalifa bin Zayed Al Nahyan. When women get married, they do not change their name.

Muslims are required to pray five times a day (facing Mecca), and times vary according to the sun. Most people pray at a mosque, but it's not unusual to see people kneeling by the side of the road if they are not near a place of worship. It is considered impolite to stare at people praying or to walk over prayer mats. The modern-day call to prayer, transmitted through loudspeakers on the minarets, ensures that everyone knows it's time to pray.

Islam is the principle religion, but the UAE is tolerant of other denominations; the ruling family has, in the past, donated land for the building of churches. There is a Christian community and churches in Abu Dhabi and Dubai, and a Hindu temple in Dubai.

BASIC ARABIC

General
Yes	na'am
No	la
Please	min fadlak (m) min fadlik (f)
Thank you	shukran
Please (in offering)	tafaddal (m) tafaddali (f)
Praise be to God	al-hamdu l-illah
God willing	in shaa'a l-laah

Greetings
Greeting (peace be upon you)	as-salaamu alaykom
Greeting (in reply)	wa alaykom is salaam
Good morning	sabah il-khayr
Good morning (in reply)	sabah in-nuwr
Good evening	masa il-khayr
Good evening (in reply)	masa in-nuwr
Hello	marhaba
Hello (in reply)	marhabtayn
How are you?	kayf haalak (m) / kayf haalik (f)
Fine, thank you	zayn, shukran (m) zayna, shukran (f)
Welcome	ahlan wa sahlan
Welcome (in reply)	ahlan fiyk (m) / ahlan fiyki (f)
Goodbye	ma is-salaama

Introductions
My name is...	ismiy...
What is your name?	shuw ismak (m) / shuw ismik (f)
Where are you from?	min wayn inta (m) /min wayn inti (f)
I am from...	anaa min...
America	ameriki
Britain	braitani
Europe	oropi
India	al hindi

Questions
How many / much?	kam?
Where?	wayn?
When?	mataa?
Which?	ayy?
How?	kayf?
What?	shuw?
Why?	laysh?
Who?	miyn?
To/for	ila
In/at	fee
From	min
And	wa
Also	kamaan
There isn't	maa fee

Driving
Is this the road to...	hadaa al tariyq ila...
Stop	kuf
Right	yamiyn
Left	yassar
Straight ahead	siydaa
North	shamaal
South	januwb
East	sharq
West	garb
Turning	mafraq
First	awwal
Second	thaaniy
Road	tariyq
Street	shaaria
Roundabout	duwwaar
Signal	sishaara
Close to	qarib min
Petrol station	mahattat betrol
Sea/beach	il bahar
Mountain/s	jabal/jibaal
Desert	al sahraa
Airport	mataar
Hotel	funduq
Restaurant	mata'am
Slow down	schway schway

Accidents & Emergencies
Police	al shurtaa
Permit/licence	rukhsaa
Accident	haadith
Papers	waraq
Insurance	ta'miyn
Sorry	aasif (m) /aasifa (f)

Numbers
Zero	sifr
One	waahad
Two	ithnayn
Three	thalatha
Four	arba'a
Five	khamsa
Six	sitta
Seven	saba'a
Eight	thamaanya
Nine	tiss'a
Ten	ashara
Hundred	miya
Thousand	alf

National Dress

Emiratis generally wear traditional dress in public, although many will dress in more western clothes if travelling abroad. For men, traditional dress means a dishdasha or khandura; a white, full length shirt dress, which is worn with a white or red checked headdress, known as gutra or sifrah. This is secured with a black chord (agal). Sheikhs and important businessmen may also wear a thin black or brown robe (known as a bisht), over their dishdasha at important events, which is equivalent to a dinner jacket in western culture. In public, women wear the black abaya; a long, loose black robe that covers their normal clothes, plus a headscarf called a sheyla.

The abaya is often of sheer, flowing fabric and may be open at the front. Some women also wear a thin black veil hiding their face, and gloves. Older women sometimes still wear a leather mask, known as a burkha, which covers the nose, brow and cheekbones. Underneath, women traditionally wear a long tunic over loose, flowing trousers (sirwal), which are often heavily embroidered and fitted at wrists and ankles. However, these are used more by the older generation and modern women will often wear the latest fashions under their abayas. At the beach, it's not unusual to see Muslim women in special bathing costumes that keep their legs, arms, bodies and head covered, with only their faces, hands and feet on show.

Food & Drink

The cultural diversity of the population is reflected in the vast range of culinary delights available in the country. Anything from Mexican and Asian fusion to an English roast dinner is available. Most of the popular restaurants are in hotels, where alcoholic drinks are also served. Some of the tastiest food can be found in the small streetside cafeterias, where two people can feast on under Dhs.50. Fast food fans will also find McDonald's, Burger King, KFC, Subway and Burger Fuel – all offering home delivery.

When it comes to food shopping, there are a number of supermarkets that stock many international brands. French chain Carrefour is one of the largest with a huge selection, while Choithrams (with Tesco products from the UK), LuLu Hypermarket and Co-op stores offer similar choice and are popular with those on a budget. Spinneys, Abela, Waitrose and Park N Shop are more expensive but sell an excellent range of British, South African and American produce.

Eat Like The Locals

While modern Arabic cuisine comes from a blend of Moroccan, Tunisian, Iranian and Egyptian cooking styles, the term invariably refers to Lebanese food. Aside from mezze, it's fairly reliant on meat, often lamb, beef or fish cooked over a charcoal grill. Meals often end with nutty Lebanese sweets and are accompanied by a variety of wonderfully fresh fruit juices.

Shawarma: lamb or chicken sliced from a spit and served in a pita bread with salad and tahina
Falafel: mashed chickpeas and sesame seeds, rolled into balls and deep fried
Mezze: a selection of dishes served with Arabic bread, a green salad and pickles
Hummus: a creamy dip made from ground chickpeas, olive oil and garlic
Tabouleh: finely chopped parsley, mint and cracked wheat salad
Fatoush: lettuce and tomato with small pieces of fried Arabic bread
Fattayer: small pastries filled with cottage cheese and spinach
Kibbeh: deep fried mince, pine nuts and bulgur
Baklava: filo pastry layered with honey and pistachio nuts
Umm Ali: a dessert with milk, bread, raisins and nuts

Emirati Specialities

Camel is eaten, but as they are highly prized for their milk and load-carrying ability, camel meat is usually saved for special occasions. You can however pick up a pint of camel milk in most supermarkets, and the odd bar of chocolate. Dates are more of a staple having been cultivated in the region for around 5,000 years, and it's said that in some countries the Bedouin way of life was sustained primarily by dates and camel milk up until as recently as the mid 20th century. Dates are also a bit of a super food, high in energy but low

Shawarma spit

Pearls & Caviar

in fat, so make a great cheap and healthy snack. Just five dates per day provide enough nutrition for one recommended daily portion of fruit or vegetables.

Pork

Pork is taboo in Islam. Muslims should not eat, prepare or even serve pork. In order for a restaurant to serve pork on its menu, it should have a separate fridge, preparation equipment and cooking area. It also needs a specific licence. In restaurants, bacon is substituted with beef or veal bacon. Supermarkets that sell pork products are also required to do so from a separate area for 'non-Muslims'. Anything you choose is immediately wrapped up and you are issued with a receipt to take to the till for payment. As pork is not locally produced you will find that it's more expensive than other meats. All meat products for Muslim consumption have to be halal, which refers to the method of slaughter.

Alcohol

Alcohol is widely available in hotels plus a few leisure clubs, such as golf clubs and sports clubs, and the very occasional non-hotel bar/restaurant. During Ramadan, alcohol is only served after sunset, and there are 'dry' nights before certain public holidays. Officially you need a liquor licence to buy, transport or even consume alcohol, whether at home or at a hotel; you must also be a non-Muslim resident. Alcohol is sold at specially-licensed stores across the UAE. Sharjah is the only dry state in the UAE, and alcohol is not sold or served in any hotels here. If drinking, always be mindful that you are in a Muslim country; drunken behaviour is not tolerated, neither is drink-driving.

Shisha

Also known as hookah pipes, hubbly bubbly or nagile, smoking the traditional shisha (water pipe) is a popular pastime throughout the Middle East. Shisha pipes can be smoked with a variety of aromatic flavours, such as strawberry, grape, mint or apple. Unlike a normal cigarette or cigar, the smoke is softened by the water, creating a more soothing effect, although it still causes smoking-related health problems (1gm of shisha smoke has 100 times the tar content of a cigarette). Smoking shisha is an enjoyable social experience but it's wise not to make it a habit. During Ramadan, when a number of Iftar tents are erected throughout cities, shisha smoking is particularly popular.

CRIME & THE LAW

While crime figures aren't officially released, the UAE is known for having a low crime rate. Serious crimes like rape and murder are infrequent and unlikely to affect the quality of life of the average expat. The most common reason for expats getting on the wrong side of the law is often alcohol. In the UAE there is a zero-tolerance policy on drinking and driving; if you are arrested for this, the usual penalty is a minimum 30 days in prison. Being drunk and disorderly in public is also something that can land you in trouble.

Should you be in any altercation, it pays to keep your calm; obscene gestures or profane language, even on the phone, are bad news. Physically or verbally abuse anyone so that it causes them harm, and you may end up in prison, unless the victim chooses to drop the charges. This includes when you're behind the wheel of a car too, so keep your road rage well in check.

10 Laws To Know

Get a liquor licence If you want to drink or buy alcohol at a hotel or at home, you'll need to have a liquor licence.
Don't live as an unmarried couple Men and women unrelated to each other cannot live together. You'd be unlucky to be pulled up for disregarding this law though.
Don't get pregnant out of wedlock At some point any hospital will ask to see your marriage certificate during the nine months up to birth. If you're unmarried and pregnant you will have issues registering the birth and may also be in hot water for non-marital sex.
Don't have one for the road The UAE has a zero-tolerance approach to drink driving. There is no safe limit.
Check illegal meds Some over-the-counter medicines from your home country may be illegal in the UAE. A list of approved drugs can be found on the Ministry of Health website (moh.gov.ae).
Respect Ramadan Eating, drinking, smoking and even chewing gum in public during the daylight hours of Ramadan is illegal. You need to wait until Iftar (breaking of the fast) to eat, drink or smoke in public.
Don't phone while driving It's completely illegal to use your phone without a hands-free device, despite being one of the most flouted laws in history.
Get your Resident ID All expats must have a national identity card. Visit eida.gov.ae for details.
Don't bounce cheques Passing bad cheques is taken seriously in the UAE, resulting in fines or imprisonment.
Look before lighting up Smoking is illegal in many public areas such as shopping malls.

Legal System

The legal system in the UAE is a mix of Shariah (Islamic) and conventional laws, implemented by the Federal Judiciary. In comparison to Saudi Arabia and other Arab nations, the laws in the UAE are more liberal, but it is a Muslim country and so more conservative than some western countries.

All emirates have Courts of First Instance and Courts of Appeal, either federal or local, in addition to the Shariah Courts which mainly deal with matters of personal status involving Muslims, such as marriage, divorce and inheritance.

Police

Abu Dhabi has a large, active, and highly respected and effective police force who take community involvement seriously. Abu Dhabi police are easily identifiable: the standard uniform is ash-grey but traffic police wear white sleeves and a white belt. Police vehicles are generally red and white with blue and red lights on the roof, but you will also see brown SUVs and pick-ups as well as some unmarked vehicles (often larger saloons). In 2014, 25 customised Mercedes-Benz were delivered to the Abu Dhabi police department.

The police are approachable; most speak some English and are generally helpful if you need to ask simple questions or for directions. If you need to call them, the number is 999 and you can use it if you are involved in a traffic accident and to report a crime.

If You're Arrested

You'll first be taken to a police station and, if applicable, a court date will be set. If you are put in a cell, and it's a weekend or a public holiday, (such as Eid) you could be kept in for a long time. If the offence is a minor one, you may get bail; the police will keep your passport and often the passport of another UAE resident who is willing to vouch for you. If you don't get bail you'll be held in the police cell until the hearing. All court proceedings are in Arabic so you'll need to hire a translator. If sentenced, you'll go straight from court to jail. It's advisable to contact your embassy as soon as possible. They won't be able to pay your legal fees, secure bail, act as lawyers or get you released, but they can liaise with family, offer advice and provide you with translators and lawyers.

Victim Support

Victims of domestic violence can contact the Family Development Foundation (fdf.ae); the UAE Red Crescent runs women's shelters in Abu Dhabi. Victims of sexual abuse can contact the National Committee to Combat Human Trafficking (nccht.gov.ae) for help.

Dos & Don'ts

You'll find that, in general, people in the UAE are patient when it comes to cultural etiquette and are keen to explain their customs to you. However, there are a few cultural dos and don'ts that you should be aware of to avoid causing offence or landing yourself in trouble with the law.

PDAs
Public displays of affection are a no-no in the UAE and anything more than an innocent peck on the cheek will at best earn you disapproving looks from passers-by.

Appropriate attire
Beach wear on the beach is fine, but in public, dress should be more conservative. Covering shoulders and knees is a safe bet if you are unsure. It's wise for women to carry a pashmina so they can cover up when necessary. That said, pretty much anything goes when out at bars and clubs.

Arabic coffee
It's likely that you'll be served Arabic coffee (kahwa) during formal business meetings. This is an important social ritual so be polite and drink some when offered. Take cups in the right hand; the signal to say you have had enough is to gently shake the cup from side to side.

Tipping
It's up to you whether you want to tip, but the norm is 10% in restaurants and cafes. It's regular practice to round up the taxi fare as a tip, and the same goes for rounding up the cost of your fuel every time you fill up. Pay valet attendants around Dhs.5; Dhs.10 is the norm in beauty salons, spas and hairdressers.

Business etiquette
Introductions and small talk usually start a business meeting, with exchanging of business cards. Treat a received card with respect, like it's an extension of the person who gave it. Being late for a meeting is considered bad manners, but punctuality doesn't mean it will start at the appointed time or that it will be uninterrupted.

Home values
When visiting an Emirati house it is customary to remove your shoes. Traditionally men and women dine separately and meals are eaten sat on floor cushions. Be careful not to point your feet at anyone or show the soles. Try everything offered, but if not sure you'll like something, just take a small amount.

Meeting people
While warm greetings and long handshakes are common, if you are meeting someone of the opposite sex a handshake may not be welcome, so it's best to wait until they offer their hand. It's considered polite to send greetings to a person's family, but can be considered rude to enquire directly about someone's wife, sister or daughter. You may on occasion see men greeting each other with a nose kiss; this is a customary greeting between close friends in the Gulf and you should not attempt to greet someone in this way.

Photography
Abu Dhabi is full of snap-worthy sights and normal tourist photography is fine. However, like anywhere in the Arab world, it is courteous to ask permission before photographing people, particularly women. In general, photographs of government and military buildings shouldn't be taken, especially if there are 'no photography' signs. Unwitting tourists have found themselves in deep trouble for this before.

Out on the town
Abu Dhabi has a good variety of nightlife and alcohol is widely available in the city's hotel bars, pubs and clubs (see the Going Out section). Remember, however, that you're in a Muslim: country and drunken or lewd behaviour is not only disrespectful but it can often lead to arrest and detention.

LOCAL MEDIA

Media is one particular area that has boomed in the UAE. Expats from around the world have been recruited to voice the radio, write the newspapers and magazines, and film the TV shows. The idea is that their knowledge from more established media markets can be passed on to Emiratis and help local media to flourish further. The upshot of this is that there are many decent local media products available in the UAE now.

Internet

Around 85% of the UAE's population is online, reflecting how easy it is to get connected in the larger cities. Internet offerings might not be quite as quick as in areas like the US or Europe, but the UAE still ranks near the top for connectivity. There are some things that expats need to remember though, particularly the despised proxy that blocks access to any site deemed offensive. What is or isn't offensive is up to the Telecommunication Regulatory Authority (TRA) which supposedly applies the same rules to both Etisalat and du subscribers, the two main providers.

Living in a Muslim community means sites containing pornography (or explicit images) or dubious religious content will be blocked. Sites that offer online dating, gambling or drugs, and, oddly, some photo-sharing websites are also out of bounds. Of course, you could access these sites with the help of a proxy blocker (VPN), but then you're technically breaking the law.

Similarly, despite VoIP (Voice over Internet Protocol) access having been blocked for a long time, regulators finally authorised it in 2010, but only to the four existing licence-holders; Etisalat, du and the satellite firms Yahsat and Thuraya. That meant making international calls through the internet were still effectively banned as authorised VoIP services weren't available from these companies. By 2013, both Etisalat and du lifted the ban on downloading the popular Skype service though, perhaps realising that the loss in revenue from calls could be made up by increased data use from customers.

Internet Entertainment

While satellite and digital TV or local radio were the only options to expats missing programmes from home, the internet now makes viewing and listening to favourites easy. Radio stations aren't blocked online, but you may need a VPN to access sources like Netflix. If you're using a tablet like an iPad, then cables can be bought to link it to your TV so you can even see it on a larger screen.

USEFUL WEBSITES

Abu Dhabi Information	**abudhabi.ae** – Abu Dhabi government portal with tonnes of information
	abudhabitourism.ae – Abu Dhabi Tourism Authority
	abudhabiwoman.com – Forums and advice for women living in Abu Dhabi
	adach.ae – Abu Dhabi Authority for Culture and Heritage
	adnec.ae – Abu Dhabi National Exhibition Centre
	adpolice.gov.ae – Abu Dhabi Police
	askexplorer.com – Essential info on living and working in the UAE
	expatwoman.com – Friendly site jampacked with useful info, jobs and events
	visitabudhabi.ae – Abu Dhabi tourism site
	timeoutabudhabi.com – Listings for Abu Dhabi
UAE Information	**7days.ae** – National newspaper
	abudhabievents.ae – Events calendar in and around the capital
	ameinfo.com – Middle East business news
	dubizzle.com – Classifieds, listings and forums across the emirates
	government.ae – UAE Government e-portal
	gulfnews.com – National newspaper
	khaleejtimes.com – National newspaper
	sheikhzayed.com – Dedicated to the life of the late UAE president
	thenational.ae – Local newspaper

USEFUL APPS

Abu Dhabi Map	A handy interactive map that offers detailed descriptions for POIs and landmarks
Abu Dhabi Police	Get updates on your fines, make emergency calls or get traffic updates
Abu Dhabi Taxi	User-friendly app to book a taxi in both Abu Dhabi and Al Ain
CityGuard	Report pot holes, rubbish or incidents with an image to the Abu Dhabi government
Salik	Keep up-to-date on your Salik toll charges (the Dubai toll system)
UAE Business	Guide to registration, licensing and costs for free zones and mainland across UAE
UAE Off-Road	Choose from a selection of off-road routes and follow the interactive GPS coordinates
Dubai Map	Navigate the city like a local with this handy and interactive map app

Radio

The UAE has a number of commercial radio stations that broadcast in a wide range of languages to reflect the emirate's diverse population. You'll find that the leading English language stations operate 24 hours a day and, while most are physically based in Dubai, they can usually be picked up with a good reception throughout Abu Dhabi. Depending on your digital or satellite TV provider, they may offer various radio channels (including Virgin Radio and the BBC World Service) as well as music television like MTV and VH1. If you miss your radio stations from back home, don't despair as Internet radio is another, and possibly the most popular option for music loving expats – you'll find that most of your favourite channels from home are available on the web.

BBC World: also available on shortwave frequencies, 1413 MW/ 639 MW Nr Business Central Twin Towers, Dubai, 04 367 8090, *bbc.com*

Channel 4 104.8 FM: contemporary music for a younger audience, 104.8FM Shk Khalifa Bin Zayed St Nr Ajman Twin Towers, Ajman, 06 746 1 444, *channel4FM.com*

Dubai 92: one of the most popular stations, '92' combines current music and popular decades-old hits from the 80s and 90s. Daily competitions and well-known chatty DJs, 92.00FM BS16 Bldg, Dubai, 04 391 2000, *dubai92.com*

Dubai Eye 103.8: quality talk radio, 103.8FM BS16 Bldg, Dubai, 04 435 4700, *dubaieye1038.com*

Radio 1: hit music broadcast across the country, 104.1FM Gulf News, Al Wasl Dubai, 04 406 2677, *myradio1.ae*

Radio 2: contemporary music broadcast throughout the UAE, 99.3FM Gulf News, Al Wasl Dubai, 04 406 2683, *myradio2.ae*

Virgin Radio 104.4: hit music along the lines of Virgin Radio in other cities, 104.4FM BS16 Bldg, Dubai, 04 391 2000, *virginradiodubai.com*

Newspapers

There's no shortage of reading material for expats, with a number of daily English language broadsheets. Abu Dhabi's The National is very popular, being one of the first to deliver real journalism in the region, but Gulf News, Khaleej Times and Gulf Today are all readily available. Most supermarkets will also have some local language newspapers if you're missing a tabloid from home. Around the city you can also find the 7Days daily tabloid newspaper and Abu Dhabi Week, a guide to events and news in the city, both for free.

There are versions of many popular international magazines, like Conde Nast Traveller, Good Housekeeping, Esquire, OK!, Hello, Lonely Planet, Grazia, Men's Fitness, Women's Fitness and Stuff. You can also keep an eye out for expat titles like Connector and Good, as well as for listings magazines such as Time Out (both Abu Dhabi and Dubai) and What's On.

Television

Channels like Dubai One and MBC4, despite being free to air, are doing a relatively good job of securing the rights to some fairly mainstream international shows. However, satellite or cable TV is a staple in most expat homes. Some shows are aired just a few days later than they are in the US or UK, while others are delayed by a few months, so it can be a little hit and miss. One of the most widely used operators, OSN (osn.com) offers a wide range of TV packages, which can include everything from sports and news to comedy and British/American favourites, although the free-to-air channels such as Dubai One, Fox Movies and MBC are improving year on year. OSN also offers a Showbox service, which allows you to pause live TV and record shows.

If you have digital or satellite TV then you probably have internet access, which is an alternative way to watch your favourite programmes.

UAE CALENDAR

The Islamic calendar starts from the year 622AD, the year of the Prophet Muhammad's migration (Hijra) from Mecca to Al Madinah. Hence the Islamic year is called the Hijri year and dates are followed by AH (AH stands for Anno Hegirae, meaning 'after the year of the Hijra').

Public Holidays

During the year there are holidays on set dates, such as National Day on 2 December. However, all other Islamic holidays are based on the sighting of the moon and therefore the dates vary each year. Often this can mean confirmation of a holiday less than 24 hours before it is due, something most companies will email employees of when it is announced.

The main Muslim festivals are Eid Al Fitr (the festival of the breaking of the fast, which signifies the end of Ramadan) and Eid Al Adha (the festival of sacrifice, which signifies the end of the pilgrimage to Mecca). Mawlid Al Nabee is the holiday which celebrates the Prophet Muhammad's birthday, and finally, Lailat Al Mi'raj marks the celebration of the Prophet's ascension into heaven.

2015 – 2016

The below list of public holidays applies mainly to the public sector; if you work in the private sector you may get fewer days holiday per year. National Day, which celebrates the foundation of the UAE, for example, is one day for private sector workers but two days for the public sector.

New Year	1 Jan 2015 (fixed)
Mawlid Al Nabee	2 Jan 2015 (moon)
Lailat Al Mi'raj	15 May 2015 (moon)
Eid Al Fitr (3 days)	18 July 2015 (moon)
Arafat Day	24 Sept 2015 (moon)
Eid Al Adha (3 days)	25 Sept 2015 (moon)
Islamic New Year	15 Oct 2015 (moon)
UAE National Day	2 Dec 2015 (fixed)
New Year	1 Jan 2016 (fixed)
Mawlid Al Nabee	11 Dec 2016 (moon)
Lailat Al Mi'raj	5 May 2016 (moon)

Featured here are some of the key dates in the UAE calendar; specific dates vary so always check the website. Also, visit askexplorer.com throughout the year to find out what's on each month.

Annual Events & Exhibitions

Abu Dhabi HSBC Golf Championship
January

Abu Dhabi Golf Club Khalifa City
abudhabigolfchampionship.com
Expect the unexpected with the battle for the coveted Falcon Trophy in this curtain-raiser to the European PGA Tour at Abu Dhabi Golf Club's National Course. Fans can expect to see some of the world's top golfers compete and an astounding array of off-course entertainment at the Championship spectator village, which is surprisingly great for kids.

Mubadala World Tennis Championship
January

Tennis Complex Zayed Sports City
mubadalawtc.com
World number 1 and Wimbledon champion Novak Djokovic returned along with world number 2, Rafael Nadal for the eighth Mubadala World Tennis Championship. Top players competed for the whopping US $250,000 prize. The Tennis Village's off-court action was great entertainment too.

Gourmet Abu Dhabi
February

Various locations
gourmetabudhabi.ae
This is a 'lifestyle gastronomic extravaganza' featuring a star-studded cast of world-renowned Michelin-starred chefs and special guests, master classes, industry insights from hospitality experts, and Chateau and gourmet dinners hosted by a range of the UAE capital's top hotels. One of the region's most significant festivals for foodies.

Symphonic Concert 'Strauss-Bruckner'
February

Emirates Hotel Auditorium
abudhabievents.ae
A classics highlight, expected to be the outstanding musical event of year. Voted 'Orchestra of the Year' by a panel of 50 international music critics in 2013, this is a debut for the capital. Featuring renowned principal conductor Christian Thielemann.

Abu Dhabi Desert Challenge
March

Empty Quarter Mezairaa
abudhabidesertchallenge.com
One of the world's most prestigious annual international cross country events, running for five days in unspoilt Liwa, Abu Dhabi's vast Rub Al Khali desert. This ever-popular motorsport spectacle is the season-opener for both the FIA Cross Country Rally World Cup and the well-attended FIM Cross Country Rallies World Championship.

UAE NATIONAL DAY

Every 2 December, the country turns green, black, red and white all over. In fact, the flag becomes as ubiquitous as traffic jams as residents throughout the emirates celebrate the birth of the UAE. Cars, trucks and taxis are decorated with flags and pictures of the country's rulers to show their patriotism. In Abu Dhabi, military bands and folklore exhibitions entertain the crowds along the Corniche and in public parks and markets. It wouldn't be an independence celebration without fireworks, and Emirates Palace traditionally holds the city's biggest display, set to music lighting up the night sky to dramatic effect – it's almost impossible not to feel patriotic. In 2015, the UAE will celebrate 44 years of independence.

Abu Dhabi Festival — March
Various locations
abudhabifestival.ae
This highly successful international festival advances classical music and fine arts among Abu Dhabi residents and visitors. A culturally-rich and diverse event, it features world-class performances and has seen performances from the likes of the Bolshoi Ballet, Andrea Bocelli, Natalie Cole and Sir James Galway.

Abu Dhabi International Triathlon — March
Abu Dhabi Corniche Al Danah
abudhabitriathlon.com
This annual event attracts the world's best triathletes and international amateurs. The race takes place across three distances – the 223km main 'long course' boasts a gruelling 3km swim, a 200km cycle and 20km closing run. There's also a 'short' course and a sprint course which can be run as a team relay.

Dubai World Cup — March
Meydan Racecourse Dubai 04 327 0077
dubaiworldcup.com
The world's richest horse race takes place at the state-of-the-art Meydan racecourse. The huge prize fund (of over $27 million), a buzzing, vibrant atmosphere, and the star-studded entertainment line-up ensure that the Dubai World Cup is one of the year's most-anticipated social occasions.

Abu Dhabi International Book Fair — May
Abu Dhabi National Exhibition Centre (ADNEC)
Al Safarat
adbookfair.com
Held annually at Abu Dhabi National Exhibition Centre, this is the Arabian Gulf's fastest growing book fair with in excess of 600,000 titles on display. Digital publishing, creative engagements with reading for children and even illustrators are all represented.

Al Gharbia Watersports Festival — April
Mirfa Public Beach Al Gharbia
algharbiafestivals.com
An all-watersports extravaganza in the charming fishing town of Mirfa in Al Gharbia, Abu Dhabi's Western Region. The festival is filled with wonder, water and world-class athletes. From kiteboards and surf ski kayaks in the waves to chilled-out camping and concerts on shore – the UAE's wettest week.

Dubai Fashion Week — April
Dubai World Trade Centre Dubai
One of the glitziest and most stylish events on the calendar, in which the top regional fashion designers present their collections to the world's fashion media. The event now attracts some of the world's most famous fashion houses.

SummerFest Abu Dhabi — June-August
Various locations
summerfestabudhabi.ae
A mega summer promotion with spectacular flight, attraction and hotel deals, this is an extravaganza spanning mid-summer, the Holy Month of Ramadan, Eid Al Fitr and the destination's traditional EidFest celebrations. SummerFest Abu Dhabi revolves around a family-friendly hub of education and entertainment activities, world-class theatrical performances and exciting international performances spread over four action-packed halls at the Abu Dhabi National Exhibition Centre (ADNEC).

Liwa Date Festival — July
Al Gharbia Mezairaa
algharbiafestivals.ae
This annual event explores the intricacies of date production and the varied products this desert fruit is now lending itself to. A fascinating insight into many desert traditions, the festival includes a date beauty contest, a date auction and educational sessions on how to care for palm trees. While it is a little bit of a trek out of the city centre to reach Al Gharbia, you are sure to come back with a new found appreciation for this delicious fruit of the desert.

Abu Dhabi International Hunting & Equestrian Exhibition — September
Abu Dhabi National Exhibition Centre Al Safarat
adihex.net
This is the Arabian Gulf's most renowned and most popular hunting and equestrian exhibition where visitors can witness camel auctions, saluki shows and falcon beauty contests as well as art and coffee-making competitions and a variety of traditional hunting and equestrian activities.

Abu Dhabi Film Festival — October
Various locations
abudhabifilmfestival.ae
The Abu Dhabi Film Festival, sponsored by twofour54, presents an exciting programme showcasing the best Arab filmmaking alongside the best of world cinema. The 2014 Film Festival featured seven world premieres of Arab films, including some in direct competition with international titles. The festival also showcased short films from all over the world, with nine days of cinema screenings, red carpet premieres, filmmaking classes and events. Stars on the red carpet have included Forest Whitaker and Richard Gere.

EidFest Abu Dhabi — October
Various locations
visitabudhabi.ae
Our Eid. Your Eid. This concept – in its fifth edition in 2015 – brings together a collection of celebratory

Dubai World Cup

activities and the spirit of sharing to Abu Dhabi, centred on the Islamic festivities of Eid Al Adha. It's the final part of SummerFest, which sees a whole host of family-friendly activities and shows.

Gulf Bike Week October

Dubai Media City Amphitheater Dubai
Over 50,000 visitors attended last year's event, enjoying stunt shows, motorbike displays, test rides and rock concerts, with previous acts including Nickelback, N.E.R.D and Megadeth. JW Marriott even hosted a Biker Brunch in 2014, which included a 'fire water' option.

Abu Dhabi Art November

UAE Pavilion & Manarat Al Saadiyat
Saadiyat Island
abudhabiartfair.ae
A popular art fair and a modern and contemporary art platform with public programmes, Abu Dhabi Art brings together leading galleries from across the world. Showcasing a variety of artwork, from museum-quality pieces to those by emerging artists, the event is at the UAE Pavilion and Manarat Al Saadiyat on Saadiyat Island. Participants have to register and some

areas have age restrictions. Entry is free but workshops are charged.

Dubai International Motor Show November

Dubai World Trade Centre (DIFC) Dubai
dubaimotorshow.com
Possibly the most influential car show in the Middle East region, the Dubai event attracts not only the major automotive manufacturers but also sees global and regional new car reveals. There are always added attractions like pit-stop challenges and demonstrations making for a great day out even if you're not bothered about the futuristic concept cars. The show returns this 2015.

Yasalam – Pulse Of The Capital November

Various locations
yasalam.ae
Abu Dhabi will be alive with another packed Yasalam Festival programme of free events, concerts and activities surrounding the Abu Dhabi Grand Prix. Join the F1 FanZone™ on Abu Dhabi Corniche for free concerts during the Beats on the Beach weekend and a host of activities at both Yas Marina and Yas Plaza.

Volvo Ocean Race

bin Zayed Global Arabian Flat Racing Festival – a globetrotting 10 race series. Launched to increase the global diversity of purebred Arabian horse racing, this year's event also includes the finale of the inaugural Sheikha Fatima bint Mubarak Ladies World Championship – the first international purebred Arabian series specifically created for female jockeys.

Al Dhafra Camel Festival   December
Madinat Zayed
aldhafrafestival.ae
Held in Madinat Zayed in Abu Dhabi's Al Gharbia (Western) region, this annual festival celebrates the importance of the ship of the desert in Emirati society. An intriguing insight into the relationship of this crucial desert animal and man, the festival is a visitor experience with a difference and includes the world's only camel beauty contest.

Dubai International Film Festival   December
Madinat Jumeirah, Al Sufouh 1 Dubai
dubaifilmfest.com
A hotly anticipated annual event showcasing Hollywood and international arthouse films, as well as work from the Middle East region. Premieres are generally held at Madinat Jumeirah, while screenings take place in cinemas across the city, with a giant screen beneath the Burj Khalifa serving up some free cinematic experiences in the evenings. It's a great opportunity to catch non-mainstream films and do a bit of celebrity spotting. Past events have seen big names such as Cate Blanchett, Freida Pinto, Martin Sheen and Tom Cruise hit the red carpet.

Emirates Airline Dubai
Rugby Sevens   November
The Sevens Stadium Dubai
dubairugby7s.com
Arguably the biggest social event on the sporting calendar and, with a mention on SKY News in December 2014, it has also grabbed the world's attention. Over 140,000 spectators from die-hard rugby fans to families with young children make their way to Dubai's The Sevens Stadium to watch top international teams compete for the 7s trophy. With friendly rivalry and prizes for the best fancy dress, the party atmosphere carries on well into the small hours.

Mubadala World Tennis
Championship   January
Zayed Sports City Al Madina Al Riyadiya
mubadalawtc.com
Six of the world's top 10 players compete for the 'winner takes all' US $250,000 prize. Staged yearly at Abu Dhabi International Tennis Complex, Zayed Sports City, and presented by FLASH Entertainment, this is one of the Arabian Gulf's fastest-growing and most popular sporting events.

Formula 1 Etihad Airways
Abu Dhabi Grand Prix   November
Yas Marina Circuit Yas Island West
yasmarinacircuit.com
Whether you're a first timer or a Grand Prix veteran, there's more to Formula F1 in Abu Dhabi. Held yearly at Yas Marina Circuit on Yas Island, this is where fans get a close view of the action. The new Yasalam Y1 Access gives ticket holders a year-round package of value-added benefits and concert ticket discounts.

Volvo Ocean Race   December-January
Abu Dhabi Theater Rd, Nr Marina Mall Breakwater
volvooceanraceabudhabi.com
Abu Dhabi hope to host the 2015-16 Volvo Ocean Race stopover in mid-December 2015 until early January, 2016, with an In-Port Race in January. Since Abu Dhabi has hosted the race for three successful years, they are aiming for this to become a regular fixture on the Middle East's sailing schedule. Meanwhile, during the event, as Destination Village on the Breakwater holds concerts, any future events are sure to attract large crowds.

HH Sheikh Mansoor Bin Zayed
Al Nahyan Global Arabian
Flat Racing Festival   November
Abu Dhabi Equestrian Club Al Mushrif
sheikhmansoorfestival.com
Suit up in your Sunday best and head to Abu Dhabi Equestrian Club for the finale of the Sheikh Mansoor

ABOUT ADNEC

The Abu Dhabi National Exhibition Centre (ADNEC), which opened in 2007, has contributed greatly to the number of business events held in the capital. This sophisticated, avant-garde convention centre, which is rapidly becoming a premier trade show location in the Middle East, now welcomes well over one million visitors each year.

In addition to trade fairs that attract an international audience, large-scale popular events such as the Abu Dhabi International Book Fair, The Life & Style Show UAE, and the most recent family-friendly Cinderella on Ice performance help keep the local public involved too. For a complete list of the upcoming shows, check out adnec.ae.

دائــرة الـشـؤون الـبـلـديـة
DEPARTMENT OF MUNICIPAL AFFAIRS
بـلـديـة مـدينـة أبـوظبي
ABU DHABI CITY MUNICIPALITY

Committed to Development Since

1962

@AbuDhabi_ADM   AbuDhabiADM   AbuDhabiADM   AbuDhabiADM

LIVING IN ABU DHABI

LIVING IN ABU DHABI

Deciding to move to Abu Dhabi is the first step, now it's time to discover all you need to know to start a new life in the sun.

World Trade Center

Making the decision to live in Abu Dhabi can be as daunting as it is exciting. There are idiosyncrasies to living in the United Arab Emirates that make getting things done frustrating, but get your head around these tasks quickly and you'll reap the rewards of your efforts. Fortunately, as a city, Abu Dhabi is well-versed in hosting expats so there's plenty of help to be had, much of it offered in this very chapter.

It's Not Dubai

When you tell people you're moving to Abu Dhabi, you'll probably find them wishing you luck in Dubai. Correcting them is likely to be the first thing you need to do, if for no other reason than they come to visit you in the correct city. Dubai's prominence on the world stage – thanks to audacious buildings and well-documented excesses – makes the confusion understandable; for many who don't know better, Dubai is the only place of note in the UAE. However, as the capital city, Abu Dhabi is critical to the UAE and the reasons for settling here are growing all the time. In fact, many who live here prefer the relaxed pace, local culture, greenery and choice of restaurants, bars and activities. Unique events like the Formula 1 every November make it that extra bit special too.

This chapter is here to help you, whether you're still making the decision to move, you've just arrived and don't know where to start, or you find yourself faced with an overwhelming amount of red tape. Just remember, procedures and laws do change regularly, sometimes in quite major ways. While these changes are generally announced in the newspapers, they are often implemented quickly, so it's a good idea to be prepared for the unexpected.

City Profile

Abu Dhabi is the capital city of the UAE, despite Dubai generally being the more recognised name globally. As with all other emirates in the country, the largest city also gives its name to the emirate, so Abu Dhabi is a city as well as the country's largest emirate, which incorporates Al Ain and Al Gharbia. The emirate shares borders with the emirate of Dubai to the north-east and the countries of Oman and Saudi Arabia to the south-east and west respectively. The name Abu Dhabi literally means 'father of the gazelle'.

Pearl trading was a huge part of the city's fortunes, but the subsequent discovery of oil is what really put Abu Dhabi on the map. In a relatively short period of time, it has transformed from a quiet coastal village into one of the most recognised cities in the region, with some considerable prominence on the global stage thanks to its financial firepower.

City Of Opportunities

Most expats who move to the emirate of Abu Dhabi settle in Abu Dhabi city, a place that has evolved rapidly since oil was found in 1958. Abu Dhabi city started on one island, but its reach now spreads to adjacent islands and beyond the mainland. Every year, new residential areas, new hotels and new attractions make it an exciting place to live, plus there's the added bonus of tax-free living.

Excellent career opportunities, fantastic weather (aside from a few sweaty months in summer), a readily available network of social contacts and some unique activities help make the quality of life an alluring reason to come to and to stay in the city. In fact, many expats live the sort of high life in Abu Dhabi they would unlikely be able to afford in their home countries; five-star dining, fast cars and 4x4s, lavish holidays and regular spa treatments – a luxury lifestyle that may prove difficult to leave behind!

Top 5 City

In a survey conducted by Ipsos Mori in 2013, Abu Dhabi was placed fourth in the world's top cities. The survey included participants' responses on the best cities to conduct business in, live and visit. Only Paris, London and New York were rated higher.

Even those on less generous packages can make the most of the great weather, and there are fantastic destinations in the Middle East to explore. From a road trip into the rocky landscape of Oman to a short haul flight to Asia, Abu Dhabi is ideally placed to give expats an unforgettable experience.

BEFORE YOU ARRIV

There are several things you can do before arriving in Abu Dhabi to help you get prepared. Be sure to run through this checklist a few weeks ahead of your planned trip to ensure a smooth move:

Checklist

- Qualification certificates and important documents attested (see below)
- Inform banks, building societies and the tax office about your move abroad
- Speak to your pension company to see if moving to Abu Dhabi affects your pension plan
- Research schools for children well in advance and get your child's name on the waiting list
- Get information about different neighbourhoods you might want to live in
- If accommodation is not provided by your employer, arrange temporary accommodation for when you arrive
- Have at least six passport-size photographs taken to bring with you for visa applications, etc
- Organise a shipping company to move your goods, and bear in mind it can take two to three months

Attested Certificates

To be accepted by the authorities here, your education certificates must be verified by a solicitor or public notary in your home country, then by your foreign office to verify the solicitor as bona fide, and finally by the UAE embassy. It's a good idea to have this done before you come to Abu Dhabi. There are private attestation companies in the city offering a verification service, but it's likely to take a minimum of two weeks.

Customs

Before you fly into Abu Dhabi, be aware that several prescription medications are banned, especially anything containing codeine or temazepam. The UAE maintains a zero-tolerance policy on recreational drugs, and even microscopic amounts could land you in jail. Your bags will be scanned on arrival to ensure you have no offending magazines or DVDs. Each passenger is allowed to bring in 400 cigarettes, 2kg of loose tobacco or cigars worth up to Dhs.3,000. Non-Muslims are also allowed five bottles of wine, four bottles of liquor or 24 cans of beer. There is a value limit of Dhs.3,000 on gifts being brought into Abu Dhabi by travellers.

ARRIVE

...ng an international move to any new city, ...ikely to find a long 'to do' list waiting for you when you arrive in Abu Dhabi. You'll be doing a lot of driving around, form filling, and waiting in queues in government departments. Just keep your sense of humour handy and soon all the boring red tape will be a distant memory.

Becoming 'Legal'

To get you started, here's a checklist of everything you need to do to become 'legal' in Abu Dhabi – and read on to find out how to tick each one off the list. Easy!

- ☐ Get a visit visa
- ☐ Apply for a residence visa
- ☐ Organise sponsorship for any family members who are not working
- ☐ Go for a medical test
- ☐ Apply for a Resident Identity Card
- ☐ Get a UAE driving licence
- ☐ Apply for a liquor licence
- ☐ Open a bank account

Abu Dhabi city

Visit Visas

Everyone entering the UAE needs a visit visa (also known as an entry permit) except for citizens of GCC countries; this must then be transferred to a residence visa if you plan to live and work here. The procedures for obtaining a visit visa vary depending on your nationality. Check the regulations before travelling as details can change. Currently, nationalities from 33 countries (including UK, USA, Australia and Canada) can obtain a 30 day visa on arrival at no cost. The 30 day visa can be renewed once for a further 30 days at a cost of Dhs.625, but it works out a lot cheaper to do a 'visa run' to the border of Oman, where you leave the country and re-enter on a new visit visa.

All other nationalities can apply for an entry visa sponsored by someone who is resident in Abu Dhabi (visit visa), or by a hotel or tour operator (tourist visa). There are minimum income levels for expatriates wanting to sponsor a visitor (or a home help) and the visitor can only be a first or second degree family member, not just a friend.

Visa On Arrival

Citizens of the following countries receive an automatic visit visa on arrival: Andorra, Australia, Austria, Belgium, Brunei, Canada, Denmark, Finland, France, Germany, Greece, Hong Kong, Iceland, Ireland, Italy, Japan, Liechtenstein, Luxembourg, Malaysia, Monaco, Netherlands, New Zealand, Norway, Portugal, San Marino, Singapore, South Korea, Spain, Sweden, Switzerland, United Kingdom, USA and Vatican City.

Residence Visas

To work or live in Abu Dhabi you need a residence visa, and there are three main types: employment, family and domestic worker. You either need to have a job in Abu Dhabi and be sponsored by an employer, or be married to, or the child of, someone who has a job here and they will sponsor you. As part of any residence visa process you will need to take a medical test and apply for your Resident ID (formerly known as the Emirates ID). Once you have your visa – and this process can be completed in less than a month if your employer is on the ball – you can legally live and work in Abu Dhabi. Well, for two years anyway (or three years in some free zones and government jobs).

Once you enter the UAE, you have 60 days to complete the visa application process – but it's unlikely to take that long. While your visa is being processed you should be able to leave the country as long as you have your passport. The residence visa permits you to live in the UAE, and you can live and work in different

INTERNATIONAL PAPERWORK OUT OF CONTROL?

SIRVA® Worldwide Relocation & Moving

Applications. Background checks. Legal documents. Managing global relocation is a daunting task. That's where we come in. As the largest globally-integrated relocation and moving provider, the experts at SIRVA deliver complete corporate relocation and moving solutions — all under one roof. From North America to the Middle East to Africa, we take the fear out of global relocation so that you can feel calm, confident and in control.

EVERYTHING YOU NEED. EVERYWHERE YOU NEED IT.

Call +971.2.677.9765 (Abu Dhabi), +971.4.818.0400 (Dubai) or visit SIRVA.com to learn more.

emirates. Conditions can vary between emirates though. For example, public sector employees working in Abu Dhabi are required by law to also live in the emirate or lose their housing allowance.

Visa renewal is a simpler procedure usually looked after by your Public Relations Officer (PRO), although you will need another medical. If you're out of the UAE for over six months you'll also find your residence visa cancelled. See Explorer's *How-To* Guide or visit askexplorer.com for procedures and advice on all residency applications, renewals and transfers.

Passport Photos

If you need passport photos (and you will need them) then you also need to know where to go. Grand Stores (grandstores.com), Golden Lens, and any of a number of independent studios are well aware of the required dimensions and can take and print photos on the spot. The best place to find them is in older buildings in Khalidiya, City Centre or near Wahda Mall. Some even offer full on photo sessions.

Employment Visa

To work in the UAE you need be under 65 years of age and pass the medical test. For those being sponsored by an employer for their residence visa, the majority of the legwork will be done by the company or their Public Relations Officer (PRO). Your company PRO will submit your medical certificate, passport, Resident ID application form, and attested education certificates to the General Directorate of Residency and Foreigners Affairs – Abu Dhabi (GDRFA), and pay the required fees. At the same time, they will also apply for your labour card; the Ministry of Labour website (mol.go.ae) has a facility to check the status of your labour card application online. Your employer will typically start the visa application process during your probation period. They will also be responsible for renewing the card when needed.

Labour Card

If you are sponsored by your employer, the company will apply for your labour card, which is technically a permit to work. If you are on a family sponsorship and decide to work, your new employer, not your visa sponsor, will need to apply for a labour card. You'll need to give your employer a No Objection Certificate (NOC) from your sponsor, your passport with residence visa, attested education certificates, passport photos, and a copy of your sponsor's passport. All labour cards must be renewed every two or three years in line with your residence visa; eventually, the Resident ID will replace this card.

PROs and NOCs

In Abu Dhabi, a Public Relations Officer, or PRO, is your company's 'man who can' who liaises with various government departments and carries out admin procedures. The PRO will take care of all visa, residency, health card and labour card applications. An NOC is a No Objection Certificate, and is essentially a letter stating that the person in question permits you to carry out a particular procedure. You'll find you need one of these in a variety of situations, whether it's from your employer allowing you to switch jobs, or your own NOC permitting a family member to work. You'll also need an NOC when applying for a driving licence transfer.

Family Visa

If you have a UAE residence visa (employment) you should be able to sponsor your family members (wife, husband, children), allowing them to stay in the country as long as you are here. If the family member is already in the country on a visit visa you can still apply for their residency. If the family member ends up getting a job, they don't need to change to employer sponsorship, but the company will need to apply for a labour card for them.

You will need a minimum monthly salary of Dhs.3,000 plus accommodation, or a minimum all-inclusive salary of Dhs.4,000. If that's all in place, take your passport, the passports of all family members, your employment contract, bank statement as proof of salary transfer, tenancy contract, and attested marriage and birth certificates to the GDRFA. The family members will also need to pass the medical test and apply for a Resident ID; proof of both must also be submitted with their visa application. Typically, you will be responsible for making this visa application – not your employer – and for paying the required fees (Dhs.310 per family member, plus medical and Resident ID charges). For advice and guidance on applying for a visa or for up to date fees, contact the Abu Dhabi Ministry Of Current Affairs at mofa.gov.ae.

The family member's passport with residence visa stamp can be collected within three to five days, or you can pay Dhs.15 to have it couriered to you. You will be responsible for renewing their visa; this will be valid for two or three years in line with your employment visa. For anyone switching jobs, and therefore sponsorship, you will have to cancel your spouse and/or children's residence visas and then reapply for new visas once you have yours.

If you want to bring your parents over, you must have a minimum salary of Dhs.20,000 and an apartment with at least two bedrooms here. Your parents must prove they can't support themselves financially and will need to relocate to the UAE.

10 REASONS TO LIVE HERE

Abu Dhabi – simply put – is a great place to live. Have a look at our top 10 reasons to live here and you may just agree. You could even grab a copy of Explorer's Abu Dhabi Top 10 for good measure.

1. **It's ready-made for outside living** Sunshine all year • More than 2,000 parks and gardens and over 400km of coastline • **14 Blue Flag** beaches to lounge on
2. **High standard of living** Spacious villa/apartment lifestyle with private/shared pool • Live-in nanny or maid an affordable option • Access to world-class restaurants, attractions and hotels
3. **It's all about the money, money, money** Competitive, tax-free salaries • Expat packages including housing, education and health allowances, if you're lucky • Cheap as chips fuel
4. **Very low crime rate** It's a safe place to live and raise a family
5. **It's a melting pot of old and new** Middle Eastern traditions are well and truly alive in the local food, architecture, dress and museums • Where else can you watch camel racing and the F1 in one weekend?
6. **Access to world-class education** Highly rated public schools and universities
7. **Developing arts and cultural centre** The capital will be home to the Guggenheim and the Louvre – it doesn't get artier than that • International superstars with the likes of Muse, The Rolling Stones, Rihanna and Madonna, come to town – and you can get tickets!
8. **Meet and work with many nationalities** With over 120 nationalities, it's a mini United Nations
9. **You're at the centre of everything – literally** It's only a 30 minute drive maximum to any attraction, restaurant or beach from home • Abu Dhabi airport is less than a five-hour flight away from Goa, Seychelles, parts of Africa, Asia, Europe and the Maldives • Depending on traffic, it's just over an hour's drive to Dubai
10. **It's the future** Forward-thinking companies • Fast-developing landscape • Growing economy

Sponsoring Your Husband

If you are a woman, you can sponsor your husband and kids if you have a minimum salary of Dhs.10,000 per month. If you are in this situation you should contact the GDRFA and present your case. However, a husband sponsored by his wife must renew his visa annually, while a woman sponsored by her husband need only renew every two or three years.

Older Children

For parents sponsoring children, difficulties arise when sons (not daughters) turn 18. Unless they are enrolled in full-time education in the UAE, they must transfer their visa to an employer. Alternatively, parents can pay a one-off Dhs.5,000 security deposit and apply for an annual visa. Daughters can stay on their father's sponsorship until they get married.

Property Owners

Owners of UAE properties worth at least Dhs.1 million can apply for a six-month multiple-entry permit, which is renewable for Dhs.1,100 provided the owner leaves and then re-enters the country. This is a permit, and doesn't give the holder as many rights as residency, such as being able to apply for a UAE driving licence, bank account, etc.

Domestic Worker Visa

A domestic worker residence visa allows a maid or nanny to legally live and work in the UAE and is valid for one year.

To sponsor a domestic worker visa, you must have a salary above Dhs.6,000 per month and be able to provide the maid with monthly salary, housing, food, medical insurance and a biannual airfare back to their home country. The process is very similar to sponsoring a family member, the main difference being a higher visa fee of 12 times the worker's salary. He/she must be a national of Bangladesh, India, Ethiopia, Indonesia, Philippines or Sri Lanka, be under 58 years, and must have passed the medical test and applied for a Resident ID card. The process is then the same as for a family visa, although you'll be asked to sign a contract stating the domestic worker's salary.

Medical Test

Any expat over the age of 18 must pass a medical test in order to get any type of residence visa. You will be tested for communicable diseases such as tuberculosis and HIV; if your tests are positive you will be deported to your home country. If you are sponsored by your employer, your PRO will arrange for you to take the medical test at a government clinic, known as screening centres. Otherwise, it's up to you to get yourself to a screening centre with the following: test form completed in Arabic (there are typing offices near the screening centres that can do this for you for around Dhs.20), passport and visit visa, proof that your Resident ID application is underway, and the test fee of Dhs.250.

Once you have taken the required tests (expect to wait for around one to three hours, although you can pay Dhs.500 for a VIP/same-day service) you will be given a receipt, which will tell you when to collect your medical certificate (usually three days later). Check haad.ae to see your medical results online.

Female domestic workers must take a pregnancy test as part of the medical exam. All domestic workers, as well as those working at nurseries, salons and health clubs, must also complete a course of Hepatitis B vaccinations, which costs Dhs.50; this is then valid for 10 years, so keep the certificate as proof.

You will need to take a medical test every two or three years depending on when you need to renew your residence visa; domestic workers must take the test annually in line with their visa.

Screening Centres

There are three centres in the city, located near Al Jazira Sports Stadium (02 496 9666); near Sheikh Khalifa Medical City on Hazaa Bin Zayed St (02 6331300); and in the Mussafah area (02 651 0555).

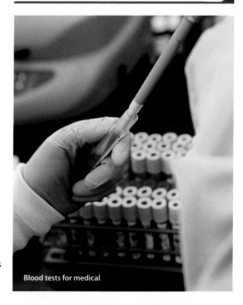

Blood tests for medical

Cost Of Living

According to the 2014 Cost of Living survey by Mercer, Abu Dhabi was ranked 68th in the world, an increase of fifteen places since 2013. Many expats still find they enjoy a higher quality of life here than back home, but it's worth calculating just how far that salary can take you.

Bargain Hunters

Residents soon learn that there are many ways to get discounts on everything from restaurant meals to beauty treatments. There are several online companies offering special deals, such as groupon.ae and cobone.com, as well as books of discount vouchers such as The Entertainer, which is available at most supermarkets and book shops and also now as an app.

Hidden Costs

Fortunate expats will have housing, health, visas for spouses, a return flight home every year, a car and even their child's education paid for. However, not all employers offer this, so an attractive looking tax-free salary can soon be eaten up. There are also set-up costs for things like internet, water and electricity which aren't taken into account in most cost of living reports.

Housing

Housing is one of the biggest outlays. If you're paying rent for yourself you may need a personal loan to find the annual rent, which is usually paid in four or fewer cheques. A one-bedroom apartment in a good area is likely to cost upwards of Dhs.90,000 per year, so you'd need around Dhs.7,500 per month, plus budget for internet, electricity and water bills if not included. Expect to pay roughly one third of your salary on your accommodation.

Maids & nannies

A maid may cost Dhs.2,000 to Dhs.3,000 a month plus a food, clothes and toiletries allowance. You'll also need to cover their flight home at least every two years, their annual visa costs and basic health insurance.

Transport costs

A 15 minute taxi journey comes in at as little as Dhs.25. Likewise, an inner city bus fare is just Dhs.2 with an additional 5 fils per km to the suburbs. Petrol is extremely cheap too, costing around Dhs.100 to fill up an average-sized family car. You can rent an older car from as little as Dhs.1,400 per month, but Dhs.2,200 will get you something new and well insured. If you buy a car, expect to pay around 20% less than the equivalent in Europe.

Food & drink

The majority of fruits and vegetables are imported so cost a premium; a bag of lettuce can cost Dhs.25. It's a similar story for many of the familiar brands from your home country. However, there are more affordable supermarkets and markets, plus other items are much cheaper in the UAE so it can balance out. Eating out and drinking in hotels can be very expensive as alcohol incurs added tax on top of the tourism tax and service charge. Many bars have discounted happy hours or ladies' nights, otherwise, it can cost as much as Dhs.50 for a pint of beer.

Education

For an international school you can expect to pay Dhs.30,000-50,000 per year for nursery and primary education, and upwards of Dhs.60,000 per year for secondary school. Ouch! On top of this you will usually need to pay around Dhs.500 to put your child's name on a waiting list, and a registration fee (around Dhs.2,000), which comes off your fees. Like housing, expect to pay about one third of your salary on education.

Health insurance

All employers must provide employees with basic health insurance. However, you may want to pay extra for more comprehensive health insurance, with extra cover for dental, maternity etc. This can cost about Dhs.180 a month. Without insurance, a medical consultation will cost you around Dhs.150-300, a dental check-up Dhs.250, and a hip replacement Dhs.50,000.

Health Card

Anyone on an employment residence visa is entitled to a Daman health insurance card, paid for by their employer; this may also cover family members. The card grants you medical treatment at government and private hospitals and facilities across the UAE. Alternatively, your employer may offer you private medical insurance. See Health for more information.

Resident Identity Card

All residents of Abu Dhabi need to register with the Emirates Identity Authority (EIDA) for a Resident Identity Card (previously known as the Emirates ID). The card contains the holder's address, photo, date of birth and fingerprints and is now an official source of identification in the UAE. It will eventually replace all other cards, such as health and labour cards. You need to apply for this before applying for your residence visa, and those without proof of an application in process will not be able to complete the medical test required for a visa. Additionally, if you fail to sign up for one, you will face daily fines.

The Resident ID costs Dhs.100 per year of visa validity (so from Dhs.100-300) plus Dhs.80 typing cost; it must also be renewed in line with your residence visa, so every two or three years. Children under the age of 15 also need one, but the fee is halved. If on an employment visa, the application is wrapped up in the visa process and taken care of by your company PRO. If not, you can find a list of registration centres and further details at id.gov.ae – and easily apply yourself.

If you're registering yourself you'll need to take your passport to an authorised typing centre to get the forms processed. You'll then receive an SMS confirmation of your appointment to get your fingerprints and photograph taken at an EIDA centre. Another SMS will be sent when your Resident ID is ready to collect.

UAE residents who wish to bypass immigration lines when entering and exiting the country can now activate the eGate service on their Resident ID. It costs Dhs.150 to register or renew, and the service is valid for two years. You can apply at the eGate shop at Terminal 1 in the airport.

Apply Online

You can apply online at id.gov.ae and pay by credit card for first-time registration, renewals and replacement ID cards. This not only speeds up the process, it saves the need to visit a typing centre. If applying for a new card, you'll then be able to reserve an appointment to visit a Resident ID registration centre where your fingerprints and a photograph will be taken. Once it's time to renew your ID, you should be able to complete the entire process online.

Driving Licence

If you're in Abu Dhabi on a visit visa you can drive a rental car so long as you have a valid driving licence from your home country and an International Driving Permit (IDP). Some other emirates only require your national licence. Once you have your residence visa, however, you must apply for a UAE driving licence (apart from GCC nationals who are allowed to drive on their existing GCC licences). This licence is valid for 10 years. Many countries are given the option of a straightforward UAE conversion (see below). However, if you are not eligible, you will have to completely re-sit a theory and practical driving test.

Traffic Police
Traffic & Patrols Departments 02 419 6666
Traffic & Licensing Department 02 419 5555
adpolice.gov.ae

Automatic Licence Transfer

Citizens with licences from the following countries are eligible for automatic driving licence transfer: Australia, Austria, Belgium, Canada, Denmark, Finland, France, Germany, Greece, Ireland, Italy, Japan, Netherlands, New Zealand, Norway, Poland, South Africa, South Korea, Sweden, Switzerland, Turkey, United Kingdom, and United States.

Licence holders from some countries require translation or consulate letters: Canada, Greece, Cyprus, Poland, Turkey, Japan and South Korea.

Speed bumps are common

The full procedure to get your UAE driving licence, is explained in Explorer's *How-To* Guide. In short, you need to submit the following documents to the Traffic & Licensing Department on Al Dhafra Street: existing foreign licence, passport with residence visa, NOC from sponsor or employer, passport photo, and Dhs.200. You'll get an eye exam and have another photo taken at the department. The licence is produced within minutes and is valid for 10 years; it costs Dhs.100 to renew it.

Always keep your UAE driving licence in your vehicle; if you fail to produce it during a police spot check, you will be fined Dhs.200. It's not a bad idea to have a photo of the licence on your phone, on the off chance you don't have the physical licence when pulled over, this might earn you some leniency.

Liquor Licence

Abu Dhabi has a fairly liberal attitude towards alcohol, but, if you're here on a residence visa, you can only buy it for home consumption from a licensed liquor store, and only if you have a liquor licence. Hotels and sports clubs are allowed to serve alcohol in their bars or restaurants (the restaurant/bar Ornina at Al Bandar in Al Raha Beach and the O1NE Yas Island nightclub seem to be a few of the exceptions).

There's some confusion about what the legal situation really is, so let's clear a few things up. You should have a liquor licence to buy alcohol from a liquor store in Abu Dhabi, but in some other emirates this is not the case. However, even if you buy alcohol elsewhere you need a liquor licence in order to transport it. The reality is that it's very rare for people to be stopped and searched, and as long as you're driving carefully you should be ok. Have an accident though and it's likely to be a very different story.

Getting Your Licence

Applying for a liquor licence is straightforward, as long as you are non-Muslim and a resident of Abu Dhabi. The whole process can be carried out online at auhsl.ae, although some distributors like Gray Mackenzie & Partners (GMP) will do it for you if you take the necessary documents along. To apply online you'll need: a passport photo (JPEG), Resident ID scan (front and back both shown on a PDF), passport (PDF), passport visa page (PDF), a salary certificate addressed to 'Abu Dhabi Special Licence Office' or bank statements from the previous six months (PDF) and, if you hold a passport from a Muslim country but are non-Muslim, a Certificate of Religion (PDF).

Once all of those details are put into the system, select the beverage shop from the list that you'd like to collect your licence from and you'll be called when it's ready to pick up. It should take around 10

days to process your licence. Be aware that you're given a monthly allowance that you can spend on liquor, which is 20% of your monthly salary up to a maximum amount of Dhs.5,000. You also need to have a minimum salary of Dhs.2,500 per month. The limit is usually enough to last you a month, although if you've got a big party planned you might need to stockpile over a few months, since you can't overspend on your limit. The retailers in Abu Dhabi are African & Eastern, Cheers (NCTH), Eurostar Cellar, GMP, High Spirits (ADNH) and Spinneys Liquor (see Shopping).

Temporary Accommodation

If you're lucky, you've secured work before coming out here and your company will put you up in a hotel for a week or more while you secure living accommodation (if they don't provide their own accommodation for you). Compared to many other countries where a hotel is somewhere to sleep, eat a mediocre breakfast and host the odd business meeting, in Abu Dhabi you'll soon find that hotels are central to most things. Their restaurants and bars are some of the best in town, and as they are licensed, they become a bit of a hub for expats.

Hotel Apartments & Hostels

While it is famed for its opulent array of five-star hotels, Abu Dhabi can also cater for those on tighter budgets too, with some excellent options. This is particularly useful if your company is only willing to put you up for one week upon arrival, or if you've arrived with no accommodation provided. A cheaper alternative is to rent furnished accommodation on a daily, weekly or monthly basis. The often have a maid service as well as a gym and pool. There are also some hostels around the country which are listed online at uaeyha.com.

Al Ain Palace Hotel Corniche Rd, Al Danah, 02 679 4777, *alainpalacehotel.com*
Al Diar Regency Hotel MeenaSt, Al Meena, 02 676 5000, *aldiarhotels.com*
Cassells Hotel Apartments Shk Zayed The First St, Al Danah, 02 610 7777, *cassellshotelapartments.ae*
Centro Al Manhal Shk Rashid Bin Saeed St, Al Karamah, 02 811 5000, *rotana.com*
Centro Yas Island Yas Leisure Drive, Yas Island West, 02 656 4444, *rotana.com*
Holiday Inn Downtown Shk Zayed The First St, Al Markaziah, 02 615 6666 ihg.com
Howard Johnson Diplomat Hotel Fatima Bin Mubarak St, Al Danah, 02 671 0000, *hojo.com*
Park Inn By Radisson Abu Dhabi, Yas Island Hotel Yas Leisure Drive, Yas Island West, 02 656 2222, *parkinn.com*

SETTLING IN

Relocating to a new country is a major upheaval, especially if your support network of family and friends is left behind. It's important to build an Abu Dhabi network as soon as possible, as it will make the transition much easier and less stressful. You may already know friends-of-friends or old coworkers who have relocated to the UAE and it can be helpful to get in touch with them before your arrival so that you can start establishing a social life from the beginning.

For those who know no one, fortunately Abu Dhabi is an easy place to meet people. The transient nature of the society, with expats coming and going all of the time, means those who are here tend to be open, friendly, and accustomed to meeting new people. Your new friends will be an invaluable source of 'local knowledge' about the best restaurants, hairdressers, schools and more. As they have been in your shoes, they'll know exactly how you feel and most aren't shy when it comes to offering their pearls of wisdom. If you're finding it difficult to meet new friends, joining a local club or group may give you a good starting point. Here are a few to get you started.

National Groups

Abu Dhabi offers opportunities to meet people from across the world, but it can also be reassuring to have a network of friends from your own country. Below are just a few of the city's nationality-based groups.

Abu Dhabi Irish Society
irishsocietyabudhabi.com
The Abu Dhabi Irish Society is open to all Irish people and anyone wanting a taste of Irish culture in Abu Dhabi. Regular events include society outings, social evenings, Irish dancing classes and Gaelic games. The society also hosts the Irish Business Forum meetings.

American Women's Network
awnabudhabi.com
This well-organised women's group is one of the largest in the city and their regular coffee mornings are a great way to meet people. Though founded by North Americans, they welcome anyone.

Aussies Abroad
aussiesabroad-abudhabi.com
An organisation dedicated to the promotion of Australian culture in the UAE. Social and recreational events include regular drinks nights, annual Anzac Day functions and balls. No doubt there's a shrimp thrown on a barbie here and there too.

German Speaking Ladies of Abu Dhabi
gladies.de
This friendly group with over 200 members is happy to welcome anyone who speaks their language. Activities include cooking classes, coffee mornings, and trips to Dubai.

Royal Society of St George Abu Dhabi
rssgauh.com
An English-based society dedicated to raising money for charities through organised events and social evenings. Established in Abu Dhabi for over 30 years, the worldwide society was bestowed with its own Royal Charter in 1963.

The Scottish St Andrews Society of Abu Dhabi
scottishsocietyabudhabi.com
This group of expat Scots, joined by more than a few 'foreigners', enjoys getting together for social gatherings and Scottish cultural activities, including the Burns supper in January.

Social Networks

These social networking groups are great for meeting like-minded people in a friendly, social setting.

Meet-Up
meetup.com is a popular forum for finding friends with similar hobbies where you can arrange times for sessions in an easy-going manner, rather than having to stick to a rigid routine.

Online forums
Sites abudhabiwoman.com and expatwoman.com are invaluable sources of advice as well as ways to connect to fellow AD residents. Facebook has a bigger social presence in the Middle East than in other areas, and most active social groups maintain a page. You'll be able to find thousands of pages and groups just by typing 'Abu Dhabi' into the search box.

Internations
Active in over 390 global communities, Internations (internations.org) is a social network that 'connects global minds.' In practice, this translates to a number of well-attended social events held on a regular basis throughout the year. This specialised group encourages you to find others that share your passion for activities such as learning Arabic, golfing and more.

Places Of Worship

The UAE has a liberal and welcoming attitude to other religions. For example, there are several active churches established across Abu Dhabi. Even if you are not a regular church-goer, the churches here tend to also act as good community hubs, so it might be worth checking out any scheduled events or activities.

Evangelical Community Church Nr The British School Al Khubairat, Al Mushrif, 02 446 4563, *eccad.org*
St Andrew's Church Abu Dhabi Nr The British School Al Khubairat, Al Mushrif, 02 446 1631, *standrewauh.org*
St George's Orthodox Cathedral Nr The British School Al Khubairat, Al Mushrif, 02 446 4564, *stgeorgeorthodoxcathedralabudhabi.com*
St Joseph's Cathedral Abu Dhabi Nr The British School Al Khubairat, Airport Rd, 02 446 1929, *stjosephsabudhabi.org*
St Stephen's Syrian Orthodox Church Nr The British School Al Khubairat, Al Mushrif, 02 446 0711, *ststephensauh.org*

BEFORE YOU LEAVE

Whether you've been in Abu Dhabi for months or for years there's a checklist of things you'll need to take care of before getting on the plane for home. The main thing is to settle your debts, as you can get into serious trouble if caught trying to leave the country with outstanding loans or bills. Get electricity, water and other utilities disconnected and remember that most providers (ADDC and Etisalat) will need at least two days' notice to take a final reading and return any security deposits you have paid (keep hold of the original deposit receipt to smooth the process). You will need to settle the final bill before you'll be able to get the security deposit back.

If you're renting, your landlord may require a clearance certificate from ADDC to show you've paid all of your bills, so leave enough time for all the red tape. They will also want your apartment left as you found it in order to refund all of your deposit.

You'll need to go through all the official channels to close any bank accounts you have set up in the UAE. Be aware too, that banks have been known to freeze an individual's account once they have been informed by the sponsor of the visa cancellation, so it's a good idea to get your finances in order before you leave. For advice, check out askexplorer.com or Explorer's informative How To publication.

You may also need to sell your car and any other belongings you have that you're not taking back. Cars can be tricky if you still owe money on them, as you'll have a minimum amount you'll need to sell it for in order to clear the debt. Allow plenty of time to make the sale. Alternatively, if you can afford to take a bit of a hit then offloading it to a dealer can be a quicker option. As with other unwanted items, classifieds boards in supermarkets or adverts on dubizzle. com or facebook.com are helpful (the 'Abu Dhabi Marketplace' page is particularly popular). Personal adverts and house clearances can be fantastic for making a sale with as minimal fuss as possible. It's also a good idea to tell your friends and colleagues in the city that you have items for sale and spring cleaning your home before you leave the country.

Many expats moving to Abu Dhabi would rather buy from a fellow expat, especially when it comes to cars, as any questions can be more readily asked and answered. If your friends and colleagues aren't interested, they may well know somebody who is.

Organise your shipping and try to give your chosen shipping company as much notice as possible. It can be worth shopping around different companies to get the best rate. Finally, if you have pets then make sure their vaccinations are up to date before travelling, particularly the rabies vaccination. There are other procedures involved that are covered in the Pets section later. Ideally though, you need six months to prepare for taking a pet home. The other option is to rehome them with a new family residing in the city.

Cancelling Your Visa

Different visa types require slightly different cancellation procedures. If your residence visa was sponsored by your employer, then they will be responsible for cancelling it once you cease to work for them. It's a simple process – you'll have to submit your passport and sometimes sign a document saying you've received all monies owed to you. You'll need to hand in your Resident ID card too.

The visa should only take five days to be cancelled (longer during Ramadan), and your employer can pay to have the process fast-tracked if you need your passport back in a hurry. Once the visa is cancelled you have 30 days before you have to leave the country – if you stay after this, you'll be fined at a rate of Dhs.25 per day for the first six months, Dhs.50 per day for the next six months, and Dhs.100 after that.

If you are in Abu Dhabi on a family visa and have separated, then your husband or wife will need to help with the visa cancellation, even if that's a tricky thing to ask. If your spouse's company completed the paperwork, they will need your husband or wife to sign the cancellation papers.

Downtown Abu Dhabi

HOUSING

Housing is one of the great challenges of setting up in Abu Dhabi. Expat packages either include housing or an allowance to cover at least part of your accommodation costs, although the amounts are much smaller than in the boom days so it's likely that you'll need to top up from your own pocket to cover the rent or mortgage.

The first question to answer is: to rent or to buy? Most expats opt for renting as it gives more flexibility, particularly when you first arrive in the capital and are unsure of the best location to live in. Also, you need to have lived in Abu Dhabi for a minimum of six months before you can apply for a mortgage here, so your first year at least is likely to be in rented accommodation.

However, an increasing numbers of expats living in Abu Dhabi are now choosing to buy rather than rent property as they plan to put down longer term roots. Unfortunately, the days of getting a 90% mortgage are

over, and at the end of 2013 Central Bank announced a new ruling to cap mortgages. As restrictive as it sounds, the good news for those wanting to buy a home is banks have dropped interest rates to attract borrowers.

Property Search

All your property questions are answered in this section, from the legalities involved in purchasing a property to the amenities of each neighborhood in Abu Dhabi.

Like any major city, there is a varying scale of property: from labour camps for lower-paid workers and maid's rooms for domestic workers to modern high-rise apartments and spacious villas in affluent or up-and-coming areas across the capital. And, whether you're single or moving here with a family in tow; whether you're living on a budget or got cash to splash, there *is* a place for you to call home.

ACCOMMODATION

When You Arrive

Apart from securing your new job, getting your accommodation satisfactorily sorted out is probably the most crucial factor in making your move to Abu Dhabi a success. This section covers the procedures and practicalities involved in both the rental and ownership markets.

Companies are legally obliged to provide employees with either housing or an accommodation allowance. This really varies as there are no official guidelines as to what this should be. Some large organisations have complexes for employees, other companies have arrangements with particular developments and reserve a percentage of their properties for workers. If you're not keen on the housing you're offered, your company may let you have the money to find your own place instead.

If you haven't heard the words 'company accommodation' thrown around, it's worth double checking a prospective job offer. Companies who don't provide specific accommodation generally include the housing allowance in your salary, so don't expect any additional help. Your actual base salary will only be a percentage of your monthly pay packet, with the remainder a 'living allowance' made up of transport and housing. You can use your housing allowance on either rent or a mortgage.

Public sector employees working in Abu Dhabi are now required by law to also live in the emirate, or forfeit their housing allowance; they must show their tenancy contract when renewing their residence visa. There are some (not yet published) exceptions to this rule, and applications are reviewed on a case by case basis. Happy house hunting!

Apartments

Abu Dhabi has an extensive range of apartments available, from studio flats to larger four-bedroom offerings. There's also an extensive price range, with posh one-bedroom apartments in new developments costing in excess of Dhs.130,000 per year. Elsewhere you can find a two-bedroom apartment for half that price. However, many of the cheaper properties are older and have noisier air-conditioning units built into the walls rather than the centralised air conditioning (C/AC) of the more modern builds. C/AC can be more expensive, but is much quieter and less intrusive.

C/AC cost is generally included in the ADDC electric bill, but residents in some apartments may need to pay cooling provider Tabreed directly. In winter months you won't need air conditioning much, so make sure it's possible to turn it off.

Expats with families tend to prefer villas to apartments, but facilities in the larger apartment complexes can make for fun, comfortable and safe family living. Make sure to evaluate all your options.

No Place To Park

Many apartment buildings will provide only one spot in basement parking garages, even for 3-bed flats. In some areas, this can be a big issue, as street parking can be hard to come by. Make sure to check out a prospective building's parking situation, as circling the block for an hour each evening is no one's idea of fun.

Hotel & Serviced Apartments

Hotel apartments are ideal if you need short-term, furnished accommodation, but they can be expensive. Apartments can be rented on a daily, weekly, monthly and annual basis and rates can vary depending on time of year. Prices will also vary greatly according to the area and facilities provided, although they will usually have satellite TV, a maid service and decent leisure facilities. Water, electricity and sometimes internet are included in the rent, which saves a lot of administration.

Villas

Villa living is an attractive prospect, but the best villas don't come cheap. However, if you shop around you might be able to find a villa for less than a higher-end apartment with the same number of bedrooms. Independent villas tend to have more space and larger gardens, but if you're after a swimming pool or gym then community complexes with shared facilities may be the best bet. It's worth remembering that air conditioning charges will be higher in a villa than in an apartment.

Step By Step Guide

Like it or not, living and working in Abu Dhabi involves paperwork and bureaucracy. But help is at hand. Explorer's How-To Guide tells you – in plain and simple language – what you'll need, where to go and how long it's likely to take. From visas and licences, to housing, cars and doing business, this guide provides you with step-by-step instructions and useful tips to make your life easier. See also askexplorer.com.

Villa Sharing

Sharing a villa is a popular option with young professionals for economic and lifestyle reasons. The downside is the lack of privacy and the chore of finding a new housemate when someone moves out. If you're looking to share an abode, dubizzle.com is the best place to start. The legality of sharing shouldn't be ignored though. Unmarried couples may not live together and neither can unrelated people of the opposite sex, yet it's a difficult law for the authorities to monitor and only likely to cause an issue if there are other reasons for police to get involved in your affairs. Subletting is also illegal without landlord consent.

Home Address

Abu Dhabi is undergoing a dramatic change in how addresses are assigned to buildings, thanks to the Onwani project. Despite the city having an American-style grid system, current addresses are confusing and often rely on local landmarks. However, throughout 2014 some 200,000 unique building addresses and 12,000 new street signs were installed. All residents of the Abu Dhabi emirate are scheduled to get a distinct postal address with house number, building number and street name by the end of 2015. The new system has also eliminated any duplicate address references to clear up any confusion. These reforms will also mean emergency calls, taxi bookings, arranging utilities, home deliveries and online shopping will become much easier. In the meantime, it's possible to rent a PO Box from the main post office, but most expats find it easier to have incoming post directed to the PO Box number at their work.

Real Estate Agents

Asteco Property Management SJ Tower, Shk Rashid Bin Al Maktoum St, Al Karamah, 02 626 0088, *asteco.com*
Aztec Properties Al Zubara Tower, Al Salam St, Al Danah, 02 645 1672, *aztecproperties.ae*
Better Homes Block D, Al Raha Blvd, Al Raha, 600 522 212, *bhomes.com*
Cassells Real Estate Corniche Tower, Al Khubeirah, 02 681 7666, *cassellsrealestate.org*
Cluttons EMC Bldg, Shk Rashid Bin Saeed St, Al Madina Al Riyadiya, 02 441 1225, *abudhabi.cluttons.com*
Crompton Partners Estate Agents Zayed Sports City, Al Madina Al Riyadiya, 02 441 7780, *cpestateagents.com*
Finders & Keepers Regus Al Bateen Business Centre, Al Bateen, 02 406 9428, *findersnkeepers.com*
Future View Real Estate Shaheen Air International Bldg, Liwa St, Al Danah, 02 627 2992, *futureviewproperty.com*

Hayatt Real Estate Sultan Bin Zayed The First St, Al Nahyan, 02 4918 790, *hayattrealestate.ae*
Homestyle Property Nr Lulu Centre, Al Salam St, Al Danah, 02 672 3220, *homestyle-property.co.ae*
Khidmah > *p.xiv, p.47* 10th Floor, Mazyad Mall, Mohammed Bin Zayed City, 02 408 0800, *khidmah.com*
Sherwoods Gibca Tower, Nr Al Noor Hospital, Shk Khalifa Bin Zayed St, Al Danah, 02 626 6887, *sherwoodsproperty.com*
Silver Lake Property Management Seven Star Rent A Car Bldg, Hamdan Bin Mohammed St, Al Danah, 02 676 2465, *silverlakeuae.com*

Renting A Home

Paying for rental accommodation in Abu Dhabi may be very different to what you're used to. Most landlords demand one cheque, and if you manage to negotiate two or three cheques expect to pay a slightly higher rent. Some landlords accept post-dated cheques that are cashed on their due date, while some employers will arrange to pay your rent payments directly from your salary, which can save a lot of hassle. Rental contracts are typically one year, and 60 days' notice must be given if you or the landlord want to cancel or amend the contract. Due to the pay-upfront system, it's not usually possible to get a refund if you break your lease early.

Finding A Rental Home

Using a real estate agent is the easiest and often best option, although they will charge you for their services, usually around 5% of the annual rent or Dhs.5,000. Only ever deal with an Abu Dhabi Municipality-registered broker or agent to avoid being the victim of any rental scam. Ask the agent for their trade licence number, which verifies that their office is licensed by the government to manage, rent and sell real estate. If you do not use a registered agent, you will not be protected if there are any problems. Alternatively, you can check out classified adverts in local newspapers or look online at sites like dubizzle. com or propertyfinder.ae. It can also be useful to drive around the areas you fancy living in. Often there will be 'To Let' signs on vacant villas. If you like a certain apartment building or villa complex then ask the security guards if there are any available units, if they don't know the answer, they'll give you the number of the property manager.

Once you find a property, ask for proof of ownership of the property being rented; a licensed agent will be able to present the owner's documents (including a copy of the landlord's passport and proof of ownership). Always demand a receipt for payments made by cash or cheque. For advice, contact the Abu Dhabi Ministry Of Current Affairs (mofa.gov.ae).

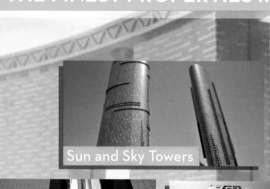

Tenancy Contract

All landlords must register their properties and all tenancy/rental contracts through the government's Tawtheeq online system which is overseen by the Abu Dhabi Ministry Of Current Affairs. If a dispute does arise between you and the landlord, no application can be submitted to the Rent Dispute Settlement Committee unless you have this in place.

In order to complete the contract for a rental, the agent will need a copy of your passport and visa, and a rent cheque or cheques. To rent through your company you will need a copy of the company's trade licence, a passport copy of whoever is signing the rent cheque, and the cheque itself. In addition to the financial terms, your lease will state what you are liable for in terms of maintenance and what your landlord's responsibilities are. Do check that the landlord provides you with maintenance cover, ideally 24-hour, to ensure that common problems with the AC, plumbing etc are dealt with and paid for.

Rent Renewals

Since the government removed the 5% rent cap at the end of 2013, landlords can now raise rents based on prevailing market conditions. If a landlord wishes to raise the rent, he must inform tenants in writing 60 days before the end of the rental period. If he fails to do so, you can dispute the increase through Abu Dhabi Rent Dispute Settlement Committee.

Before signing on the dotted line, check the following:

- **Rent payment:** Do you have to pay a whole year upfront or in a series of post-dated cheques? If you can afford to provide fewer cheques, you can use that as a bargaining chip to lower the rent.
- **Maintenance:** Who is responsible for day to day maintenance and repairs? Some rents may be fully inclusive, or you may be able to negotiate a cheaper rent if you carry out repairs yourself.
- **Water and electricity:** Some apartments have a standard fee for electricity, some rents even include electricity and water. Most don't. If yours doesn't, you'll need to pay a Dhs.1,000 water and electricity deposit to Abu Dhabi Distribution Company (ADDC).
- **Parking:** Landlords do not have to provide parking, so check first if there is an additional fee for underground or covered parking.
- **Security deposit:** Is one required and if so, how much? The standard is usually between Dhs.3,000 and Dhs.5,000 or between 2% and 5% of the annual rent. Some landlords stipulate a fixed amount of around Dhs.5,000. This is a one-off payment and fully refundable if there are no issues.
- **Home improvements:** Is DIY and decorating allowed in the property?
- **Pets:** Are they permitted and are there any restrictions on the type of pet? In some apartments, cats are permitted but dogs are not; there are seldom such restrictions in villas.

HOUSING ABBREVIATIONS	When looking for property to rent in newspaper classifieds or online, there's a whole new language to learn. Here's our guide to some of the most common abbreviations used by landlords and agents.

BR	Bedroom
C A/C	Centralised air conditioning (sometimes included in the rent)
C/port	Car port (usual in compounds)
D/S	Double-storey villa
Eff	Efficiency
Ensuite	Bedroom has private bathroom
Ext S/Q	Servants' quarters located outside the villa
Fully fitted	Includes appliances (oven, kitchen, refrigerator, washing machine)
Hall flat	Apartment has an entrance hall
HWS	Hot water system
L/D	Living/dining area
M/a	Mature age (either you or the building)
Ns/prof	Non-smoking professional
OSP	Off-street parking
PWK	Per week
S/S	Single-storey villa
Shared pool	Pool is communal for all villas on compound
Spac	Spacious
W A/C	Window air conditioning (often indicates an older building)
W/robes	Built-in wardrobes (closets)

Abu Dhabi New Unified Addressing and Wayfinding System

Benefits

 Improving emergency response times

 Reducing travel time with more effective signage

 Helping to reduce environmental impact

 Expanding exploration by residents and tourists

 Delivering goods, simpler and quicker

 Tapping into the growth of local and global online commerce

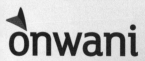
onwani

DEPARTMENT OF MUNICIPAL AFFAIRS دائـرة الـشـؤون الـبـلـديـة

بلديـة المنطقـة الـغـربيـة
WESTERN REGION MUNICIPALITY

بلديـة مدينـة العين
AL AIN CITY MUNICIPALITY

بلديـة مدينـة أبوظبـي
ABU DHABI CITY MUNICIPALITY

- **Gardens:** If in a villa, are you responsible for the maintenance? This can become costly due to arid conditions and the amount of water needed. A well and pump can be installed for between Dhs.1,500 and Dhs.3,000, which may work out more cost effective in the long run.

It's also worth noting that even if you find a property to rent yourself, a real estate agent will likely be needed to secure the deal. You can expect the fee for this to still be around 5% of the annual rent or between Dhs.2,500 and Dhs.5,000.

Early Termination Penalties

Most leases are usually fixed for one year. If you leave early you will probably have to pay a substantial penalty. If you really want to get out of your lease, you may be able to sublet it to new tenants, but this can only be done with your landlord's consent.

The Rent Committee

The Abu Dhabi Rent Dispute Settlement Committee (800 2353) was created to oversee rent disagreements between landlords and tenants. The committee also oversees rental prices and, where necessary, can impose increase caps. Any tenant that has a dispute regarding rent increases, eviction and breaches of contract, can take their case to the committee; in many cases, the committee rules in favour of the tenant. If the case goes to court, the Arabic copy of your lease will be the version referred to, so make sure you get it translated before you sign your lease agreement in case there are any hidden extras. Full details about settling rental disputes are available on Abu Dhabi Government's website, abudhabi.ae (under 'Land Transactions') or you can call the committee directly. If your property is managed by Abu Dhabi Commercial Properties, you can lodge a complaint with them (adcp.ae).

Khidmah Asset Management > p.xiv, 47

Emirati company Khidmah was founded in 2009 and has established itself as a leading property service provider with prestigious clients across the Middle East, GCC region and globally. As well as sourcing lease and sale properties for clients, Khidmah offers housekeeping and property management solutions. Call 02 408 0800 or visit khidmah.com for details.

Buying A Home

Expats can't own property on Abu Dhabi island, but the government set aside 'investment zones' away from the main island where expats from outside GCC countries can buy on 99-year leasehold leases (known as an Usufruct lease). Some of these areas have the newest buildings and apartment blocks in the city. The main investment zone areas are: Saadiyat Island, Al Raha Beach, Al Reem Island, Al Maryah Island, Yas Island and Al Reef. Expats can also lease and build on undeveloped land on a 50 year development lease (known as a Musatahah lease), but it is very uncommon for individual expatriates to do so as few undeveloped plots are even released for private ownership/leasing.

Property prices in Abu Dhabi weren't hit quite so badly as in neighbouring Dubai during the economic crisis, but they still took a bit of a bashing. They have recovered remarkably well since that point, and in the third quarter of 2014, the average sale price for residential units was Dhs.16,000 per square metre. At the height of the market in 2009 that figure was Dhs.17,222 per square metre.

The residential developments where expats can buy are large-scale projects created by Abu Dhabi developers. Generally they are extremely reputable, but the level of finish and facilities management capability will vary from development to development. When considering buying, it is essential to research the development company thoroughly before jumping in and making a binding commitment.

Major Developers

Aldar Properties (aldar.com): Projects include Yas Island, Al Raha Beach, World Trade Center, their iconic HQ building (the round one), Al Gurm Resort and Al Raha Gardens. Merged with Sorouh in 2013, the company behind Shams Abu Dhabi on Reem Island.
Tourism Development & Investment Company (TSIC) (tdic.ae): Responsible for many of Saadiyat Island's cultural, residential, commercial and tourism projects; developer of Sir Bani Yas and Delma islands, plus a number of Abu Dhabi's hotels and resorts.
Mubadala Development Company (mubadala.com): Owned by the Abu Dhabi government, this is the company behind the development of Al Maryah Island.
Tamouh (tamouh.com): This company is the main force behind the huge Reem Island development and they recently resumed work on Meena Plaza, a huge complex set to revolutionise the port area.

House Hunting

The list of real estate agents earlier is a great place to start, but it's also possible to trawl through the property listings in Gulf News (gnads4u.com) or on dubizzle.com. If you're already in touch with a real estate lawyer, it's worth asking for names of reputable agents. In general, expect to pay around 2-5% of the purchase price to the agent upon completion of sale.

Mortgages

Before you go house hunting, it's advisable to get a mortgage in place, or 'approval in principle', so you're in a position to make an offer should you find the place of your dreams. A 10% deposit is required to secure a property and this could be money wasted should you then find nobody is willing to lend to you.

At the end of 2013, the UAE Central Bank announced a new ruling to cap mortgages (also known as home loans here). For properties valued at less than Dhs.5 million, expat first-time buyers can get a mortgage of 75%. For properties valued above Dhs.5 million, expats can only get a mortgage of 65%. Expats taking out a 'home loan' for a second or subsequent property will be able to get a 60% mortgage. Financing for off-plan property, meaning it hasn't yet been built, is restricted to 50% regardless of the value of the property or the nationality of the applicant.

A mortgage can be calculated on more than one salary, providing they are listed as co-borrowers in the loan contract. Central Bank rules also state that your monthly mortgage instalments and other debts should not consume more than 50% of your income. Expats may also find it more difficult to get a mortgage if they are single and have been here less than six months. If you have a family, a stable job and have been in the country for a few years then they presume you are committed to the country and are happier to lend you money.

The amount financed by the lender also varies and depends on whether the property is a villa or an apartment, where they are and who built them. It's also worth noting that some banks and lenders will only provide mortgages for select developments. Additionally, they may also have different acceptance criteria and mortgage processes, which change frequently, so it's advisable to do your homework. There are international names such as HSBC, Barclays, Standard Chartered and Citibank alongside local financial houses, including Emirates NBD, Mashreq, Abu Dhabi Commercial Bank (ADCB) and the National Bank of Abu Dhabi (NBAD). Fortunately, interest rates are currently much lower than the 9% highs of the pre-financial crisis era, with fixed rate deals available at around 2-4% depending on the term.

Islamic Mortgages

Shariah-compliant or Islamic mortgages are alternative financing options available to both Muslims and non-Muslims. The bank purchases the asset on behalf of the buyer who then effectively leases it back from the institution at a marked-up price but with zero interest. The bank owns the title deeds of the purchased property until the full amount is repaid.

Equity release and mortgage transfers are now available on the market too, offering investors the opportunity to secure better rates; international mortgages offering loans in currency denominations other than dirhams are also available.

Purchase Costs

Make sure you budget for the additional costs associated with buying a house, as they can add up to significant amounts. The obligatory amounts equate to around 6% of the purchase price, not including any cash deposit.

Solicitor fees: By law there is no requirement to have a solicitor act for you when buying property in Abu Dhabi, but you may wish to employ legal help to see you through the process. Legal costs will vary depending on whose services you use.
Real estate agent/broker's fees: The flat fee to the agent is usually 2-5% of the purchase price, upon completion of sale.
Mortgage broker fee: Often 0.5% of the purchase price or a pre-determined flat fee.
Arrangement fee: Dhs.3,000, but can often be offset against the processing fee.
Processing fee: Often around 1.5% of purchase fee, but minimum amounts of around Dhs.3,000 are common.
Valuation fee: Expect to pay around Dhs.3,000.
Life and household insurance: Life insurance to the value of the property is mandatory for a mortgage. Shop around for the best deal.
Land registry: Payable to the Abu Dhabi Department of Municipal Affairs (dma.abudhabi.ae, 02 678 5555), the fee is 1% of property price and establishes legal ownership of the property.

The Buying Process

Once you've found your dream home and your offer has been accepted, a Sales & Purchase Agreement (SPA) will be drawn up by the real estate agency, which defines all the terms and conditions for the transfer of property. If you require a mortgage, the lender will issue an unconditional offer letter, which states the terms and conditions of the mortgage.

To process the mortgage, you will need your passport plus copies, six months of bank statements, salary confirmation from your employer and six months of salary slips. Mortgage terms are usually for 25 years, and while age restrictions are in place they do vary. Many lenders will normally finance individuals up to 65 years of age.

Once the paperwork is signed and sent back to the lender, the settlement process can begin. This is when the lender transfers the mortgage payment to either the seller or to the existing lender who has the first charge over the property. This usually occurs on

Al Raha Gardens

the day of the transfer or as per the conditions of the lender. Equal instalments are then taken from your bank every month. When you buy a property, in order for the full transfer of ownership to take place, you will need to register the property. And then? It's time to collect your keys and call the removal van.

Maintenance Fees

Maintenance fees are payable by the property owner and cover the cost to the developer of maintaining all the shared facilities and communal areas such as the gym, pool and security personnel. Fees are typically paid annually. The amount varies between developers and may be written into your contract fine print as 'subject to change', so try to get as much clarity on this issue as possible before you sign.

Real Estate Law

There's no requirement to have a solicitor act for you when buying a property, or selling one, but it will give you peace of mind. You're strongly advised to organise a local will if buying a property as inheritance can be a legal minefield here in the UAE. Without a relevant will in place you may find your assets don't automatically go to the right person. The One Group will give you advice on preparing your will (theonegroup.co).

Land Registry

The government of Abu Dhabi's Department of Municipal Affairs (dma.abuhabi.ae, 02 678 5555) is the emirate's land registry and transaction agency. Upon completion of a sale, a land registry fee (1% of the property price) must be paid by both the buyer and seller. Registering the property establishes legal ownership and provides the new owner with a title deed, safeguarding against future disputes.

Selling A Home

Finding a good agent to help you sell your home is important, as private property sales here are quite rare. Agents can charge up to 2% of the property price to cover the costs of marketing your property through print and online media, as well as at open days. The list of estate agents towards the beginning of the section can be your best bet as they will have experience of the process and know the best places to advertise. You can do this by yourself as advertising property online has become increasingly popular. However, be prepared for plenty of calls from bargain hunters offering way below the asking price. There is no legal need for a property survey, assessment or solicitor so these fees are negated. However, if you do decide to go it alone, it is advisable to appoint a solicitor.

Rental And Buying Costs

For Abu Dhabi residents the decision to rent or to buy can be a tough one, so it makes sense to carefully consider all financial aspects.

Housing is usually an expat's biggest monthly expense, so it pays to be aware of the local market. Two decisions have greatly affected housing prices in Abu Dhabi: the location mandate for public employees and the removal of the rent cap.

A 5% cap on rental price increases was abolished in 2013, allowing landlords to charge as they see fit. This has meant some residents who were long-time tenants in a property have seen rents rise dramatically – the cap meant their rents hadn't moved in line with the market, so they were living in artificially cheap accommodation for a long time.

Also in 2013, a new law required that Abu Dhabi Government employees live in the emirate in order to receive their housing allowance. This forced an estimated 15,000 workers to relocate to the capital (many had been commuting from Dubai) and raised demand for housing.

As a result of these two events, the housing market soared during the first half of 2014, leading some analysts to wonder if prices were in a bubble similar to that of 2009. By the third quarter of the year, however, the rapid pace of growth had already slowed, leading most to foresee market stabilisation in the near future.

The reality is that rental and buying costs vary widely depending on area and building. Luxury buildings in Raha Beach, Reem Island and Saadiyat Island are popular with wealthy locals and expats and rents have risen accordingly. In other areas, and especially in the older parts of the city, rents have actually fallen.

Some employers provide accommodation free of charge. Others provide a housing allowance which may or may not cover the rent for where you'd like to live. With their employer's permission, expats may also use their allowance to buy a property. Whichever option you take, you should still aim to keep the cost of your accommodation to a maximum of a third of your income, as utilities and living costs soon add up.

Renting

While the recent volatility might seem worrying, the plentiful supply of new properties and the ample land supply for future developments mean that rental prices are likely to regain stability. It's unlikely that prices will escalate beyond control as landlords are likely to find a lack of willing tenants should they price rental properties too high.

This is particularly true as the number of expats who have their accommodation paid for entirely by their employers is reducing all the time, so your rental costs really do need to be a consideration. Generally, rent is paid in full for the year at the beginning of the term too, so you may have to factor in the interest charged on a personal bank loan.

Buying

If you're considering buying in Abu Dhabi, it's worth being armed with as much information as possible, as some things can be quite different in the UAE compared to your home country. Many of the associated costs are covered elsewhere in this chapter, so the questions here are whether and what to buy.

More residents are certainly deciding to buy, judging by recent figures. Apartment sale numbers were up 28% in the first half of 2014 over the previous year, according to Jones Lang Lasalle. Villa sales increased 27% year on year. More market supply has buoyed these numbers, as have relaxed mortgage restrictions.

Prices are also up: bayut.com reported a 16% increase in property sale prices in the first half of 2014. The release of several luxury property developments helped to boost these numbers. There are no signs that housing values will increase dramatically, which should be a good thing for the economy as whole.

Buying can mean either freehold or leasehold property, which depends hugely upon your location. Freehold gives non-GCC nationals the opportunity to own entirely, while leasehold offers a lease on the property which would usually run from a period between 30 and 99 years. Leasehold means that the land or the property is never entirely owned by the buyer in full, which can cause some insecurity.

Traditionally, non-GCC nationals could only buy on a leasehold basis but, since 2002, expats have freehold property rights within designated zones. Now, the majority of purpose-built, community style developments in Abu Dhabi boast freehold units, especially the new off-island developments. However, check at the time of buying what the visa status is for property owners, as this often changes.

Off-Plan Buying

The rapid buying and selling of off-plan properties, or properties that aren't yet constructed, was one of the contributors to the 2009 property bubble explosion. Since then, off-plan buying has come under more government regulation and scrutiny. It still remains a popular option for some developments, particularly in luxury areas such as Saadiyat which are developed by well-known companies. But many buyers are more interested in completed or near-completed properties as they want to see the finished product before purchasing. This can provide additional peace of mind and reassurance that the specifications are to their liking.

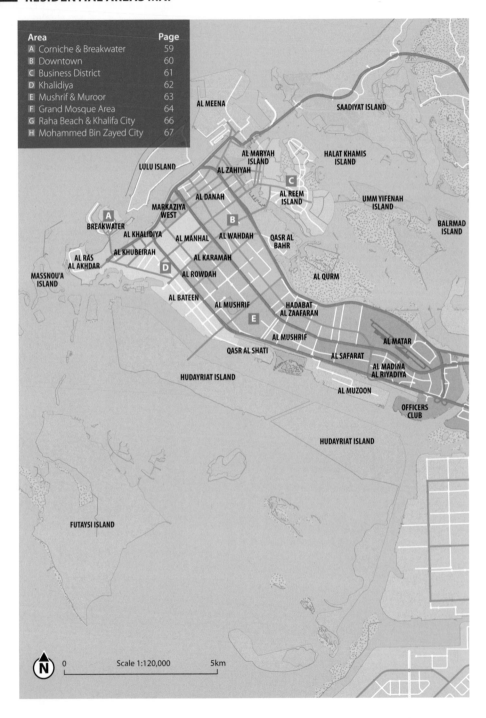

Area	Page
A Corniche & Breakwater	59
B Downtown	60
C Business District	61
D Khalidiya	62
E Mushrif & Muroor	63
F Grand Mosque Area	64
G Raha Beach & Khalifa City	66
H Mohammed Bin Zayed City	67

AL MEENA

SAADIYAT ISLAND

LULU ISLAND

AL MARYAH ISLAND

HALAT KHAMIS ISLAND

AL ZAHIYAH

C AL REEM ISLAND

UMM YIFENAH ISLAND

AL DANAH

MARKAZIYA WEST

A BREAKWATER

B

AL KHALIDIYA

AL MANHAL

AL WAHDAH

QASR AL BAHR

BALRMAD ISLAND

AL RAS AL AKHDAR

AL KHUBEIRAH

AL KARAMAH

MASSNOU'A ISLAND

D

AL ROWDAH

AL QURM

AL BATEEN

AL MUSHRIF

HADABAT AL ZAAFARAN

E

AL MUSHRIF

AL MATAR

QASR AL SHATI

AL SAFARAT

AL MADINA AL RIYADIYA

HUDAYRIAT ISLAND

AL MUZOON

OFFICERS CLUB

HUDAYRIAT ISLAND

FUTAYSI ISLAND

N

0   Scale 1:120,000   5km

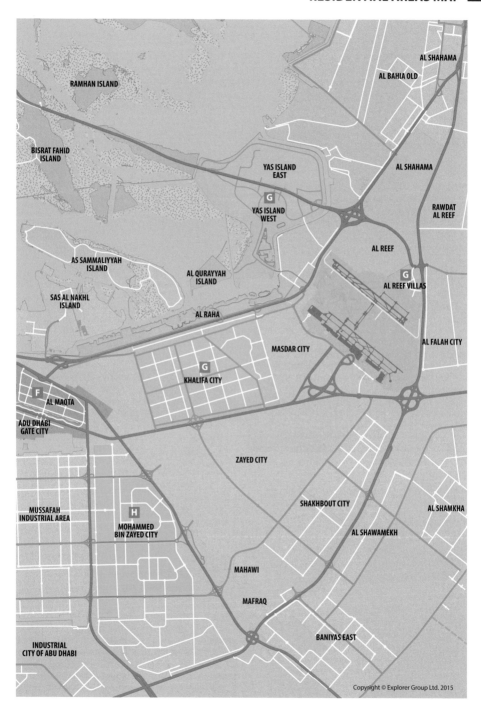

Al Bandar at Raha Beach

RESIDENTIAL AREAS

Picking the place to live that best suits your needs can be a particularly tricky task. This chapter gives an overview of the main residential areas (see map on previous page), including rental price ranges and descriptions of specific developments, to help you find the perfect place to move to. For further information on the schools, shops, attractions and healthcare see the relevant sections within this book.

Where To Live?
Abu Dhabi isn't short of interesting places to live and new options are constantly arriving on the market. From family-friendly compounds in the Khalifa Park area to the hustle and bustle of apartment living along the Corniche, Abu Dhabi has something for everyone. Many expats who work in Dubai find the newer developments near Abu Dhabi Airport (Al Raha Beach, Al Reef and Khalifa City) are convenient as they can

cut 30 minutes or more from the commute compared to central island locations. Whichever place you pick to live you're sure to find many great features, and the rest of the city's attractions will be just a short drive or taxi ride away.

Icon Key
You'll find these icons throughout the following section. They're a handy way to understand at a glance the main differences between housing developments in the same area, or to quickly compare the dominant housing types in different areas of the city.

 By the beach   Family friendly

 High-rise living   On a budget

Corniche & Breakwater

The Corniche stretches along the Arabian Gulf coast, from the 'seven-star' Emirates Palace right up to Port Zayed. Looking across the water, the Breakwater peninsula can be seen; it's home to the popular Marina Mall and the largest UAE flag in the city. The Corniche has traditionally been one of the most sought after areas to live, thanks to the expansive beach backed by green parks, abundance of shopping options and the multitude of restaurants and hotels that all bustle for a prime position.

Abu Dhabi's Corniche seems to be constantly changing, with even more beachfront access and further apartment tower developments planned for the Port Zayed end. Easy access to the Sheikh Khalifa Highway via Al Meena and Saadiyat Island makes travelling to Yas Island and onwards to Dubai even easier now too, avoiding the traffic lights through the city. Parking at some of the older buildings can still be an issue though.

Schools

Behind the Corniche is the popular American Community School (ACS). There are also some post-secondary establishments like the Higher College of Technology and Syscoms College. Schools in Al Bateen and Al Dhafrah are a 10-15 minute drive away.

Healthcare

Corniche Hospital at the northerly end of Corniche Road specialises in obstetric and neonatal care (it sees an average of 20 births every day). Al Noor Hospital, which is affiliated with the UK's National Health Service, is on Khalifa Bin Zayed The First St.

Shops

The impressive Marina Mall is a big draw to the area and has a Carrefour for the weekly shop. The World Trade Centre Mall And Souk is another new hotspot that boasts the country's first House of Fraser department store. There are also a lot of independent shops in the streets behind the Corniche. At the Al Meena end near Port Zayed you'll find the Mina fish market, Iranian Souk and Al Mina vegetable market.

Bars & Restaurants

With hotels like Sofitel, Sheraton, Hilton, Le Royal Meridien, Jumeirah At Etihad Towers and Emirates Palace stretching along the length of the Corniche, residents are spoilt for choice when it comes to eating out or meeting friends for a drink. There are small restaurants along the beach and just off Corniche Road too, and you'll find many fast food chains in this area. For a relaxed night out head to The Beachcomber at the Sheraton, while Jumeirah At Etihad Towers' elevated restaurant, Quest, oozes elegance.

Attractions

Heritage Village, with its representation of traditional Emirati life, and the Abu Dhabi Theatre are reasons to visit Breakwater. The vast promenade along the Corniche attracts runners, roller skaters and other active types, although there are also parks and cafes to enjoy. Emirates Palace and Jumeirah At Etihad Towers are exclusive dining destinations.

Marina Villas

Exclusive development of five to eight-bedroom villas behind Marina Mall looking out to the Arabian Gulf. Some even have their own private beaches.
Annual rental cost: Five-bedroom villa from Dhs.700,000

Corniche

Some of the older buildings in the city can be found along the Corniche, often meaning more space. Expats may fancy the more exclusive and newer Etihad Towers or Nation Towers at the Emirates Palace end, although they cost more than the average.
Annual rental cost: One-bedroom apartment from Dhs.90,000; three-bedroom apartment from Dhs.110,000

Abu Dhabi Corniche

Downtown

Downtown Abu Dhabi is a busy melting pot that thrives with life. Some of the city's more affordable apartments and hotels can be found here, mixing it up with five-star hotels towards the Corniche in the west and a few villas heading towards Al Nahyan and Al Wahda to the east. There's a wealth of smaller shops, cafes and restaurants to explore and some of the city's most lively nightlife is here. If you need to be in the cut and thrust of the city, this is the place for you, although noise and delays from traffic can be frustrating. If you have a car, you'll also want to check out the parking situation before signing a lease, as it is very limited.

Al Zahiyah

Schools

Al Muna Primary and Pearl Primary School, along with GEMS World Academy, are all in the area. There are numerous options in neighbouring areas of Al Karamah, Al Bateen and just past Al Nahyan that would be easily commutable.

Healthcare

There are a host of hospitals in the area; Burjeel Hospital, Dar Al Shifa Hospital, National Hospital, Al Noor and more. Corniche Hospital and Cleveland Clinic are also both easily accessible.

Shops

One of the best areas for shopping you will find Abu Dhabi Mall, Al Wahda Mall and Madinat Zayed Shopping Centre here. The high-end Galleria Mall can be found at Al Maryah Island, while Mariah Mall and Hamdan Center are both small but their great range of stores sell everything from watersport equipment to pet shops and interior design.

Bars & Restaurants

Some of the more lively nightlife spots can be found in Al Zahiyah, it also has some of the best value and tastiest restaurants, particularly if you like Indian food. Beach Rotana, Le Meridien and Abu Dhabi Marina & Yacht Club are popular and many excellent restaurants and bars. Cafes, restaurants and chocolatiers can be found all along Sultan Bin Zayed The First St.

Attractions

Much of the attraction of this area for visitors is the shops, and it's a fascinating neighbourhood for a stroll. Abu Dhabi's most historic building, Qasr Al Hosn is next to the Cultural Foundation, although due to renovations it's not always accessible. More recently the views across to Al Maryah Island have become an impressive sight, something guests at Beach Rotana and Le Meridien can enjoy.

Al Zahiyah

Formerly known as the Tourist Club Area, there are lots of older high-rise apartments here, but it is not so great for families. Parking can also be difficult.
Annual rental cost: One-bedroom apartment from Dhs.68,000; three-bedroom apartment from Dhs.95,000

Madinat Zayed & Markaziya

A busy area with easy access to the Corniche, although availability is slim. Some nice, newer towers towards Al Markaziya area.
Annual rental price: One-bedroom apartment from Dhs.80,000; three-bedroom apartment from Dhs.110,000

Al Nahyan

A little quieter but still close to the action with plenty of coffee shops, cafes and a new park. Some cheaper rentals, but also newer buildings with amenities.
Annual rental cost: One-bedroom apartment from Dhs.65,000; three-bedroom apartment from Dhs.105,000

Business District

The newly developed Al Reem and Al Maryah islands form an impressive skyline of residential, commercial and business properties for Abu Dhabi. Al Maryah Island is the officially designated Central Business District and Sowwah Square is at the heart of that. Buildings on both islands have been nominated or have won their categories in the Council on Tall Buildings and Urban Habitat awards, which highlights the kind of impressive development you'll be living in. At the moment it's very much a destination for professionals with younger families and while amenities are still a little limited, it's set to become a real hub for Abu Dhabi. If you're happy to take a short drive or cab ride, the endless entertainment of Downtown is just a bridge away.

Schools

Repton School will be joined by a number of schools and universities set to open on Reem Island. Paris-Sorbonne University of Abu Dhabi is also already up and running there.

Healthcare

Cleveland Clinic is a huge building offering specialist treatment in everything from dermatology to neurology. Abu Dhabi National Hospital in Al Baladia is also a short drive away.

Shops

The luxurious Galleria Mall offers many of the finest designer names. For more day-to-day needs, Boutik

Sowwah Square

Mall between Sun & Sky Towers on Reem Island is the place to go; there's even a Waitrose. Reem Mall and Paragon Bay Mall are due to open before 2018.

Bars & Restaurants

The five-star Rosewood houses the fantastic rooftop Glo bar and Lebanese restaurant, Sambusek, while Catalonian restaurant, Catalan, are also highly regarded. The Galleria has a selection of upscale restaurants and cafes, including the Emporio Armani Cafe, but also offers more casual choices like burrito bar Taqado and New York City import Magnolia Bakery. Japanese stand-out restaurant Zuma can be found in The Galleria mall.

Attractions

Aside from the impressive high-rise architecture, high-end hotels and the shopping at the Galleria Mall, there's lots more to see or do in this area. However, new beaches, a marina and sports facilities are also in the pipeline and will make this district more interesting.

Al Reem Island

Most residential buildings on the islands at the moment are on Reem Island, in any one of a number of developments such as Gate Towers, Sun & Sky Towers, Marina Square, or The Arc. All are less than four years old and offer excellent pools and gyms.
Annual rental cost: One-bedroom apartment from Dhs.90,000; three-bedroom apartment from Dhs.145,000

Neighbouring Community: Saadiyat Island

Across the water to the north of Reem Island is Saadiyat Island, a natural outcrop that is destined to be the cultural centre of Abu Dhabi and the UAE. The Louvre and the Guggenheim museums are expected to open in the near future. If early off-plan sales are any indication, by 2018, Saadiyat will be the place to live in Abu Dhabi. At the moment there's still construction, but the stunning beaches, popular Saadiyat Beach Club and easy access into the city – and also away from it along the E12 highway for Dubai-bound traffic – are creating big demand for existing residential areas like Saadiyat Beach Villas, Saadiyat Beach Residences and Saadiyat Beach Apartments at the St Regis hotel.
Annual rental cost: One-bedroom from Dhs.80,000; three-bedroom from Dhs.170,000

Khalidiya

One of the most popular and upscale areas in the city, it treads that fine line between being quiet and established yet offering plenty to do. To the bottom of Khalidiya it stretches out to Al Bateen, an extremely affluent and well-groomed area popular with Emirati residents. In the heart of Khalidiya though there's a good mix of Arab and expat communities, who enjoy it for the family feel and close proximity to the Corniche and city centre. The area stretches out to the borders of Al Mushrif to the east and Downtown to the north, encompassing an eclectic area of residential and commercial zones.

Schools

German International School, Al Bateen Secondary School and American Community School are just some of the international schools in the area. There are lots of high quality nurseries available.

Healthcare

Khalidiya Urgent Care Centre is by Khalidiya Mall, while Sheikh Khalifa Medical City has an emergency department. The American Hospital is near as is the Gulf Diagnostic Centre Hospital in Al Bateen.

Shops

Khalidiya Mall was the neighborhood's major shopping centre until Mushrif Mall opened close by with over 200 shops and a LuLu Hypermarket. Marina Mall and Al Wahda Mall are nearby and supermarkets Choithram, Spinneys, Spar and Abela are here, too.

Khalidiya Kids' Park

Bars & Restaurants

The block of Khalidiya adjacent to Al Khaleej Al Arabi St offers a global selection of restaurants, from Spanish tapas and Japanese fusion to one of the city's best bets for Lebanese shwarma. Several artsy coffee shops, housed in converted villas, are also in the area. Popular nightspot The Jazz Bar can be found at the Hilton Corniche.

Attractions

Khalidiya Kids Park and Khalidiya Public Park are both popular family hangouts. Al Bateen dhow yard is an insight into traditional Emirati boat building, although access has been limited in recent times. Most of the big attractions are just a short drive away, including the relatively new Bateen public beach.

Place Names

You will see many places with the prefix 'Al', such as Al Khalidiya or Al Raha Beach. The use of this prefix essentially translates as 'the'. However, it is not a permanent part of the noun and can be dropped or added where appropriate. You'll also see 'Madinat' in place names, which means 'city'.

Khalidiya

You might be able to find a bargain studio in the busy Khalidiy vicinity, but it's mainly one to three-bedroom apartments or good sized villas in compounds like Khalidiya Village that you will be offered. If you have the chance, make sure you snap rentals up quickly as this area is very popular thanks to its family feel and urban twist.

Annual rental cost: One-bedroom apartment from Dhs.75,000; three-bedroom apartment from Dhs.120,000; five-bedroom villa from Dhs.200,000

Marasy Al Bateen

Marasy is part of a redevelopment of the older Al Bateen marina area that also includes exclusive compounds aimed at Emirati residents. The eight apartment blocks at Marasy are relatively new to the market and are designed with short walks or cycle rides to the Corniche as a huge selling point. There is also a convenient marina nearby where you can dock your very own boat.

Annual rental cost: One-bedroom apartment from Dhs.75,000; three-bedroom apartment from Dhs.180,000

Mushrif & Muroor

This is the 'middle bit' of Abu Dhabi island that most drive through to get to the 'action' at the Corniche end of the city. However, it's not without charm and there are plenty of villas for rent in this more leafy part of town. While it might not seem particularly vibrant, take time to explore this large section of the city and you'll find plenty to keep you entertained.

Al Gurm

Schools

The British School Al Khubairat (BSAK) is very popular with British expats and is close to an enclave of Christian churches. Lycee Louis Massignon and American International School (AIS) are also in the area.

Healthcare

The Middle East Specialised Medical Centre is in Hadabat Al Zaafaran and the government hospital, Mushrif Primary Health Care, is near Mushrif Mall.

Shops

Mushrif Mall (with over 200 shops) is the main shopping destination, and there's a large fruit, vegetable, meat and fish market in the basement. There are some smaller shops dotted around on service roads. There's a Carrefour heading out of town near Al Zaafaranah Park.

Bars & Restaurants

Hotels like Dusit Thani near the city end and Holiday Inn, Aloft and Hyatt Capital Gate near the mainland end have superb dining and nightlife options. As in most of the city, there are good cafes and restaurants tucked in amongst residential and business areas.

Attractions

The Eastern Corniche runs alongside Sheikh Zayed Bin Sultan St and looks out over the mangroves, and is close to the Eastern Mangroves Promenade. It has gardens and gazebos for picnics and is popular with joggers and cyclists. Abu Dhabi City Golf Club, Abu Dhabi Equestrian Club and Al Jazira Football Club are all at the city end. Abu Dhabi National Exhibition Centre (ADNEC) is a big draw with cultural, business and entertainment events on throughout the year.

Mushrif

A quiet, central location which was one of the most sought-after areas of the city for years. Most villas are huge, although some have been legally split into smaller units.
Annual rental cost: One-bedroom apartment from Dhs.65,000; three-bedroom villa from Dhs.170,000

Muroor

From the busier city end to the quieter communities towards the Sheikh Zayed Bridge, Muroor is a fine option for families with some good sized accommodation for rent.
Annual rental cost: One-bedroom apartment from Dhs.65,000; three-bedroom villa from Dhs.120,000

Al Gurm

A super-luxurious development of waterside apartments, Al Gurm Resort Villas is one of the exclusive addresses in the city on the southern side of the island.
Annual rental cost: Four-bedroom villa from Dhs.700,000

Al Qurm

You'd be hard-pushed to find anything but a large villa in the Al Qurm area, which makes it popular with families. Al Qurm Gardens and Al Dhabi Complex are two of a number of compounds in the vicinity. The Eastern Corniche with views over the mangroves is nearby and it has good access in and out of town.
Annual rental cost: Five-bedroom villa from Dhs.200,000

Grand Mosque Area

Around the stunning Sheikh Zayed Grand Mosque there are some of the most interesting neighbourhoods in the city. From the Rihan Heights towers near the Zayed Sports City complex and the established expat community around Mangrove Village, to the numerous villa and apartment compounds heading towards the city, there really is something for everybody. The Qaryat Al Beri (Between the Bridges) area is an attraction in itself; The Ritz-Carlton on the city side of the canal and Shangri-La and Fairmont Bab Al Bahr hotels on the mainland side create a hub of evening activity.

Schools

Brighton College is in Khalifa Park next to the Bloom Gardens Compound. Aside from that, on the island near Mushrif or off the island towards Raha Beach and Khalifa City there are a number of options.

Healthcare

There's a Healthpoint multi-speciality hospital by Zayed Sports City. A newer branch of Al Noor Hospital is by Al Zaafaranah Park.

Shops

The Souk adjacent to the Shangri-La hotel is an interesting place to visit. There are a number of small supermarkets amongst residential developments and a large Carrefour near Al Zaafaranah Park. Mushrif Mall is a short drive away.

Bars & Restaurants

'Between the Bridges' is the place to go for good nights out, with Shangri-La, Traders and Fairmont Bab Al Bahr hotels full of top restaurants and night spots. The Ritz-Carlton on the other side of the canal is also recommended. Park Rotana Complex near Khalifa Park offers a choice of restaurants and a pub that is extremely popular with expats.

Attractions

Sheikh Zayed Grand Mosque and Khalifa Park (with a splash park for kids and aquarium) are firm favourites. Al Maqtaa Fort is a historical site which looks impressive at night when the stunning Sheikh Zayed Bridge is lit up nearby, take a free evening abra ride across the Grand Canal to get a better view. The top leisure and sports facilities at Zayed Sport City and Armed Officer's Club are also in the area.

The Hills

A fairly new development and well sought after, offering modern villas with sea views and easy access to a park and Armed Officer's Club. Good for getting into the city quickly or out of it with equal haste.

Annual rental price: Five-bedroom villa from Dhs.280,000

Mangrove Village

A well-established, family-friendly compound of villas by the water with good shared facilities. Neighbouring this is the similar, if slightly more packed-in, Seashore Villa compound.

Annual rental cost: Two-bedroom villa for Dhs.165,000; four-bedroom villa from Dhs.215,000

Bain Al Jessrain

A popular place with locals consisting mainly of larger villas, with some local amenities and easy access to the area's hotels.

Annual rental cost: Four-bedroom villa from Dhs.225,000

Khalifa Park

Plenty of smart compounds in the area with the Park Rotana complex and Khalifa Park all in close proximity. Property near the capital's biggest park is popular as there is so much on offer, including a library, museum, mini railway, water park and farmers' markets.

Annual rental cost: One-bedroom apartment from Dhs.85,000; three-bedroom apartment from Dhs.125,000

Sas Al Nakhl

A newer gated development with pool, tennis court and kid-friendly facilities. A little set alone, but a short drive to many local attractions and amenities.

Annual rental cost: Three-bedroom villa from Dhs.165,000

Golf Gardens

An attractive compound with guaranteed greenery and plenty of wildlife thanks to the popular and neighbouring Abu Dhabi Golf Club. There are 395 residential units in total to choose from.

Annual rental cost: Three-bedroom villa from Dhs.225,000

Golf Gardens

Sas Al Nakhl Village

Mangrove Village

Raha Beach & Khalifa City

This large area on the edge of Abu Dhabi is perfectly placed for access to Abu Dhabi International Airport, Yas Island and the E10/E11 highway to Dubai, yet you can still get into Abu Dhabi city centre in under 30 minutes if the traffic is flowing. Aside from limited shopping options, it's well serviced for nearby beaches, sports and leisure activities. Raha Beach is one of the areas where expats can buy property and the waterfront complexes of Al Bandar, Al Muneera and Al Zeina are some of the most desirable locations in Abu Dhabi. The sprawling Khalifa City offers larger accommodation for the money and is popular with families after more space and some peace and quiet. It can be a bit dusty and isolated, but with the 'New Khalifa City' set to be built between Khalifa City and the more local-friendly Shakhbout City, this area could become even more desirable.

Yas Island > p.191

> p.191

With some of Abu Dhabi's hottest tourist and visitor attractions, including the country's second largest mall now at Yas Mall, the impressive Yas Island continues to grow with some excellent housing developments. With the Sheikh Khalifa Highway linking Yas Island to Saadiyat Island and then into the city centre, Yas Island could be a future address of choice and not just a great destination for dining, nightlife and family fun.

Schools

Take your pick of nurseries; Humpty Dumpty, Stepping Stones, Windsor, Teddy Bear American or Redwood Montessori. GEMS American Academy, Canadian International School, Al Yasmina and Al Raha schools make the area something of an education hub.

Healthcare

There's HealthPlus Family Health Care Center at Al Bandar or Al Noor Hospital on the island near Al Zaafaranah Park. Otherwise, out on Sheikh Zayed Road towards Dubai is the Al Rahba Hospital.

Shops

Al Raha Mall has the excellent Party Center store while the Lulu Hypermarket is one of the best stores open at the newish Deerfields Townsquare shopping centre. Abela, Spinneys, Waitrose, Geant and Spar are all in the vicinity. However, your best bet may be to head to the massive Yas Mall, the country's new and second-largest mall, for the weekly shop.

Bars & Restaurants

Westin Abu Dhabi to the west, Yas Plaza hotels on Yas Island and Yas Mall offer plenty of food options.

Ornina at Al Bandar is a licensed restaurant and the cool O1NE Yas Island nightclub adds to burgeoning nightlife options. Cafes and restaurants at Etihad Plaza, Al Bandar, Yas Viceroy and Yas Marina are great.

Attractions

Al Forsan International Sports Resort and Abu Dhabi Golf Club are great for sporty types, while Yas Island boasts Ferrari World Abu Dhabi, Yas Waterworld and Yas Marina Circuit. Eco-friendly Masdar City, near the airport, offers a glimpse into a carbon neutral future.

Raha Beach

Al Bandar, Al Muneera and Al Zeina offer mainly apartments, but exclusive duplexes, townhouses and villas make the price range huge. Al Zeina is the newest development.
Annual rental cost: One-bedroom apartment from Dhs.95,000; three-bedroom apartment from Dhs.180,000; three-bedroom townhouses from Dhs.240,000

Khalifa City

Lots of compounds as well as individual villas, most with large accommodation. Popular with locals and expats who have families.
Annual rental cost: Three-bedroom villa from Dhs.160,000

Raha Gardens

A popular long, narrow stretch of three to five-bedroom villas, segmented into 11 gated communities with 24 hour security.
Annual rental cost: Three-bedroom villa from Dhs.190,000

Neighbouring Community: Al Reef

Made up of four villages and a downtown area, it's a community on the Dubai side of Abu Dhabi airport. Rents are cheaper and it's very expat friendly, but consider your commute times carefully: it's 40 minutes to the Corniche and only slightly longer to Dubai.
Annual rental cost: One-bedroom apartment from Dhs.65,000; three-bedroom villa from Dhs.110,000

Mohammed Bin Zayed City

Mohammed Bin Zayed City

To the south of the city, Mohammed Bin Zayed City (MBZ as it's known to locals) runs alongside the industrial area of Mussafah and continues eastward towards more local-dominated neighbourhoods. It's often not the first choice for Western expats, but there is relatively easy access into the city and for your rental allowance you're likely to find a larger living space. In fact, it's probably better serviced for accessible shopping and healthcare than many other areas of the city. There are new amenities being built all the time, and nearby Capital Mall has the city's largest Lulu Hypermarket. If you enjoy desert adventures then the easy access to the motorways to the south and west opens up a world of sand-based fun.

Schools

British International School Abu Dhabi (BISAD) is on the outskirts, next to Abu Dhabi University. The Australian School is a short drive away in Shakhbout.

Healthcare

Abu Al Abiad Hospital is in the centre of Mohammed Bin Zayed City with NMC Hospital and a branch of Al Noor Hospital by the E22 road. Nearby, the large Al Mafraq Hospital has a new emergency maternity ward.

Shops

Mazyad Mall and Capital Mall in the northern part of MBZ offer the usual brands, and Mazyad also has a popular Gold's Gym. Dalma Mall is an extremely large mall on the border with Mussafah with an excellent choice of shops and eateries, plus a popular kids' play zone. Bawabat Al Sharq Mall in Baniyas East is a huge and impressive spot that is well worth the trip. Mind the posted dress code in all of these malls; with the amount of locals residing in the area, tastes tend to be more conservative than what you'd see on the island.

Bars & Restaurants

A mix of Indian, Arabic and fast food restaurants can all be found alongside villas and in small shopping centres. Inside the malls you'll see the usual restaurant chains, burger joints and bakeries. A lack of hotels means a taxi ride to the Between the Bridges area or further into Abu Dhabi for licensed venues.

Attractions

There's not a lot to see in the immediate area. A quick drive on the E11 toward Al Rahba brings you to the small but decent Emirates Park Zoo. Over in Mussafah, unusual finds like the Abu Dhabi Art Hub (a gallery and residence for guest artists) suggest the area might yet grow its own sense of identity.

Mohammed Bin Zayed City

Being close to the industrial zone keeps the large villas in quiet streets remarkably well-priced.
Annual rental cost: Three-bedroom villa from Dhs.120,000; four-bedroom villa from Dhs.130,000

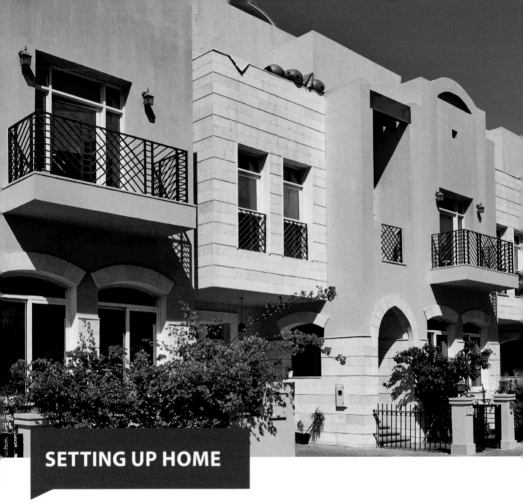

SETTING UP HOME

Keys in hand and foot through the door; now the fun really begins. There's a fantastic selection of places that can supply furnishings for your new place and expats often find some unusual styles to try out that they can't get back home. However, there are familiar companies like IKEA, as well as many other furniture stores, that can give that modern feel to your new apartment or villa. See the Shopping chapter for more.

First Things First

For all the joy of moving in, there's also an array of phone calls to make and services to set up. Rarely does anything happen quickly or easily when it comes to this sort of thing, but being armed with the right information and approaching it all with a calm attitude can certainly help.

Don't forget that once you've moved in, the regular utility bills will need to be paid on time or you risk being cut off. No notice is given, you'll simply find your internet has stopped working or there's no water coming from the taps. Often you can get these reconnected quite quickly, but it can depend on the provider. Direct debits are only just starting to be employed in the country, so it can sometimes mean a one-off monthly payment and even a trip to a counter to pay the bill in person.

However, there isn't much else that you should be too worried about, aside from the slowness at which things can take to get done. For everything else, this chapter should point you in the right direction. Once you're settled in you'll find domestic life in Abu Dhabi is likely to be remarkably similar to the one that you left back at home. The dining, nightlife, sunshine and vast array of activities you'll be enjoying may be different, but you'll probably still find time to slouch on the sofa and catch up with your favourite TV shows.

Moving Services

If you're moving to Abu Dhabi with much more than a few suitcases, then you may need to ship some of your possessions from home, either by air or by sea. Air freight is fast but quite a lot more expensive than shipping, so it's a good option if you are only bringing in smaller amounts. Gulf Air (gfcargo.com) and Etihad (etihadcrystalcargo.com) both have dedicated handling departments and fly direct to Abu Dhabi from multiple global destinations. For a larger consignment, shipping by sea is comparatively cheap, although it can take longer (on average, six weeks from UK to Abu Dhabi).

There are removal companies that can help with shipping your things and it's often best, and safest, to opt for one with a wide international network as they will have a reliable local contact in both your departure and arrival locations. Most companies offer free quotes, so make sure you shop around. Once your belongings arrive in Abu Dhabi and are ready to be collected you'll be notified by phone or letter. Some agencies carry out the customs clearing process for you. However, even if they do, you may be called to be present while customs officers open your boxes to ensure that you're not bringing anything illegal or inappropriate into the country. It might be easier to carry customs-restricted goods, like DVDs or books, in your checked luggage on the airplane; it's easier to open a suitcase at the airport than empty a box outside in the sun!

If your shipping company is not delivering your things from the customs centre to your new home, you can find removal companies advertised in the classified sections of the local papers. You could also head to the car park next door to the Central Post Office in Madinat Zayed. Drivers with small trucks wait to transport goods for a fee (be sure to negotiate). You'll need to pack your own goods and they won't be insured by the drivers during transport, so you'll want to pack them well.

One-Stop Shops

Larger international removal companies, such as Allied Pickfords (alliedpickfords.com), Bishop's Move (bishopsmove.com), Santa Fe Relocation Services (santaferelo.com) and Writer Relocations (writercorporation.com) can take a lot of the stress out of moving to Abu Dhabi. In addition to packing, shipping and storing your possessions (and even your car, if you're particularly attached to it), some firms can help speed up the visa process, find you rental accommodation in advance, organise travel for your pets and even find suitable schools for your children.

Abu Dhabi Shipping Agency Salem Saif Saqer Al Mehairbi Bldg, Nr Cristal Salam Hotel, Al Zahiyah, 02 644 9100, *adsa.ae*

Al Futtaim Logistics 8th Street, Mussafah Industrial Area, 02 555 9635, *aflogistics.com*

Allied Pickfords > *p.iv, 35, 77* Arab Tower, Shk Hamdan Bin Mohd St, Al Danah, 02 677 9765, *alliedpickfords.com*

Crown Relocations Mina Centre, Al Meena, 02 673 3076, *crownrelo.com*

Delight International Movers 8th Street, Mussafah Industrial Area, 02 690 2900, *delightmovers.com*

National Shipping Gulf Agency Nr Mina Centre, Al Meena, 02 673 0500, *gac.com*

Move One Relocations Costa Coffee Bldg, Shk Rashid Bin Saeed Al Maktoum St, Al Karamah, 02 658 4696, *moveoneinc.com*

Santa Fe Relocation Services > *p.71* Shk Hazza Bin Zayed St, Al Dhafra, 02 815 2820, *santaferelo.com*

Smooth Moves

- Get more than one quote – some companies will match lower quotes to get the job.
- Make sure all items are covered by insurance.
- Keep an inventory and ensure each item is listed.
- Don't be shy about requesting packers to repack items if you are not satisfied.
- Take photos of the packing process to use for evidence if you need to make a claim.

Furnishing Accommodation

Most properties, including rentals, come unfurnished which can be quite a surprise for a lot of expats. Closets and cupboards are not standard in all places, especially in older buildings, and basic white goods like an oven or a fridge are often not included. Unless you're moving into a new building that specifically states it includes appliances, plan on some appliance shopping as well as the more enjoyable furniture shopping. Abu Dhabi is home to many furniture stores, ranging from Swedish simplicity at IKEA on Yas Island to modern designs at THE One in Khalidiya (see the Shopping chapter for more options).

Areeca Furniture & Curtains Nr Al Diar Capital Hotel, Al Zahiyah, 02 679 0010, *areeca.com*

Gemaco Interiors Gemaco Bldg, Shk Rashid Bin Saeed Al Maktoum St, Al Manhal, 02 633 9100, *gemacointeriors.com*

Indigo Living Sheikh Zayed Rd, Dubai, 04 339 7705, indigo-living.com

Saraya Interior Design & Contracting Nr Hamdan Post Office, Shk Khalifa Bin Zayed The First St, Al Danah, 02 674 7433, *sarayaid.ae*

Second-Hand Furniture

With an expat community constantly coming and going there's no shortage of good quality, inexpensive second-hand furniture for sale on local websites. Facebook has several pages dedicated to the purpose, and the classifieds section of dubizzle.com can provide some great deals. If you're in a fixer-upper mood, watchmen from buildings that are about to be torn down will often set up shop on the ground level to sell furniture that was left behind by departing tenants so you can bag a bargain.

Furniture Leasing

If you're only planning to be in Abu Dhabi for a short time, acquiring a household full of furniture and appliances may not make sense in terms of hassle and cost. Furniture leasing is an alternative option. Some real estate companies offer this service, so it's worth asking them when looking for your rental accommodation. Alternatively, Indigo Living (indigo-living.com) offers short and long-term leasing options across the UAE.

Curtains & Blinds

You'll need good blinds to block out the bright morning sun, but again, most rentals don't come with them included. If you have windows built to a standard size then shops like IKEA or Pan Emirates should have off-the-shelf options. If not, there are several companies that will tailor-make curtains and blinds, and even come and install them for you. Ask the building's security guards, they will know good tailors in the area that have experience with fitting curtains for your building.

Interior Design

Starting with an empty apartment can be a great opportunity to create a home from scratch. Whether you need help with choosing colours for the walls, decorative art to hang on them, or the furnishings throughout, there are an increasing number of specialists just a phone call away. A good interior designer will pick options that suit your lifestyle, making it easier for you to get settled quickly. The listings on the previous page are a good place to start, or ask friends for recommendations.

Utilities & Services

Electricity & Water

Electricity and water services are provided by the government and run by the Abu Dhabi Distribution Company (ADDC). The service is excellent and power cuts and water stoppages are rare. When you register, you'll need to pay a deposit of Dhs.1,000. If the property has been leased through your company, they may arrange the deposits and settle the bills for you.

Water and electricity deposits, as well as monthly bills, can be paid at any ADDC outlet, online (addc.ae) or through various banks listed on the reverse side of the bill. ADDC charges a standard rate per unit, currently five fils per unit of electricity and Dhs.2.2 per unit of water for non-UAE nationals. Your bills are likely to be significantly higher in the hot summer months as air-conditioning is essential, as is a good hose down for any garden you may have.

Electricity

The electricity supply in Abu Dhabi is 220/240 volts and 50 cycles. The socket type is identical to the three-point UK system but most appliances here are sold with two-pin plugs. Adaptors can be bought from any grocery or hardware shop.

Drinking Water

Tap water is safe, but as it is desalinated and treated sea water, most expats go for the cleaner taste of bottled water. To save on plastic waste, these companies deliver and replace five-gallon refillable bottles, and can also provide a water cooler.

Awafi Mineral Water Nr Toyota Bldg, Mussafah, 02 555 5762, *awafiwater.com*
Masafi Various locations, 800 5455, *masafi.com*
Nestle Pure Life Various locations, 800 4404, *nestle-family.com*
Oasis Water Various locations, 600 522 261, *oasiscome2life.com*

Gas

There is no main gas supply in Abu Dhabi, but some newer apartment buildings supply gas for cooking from central storage tanks on the roof or underground. Gas canisters can be bought for cooking, which generally cost about Dhs.250 for a new canister and around Dhs.75 for a refill, depending on size. Canisters can be bought from local shops, and if you live out of town you'll hear the gas delivery van's bell ringing in the morning as it goes on its rounds. You can flag these down or contact companies like Al Ruwais Industrial Gases (02 555 9295) or Tarish Ateeq Al Qubaisi Gas (02 559 9477). These companies will often be able to install your canister too.

Sewerage

The Mafraq Wastewater Treatment Works receives and treats the municipal and industrial sewage and waste water of Abu Dhabi and the surrounding areas. The treated 'grey' water is reused for irrigation, landscaping

THINKING RELOCATION?
THINK SANTA FE.

We make it easy

SANTA FE
RELOCATION SERVICES

Relocation | Storage | Moving | Immigration

Santa Fe Relocation Services
T: +971 (2) 815 2820
T: 800 32800
F: +971 (2) 815 2815
Email: UAE@santaferelo.com
www.santaferelo.com

and agricultural activities. This is part of the city's efforts to protect the environment from pollution. The sewage is collected on a regular basis from septic tanks by sewerage trucks. It is then pumped to the plant through more than 15 pumping stations. The sewerage undergoes complex treatment to free the water from bacteria and is regularly tested by the Environment Agency (ead.ae).

Rubbish Disposal

If you live in an apartment then generally you'll have a rubbish chute to dispose of your garbage. In some areas though, there will be dumpsters on the street where all rubbish must be placed. While these are emptied by the municipality on a regular basis and taken to a landfill in the Mussafah area, sometimes they can attract street cats and the occasional rat. You can call the municipality (800 22220) if these are bothering you. Villas have their own bins, and there's a continuing rollout of a scheme to add extra bins for recyclable waste. There is also a growing number of recycling points near government buildings, supermarkets and schools if you don't have the facilities at home.

Landline

There are two home phone providers for the UAE; Etisalat and du. Etisalat is the original offering and previously if you subscribed to du's call plans you had to pay the Etisalat line rental charge still, plus a Dhs.50 activation fee. You also had to dial 08888 before the number you wanted to dial. While this set-up is still available, du can now also supply a landline to your property in its Homephone Plus package, doing away with the 08888 prefix on numbers and customers paying a line rental straight to du instead.

To install a landline from either apply directly; Etisalat requires an application form, a copy of your passport, residence visa (or Resident ID) and an installation fee of Dhs.180; du needs your passport or Resident ID, a copy of your tenancy agreement and an installation fee. You may also need a salary certificate with minimum monthly salary of Dhs.2,500, your last three bank statements or valid UAE credit card.

Once you've chosen your provider, there are numerous packages you can opt for that best suit your needs and wallet; they also both offer broadband and TV which can be included in the package too. Installation of a landline can be quick, within a few days of ordering, but it's worth politely following up on your order as sometimes it can take a few frustrating weeks to get sorted.

Payment of du bills can be done by phone, internet, through partnered banks and outlets, via quickpay machines or through a regular debit from your credit card. Etisalat bills can be paid at their business centres or payment machines (EPMs), online, through autopay, direct debit or mobile pay, eZeepay online payments through banks, Emirates Post and exchange houses, offline payments in banks, payments through mail or with a cheque deposit at drop boxes.

Codes & Prefixes

Abu Dhabi	02	Ajman	06
Al Ain	03	Dubai	04
Fujairah	09	Ras Al Khaimah	07
Sharjah	06	Umm Al Quwain	06
UAE Country Code	971		

Mobile Phone

Mobile phone users can choose between du (prefix 055) and Etisalat (prefix 050 or 056). Both providers offer monthly pay-as-you-go packages. You can register for a pay-as-you-go SIM card for either Etisalat or du from any of the company kiosks located in malls, or from the many mobile phone shops scattered throughout the city.

Missing Mobile

Lost your mobile? For Etisalat, call 101, or for du call customer care on 055 567 8155 to temporarily disconnect your number (you will need your passport number for security). You SIM card can be replaced and you can keep the same number, but you'll lose the numbers you had saved in your phone's memory. SIM replacement with costs Dhs.55 with du and Dhs.25 with Etisalat. You can also cancel your number permanently by simply filling out and submitting a cancellation form.

Call Costs

Etisalat charges Dhs.39 per month rental for a post-paid line but that includes free calls to local and national landline numbers. International call charges vary depending on the country calling, although calls to some countries where Etisalat operate in can be made cheaper on special plans. For others, the off-peak times are 9pm to 7am from Saturday to Thursday, all day on Fridays until 7am on Saturdays and on national public holidays declared by the federal government.

Either a du or an Etisalat pay-as-you-go line costs Dhs.55 and includes Dhs.10 credit to get you started. As long as you use it regularly, the number will be valid for life.

Post-paid monthly contracts are also available. For du you will need your Resident ID and residence visa, as well as one of the following: a UAE credit card, a recent utility bill with your physical address, your tenancy agreement or a salary certificate that shows a minimum monthly income of Dhs.2,500. For

Etisalat you need your Resident ID and the salary certificate, again showing a minimum salary of Dhs.2,500 per month.

Internet

All internet usage is regulated by the Telecommunications Regulatory Authority (TRA). This means that sites that are deemed to be offensive, either religiously, culturally or politically, are blocked and can't be accessed. Although both Etisalat and du provide internet services in the UAE, only Etisalat provides internet in Abu Dhabi at present. However, there is an ongoing dispute over 'bitstream access' – the technology that allows the leasing of an internet provider's infrastructure to other operators – and Etisalat may open up this access to du in the future which should increase competition.

For home broadband Etisalat charges a Dhs.199 installation fee and offers either 512kbps internet for Dhs.199 per month or 1mbps for Dhs.259 per month. For faster internet you need to sign up to an eLife Triple Play bundle, with TV, internet and telephone services. With these the megabits per second of information you can receive are as high as 300 million, but that top package costs Dhs.2,999 per month.

Only existing licence holders Etisalat, du and satellite firms Yahsat and Thuraya may offer Voice over Internet Protocol (VoIP) phone services. None of them do yet. Despite access to popular VoIP website Skype being unblocked in 2013, it is still technically illegal to use the service for voice communications as it is unregulated by TRA. Using Skype for calls between two computers generally works, although a Virtual Private Network (VPN) or other proxy blocker is needed to call other phones.

Etisalat On The Go

When out and about, look out for Etisalat's Wi-Fi hotspots to get online. These are located all over town at various malls, cafes and restaurants and you can connect by purchasing a prepaid card. See izone.ae for listings. Existing broadband customers can get a period of free time in these hotspots, depending on what package they hold.

Postal Services

There is currently no traditional postal delivery service to home addresses, although that will hopefully change in the near future with Abu Dhabi's new street naming scheme. For now, mail has to be delivered to a PO Box. Emirates Post can offer individual PO box bundles, with installation of a box to a specific villa, to a building or in a residential compound. Customers can also use the traditional method of having a PO Box at one of Empost's own post offices.

Online Shopping

If you miss your favourite stores from home or aren't in the mood to head to the mall, check out Aramex's shopandship.com. After you sign up for an account, you can ship your online purchases to Aramex's forwarding facility in the UK, US, South Africa, Spain, France, or any of eight other countries. Then, the package will be sent to your address in the UAE for a reasonable rate.

To get your own PO Box, fill in an application form at your nearest post office and pay the annual fee of Dhs.200. You will be given a set of keys (Dhs.10 per key) to access your own box. Empost will send you a notification by email when you receive registered mail or parcels in your PO Box. Be warned that you might have to pay customs charges on international packages. Many people have their post sent to their work PO Box instead of arranging a private one.

Letters and packages do occasionally go missing and, if the item has not been registered, there's little that you can do apart from wait – some turn up months after they're expected, others not at all.

Empost offers a courier service for both local and international deliveries, with delivery times guaranteed and packages that can be tracked. Registered mail is a relatively inexpensive alternative and can also be tracked via a reference number. All the major international courier services deliver to Abu Dhabi, including DHL (800 4004), FedEx (800 33339), UPS (800 4774) and Aramex (02 555 1911), and all of them will deliver to your door. If you are expecting a package, make sure the person sending it has included the correct phone number, as that is often the only way for a courier to find your location.

Television

There are a number of free television channels available in the UAE, but English language channels are limited. Most expats opt for paid TV from one of the satellite services like Orbit Showtime Network (osn.com), but if you don't fancy a satellite dish or your rental terms don't allow one, then the likes of Etisalat and du offer digital TV. Digital TV providers can also provide your broadband and landline phone services, with bundles offering various levels of broadband speed, call time and channel choice available. It can get expensive if you want the best of each.

High Definition (HD) channels are now commonplace and there are plenty of the 'on demand' options available that many expats are used to. For example, OSN customers can purchase a Showbox (a recordable digital receiver) that allows them to pause live television and record favourite shows, and they can also watch movies and series online through OSN Play, which is free to subscribers. Digital TV subscribers also get the benefits of recording and pausing live television, with Etisalat also launching its eLife TV iPad App to let subscribers watch on their tablet via Wi-Fi or Etisalat's super-fast Mobile Internet.

Football Fans

If you're after English Premier League, Spanish La Liga, Italian Serie A or the UEFA Champion's League then you'll need to subscribe to the BeIn Sports package. If you're an existing Etisalat or du subscriber you can add on the package for Dhs.78 or Dhs.77 a month, respectively.

Maids & Cleaners

Domestic Help

You'll find many expats use housemaids in Abu Dhabi as they're readily available and generally much more affordable than in their home countries. Some choose to sponsor a full-time, live-in housemaid, who will also work as a nanny. However, through an agency, you can have a maid for around Dhs.35 per hour (usually a minimum bookable time of two to three hours per visit), and they'll take care of your sweeping, mopping, dusting, washing and ironing.

Abu Dhabi Maids 055 222 9800, *abudhabimaids.ae*
Exiles Maid Service 02 557 1542,
exilesmaidservice.ae
Queen's Beez 050 229 2998

Carpet Cleaners & Laundry Services

While wall-to-wall carpets are rare here, loose rugs and carpets are commonplace and get mucky pretty quickly. Carpet cleaners will come and take these away, returning them like new a few days later. They often offer an upholstery cleaning service too for items that can't be moved, such as sofas.

There's no shortage of laundry shops in Abu Dhabi; they also do dry cleaning and ironing. Make sure you note any specific ironing requirements though - creases in trousers are standard, so speak up if you don't want them. Dry cleaning can cost Dhs.5 to Dhs.8 for a man's shirt, while regular laundry will be even cheaper.

Aroma Cleaning Nr Grace Home Bldg Materials, Musaffah Industrial Area, 02 671 5330
Jeeves of Belgravia Nr Sheraton Khalidiya Hotel, Markaziya West, 02 666 3755
Modern Cleaning Methods 02 645 2825, *modernmethodsco.com*
Sparkle Laundry & Dry Cleaners Mussafah Industrial Area, 02 554 7080

Homes & Gardens

Builders & Decorators

If you're an expat with your own home in Abu Dhabi then you'll be in a relatively new development. However, should you decide that either interior or exterior alterations are needed you need to be a little careful. While the Municipality of Abu Dhabi allows you to seek architectural approval for modifications to existing buildings as well as for pathways and car shades, you may find that your property developer will have its own ideas on what can and cannot be done.

In master developments, for instance, there are strict rules regarding the consistency between properties and changes may have to remain within the general layout of the design. And if you are given permission to carry out your alterations then you may be required to use one of the companies that your developer already works with. Often, for smaller projects, the contractor you hire can arrange approval itself, saving time and effort on your part. Just make sure you've got a reputable contractor on your side. Ask people you trust for references or start with the following options: Dwellings Group (dwellingsgroup. ae) and Mplus+ (abudhabi.mplus.ae).

Maintenance

Thanks mainly to the climate, Abu Dhabi homes can need a fair bit of maintenance; from servicing of air conditioning units and getting rid of unwelcome creepy crawlies, to fixing haywire electrics or sorting out the all-too-common plumbing issues.

General maintenance, such as plumbing and electrical, is the responsibility of the landlord. Your contract may specify who is liable for additional services such as pest control or A/C cleaning. If it falls under your realm of responsibility, there are two main options; employ maintenance services on an annual contract or get issues fixed as they crop up.

Annual contracts are not cheap at between Dhs.7,000 to Dhs.11,000 per year, but they cover most things you'll need; regular air-conditioning servicing, seasonal pest control, basic masonry work and 24 hour emergency call out services. Most companies offer extra services, such as swimming pool maintenance and gardening for an add-on fee.

Taking the approach of fixing problems as they happen means it's a good bet to speak with colleagues and friends for recommended tradesmen. For A/C problems, try companies like York Air Conditioning (02 641 4277) or Duct Doctor (050 235 1513) ; for pest problems try National Pest Control (02 550 2361) or Delight International Facilities Management (02 690 2800). There are dozens of options for each service you might need, so it's always good to do your own research first. At some point your apartment or villa

Where the World comes to School

Authorised to deliver the **International Baccalaureate Primary Years, Middle Years** and **Diploma Programme** to students of over 75 different nationalities.

Fully accredited by the **NEASC**
(New England Association of Schools and Colleges)
and the **CIS** (Council of International Schools).

Abu Dhabi Education Council (ADEC) rating: high performing school/Band A

Visit **www.ris.ae** to apply online or call **+971 (0)2 556 1567**
Khalifa City 'A', Al Raha Gardens, Abu Dhabi

RAHA
INTERNATIONAL
SCHOOL

will need a little help, so being prepared is something that can save you a lot of stress when the roof starts leaking or the patio door gets jammed.

A fresh lick of paint in your new apartment or villa is always welcome and may be well needed. If renting, check with the landlord that decorating is allowed as they don't need much excuse to keep hold of your security deposit when it's time to move out. An excellent range of paints and associated implements can be found at Jotun Paints (02 691 0700) and Ace Hardware (02 673 1665). Companies like Evershine (02 553 1851) offer painting services. The cost of internally painting a whole villa, if you don't fancy the task yourself, can vary between Dhs.3,000 and Dhs.8,000, depending on size, materials and contractor.

Gardens

If you are buying a brand new house, the garden you have may be nothing more than a sandy pit. Even landlords of rental properties aren't obliged to landscape the gardens of new villas before they rent them out. However, a green garden is not out of the question, you only have to look around at some of the parks and lawns around the city to see that. The secret to this is irrigation.

Once you have grass laid and plants planted you'll need to be diligent about watering; in the hot summer months that might mean giving them a drink twice a day. It might be worth using the services of a gardener or having a simple irrigation system installed. Some keen gardeners opt to have a borehole dug in their back yards to reduce their water bills, such is the need for large amounts. As expats do not enjoy land rights though, you will need to get the permission of the land owner. In any case, the general rule of thumb is the further from the sea you are, the further you will have to drill down. The upside of this is you'll have to worry less about the salinity of the water.

Adding extra greenery with plants is the next step, and it's a wise move to plant hardy native species as they generally need less water. The plant souk at Meena Port sells a wide array of plant types including these desert-hardened foliages. There are also stores here offering landscaping services at very reasonable rates. Elsewhere, Carrefour, Spinneys, IKEA and Ace Hardware have a selection of plants as well as a small amount of essential gardening tools.

If the thought of all that gardening and watering is too much, but you can't stand looking at a sandpit then a fake lawn could be the way to go. They stay green all year and, aside from an occasional hosing down, they don't need watering. You can buy astroturf in Ace (aceuae.com), while Clearview (clearview. ae) installs fake lawns. Alternatively, opt for block paving or decking. Ace also sells decking, while Alomi (alomirealwoodflooringllc.com) is a specialist wood merchant with experienced carpenters to lay decks.

If you head to Plant Souk, adjacent to the Iranian Souk in Al Meena Port, you can buy plenty of trees, shrubs and flowering plants to really liven up your lawn. Prices here are also a good deal cheaper than anywhere else.

Swimming Pools

A lot of properties in Abu Dhabi have private pools or at least access to a shared development pool. If you don't have one in your villa, you can always pay to have one installed – but it doesn't come cheap. Another option is to have a custom-made, free-form fibreglass and ceramic pool fitted. As tough and durable as a concrete version, these pools are effectively portable, although it would be a massive job. Allow for around four weeks for delivery, 10 days for installation and an invoice upwards of Dhs.110,000 (including labour costs, pumps and filtration). Try Pools by Design (poolsbydesign.net) or, for a more traditional pool, Absolute Pools (absolute-pools.com).

Home Insurance

There are a number of locally and internationally recognised insurance companies operating in the UAE that offer coverage against theft (which is a relatively uncommon crime), fire, natural disasters and water damage. To apply, you will need to submit a declaration estimating the value of your household contents. In the event of a claim, you must provide receipts and proof of loss/damage. Good coverage will include periods that you are away, though insurers may stipulate minimum security requirements in the policy. These companies are generally the best bet for life, car and pet insurance too.

Abu Dhabi National Insurance Company (ADNIC)
Al Danah, 02 408 0100, *adnic.ae*
Orient Insurance Company Business Avenue Tower,
Shk Zayed Bin Sultan St, Al Danah, 02 676 3222,
insuranceuae.com
AXA Insurance (Gulf) National Consultative Council
Complex, Delma St, Al Nahyan, 02 495 7999,
axa-gulf.com
Emirates Insurance Company Al Firdous St,
Al Zahiyah, 02 644 0400, *eminsco.com*
Gargash Insurance Al Yasat Tower, Nr Al Raha
Hospital, Fatima Bint Mubarak St, Al Danah,
02 671 7100, *gargashinsurance.com*
Guardian Insurance Brokers Nr Red Crescent
Authority, Sultan Bin Zayed The First St, Al Nahyan,
02 491 3777, *gib-uae.com*
National General Insurance Co (NGI) Al Otaiba Tower
Fatima Bint Mubarak St, Al Danah, 02 622 0223, *ngi.ae*
RSA Habib Bank Bldg, Hamdan Bin Mohammed St,
Al Danah, 02 635 1800, *rsadirect.ae*

A good move delivers the biggest. smile.

Eastern Ring Road

GETTING AROUND

Abu Dhabi is a city geared up for cars, and it has a good and continuously improving infrastructure. With a grid-like street system it shouldn't take you too long to find your way around. However, if you're planning on using satellite navigation systems, it can be confusing. Streets are generally well-signposted with bilingual blue or green signs indicating the main areas or roads in and out of the city and a new and official street name and numbering system was implemented in 2014, but people often refer to streets by their colloquial name or rely on landmarks to give directions.

There are some good public transport options (bus routes carry passengers all over the emirate), but most people do travel by car, whether that's driving themselves or using generally excellent and inexpensive taxis. Driving is probably the best way to get the measure of the city's numerous districts. Traffic during rush hours can get heavy, especially if

there's even a minor accident, but you'll soon learn where the hotspots are and either avoid or leave for your destination at an appropriate time. There are other idiosyncrasies you'll find too; traffic lights spring up everywhere and you can find yourself sat at a red light in an empty building site for ages. You'll also encounter plenty of speed bumps that even the largest 4WDs will take at crawling pace.

Other sights you may find unusual are the number of cars that pull over and stop on the hard shoulder. This is particularly obvious at sunset when some drivers will stop to answer the call to prayer by the side of the road. And once it's dark, watch out for workers who loiter by the side of motorways waiting for lifts. Sometimes they can be quite close to the road and difficult to spot. Despite government guidelines on driving, don't count on other road users. Being cautious is the best approach to stay incident free.

Abu Dhabi Road Network

Abu Dhabi's road network is excellent, and most roads have at least three lanes. A new naming system, Onwani, is being completed and should be fully operational by 2015. It will make navigation even more straightforward as all buildings in Abu Dhabi will have actual addresses. At the moment you will have to give your taxi driver a landmark near your destination or, if you're driving, be guided by vague directions.

Abu Dhabi island is linked to the mainland by three bridges; each holds one of the three main roads into and out of the city. Mussafah Bridge sees Al Khaleej Al Arabi Street at the south side; Al Maqtaa Bridge holds Rashid Bin Al Maktoum Rd, which runs through the middle of the city; and the Sheikh Zayed Bridge carries Shk Zayed Bin Sultan St to the north. In addition, the Sheikh Khalifa Bridge and Expressway links to the north end of the Corniche, provide alternative routes to and from the city through Saadiyat and Yas islands.

Historically, all Abu Dhabi roads were numbered. Odd numbered streets ran eastwards from First Street (the Corniche) to 31st Street, while even numbered streets ran south from Eighth Street (Shk Zayed Bin Sultan St) down to Second Street and then suddenly from 22nd Street to 32nd Street. Although you will still hear residents refer to streets by their numbers, these have been removed from the new street signs. Also missing from the new signs are the colloquial names of the roads, which are used more often than the proper names. Following are some of the new signposted street names, with colloquial names and numbers in parenthesis: Rashid Bin Al Maktoum Rd (2nd, Airport); Khalifa Bin Zayed The First St (3rd); Sultan Bin Zayed The First St (4th, Muroor); Hamdan Bin Mohammed St (5th); Fatima Bint Mubarak St (6th, Najda); Shk Zayed First St (7th, Electra); Shk Zayed Bin Sultan St (8th, Salaam); Al Falah St (9th); Hazaa Bin Zayed St (11th, Defence); Delma St (13th).

Road Signs

Signposting in Abu Dhabi is generally very good once you understand the system. Blue or green signs indicate the roads, exits or locations out of the city, while brown signs show heritage sites, places of interest and hospitals.

Maps

With new roads popping up on a weekly basis, finding your way around Abu Dhabi can be made a little more difficult. Explorer produces several of the most up-to-date street maps available, including the fully indexed *Abu Dhabi Street Atlas*, the pocket-sized *Abu Dhabi Mini Map* and the handy *Abu Dhabi Tourist Map*. Visit askexplorer.com/shop.

If the signage gets confusing, remember that Al Maqtaa, Al Mussafah and Sheikh Zayed Bridges all lie at one end of the island, while following any sign for the Corniche will lead you to the other end of the island. Road signs for the Sheikh Khalifa Highway will direct you to the giant ringroad that joins Abu Dhabi's stretch of Corniche with the E11 road north to Dubai or south toward Ruwais.

Abu Dhabi taxis

Once you get off the island, simply put, Dubai means north, Al Ain means east, and Tarif, Al Gharbia and Madinat Zayed all mean south.

Address System

The current overhaul of addresses in Abu Dhabi will see a format similar to that used in the UK. An address will have a building number, street name, city name, emirate and postcode. It will be a landmark achievement in the city when completed as official addresses have never existed here before.

While this is still being rolled out though, your address is essentially given by landmarks. This means companies will often list their building name, road and nearest landmark when giving you their location.

Explorer's *Abu Dhabi Street Atlas* makes locating particular building much easier with an index of almost 5,000 roads and buildings.

Driving In Abu Dhabi

Vehicles in Abu Dhabi have the steering wheel on the left and they drive on the right-hand side of the road. If you're from a country like the UK or India where the steering wheel is on the right, don't worry about having to learn changing gears with the other hand – the vast majority of cars here have automatic transmissions.

Despite the good roads, driving in Abu Dhabi can be a bit of a culture shock. Road manners are in short supply and drivers generally have a one-tracked mind about where they want to get to, giving little thought to cars behind them. Some of the worst offenders will take to the hard shoulder to avoid queues or tailgate excessively to force others to change lanes. It can be a frightening experience for first-time drivers in the city.

Abu Dhabi road accident statistics are improving every year, with an 18% drop in fatalities recorded in the first 8 months of 2014 versus the same period in 2013. Still, it's essential to be an aware, defensive driver. The five main causes of accidents in the emirate in 2014, according the Abu Dhabi Police Traffic and Patrols Directorate, were: speeding; sudden swerving; negligence and general inattention to the road; tailgating; and jumping the red light.

Automatic Licence Transfer

Citizens with licences from the following countries are eligible for automatic driving licence transfers: Australia, Austria, Belgium, Canada, Denmark, Finland, France, Germany, Greece, Ireland, Italy, Japan, Netherlands, New Zealand, Norway, Poland, South Africa, South Korea, Sweden, Switzerland, Turkey, United Kingdom and United States. Citizens of GCC countries do not need to apply for licence transfer.

Licence To Drive

Tourists can drive hire cars on their domestic licence or an International Driving Permit. If you have a residence visa then you must have a UAE driving licence – it is illegal to drive without one. Some nationals qualify for an automatic licence transfer, so long as their original licence has not expired (see above and Moving To Dubai).

To apply for a permanent driving licence, submit the necessary documents (your existing foreign licence, passport with visa page or Resident ID, NOC from your employer or sponsor and a passport photo with Dhs.200) to the Traffic & Licensing Department (adpolice.gov.ae). The licence is produced within minutes and is valid for 10 years, with renewal being a straightforward process.

If you're from a county that qualifies for automatic licence renewal but your domestic licence has expired, you will either need to sit a full driving test, or you can return home and renew it there to save some hassle.

Always carry your driving licence with you in the vehicle, along with the registration card – you could be fined if stopped by the police otherwise.

Parking

The majority of hotels in the centre of Abu Dhabi have underground parking, which is useful if you're heading for an evening out. On the streets, it can be a little more problematic. The busy city has car parks dotted all over, but they are often full. The city-wide Mawaqif pay & display system charges between Dhs.2-3 per hour with a maximum charge of Dhs.15 in 24 hours. Parking is generally free between 10pm and 7am and on Fridays and official holidays. The pay machines, which are powered by inbuilt solar panels, accept one dirham coins. You can also purchase a Mawaqif prepaid card at local minimarts. The most convenient option, though, is to pay via your mobile phone. The system sends you a text message 10 minutes before your time expires which allows you to easily renew for an additional hour; it's very convenient when you're in the middle of a meeting and don't have time to pop more coins in the meter. Sign up at mawaqif.ae.

Should you be prepared to walk a short distance you'll usually be able to find a parking space. Due to the sweltering heat, however, most Abu Dhabi drivers try to park as close to their destination as possible, oftentimes with fairly creative results. Don't be tempted to follow suit and park illegally though, as the patrolling Mawaqif agents do hand out tickets.

There are specially designated parking spaces for people with disabilities in most malls and supermarkets – to use these spaces you will need to obtain a permit from the Abu Dhabi General Police Directorate (02 446 1461).

Residents' Parking

Residential permits are available from Mawaqif and allow residents to park in any available standard parking bay in the area where they live. The annual fee for a parking permit is Dhs.800; add another vehicle and it's a discounted Dhs.1,200 total fee. To apply you need a passport copy with residence visa, a lease or ownership contract, your last electricity bill and vehicle ownership documents. The verification and processing of residents permits takes a minimum of three working days.

If you're visiting friends, be mindful not to park in residents' parking spots any time after 9pm. These spots, located in the interior of each block rather than on the street side, are generally well-indicated with blue signs. Non-residents parked in these spots will face a hefty fine and possible removal and towing of their cars – you've been warned!

For more information visit mawaqif.ae or the Customer Service Centre on the corner of Hamad bin Mohamed Street and Shk Zayed Bin Sultan St (open 7am-9pm Sat to Thur, and 5pm-9pm Fri). You may want to catch a cab there, as coincidentally, parking is a nightmare.

Road Tolls

Abu Dhabi doesn't charge you to use its roads, although there is a car registration fee of around Dhs.200, payable annually when your vehicle is inspected for safety and roadworthiness. If you're driving to Dubai, there is an automated toll system along Sheikh Zayed Road/E11 Highway. It has six gates that will charge you Dhs.4 as you pass through each, to a maximum charge of Dhs.20 per day.

There's no toll booth, instead you must purchase a Salik tag, register it and add prepaid credit to it. The tag goes on your windscreen and the system automatically recognises your tag and car then charges your account accordingly. If you drive through the gates without enough credit, fines start at Dhs.50; if your car is not registered with Salik and you drive through a gate you'll be charged Dhs.100 in the first instance. In both cases, the maximum fine is Dhs.10,000 per calendar year. The Salik system is very well-run across the UAE. Although you will incur violations if you fail to keep your account charged it, it is a straightforward thing to do. Salik sill also SMS you reminder texts when your balance is running low.

If you're heading to Dubai, the fourth petrol station past Abu Dhabi airport on the E11, around 40 minutes into your journey, sells the Salik tags. If you've forgotten to pick one up, be on the lookout for helpful signs that warn of impending Salik gates; take the exit before the gate to avoid it. For more information visit salik.ae or call 800 72545.

Traffic Fines & Offences

Speed limits in the city are generally 60kph or 80kmph, and 100kmph or 120kmph on highways. Signs displaying speed limits appear regularly, so you have little excuse if you're caught. Any traffic violation, including speeding, will come with a fine and could mean black points. You start with 24 points and black points are subtracted from that. The number of points and level of fine handed out depends on severity of violation; speeding at more than 60kmph over the speed limit will see you receive 12 black points, a 30 day vehicle confiscation and a Dhs.1,000 fine, exceed the limit by less than 30kmph and it's a Dhs.600 fine. A full black points table is on adpolice.gov.ae.

You won't be notified if you're caught on a speed camera – but you will be expected to pay all outstanding fines when you come to re-register your vehicle at the end of the year. To avoid any nasty shocks keep a check on your offences by visiting adpolice.gov.ae and entering your vehicle registration plate; you can then pay online.

If you are pulled over by the police or are involved in an accident you'll need to show your driving licence or risk being fined. You will be given a grace period in which to present your licence at the police station; if you fail to do so, you risk having your car impounded and facing a court appearance.

It's worth remembering that children under 10 years old are not allowed to sit in front seats and passengers in front seats must wear seatbelts. It goes without saying that drink-driving is illegal, and Abu Dhabi has a zero-tolerance policy – get caught and you'll face jail and deportation. Also, in the event of road rage, keep your cool and avoid making any rude gestures or swearing as it's considered highly offensive and you could be prosecuted.

To get totally up to speed, you can find the UAE Federal Traffic Law online. However, it may end up creating more questions than it gives answers, with the rules of the road relatively vague.

Blood Money

Part of Shariah law is the awarding of blood money or 'diya' if one causes death or injury to another person. This is commonplace after fatal road accidents. The blood money is paid to the victim's family as compensation, and in the UAE that's Dhs.200,000 for the death of a male and Dhs.100,000 for a female, although the judge in charge of the case can decide on the final amount. Injuries are a percentage of the total, so multiple injuries can add up to much more. If a person kills someone to protect himself, his family, his property or other individuals and their property from harm, then blood money is not paid.

U-turns are frequent

contracted by the police to process minor accidents; their cars are white with black and orange markings. Motorists involved in minor traffic accidents will be asked to pay Dhs.300 for their attendance, payable by the party at fault.

Road Service Patrol

Abu Dhabi's Department of Transport launched the free Road Services Patrol service in late 2011. The Road Service Patrol is contactable by calling 999, and offers recovery of broken down vehicles, assistance with issues like flat tyres and can apply first aid support to the police in accident situations.

A nominal fee of Dhs.50 will be charged to get a report and diagram in accidents caused by unknown persons. When Saaed arrive, have your vehicle, driver's licence and insurance papers ready for them and follow their instructions. They will ask your opinion of what happened and then decide who was at fault. Make sure you call Saeed too, even if the other party has. If they decide it's your fault you get a pink/red form; the other driver, who is given a green form, can then claim on your insurance for any required repairs. The insurance company will need a copy of your green or red form; without it a garage cannot legally carry out repairs.

If the accident is serious, call 999 immediately. The call centre can dispatch emergency services to the scene. In the case of serious accidents, cars should not be moved from the scene until the police have arrived.

Breakdowns

Although Abu Dhabi motorists don't have a reputation for being exceptionally courteous or helpful, in the event of a breakdown you will usually find that passing cars will stop to lend a hand. If help isn't forthcoming, you can call 999 to request the Road Service Patrol to come to the scene. Pull your car over to a safe spot if possible, and evacuate the vehicle until help arrives.

The Arabian Automobile Association (800 4900) offers a 24 hour roadside breakdown service for an annual charge. This includes help for minor mechanical repairs, battery boosting, if you run out of petrol, get a flat tyre or lock yourself out. The more advanced service includes off-road recovery, vehicle registration and a rent a car service. For more information go to aaauae.com. Other useful breakdown or recovery services include Abrat Al Sahraa Transport & Recovery (02 555 5848) and Lucky Recovery (02 555 5522). Some car dealers offer a free breakdown service for the first year after buying a new, or sometimes used, car; most insurance companies also offer the option of including breakdown and recovery in your cover package.

Traffic Accidents

In the case of a non-serious road accident, if no one is hurt and vehicle damage is minor, you must move your vehicles to the side of the road to avoid blocking traffic. Failure to do this can result in a Dhs.200 fine. If emergency services are not required, call Saaed on 800 72233. Saaed is an independent agency

Petrol Stations

Petrol stations in Abu Dhabi are run by the Abu Dhabi National Oil Company's distribution division, ADNOC-FOD, and are usually open around the clock. There are plenty of petrol stations on the main roads around the Abu Dhabi emirate; you'll find at least four each way between Abu Dhabi and Dubai on the Sheikh Zayed Road (E11). In the city most petrol stations line either Rashid Bin Al Maktoum Rd or Al Khaleej Al Arabi Street, with others dotted around Downtown and Khalidiya areas. Off the island, there are not as many options and you may need to plan your petrol stops.

Petrol pumps are manned by attendants, meaning you only have to drive up, pop open the fuel cap and tell them what you want. In the hot summer months, this means you don't have to get out of your cool air-conditioned car. ADNOC has tried introducing self-service pumps before and may yet attempt it again, but if they do there will still be manned pumps too. Filling up a car like a Toyota Yaris should cost you no more than Dhs.70, including a small tip for the attendant, who will also wash your windshield upon request. In Abu Dhabi, all ADNOC stations accept both cash and credit cards.

Most petrol stations offer other services like car washes, oil changes and even tyre replacement. They also generally have a fast food establishment or two attached to them, as well as a shop selling all those things you may have forgotten on your weekly grocery run. If you can avoid filling up at commuting times it's worth doing, as queues at petrol stations can be frustratingly long – and don't be surprised to see some interesting queue jumping from fellow drivers.

Learning To Drive

For those needing to sit a test, or learn to drive while in the UAE, a learning permit is required from the Traffic Police. You will need your essential documents, the driving licence documents and Dhs.40, and to take an eye test at the Drivers Licensing Department at Abu Dhabi Police.

For a driving licence, applicants must open a traffic file with the licensing department before heading to the Emirates Driving Company, or EDC, (edcad.ae or 02 551 1911) for training; a branch of the department can be found at the EDC.

After the traffic file initiation, applicants will register at the EDC, where you'll need: two recent personal photos, a passport copy with valid residence visa, valid Resident ID, an applicant's driving test appointment (created at traffic file opening stage) and a previous driving licence – if any.

Emirates Driving Company

Emirates Driving Company (EDC) was established in 2000 in Abu Dhabi, as a public joint stock company partially owned by Abu Dhabi government, with the aim of reducing the frequency of traffic accidents, increasing training competencies and developing the skills of the drivers.

The first stage is to get a theory training and theory test (orientation courses and intensive bookings are available at the special service centre upon request). Applicants with a valid previous driving licence will then have practical road lessons with an external private school before taking a 'one chance' road test with the Traffic & Licensing Department, at Abu Dhabi Police.

If you've never had a driving licence before or you've failed the above test you'll need to book a personal assessment plan (PEP) in order to identify your ability level for the practical yard training (four levels are available). Based on the PEP test results, the practical yard training in EDC should then be booked (which includes simulator training) and finally you'll sit the yard test in EDC. The final stage before the road test (three chances to pass) will be training on the road with private driving schools.

Al Harbi Driving School Nr Electra Park, Al Zahiyah, 02 671 6177
Delma Driving School Delma Island, 02 878 1838
Emirates Driving Company Street 17, Mussafah Industrial Area, 02 551 1911, *edcad.ae*

Etihad Plaza

Hiring A Car

Whether you're waiting for your residence visa to be processed, aren't sure how long you'll be in the UAE or simply don't want the hassle of buying a car, long-term renting is the best way forward. Reputable companies will include registration, maintenance, replacement, 24-hour assistance and insurance in their fee, meaning you just have to drive it and fill it with petrol.

The longer you book your rental car for, the cheaper the rate you receive will be; a small economy car should cost you around Dhs.1,700 per month, but it's worth shopping around to get the best deal. See if your company is affiliated with a particular agency; this might also help keep the price down. For peace of mind it's worth paying more to ensure a high-level of comprehensive cover, including personal accident coverage, and cover for Oman should you be planning on a spot of exploring. If you'll only be traveling to Oman occasionally, though, you can buy relatively inexpensive coverage at the border.

MAPPING SOLUTIONS

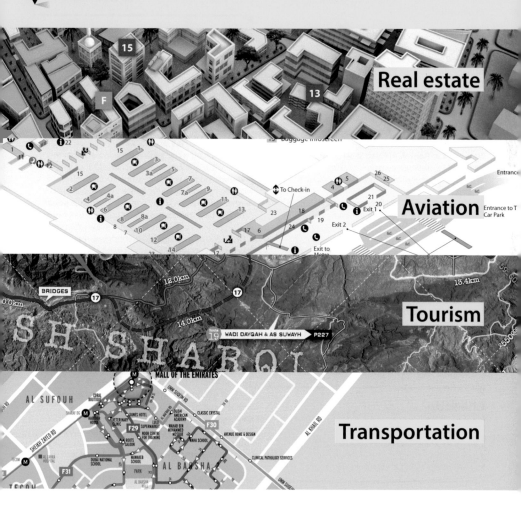

Real estate

Aviation

Tourism

Transportation

From our best-selling products to our innovative and fully client-integrated custom mapping solutions, we deliver maps of the highest quality that meet the exact needs of our customers, our clients, and their customers.

ask explorer.com

     askexplorer

If you drive to Dubai regularly the Salik charges will be added to your monthly bill, but be aware of any monthly or yearly mileage limits put in your agreement. You need a UAE driving licence to drive a hire car if you're a resident; tourists can drive them with their domestic licence and an International Driving Permit.

Avis Abu Dhabi, 02 575 7180, Al Ain, 03 768 7262 *avisuae.ae*
Budget Rent A Car Sultan Bin Zayed The First St, Al Wahdah, 02 443 8430, *budget-uae.com*
Dollar Rent A Car > *p.79* Hazza Bin Zayed St, Al Dhafrah, 02 641 9002, *dollaruae.com*
Europcar Nr NBAD, Khalifa Bin Zayed St, 02 626 1441, Al Ain, 03 721 0180 *europcar-middleeast.com*
Hertz Rent A Car Al Falah St, Al Danah, 02 672 0060, *hertzuae.com*
National Car Rental Al Falah St, Al Dhafrah, 02 642 5115, *national-ae.com*
Sixt Rent A Car Musaffah Industrial Area, 02 550 3723, *sixt.com*
Thrifty Car Rental Shk Hamdan Bin Mohammed St, Markaziya West, 02 634 5663, *thriftyuae.com*

Buying A Car

The UAE is a good place to be if you like cars. Petrol is cheap, big engines are commonplace and, when there are roads, they are generally flat and smooth. New residents may also be surprised at how affordable a brand new vehicle can be. A new BMW 3-series in Abu Dhabi is likely to cost around 20% less than the same car in the UK. This price gap and low running costs can tempt expats into opting for something a bit more extravagant than they would buy back home.

Check Up

Before buying a used car, it's a good idea to get it checked by a reputable garage, especially if it's a 4WD, which might have been driven off-road a lot. The major garages are located out of the city in Mussafah, and will charge around Dhs.400 for this service.

There are bargains to be had on the second-hand market too, with expats often keen to shift a car below market value to ensure a sale before leaving the country. Online sites like dubizzle.com or autotraderuae.com are useful, as are the notice boards of your local supermarket for bargain buys.

Motor World Abu Dhabi in Shamkah near Abu Dhabi Airport is the dedicated area for car dealerships. It's been a little slow to take off due to the out of town location, but if you want choice and the chance

to haggle, this is the place to go. Most of the big dealerships from the island have already relocated there. Just don't expect a good price for your car if you're selling. Some locals gather on a nearby roundabout at weekends to sell their cars, which can offer considerable savings for buyers.

Gulf Spec

Try to check any second-hand car you're buying is 'Gulf Spec', particularly European or American marques. This means the manufacturer has taken measures to reinforce the vehicle against the harsh climate such as an electric fan over oil coolers and air filters better suited to dealing with the sand in the air.

Second-Hand Sales

As well as getting the vehicle tested, check that the engine plate number on the car corresponds with that given on the vehicle registration card. Also, check with the Abu Dhabi Traffic Police that the vehicle is neither stolen nor has any fines; visit adpolice.gov.ae. After you have purchased the vehicle, you will need to insure it, then transfer ownership/vehicle registration, A Dhs.3,000 fine is imposed on both buyer and seller for cars sold unofficially. You will need to collect an application form from the Traffic Police and submit it, along with an NOC from the seller's finance company (if applicable), the previous owner's registration card, your new insurance certificate, your UAE driving licence and a Dhs.100 transfer fee. The previous owner must also be present to sign the form.

Importing A Car

It is possible to import or export your car, but be prepared for paperwork, and a bit more paperwork. If you're keen to hang onto your chosen four wheels, the best thing to do is to contact Kanoo Shipping (kanooshipping.com) or Khalidia International Shipping (khalidiashipping.com) for more details.

If you're buying a car from outside of Abu Dhabi you will need to complete export and import procedures. Both buyer and seller will need to be present at the licensing department in the seller's emirate. The department will ask for copies of a passport and driving licence, the vehicle registration card, an insurance policy in the new owner's name (three day policies can be available at the site) and a technical inspection certificate. The seller may also need a no objection certificate from their bank if there is an outstanding loan amount. In all emirates aside from Dubai you will be issued with export plates to drive the car home on. You will then have to register it in Abu Dhabi. If buying from Dubai, the car will have to be transported to Abu Dhabi on the back of a truck, which costs between Dhs.400 to Dhs.600.

TAKE FREEDOM TO THE NEXT LEVEL
2015 JEEP® RANGE

Jeep® Grand Cherokee Limited
- 3.6 L V6 Pentastar™ Engine, 290 HP
- 8-Speed Automatic transmission

Jeep® Wrangler Unlimited
- 3.6L V6 Pentastar engine, 285hp
- 4x4 command track system

Jeep® Cherokee
- 3.2L Pentastar™ V6 Engine, 271 HP
- NEW 9-Speed Automatic Transmission

Jeep® Wrangler Rubicon
- 3.6L V6 Pentastar engine, 285hp
- Hill Start Assist and Hill Descent Control

Jeep® Compass
- 2.4L, 4 Cylinder Engine, 172 HP
- 6 Speed Automatic Freedom Drive 4x4 system

INCLUDES 5 YRS OR 100,000 KMS WARRANTY

Jeep®

f www.facebook.com/JeepAbuDhabi   www.twitter.com/JeepAbuDhabi   www.youtube.com/JeepAbuDhabi   www.instagram.com/JeepAbuDhabi

SOLE DISTRIBUTOR FOR JEEP IN ABU DHABI AND AL AIN

الغربيــة للسيارات ذم م
Western Motors LLC

Airport Road Showroom: 02-652 2510
Corniche Showroom: 02-499 5333
Al Ain: 03-715 7477

For more information, call:
800 JEEP(5337)
www.**jeep**abudhabi.com

Lamborghini Murcielago

Vehicle Finance

Many new and second-hand car dealers will be able to arrange finance for you, often through a deal with a preferred banking partner like ADCB or NBAD. Most official dealers and main financial establishments should be able to sort out monthly automatic payments for you. Alternatively a personal loan often offers lower interest rates and better terms. If you go with the bank that receives your salary, the application is often easier. Just make sure you can afford the payments as bad debt is not good news.

New Car Dealers

Abu Dhabi Motors (BMW, MINI, Rolls-Royce) Nr Maqta Bridge, 02 507 5800, *bmw-abudhabi.com*
Al Fahim Motors (Central Motors), Mussafah M5 intersection, 02 656 7000, *alfahim.com*
Al Futtaim Motors (Toyota, Lexus) Nr Carrefour, Shk Rashid Bin Saeed St, Al Madina Al Riyadiya, 02 419 9999, *alfuttaimmotors.com*
Al Habtoor Motors (Bentley, Bugatti, McLaren, Mitsubishi) Al Falah St, Al Danah, 02 698 9600, *habtoormotors.com*
Al Jaziri Motors (Lamborghini) Nation Towers, Corniche Rd, Al Dhafrah 02 641 7611, *Lamborghini-abudhabi.com*
Al Masaood Automobiles (Infinity, Nissan, Renault) Fatima Bint Mubarak St, Al Danah 02 677 2000, *masaood.com*
Al Yousuf Motors (Daihatsu), Abu Dhabi – Al Ain Rd, Sas Al Nakhl Island 02 558 8890, *aym.ae*

Audi Abu Dhabi Al Sawari Tower A, Corniche Rd West, Al Khalidiya, 02 665 8000, *audi-abudhabi.com*
Bin Hamoodah Automotive (Chevrolet, GMC) Nr Holiday Inn Hotel, Shk Rashid Bin Saeed St, Hadabat Al Zaafaran, 02 444 8888, *binhamoodahauto.com*
Emirates Motor Company (Mercedes-Benz) 10th St, Truck Rd, Mussafah Industrial Area, 02 656 7777, *abudhabi.mercedesbenzme.com*
Galadari Automobiles (Mazda) Al Mamda Plaza Residence, Fatima Bint Mubarak St, Al Danah, 02 677 3030, *mazdauae.com*
Juma Al Majid Est (Hyundai) Shk Zayed The Second St, Al Danah, 02 644 0233, *hyundai-uae.com*
Liberty Abu Dhabi Automobiles (Cadillac) Nr Maqta Bridge, Al Maqta, 02 558 9988, *libertyautos.com*
Mercedes-Benz Main Showroom, Mussafah M5, 02 656 7755, *abudhabi.mercedesbenzme.com*
Peugeot Nr HSBC, Shk Rashid Bin Saeed St, Al Danah, 02 633 3000, *peugeotabudhabi.ae*
Porsche Centre Al Salam Tower, Salam St, Al Zahiyah, 02 674 5600, *porscheabudhabi.com*
Premier Motors (Ferrari, Ford, Jaguar, Land Rover, Lincoln, Maserati) Zayed the First St, Al Khubeirah, 02 493 5000, *premier-motors.ae*
Trading Enterprises (Chrysler, Dodge, Jeep, Volvo) Nr Etisalat, Shk Zayed The First St, Al Danah, 02 633 3408, *tradingenterprises.com*
Volkswagen Nr NBAD, Corniche Rd, Al Khalidiya, 02 681 7770, *volkswagen-abu-dhabi.com*
Western Motors > *p.87* (Fiat, Jeep) Al Sawari Tower B, Al Khalidiya, 02 667 6000, *jeepabudhabi.com*

Used Car Dealers

501 Cars Nr National Theatre, Shk Rashid Bin Saeed St, Al Mushrif, 02 666 6501, *501cars.com*

Al Fahim Motors (Central Motors), Mussafah M5 intersection, 02 656 7000, *alfahim.com*

Al Futtaim Automall Nr Mina Centre, Al Meena, 02 673 3504, *automalluae.com*

Al Hilal Auto Al Sahel Tower, Al Khubeirah, 02 417 4720, *alhilalbankauto.ae*

Ali & Sons Used Cars Division Al Sawari Tower A, Al Khalidiya, 02 665 8000, *asusedcars.com*

Porsche Centre Mussafah Al Salam Tower, Al Zahiyah, 02 619 3911, *porscheabudhabi.com*

Prestige Cars Al Khaleej Al Arabi St, Al Khalidiya, 02 681 0111, *prestigecars.ae*

Reem Automobile Showroom Motor World, Al Shamkha, 02 586 2121, *reemauto.ae*

Western Motors > *p.87* (Fiat, Jeep) Al Sawari Tower B, Al Khalidiya, 02 667 6000, *jeepabudhabi.com*

Insurance

Annual insurance policies last for 13 months (allowing a one-month grace period for when registration expires). It's best to get fully comprehensive cover with personal accident cover, and advisable to be covered for 'blood money'. Rates depend on age and model of your car and your previous insurance history, although no-claims bonuses accrued in your home country are rarely recognised. Expect to pay between 4-7% of the vehicle's value, or a flat rate of 5% for cars over five years old. If you feel your car is worth more than you paid for it, make sure the insurance company covers it at the market value. Insurers will need to see copies of your UAE driving licence, passport and vehicle registration form.

Most insurance agencies now let you request a quote online, and there's a multitude of choice out there from local companies such as AWNIC (awnic.com) to international favourites, AXA (axa-gulf.com), RSA (rsadirect.ae) and Zurich (zurich.ae). If you're driving to Oman you will need additional cover, which can be part of your annual insurance or purchased ad hoc.

Registering A Vehicle

All cars must be registered annually with the Abu Dhabi Police department; if you're buying new, then the dealer should do this for you. All cars over three years old must also have an annual vehicle inspection test, which is part of the registration process.

Vehicle registration, vehicle testing and the renewal of annual car insurance generally take place at the same time. To start the process, first check you have no outstanding traffic offence and fines against your car at adpolice.gov.ae as registration renewal can't be completed until they are cleared. Then, renew your insurance as you will be asked to show a valid 13 months certificate. With this done, take your vehicle to a Vehicle Licensing Department-approved service centre; the vehicle test centre at Al Salama main building in Abu Dhabi operates 24 hours from Sunday to Thursday, for example. (See adpolice.gov.ae for a list of service centres).

Pay the Dhs.120 test fee, wait for around 20-30 minutes for the test, and hopefully it should pass and you'll receive a test certificate. If your vehicle fails the inspection, have it repaired and retested within 30 days for no additional fee. Some insurance companies offer to collect your vehicle and handle the test and registration for you – often within a couple of hours.

Once passed and with test certificate in hand, go to a registration office and submit your insurance certificate, current registration card (or that of the previous owner if you are transferring ownership), UAE driving licence and Resident ID, plus the Dhs.100 fee. You'll receive a new registration card plus a new sticker for your vehicle's rear plate. Now you're all legal to drive the vehicle for another year.

You have one month's grace for renewal of your car registration, hence the 13 month insurance policy. This keeps you legal if it's inconvenient to get the car registration renewed at the specified time. After that month though, you will incur fines of Dhs.10 for each month you delay. If renewal hasn't happened for over a year, the charge for re-registration is Dhs.325.

Vehicle Repairs

Major repairs can only be completed with an accident report form from the Traffic Police. However, minor repairs like dent and scratch removals do not need one. Your insurance company will send you to a particular garage or give a selection of preferred garages, and you will likely have an excess to pay of around Dhs.250-500, depending on your policy. If your car is new or still within warranty, make sure the insurance covers 'agency repairs' – repairs at the workshop of the dealer selling the car. Non-agency repairs may invalidate your vehicle's warranty. Like in any country, it's also worth keeping your new car serviced regularly as your dealership advises, as this keeps your vehicle desirable for prospective buyers.

For older cars, many ADNOC service stations and other petrol stations offer a range of basic car maintenance procedures, such as lubrication service and air inflation for flat tyres. There are some where you can get a drive-in, drive-out oil change. Mussafah also has a concentration of small workshops where tyres, oil changes, air-conditioning re-charges and new batteries can be found. In fact, car batteries don't always cope well with the heat in the UAE and it's not uncommon to return to your car and find the battery completely dead. Dial-A-Battery (800 247 365) can come to you 24 hours a day in Abu Dhabi and replace your dead battery with the right new one.

ADM Abu Dhabi Motors Nr Maqtaa Bridge, Airport Rd, Al Maqta, 02 507 5800, *bmw-abudhabi.com*
Al Habtoor Motors Nr Al Futtaim Workshop, Al Safa Industrial Area, Mussafah, 02 555 3344, *habtoormotors.com*
Al Mazroui & Clevy Auto Services Mussafah Industrial Area, 02 555 4589, *mazautouae.com*
Ali & Sons Nr ADNOC, Mussafah Industrial Area, 02 502 6564, *ali-sons.com*
Bosch Service Centre ADNOC, Hadabat Al Zaafaran, 02 449 8060, *cmeuae.ae*
Central Motors & Equipment Mussafah Industrial Area, 02 554 6262, *cmeuae.ae*
Elite Motors Nr Al Falah Plaza Shopping Centre, Al Dhafrah, 02 642 3686
Trading Enterprises Nr ADNOC, Mussafah Industrial Area, 02 698 4000, *tradingenterprises.ae*

Tinted Windows

Many drivers choose to block out the sun's glare and get their vehicle windows tinted. The legal limit is 30% and there is a fine for those who get caught in the dark. Tinting can cost from Dhs.200 for an average car. Having tinted windows will also help to keep your car interior cool while parked in the searing heat of summer, although it'll still get warm in there. Folding screen visors that you put in your windscreen while parked can also help deflect some of the sun's rays.

Cycling

Cycling is a popular leisure pursuit with expats in Abu Dhabi, but it's not a particularly effective method of transport. There are clubs that meet in the early hours and go for long rides around the city's major roads, while others head out to the desert with their mountain bikes. Unfortunately, the city is not geared up for bicycles and there are very few safe areas for cyclists. The Corniche and some of the newer developments off the island do, however, have dedicated cycle lanes with more planned throughout the city. It's advisable to keep your helmet on; there have been several high-profile fatal accidents in the UAE in recent years. The lack of lock-ups outside buildings or offices, the sweat-inducing heat and busy roads with unpredictable traffic means commuting by bike is not really a viable option.

Cycle Tracks

The Corniche is one of the most popular spots for leisure cycling for people of all ages, with Fun Ride Sports (funridesports.com), based at the Hiltonia Beach Club, on hand to rent out bikes for Dhs.25 per hour for adults, Dhs.20 for kids. They have five other stations throughout the city too, including at Abu Dhabi City Golf Club and Yas Plaza on Yas Island.

On Tuesday nights from 6pm to 9pm, cyclists can attend TrainYAS at Yas Marina Circuit and pedal around the 5.55km track for free; Wednesdays are ladies night. The Cleveland Clinic provides complimentary use of 50 bikes each week. If you're too late to snag one of those, rental is available onsite and costs Dhs.30 for a bike and mandatory helmet.

PEDALS & PEDESTRIANS	For walking and cycling enthusiasts there are a few quieter spots around the city. Head to any of these on a cooler day, or in the evening, and enjoy exploring.
Al Mushrif Park	Situated in Mushrif, this is one of the most popular parks for jogging and walking, depsite being one of the smaller parks.
Khalifa Park	At the base of the island is the capital's largest park. Its size makes the park a favourite among walkers. The trees, pergolas and gazebos offer shade from the hot sun, and fountains add to the park's pleasant feel;
Al Khalidiya Public Park	This park boasts lots of grass and space, so is perfect for walks and another favourite for families with children. There's a charge of Dhs.1 in the evenings and on Fridays.
Family Park	Located along Corniche Road, this is a great place to pedal along tree-lined walkways, picnic in the sun, or explore the themed play areas.
Yas Gateway Park	The well-landscaped paths lining yas Leisure Drive and the nearby Yas Gateway Park are ideal for walkers and cyclists seeking a bit of solitude. When there's a concert at the nearby du Arena, this spot comes with a soundtrack.
Al Zahiyah	Formerly the Tourist Club Area, for sheer activity this park can't be beaten. The sights, sounds and smells promise something new with every visit.

Walking

It's best to keep walking outside to a minimum in the height of summer; a five-minute stroll in 45°C temperatures can have you sweating like you've just run a marathon. In the cooler months though, walking around Abu Dhabi can be the best way to explore it, especially in the relatively compact Downtown area. Often there are good pavements, albeit with some large drops to the kerbs, but watch out for haphazard parking blocking the path, or construction areas that don't give pedestrians many options aside from walking in the road. Bear in mind that crossing a main road anywhere but on a marked crossing is illegal, not to mention extremely dangerous. There are Dhs.200 fines for jay-walking, and police have recently been handing out more tickets in an effort to reduce pedestrian fatalities. The subways or overpasses that are located in the middle of most major blocks are a safe and easy place to cross the street, or you can always walk to the next corner. Walking along the Corniche with its retail kiosks, outdoor cafes and beach is a popular pastime as is the Yas Mirina Circuit on Tuesdays.

Abu Dhabi-Dubai Emirates Express

Public Transport

The car is the most popular and practical way of getting around Abu Dhabi. However, with the lack of trains and trams – and with cycling and walking limited during the hot summer months – the most popular form of public transport is the city's bus service.

Plan Abu Dhabi 2030 features a Surface Transport Master Plan, which will include an integrated tram, rail, metro, bus and ferry systems, along with dedicated cycle and pedestrian lanes across the city – so watch this space.

Boat

Despite being located on an island, opportunities for getting around by boat in Abu Dhabi are limited. A free abra crosses the Grand Canal in the evenings, making stops at the Shangri La, Fairmont, and Ritz Carlton hotels, but it's a tourist attraction rather than a mode of transportation. Similarly, there are various boat trips in the form of dinner dhows (traditional Arabic vessels), tours and sightseeing day trips. These can be found departing from the Meena Port or Marina Mall marinas.

Some expats here in Abu Dhabi invest in a boat for regular weekend jaunts to one of the 200 different islands scattered offshore. The climate makes boating a popular hobby, with a number of marinas to berth your boat. Check out uaeboats4sale.com for boat bargains, or the Activities chapter for more information on exploring Abu Dhabi by water.

Bus

Taking a bus is the most affordable option. Inner city fares are a flat Dhs.2. To ride from the city to one of the suburbs adds an additional five fils per kilometre, which averages at about Dhs.5 for each journey.

'Ojra' bus passes can be purchased at the central bus station next to Al Wahda Mall or at any Red Crescent kiosk on the island. An inter-urban pass costs Dhs.80 for one month of unlimited use. For more information on Ojra call 800 55555 or visit ojra. ae where comprehensive bus route maps can be found and easily downloaded in PDF format. Those without passes can simply deposit a Dhs.2 in the silver box upon entering the inter-urban bus; drivers can't provide change, so be sure to have coins handy.

The main bus station in Abu Dhabi is on Hazza Bin Zayed Road next to Al Wahda Mall and there are clearly marked bus stops with air-conditioned shelters on nearly every major road on the island.

The Abu Dhabi-Dubai Emirates Express is a two-hour bus service between the emirates, costing Dhs.25 for a one-way ticket. The bus runs every 30 minutes between 6.30am and 9.30pm from the central bus station in Abu Dhabi, and from Dubai's Al Ghubaibah station from 6.20am to 11.40pm, although they start slightly later at the weekends. Buses to Al Ain leave less frequently and are also Dhs. 25.

For those that want to go to the Al Gharbia region, private vans located in the area in front of the central bus station will transport you for around Dhs.30, depending on your exact destination. Other vans make the trip to Dubai or Al Ain, often leaving you closer to your final destination than the big bus would.

Taxi

Inside the city, taxis are the most popular form of public transport. The city has a 7,000 strong taxi fleet that is overseen by TransAD (transad.ae). In 2015, TransAD will launch 260 new Mercedes taxis on its roads, while an I-phone taxi App was introduced in 2014. You can call TransAd (600 535353) directly and ask them to pick you up. They arrive quickly and you can ask them to remember your home address to make future booking even faster. The starting fee is Dhs.3.50 during the day, Dhs.4 after 10pm and Dhs.20 for an event pick-up. If you use the call centre add Dhs.3 during the day and Dhs.4 at night. Journey costs up to 50km are charged at Dhs.1.6 per kilometre, or Dhs.1.69 per kilometre between 10pm and 6am. There is also a minimum fee of Dhs.10 for taxi rides in the evening period. Tawasul Transport (02 673 4444) provides wheelchair accessible taxis on request.

Transport providers Lyft and Uber also operate in Abu Dhabi, though they are a bit more expensive than TransAD taxis. You can book a ride through either company's eponymous app, and the driver will be given the exact GPS coordinates of your location. This can be very convenient if you're in a maze of villas and it's difficult to explain your location.

Air Travel

Abu Dhabi is well placed to reach destinations in Africa, Asia and Europe. In fact, 100 capital cities are within a six-hour flight from Abu Dhabi. Most European capitals and major cities have direct flights to Abu Dhabi International Airport (code: AUH), with Etihad Airways, the national airline of the UAE, one of the key providers.

The airport is undergoing a dramatic transformation, with a multi-billion Midfield Terminal due to be open in mid 2017. The extension will have a maximum capacity of 40 million passengers and will be among the world's biggest single-capacity buildings. This expansion is linked to Etihad's own expansion as the company aims to increase its fleet of aircraft to 159 by 2020. At the moment, Terminal 3 is exclusively for Etihad Airways.

The airport is well equipped for travellers with disabilities, with a special check-in gate that has direct access from the car park, dedicated lifts and a meet and greet service. This is known as 'Golden Class' (02 575 7466). On leaving the airport you'll find taxis are freely available. There is an hourly round-the-clock bus service between the airport and Abu Dhabi's central bus station. It costs just Dhs.3 each way. Etihad also runs its own private bus service to Dubai, it's free for those with a boarding pass.

Terminals 1 and 2 (Terminal 3 is adjacent to Terminal 1) have short and mid-stay parking, as well as a SKYPARK, while Terminal 2 also has long-stay parking and a free shuttle bus to all other terminals. See abudhabiairport.ae for rates. If you fly with Etihad you can often be eligible for seven days free parking too.

You may notice signs to 'Royal Jet' around the airport. This is an international luxury flight operator based in Abu Dhabi, with a fleet of private charter planes. On Abu Dhabi island you'll also find Al Bateen Executive Airport (code: OMAD), which focuses on private jets. Flying from here can give spectacular views of Sheikh Zayed Grand Mosque.

Checking In

There are two options for early check-in to Abu Dhabi International Airport. Passengers can check-in to the City Terminal, located in Al Zahiyah, up to 24 hours before a scheduled flight, depending on airline. ADNEC, Abu Dhabi National Exhibitions Company, also offers round-the-clock check-in services. Contact the City Terminal (02 644 8434) or ADNEC (02 444 9671) to see if you're eligible for early check-in.

Air Arabia 02 631 5888, *airarabia.com*
Air Blue 02 622 3112, *airblue.com*
Air France 800 23823, *airfrance.ae*
Air India 02 632 2300, *airindia.com*
Air Seychelles 02 611 8640, *airseychelles.com*
Alitalia 02 6222 888, *alitalia.com*
Austrian Airlines 02 677 6621, *austrian.com*
British Airways 02 611 8600, *britishairways.com*
Cathay Pacific 02 617 6000, *cathaypacific.com*
China Airlines 02 626 4070, *china-airlines.com*
CSA Czech Airlines 02 491 5288, *czechairlines.ae*
Delta Airlines 02 671 3033, *delta.com*
Egypt Air 02 634 4777, *egyptair.com*
Emirates 02 60055 5555, *emirates.com*
Ethiopian Airlines 02 627 3333, *ethiopianairlines.com*
Etihad Airways 02 511 0000, *etihadairways.com*
flydubai 04 231 1000, *flydubai.com*
Gulf Air 02 651 6888, *gulfair.com*
Jazeera Airways 04 224 4464, *jazeeraairways.com*
KLM Royal Dutch Airlines 800 556, *klm.com*
Kuwait Airways 02 631 2230, *kuwait-airways.com*
Lufthansa 02 639 4640, *lufthansa.com*
Middle East Airlines 02 622 6300, *mea.com.lb*
Pakistan International Airlines 02 635 2611, *piac.com.pk*
Qatar Airways 02 621 0007, *qatarairways.com*
RAK Airways 02 633 8700, *rakairways.com*
Rotana Jet 02 444 3366, *rotanajet.com*
Royal Air Maroc 02 505 2024, *royalairmaroc.com*
Royal Brunei Airlines 02 611 8630, *bruneiair.com*
Royal Jordanian 02 622 5335, *rj.com*
Saudi Arabian Airlines 02 635 1400, *saudiairlines.com*

National airline Etihad Airways

Shaheen Air 02 626 5111, *shaheenair.com*
Singapore Airlines 02 622 1110,
singaporeair.com
SriLankan Airlines 02 633 7125,
srilankan.com
Sudan Airways 02 833 3967, *sudanair.com*
Turkish Airlines 02 6267 771, *turkishairlines.com*
Yemen Airways 02 633 8700, *yemenia.com*

Low Cost Airlines

There's an ever-increasing choice of budget airlines based in the UAE including Rotana Jet, flydubai and Air Arabia. Each offers no-frills, cheap flights to a wide variety of international destinations.

Outside The City

The UAE's biggest airport is Dubai International Airport (code: DXB), which has three terminals including one dedicated to Emirates. The Dubai World Central Al Maktoum International Airport (code: DWC) is located closer to Abu Dhabi, near Jebel Ali Free Zone and will eventually be the biggest airport in the world, with four terminals and an annual passenger capacity of 160 million. Budget airline Wizz Air was the first to take off from the airport, and other airlines have temporarily relocated there due to ongoing maintenance at DXB. Meanwhile, Al Ain airport flies to nine destinations and is served by seven airlines.

eGate

The eGate is a way for frequent flyers to get through passport control in a matter of seconds, with just a quick swipe of an eGate card and scan of your fingerprint. You can apply for the card at Abu Dhabi Airport or the Abu Dhabi Naturalization Department. To qualify, your passport must have at least six month's validity and you must be a UAE citizen or an expat with a residence visa. Take your passport and a passport photo to either place, submit your fingerprints and pay Dhs.200, and you should have your eGate card in around 15 minutes.

The Future

Etihad Rail is establishing a nationwide network of train lines covering 1,200km and connecting Abu Dhabi with Al Ain, Dubai, Sharjah, Fujairah, Ras Al Khaimah and Khor Fakkan by 2018. Initially this will be aimed at freight transport, but a passenger service between Abu Dhabi and Dubai is likely to be part of future plans. Etihad Rail also plans to extend the train connections into other GCC countries and is even looking at expanding its reach as far as Turkey.

As part of the Surface Transport Master Plan (STMP), which is an extension of the grand Plan Abu Dhabi 2030, the Department of Transport is also planning a metro and light rail system for the capital. The underground section will run from Zayed Sports City to Mina Port, with 17 stations on the line. A light rail 15km blue line is expected to run from Marina Mall to Reem Island with a 13km green line connecting the capital's Central Bus Station to Saadiyat Island. Initial plans had a metro and light rail system operational by 2016, but since construction isn't yet underway, it seems Abu Dhabi metro rides won't happen for at least a few more years.

Central Business District, Al Maryah Island

FINANCE

Money is a big reason for expats to be in Abu Dhabi, so it makes sense to be smart with it when those first tax-free pay cheques come in. From setting up a bank account to credit cards and debt, this chapter will give you the information you need to know in order to watch those dirhams grow.

Main Banks

To open an account in most banks, you will need a residence visa or to have your residence visa application underway. To apply, you will need to submit your original passport, copies of your passport (personal details and visa pages) and an NOC from your sponsor. Some banks set a minimum account limit – this can be anything from Dhs.2,000 for a deposit account and as much as Dhs.10,000 for a current account.

This means at some point during each month your account balance must be over the minimum limit; but if your wages are paid into this account then for most expats that shouldn't be a problem.

There are plenty of ATMs (cash points) available all around Abu Dhabi, even the odd drive-through one, and most cards are compatible with the Central Bank network (some also offer global access links). You may pay a small fee for if you have to use another bank's ATM but it should never be more than a few dirhams. Even if you use your bank card from your home country, you shouldn't have too many issues using an ATM, although the exchange rate given may not always be favourable.

Banks are open from 8am to 1.30pm, Saturday to Wednesday, and 8am to noon on Thursday. Mall branches have more flexible hours; some are open until 10pm. All banks are closed on Fridays.

Abu Dhabi Commercial Bank (ADCB) Shk Zayed Bin Sultan St, Al Danah, 02 696 2576, *adcb.com*
Abu Dhabi Islamic Bank Shk Rashid Bin Saeed St, Al Matar, 02 610 0600, *adib.ae*
Al Hilal Bank Abdulla Al Mahry Bldg, Al Danah, 02 499 4444, *alhilalbank.ae*
Al Masraf Al Masraf Tower, Hamdan St, Al Zahiyah, 02 588 9300, *arbift.com*
Bank of Sharjah Al Mina St, Al Zahiyah, 02 679 5555, *bankofsharjah.com*
Barclays Bank Al Jazeera Tower, Hamdan Bin Mohammed St, Al Danah, 02 429 6902, *barclays.ae*
Citibank Fatima Bint Mubarak St, Al Danah, 02 494 3000, *citibank.com*
Commercial Bank International Corniche St, Al Khalidiya, 600 5 4440, *cbiuae.com*
Commercial Bank of Dubai Baniyas Tower, Al Danah, 02 800 223, *cbd.ae*
Crédit Agricole Corporate & Investment Bank Al Muhairy Centre, Al Manhal, 02 631 2400, *ca-cib.com*
Dubai Islamic Bank Nr Baby Shop, Shk Rashid Bin Saeed St, Al Danah, 02 634 6600, *dib.ae*
Emirates Islamic Bank Shk Rashid Bin Saeed St, Al Karamah, 02 446 4000, *emiratesislamicbank.ae*
Emirates NBD Al Neem Tower, Liwa St, Al Danah, 600 540 000, *emiratesnbd.com*
HSBC Omeir Bin Yousuf Bldg, Shk Rashid Bin Saeed St, Al Danah, 600 554 722, *hsbc.ae*
Mashreq Bank Blue Tower, Khalifa Bin Zayed The First St, Al Danah, 02 627 4737, *mashreqbank.com*
National Bank of Abu Dhabi (NBAD) Nr Al Noor Hospital, Sultan Bin Zayed The First St, Al Danah, 02 611 1111, *nbad.com*
The Royal Bank of Scotland Hazza Bin Zayed St, Al Karamah, 02 408 4005, *rbsbank.ae*
Standard Chartered Crystal Tower, Shk Zayed The First St, Al Khalidiya, 600 522 288, *standardchartered.ae*
Union National Bank Shk Zayed Bin Sultan St, Al Danah, 02 674 1600, *unb.ae*

Best Mobile Banking

Well known city banks, such as the National Bank of Abu DHabi (NBAD) and the Abu Dhabi Commercial Bank (ADCB), offer banking by SMS. Access your account balance, check transactions, or request a chequebook, simply by sending a text. You'll also get SMS messages to your phone whenever money is paid in or leave your account.

Online Banking

Online banking, where you can check your balance, transfer money and pay bills online, is commonplace with the majority of banks. Some, like the National Bank of Abu Dhabi (NBAD, nbad.com) and Abu Dhabi

Commercial Bank (ADCB, adcb.com) offer excellent financial advice and online services for companies and individuals as well as free banking apps that you can download to your smartphone or tablet. These offer the same functionality and make keeping track of your finances even easier.

Money Exchanges

Money exchanges re available all over Abu Dhabi, they offer good service and reasonable rates and are often better than the banks. UAE Exchange (uaeexchange.com) has a trusted network of branches which offer a unique Express Money service. Many hotels will also exchange money and travellers' cheques at the standard (poor) hotel rate. Be aware that exchanges tend to close between 1pm and 4.30pm.

Credit Cards

Credit cards are widely available and banks are becoming more open to new applications following the global crisis. Eligibility usually depends on a minimum salary, and to apply you'll need a salary certificate detailing your earnings (provided by your employer) and a copy of your passport with your residence visa and work permit. Once you have your card you'll find it's accepted at most shops, hotels and restaurants. Many banks offer credit cards with loyalty programs; you can redeem points for gifts, dining or entertainment vouchers or airline miles.

Prepaid Cards

Prepaid cards are available from a number of national banks. These are great for under 18s, as they can shop safely online, can stop the card if it's lost which means they don't lose the money, and parents can track online what they've been spending money on. Using prepaid cards means two for one deals in some eateries can be taken advantage of too.

Cheques

To date, post-dated cheques have mainly been used to secure finances and pay rent, with a year's rent being 'paid' upfront in several cheques. Since 2013, Abu Dhabi's direct debit system has reduced the need for cheques to guarantee loans and could replace a reliance on post-dated cheques for rental payments. It is a criminal offence to bounce cheques, even if you had written them months earlier. More than four bounced cheques a year will get you blacklisted by the UAE Central Bank, and your account may be closed. A cheque cannot be cancelled unless it is lost or stolen, so think ahead when writing post-dated cheques. Your bank will provide you with a free starter chequebook when you open an account. Replacements must also be ordered through the bank.

Financial Planning

With some steep start-up costs when you first arrive in the country it's important to plan your finances straight from the off. Unexpected costs, even innocuous home or car repairs, can put a strain on your bank account and make having a financial safeguard in place essential and there may be little support if you are struggling with debt. Financial advisors can help but check that they are licensed by the Central Bank of the UAE. Companies such as The One Group (theonegroup.co) are a solid choice. Consider the company's international presence too, as you'll still want the same access to advice if you return home.

Planning Ahead & Writing A Will

The tax-free lifestyle offers a great opportunity to save money. If you have a pension scheme in your home country, it may not be worth continuing your contributions when you move. Or you may prefer to set up a tax-free, offshore savings account.

Establishing you and your family abroad financially makes it more sensible than ever to plan for the unexpected. The One Group (theonegroup.co) can help you to write a will to secure your financial future against any eventuality.

Financial Advisors

Globaleye Sultan Towers, Rashid Bin Al Maktoum Rd, Hadabat Al Zaafaran, 02 443 8638, globaleye.com
Holborn Assets Al Shafar Tower, Dubai, 04 457 3800, *holbornassets.com*
KPMG Falcon Tower, Hamdan Bin Mohammed St, Markaziya West, 02 634 3318, *kpmg.com*
Mondial (Dubai) Pinnacle Bldg, Al Barsha 1, Dubai, 04 399 6601, *mondialdubai.com*
PIC Middle East Etihad Towers, Al Bateen, 02 676 5588, *pic-uae.com*
The One Group Aspect Tower, Business Bay, Dubai, 04 363 6100, *theonegroup.co*

Debt

Unlike some countries where you will receive several reminders for missed payments, if you are late paying for basic household bills such as electricity or water, your services may be disconnected. Missed payments on credit card bills will often incur fines or restrictions to services, and it is also considered a criminal offence to write a cheque and have insufficient funds. There are no bankruptcy laws in the UAE, so individuals who fall into financial difficulties are fully liable for their debt. If you are unable to keep up with repayments for your bank loans or credit cards and your bank files a complaint against you, you may be faced with prosecution, a visa ban or an extended term in jail.

Tax

The UAE levies no personal income taxes, residential property taxes or withholding taxes. The only noticeable taxes you pay as an expat are a 30% tax on alcohol bought at liquor stores and 50% tax on tobacco (although cigarettes are still comparatively cheap). There are also less noticeable taxes in the form of 'fees' that you have to pay to get almost any piece of administration completed in Abu Dhabi, which can add up quite significantly.

In hotel food and beverage outlets, there is a 6% Abu Dhabi Tourism Authority tax and a 10% service charge. Sometimes these is included in the displayed price, check the menu to be sure. Outside of hotels you won't pay Tourism Authority tax although individual outlets may add a service charge. Note that this service charge doesn't necessarily go to the staff's pockets, so it's always nice to leave an additional tip.

Taxing Issues

You may need to register your residency in the UAE with the government in your home country to avoid paying income tax or capital gains tax. It's best to check with your consulate for exact details. There are also rumours that income tax or taxes on remittances abroad will be introduced in the UAE, although experts tend to think this is unlikely or, at least, not imminent.

Offshore Accounts

Offshore accounts work in much the same way as a conventional account, but it can be adjusted specifically for you. Money can be moved to where it will produce the best rewards, and cash can be accessed whenever and wherever you need it, in your desired currency. Offshore accounts allow for management through the internet and over the phone, in a range of currencies (most commonly in US dollars, euros or pounds). Local and global firm, The One Group (theonegroup.co) offer specialist financial advice to help you establish an overseas bank account.

If you are travelling outside the UAE, try to make sure that your account comes with 24 hour banking, internationally recognised debit cards, with the ability to write cheques in your preferred currency. To open an account, there is usually a minimum balance of at least $10,000 and you will need certain reports or documents from your chosen country. HSBC (hsbc.ae) is a good starting point but do your research and check the potential tax implications first. Expats set up an offshore account to avoid their money being frozen in a UAE bank, which can occur when leaving a job, cancelling a visa, or going to prison.

Giving children back their childhood

GET INVOLVED

Each year the Christina Noble Children's Foundation supports thousands of vulnerable children and their families in Vietnam and Mongolia. Focusing on health, education and community support, the Foundation seeks to maximize the potential of each child. We believe that every child has the right to a childhood free of risk, exploitation and poverty.

None of this would be possible without your support and there are plenty of ways get involved, for example:

SPONSOR A CHILD

For the price of a daily cup of coffee you can give a child an education that can take them from Primary School to University and help break the cycle of poverty.

GIVE A GER

$3,500 is all it takes to provide a family in Mongolia with a traditional home. This not only provides a roof, but offers security and relief allowing parents to focus on their children's well being.

CHALLENGE YOURSELF

We are proud of our partnership with Gulf 4 Good and encourage you to take part in one of their life changing challenges.

CORPORATE SUPPORT

If your company has a dedicated CSR programme or nominates a 'Charity of the Year' we would love to talk to you about supporting the Foundation and the value it can bring to your employees and stakeholders.

To get involved and for more ideas visit www.cncf.org or contact tammy.urwin@cncf.org

HEALTH

Both private and government healthcare services are available in the UAE. General standards are high, with English speaking staff and internationally trained medical staff in most hospitals and medical centres. The main differences between public and private facilities are a higher level of personal service and dorm style rooms versus private hotel-style rooms (and the food!). Most hospitals offer a comprehensive range of inpatient and outpatient services.

Government Insurance

Abu Dhabi was the first emirate to introduce a compulsory medical insurance scheme for expatriate workers back in 2006 – and it's only now that Dubai is following suit. By law, employers are responsible for providing annual basic health insurance. This can be a public Daman policy or a private policy, and benefits can be extended to family members.

Daman's Abu Dhabi Basic Health Plan covers consultations, hospital stays, treatments, medicines and maternity. You can use your Daman card for direct billing at health service providers across the plan's network, which includes hospitals, clinics, pharmacies and diagnostic centres; in most cases, you will just pay a non-refundable charge of Dhs.50-150 at each consultation.

All expats can upgrade this to an Enhanced Health Plan should they require a customised policy, but they must pay the difference. Health insurance is organised as part of the residence visa application process and renewed in line with the visa. Keep your insurance card with you at all times, as you will need to provide insurance details in order to book an appointment at some hospitals.

RK41590

Delivering Better Health in the Middle East

The first hospital in the Middle East to be awarded Joint Commission International Accreditation (JCI)
The first private laboratory to be certified by the College of American Pathologists (CAP)

Scope of Services at American Hospital Dubai

- Ablation Therapy
- Anesthesia
- Audiology
- Cochlear Implant
- Cardiac Surgery
- Cardiac Catheterization
- Cardiology
- Cardiopulmonary
- Dermatology
- Diabetes / Endocrinology
- Dietary Counseling
- Endoscopy
- ENT Surgery

- Gastroenterology / Hepatology
- Hematology
- General Surgery
- Internal Medicine
- Medical Imaging
- Minimally Invasive Surgery
- Nephrology / Dialysis
- Neurology
- Neurosurgery
- Obstetrics / Gynecology
- Oncology / Chemotherapy
- Ophthalmology

- Orthopedics
- Pathology & Laboratory
- Palliative Medicine
- Pediatrics (Children)
- Pediatric Allergy and Asthma
- Pediatric Surgery
- Primary Care
- Rheumatology
- Sports Medicine and Physical Therapy
- Urology
- Vascular Surgery
- 24 Hour Emergency Service

المستشفى الأمريكي
AMERICAN HOSPITAL
D U B A I دبي

cap
ACCREDITED™

ahdubai.com

Organization Accredited
by Joint Commission International

American Hospital Dubai accepts most major insurance plans 800 - 5500

The Basic Health Plan gives you access to any of Abu Dhabi's government hospitals and clinics, as well as to select private hospitals and health clinics – up to an annual limit of Dhs.250,000. There are also limitations on private hospitals; for example, you are only covered for emergency treatment at Tawam and Sheikh Khalifa Medical City hospitals. You are also covered for emergency care and treatment outside of the UAE. There is a selection of Enhanced Health Plans to choose from, which offer varying levels of worldwide cover at government and private hospitals.

Nannies & Maids

It is compulsory by law for sponsors to provide a domestic worker in Abu Dhabi with basic Daman health insurance. The sponsorship process cannot be completed without it. The government subsidises the cost of health insurance for domestic workers, so sponsors just pay an annual flat fee of Dhs.600. Take your domestic worker's work permit (or residence visa if you are in the process of renewing the permit) to Daman National Health Insurance Company. You'll also need copies of passports, proof of your own health insurance policy, and proof of the maid's salary.

Daman National Health Insurance Company
Millennium Tower, Nr Hamdan Centre,
Shk Hamdan Bin Mhd St, Al Danah,
02 614 9555, *damanhealth.ae*

Private Insurance

Many employers provide staff with private health insurance that will give them access to the rapidly growing network of private hospitals and clinics. Waiting times are generally shorter in private clinics. If you have private health insurance, it's worth checking what you are entitled to as cover varies depending on the policy.

Dental care, maternity and screening tests aren't usually covered as standard, and you may need to have been on the policy for a year before you can receive maternity cover. Before making an appointment to see a healthcare professional, always check if the clinic or hospital is part of your insurer's network. Otherwise, you will need to pay the full costs by yourself.

Some companies offer direct billing, which means the insurer pays the hospital or clinic directly and you only pay a nominal fee each time you visit. Others require you to pay the cost of the consultation, treatment and medication up front and then file a claim to the insurer. If your employer is paying for your private medical insurance, your employment contract will state whether your spouse and dependants are included in the policy. If you plan to insure your family yourself, you may need to buy a separate policy for them as it's not always possible to extend existing policies. For a list of healthcare insurance providers, see Insurance Companies in the Setting Up Home section.

Government Hospitals

Abu Dhabi Health Services Company, SEHA (seha.ae), owns and operates 12 government hospitals, with more than 2,600 beds in total.

Al Ain Hospital

Shakhboot Bin Sultan St Al Ain **03 763 5888**
alain-hospital.ae
The Al Ain Hospital is one of the two major government-run hospitals in the city of Al Ain (the other being Tawam Hospital). It has 30 departments including cardiology, orthopaedics, paediatrics, urology and ENT. The focus is on emergency and acute care.

Al Rahba Hospital

Shk Maktoum Bin Rashid Rd Al Rahba
02 506 4444
alrahba.ae
Al Rahba is another government hospital and it is just off the island on the Abu Dhabi-Dubai highway. Outpatient departments include dermatology, diabetic education, dialysis, ENT, endocrinology, nephrology, neurosurgery, obstetrics and gynaecology. Al Rahba also has a neonatal intensive care unit.

Behavioural Sciences Pavilion

Sheikh Khalifa Medical City (SKMC) Al Dhafrah
02 610 4962
skmc.gov.ae
Map **2 K7**
This is a government-run specialist psychiatric hospital within Sheikh Khalifa Medical City. It offers across-the-board psychiatric diagnosis, treatment and support for adults, adolescents and children. In total there are 125 beds for patients.

Corniche Hospital

Nr Sheraton Abu Dhabi, Corniche East St,
Al Zahiyah, **02 672 4900**
cornichehospital.ae
Map **2 Q2**
Owned by the government and run by the renowned Johns Hopkins Medicine group, this is a purpose-built obstetrics and gynaecology hospital with the largest maternity department in the capital. If you're pregnant during your time in Abu Dhabi, chances are you'll come through these doors at some point, and with welcoming staff, you can arrange a visit.

MEDECINS SANS FRONTIERES
DOCTORS WITHOUT BORDERS

DOCTORS
WITHOUT
HESITATION.

BUT NOT WITHOUT YOU.

EVERY DAY OUR TEAMS ON THE GROUND ARE WORKING TO SAVE LIVES IN POVERTY-STRICKEN,
WAR-TORN, AND DISEASE AFFECTED AREAS.THE CONDITIONS ARE ALWAYS CHALLENGING,
SOMETIMES DANGEROUS. BUT THANKS TO THE GENEROSITY OF OUR SUPPORTERS, WE CONTINUE TO
OFFER MEDICAL AID TO THOSE WHO NEED IT MOST, REGARDLESS OF RACE, RELIGION OR

Delma Island Hospital
Delma Island Western Region
02 878 1888
The small but comprehensive government hospital provides emergency services, internal medicine, paediatrics, obstetrics and gynaecology, general surgery, and dialysis to residents and tourists on the 45 square kilometre island off the coast of Al Gharbia.

Ghayathi Hospital
Silla Rd, Ghayati Ruwais **02 874 1666**
The government-run Ghayathi Hospital provides basic medical services for people in the small towns of Ghayathi and Bida Mutawa in the Western Region. It has an ICU and emergency department as well as access to digital x-ray and CT scan machines.

Madinat Zayed Hospital
Madinat Zayed **02 884 4444**
seha.ae
Map **3 C3**
Madinat Zayed Hospital is a mid-sized government hospital serving the Al Gharbia western region of Abu Dhabi emirate. Given its remote location, this facility offers surprisingly extensive medical services that include an emergency department, general medicine and an advanced ophthalmology department.

Mafraq Hospital
Shk Maktoum Bin Rashid Rd Mahawi
02 501 1111
mafraqhospital.ae
Map **1 T13**
Around 35 kilometres from the city centre, it's one of the UAE's biggest and busiest hospitals. It has more than 500 beds, 36 clinical and non-clinical departments and a host of tertiary and day-visit medical facilities. It's best known for its expertise in complex surgery and also has a well-equipped emergency department. Its Neonatal Intensive Care Unit (NICU) is a fully closed unit that provides the fullest possible range of critical care facilities.

Sheikh Khalifa Medical City (SKMC)
Al Karamah St Al Dhafrah **02 819 0000**
skmc.gov.ae
Map **2 K7**
Managed by the Cleveland Clinic, SKMC encompasses several Centres of Excellence and is the flagship institution for Abu Dhabi's public health system, including a 568 bed acute care hospital, 14 specialised outpatient clinics and a blood bank. It also manages six family medicine clinics, two walk-in clinics, an urgent care centre and two dental centres. The emergency room is excellent and patients rarely have to wait more than a few minutes before being seen.

Private Hospitals

You will need private health insurance to be treated at one of the growing number of excellent private healthcare facilities in Abu Dhabi. However, even if you have private health insurance you'll need to check your policy to see exactly which hospitals and treatments are covered, as not all will be on the approved list.

Ahalia Hospital
Hamdan Bin Mohammed St Al Danah
02 626 2666
ahaliagroup.com
Map **2 M3**
The flagship facility of the large Ahalia group has 24 hour casualty and ambulance services along with specialists in cardiology, homeopathy, neurology, radiology and many other medical disciplines.

Al Noor Hospital
Khalifa Bin Zayed The First St Al Danah **800 55666**
alnoorhospital.com
Map **2 N3**
Al Noor Hospital is one of the best known private hospitals and offers specialist care in fields including cardiology, gynaecology, paediatrics, dermatology, and dental. The hospital also offers less conventional medical care with its Chinese medicine clinic, a Lasik centre and a sleep laboratory. A fertility centre is also on site that can help overcome infertility issues. A second branch on Rashid Bin Al Maktoum Rd is commonly referred to as 'new Al Noor' (02 444 6655).

Al Raha Hospital
Fatima Bin Mubarak St Al Danah
02 633 0440
alrahahospital.com
Map **2 P4**
Al Raha Hospital is a private general hospital in the centre of the island (not in the more well-known Al Raha Beach area). The comprehensive facilities cover urology, gynaecology, ENT, dentistry, internal medicine, paediatrics, anaesthesia, radiology and pathology disciplines. It also has a dermatology unit and offers laser treatments.

Al Salama Hospital
Hamdan Bin Mohammed St Al Zahiyah
02 696 6777
alsalamahospital.com
Map **2 R3**
This private hospital in the Al Zahiyah area provides inpatient and outpatient treatments in fields including obstetrics, infertility, cardiology, neurosurgery, pathology, sports medicine and physiotherapy. It also has the facilities to offer advanced keyhole surgery.

American European Medical Center

Dalma St Al Karamah
02 445 5477
aemcare.ae
Map **2 L10**
Opened in 2006, it has emerged as one of the city's top outpatient clinics offering a wide range of health services. The clinics and faculties offer general and internal medicine as well as cardiology, dental surgery, gastroenterology, general surgery, obstetrics and gynaecology, pediatrics and radiology. House calls can also be arranged through the Home Healthcare service.

Burjeel Hospital

Fatima Bint Mubarak St Al Dhafrah **02 508 5555**
burjeel.com
Map **2 P7**
This tertiary care centre is Abu Dhabi's biggest private hospital and offers care in more than 30 specialist areas. Burjeel specialises particularly in reproductive health and IVF treatments. The hospital is linked to Brussels University, an acknowledged leader in the science of reproduction.

Cleveland Clinic

Al Maryah Island **02 659 0200**
clevelandclinicabudhabi.ae
Map **2 T5**
Set to open in 2015, this world-class multi-speciality clinic has five centres of excellence in heart and vascular, neurology, digestive disease, critical care and eye and respiratory. You can expect top notch care: 5500 doctors applied for 175 open positions and 80% of the accepted applicants were trained in the US. Five of the floors of its distinctive building on Al Maryah Island are purely for clinical use.

Dar Al Shifaa Hospital

Hazza Bin Zayed St Al Dhafrah **02 641 6999**
daralshifaa.net
Map **2 P7**
Services here include a 24 hour emergency department, neonatal intensive care, paediatric and neonatology, obstetrics and gynaecology, maternity and delivery, ENT, urology and lithotripsy, cardiology, as well as physical medicine and rehabilitation.

Emirates International Hospital

Nr Safeer Centre, Al Jimi Al Ain
03 763 7777
This private hospital in Al Ain has specialist departments including accident and emergency, physiotherapy, dermatology, venereology, cardiology, cardiovascular, ENT, internal medicine, obstetrics and gynaecology, ophthalmology, general surgery, laparoscopy and urology. It also offers extensive maternity facilities, including a special care baby unit.

Gulf Diagnostic Center Hospital

Al Khaleej Al Arabi St Al Bateen **02 417 7222**
gdc-hospital.com
Map **2 G10**
In addition to specialist areas including tropical medicine, pathology, psychology and a range of surgeries, the centre offers a full range of outpatient medical services including GP services and dentistry.

King's College Hospital Clinics

Shining Towers, Khalidiya 02 501 4000
kchclinics.com
Map **2 H5** xxx
Located in the heart of the capital close to Khalidiya Mall, the clinic runs in tandem with the renowned King's College Hospital London. The leading clinic is a centre of excellence for hepatology, gastroenterology, fetal medicine, family medicine, internal medicine, paediatrics, obstetrics, gynaecology and dietetics. The state-of-the-art clinic has 21 treatment rooms, xray suites, scanning facilities and specialist staff.

LLH Hospital

Zayed The Second St Al Danah **02 633 5522**
llhhospital.com
Map **2 N4**
This hospital is a top-class and extremely well-equipped private hospital in the city centre. It offers a 24 hour emergency department (with ambulance service), a diagnostics clinic, maternity ward and an in-house pharmacy, plus specialist MRI and mammography departments. LLH Healthcare Services also manages the Burjeel Hospital mentioned earlier in this listing.

Cleveland Clinic

National Hospital
Nr Honda Showroom Al Danah **02 671 1000**
hcmena.com
Map **2 P5**
This state-of-the-art, private hospital offers general medicine and surgery, in addition to a wide range of specialised medical disciplines including IVF treatment, sports physiotherapy and holistic health. It also has its own radiology department with an open magnetic resonance imaging (MRI) system.

NMC Specialty Hospital Abu Dhabi
Zayed The First St Al Danah **02 633 2255**
nmc.ae
Map **2 L4**
One of the city's biggest private hospitals, it offers a comprehensive range of medical services plus a general outpatient unit open 24 hours a day. Specialist departments include paediatrics, cardiology, orthopaedics, dentistry, neurology, gastroenterology, urology, eye care, psychiatry, dermatology and ENT. A private ambulance service is also available.

NMC Specialty Hospital Al Ain
Nr UAE University, Al Mutaredh Al Ain **03 755 5999**
nmc.ae
The Al Ain branch of this hospital offers extensive outpatient and inpatient services. There are several family doctors based out of the hospital, as well as a dental surgery, an in-house pharmacy and a state-of-the-art diagnostics centre.

Oasis Hospital
Hessa Bint Mohamed St Al Ain **03 722 1251**
oasishospital.org
The Oasis is a small, private hospital in Al Ain, which is locally renowned for its maternity and specialist baby care units. Outpatient services include a diabetes clinic, physiotherapy, infectious diseases and pre-natal care.

Specialized Medical Care Hospital
Sultan Bin Zayed Al Awwal St Al Ain **03 755 2291**
smchosp.com
The Specialized Medical Care Hospital is a private facility in the Al Jahili area offering a 24 hour emergency care service and a wide range of services with a particular emphasis on minor and one-day surgical procedures. The outpatient care manifesto includes healthcare services in paediatrics, dentistry, cardiology, obstetrics and gynaecology.

Tawam Hospital
Khalifa Bin Zayed St, Al Maqam Al Ain **03 767 7444**
tawamhospital.ae
Affiliated with the prestigious American Johns Hopkins Medicine group, it's best-known for the expert maternity clinic. Other specialised areas include

an oncology department, an emergency trauma department, a diabetes centre, an infertility clinic providing treatments including IVF, and a pain clinic that offers treatments such as acupuncture.

Accidents & Emergencies

Abu Dhabi Police receives all 999 calls but you can dial 998 to be put straight through to ambulance services. Private medical firms such as NMC (nmc.ae) run fleets of ambulances. You will need to subscribe to access their services or pay for one-off use.

Sheikh Khalifa Medical City and off-island Al Rahba Hospital have the best accident and emergency (A&E) departments in Abu Dhabi, although Al Mafraq and Al Noor Hospitals also have good A&E departments. Part of Sheikh Khalifa Medical City, the Khalidiya Urgent Care Center (02 819 1451, skmc.ae), treats minor emergencies such as abdominal pain, cold and flu, minor bone breaks, ear, nose and throat issues, asthma attacks, rashes, vomiting and diarrhoea.

In Al Ain, Al Ain Hospital deals with general accidents and emergencies, while Tawam Hospital specialises in emergency traumas. The A&E departments at both these hospitals are efficiently managed and you rarely have to wait long. While finding a place for emergency treatment is easy, getting there can be more problematic as Abu Dhabi's paramedic services are developing.

General Medical Care

For general non-emergency medical care, most hospitals have a clinic where you can turn up, present your insurance card and wait to see a general practitioner. Call ahead to check that there is a clinic, and its hours of operation. Often a triage nurse will take down the details of your medical history and ailment before you see a doctor. These services usually operate on a first-come-first-served basis so waiting times can vary dramatically. Early evenings and Sunday mornings are generally a busy time and best avoided if possible.

Whether you have Daman or private health insurance, check in advance that the hospital is on your insurer's network. Most hospitals and clinics offer family medicine as part of outpatient services. You can usually call to make an appointment but if they can't see you that day and you need immediate non-emergency medical care, they may treat you in the A&E department.

Al Aahed Medical Centre Nr Lulu Hypermarket, Hilton Rd, Al Ain, 03 764 2791
Al Dhahery Clinic Saeed Hillal Abdulla Al Kuwaiti Bldg, Zayed Bin Sultan St, Al Ain, 03 765 6882

Al Maqtaa Healthcare Center Al Khaleej Al Arabi St, Al Maqta, 02 558 4611, *ahs.ae*

Bani Yas Primary Health Care Centre Nr Mafraq Hospital, Baniyas East, 02 583 5599, *mafraqhospital.ae*

Dawn Medical Centre Hamdan Bin Mohammed St, Al Danah, 02 626 2666, *ahaliagroup.com*

Dr McCulloch Clinic Al Noor Hospital, Al Danah, 02 626 2677, *dr-mcculloch.com*

Family Medicine Centre Al Ain Hospital, Al Ain, 03 763 5888, *alain-hospital.com*

Gulf Diagnostic Center Hospital Al Khaleej Al Arabi St, Al Bateen, 02 417 7222, *gdc-hospital.com*

Hamdan Medical Centre Hilton Rd, Al Ain, 03 765 4797

Ibn Sina Medical Centre New Al Manara Pharmacy Bldg, Shk Zayed The First St, Al Khalidiya, 02 681 6400, *ibnsinauae.com*

New Al Ain Medical Clinic 137 Shk Zayed Bin Sultan St, Al Mutawaa, Al Ain, 03 764 1448

Swedish Medical Centre Zayed The First St, Al Khubeirah, 02 681 1122

One-Stop Clinics

The Abu Dhabi Health Services Company – SEHA runs a network of one-stop-shop ambulatory care clinics, which offer easy access to primary and specialist care. There are over 30 clinics across Abu Dhabi listed at ahs.ae, with most covered by your Daman card. Services offered include family medicine, x-rays, dentistry, urgent care, maternity and well woman, physiotherapy and paediatrics.

Specialist Hospitals & Clinics

Whatever your ailment, chances are you'll find the right specialist doctor in one of the many Abu Dhabi hospitals or clinics. Sometimes you don't need a referral, but it is recommended that you discuss your condition with your regular doctor who will advise you who to see. Most hospitals offer a range of outpatient specialist services as well as walk-in clinics; the NMC Speciality Hospital prides itself on providing the best care as does the renowned King's College Hospital Clinics (kchclinics.com). Small, specialist practices can diagnose and treat a range of conditions. Many general practices also have resident specialists and others offer a maternity service, screening for childhood diseases, treatment for acute illness and occupational medicine (specialising in aviation). It also specialises in medical care for divers; offering training for dive tour operators as well as the medical required for all professional divers. Always check what your local clinic can offer before seeking specialists though.

Maternity

The standard of maternity care in Abu Dhabi is very good. The most popular maternity hospitals for expats are Al Noor and Corniche. Before you decide on a government hospital, check its policy on husbands and family members being present in the labour ward. Some hospitals may not allow your husband to be with you in the labour ward, although he can be present at delivery if it is not by caesarean. If you are persuasive and there are no local ladies admitted, your husband may be allowed access to the ward.

All government hospitals now charge expatriates for maternity services, and costs vary dramatically. Private hospitals will be more expensive but not always as much as you think. Check that your medical insurance covers maternity as some require you to have been with the insurer for at least 12 months prior to conception. And some may not cover maternity at all. You may find insurers need prior written advice of your expected delivery date and method as well as the last scan before birth. It is best to check your insurer's requirements well before your due date.

Most private hospitals offer maternity packages that include prenatal care, delivery and postnatal care for you and the baby, but be aware that the hospital's quote is for the most basic 'best case scenario' delivery. If you have an epidural or an assisted delivery, you will be charged extra. If you go to an independent gynaecologist for your prenatal care, you will usually be offered a choice of hospitals and delivery packages where your doctor can attend the birth.

Water births are now possible at the Al Ain Cromwell Hospital (alaincromwell.com). Meanwhile, Corniche, Al Rahba and Dar Al Shifa hospitals all have neonatal intensive care units and Oasis Hospital has a special care baby unit; Mafraq Hospital's Neonatal Intensive Care Unit (mafraqhospital.ae) is a fully closed unit that provides the fullest possible range of critical care facilities.

Antenatal Classes

Mama Care is a maternity care educational programme for expectant and new mothers held at NMC Specialty Hospital Abu Dhabi. Antenatal sessions are held every Saturday for mums and dads, while women in their first to third trimesters can also receive prenatal and postnatal advice from expert medical professionals including nurses, dieticians and exercise physiologists. Call 02 633 2255 for further information and to book.

Corniche Hospital has a Parent Education Centre, offering classes on prenatal care, exercise during pregnancy, preparation for birth and birthing techniques, birth by caesarean section, and feeding and caring for newborns and infants. Classes are taught in Arabic, English, Malayalam, Hindi and

Urdu by a qualified parent education expert, and are available to all hospital patients and their families. Enquire at your chosen hospital to see what antenatal classes they may offer.

Obstetrics & Gynaecology

Most hospitals and general practices in Abu Dhabi offer gynaecological and obstetrics services. In your home country, you may have received a reminder from your doctor when you were due for a smear test or mammogram. In the UAE it will be up to you to remember when you are due for a test. 'Well Woman' check-ups (usually annual) can take care of your usual tests in one go and include a general health check. These are often promoted through the media to encourage women to get checked up. Most forms of contraceptive are available in Abu Dhabi (although the morning-after pill is not).

A gynaecologist can recommend the most suitable form of contraception for you. If you take oral contraceptives, a variety of brands are available but you will need a prescription, especially when buying from major pharmacy chains. Be aware that although it's rarely enforced, the law states you should be married to be prescribed or to buy contraceptives as sexual relations between unmarried couples is illegal, so you do need to be careful.

The British Clinic
Al Hamra Plaza, Zayed The First St Al Danah
02 677 1252
thebritishclinic.net
Map **2 P4**
A specialised independent clinic, established back in 1994, offering fertility techniques and minimally invasive therapy, as well as general obstetric services, maternity care and antenatal counselling.

Dr Amal Al Biely
Damas Jewellery Bldg, Zayed The First St Markaziya West **02 632 4934**
Map **2 K4**
Well-regarded, independent gynaecology and obstetrics specialist. The clinic is located near to the Corniche and not far from the Corniche Hospital.

HealthPlus
Hazaa Bin Zayed St Al Karamah **02 643 3494**
hplus.ae
Map **2 J8**
This centre of excellence covers general obstetrics and gynaecology, maternal-foetal medicine, minimally invasive surgery, urogynaecology and reproductive medicine. It was the first of 20 such centres set to open across the emirate.

Paediatrics

Most government and private hospitals and medical centres have full-time paediatricians. Sheikh Khalifa Medical City (skmc.gov.ae) offers excellent facilities and they are a growing number of private paediatric departments. Abu Dhabi is also well served for neonatal care. The Corniche, Al Rahba, Dar Al Shifaa and Oasis hospitals have facilities to care for newborns with health problems, but don't be afraid to ask around to find the doctor who is best for your needs. Dr McCulloch Clinic, Gulf Diagnostic Center Hospital and Advanced Cure Diagnostic Center are all popular with expats. There are also paediatric surgeons, neurodevelopment therapists, and specialists for children with special needs and learning difficulties.

Compulsory Vaccinations

By law, parents are required to ensure that their baby's immunisation shots are up to date. While the first vaccines are given as soon as your baby is born, you will be required to return to your hospital or clinic every two months until the baby is one year old. At 18 months, babies receive three booster shots and then do not have any more until they are aged five.

The UAE's national immunisation programme includes Hepatitis A + B, polio, MMR (measles, mumps and German measles), chickenpox, Hib and whooping cough. Bring copies of your child's vaccination records from your home country when you move to Abu Dhabi as you will also need these for nursery and school applications. Your child will also be given a mandatory annual eye test at school age.

Dr Abdullah Azzam Paediatric Clinic
Al Bu Qubai Tower, Zayed The Second St
Al Khalidiya **02 634 4185**
Map **2 K4**
An independent paediatric clinic located conveniently in Al Khalidiya.

Dr Ahmed Al Hilfi Clinic
Al Hamra Plaza,
Zayed The First St Al Danah
02 674 4438
Map **2 P4**
A friendly and professional independent outfit ideally located in the city centre. Dr Al Hilfi specialises in paediatric surgery.

Dr Ghiath Sandouk
Gulf Diagnostic Center Hospital Al Bateen
02 417 7222
gdc-hospital.com
Map **2 G10**
A French Board Certified paediatric allergist based at Gulf Diagnostic Center for more than a decade.

Abu Dhabi healthcare

Dr Raad Al Khayat
Aster Medical Centre Al Zahiyah **02 645 6100**
Map **2 R4**
An independent general paediatrician.

Dr Sami Kanderian Clinic
**Imperial College London Diabetes Centre,
Al Khaleej Al Arabi St** Al Safarat **02 404 0800**
Map **1 H8**
A general paediatrics clinic located near ADNEC.

Ghaleb Khalayli Paediatric Clinic
**Al Hamiri Bldg, Shk Khalifa Bin Zayed St,
Al Mutawaa** Al Ain **03 766 3998**
A general paediatrics clinic in Al Ain.

Physiotherapy

Many Abu Dhabi residents work hard and play harder,
but accidents and injuries happen so you'll be pleased
to know the city has some excellent specialists to help
you on the road to recovery.

Physiotherapy is well known for its role in
sports injury rehabilitation but it can also help
with neurological disorders, musculoskeletal pain
and cardiopulmonary disorders. Most of the main
hospitals have a rehabilitation department of some
sort which includes physiotherapy services, and
some general practice clinics also have resident
specialists. Al Mafraq Hospital, for example, has a
physical medicine department with all the facilities
and expertise for physiotherapy and rehabilitation. Al
Noor Hospital boasts a state-of-the-art physiotherapy
and rehabilitation department specialising in sports
injuries, spinal injuries and ligament injuries. The
latest techniques such as short wave and microwave
diathermy, ultrasonic massage, magnetotherapy,
paraffin therapy and hydrotherapy are all on offer.

The Gulf Diagnostic Center Hospital has a dedicated
physiotherapy department, while in Al Ain, the NMC
Specialty Hospital offers a range of rehabilitation
services. Oasis Hospital has a physical therapist
who combines manual therapy, ultrasound, electric
current, and hot or cool compresses to treat a variety
of conditions and sport or muscular injuries. If you're
a member of a sports club they may also have a list of
good tried and tested physiotherapists.

Pharmacies

Many prescription drugs from your home country are
sold over the counter here. Also, many prescriptions
are covered by your health insurance, so do check
before paying.

Tell the pharmacist if you have a pre-existing
condition, allergy or take other medications, and make
sure you understand the administration instructions.
Some common medications are not available here
(such as Gaviscon for infants and Pepto Bismol).
However you can bring these into the UAE with you
and often a similar medication is available (such as
Infacol instead of infant Gaviscon). Pharmacies are

common, including a number of Boots chemists in malls around the city, and several are open 24 hours such as Urban Pharmacy (02 445 8584), Lifeline (02 633 2255), Al Noor (02 672 2117) and Al Ain Pharmacy (03 765 5120). Supermarkets and convenience stores sell basic medications, although sometimes finding a simple ointment like antiseptic cream still requires a pharmacy. A local pharmacy will often deliver for free, but be sure to tip the driver.

Medication

Certain medications do require a prescription in the UAE and some medications widely available in other countries such as codeine, diazepam and temazepam, are banned here. It's a crime to have these medicines in your possession unless you can produce an official prescription from your doctor in your home country. Even then you might end up at the police station while it is translated into Arabic.

It's best to avoid medications that are banned in the UAE unless it is absolutely necessary and there's no locally available alternative. The list of banned drugs does tend to change quite regularly so it's advisable to check with the Drug Control Department at the Ministry of Health (moh.gov.ae) before travelling to avoid any unwelcome problems on arrival.

Dentists

Dentistry in Abu Dhabi is of a very high standard with prices to match. Standard health insurance generally doesn't cover dentistry unless it's emergency treatment after an accident. You may be able to pay an additional premium for dentistry but the insurer may first want proof you've had regular recent check-ups.

If you receive medical insurance through your employer, the card you are issued with, will point you in the direction of dentists you are eligible to use. You can also ask friends and colleagues if they recommend a good, reasonably priced dentist as a filling could set you back anywhere between Dhs.50 and Dhs.1,000, and a root canal might cost between Dhs.600 and Dhs.3,000. Cosmetic dentistry is also big business, with a basic whitening treatment costing Dhs.1000. Many general practices and hospitals also offer dental services, such as the Sheikh Khalifa Medical City.

Advanced American Dental Clinic

Nr American Community School Al Bateen
02 681 2921
americandentalclinic.com
Map **2 E5**
The Advanced American Dental Clinic is a well-known dental practice that offers everything from orthodontic dentistry and periodontal treatments to endodontic treatments, teeth whitening services, neuromuscular dentistry as well as some cosmetic dentistry should you need it.

Al Ain International Dental Clinic

Ahmad Khalaf Al Otaiba Bldg, Nr Commercial Bank Of Dubai Central District Al Ain **03 751 1660**
alainden.ae
A Swedish-run dental clinic offering a range of services, including laser dentistry, preventive treatment, dental care for children, and cosmetic dentistry. It specialises in the prevention of gum and jaw disease.

Barbara Orthodontic & Dental Polyclinic

Etihad Tower, Khalifa St Al Bateen **02 626 9898**
barbaradentalclinic.ae
Map **2 B3**
Barbara Orthodontic & Dental Polyclinic is a well-established practice. Services include implants and orthodontic treatment including ceramic braces. Service such as laser teeth whitening are available and there is also an in-house GP.

British Dental Clinic

Hamdan Bin Mohammed St Al Danah **02 677 3308**
Map **2 Q3**
Expert dental surgeons provide emergency, preventive general care and cosmetic dentistry at this friendly, well-known clinic. Popular with many expats.

City Dental & Medical Centre

Shk Khalifa Bin Zayed St Al Ain **03 764 2252**
Map **4 C2**
City Dental & Medical Centre provides a full range of dental procedures and treatments with the aim of being affordable while still providing a quality service.

Dr Elisabeth Dental Clinic

Hilton Corniche Hotel Apartments, Corniche East St Al Danah **02 626 7822**
Map **2 N3**
The Dr Elisabeth Dental Clinic offers general dentistry and the full range of dental care in a friendly environment. The practice is in the city centre just behind Pizza Hut.

Dr Firas Dental Clinic

Marina Village Breakwater **02 633 5990**
Map **2 D1**
Patients of all ages are taken care of at this practice which offers everything from cosmetic dentistry, veneers, fillings, crowns and bridges, to root canals, gum treatment, teeth cleaning, extractions and emergency care.

Gulf Dental Clinic
Nr Bank Melli Iran Al Ain **03 765 4373**
A general dental and orthodontic clinic that is popular and well-regarded among expats living in Al Ain. Its 'Dentistry With a Smile' strapline highlights the sort of friendly service you can expect.

International Center for Dental Excellence
Centro Business Tower, near ADNEC Al Saafarat **02 447 7752**
Map **1 H8**
This shiny new centre, the only one in the capital to be affiliated with an American dental school, boasts the latest technology to carry out all the usual services with ease and accuracy.

International Dental Clinic
Arabian Home Pharmacy Bldg, Shk Rashid Bin Saeed St Al Manhal **02 633 3444**
Map **2 L7**
The International Dental Clinic is a high-quality dental practice which provides a comprehensive range of general dentistry services. It is based near Sheikh Khalifa Medical City.

Maher Medical Centre
Al Zawari Tower B, Corniche West St
Al Khalidiya **02 666 3588**
Map **2 H4**
Maher Medical Centre is a larger general medicine practice which includes a dental clinic. Dental services include the full spectrum of check-ups and treatments.

Modern German Dental Center
Bateen C6 Tower Al Bateen **02 667 3235**
Map **2 D6**
The Modern German Dental Center is a general dentistry practice. Its staff of dentists specialise in outpatient surgery with procedures such as root canal treatment, tooth bleaching, crowns and implants.

Paris Dental Clinic
Abu Dhabi Co-op Bldg, Hamdan Bin Mohammed St Al Danah **02 677 3373**
Map **2 P3**
The Paris Dental Clinic's well-regarded team of specialists provides general dental care including endodontic treatment, cosmetic procedures, implants, as well as orthodontic treatment.

Petra Dental Care Centre
Euro Hotel Apartment Al Dhafrah **02 641 1899**
Map **2 M7**
Petra Dental Care Centre is a good dental clinic which offers a wide range of treatments and services including general orthodontic work as well as dental implants, zircon bridges and veneers.

Royal London Dental Clinic
Al Bhadi Bldg, Al Muwaiji Al Ain **03 755 7155**
theroyallondondentalclinic.com
A qualified and experienced team offers a full range of dental services including examinations, preventive treatments, restorative dentistry, gum disease treatment, root canal treatment, children's dentistry and cosmetic dentistry.

Swedish Dental Clinic
Swedish Medical Centre Al Khubeirah **02 681 1122**
Map **1 B5**
The Swedish Dental Clinic offers expert care and treatment in a well-equipped city centre general dental clinic. It has many loyal patients who rate it highly.

Opticians

There's at least one optician in nearly every shopping mall in Abu Dhabi with a full range of prescription frames, sunglasses and contact lenses. Many larger outlets can do eye examinations and make glasses on the premises. Abu Dhabi's dry, dusty environment and air-conditioned lifestyle can cause problems for eyes which can be eased with special drops. Sunglasses are essential. If you need a specialist, there are ophthalmology departments at Sheikh Khalifa Medical City, Magrabi Eye & Ear Center and Madinat Zayed Hospital. Magrabi Eye & Ear Centre has a paediatric ophthalmology unit too. Several hospitals and clinics offer laser eye surgery with prices from Dhs.4,000 to

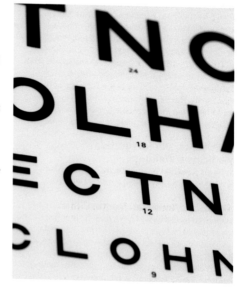

about Dhs.7,500 per eye. All laser surgery packages include a year's follow-up care.

Elite Optic Zayed The First St, Al Khalidiya, 02 666 6019, *eliteoptic.com*
Kattan Opticians Nr Spinneys, Shk Hamdan Bin Mohammed St, Al Danah, 02 678 0818
Magrabi Eye & Ear Specialized Hospital Al Nakheel Tower, Fatima Bint Mubarak St, Al Danah, 02 634 5000, *magrabihospitals.com*
Magrabi Optical Al Jimi Mall, Al Ain, 03 763 0680, *magrabioptical.com*
Moorfields Eye Hospital Dubai Healthcare City, Dubai, 04 429 7888, *moorfields.ae*
Vision Express Al Wahda Mall, Al Dhafrah, 02 443 7015, *alshaya.com*
Yateem Optician Crystal Tower, Al Danah, 02 677 6222, *yateemgroup.com*

Alternative Therapies

The UAE Ministry of Health licenses alternative medicine practitioners through its department for Traditional, Complementary & Alternative Medicine. Prices are comparable to western medicine but most insurance companies will not cover the costs. Some main hospitals have departments for alternative treatments: National Hospital has a holistic health clinic offering drugless treatments such as hydrotherapy, mud therapy, dietetics, fasting therapy, acupressure, acupuncture and yoga.

Al Noor Hospital has a Chinese medicine clinic, and Tawam Hospital offers acupuncture, while elsewhere Ahalia Hospital has a homeopathy department. Yoga and pilates can also be helpful in achieving balanced health and there are classes to be found at studios and health clubs around the city.

There are a number of good spas and salons who offer aromatherapy and some even have colour therapy services, including in the Espa Spa at the Yas Viceroy. The different use of coloured lights is something that many feel has beneficial results for general well-being and treating seasonal depression.

DNA Center For Integrative Medicine & Wellness
St Regis Saadiyat Island Resort Saadiyat Island
02 610 9000 dnahealthcorp.com
Map1 G1
With the latest technology, including CAT scans, to assess and treat illnesses, DNA goes further by offering personalised lifestyle medicine. Rather than just curing, they use advanced techniques as well as Eastern and Western practices to assess potential health issues and create plans to avoid future problems, creating wellness and inner peace in the process.

Gulf Chinese Medical Centre
Al Hamad Bldg, Rashid Bin Saeed St Markaziya West
02 634 3538
gulfchinesemedical.net
Map **2 L3**
This clinic is one of the best alternative medicine centres in town, thanks to its popular Dr. Hu. He offers traditional Chinese treatments such as acupuncture, acupressure, reflexology and therapeutic massage for conditions including headaches, insomnia, arthritis, asthma, gastrointestinal problems, diabetes, hypertension and prostatitis. It also has a unique herbal centre.

Homeopathic Medical Specialized Clinic
Lufthansa Bldg, Nr Lifeline Hospital, Zayed The Second St Al Danah **02 621 0400**
hmcuae.com
Map **2 N4**
This clinic offers curative and preventive treatments based on the healing properties of natural elements. Working to international standards with medicines from Germany, the trained doctors use homeopathy to stimulate immunity in their patients' bodies in order to treat illness or to increase wellness.

Cosmetic Treatment & Surgery

The UAE is building a reputation as a luxury healthcare destination in part due to a concerted effort by the government to attract top surgeons to centres such as Sheikh Khalifa Medical City. Cosmetic surgery is driving this growth and the city now boasts several establishments that specialise in the permanent alteration of various parts of your anatomy. Private hospitals and independent clinics also offer aesthetic and reconstructive surgery. Standards are generally high, but it's always advisable to look into a few clinics. A number of cosmetic clinics also offer non-surgical alternatives. See sections on Hospitals, General Medical Care and Specialist Hospitals & Clinics in this chapter.

American Surgecenter
Nr Italian Embassy, Mubarak Bin Mohammed Al Nahyan St Al Rowdah **02 443 0909**
theamericansurgecenter.com
Map **2 J9**
The American Surgecenter is a state-of-the-art medical facility offering the latest available medical, surgical, dental and aesthetic services. From plastic surgery to laser hair reduction, and from fetal medicine to bariatric surgery, facials and spa services, it offers the most up-to-date American medical technology. Its Americare Home Health Service helps patients

of all ages, from newborn to the elderly, to receive professional, compassionate healthcare services in the comfort of their home. They provide home visits from physicians, skilled nursing and therapy sessions in addition to assisted transportation, pharmaceutical services and in-home diagnostic services.

Bodyworx Aesthetics Clinic
Fatima Bint Mubarak St Al Dhafrah **02 641 9961**
bodyworx.ae
Map **2 Q7**
Dr Thomas Berger, one of the most trusted dermatologists in the capital, heads up the team at this boutique facility. They offer all types of dermatological procedures, treating ageing skin, spider veins, rosacea, and acne, as well as laser hair removal, permanent makeup application and plastic surgery for face and body.

CosmeSurge & Emirates Clinics
Nr Polish Embassy, Dalma St Al Karamah
02 446 6422
cosmesurge.com
Map **2 K9**
A team of experienced sub-specialist cosmetic surgeons offer surgical and non-surgical cosmetic procedures, non-invasive beauty therapy and cosmetic dentistry. A branch has recently opened in Khalifa City (02 557 2220).

Kaya Skin Clinic
Al Karamah St Al Karamah **02 445 9923**
kayaskinclinic.me
Map **2 K8**
This specialist skin clinic offers a range of aesthetic treatments including laser hair removal, Botox, anti-ageing therapies and chemical peels. They have 18 clinics in the Middle East, making them one of the largest operators in the region.

Obagi Dermatology & Cosmetic Centre
Nr Sheikh Khalifa Medical City, Hazza Bin Zayed St
Al Karamah **02 445 7100**
obagi-uae.com
Map **2 K8**
Skincare experts provide surgical and non-surgical skin and cosmetic treatments, including fillers, Botox, laser, weight control, cosmetic enhancements and reductions, and aesthetic medical spa treatments.

Nutritionists & Slimming

It's easy to pile on the pounds with so many good dining options in Abu Dhabi. Al Falah Natural Treatment Centre and Ibn Sina Medical Centre offer clinical nutrition and medical weight loss

programmes. Imperial College London Diabetes Centre has a nutrition team, as does the DNA Center and Sheikh Khalifa Medical City. NMC Specialty Hospital specialises in individual health plans; the hospital also runs the BiteRite Cafe. Eat there, where all calories are helpfully listed on the menu, or make use of its tailor-made healthy eating delivery service. Live'ly (lively.ae) also has a meal delivery service that can help you chisel your abs or lose a few pounds. Weight Watchers is not in the UAE but many still use weightwatchers.com and its online forums for a bit of support. A personal trainer can also advise on exercise and diet and give you that dose of motivation.

Counselling & Therapy

Moving to another country can be very stressful and it sometimes helps to talk through the issues and anxieties you are facing. Mental health services are increasing all of the time in the UAE, so your family doctor should be able to refer you to a suitable service should you feel the need for some extra support.

A growing number of psychiatric and neurology specialist services have sprung up in Abu Dhabi and as you don't always need a referral, you can contact them directly. The American Center for Psychiatry and Neurology (02 697 9999, americancenteruae. com) is at the forefront. It is near Al Khalidiya Mall and offers psychiatric evaluation, assessment and treatment for all ages. It offers therapy for adjustment, post-traumatic stress, eating or panic disorders. It treats alcohol abuse and offers anger management, and counselling for couples, children, adolescents and families. It also offers academic assessment and treatment. There is also a corporate employee assistance programme with seminars, workshops and in-house consultations. Gulf Diagnostic Center has a specialist mental health department with services including the treatment of eating disorders.

The Behavioral Science Pavilion at Sheikh Khalifa Medical City is dedicated to the assessment, management and treatment of psychiatric disorders, and the NMC Specialty Hospital psychiatric department offers emergency evaluation and treatment, crisis intervention and resolution. It also offers outpatient and inpatient services for adults, adolescents and children to treat schizophrenia, mood disorders, depression, anxiety, phobia, eating disorders, compulsive disorders, emotional problems, psychosexual dysfunctions and developmental disorders. The National Rehabilitation Centre specialises in treating substance addiction. However, check your insurance policy before making appointments as most insurers will not cover anxiety or stress-related illnesses.

Family fun in the desert

FAMILY & PARENTING

Bringing your family out to Abu Dhabi, or starting one while you're here, can be a fantastic experience. There's plenty of help, great educational facilities and a whole range of activities for the kids. This section covers much of that, but also takes a look at some of the more sobering topics like bereavement and divorce; issues that you may be faced with during your time here.

Marriage

When living in the UAE under Shariah law, marriage is the only legal bond for a man and a woman to establish a relationship and have children. It is illegal to live together as a couple if you are unmarried and you cannot have children out of wedlock.

If you're Christian or Catholic, you can marry in a church; if you'd prefer a non-religious marriage, you can tie the knot at your embassy. Muslim weddings take place before a Shariah court; the man must be a Muslim while the woman can be non-Muslim. A Muslim woman cannot marry a non-Muslim man in the UAE. Whatever your nationality, you should contact your embassy to notify them of your intent to get married and find out the exact process and paperwork necessary. Once wed, you will need to register the marriage with your embassy to get it validated internationally.

The Wedding Planner
One of the challenges of getting married outside your country of origin is being far away from your support network; if this is the case, a wedding planner can provide invaluable assistance and ensure that the big day runs smoothly. Try C'est La Vie (clvweddings.com), wedding.ae or Fonoon (fonoon-uae.com).

The Ceremony

While the wedding must be conducted in either a church, court or at your embassy, you have a large choice of where to have a wedding blessing and the reception. Many couples choose to have a small church ceremony and then celebrate at one of the luxury hotels, on the beach or even aboard a yacht.

Christians living in Abu Dhabi can get married at St Andrew's Church, near The British School in Al Mushrif (02 446 1631, standrewuah.org). The chaplain is registered with the UAE government as authorised to conduct legally recognised wedding ceremonies. Anglican wedding ceremonies can also take place at the Holy Trinity Church, Dubai, at Christ Church in Jebel Ali, Dubai or St Martin's Church in Sharjah, all of which are recognised by the UAE government. Ministers from the Anglican Church can also marry people at other approved locations.

Roman Catholic marriages can take place at St Joseph's Cathedral on Rashid Bin Al Maktoum Rd in Abu Dhabi (02 446 1929, stjosephsabudhabi.org). To marry in a Roman Catholic church, at least one of the partners must be Roman Catholic, and both of them must be resident in Abu Dhabi. Women must be at least 18, men must be over 21.

Hindu marriages are conducted by the maharaj at Dubai's Hindu Temple in Bur Dubai. Both parties must be Hindi and at least one of the couple should be an Indian citizen with a UAE residence visa.

Fees for a church wedding are around Dhs.2,000 and you can get married on any day of the week if a minister/vicar is available. You will typically need two or three witnesses who are UAE residents.

Couples from any religion can also get married at the Abu Dhabi Judicial Department (adjd.gov.ae).

There are certain conditions you have to meet for a church wedding:

- At least one member of the couple has to have been baptised
- At least one of the couple must have a UAE residence visa; expats on a visit visa cannot get married in the UAE
- Both people must be aged 18 or over

Depending on your faith and denomination, you may have to go for counselling sessions and regular church services. You will also need to register certain documents including birth and christening certificates, and written evidence that each is single and free to marry (divorce papers or a letter from your embassy). You will need a Banns certificate or certificate of no impediment, which takes up to three weeks to process and needs to be applied for at your home embassy. For example, the British embassy will display a notice of marriage for 21 days and, assuming no one objects, you are then free to tie the knot.

In nearly all cases, a marriage that is legally performed in the UAE will be recognised elsewhere in the world, but it's always best to check. In order to register the marriage, marriage certificates have to be translated into Arabic before being submitted to the Abu Dhabi Judiciary Department, Ministry of Justice and the Ministry of Foreign Affairs for attestation and finally taken to your embassy to record and legalise the marriage in the home country.

In Preparation

Visit the Abu Dhabi Bride Show (thebrideshow.com/abudhabi), held every February at the Abu Dhabi National Exhibition Centre; it covers everything you'll need for your big day.

The Reception

When it comes to your reception, any one of Abu Dhabi's stunning hotels would make the perfect venue and they will assist you with everything from the music and menus to floorplans and florists.

Jumeirah At Etihad Towers

Nr Emirates Palace, Corniche Rd
Al Bateen **02 811 5555**
jumeirah.com
Map **2 B3**

This luxury destination was named the Middle East's Leading Wedding Venue 2012 in the World Travel Awards and with good reason. There's a dedicated team of planners to make sure your event runs smoothly, and everything from the bridal suite to the ballroom is suitably elegant and awe-inspiring.

Ritz-Carlton Abu Dhabi Grand Canal

Nr Maqtaa Bridge Al Maqtaa **02 818 8888**
ritzcarlton.com
Map **1 L8**

For flawless elegance and fantastic views of the emirate, you can't go wrong with The Ritz. There's a range of romantic venues to choose from, including tranquil beaches, intimate gardens and a grand ballroom. Catering includes custom-designed wedding cakes.

Shangri-La Qaryat Al Beri

Qaryat Al Beri Complex, Nr Al Maqtaa Bridge
Al Maqta **02 509 8888**
shangri-la.com
Map **1 L8**

At the luxurious Shangri-La, the gleaming Sheikh Zayed Grand Mosque across the creek provides a stunning backdrop to your big day. There's also an impressive ballroom and a picturesque stretch of private beach. The events team will ensure that your day runs smoothly.

Westin Abu Dhabi Golf Resort & Spa
Nr Abu Dhabi Golf Club Khalifa City **02 616 9999**
westinabudhabigolfresort.com
Map **1 N8**
Set across more than 160 acres of parkland, the lush greenery of the Westin Abu Dhabi Golf Resort & Spa makes for a gorgeous setting for your nuptials. The hotel offers bespoke wedding services to ensure your every need is catered for.

Family Law

It is essential that you have a will in place, and it's especially important to seek legal advice if you become a property owner in Abu Dhabi. That's because, under Shariah law, the rules for who inherits property after someone's death differ from those in other countries. For example, in the event of a man's death, it may be that his sons (or brother, if he doesn't have any sons) are first in line for inheritance and his wife could end up with nothing. Fortunately, the UAE does claim to guarantee a woman's right to inherit property, but it's worth making your will watertight.

Also, if a family member dies, the government can freeze his/her accounts until all of their liabilities are cleared, such as loans, credit cards and business debts; this can happen very quickly but can easily be overturned if a UAE will is in place. Providing each other a 'Power of Attorney' document in addition to a will is also recommended to prevent this.

An Abu Dhabi-based lawyer can assist you with a locally viable will (do check that they are authorised by the government to write wills), or contact Just Wills (just-wills.net), part of a UK-based estate planning organisation with a UAE presence. In addition to the lawyers listed, your embassy may be able to recommend a firm with experience in the laws of your home country as well as those of the UAE.

Afridi & Angell Al Ghaith Tower, Shk Hamdan Bin Mohammed St, Al Danah, 02 627 5134, *afridi-angell.com*
Al Tamimi & Company Al Sila Tower, Al Maryah Island, 02 813 0444, *tamimi.com*
Clyde & Co West Tower, Abu Dhabi Mall, Al Zahiyah, 02 644 6633, *clydeco.com*
Consolidated Consultants (Jafar Tukan & Partners) Nr City Terminal & Saba Hotel, Al Zahiyah, 02 644 2955, *ccjo.com*
DLA Piper Middle East Penthouse C2 Bldg, Al Bateen, 02 494 1500, *dlapiper.com*
Emirates Advocates Abu Dhabi Islamic Bank Bldg, Zayed The First St, Al Danah, 02 639 4446, *emiratesadvocates.com*
Baker & Mckenzie Sila Tower, Al Falah St, Al Maryah Island, 02 676 6003, *habibalmulla.com*

Hadef & Partners Blue Tower, Khalifa Bin Zayed The First St, Al Danah, 02 627 6622, *hadefpartners.com*
International Advocates & Legal Consultants Bin Hayai Bldg, Shk Zayed The First St, Al Khalidiya, 02 633 5000
Reed Smith Silah Tower, Al Falah St, Al Maryah Island, 02 622 2636, *reedsmith.com*
Simmons & Simmons ADNIC Bldg, Khalifa Bin Zayed St, Al Danah, 02 651 9200, *simmons-simmons.com*
SNR Denton Al Ghaith Tower, Shk Hamdan Bin Mohammed St, Al Danah, 02 626 6180, *snrdenton.com*
Trowers & Hamlins Tower C1, Al Bateen Towers, King Abdul Aziz St, Al Bateen, 02 410 7600, *trowers.com*

Making A Will
Firstly, make an appointment with a licensed estate planner, preferably one with knowledge of the law of your home country. Locally based and global company, The One Group (theonegroup.co), can help you prepare a document. You'll need passport copies, contact details of executors and proof of assets. A will can be drawn up and needs to be attested at your embassy or consulate. Have this attested document translated at an authorised typing centre and then attested by a notary public in the emirate you live in.

Divorce
Divorce, like other matters of family law, is either governed by UAE law, Shariah law, or by the laws of the individuals' originating country. If the parties are from different countries, the applicable law is that from where the marriage was solemnised.

The first step in any divorce hearing is to look at reconciliation with the aid of the Family Guidance and Reformation Centre, which functions under the Abu Dhabi Judicial Department (02 651 2222, adjd.gov.ae). Anyone experiencing marital problems or family disputes can use this service, and you can file a complaint against your spouse by simply providing the centre with copies of your ID (passport or Resident Identity Card) and your marriage certificate. If counsellors at the centre are unable to help a couple to reach an amicable settlement then the case may get referred to court for legal proceedings to take place. This is when you need to seek legal advice.

You'll now need the services of an expat law firm, who can advise you which 'jurisdiction' (UAE or your home country) is most appropriate for you in terms of cost, timescale and outcome. If the case is simple and uncontested you may not even need to attend court, and you can expect to pay around Dhs.10,000, inclusive of all court fees and other expenses. In custody of children, the court's paramount concern is the child's welfare. In Shariah law, the custody of a child while a minor will be the mother's unless there are compelling reasons to decide otherwise.

Death

In the event of the death of a friend or relative, the first thing to do is to notify the police by dialing 999. The police will file a report and the body will be taken to a hospital where a doctor will determine the cause of death and produce a report. The Abu Dhabi authorities will need to see the deceased's passport and visa details and the Abu Dhabi Police will investigate in the case of an accidental or suspicious death, and it's likely that an autopsy will be performed at a government hospital.

Death Certificate

After the deceased has been taken to the mortuary, the hospital will issue a report determining the cause of death. You need to submit this report to the mortuary to obtain a death certificate of declaration, which needs to be stamped by the police.

Take this declaration, along with the deceased's original passport and residence visa (and copies) to the Department of Preventive Medicine, where the death certificate will be issued and then attested. If the deceased is being sent home, request a certificate in English or the appropriate language.

Inform your embassy so that they can register the death, provide a letter of no objection if you wish to fly the body home, and cancel the deceased's passport. The cost for this ranges from free with the South African embassy to Dhs.1,000 with the British embassy.

Then, return with all documents to the police station where you will be issued with three letters for releasing the body from hospital, embalming the body and transporting the body to the airport (in the case of repatriation).

In terms of costs, you will need Dhs.60 for the death certificate, Dhs.100 for English translation (optional) and up to Dhs.1,000 for the embassy letter and registration fee.

Death Registration

Once the official UAE and embassy death certificates have been issued, the death must be registered with the Ministry of Health. The Ministry of Foreign Affairs must then attest the death certificate and the translation; the General Directorate of Residency and Foreigners Affairs cancels the visa.

Once the death has been registered with the appropriate authorities, it is then possible to organise either funeral arrangements within Abu Dhabi or repatriation to your home country.

Local Burial Or Cremation

When someone dies, one of the key things for relatives to decide upon is where the body should be buried. Will it be repatriated to the deceased's country of origin or will the body be buried here in the UAE?

More often than not, the deceased will be repatriated to their home country. However, Abu Dhabi does have mortuary, cremation and burial sites all equipped with modern and proper facilities (note that cremation is available only to Abu Dhabi residents). Local burials take place at the Abu Dhabi Christian Cemetery, with all arrangements for the funeral done through St Andrew's Church. Alternatively, contact Al Foah Funeral Services (alfoahfuneralservices.com), which runs a multi-faith crematorium and can take care of all funeral arrangements, including repatriation of human remains, thanks to a partnership with Etihad Cargo. Another useful contact is Middle East Funeral Services (mefs.ae) which is based in Dubai but operates throughout the UAE.

Abu Dhabi Christian Cemetery Sas Al Nakhl Island, 02 446 1631
Al Foah Funeral Services Al Danah, 056 737 3618, *alfoahfuneralservices.com*
St Andrew's Church Abu Dhabi Al Mushrif, 02 446 1631, *standrewauh.org*

Returning The Deceased Home

Before repatriation, it is an international requirement that the deceased be embalmed, which can be arranged through the Sheikh Khalifa Medical City or the Muhaisna Medical Fitness Centre (04 502 3939) for around Dhs.1,000; this includes the embalming certificate. The body must be identified before and after embalming, and a casket then selected.

The following documents will need to accompany the deceased overseas: the local death certificate, a translation of the death certificate, the embalming certificate, NOC from the police, the embassy death certificate and NOC, and the cancelled passport. Have at least seven copies of each document with you.

If the body is not travelling on the same flight as the next of kin, you will need to make arrangements for the remains to be collected at the airport of arrival. Details of the undertaker will normally be required by the airline before departure.

Omeir Travel Agency (omeir.com, 02 612 3456) has experience in repatriation and will give you all the necessary information, along with the procedures to follow for returning the deceased home.

Having A Baby

There are a number of advantages that make having a baby in Abu Dhabi easier than in your home country. For one thing, the standard of maternity healthcare – both private and government – is excellent. For another, there's a better chance that you can get by on a single income, meaning that one parent (in practice, usually the mother) can stay at home with the baby, rather than having to return to work for financial reasons. Add to that the inexpensive healthcare and babysitting services, which allow you to be a little more independent than your counterparts back home. Pregnant women are generally treated exceptionally well here, too – expect priority access to seats on buses and airplanes and even be able to use special supermarket lanes.

However, there are a few disadvantages to be aware of. Maternity leave is paltry: just 45 days' paid leave, and no paternity leave whatsoever. Plus, there's the absence of the social support network of family and friends you may have had back home. Fortunately, there are heaps of expats with children in Abu Dhabi, and many meet up regularly and offer plenty of support to each other. See a partial list on the following pages.

Let's just clear up some of the misunderstandings and urban myths about having a baby in Abu Dhabi. Here we go:

Your baby's birth certificate will be written in Arabic
- He/she will not have UAE citizenship or a passport
- Breastfeeding is allowed in the UAE, just be discreet
- Home births are not permitted in the UAE
- You must be married before giving birth
- The husband is allowed to be present at the birth at most private hospitals

Overseas Births

If you have your baby back in your home country, you will need to organise their residence or visit visa before entering the UAE. The application should be filed by the father along with his passport and residence visa, salary certificate, and a copy of the birth certificate.

From Bump To Birth

As soon as you find out that you're going to have a baby, you need to choose where to go for your maternity care. Most expecting expat mothers opt for a private hospital rather than a government hospital, and as long as you have private health insurance this should be affordable, if not free.

Bear in mind that some hospitals may charge extra for certain procedures, such as caesarean sections, costing upwards of Dhs.20,000, and epidurals, which normally cost about Dhs.2,000. Having twins, triplets or more will cost you more, too. There are also hidden costs for resuscitation after the birth, your husband staying overnight in the room with you, and, in some hospitals, baby's nappies and wet wipes. Finding out all of these costs before you decide on where to have your baby can help ensure those first days with your new baby are not blighted by financial headaches and stress.

There are two specific maternity hospitals in Abu Dhabi – The Corniche (which has a neo-natal intensive care baby unit and runs a breastfeeding clinic) and Al Noor, although you can give birth at other hospitals too. Several hospitals in Abu Dhabi also offer popular antenatal classes, including Cleveland Clinic, Corniche Hospital, Al Noor Hospital and Burjeel Hospital.

Water Births

Water birth delivery is available at the Al Ain Cromwell Women and Children's Hospital (alaincromwell.com). However, you'll need to sign up to their whole delivery package which will cost you between Dhs.12,000 and Dhs.14,000 if you don't have insurance, or if your insurance won't cover it.

Maternity Care

Unlike some other countries, in the UAE the delivery will be performed by the doctor who treats you throughout your pregnancy, rather than a midwife. Therefore, it's important to find a doctor that you are comfortable with from the beginning, as he or she will be with you 'from bump to birth'. You can choose to have all your antenatal care at a local clinic, as many obstetricians are then authorised to deliver at a certain hospital. It's also more than likely that you will be able to receive more frequent check-ups and scans in the run up to the birth as part of your care, including a 4D scan.

In many countries caesarean sections are only an emergency option, but here elective C-sections are more common. Keep in mind they may not be covered by health insurance, and require a longer hospital stay.

Marriage And Babies

It's illegal to have a baby out of wedlock while resident in the UAE. Therefore, if you are unmarried when you fall pregnant, you need to a) get married quickly or b) leave the country. You will be asked for your marriage certificate when you give birth, or at prenatal checks, and if there is a significant discrepancy in your dates you will face some tricky questions and a lot more paperwork.

Health

For many women, fitness is an important part of their lifestyle that they are keen to maintain during pregnancy. It's essential to consult your doctor before embarking on any exercise programme while you're expecting, but most agree that gentle, low impact exercise is beneficial to mum and bump. It can also make getting back in shape later a little easier. Look for classes in prenatal yoga and pilates – try Bodytree Studio (bodytreestudio.com) for both.

Registering Your New Baby

If you're planning to have a baby in Abu Dhabi, the following is an essential checklist to ensure your child is properly registered once born.

Get a UAE birth certificate

You have 14 days after the birth to get your newborn's UAE birth certificate, which is needed to apply for a passport and residence visa. The hospital will issue a 'notification of birth certificate' in Arabic. Take this to the Department of Preventive Medicine along with your marriage certificate, both parents' passports, and copies of their photos and visa pages. The Arabic birth certificate will then be issued for Dhs.50, and you get an English translation on the same day. You need to get both attested at the hospital, and then by the Ministry Of Foreign Affairs.

Register the birth with your embassy

Once you have the UAE birth certificate, you can register the birth with your embassy. The embassy will issue you with a registration of birth certificate that can be used to apply for the passport. Fees will vary depending on nationality.

Apply for your baby's passport

To apply for a passport, you'll need to provide the birth certificate (UAE or home nationality), the registration of birth certificate (issued by embassy) and two new photos. The procedure will vary from nationality to nationality. British nationals should visit gov.uk, download the application and then send it along with the documents to Her Majesty's Passport Office (see website for details). The baby's passport should arrive in between four and six weeks.

Apply for birth certificate from your home country

You can apply for a birth certificate from your home country too. The process will vary depending on your nationality. British nationals, for example, must wait until six months after they register the birth, because it takes that long to process the registration. However, they can then apply for a British birth certificate for their child online.

Get a residence visa for your baby

You have 120 days from the birth to get a UAE residence visa for your newborn baby (or risk being fined Dhs.100 a day). To qualify, the parent (sponsor) must earn at least Dhs.4,000 (or Dhs.3,000 plus accommodation) per month. You'll need the following documents:

- Typed application form
- Baby's passport
- Original + copy of the baby's attested birth certificate in English and Arabic
- Three passport photos of the baby
- Original and copy of the attested marriage certificate
- Passport copy of sponsor (the parent)
- Copy of mother's passport and visa page
- Marriage certificate
- Copy of job contract for the sponsor or a salary certificate
- Attested tenancy contract
- Three months' worth of bank statement for long-time residents. New residents can submit one-month bank statement or bank letter confirming salary transfer
- Resident ID of the sponsor
- Resident ID application form for the baby
- Dhs.310 application fee and typing fee

Pick up an application form from a typing office and have them complete it for you. Then, visit the residency section of the General Directorate of Residency & Foreigners Affairs, hand in the completed form and supporting documents. The residence visa will be sent to you through a courier service.

Born Back Home

Babies born abroad to expat mums with UAE residency are required to have a residence visa or visit visa of their own before entering the UAE. The application should be filed through the usual channels by the father or family provider, along with the essential documents, a salary certificate and a copy of the newly born child's birth certificate.

Maternity Leave

A working mother will be given just 45 days of paid maternity leave (60 days for government employees) so long as they have been with the company for a year already (it's half pay otherwise). You can also take an additional month of unpaid leave with your employer's permission. If you need extra time for medical reasons, you can take up to 100 days, although this is only granted upon production of a medical certificate from your doctor. These days can be consecutive or non-consecutive. New mothers are still entitled to their annual paid holiday.

Breastfeeding time is granted until the baby is 18 months old; it is two daily breaks, maximum 30 minutes each. In practice, this means most new mums arrange to come to work an hour late or they can leave an hour early.

Adoption

While you can't adopt a UAE National baby, many couples in Abu Dhabi adopt children from Africa, Asia and the Far East. Adoption regulations vary according to which country the child is from, but once you clear the requirements of that country and complete the adoption process, you'll have no problems bringing your new child into the UAE on your sponsorship. You may also want to check with your embassy about the procedure for applying for citizenship for your new child in your home country.

You are advised to go through the Hague Adoption Convention, an internationally recognised process. You'll be required to provide a file of essential documents, undergo a police check, and complete a 12 hour home-study programme – which involves psychological analysis and parental preparation. After a home visit and final interview, you will receive 'approval', and your home study file can be handed over to any international adoption agency recognised by the UAE, and your name added to their adoption list. It is then a matter of waiting for the phone to ring...

Single Parents

It is possible to be a single parent in Abu Dhabi and sponsor your child. There are additional requirements to meet, including a minimum salary level and letter of no objection from the other parent (or death certificate, in the case of a deceased spouse). Visit the Immigration Department to find out the exact requirements. Although it can be daunting, the high standard of living and affordable childcare offers distinct advantages to raising a child on your own in the UAE, although single males may struggle hiring female nannies or maids.

Mother & Baby Groups

A number of mother and baby or toddler groups offer invaluable support and camaraderie for new mums feeling a million miles from friends and family. Groups like this are a great way to meet other expat parents, make friends, and build up a support network. Although most are aimed primarily at women, in general dads are welcome to attend too. You can expect to get connected with social activities, information on useful services and word-of-mouth advice on resources and events around the emirate.

Abu Dhabi Mums
abudhabimums.ae
This popular group boasts 600 members from more than 70 countries and has been going since 1994. With regular social events and age-based playgroups, it's a great way to make friends and meet other parents. Plus, the website alone is an invaluable source of family-focused information.

Abu Dhabi Woman
abudhabiwoman.com
Although not strictly a mother and toddler group, this popular expat online resource has plenty of relative information, as well as an active discussion forum called The Parent Place where mums and dads can swap tips on everything from pregnancy and giving birth to nurseries and schools.

Moms Guide Abu Dhabi
050 259 4019
momsguidead.com
Launched in 2012 as a collaboration between expat and Emirati mums, this organisation aims to inspire and empower mums while building a strong community spirit. It's a great resource for information on relevant news, discount deals and child-friendly events in the emirate and offers a comprehensive listing of kid-friendly events.

Hiring A Nanny

Having a baby outside of your home country will most likely mean that you don't have access to your family support network. Fortunately, childcare is generally affordable and hiring a nanny is quite common. Many people hire a full-time maid who will cook and clean alongside taking on childcare duties. If you want to sponsor a maid, you must have a salary above Dhs.6,000 per month and be able to provide her with housing (many apartments and villas in the emirate have a maids room inside or outside), medical insurance and the usual benefits, which include an airfare back to her home country at least once every two years, food, clothing and toiletries. You'll also have to pay a 'maid tax' to the government of around Dhs.5,200.

If you employ a full-time live-in maid you will need to sponsor her for a residence visa. You can only sponsor a maid from the following countries: India, Sri Lanka, Philippines, Ethiopia, Bangladesh, and Indonesia. This requires taking the following documentation to the Residency Department at the General Directorate of Residency and Foreigners Affairs: a prepaid application form, medical certificate, the maid's passport (showing an entry stamp and visit visa), her Resident ID (or application), passport photos of the sponsor and the maid, a passport copy and visa page for the sponsor and wife, sponsor's salary certificate, attested tenancy agreement from Tawtheeq, copies of your electricity and water (ADDC) bill, and the maid's labour contract, which states her salary (signed by both).

Once the maid is given her residence visa stamp in her passport, which has to be renewed annually, she will also receive a Domestic Worker Permit (equivalent to your labour card).

Renewing A Maid's Visa

This is a quick and easy process that shouldn't take as long as the initial process: just take copies of yours and the maid's passport and visa, your tenancy contract and salary certificate, medical test results and insurance certificate to the Residency Department. The maid will then be issued a new residence visa, Domestic Worker Permit and Resident ID. If you need more advice, visit askexplorer.com for details.

Pros & Cons

There are plenty of advantages to having a live-in nanny. Not only is it relatively inexpensive – generally much cheaper than childcare in many expats' home countries – but having someone to look after your child means that parents can enjoy more support and independence. This is particularly true for working mothers and single parents.

On the other hand, you should keep in mind that first aid and childcare qualifications are not legally required for your babysitters or childcare workers in the UAE, so it's worth doing your research to find one that suits you.

Check out Majestic Nannies (majesticnannies.com) which has been going since 2003 and specialises in providing qualified, internationally trained and experienced childcare staff for 'discerning' parents. Networking and word-of-mouth can also pay dividends as many parents with young children will be in the same boat as you. Check out Abu Dhabi Mums (abudhabimums.ae) for recommendations from other parents and expatwoman.com for a long list of ads from maids looking for work.

Can You Afford It?

Once you've made the decision to employ a nanny, you'll need to work out if you can actually afford to do so. The average monthly wage is around Dhs.2,000 but allow an extra Dhs.400 for things like phone credit, food, clothes and toiletries. With annual visa costs, health insurance and flights home that could mount up to around Dhs.35,000 per year or more.

Activities For Kids

Abu Dhabi is a veritable playground for every child, from tots to teens, with a huge range of different activities on offer. The cooler months make for a wonderful, outdoorsy lifestyle; you can picnic in the park, splash about at a waterpark, spend a day at the beach or even learn how to sail. As the weather heats up, you can visit one of the many indoor play and edutainment centres dotted around the city.

The city is also a remarkably safe place, aside from some of the obvious things such as traffic. If you find yourself living in one of the quieter villa compounds or one of the newer, purpose-built apartment complexes, there's often a lot of safe outside space and many expat parents don't mind letting their kids run around with their friends unsupervised.

Keep an eye on the local press too as, most months, there's something going on for families whether that's ice shows, exhibitions or one-off entertainment. Many malls have specific kiddie entertainment like face painting or some kind of craft activity in the early evenings at weekends too.

Outdoor

When the temperatures drop around October, enjoying the many outdoor activities is a welcome relief. Until May time, the below can keep your little ones well entertained while teaching them some fun new skills. You may find you'll want to join in too.

Abu Dhabi Equestrian Club
Shakhbout Bin Sultan St Al Mushrif **02 445 5500**
adec-web.com
Map **2 J13**
The Abu Dhabi Equestrian Club is a must-visit for anyone who loves horses, with equestrian sports being a highly revered traditional pastime in Emirati life. As well as races and show jumping events held throughout the cooler winter months, the club also offers instruction for riders of all ages and abilities. These start with riding for beginners and advances right through to show jumping. Private riding lessons start from Dhs.200 for members while non-members are charged Dhs.350.

Abu Dhabi Sailing & Yacht Club
Abu Dhabi Theater Rd, Breakwater **02 658 3333**
adsyc.ae
Map **2 E2**
The Abu Dhabi Sailing & Yacht Club offers sailing lessons for youngsters aged six and over. The experienced instructors will guide them through basic techniques although kids need to be confident swimmers to join the school. There are plans to ensure that staff, equipment and facilities are subject to the standards of the UK Royal Yachting Association too.

Al Mahara Diving Center
Nr Main Taxi/Bus Station Al Nahyan **02 643 7377**
divemahara.com
Map **2 N8**
These dive specialists have a range of youth programmes including the popular PADI Bubblemaker; a course aimed at giving kids aged eight and over their first taste of scuba diving in a safe environment. They don't have to be super swimmers although they should be comfortable in the water (maximum water depth is just two metres). A great first dip into exploring the sea's treasures.

Indoor

From around May to September, having fun in air-conditioned venues like these is often the best option.

Action Zone
Meena Centre Al Meena **02 673 4577**
actionzone.ae
Map **1 D2**
Action Zone is a kid's paradise: big, bright and noisy, with enough games, activities and rides to keep even the most energetic little ones entertained. Located at Mina Centre in Abu Dhabi and covering over 3,000 square metres, the park has themed carousel rides, amusement park rides including bumper cars, and a wide range of video and arcade games. For more adventurous visitors, there's also a bungee trampoline and a climbing maze to tackle.

Art Beat
Nr Mushrif Mall Al Mushrif
02 444 5135
Map **1 G7**
In contrast with the usual playplaces, Art Beat doesn't engage kids through pulsating lights and raucous games. Instead, paint, glue and glitter are the attractions. Kids can first select a 'canvas', anything from cardboard letters to clay animals. Then they can decorate it using any of the many available materials. Friendly staff will answer questions and help your child construct a masterpiece.

Kool Kidz
WTC Mall Al Markiziya **02 677 0954**
koolkidz.ae
Map **2 L3**
This playzone is geared towards slightly younger age groups, with a range of different zones for arts and crafts, video games, traditional blocks and trains and climbing sets. Kids will love running around the safe foam floors from one area to the next. Children age three and over can be left alone while parents shop or have coffee in the mall; Kool Kidz charges per hour, starting at Dhs.60 for the first hour. It is a perfect entertainment option for hot summer months.

Sparky's Family Fun Park
Khalidiya Mall Al Manhal **02 635 4316**
sparkysme.com
Map **2 H5**
Located on Khalidiya Mall's top level, Sparky's is a family fun centres and boasts enough attractions to keep even the most energetic of kids entertained. As well as fun fair-style rides, including an ever-popular rollercoaster, there are also bumper cars, a football striker zone and bowling alley. Arcade games and a 3D and 4D cinema provide gentler entertainment for kids and grown-ups. There's even an ice rink providing lessons in skating, ice hockey and curling, where you can cool down during summer.

Classes
Learn something new or perfect an existing skill with classes and courses from these useful places. In addition to the places listed below, Manarat Al Saadiyat often offers one-off art classes to accompany the launch of new exhibits; these are usually offered for kids as well as teenagers, so check saadiyat.ae for details. It's also worth keeping up with the events listings in The National or Gulf News for additional classes that are offered throughout the year.

Abu Dhabi Pottery
Nr Khalidiya Park, Zayed The First St
Al Manhal **02 666 7079**
abudhabipottery.com
Map **3 C3**
For a change from the usual sports or dance-related activities, why not have a go at something more creative and crafty? Abu Dhabi Pottery offers classes for adults and children over five years old, and gives you the chance to try both hand building and the wheel technique. With supportive, knowledgeable instructors on hand, your youngsters are sure to create something original to take home. Classes cost Dhs.185 for adults and Dhs.100 for children.

Arabian Swim Academy
Various 050 883 8091
arabianswimacademy.com
Swimming is a key skill to have when living on an island, and aspiring mermaids and mermen can develop their abilities at the Arabian Swim Academy's sessions. Nine levels of classes, from seahorse to dolphin, teach children the necessary strokes to glide easily through the water, while varying student-teacher ratios ensure that little ones are safe and supported. Parent-child swim sessions are available for kids under the age of 3. Lessons cost Dhs.70 per session and a yearly registration fee is Dhs.150.

Bodytree Studio
Hazaa Bin Zayed St Al Manhal **02 443 4448**
bodytreestudio.com
Map **2 J7**
You're never too young to get into yoga, and Bodytree Studio offers a valuable opportunity for kids to be introduced to yoga in a fun and relaxed environment. There's a wide range of classes for participants of all ages, with special classes just for little ones. Kids yoga classes run for 30 minutes, and you can purchase a package of four classes for Dhs.140. The centre also

Outdoor adventure

offers children's music classes and ballet lessons, as well as mum-and-baby yoga classes for new mums.

Royal Institute of Music & Arts
National Printing Centre Bldg, Shk Rashid Bin Saeed St Al Danah **02 622 5410**
royalinstituteofmusic.com
Map **2 L3**
If your kids dream of performing on stage – whether they want to be a rock star or a concert pianist – then the Royal Institute of Music & Arts is a great choice. There are classes to suit all levels here, and experienced, certified teachers will guide your children from theory to practical lessons in guitar, keyboard, piano, drumming, violin and vocals. The institute is recognised by the Ministry of Education and it also prepares students for the music examinations conducted by Trinity Guildhall and ABRSM Colleges of Music, London.

Dib Dib
Brownies, Girl Guides, Cubs and Scouts Groups are all well established in the region. All children from five to 18 years old can join in and parents can always volunteer. The phrase 'Be Prepared' in Arabic is *kun mast'idan*, which might come in useful for any budding Cub.

Summer Camps
Soaring temperatures that have everyone cooped up indoors can make summer a challenging time to entertain the kids. To help keep boredom at bay, there are a number of summer camps around Abu Dhabi to help keep your children busy doing something productive, whether that is learning a new language, painting a masterpiece or playing some indoor sport. Various schools and organisations throughout Abu Dhabi run summer camps during the hottest months, while several nurseries also offer summer day care for younger children. While many activities will be inside air-conditioned buildings there are plenty that will have your little ones getting a good dose of fresh air.

You will be keen to find out if the activities are age appropriate to your child beforehand or if there are any other restrictions you might need to know about. So, it's best to do your research first and plan ahead. You should book early, too as the most sought after places will fill up quickly. Keep your eyes open nearer to the onset of summer as a lot of the hotels and malls realise the need for help with kids during this time. Many well known hotels have held summer camps in the past, but check each summer with your favourite hotels as it does vary each year. It is also worth asking for sibling discounts as these are often given.

Al Forsan International Sports Resort
Abu Dhabi - Al Ain Rd, Khalifa City **02 556 8555**
alforsan.com
Map **1 P9**
In many ways, Al Forsan is the ultimate amusement and activity centre, offering everything from horse riding, archery and paintballing to clay pigeon shooting, wakeboarding and cable boarding. It's a great venue when it comes to catering for all ages, and its yearly summer camps help kids to stay active, have fun and try out new things. The camp activities tend to be organised around the many excellent on-site facilities, and kids can expect to try out everything from watersports to go karting. The addition of a new hotel is sure to increase the appeal as parents can perhaps link their child's summer camp with their own little sporting break.

Beach Rotana Abu Dhabi
Nr Abu Dhabi Mall, Al Zahiyah **02 697 9000**
rotana.com
Map **2 S5**
Many hotels organise fun summer camps during the hotter months, and the Beach Rotana's schedule tends to be one of the most popular. The season usually kicks off with a meet and greet attended by the children and their parents, where the camp leaders will talk through what they can expect over the coming weeks. There's a wide variety of activities on offer, from sports like badminton and basketball to music, art and dance.

The Club
Shk Khalifa Hwy, Al Meena **02 673 1111**
the-club.com
Map **2 V3**
This private members' leisure club is open to applications from UAE residents, and families who join get access to the excellent summer holiday clubs. There's a wide range of fun new experiences to try out at the multi-activity camp, which combines sports, watersports like kayaking and stand up paddle boarding, and arts and crafts, plus there are camps devoted to dance and musical theatre for Glee fans.

M & S Sports Services
Various locations
mandssports.com
This popular organisation hosts regular holiday camps for kids, with a strong emphasis on having fun while playing sports and getting fitter. Each day of the summer camp has a different theme; while the main sports are football and swimming, there's also a broader focus on developing agility, balance and co-ordination. Experienced, well-trained coaches ensure that everything runs smoothly, and there are other non-sporting activities like arts and crafts too.

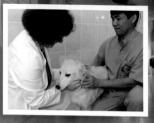

PETS

If you plan to have a pet in Abu Dhabi, keep in mind that most housing contracts state that pets are not allowed. You may, however, be able to chat to the landlord and find some leeway. Keep in mind that pets are banned from parks and beaches, so you're limited to walking your dog on the streets of your neighbourhood. Dogs must always be on a lead (some breeds need to be muzzled) – however, you could always head into the desert and let Rover enjoy the wide, open spaces freely.

Moving Your Pet

You can bring pets into the UAE without quarantine as long as they are microchipped and vaccinated in your home country with verifying documentation. They must also be older than four months and have had their rabies injection at least 21 days prior to travel. However, do your research as certain breeds and cross-breeds are banned. Your pet should have an import permit and, depending on the country of origin, may need an additional RNATT (rabies) blood test. See the pet import pages at moew.gov.ae for more information.

Buying A Pet

If you're thinking about getting a pet, the hard-working Abu Dhabi Animal Shelter (abudhabianimalshelter.com), set up by the municipality itself, is a rescue centre for stray cats and dogs that aims to rehabilitate them and find new homes. The shelter also runs a fostering programme for pet-lovers that can't offer a permanent home. Check out the website to see which furry friends are househunting. Other shelters for adopting a pet include Animal Action and Feline Friends, while there are a number of pet shops around the city.

Sleek Salukis

The saluki is the breed of dog most commonly associated with the region; they are used in traditional forms of hunting and resemble a greyhound in many ways. The Arabian Saluki Centre (02 575 5330) offers a wealth of information and care for these thoroughbred dogs and even welcomes visitors to learn about them.

Vaccinations & Registration

If living in Abu Dhabi, you must inoculate your cat or dog and register it with the Abu Dhabi Municipality, which will then microchip your pet and provide you with a plastic neck tag for them. If the municipality picks up an animal that turns out to not have a tag and microchip, it is treated as a stray and will be kept for a short time before being put down. Officially, vets should not provide any treatment for your cat or your dog if it has not been microchipped, although this may not always be the case.

Also, all dogs in the emirate have to be vaccinated against rabies, distemper, canine hepatitis, leptospirosis and parvovirus; cats have to be vaccinated against rabies, feline rhinotracheitis, calicivirus and panleukopenia.

It's recommended that cats and dogs be kept inside, which may seem like unusual advice. However, the main threat is in picking up diseases from a stray animal; in addition, the hot summer months can also become as unbearable outside for these furry friends as it is for their owners.

Flight Of The Falcon

The Abu Dhabi Falcon Hospital (falconhospital.com) helps keep the impressive birds in top shape for falconry, from owners across the country (including royalty). It's also a fascinating place to visit.

Vets, Kennels and Boarding

Abu Dhabi Animal Shelter Nr Abu Dhabi Falcon Hospital, Al Shamkha, 02 575 5155, *abudhabianimalshelter.com*
Abu Dhabi Falcon Hospital Sweihan Rd, Al Shamkha, 02 575 5155, *falconhospital.com*
American Veterinary Clinic Al Falah St, Al Khalidiya, 02 665 5044, *americanvet.ae*
The British Veterinary Centre Arabian Gulf St, Al Khalidiya, 02 665 0085, *britvet.com*
Cloud9 Pet Hotel & Care Khalifa City, 02 556 4111, *cloud9pethotel.com*
Dubai Kennels & Cattery > p.125 Al Rebat St, Umm Ramoul, Dubai, 04 211 4800, *dkc.ae*
Feline Friends Various locations, 050 823 1569, *felinefriendsuae.com*
German Veterinary Clinic 39th St, Khalifa City, 02 556 2024, *germanvet.ae*
National Veterinary Hospital Shk Rashid Bin Saeed St, Al Mushrif, 02 446 1628, *nationalvet.com*
New Veterinary Clinic Nr Adnoc Petrol Station, Zayed The First St, Markaziya West, 02 672 5955

Dubai Kennels & Cattery

Animal Care • Animal Relocations • By Animal People

Since 1983

Boarding.
Daycare.
Relocations
AND Veterinary!
Wow! That's better
than sniffing butt?

DKC Veterinary Clinic

Animal Care • Animal Relocations • By Animal People

www.dkc.ae

 /dubaikennelscattery

04-211-4800

FITNESS

Gyms & Fitness Clubs

With the world's sporting eyes now on Abu Dhabi, the emirate is on a fitness drive with healthy living campaigns and more sports going into schools. On Yas Island, Yas Marina and Yas Beach are bursting with clubs and activities, and the new Vogue Fitness gym has raised the bar when it comes to working out in the capital. However, finding accommodation with a gym can be difficult. New houses and flats generally have fitness centres unless they are older. Thankfully, there are plenty of gyms to join and many hotels have health club memberships and run exercise classes if your home doesn't have facilities. Independent gyms and health clubs usually offer day passes for Dhs.100 to Dhs.250. Try Hiltonia Health Club & Spa at the Hilton Corniche or Saadiyat Beach Club, both of which have excellent gyms, beaches and swimming pools.

My First Gym

If you want to give your kid a mind, body and soul workout, then My First Gym (myfirstgymuae.com) is the place to go. Mommy and Me classes, yoga, ballet and gymnastics aim to help the development of bright and active children. You can even have a kid's birthday party there.

Abu Dhabi Country Club

Shakhbout Bin Sultan St Al Mushrif **02 657 7777**
adcountryclub.com
Map **2 J13**
Extensive facilities include two gyms (one women-only), as well as nine tennis courts, two squash courts and a basketball court. There's a swimming pool and

two Jacuzzis, and several outdoor all-weather football pitches. Personal trainers and coaches are on hand for group and private lessons. Classes are free to members and Dhs.50 for non-members.

Al Forsan International Sports Resort
Abu Dhabi - Al Ain Rd, Khalifa City **02 556 8555**
alforsan.com
Map **1 P9**
In addition to all the other activities on offer at Al Forsan such as shooting and paintballing and every watersport you could possibly think of, there is a gym and swimming pool with memberships available, as well as single day access for Dhs.120.

Armed Forces Officers Club & Hotel
Nr Shk Zayed Grand Mosque, Al Khaleej Al Arabi St, Officers Club **02 441 5900**
afoc.mil.ae
Map **1 K9**
A fantastic, spacious and complete gym with all the advanced equipment and specially equipped sections for cardiovascular fitness and aerobics. It also has one of the capital's only indoor tennis courts.

The Club
Shk Khalifa Hwy, Al Meena **02 673 1111**
the-club.com
Map **2 V3**
Open to private members only, it has a private beach, various swimming pools, tennis, squash, badminton and a well-equipped gym. Classes are reserved for members only. Annual adult membership starts at Dhs.3,450 although it is subject to a Dhs.3,750 joining fee, plus extras depending on which facilities you use.

Fit Studio
Skh Zayed Bin Sultan St, Al Matar **02 444 3012**
fitstudio.ae
Map **1 J7**
A great option if you prefer social classes to going it alone in a gym, Fit Studio offers the full range of Les Mills disciplines (Bodyattack, Bodycombat, Bodystep, TRX, RPM, Yogalates etc) from around Dhs.50 per class. You can see timetables and book classes online.

Fitness First
Marina Mall Breakwater
02 666 2116
fitnessfirstme.com
Map **2 D1**
The ladies-only outlet of Fitness First at Marina Mall has machines, free weights, and group exercise studios. They offer the Les Mills series of cardiofitness classes as well as several varieties of yoga. There are numerous mixed and ladies branches around the city at Abu Dhabi Mall, Dalma Mall and Al Seef Mall.

Golds Gym
Al Wahda Mall Al Wahdah
02 672 7220
goldsgym.ae
Map **2 M7**
This outlet of the popular gym chain is one of the capital's most popular options for getting fit. There are mixed and ladies only parts to the gym, as well as very well-attended classes whose participants have varying levels of fitness; it's a safe choice for those who are a little shy and would prefer to hide at the back.

Haddins Fitness
Zayed Sport City Al Madina Al Riyadiya **02 403 4233**
haddins.com
Map **1 J8**
Haddin's Fitness at Zayed Sports City offers a broad range of group fitness classes, gym, tennis lessons and personal training, as well as their popular boxing programme. Professional staff also run a popular Primal Fitness Programme. Tiered access memberships and package deals offer good value.

Original Fitness Co
Bateen C6 Tower, Al Bateen **02 406 9404**
originalfitnessco.com
Map **2 D6**
This company's claim to fame is its fitness boot camps. The four-week military-style training programmes are guaranteed to jump-start you on the road to fitness by combining cardiovascular, strength and mental conditioning. The company offers individual, group and corporate training sessions.

The Room Abu Dhabi
Zayed Sports City Al Madina Al Riyadiya
056 331 0310
theroom.ae
Map **1 J8**
Taking a wellness approach to fitness, The Room has lots of classes, including spinning with certified instructors. Based at Zayed Sports City, its Care Team helps the most gym-phobic guest get to a healthier lifestyle. If the idea of a traditional gym is intimidating then the friendly team and ethos here will put you at ease and help usher you to improved fitness.

Vogue Fitness
Building 2, Yas Marina Yas Island West
050 639 5997
vfuae.com
Map **1 T5**
Raising the bar for fitness in Abu Dhabi, the new Vogue Fitness gym offers outdoor training sessions and motivational fitness classes for Yas Marina fitness enthusiasts. An indoor gym opens soon with group classes and a unique CrossFit class.

Boot Camps

CrossFit, which pushes the super fit to their limits, is still in its infancy in Abu Dhabi. But if you like a good, hard, military-style workout with the added bonus of someone shouting at you, say, on the beach at dawn, then boot camp is for you. Some fitness companies specialise in boot camp training, otherwise ask at the larger gyms or hire a personal trainer. Original Fitness Co runs boot camp-style group and individual training classes for all fitness levels and ages. Women's only courses are also available.

Outdoor Workouts

There's a great list of places you can swim, walk and jog in Abu Dhabi – and all for free, or just a few dirhams. The Corniche provides ample room for a morning swim or a jog, and there are plenty of exercise stations along the way, including pull-up bars and push-up areas, as well as vending machines for water. Alternatively, you can run at Khalifa Park or Al Mushrif Ladies Park. The best place for cycling is along the Corniche's dedicated cycle lane from Marina Mall to Mina Port, or around Yas Island.

Primal Instinct

For those after a different kind of fitness challenge, keep an eye out for the Haddins Primal Fitness Programme, run by Haddins Fitness (haddins.com). The challenging programme has you pulling, running, dragging and pushing things like huge truck tyres; basically mimicking many of the natural movements your body would have made in primitive times.

Yoga & Pilates

Yoga is a low-impact yet challenging holistic exercise that has been practised in the East for centuries. It involves sequences of poses, or 'asanas' that, combined with breathing exercises, gently but powerfully help your body become stronger and more flexible. In addition to the studios below, many health and fitness clubs offer yoga, as do some of Abu Dhabi's alternative therapy centres. You can even try Bikram yoga, which takes place in a heated room for faster results, at the Hot House in Al Zeina.

Bodytree Studio

Hazza Bin Zayed St Al Manhal **02 443 4448**
bodytreestudio.com
Map **2 J8**
Great for yoga and pilates enthusiasts with individual and partner training sessions, pre-natal and natal yoga, Hatha, Kripalu Flow, Ashtanga and Vinyasa practices, children's yoga and belly dancing. Drop-in classes cost Dhs.80 an hour. A 10-class package is Dhs.540; private classes are Dhs.280 per hour.

Eden Studio

Le Meridien Abu Dhabi Al Zahiyah
02 697 4354
lemeridienabudhabi.com
Map **2 S4**
Yoga classes are usually at 9.30am, 6pm and 7pm, Saturday, Monday and Wednesday. Some classes are mixed and there is a good number of women-only classes. Outside of yoga you can also participate in the Ballerina Bum Bootcamp, or get the kids involved in a children's Capoeira lesson.

Personal Training

Whether your goal is a great six pack, to run a marathon, or just to feel fitter, the support and encouragement from a good personal trainer might be just the shot. A personal trainer will assess your fitness, design the perfect regime for you and, crucially, motivate you to show up. Even one session can have benefits, especially as you can learn some expert tips and take them into your own gym sessions.

There are a number of indoor and outdoor personal trainers in Abu Dhabi, some attached to gyms or health and fitness centres, others employed by fitness companies, and some working for themselves. The UAE recently introduced the REPS database for qualified Personal Trainers. Its also a good idea to ask friends for a recommendation or look on websites like abudhabiwoman.com or facebook.com's 'Abu Dhabi Q&A' page to see who others have used.

Yoga classes

WELL-BEING

Beauty Salons & Nail Bars

Beauty is big business in Abu Dhabi, and you're never far from a salon where you can pop in for a quick mani-pedi, massage or facial. With all of these treats available at comparatively cheaper prices than many other cities – you can expect to pay around Dhs.50 for a manicure and Dhs.60 for a pedicure – most expats find themselves indulging in a spot of pampering more often than they would back home. Fridays tend to be the busiest day for salons, with customers prepping for the weekend ahead, so be sure to book in advance. Salons specifically for kids and others aimed at gents are also available throughout the city.

Maven Spa
Al Wahda Mall Al Wahdah
02 443 3700
Map **2 M7**
If you need a little relaxation along with your polish, this is the place to be. It's a bit pricier than other salons, but the sense of serenity in the midst of a busy mall definitely feels priceless.

The Nail Spa
Al Wahda Mall Al Wahdah **6005 44001**
thenailspa.com
Map **2 M7**
The revamped UAE chain has branches at Al Wahda Mall, Eastern Mangroves and the World Trade Center Mall and Souk. Expect a warm welcome and plenty of pampering; manicures and pedicures come with optional add-ons like foot scrubs and massages.

NStyle Nail Lounge
Marina Mall Breakwater **02 681 6333**
nstyleintl.com
Map **2 D1**
Nail Lounges are located throughout the UAE and are a popular place to go for manicures, pedicures, waxing and threading. Also runs the Urban Male Spa.

Tips & Toes
Villa 365-1, Al Khaleej Al Arabi St Al Bateen
02 445 8834
tipsandtoes.com
Map **2 G11**
These ubiquitous spas are a byword for easy indulgence, and offer everything from gelish mani-pedis to Turkish and Moroccan hammams.

Henna

The traditional art of henna painting, a decorative temporary tattoo, is widely available in the city. It's a great memento for visitors, costs around Dhs.40 and will fade after two to three weeks. The Beautiful Henna Centre (noqooshaljameela.com) offers a huge selection of Indian and Arabic patterns for hands, feet and ankles at their Al Dhafrah studio; if you'd rather relax in the comfort of your own armchair, they also offer a home service.

Kids

It's not just grown-ups that can be pampered. Other salons and spas may accommodate kids too, if asked nicely.

Anahata Spa
Street 35 Khalifa City
02 5577 722
anahataspa.ae
Map **1 R8**
The Mini Children's Spa here caters extremely well for little VIPs, from signature massages and facials for troublesome teenage skin, to princess make-overs, mini manicures, and hip hair styling. There are also some special mother-daughter treatment packages. Add into the mix beanbags to lounge on, girlie treats and Barbie DVDs on tap, and you have the perfect princess pampering experience.

Hairdressers

In Abu Dhabi, you'll find ladies and gents hairdressers to suit every budget, from small salons where you could pay as little as Dhs.30 for a simple cut to larger, branded salons where prices start at around Dhs.100. For higher quality styling and chopping, you can expect to pay upwards of Dhs.300, and many salons offer colouring (from Dhs.300), straightening (from Dhs.1,000) and extensions (from Dhs.500). Recommendations from friends and colleagues are a good way to find a stylist that you like; the following salons are all popular spots with the capital's expats.

Changes Liwa Centre, Al Danah, 02 634 1147
Glamour Salon Nr Dazeera Tower, Khalifa Bin Zayed The First St, Al Danah, 02 626 3002,
glamoursalonuae.com
Hairworks Spinneys, Al Khubeirah, 02 681 6678,
hairworksbeauty.com

Barbers & Male Salons
Barbershops are dotted throughout the city (some offer cuts for less than Dhs.10), but for men in search of something more than a simple chop then male spas generally offer a greater breadth of options.

Aziz Hairdresser Abu Dhabi Mall, Al Zahiyah,
02 645 1505
The Lounge Al Khaleej Al Arabi St, Al Bateen,
02 667 7377, *thelounge.ae*
Man/Age Luxury Men's Spa Marina Mall, Breakwater,
02 681 8837, *managespa.com*

Kids

Children are also well catered for, with specialist
children's hairdressers like Kids Land Salon Abu Dhabi,
where eye-catching designs, racing car seats and
movies on tap all help to distract the little darlings for
a tantrum and meltdown-free haircut. A kiddie cut will
cost you around Dhs.100.

Chic Baby Salon Nr Crowne Plaza Hotel, Hamdan Bin
Mohamed St, Al Danah, 02 632 3030
Kids Land Salon Marina Mall, Breakwater, 02 681 6316

Spas

Whatever your pampering budget, you'll find a spa
to suit you in Abu Dhabi. The UAE capital is blessed
with world-class luxury spas within five-star hotels as
well as small, independent establishments that offer
fewer bells and whistles but better value for money.
As well as the usual massages, body scrubs and wraps,
you'll also find more unusual treatments such as the
ancient practice of Ayurvedic massage, reflexology and
traditional hammams.

Budget and mid-range spas are perfect for regular
indulgence, but if you want to splash your cash for a
special occasion, there are some amazing treatments
– think royal hammams and 24 carat gold facials – to
leave you feeling like a million bucks. Expect to pay
around Dhs.700 for a 90 minute treatment at a hotel
spa or about Dhs.300 at smaller spas. However, at
certain times of the year, such as during Ramadan,
you'll find lots of deals being offered on treatments.
Keep a look out on sites like groupon.ae or 'like' your
favourite spa on Facebook to find out the deals first.

Budget

There are spas of all sizes and styles ready to rub, scrub
and knead you into relaxation. And here are a handful
of the more independent places that offer better value
for money, but you may have to forego some of the
most luxurious facilities.

Cristal Spa

Cristal Hotel Abu Dhabi Al Danah **02 652 0079**
cristalhospitality.com
Map **2 M4**
Cristal Spa has an understated feel compared to some
of the more opulent spas in the city, but therein lies its
appeal. The focus is on excellent treatments delivered

by highly skilled therapists using organic products. If
you have time to spare, use the swimming pool, sauna
and Jacuzzi – alternatively, sneak the superb Express
Facial into your lunch break.

Eden Spa & Health Club

Le Meridien Abu Dhabi Al Zahiyah **02 697 4354**
lemeridienabudhabi.com
Map **2 S4**
This spa might not be the fanciest in town but the care
from the therapists is impeccable and the treatment
menu is extensive – there's a huge array of massages,
facials, body wraps and body scrubs to choose from, as
well as various Ayurvedic therapies on offer too. Try the
balneotherapy, a hydro massage bath.

Polish Nails Care & More

Shk Rashid Bin Saeed St Al Karamah **02 445 2053**
Map **2 L10**
This popular salon offers a wide range of treatments at
prices that won't break the bank. You'll find
an array of massages, scrubs and facials on offer, and
there are regular discounts on packages. Plus, there's
a cosy kids room with DVDs, toys and games to keep
little ones entertained.

Zari Spa & Beauty Centre

Nr NMC Hospital Al Danah
02 617 9150
Map **2 M4**
Zari is a long-standing favourite among Abu Dhabi's
ladies. While it was initially a hair salon, it now offers a
broad range of treatments including facials, massages,
threading, eyelash extensions, pedicures and
hydrotherapies, all at reasonable prices. The treatment
rooms and their trio of semi-private cubicles aren't to
everyone's taste though.

Mid-range

Plenty of hotels and boutique spas dotted around
Abu Dhabi have pitched mind and body treatments
somewhere in the middle – with a few personal
touches, smaller but well-equipped to meet the
beauty needs of residents everywhere; more
affordable, they offer 'me' time as and when required.

Anahata Spa

Street 35 Khalifa City A **02 5577 722**
anahataspa.ae
Map **1 R8**
Offers a huge range of treatments, from massage and
Ayurveda to hair, nail and beauty care. Located in a
spacious converted villa, the salon also holds Vinyasa
Flow and Kundalini yoga classes, plus pilates and
positive-thinking meditation. The therapists are well-
trained in their particular treatments and the location
makes it a popular choice for ladies living off-island.

Body & Soul Spa & Recreation Club
Al Raha Beach Hotel Al Raha **02 508 0486**
danahotels.com
Map **1 R7**
Offers a range of reasonably priced massages, facial and body wraps, with regular seasonal promotions to provide even better value. The treatment rooms are small but cosy, and there's a pool, sauna and Jacuzzi to relax in either before or after your treatment.

Bodylines
Yas Island Rotana Yas Island West **02 656 4000**
rotana.com
Map **1 T5**
With full body, hot stone or area-specific massage, the facility is spa-like in appearance with its cool slate walls, aromatherapy scented air and serene, spacious layout. Enjoy the option to relax in the steam, sauna and Jacuzzi facilities before your fully qualified therapist offers you the massage pressure of your choice with a selection of fragrant oils.

Hiltonia Beach Club
Nr Hilton Abu Dhabi Al Khubeirah **02 692 4205**
abudhabi.hilton.com
Map **2 C3**
Soft decor and spacious treatment rooms make Hiltonia Spa a soothing space to unwind. The menu includes aromatherapy and reflexology plus a signature Indian head massage and various forms of hydrotherapy. Make a day of it by opting for a package including use of the sauna, steam room and Jacuzzi.

Namm Spa
Dusit Thani Abu Dhabi Al Wahdah **02 698 8300**
dusit.com
Map **2 N12**
This cool, airy spa in the heart of the Dusit Thani has an extensive menu with a special emphasis on massage. The 90 minute traditional Thai massage is guaranteed to knead all your knots into submission. Natural ingredients such as Dead Sea mud, seaweed, cardamom and lemongrass are incorporated into various wraps and scrubs to leave your skin super fresh.

Oriental Spa & Fitness
Al Bateen St Al Bateen **02 665 5707**
Map **2 F6**
This small spa in a converted villa has a home-made feel to it but offers a good range of services, like massage, beauty, haircare and nail treatments. Makeup courses are also available, as are a small swimming pool, a fitness room, aerobics classes and a range of slimming and body-conditioning machines.

The SPA at Radisson Blu
Radisson Blu Hotel, Abu Dhabi Yas Island
Yas Island West **02 656 2494**
radissonblu.com
Map **1 T5**
Arrive early to enjoy the Jacuzzi, steam room and sauna. The aromatherapy massages and Anne Semonin facials are all a cut above; try the signature Radisson Blu Formulation which will leave you feeling truly and utterly pampered.

CHI, The Spa

Luxury

These hotel spas will customise every detail of your treatment for a blissful experience – and a massage or facial at one of these havens usually means you can wallow in Jacuzzis, saunas and steam rooms before and after your treatment – but you'll pay top dollar.

Emirates Palace Spa

Emirates Palace Al Ras Al Akhdar **02 690 7978**
spa.anantara.com
Map **2 B2**
The stunning Moroccan-influenced spa at the Emirates Palace is the epitome of luxury. Boasting two steam rooms, two Jacuzzis and a unique ice cave, as well as a deluxe hammam, the facilities are flawless and the treatments are out of this world. Spoil yourself with the caviar facial or the royal hammam ritual.

ESPA

Yas Viceroy Abu Dhabi Yas Island West
02 656 0862
viceroyhotelsandresorts.com
Map **1 T5**
Espa is a gorgeous haven of luxurious indulgence in the Yas Viceroy. The menu is vast – with more than 30 massages, scrubs and 'escapes' – and the service is exceptional. All signature treatments start with a welcoming foot cleanse and rosehip exfoliation. Unwind in the relaxation areas and try the Metronap – 20 minutes in a recliner pod that's apparently equal to eight hours of sleep.

Heavenly Spa

The Westin Abu Dhabi Golf Resort & Spa
Khalifa City **02 616 9999**
westinabudhabigolfresort.com
Map **1 N8**
The aptly named Heavenly Spa is a haven of tranquillity in the busy capital. Be pampered by highly skilled therapists in a gorgeous space, with stunning indoor and outdoor relaxation areas where you can soak up your post-treatment bliss. Massages are impeccably tailored to suit your needs, with natural aromatherapy oils to leave you feeling rejuvenated.

Iridium Spa

St Regis Saadiyat Island Resort Saadiyat Island
02 498 8996
stregissaadiyatisland.com
Map **1 G1**
A visit to Iridium Spa on Saadiyat Island feels a bit like escaping into woodland retreat, thanks to the rustic, earthy tones of the decor. Be prepared to feel thoroughly looked after as your knowledgeable therapist leads you through a detailed consultation to find the scrub, wrap or massage tailored to suit your needs and wants.

Mizan

Hilton Capital Grand Abu Dhabi
Al Madina Al Riyadiya **02 617 0014**
hilton.com
Map **1 J8**
Don't be fooled by the business hotel location – Mizan is one of the biggest and best spas in Abu Dhabi, with its lovely plunge pools, deluxe hammam and wet areas, and Vichy shower suite. The spacious treatment rooms create a soft, relaxed feel – try the Thai or Swedish massage and sink into pure bliss.

The Spa at Saadiyat Beach Club

Saadiyat Beach Saadiyat Island **02 656 3500**
saadiyatbeachclub.ae
Map **1 H1**
Located at the stunning beach club, you can't go wrong with a trip to The Spa at Saadiyat Beach Club. The treatment rooms are luxurious and the therapists pay meticulous attention to your every need. Try the Sodashi Sun Soother if you've overdone the sunbathing or the indulgent Signature Facial to leave you glowing.

Talise Spa

Jumeirah At Etihad Towers Al Bateen
02 811 5858
jumeirah.com
Map **2 B3**
Talise is Jumeirah's own spa brand, and the cavernous yet luxurious Talise Spa at Etihad Towers is the place to spoil yourself with indulgent wraps, scrubs, baths and massages delivered by outstanding therapists. To truly splash out – perhaps for a special occasion – opt for one of the signature rituals.

Top Treatments

In a country known for its luxury and lavishness, it should come as no surprise that the UAE is home to some of the most extravagant spa treatments imaginable. For the ultimate budget busting treat, opt for a gold facial – this precious metal is known for its brightening, anti-ageing properties. Try the Kaya Gold Radiance Facial at Kaya Skin Clinic (kayasskinclinic.me) at one of the five Abu Dhabi locations, which uses a 24 carat gold peel, moisturiser and mask.

Zen The Spa At Rotana

Beach Rotana Al Zahiyah
02 697 9333
rotana.com
Map **2 S5**
Descending into the aptly named Zen feels like disappearing down a rabbit hole of relaxation. Signature treatments for pregnancy, rejuvenation and

immune boosting massages are all reasonably priced as is the rest of the menu, which includes a wide range. Try the indulgent Rasul Mud Extravaganza, which is deeply relaxing as well as detoxifying.

Day Spas

If you fancy more than a quick treatment, these places can help you make a day of it. Most spas will actually offer some kind of day-long service which generally involves use of pool areas, saunas and steam rooms.

CHI, The Spa

Shangri-La Hotel Qaryat Al Beri Al Maqtaa
02 509 8900
shangri-la.com
Map **1 L8**
As you'd expect from a spa situated in the Shangri-La, CHI, The Spa is a haven of tranquillity. There's an extensive range of luxurious scrubs, massages, facials, signature treatments and relaxation rituals inspired by the Middle East. Be sure to arrive early to make the most of the spa room, steam room, sauna and Jacuzzi.

Remede Spa

St Regis Corniche Abu Dhabi 02 694 4444
Map **2 D3**
This fabulous, indulgent spa offers a special day package, the St Regis Splendour. The 4.5 hour package starts with a diamond microdermabrasion performed on the entire body followed by the application of a moisturizing paraffin mask. Then, enjoy a healthy lunch at the Spa Cafe before wrapping up the blissful day with a hot stone massage.

Hammam

The Oriental Hammam is a traditional pampering experience in the Middle East, which shares similarities with Turkish baths. It typically involves being bathed, steamed, washed with black soap, scrubbed with a loofa and massaged on a hot marble table – an intense treatment that leaves your skin squeaky clean and flowing. Try the extravagant Royal Hammam Ritual at the Talise Spa for an indulgent 165 minutes.

Zayna Spa

Grand Millennium Al Wahdah **02 495 3822**
millenniumhotels.com
Map **2 M8**
With packages available that last from 30 minutes to five hours, Zayna Spa is the perfect destination for a full-blown indulgence day. Soft music, the scent of aromatherapy oils and warm south-east Asian hospitality set a relaxing scene. There's a wide range of treatments on offer, from a bliss-inducing massage to an extravagant caviar facial.

Male Spas

While there are some unisex spas, it's often easier for men to head to a special male spa for a treatment. Regardless, this may seem like an unusual thing to do for a lot of male expats as spa treatments are generally seen as something more favoured by ladies. However, the damaging sun, skin-drying air conditioning and usual daily stresses can make the world of massages, facials and spas start looking like a good idea.

Cocopilla Men Relaxation and Massage Center

Al Raha Mall Al Raha Beach **02 555 4677**
cocopillaspa.com
Map **1 R7**
Whether you're after a haircut, shave or massage, Cocopilla has the answer. From deep cleansing and Vita-C facials, to a massage with banana leafs or suction cups, the Asian inspired spa offers a wealth of treatments. They even have a Moroccan bath or for the more adventurous, try the butter glitter scrub, coffee scrub or even Cocopilla's milk bath.

The Lounge

Al Khaleej Al Arabi St Al Bateen **02 667 7377**
thelounge.ae
Map **2 G6**
Any man who has avoided pampering themselves for fear of ending up in a 'girly' spa will find much to love about The Lounge. The decor of the men-only spa is all earthy, masculine tones, the menu offers everything from a traditional shave and a haircut to a Morrocan or Turkish hammam, and the service is fit for a king.

Man/Age Luxury Men's Spa

Marina Mall Breakwater **02 681 8837**
managespa.com
Map **2 D1**
This luxury men's spa located in Marina Mall is the perfect pitstop for weary gents looking to take a break from their shopping trip. There are a number of signature treatment combinations that offer excellent value for money, and the extensive menu covers your every grooming need, from shaving and haircuts to manicures, massages and facials.

Vintage Men's Spa

Al Wahda Mall Al Wahdah **02 445 2127**
vintagemenspasalonabudhabi.com
Map **2 M7**
This new addition to Abu Dhabi's male spa scene is proving a firm favourite with the capital's gents. Located in Al Wahda Mall, the spa offers a wide range of personal grooming services on its extensive menu, which is very reasonably priced. Channel your inner Don Draper with a retro-inspired treatment like the luxurious 30 minute Vintage Hot Lather Shave.

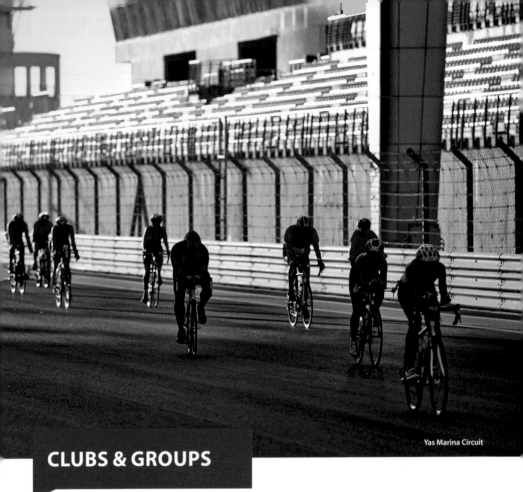

Yas Marina Circuit

CLUBS & GROUPS

With so many people from all corners of the globe calling Abu Dhabi home it should come as no surprise that the emirate and city now offer a wide range of sports and hobbies to be enjoyed. Everything from triathlon to tango dancing is covered in this section. You'll find organisations offering competitive cricket, tennis, basketball and netball, to name a few, plus local representations of football codes from around the world. Plus, the great climate for most of the year and miles of stunning coastline means outdoor pursuits and adrenaline activities such as cycling, dune bashing and watersports are well supported. See the Things to See & Do chapter for more information.

From dance classes to photography, there are like-minded people in the city and emirate who will be more than happy to hear from you. How these activities are organised vary from regular meetings and paid-for classes to forum or social media based groups. The popular Yas Marina at Yas Island (yasmarina.ae) has injected the capital with a wealth of fitness clubs and activities. Vogue Fitness has raised the bar when it comes to working out in the city.

There's also nothing to stop you from starting your own group or club either. Alternatively, a trip to Dubai can often help you find clubs and groups that aren't available in Abu Dhabi, and it's just over an hour away.

Team Spirit
More than 10,000 members are signed up for Duplays (duplays.com) recreational sports leagues in Abu Dhabi and Al Ain – an organisation set up in 2009. It's a great way to keep fit, meet new people and settle in to a new city. Players of all skill levels are welcome. Get stuck into five or seven-a-side football, beach volleyball, kickball or badminton, to name a few. Individuals joining can be assigned a team.

American Football

'Monday Night Lights' – Duplays' Abu Dhabi flag football league – holds games every Monday night between April and June with cross-city games against Dubai's best ball players coming soon. Cost of joining is Dhs.400 for individuals and Dhs.3,600 for teams. For more information, visit duplays.com.

Badminton

Badminton is surprisingly popular in Abu Dhabi with a competitive league and a number of die-hard fans of the sport. Members of The Club (the-club. com) can enjoy weekly matches in the indoor court with occasional leagues introduced, while Duplays (duplays.com) runs a recreational co-ed eight-week season for those who want to meet new people and work up a playful sweat in the process. Drop-in games are played on Sunday evenings at GEMS World Academy and cost Dhs.50. Alternatively, if you already have the gear and a partner, Mafraq Hotel has a court that can be hired on an hourly basis.

Basketball

There are a number of public courts around town and many of Abu Dhabi's hotels have a basketball court (usually outdoor) that's free for members to use. While there aren't any regular leagues in Abu Dhabi at this time, MPac sports (mpacsports.com) has tournaments in Dubai every Friday.

Climbing

See Activities, Things To See & Do.

Cricket

Cricket is a passion shared among many communities in Abu Dhabi. Many firms have their own cricket teams for inter-company competitions and the sport is becoming more popular in schools. Car parks, vacant land and parks all sprout stumps at weekends and evenings. Abu Dhabi regularly hosts international matches.

Abu Dhabi Cricket Council

uaecricket.com

The council was established to promote and run cricket affairs in the emirate. There are currently 65 local clubs registered, with over a thousand players of many nationalities. If you want to play cricket, the council will put you in contact with a suitable club. The council also runs a cricket academy and organises local and international matches at the purpose-built cricket stadium near Khalifa City.

Cycling & Mountain Biking

Abu Dhabi is not the most bike-friendly of places but if you're willing to brave some crazy drivers there are plenty of areas to ride including the Corniche where

there are cycle paths. It's even possible to hire bikes (q8byky.com). The Saracens offer weekly offroad rides. Both government and enthusiasts strive to improve cycling in the city and there are a number of bike rental stations provided by ADCB bank. For further information about Biking see Activities, Things To See & Do and also the Getting Around sections.

Al Wathba Cycle Track

Al Wathba
abudhabitriclub.org

The Al Wathba cycle track opened in 2014 to rave reviews by local cyclists. The 16km track is floodlight for night riding, and plans are in place to extend it to 100km. The Abu Dhabi Tri Club website has a detailed explanation of how to get there.

Abu Dhabi Tri Club

Various locations **050 610 9506**
abudhabitriclub.org

The Abu Dhabi Tri Club runs weekly rides on a number of different routes and maintains an informative website about local cycling opportunities.

Yas Marina Circuit

Yas Island West **02 659 9800**
yasmarinacircuit.com
Map **1 T5**

Yas Marina Circuit opens up for cyclists on Tuesday nights. It's a great place to ride safely under the floodlights. Helmets are required.

Dragon Boat Racing

The ancient sport of dragon boat racing involves crews of 20 in long boats adorned with dragon heads and tails, paddling furiously in short-distance races. Abu Dhabi's pristine turquoise waters and year-round warm weather make the perfect setting for dragon boat racing. The UAE Dragon Boat Association (dubaidragonboat.com) lists all of the country's dragon boating crews.

Al Bandar Dragons

Al Bandar Marina Raha Beach **050 901 1081**
Map **1 S6**

For dragonboaters residing on the mainland, Al Bandar Dragons is your best bet to get on the water. A friendly, well-organized team, they have several weekly practices.

Capital Dragons

Nr Heritage Village Breakwater **050 571 1208**
Map **2 F2**

This competitive group welcomes all new paddlers. Training sessions run on Monday, Wednesday and Saturday evenings as well as Friday mornings. Look for the bright yellow boat near Heritage Village.

Fishing

See Activities, Things To See & Do.

Football

Football (or soccer for any American expats) is, as in most of the rest of the world, the most popular sport in the United Arab Emirates and it enjoys a large number of spectators as well as plentiful players.

If you have the team but need a place to play, there's a football field at Abu Dhabi Country Club (adcountryclub.com), indoor and outdoor pitches at The Dome @ Rawdhat (thedome.ae) and Zayed Sports City (zsc.ae) boasts 14 multi-purpose pitches in full and half sizes, all with floodlights for nightime playing. If you'd rather watch than play, the UAE's national league has regular fixtures at the Al Jazira and Al Wahda stadiums in town. Or you can try Aussie Rules!

Zayed Sports City

Abu Dhabi Falcons

Zayed Sports City Al Madina Al Riyadiya
056 174 4271
abudhabifalcons.com
Aussie Rules is gaining a foothold here in the Emirates. The Abu Dhabi Falcons compete in the Middle East AFL competition from October to March each year with teams from Dubai, Muscat, Bahrain and Qatar.

Abu Dhabi Strollers

Zayed Sports City Al Madina Al Riyadiya
050 818 0685
Map **1 J8**
This club holds weekly kickabouts every Sunday in Abu Dhabi from 7.30pm to 9pm, and has a team in the seven-a-side and eleven-a-side Abu Dhabi leagues. There's also an annual trip to Phuket in Thailand for the Sevens tournament in November.

Duplays

Various locations **055 224 0186**
duplays.com
For some regular five-a-side action, the Abu Dhabi branch of Duplays' sporting community organises competitive leagues every couple of months. Games are played weekly at the Dome@Rawdhat. Costs Dhs.400 to sign up or Dhs. 2,600 per team of eight.

Manchester United Soccer Schools

The Dome@Rawdhat, Shk Rashid Bin Saeed St
Al Madina Al Riyadiya **02 449 8480**
thedome.aei
Map **1 J8**
Manchester United Soccer Schools offers courses and camps for young players aged 6 to 18 years. The courses run several times a year at the Dome@Rawdhat. All players take part in a series of skills challenges. Selected participants represent the soccer school at the World Skills Final event in the UK.

Gaelic Games

Abu Dhabi Na Fianna

Various locations
abudhabinafianna.com
Na Fianna is the sister association of Abu Dhabi Irish Society and offers a sporting programme of Gaelic games including Gaelic football and hurling. They run training and competitions and a busy social calendar.

Hashing

Hashing was started way back in 1938 when a group of British colonial officers would gather on Mondays to work off the weekend excesses with a run. A hash is based on the old paper chase idea, with a few select members running ahead and the remaining pack running after them and following their trail. Traditionally thirst was quenched with frothy brews, and nowadays the many hashing clubs around the world take that part quite seriously. In fact, the running can often take second place to the socialising.

Abu Dhabi Island Hash House Harriers

Various locations **050 669 2667**
auh4.org
If you think you need the drinking capacity of an elephant and the running ability of Sebastian Coe to join a hash, think again. Sprint, run, walk or hobble. The hash meets on Monday nights at various locations around the city. Membership costs Dhs.150 and includes a welcome pack and T-shirt. Under 16s join free with parents. Runs cost Dhs.50 for adults, Dhs.20 for under 16s, and Dhs.75 for nonmembers.

Horse Riding

The UAE has a wealth of equine talent. Recreational riding is well supported and most stables offer quality horses, whether for hacks out in the desert (with gazelles running alongside) or rides along the beach. Courses are on offer for beginners through to the advanced rider. Racing and endurance riding are also popular and races are held throughout the year.

Some clubs even have polo facilities and may be able to teach you how to play. This could be particularly useful if you fancy entering the annual British Polo Day – although it may take quite a few lessons to get to that standard.

Abu Dhabi Equestrian Club

Shakhbout Bin Sultan St Al Mushrif **02 445 5500**
adec-web.com
Map **2 J13**
As well as races and show jumping events during the cooler months, the club offers comprehensive instruction for beginners through to show jumping. Private lessons start from Dhs.200 for members and Dhs.350 for non-members. The club offers modern stables, a polo field and an equine swimming pool.

Al Forsan International Sports Resort

Abu Dhabi - Al Ain Rd, Khalifa City **02 556 8555**
alforsan.com
Map **1 P9**
This complex offers fantastic premises and lessons for all levels, indoor and outdoor training areas, show jumping facilities, and a polo field. Lessons start from Dhs.180 and package deals are available.

Sir Bani Yas Stables

Sir Bani Yas Island Desert Island Resort & Spa
02 801 5400 desertislands.anantara.com/
Map **3 B3**
This luxury equestrian complex features barns, training arenas, paddocks, lunge rings and training rings. Guests can enjoy private lessons or guided rides around the island for a unique view of the Arabian wildlife. All levels of skill are catered for. More experienced riders can tackle the Royal Bay Ride along a golden beach.

Ice Hockey

Abu Dhabi Falcons Ice Hockey

Zayed Sports City Al Madina Al Riyadiya **02 445 6732**
abudhabifalcons.wikifoundry.com
Map **1 J8**
This club aims to develop youth ice hockey in a fun, safe environment. Practice sessions are held at Sheikh Zayed Sports City and the teams play against Al Ain, Dubai, Dhahran, Doha and Muscat. The club runs an annual camp with professional Canadian coaches. Boys and girls aged 5 to 18 are welcome.

Abu Dhabi Scorpions Ice Hockey

Zayed Sports City Al Madina Al Riyadiya
050 621 6464
Map **1 J8**
All players over the age of 18 are welcome. The Scorpions play in the Emirates Hockey League against the Abu Dhabi Storms (an Emirati team), two teams from Al Ain and a team from Dubai. The league is well organised and highly competitive. For more information about either the Scorpions or the Storms, contact chairman Ali Kaddas, or visit the ice rink where the main office is based.

Kayaking & Kitesurfing

See Activities, Things to See & Do.

Martial Arts

Abu Dhabi Aikido Club

Nr Abu Dhabi Country Club Al Mushrif **050 422 0122**
abudhabi-aikido.com
Map **2 J12**
Aikido means harmony and love with the spirit of the universe, and is designed to give you the ability to defend yourself while gaining control of your assailant without inflicting injury. Classes take place at the Abu Dhabi Hilton and Asian Karate Center (behind the Russian Embassy).

Abu Dhabi Combat Club

Nr Abu Dhabi Country Club Al Mushrif **02 443 0022**
adcombat.com
Map **2 J12**
This club focuses on Brazilian jiu-jitsu but cross-trains in boxing, kickboxing, judo, and wrestling. Membership costs Dhs.200 for one month and Dhs.800 for six months for children, and Dhs.200 for one month and Dhs.1,500 for one year for adults. Classes are weekdays only from 5pm to 6pm for children and 7pm to 8pm for adults.

Baroudy's Sports Club

Golden Tower, Corniche St Al Danah
02 626 8122
Map **2 Q2**
Baroudy's teaches taekwondo, which embraces the traditional beliefs of honour, integrity, loyalty and compassion. Taekwondo is about self defence but also improves physical fitness and mental discipline.

Cobra Fitness Abu Dhabi

Nr Spinneys Al Raha **055 616 0996**
cobramuaythai.com
Map **1 S6**
Cobra Fitness teaches all students from beginners to the advanced. Chief instructor Mat Dryden runs Muay Thai lessons and traditional boxing training as well as

a Fitness for Fighters class that will push even the most in-shape participants to their limits. If you'd rather watch than fight, Dryden organises local matches.

Emirates Sports Centre
Nr Modern Bakery, Hamdan Bin Mohammed St
Al Zahiyah **02 676 6757**
emiratessportscentre.com
Map **2 R3**
Karate and kung fu instructor Master Jai has been recognised with a number of awards during his more than 15 years of martial arts experience. Kids, adults and ladies classes are available and the centre also teaches kickboxing, yoga and has fitness lessons.

The Oriental Karate & Kobudo Club
Al Zahiyah **02 677 1611**
orientalkarate.com
Map **2 R4**
This active Abu Dhabi club offers classes for all skill levels. and at various locations: Madinat Zayed (02 634 5080), Airport Road (02 445 7375), Khalifa Street (02 622 4182) and Al Khalidiya (02 621 8773). Classes are Dhs.250 per month (two sessions per week), excluding a Dhs.100 admission fee and Dhs.100 for the uniform.

Sheraton Resort Health Club
Sheraton Abu Dhabi Hotel & Resort Al Zahiyah
02 697 0272
sheratonabudhabihotel.com
Map **2 Q2**
Sheraton Resort Health Club offers classes in martial arts including judo, kickboxing and karate. The instructor is a highly experienced martial arts black belt who teaches defence and safety. Lessons – for adults or children – are for various skill levels. Individual sessions cost Dhs.40 for non-member adults and Dhs.30 for children.

Tai Chi Club
The Club Al Meena **02 673 1111**
the-club.com
Map **2 V3**
The Tai Chi Club has a trained professional leading weekly classes on Tuesdays from 5pm to 6pm. You must be a member of The Club or accompanied by a member to take part. Classes are held in the studio with Dr Hu.

Motorsports
See Activities, Things To See & Do.

Abu Dhabi 4x4 Club
Various locations
ad4x4.com
The 4x4 club, founded in 2006, arranges regular convoys for desert driving. Some activities are geared

toward families, while others involve more serious dune bashing. The comprehensive website offers a wealth of information for driving enthusiasts.

Abu Dhabi MX Club
Various locations **050 818 4668**
Abu Dhabi MX Club is a social group that meets on some weekends and some week nights (from about 4pm to 7pm) to ride in the desert. It uses several practice tracks. Riders of all standards welcome.

Netball

Abu Dhabi Netball League
Various locations **050 516 6002**
abudhabinetballleague.com
Netball is the biggest weekly women's sporting event in Abu Dhabi. Women, girls and now even men of all levels of experience take part. League teams compete in the Inter-Gulf Netball Championships. New players are welcome to join in the weekly sessions at Zayed Sports City; the yearly registration fee is Dhs.400.

Padel
This hybrid of tennis and squash, wildly popular in Spain and parts of South America, has been slowly making inroads in the capital. The Abu Dhabi Country Club and Zayed Sports City both have specialised glass-walled outdoor courts that are available to rent from Dhs.50 per hour. PSS-Emirates (pss-emirates. com) also offers lessons at ZSC. Although there are no leagues as of yet, the Padel Abu Dhabi facebook page actively organises tournaments. It's also a great place to find fellow players.

Polo

Ghantoot Racing & Polo Club
Ghantoot **02 562 9050**
grpc.ae
Map **3 E2**
The Ghantoot Racing & Polo Club's calendar features regular chukka tournaments and high-profile international games, as well as the popular Pink Polo match each autumn. The club sprawls over 300 hectares close to the Abu Dhabi-Dubai highway. The quality of horses and play is high and spectators are welcome. There is also a restaurant and library.

Rugby
Men, women and children play rugby throughout the UAE, with the larger teams taking part in Gulf league and cup competitions. The highlight of the year is the Emirates Airlines Dubai Rugby Sevens Tournament at The Sevens ground in Dubai. Touch rugby is a popular option, especially for kids, and most clubs will offer this. Very few clubs train or play during the summer.

Abu Dhabi Harlequins Rugby Club
050 614 5199
abudhabiquins.com
Formerly the Abu Dhabi Rugby Football Club, the Abu Dhabi Harlequins is a busy club boasting over 400 members, including men, women and children. All are definitely welcome. They train and play on the fantastic pitches at Zayed Sports City and have touch rugby matches too, with a good social setup.

Ecole Française de Rugby
Zayed Sports City Al Madina Al Riyadiya
050 813 0382
efrabudhabi.com
Map **1 J8**
This club welcomes beginners and players of all nationalities aged 6 to 19 years. They have around 250 players with roughly 40 volunteers helping with the coaching and training, as well as the management and reporting of the club. Training is on Tuesdays at Zayed Sport City, with special groups depending on age and gender.

Running
The weather is ideal for running for more than half the year, even though you'll find dedicated types pounding the streets even in the height of summer. Evenings and early mornings are the best times to run in the hottest months. Clubs and informal groups meet for casual and competitive runs and to train for events. Regular, short distance races are held, as well as biathlons, triathlons and hashes. A favourite competition is the epic Wadi Bih Run, where teams of five run the 70km from Ras Al Khaimah to Dibba over mountains topping out at more than a thousand metres. The Dubai Marathon is held each January.

Abu Dhabi Striders
Various locations
abudhabistriders.com
The Striders come from all walks of life with varying fitness levels. They run every Wednesday and hold interval training sessions on Sundays. Each year the club holds 10km, half marathon, full marathon and cross-country races. Members take part in races across the UAE and organise social events.

Sailing
See Activities, Things To See & Do.

Skating & Rollerblading
The best places to skate have few people and enough slopes and turns to make it interesting and to improve your balance and skill. The Corniche and Breakwater have long paved areas, best when they're not too crowded. Although it gets busy in the evenings, the New Corniche is another good spot and has views across the mangroves. Prepare for the inevitable falls by wearing the necessary safety gear: a helmet and elbow, knee and wrist pads. For more serious skaters, there is a skate park behind the British Embassy with plenty of ramps and jumps. Skate Arabia (skatearabia.com) is an online skating community which posts blogs and information about events being held in the

Abu Dhabi Corniche

region. It also occasionally organises competitions and events in Abu Dhabi. In Dubai, there's a great park at Tashkeel where you'll find like-minded skaters.

Skiing

World-famous indoor snow dome Ski Dubai, at Mall of the Emirates, is an hour's drive from Abu Dhabi and is well worth the trip even if you are a beginner as it is also a great place to learn. See Dubai, Out of the City.

Snooker

Snooker here is a largely informal affair. A number of golf clubs have snooker and billiards facilities available for practising and for friendly competitions, but other than at The Club, there are no formal leagues.

The Club

Shk Khalifa Hwy, Al Meena **02 673 1111**
the-club.com
Map **2 V3**
The Club has three full size tables available for members. Weekly league matches and regular tournaments are played. In addition to membership fees, an additional Dhs.125 annual subscription is required for The Snooker Section.

Squash

Courts are available for hire at a number of hotel health clubs and private clubs. Duplays (duplays.com) has its own league at the Officers' Club, and their online board is a good place to find others looking for a game.

Abu Dhabi Golf Club

Abu Dhabi – Shahama Rd, Khalifa City **02 558 8990**
adgolfclub.com
Map **1 N8**
Squash courts are available here for members only. Members' guests are charged Dhs.100 per hour.

Hiltonia Health Club & Spa

Hilton Abu Dhabi Al Khubeirah **02 681 1900**
hilton.com
Map **2 C3**
Coaching is available here with prices for a single lesson starting at Dhs.115 for members and Dhs.125 for non-members. A discounted rate is available if you book 10 lessons: Dhs.1,035 for members and Dhs.1,150 for non-members.

Surfing

See Activities, Things To See & Do.

Swimming

Abu Dhabi's location on the Arabian Gulf means easy access to water that's relatively clean and at a pleasant temperature for most of the year. During the hottest months, the water near the beach is often warmer than a bath. Swimming in the sea is possible at public beaches, beach parks and private beaches belonging to hotels, usually with dedicated areas.

There are no public swimming pools but most hotels have swimming pools that are open for use by the public for a day entrance fee; the Abu Dhabi Marina and Yacht Club also has a pool open to day

Abu Dhabi Golf Club

guests, as does the Saadiyat Beach Club. Entrance charges vary, but range from Dhs.50 to Dhs.400 on weekdays and Dhs.100 to Dhs.600 at weekends, and sometimes include beach access if the hotel has a private beach. Pools are usually cooled for the summer months. Hiltonia Health Club & Spa offers swimming lessons for kids and adults. Prices start from Dhs.120 (members) or Dhs.150 (non-members) for a private lesson, while group lessons are on offer from Dhs.270 for a set of four sessions.

Abu Dhabi Country Club
Shakhbout Bin Sultan St Al Mushrif **02 657 7777**
adcountryclub.com
Map **2 J13**
The club has a circular temperature controlled outdoor swimming pool, open from 8am to 8pm.

Al Jazira Sports & Cultural Club
Shk Rashid Bin Saeed St Al Wahdah
050 264 9707
jc.ae/en
Map **2 M12**
The club has an indoor 50m pool, used mostly by serious swimmers. Lessons are also available.

Armed Forces Officers Club & Hotel
Nr Sheikh Zayed Grand Mosque, Khaleej Al Arabi St
Officers Club **02 441 5900**
afoc.mil.ae
Map **1 K9**
This sports club houses the other 50m pool in the emirate. It's closer than Al Jazira Sports Club if you're coming from the mainland.

Tennis
Courts are available for public use in Abu Dhabi hotels, or for members in private clubs. Nearly all courts are floodlit in the evenings. Court hire varies from Dhs.40 to Dhs.70 on weekdays and up to Dhs.100 at the weekends. Group and individual coaching is widely available. For professional tennis, the Mubadala World Tennis Championship has become an annual fixture which attracts the game's biggest names.

Abu Dhabi International Tennis Complex
Zayed Sport City Al Madina Al Riyadiya **02 403 4200**
zsc.ae
Map **1 J8**
Part of Zayed Sports City, the Abu Dhabi International Tennis Complex is home to the Mubadala World Tennis Championship each January. The state-of-the-art, Association of Tennis Professionals (ATP) standard tennis facility has six training courts and a centre court with a spectator capacity of 5,000. Family membership is available from Dhs.2,500 and individuals from Dhs.1,200. Court hire starts at Dhs.40 per hour.

The Club
Al Meena **02 673 1111**
the-club.com
Map **2 V3**
Perfect your backhand in no time with four floodlit tennis courts and a professional coach available for members. Social evenings and tournaments regularly take place. For the more competitive there are annual club championships, and teams from The Club are put forward to compete in the Abu Dhabi Tennis League.

Hiltonia Health Club & Spa
Hilton Abu Dhabi Al Khubeirah **02 681 1900**
hilton.com
Map **2 C3**
Tennis coaching is available from Dhs.180 (members) and Dhs.200 (non-members). Ten lessons for two people cost Dhs.1,000 per person (members) and Dhs.1,100 (non-members). Group lessons are also available and all groups will be divided by ability and age into Maxi, Midi and Mini tennis groups.

Triathlon

Abu Dhabi Tri Club
Various locations **050 610 9506**
abudhabitriclub.org
This club is a friendly and active group of swimming, running and cycling enthusiasts who train year round. Apart from regular training sessions, members attend competitions and events across the region. There is no formal membership; just show up.

Zayed Sports City > *p.211*
Zayed Sports City (zsc.ae) is a dedicated sports hub open seven days a week within easy reach of all parts of the city. It includes an ice rink, world-class bowling alley, tennis courts, basketball courts, gyms, lush playing fields, video games and a cafe. It's also home to the UAE's largest stadium, as well as a tennis stadium which hosts the annual Mubadala World Tennis Championship.

Watersports
For information on diving, kayaking, kitesurfing and other watersports, see Activities, Things To See & Do.

Al Forsan International Sports Resort
Abu Dhabi - Al Ain Rd, Khalifa City **02 556 8555**
alforsan.com
Map **1 P8**
In addition to all the other activities on offer at Al Forsan such as shooting and wakeboarding, there is a gym and swimming pool with memberships available, as well as single day access for Dhs.120.

HOBBIES

Arts & Crafts

Abu Dhabi Music & Arts Foundation

Makeen Tower Al Zahiyah **02 333 6400**
admaf.org
Map **2 S5**
The ADMAF organises and runs the annual Abu
Dhabi Festival and holds year-round educational
activities in everything from film and music to
poetry. Some are open to the public, others only
to professional and academic communities. Often
visiting artists, musicians or writers will lead
workshops or give lectures.

Abu Dhabi Pottery

Nr Khalidiya Garden, Shk Zayed The First St
Al Khalidiya **02 666 7079**
abudhabipottery.com
Map **2 G5**
Creative-minded adults and children aged five and
older can try hand sculpting clay models or attempt
making a pot on the spinning wheel, all under the
guidance of friendly staff. A chance to explore your
creative side costs Dhs.185 per session for adults and
Dhs.100 for children.

Creative ceramics

dssilversmith Jewellery

Cranleigh School Saadiyat Island **050 784 0509**
dssilversmith.com
Map **1 H1**
Silversmith Don Sankey holds regular courses in silver
jewellery design and creation, including pendants,
earrings, rings and cufflinks. The cost is Dhs.200 per
week of a seven week session.

National Theatre

Shk Rashid Bin Saeed St Al Wahdah
02 621 5300
Map **2 M12**
Classes include painting, sculpture, ceramics and
silk painting. They run from Sunday to Thursday, and
prices start from Dhs.500 for monthly courses.

Birdwatching

The increasing lushness of the area attracts ever
more birds, many of which are not easy to find in
Europe or the Middle East. Over 80 species breed
locally, while over 400 have been recorded on their
migration between Africa and Central Asia. Species
spotted include the socotra cormorant, chestnut-
bellied sandgrouse, crab plover, and Saunders' little
tern. Tommy Pedersen maintains a detailed and
up-to-date website with records of bird sightings and
descriptions (uaebirding.com).

Good areas for birdwatching include the eastern
lagoon on the New Corniche, the port area,
Mushrif Palace Gardens and around the Abu Dhabi
Equestrian Club. Other excellent places include the
mangrove swamps in Umm Al Quwain and at Khor
Kalba – the only place in the world where you can
spot the white-collared kingfisher. During migrating
periods (September/October and March/April),
enormous flocks of wading birds can be found.
The flamingos are a spectacular sight. Access is
restricted to permit holders, but with binoculars you
can see birds from the car if you park along the Ras
Al Khor creek.

Chess

The heart of the chess scene is the Abu Dhabi Chess
& Culture Club, which runs a host of tournaments
throughout the year.

Abu Dhabi Chess & Culture Club

Al Bateen St Al Bateen **02 633 1110**
abudhabichess.com
Map **2 F6**
Abu Dhabi Chess & Culture Club was opened in 1979
and its members compete in local and international
chess tournaments including an annual tournament
run by the Abu Dhabi Tourism & Culture Authority.
The club has sponsored numerous competitions and
enrols members of all ages. All welcome.

Cookery

Atayeb
Yas Viceroy Abu Dhabi Yas Island West **02 656 0600**
viceroyhotelsandresorts.com
Map **1 T5**
Classes cost Dhs.250 per person, including lunch and
soft drinks, but phone or email for details of dates.

Jones The Grocer
Sultan Bin Zayed The First St Al Wahdah
02 443 8762
jonesthegrocer.com
Map **2 N10**
Learn how to make pastas, breads and pastries at
Jones The Grocer's popular cookery master classes.
Cost is Dhs.375 per person and the focus is on
Mediterranean fare. You'll even come out with your
own apron so you can recreate the professional
atmosphere at home! Another Jones The Grover
recently opened in Al Muneera boosting the number
of their outlets to six.

Market Kitchen
Al Danah **02 695 0300**
leroyalmeridienabudhabi.com
Map **2 L3**
This unique class starts with a trip to the Mina fish and
vegetable markets. Choose your food, with advice
from the restaurant's chefs on how to select the
freshest fish and produce, and return to the restaurant.
The chefs will show you how to prepare the dishes
you've planned. The most innovative thing: there's
no set fee. Pay for your own food, then give the chefs
what you think the day was worth. The experience is
offered every Saturday from 10:30am to 3pm.

PartiPerfect
Nr Marina Mall, Marina Office Park Breakwater
02 681 0090
partiperfect.ae
Map **2 D1**
PartiPerfect enables you to organize your own private
cooking class. Select from a menu of options including
Middle Eastern, coffee morning cakes or, for the
health-conscious, substantial salads. There are also
school holiday classes for children and even birthday
party cooking fiestas!

Royal Orchid
Nr ADNOC Al Zahiyah **02 677 9911**
theroyalorchidgroup.com
Map **2 R4**
The Royal Orchid restaurant, located behind the
ADNOC petrol station on Shk Zayed The First St,
periodically hosts classes on Thai and Indian cooking.
Lessons are followed by a three course meal.

The Yacht Club
InterContinental Abu Dhabi Al Bateen **02 666 6888**
dining-intercontinental-ae.ae
Map **2 C4**
The Yacht Club at the InterContinental runs sushi
masterclasses, teaching you the basics of cutting and
preparing an authentic Japanese roll. It costs Dhs.185
per person, including a two course lunch.

Dance

If you love a good boogie on the dance floor then a
dance class may be perfect for you. Try Irish, tango,
salsa, ballet, African or flamenco at an Abu Dhabi
dance school or gym. Meetup.com has various groups
for dance enthusiasts, while Bodytree offers ballet.
Salsa classes are a fun option at clubs like Etoiles.

Abu Dhabi Irish Society
Various locations **050 671 8499**
irishsocietyabudhabi.com
Beginners, intermediate and advanced dancers are
taught separately and anyone is welcome to join.
Classes are held at The Dome@Rawdhat.

Eden Studio
Le Meridien Abu Dhabi Al Zahiyah
02 697 4354
lemeridienabudhabi.com
Map **2 S4**
Eden offers pure dance and dance-fitness classes,
including Zumba, belly dancing, Argentine tango, salsa
and Brazilian dance. The studio also runs yoga classes.

Expressions of Dance & Drama
Al Falah St Al Dhafrah
02 493 0115
expressions-dance.net
Map **2 P6**
The trainers here offer children and adults a fun way
to dance their way to fitness. Classes in ballet, tap, jazz,
hip hop and Argentine tango all available.

International Music Institute
Nr Grand Stores, Shk Zayed The First St Al Manhal
02 621 1949
imi-jmc.net
Map **2 K4**
For ballet, modern dance and belly dancing, the
Institute offers much more than just music.

Salsa With Brando
International Music Institute Al Manhal
050 268 4520
salsawithbrando.com
Map **2 K4**
Annual Abu Dhabi International Salsa Festival founder
Orson Brando teaches beginners and the more

advanced at the International Music Institute. Classes start Dhs.50 for an hour.

Scottish Country Dancing
The Club Al Meena **02 6731 111**
the-club.com
Map **2 V3**
Don your kilt and sporran and join this fun class for some traditional highland dancing. All welcome and it really doesn't matter if you've never danced before. Classes are held Sundays and Thursdays and cost Dhs.30 per session.

Zayed Sports City > p.211
Al Khaleej Al Arabi St Al Madina Al Riyadiya
02 403 4200
zsc.ae
Map **1 J8**
Salsa lessons and Latin music are the themes of regular nights at The Clubhouse bar and restaurant. There's always the option to dance on ice too, with figure skating lessons at Zayed Sport City's ice rink.

Drama
The performing arts are growing in terms of the number of performances in the capital and opportunities for residents to get involved, although the few new theatres remain relatively quiet. Still, while the government's major cultural developments are under way, there are already a few opportunities to tread the boards and unleash your inner performer, with some leisure clubs hosting plays and shows. For truly cutting-edge modern theatre, check out the twice-yearly free performances by New York University Abu Dhabi's Theater Mitu company (theatermitu.org) or contact Abu Dhabi Players.

Abu Dhabi Dramatic Society
The Club Al Meena **02 673 1111**
the-club.com
Map **2 V3**
The Abu Dhabi Dramatic Society is open to members only. Productions are open to the public as long as they're guests of a member. The society puts on four productions a year and offers children's programmes and workshops.

New York Film Academy Abu Dhabi
Nr Abu Dhabi TV, Sultan Bin Zayed The First St
Al Wahdah **02 446 6442** nyfa.edu
Map **2 M10**
The Abu Dhabi branch of the New York Film Academy (abudhabifilmschool.com) opened in 2008 and offers intensive four and eight-week film acting courses, as well as one and two-year acting diplomas. Evening courses are also available, and no prior experience is necessary, just a love of all things theatrical.

Environment

Abu Dhabi Eco Chicks
Various locations
abudhabiecochicks.wordpress.com
This group of 'educated, empowered and eco-minded' ladies organise various initiatives to make a difference. Their website is a great resource for all the latest issues and campaigns affecting the environment in Abu Dhabi.

Emirates Environmental Group
Nr Dubai Zoo Dubai **04 344 8622**
eeg-uae.org
Map **3 E2** Metro **Financial Centre**
A voluntary organisation devoted to protecting the environment through education, action and community involvement. Activities include lectures, recycling collections and clean-up campaigns.

Emirates Natural History Group
Various locations
enhg.org
The ENHG holds regular field trips and lectures on subjects from astronomy to zoology. The Abu Dhabi group meets in the main auditorium at Abu Dhabi Men's College of the Higher Colleges of Technology, at 7.30pm on the first and third Tuesdays of each month with the exception of July and August, when there are no meetings. Membership costs Dhs.100 per calendar year.

Emirates Wildlife Society
Abu Dhabi Chamber of Commerce & Industry
Markaziya West **02 634 7117**
uae.panda.org
Map **2 L3**
Collaborates with the World Wildlife Fund to coordinate a volunteer programme for fundraising, wildlife surveys, clean-ups, as well as educational and awareness campaigns.

International Fund For Houbara Conservation > p.iii
Mamoura Bldg A, Al Wahdah **02 693 4455**
houbarafund.org
Map **2 N10**
Established in 1989, the National Avian Research Centre (NARC), in Sweihan, Abu Dhabi, was the first centre to develop a comprehensive Houbara bustard conservation public awareness programme, mainly aimed at educating young people about the plight of these vulnerable birds and the IFHC's efforts to save them.

Flying
At present there are no private flying clubs in the Abu Dhabi emirate, however the Micro Aviation Club (microaviation.org) in Dubai occasionally offers

lessons in Abu Dhabi or, if you are really keen, you can travel north to Dubai or drive east to Fujairah. Those with a private pilot's licence can contact the Dubai Flying Association; while at Fujairah Aviation Academy (fujaa.ae) the brave can pick up the high habit and obtain their pilot's licence. If you are after a private flight but would prefer someone to fly, contact Abu Dhabi Aviation on 02 575 8000.

Music

Learn a new instrument, record an album at White Cube recording studios or join like-minded guitarists, drummers and violinists; if you have an urge to make music, these places are for you. The Juli Music Institute at Al Bandar offers a variety of music lessons.

International Music Institute
Nr Grand Stores, Zayed The First St Al Manhal
02 621 1949
imi-jmc.net
Map **2 K4**
IMI was started in 1994 to nurture music education in Abu Dhabi and offers professional lessons for piano string, wind, and percussion instruments. The official branch of A.B.R.S.M (Associated Board of Royal School of Music), it offers individual and group classes.

Royal Institute of Music & Arts
**National Printing Centre Bldg,
Shk Rashid Bin Saeed St** Al Danah **02 622 5410**
royalinstituteofmusic.com
Map **2 L3**
Established in 1999, music students can take courses here for a wide range of popular instruments as well as vocal courses. The institute can also put you through exams and get you involved in regular performances.

The Young Musician Music Institute
Al Raha Mall Al Raha **02 556 2080**
tymmi.com
Map **1 R7**
A highly trained faculty which teaches a variety of instruments and genres, including classical, rock, jazz, blues, pop, flamenco and even heavy metal. Courses recognised by the Trinity College of Music, Royal School of Music, Trinity Rock School of Music and the London College of Music are available.

Photography

Abu Dhabi Photographers
Various locations 050 958 7508
adp-uae.com
ADP organises training meetings, photography exhibitions and photography field trips for its nearly 1000 members. It also hosts three themed photography competitions each year. It doesn't matter

if you are a beginner, an amateur or a seasoned pro, just bring along your camera, equipment and your passion for photograpahy.

Gulf Photo Plus
Alserkal Avenue, 8th Street Dubai **04 380 8545**
gulfphotoplus.com
Map **3 E2** Metro **Noor Islamic Bank**
Gulf Photo Plus is the place for networking and honing your photography skills. It organises workshops and events, and has an online community where you can share images and grab a bargain in the marketplace.

Reading

Despite the lack of Western-style libraries in Abu Dhabi, the written word is alive and well at the many book clubs sprinkled around the city. Time Out Abu Dhabi launched a monthly club that meets at WTC Mall (timeoutabudhabi.com), and the AWN Book Club subset of the American Women's Network holds sessions on the fourth Monday of each month (awnabudhabi.com). The Abu Dhabi Book Club Meetup has over 500 members (meetup.com) and organises evening events.

Singing

Abu Dhabi Choral Group
Brighton College Abu Dhabi Al Matar **050 442 0029**
abudhabichoralgroup.com
Map **1 J7**
ADCG has been active for more than 30 years. All welcome. Rehearsals are Tuesday evenings at Al Muna School in Khalidiya. The four-part harmony choir stages two major performances a year – with numbers from musical theatre for the spring production and festive tunes for December concerts.

Al Reef Community Choir
Smart Learning Nursery Al Reef
Map **3 D2**
This newly formed choir, located in the popular expat community of Al Reef, holds practices on Mondays at 8pm. It is led by two voice coaches and open to men and women 18 years of age and older.

Voices of Harmony
Abu Dhabi Tourism & Culture Authority Al Matar
050 442 0029
Map **1 J7**
This all-women group sings a cappella style and has performed at various hotel events, fundraisers and at private homes. They have even been asked to perform at various special occasions around the UAE, at National Day parties for the United States Embassy and Abu Dhabi Tourism & Culture Authority. Auditions take place and a commitment to attend is crucial.

WORKING IN
ABU DHABI

Central Business District

WORKING IN ABU DHABI

The UAE capital is still a land of opportunity for skilled professionals with plenty of rewards on offer.

Expat workers come to Abu Dhabi for a number of reasons: to advance their career, enjoy a higher standard of living, or to explore new opportunities. Whatever the reason, there are various advantages to making the move.

While the biggest bonus of working in Abu Dhabi may seem to be tax-free salaries, the cost of living (or your newly acquired lifestyle) can somewhat balance out this benefit. All-inclusive packages with accommodation and education allowances are not as common as they once were, although basic benefits still apply (such as annual flights home, health insurance and 22 calendar days of leave).

That said, Abu Dhabi is still very much a land of opportunities for skilled professionals. It is comparatively easier to change industries, as skill sets are less 'pigeon-holed' than in other countries, and

jobs in certain industries (such as construction and property) are more readily available.

Expats can work in either the public (government) or private sectors; many companies in the private sector operate within Free Trade Zones (FTZs), where foreigners can work, trade or establish their business under more relaxed laws.

To work anywhere in Abu Dhabi you need to be aged 18 to 65 years old, be sponsored by an employer, and have a residence visa. The visa permits you to live and work anywhere in the UAE; it is valid for two years (or three years if working in some free zones and government jobs). All companies are governed by UAE Labour Law, although there is a noticeable gap in salaries, benefits, holidays, annual leave, and end of service payments between the government/public and private sectors.

148

EMPLOYMENT

Getting Started

If you're looking to live and work in Abu Dhabi you have three options. You can search for jobs while in your home country; you'll often be interviewed by phone or Skype, rather than here in the UAE. Once you have a job offer, your employer will start to process your residence visa. Depending on your contract, your employer may pay for your flight to Abu Dhabi (and often tickets for any family members), one month's temporary accommodation, shipping costs, vehicle hire, and the services of a relocation company to help you find a new home. Alternatively, you can arrive in Abu Dhabi on a visit visa, which means that you have 30 days (or up to 60 days if you renew it) to legally look for work and live in the country. Or, you may already be living and working in the UAE and looking to transfer jobs. In this instance, you will need to cancel your existing residence visa; your new employer will then sponsor you on a new residence visa.

Job Hunting

Whatever your situation, start by registering with one of the numerous recruitment agencies here. The agency will then set up an interview where you are usually required to fill out a form summarising your CV; you will also need a few passport photos. The agency takes its fee from the registered company once the position has been filled. It is illegal for a recruitment company to levy fees on candidates for this service, although be warned that some might try. Employers also use local newspapers and headhunters (also known as executive search companies) to advertise job opportunities, as well as their own websites. Keep it mind that it is often easier to look for a job once you are in Abu Dhabi, as not all newspaper adverts make it online. Get your hands on the Gulf News appointments supplement (gnads4u.com), published every day except Fridays and Saturdays, or the Khaleej Times Appointments (khaleejtimes.com) every day except Friday. The National has a careers section that is available to those who subscribe online.

Also, check listings on online versions of international newspapers as companies within the UAE often post jobs on these sites. Websites for The Guardian (guardian.co.uk) and The Times (timesonline.co.uk) newspapers in the UK and The Washington Post (washingtonpost.com) in the US are often a good resource. You can also upload your CV to sites like monstergulf.com, naukrigulf.com, bayt.com, gaapweb.com and gulftalent.com. Job advertisements are posted on dubizzle.com, abudhabiwoman.com and expatwoman.com. Also try contacting companies directly and start networking using sites such as linkedin.com. Word of mouth is often the best recruiting tool in the UAE, so make sure everyone you know knows you're looking for a new job.

What To Expect

According to the Bayt.com Job Index Survey (August 2014), the time is ripe for many jobseekers. More than 60% of employers were definitely hiring in the third quarter of 2014, and 60% had hired new employees in the previous quarter. The most attractive industries in the UAE for jobs were perceived to be construction (39%), banking and finance (39%) and oil, gas and petrochemicals (35%).

Recruitment agency Charterhouse lists the following average monthly salaries for key sectors:
HR Manager: Dhs.25,000
Head Nurse: Dhs.16,000-21,000
Head Of Corporate Bank: Dhs.60,000
Senior Civil/Structural Engineer: Dhs.35,000
Financial Accountant: Dhs.20,000
Chief Financial Officer: Dhs.60,000
Senior Project Engineer: Dhs.55,000
Senior Architect: Dhs.30,000
Legal Secretary: Dhs.20,000
General Manager (Construction): Dhs.75,000
Head Of IT: Dhs.20,000-30,000
Communications Manager: Dhs.22,000-35,000
Graphic Designer: Dhs.14,000-25,000
Marketing Manager: Dhs.25,000
Partner (Law Firm): Dhs.60,000-70,000 plus

Recruitment Agencies

ABC Recruitment Al Ghahedi Tower, Madinat Zayed, 02 635 5656, *abcrecruitment.ae*
BAC Middle East Liberty House, Dubai, 04 439 8500, *bacme.com*
Bayt.com Park Rotana Complex, Al Matar 02 408 9111, *bayt.com*
Charterhouse >*p.146, 151* Al Bateen Business Centre, Al Bateen, 02 406 9819, *charterhouseme.ae*
IMG Recruitment & General Services IMG Bldg, Liwa St, Al Danah, 02 626 8885, *imgrecruitment.com*
Jobscan Executive Search Shk Hamdan Bin Mohammed St, Al Danah, 02 627 5592, *jobscan.ae*
Manpower Middle East Dubai Internet City, Al Sufouh 2, Dubai, 04 391 0460, *manpowergroup.ae*
Michael Page Suite 2, Tower A, Al Jazira Sports & Cultural Club, 02 611 9200, *michaelpage.ae*
Specialist Services Nr Emirates Steel, Industrial City of Abu Dhabi 1, 02 507 4000, *specserve.com*
WTS Energy 3 Towers Bldg, Shk Zayed The First St, Al Danah, 02 6738 768, *wtsenergy.com*

Permit To Work

Once you receive a job offer, your employer, and sponsor, will start to process your residence visa with the General Directorate of Residency and Foreigners Affairs (GDRFA). All the paperwork should be taken care of by your public relations officer (PRO) (see Getting Started); you will need to take a medical test and hand over your passport and attested education certificates. Your labour card, which is effectively your permit to work, will be processed at the same time. Your PRO should also help with the application for your Resident Identity Card.

Your labour card is processed by the Ministry of Labour; if you work in a free zone, though, it is processed by the free zone authority and can be ready in as little as 24 hours. The card features your photo and details of your employer. You're supposed to carry the card with you at all times but it is highly unlikely that you will ever be asked to produce it. The labour card costs Dhs.1,000 (paid for by your company) and is valid for as long as your residence visa is.

You will need to sign your labour contract before the labour card is issued. This contract is printed in both Arabic and English. The plan is for labour cards to be phased out in favour of the Resident ID, but, for now, the labour card is still required.

Family Sponsored

If you are sponsored by your husband or wife on a family visa, you can still legally work. Your employer will simply need to apply for your labour card; you will need an NOC from your sponsor as well as passport with residence visa, your sponsor's passport and your attested education certificates.

Employment Contracts

Once you have accepted a job offer you will be asked to sign an employment contract; this should list the starting date, type of employment, location, terms and conditions, duration and the salary. This is a legally binding agreement that should be written in both Arabic and English. You can check or print your labour contract and card online at mol.gov.ae.

An employment contract can be terminated if both parties agree, provided that the employee's written consent is given; the employer will then need to cancel your residence visa. See Changing Jobs.

Probation

Probation periods can be set for a maximum of six months. Some companies delay the residency process until the probation period is up, which can make settling in difficult – no residency means you can't sponsor family members, buy a car or get a bank loan.

By law, employees are not entitled to paid sick leave during probation and most firms do not grant paid annual leave to be taken during this time – you will continue to accrue annual leave though, and you'll be able to take it over the course of the year.

Leave

While on sick leave, the first 15 days are with full pay, the next 30 days are with half pay, and any subsequent days are unpaid. Annual holiday starts at one calendar month per year, roughly 22 working days.

Working Hours

As Friday is the Islamic holy day, working weeks run from Sunday to Thursday; Friday and Saturday being the weekend. Some companies only take off the Friday; others have a five and a half day week. Working hours differ dramatically between companies; straight shifts vary from 7am to 2.30pm for government organisations to the common 9am to 6pm for private companies. Most retail outlets tend to open from 10am to 10pm but often operate shifts. Teachers start at around 7.30am and classes finish around 2.30pm.

The maximum number of hours permitted per week is 48, although some industries, such as hospitality and retail, have longer stipulated hours. Public holidays are set by the government, while the timing of religious holidays depends on the sighting of the moon. This means that it can be difficult to plan holidays, as confirmation of time off may be announced as late as the day before. All employees are entitled to a shorter working day during Ramadan, typically two hours less.

Gratuity Payments

An employee on a fixed-term contract who has completed one or more years of continuous service will be entitled to 21 days' pay for each of the first five years of service and 30 days' pay for each additional year as an end-of-service gratuity payment; this compensates for the lack of a pension system. This is based on your basic salary (not including housing, transport and utilities). The total end of service gratuity should not exceed the salary of two years. Leaving before the end of your fixed-term contract or being fired for breaking UAE Labour Law could result in the loss of your gratuity payment.

Maternity Leave

Under UAE Labour Law, women are entitled to 45 days maternity leave, on full pay, once they've completed one year of continuous service – fathers are not entitled to paternity leave. Those who have been with their employer for less than a year can claim 45 days on half pay.

UAE Labour Law

The UAE Labour Law outlines information on employee entitlements, employment contracts and disciplinary rules. The law is employer friendly, but it also clearly outlines employee rights. You can download a copy of the document from the Ministry of Labour website (mol.gov.ae); it's worth noting that the document has not been fully updated for some time. See mol.gov.ae for the most recent updates to the law.

Changing Jobs

If you decide to leave a company before the end of your contract you will require permission from your existing employer in the form of an NOC. Your employer will also need to cancel your residence visa. You will then be able to switch to a new job without any problem; your new employer will process a new residence visa and labour card.

Officially, anyone working in the private sector who breaks their contract could face a six-month ban from working for any other company in the UAE (if you are working in a free zone, this ban may be restricted to jobs within that free zone only). However, banning rules are increasingly relaxed and job transfers have become much more flexible. Stay on good terms with your employer and you shouldn't face a problem. If you complete your contract period, either two or three years, you can legally move jobs without an NOC.

Always check if there is a non-compete clause in your contract, particularly if your new role is with a direct competitor to your current employer.

There are some exceptions where you can transfer your sponsorship without the approval of your current sponsor, such as death of your sponsor, change of company ownership, company closure and cancellation of your company's trade licence.

Absconding

Anyone leaving the country or their job permanently without informing their employer and cancelling the residence visa with their sponsor will be classed as 'absconding' and may receive a ban; employers have to wait six months to report absconders who have left the country. If you remain in the country, that period is reduced to seven days.

Absconders are reported to the Ministry of Labour, who then pass information on to the GDRFA and the Abu Dhabi police. If a ban is on your computer file, any applications from a new employer for a residence visa and labour card will be refused. Also, if you leave the country or are unaccountable for seven days in a row or 20 days in total, your company can terminate your employment contract without awarding you gratuity pay or any outstanding benefits.

Company Closure

It can be complex, but if the company you work for closes, you are still entitled to outstanding holiday pay and gratuity. The Ministry of Labour would need to be involved though. An employee of a firm that has been closed is also allowed to transfer sponsorship to a new employer; if they can't find a new job their visa will be cancelled and they will have to leave the country. To transfer the visa they'll need an attested certificate of closure, issued by the court and submitted to the Ministry of Labour. If your company were to close without cancelling their trade licence, you could receive a short-term ban from taking a new role with a new employer. Consult the appropriate government offices to get your paperwork right, or consider investing in the services of a lawyer who specialises in labour issues.

Redundancy

If you are made redundant, the first thing to discuss with your employer is whether they are prepared to be flexible with your visa status. If you have a good relationship with your company, you should have room to negotiate the terms under which you are leaving, and it's a good idea to request a few months leeway so that you have the opportunity to find a new employer and sponsor. If this is not possible and your company wishes to cancel your visa immediately, you have a standard 30-day grace period within which to leave the country before incurring any fines for overstaying your visa. Similarly, if you are in company accommodation, try to negotiate the date on which you need to move out. If your company has paid for your villa or apartment up front, they may let you stay for a fixed period.

It is always a good idea to plan for every eventuality by putting money aside to act as a buffer should you lose your job; rather than incur large debts, this money can help pay for key bills like rent and car loans.

Free Zones

Free Trade Zones (FTZ) have been set up in Abu Dhabi to attract more investment from foreign companies by making setting up a business much easier and cheaper. The benefits of setting up in one are: 100% foreign ownership (elsewhere you need an equal partnership with an Emirati), no corporate taxes for the initial 15 years, 100% repatriation of capital and profits, no personal income taxes and no currency restrictions.

Each FTZ is governed by a Free Zone Authority, which streamlines the licensing process for opening a business. Many free zones offer a One Stop Service, which helps to speed up the process of obtaining permits, licences, approvals and clearances from the government bodies and licensing authorities.

An FZA acts as the sponsor for all employees within that free zone, which is good news for employees as it helps to cut red tape if you want to switch jobs within that free zone. Also, an FZA can bypass the Ministry of Labour and process your labour card in as little as 48 hours.

Abu Dhabi free zones are aimed at specific types of business or industry:

Abu Dhabi Airport Free Zone (ADAFZ) by Abu Dhabi International Airport. Aviation, freight and logistics
Abu Dhabi Global Market (ADGM) on Maryah Island. Financial services
Industrial City of Abu Dhabi (ICAD 1, 2 and 3, Mussafah). Manufacturing and engineering
Khalifa Industrial Zone Abu Dhabi (KIZAD) in Taweelah. Industry and export/import through the huge Khalifa Port
twofour54/Media Zone by Khalifa Park. Media and production. Big names in the international media arena including BBC, CNN, Thomson Reuters Foundation, and Financial Times are set up in the twofour54 free zone
Masdar City, near the airport. Renewable energy and clean technology

Business Culture

Like anywhere in the world, doing business in the UAE has its unique idiosyncrasies. Even if you work for a western company, the chances are that some of your business transactions will be with Emiratis, whether on a customer or client basis.

Family ties, friendship, honour and trust are crucial. So much so that those who have built good relationships can often see rules bent; the system of favours being given and not forgotten is an integral, if unspoken, part of things. Age, money and social connections are also significant in establishing your status, and older people are treated with respect. Often elders in a room are greeted first and served first at meals.

All of this can mean that things can take longer to get done than expats are used to. This can lead to frustrations and difficulties meeting expected deadlines if you work for a western company.

Warm greetings are commonplace, with long handshakes, effusive compliments and enquiries about the health of families. Avoid enquiring after female family members though, as this is kept extremely private. Similarly, when meeting someone of the opposite sex it's likely that a handshake will not be given and it is best to refrain unless they extend their hand to you. Always use your right hand to meet, eat or hand over items as Muslims reserve the left hand for bodily hygiene and consider it unclean. Avoid showing the bottom of your shoes

in meetings too as this is considered an insult. If you're attending a business meeting at an Arab-owned company, it's likely that you'll be served traditional Arabic coffee, or kahwa. Sharing coffee is an important social ritual in the Middle East so you should drink some when offered. Cups should be taken in the right hand and if there is a waiter standing by, replenishing your cup, there are two ways to signal that you have had enough: either leave a small amount of coffee in the bottom of your cup or gently tip the cup from side to side.

Networking & Events

With Abu Dhabi still being a relatively small city, made up of numerous communities that are smaller still, networking is critical, even across industries. Everyone seems to know everyone else, and getting in with the 'in-crowd' definitely has its plus points. Business acumen here can, at times, be more important than specific industry knowledge so it pays to attend business events and trade shows. Make friends and form connections in government departments and this will often land you in the front line for any opportunities that might come up.

Likewise, bad news is rarely made public here, so staying in tune with the grapevine can help prevent wrong decisions. Social networking sites like LinkedIn (linkedin.com) or Xing (xing.com) are great resources when looking for new jobs or contacts. There are specific sub-groups within these sites for business professionals based in the UAE.

Abu Dhabi Business Women Council Abu Dhabi Chamber Of Commerce & Industry, Markaziya West, 02 617 7495, *adbusinesswomen.ae*

Abu Dhabi Chamber Of Commerce & Industry Corniche Rd, Markaziya West, 02 621 4000, *abudhabichamber.ae*

AmCham Abu Dhabi Trade Center, Abu Dhabi Mall, Al Zahiyah, 02 631 3604, *amchamabudhabi.org*

Arab Business Club Pyramid Centre, Umm Hurair Rd, Oud Metha, Dubai, 04 358 3000, *arabbusinessclub.org*

Australian Business Group Abu Dhabi Green Tower, Khalifa Bin Zayed The First St, Al Danah, 050 264 1134, *ausbg.net*

British Business Group Cert Technology Park, Al Wahdah, 02 445 7234, *britishbusiness.org*

Canadian Business Council Abu Dhabi Cert Technology Park, Al Wahdah, 02 446 7223, *cbcabudhabi.com*

French Business Group Nr Sheraton Corniche, Mina St, Al Zahiyah, 02 674 1137, *fbgabudhabi.com*

German Emirati Joint Council For Industry & Commerce (AHK) Abu Dhabi Mall, Al Zahiyah, 02 645 5200, *ahkuae.com*

Iraq Business Council Abu Dhabi RAK Bank Bldg, Khalifa Bin Zayed The First St, Al Danah, 02 627 1570, *ibcad.com*

Lebanese Business Council Green Tower, Khalifa Bin Zayed The First St, Al Danah, 02 626 6204, *lbcuae.ae*

Luxembourg Trade & Investment Office Silver Wave Tower, Al Meena, 02 491 2446, *investinluxembourg.ae*

Philippine Business Council Of Abu Dhabi Al Dhafra St, Nr Mushrif Mall, Hadabat Al Zaafaran, 02 672 0288, *philippinebusiness.org*

South African Business Council Mitsubishi Motors Bldg, Shk Zayed Rd, Dubai, *sabco-uae.org*

Swiss Business Council Abu Dhabi Hadabat Al Zaafaran, 050 824 2931, *swissbcuae.com*

Trade Representative Of The Netherlands Al Masaood Tower, Hamdan Bin Mohammed St, Al Danah 02 695 8000, *netherlands.ae*

Freelance Work

Freelancing is legal in the UAE and you can set yourself up as a full-time freelancer. You can pick and choose the jobs you accept and work your own hours, but you will not receive benefits such as medical insurance, sick leave or holiday pay.

You will need an employment visa from the Ministry of Labour, and there are three main options. You can get a temporary work permit if you are to be employed by a company for a maximum six-month contract. Alternatively, if are working full-time you can also apply for a part-time work permit with a second employer; you will need an NOC from your existing employer though. The easiest and most flexible option is to get a freelance work permit from a free zone, which allows you to live and work in the UAE under the sponsorship of that FZA.

If you plan to start trading, you will need to apply to the Ministry of Labour for a freelance business licence – a fairly lengthy procedure. See Explorer's *Abu Dhabi How-To* guide for detailed information on setting yourself up in the UAE.

Free Trade Zone Permits

Freelance permits are available for individual media professionals at twofour54 in Abu Dhabi (twofour54. com), which is a unique free zone run by Media Zone Authority – Abu Dhabi, that allows media professionals to set up on their own. Once accepted as a sole proprietor you can carry out the specific business activities printed on your licence. There are set-up costs involved, including a Dhs.5,000 deposit, and you will have to pay the Dhs.2,500 licence fee and Dhs.2,200 visa fee. You also have to renew your licence annually.

There is no issue with an Abu Dhabi resident setting up in a Dubai free zone, so you also have the option of approaching Dubai Media City (dubaimediacity.cim) and Studio City (dubaistudiocity.com). A permit here includes a residence visa, access to 10 shared work stations and a shared PO box address. You will need to submit a business plan, spend a minimum of three hours per week at a hot desk (but less than four hours per day), and pay around Dhs.22,000 in fees.

A third option is to apply to the Virtuzone, which operates in the Fujairah Creative City free zone. Virtuzone (vz.ae) can help you to set up a small company or relocate it to the UAE. Start up costs begin

at around Dhs.10,000 and significantly there's no need for a UAE sponsor. Also, there's no requirement to take a commercial premises – something that really drives up the price of setting up in other free zones.

Part-Time Work

If you are sponsored by your spouse, you can work part-time – you will just need an NOC from your husband or wife and a part-time work permit from the company you will be working from.

Those on student sponsorship visas and teenagers between 15 and 18 are also permitted a one-year part-time work permit, although types of labour and the number of working hours are limited. In both cases, the labour laws stipulate that priority should be given to UAE and GCC citizens and, as the concept of part-time work is relatively new to the UAE, it may not always be easy to find a role.

VOLUNTARY & CHARITY WORK

There are a number of opportunities to do voluntary or charity work in Abu Dhabi. The organisations listed below are always looking for committed volunteers, fundraisers and donations. If you'd prefer to contribute in a different way, the regular Sheraton Charity Flea Markets raise money for numerous good causes and attract many supporters and volunteers.

Animal Action Abu Dhabi
Australian Veterinary Hospital Khalifa City
facebook.com/animalactionabudhabi
The mission of Animal Action is to 'save all creatures great and small'. Their dedicated volunteers take in and foster stray or abandoned animals until permanent homes can be found. Volunteers are also needed to walk the dogs that are housed at the Australian Veterinary Hospital. Animal Action also puts on fundraising events throughout the year.

Emirates Red Crescent
Sultan Bin Zayed The First St Al Dhafrah **02 641 9000**
rcuae.ae
The Abu Dhabi branch of the wide-reaching charity helps provide medical and educational assistance to those in need, responds to aid appeals and also provides sponsorship for orphans. Fundraising stations are set up at most malls; for those who prefer to donate time, their website includes a volunteer sign-up portal.

Environmental Agency Abu Dhabi
Sultan Bin Zayed The First St Al Wahdah
02 445 4777
ead.ae
As a non-profit entity, Environmental Agency Abu Dhabi (EAAD) is always keen to hear from and ready to welcome volunteers who are willing to get involved, particularly in work related to environmental education.

Ewa'a Shelters For Women & Children
Abu Dhabi Gate City **02 558 4812**
shwc.ae
A non-profit, non-governmental organisation operated under the UAE Red Crescent, Ewa'a Shelter offers help for female victims of human trafficking and other forms of exploitation. If you would like to take part, you can volunteer to help provide education, health, and entertainment services.

Feline Friends
Various locations **050 823 1569**
This non-profit organisation has been taking care of cats in the UAE for more than a decade. Volunteers rescue and re-home stray cats and kittens, promote street cat control and even provide valuable care to sick and injured cats. The centre also holds regular adoption days to try and find its cats new owners.

Gulf For Good
International Humanitarian City Dubai **04 368 0222**
gulf4good.org
Gulf for Good is a UK-registered charity that organises a variety of once-in-a-lifetime challenges – whether you fancy climbing Mount Kilimanjaro, trekking to Everest Base Camp, or cycling, hiking and kayaking through the wilderness of Borneo – with challengers' sponsorship going to local charities based in the countries where the challenges take place.

Labor Of Love UAE
Various locations
laborofloveuae.com
This group of volunteers is committed to making a difference in the lives of low income workers in the emirate of Abu Dhabi. They organise regular social activities such as art workshops and English classes for labour camp workers as well as food packs during the month of Ramadan.

Little Wings Foundation
Dubai
thelittlewingsfoundation.org
This non-profit organisation provides medical assistance to children in the Middle East and North Africa who have musculoskeletal deformities, helping them to lead a happy and successful life.

Make A Wish Foundation
Mubarak Bin Mohammed Al Nahyan St
Al Khalidiya **02 666 5144**
makeawish.ae
The local branch of this global foundation is dedicated to making a dream come true for children diagnosed with life-threatening illnesses, providing them and their families with hope and happiness.

Sheikh Khalifa Medical City Volunteers
Hazza Bin Zayed St, Al Wahdah **02 819 4505**
skmc.ae
SKMC depends on volunteers of all ages to greet and escort patients, provide wheelchair assistance and engage in other aspects of community outreach. An application form is available on their website.

Special Care Centre
Hazza Bin Zayed St, Al Wahdah **02 641 8418**
specialcentre.ae
A non-profit organisation which supports children with special needs. The centre is always in need of volunteers to help with activities and events. Register by filling in a form at the centre.

Volunteer In UAE
volunteerinuae.com
VIU was founded in 2008 with the purpose of helping to connect willing volunteers with the charities and non-profit organisations most in need of their help. There's a strong community of volunteers from all around the UAE and a host of ongoing projects. Visit their website for details of upcoming events and a list of affiliated charities.

incredible natural environment, rich resources, wonderful wildlife and biological diversity.

On Saadiyat Island, the TDIC Hawksbill Turtle Conservation Programme, active since 2010, has helped to identify and protect the nests of this critically endangered species. To date, they have helped over 700 eggs to hatch.

Sir Bani Yas Island, which is part of the Abu Dhabi emirate, is home to an internationally acclaimed breeding programme for endangered wildlife. Created as a private wildlife sanctuary by the late Sheikh Zayed, it is now an exclusive eco-resort (02 801 5400, anantara.com). Emirates Wildlife Society is a national environmental NGO that operates in association with the WWF (panda.org). Beyond Abu Dhabi, the Breeding Centre for Endangered Arabian Wildlife (06 531 1212) at Sharjah Desert Park has a successful breeding programme for wildlife under threat, such as the Arabian leopard. It is off-limits to visitors but the Arabian Wildlife Centre (06 531 1999), also at the Desert Park, is open to the public.

The International Fund For Houbara Conservation (houbarafund.org) is targeted at preserving the native bird, which has important cultural ties to the Bedouin way of life. The houbara bustard is a chicken-sized bird that was a favourite quarry of falconers. The fund works tirelessly to conserve the bird and reintroduce them into the wild, while educating people about their importance to the UAE.

Outside of Abu Dhabi, the Change Initiative (thechangeinitiative.com) is a flagship store in Dubai specialising in environmentally-friendly services and products such as solar panels and appliances.

Environmental Groups

The UAE government and the local municipalities have started making efforts towards reducing waste and consumption and raising environmental awareness. There are a number of ongoing sustainability projects taking place throughout the country, one of the most notable being Masdar City in Abu Dhabi. This innovative community lies at the heart of what is being hailed as a groundbreaking green project aiming to create one of the most sustainable places in the world to live and work.

The aim is to provide the highest possible quality of life at the lowest possible cost to the environment, with a strong emphasis on the use of renewable energy sources. The government effort is being accelerated by various organisations working to protect the environment and educate the population about environmental issues. The Environment Agency Abu Dhabi (ead.ae) assists the Abu Dhabi government in the conservation and management of the emirate's

Sir Bani Yas Island

Starting A Business

Many expats are drawn to the idea of starting their own business. If you're thinking about setting up on your own in the UAE, there are a number of things to consider including trading licences, location and the capital required, not to mention the economic climate.

If you're fed up with working for someone else or see a gap in the market, you are just a few steps (and a small bundle of red tape) away from setting up your own business and being your own boss. First things first: do some market research, either with an official market study or some personal legwork and investigation, and be aware of the business climate. There are no clearly defined bankruptcy laws here, so mismanagement of funds could result in harsh repercussions, including deportation or even jail time.

Although there is no minimum capital requirement to start a business – unless you opt for a general trading licence, in which case the capital requirement is Dhs.300,000 – there are rules to adhere to. You will need a local sponsor, who will have a majority stake in your company. However, this does not mean that 51% of profits always go to the local; the agreement could be tailored so that the expat gets the majority of the profits.

Alternatively you could set up in a free zone, where full private foreign ownership is already permitted. The licensing process for opening a business in a free zone is also more streamlined and you can get assistance from the free zone organisation.

The majority of entrepreneurs in the UAE set up as a Limited Liability Company (LLC), which offers an expat up to a 49% share in the business. Note that before you set up in any location you need to contact the Abu Dhabi Chamber of Commerce & Industry (abudhabichamber. com) and the Ministry of Economy (economy.gov.ae). Both can offer excellent advice. Embassies or consulates can also be a good business resource and may be able to provide contact lists for the UAE as well as the country of representation.

Before you can apply for a licence for business, you first need a lease or postal address. You will either need to rent or buy a premises, or simply register for a PO Box address with emiratespost.ae.

There are also various business groups in Abu Dhabi that can help facilitate investments and provide opportunities for networking, or investments in both your respective home country and within the UAE. For further information, refer to Explorer's *Working In The Gulf* or visit askexplorer.com.

Get, set, go!
The following companies can assist you with setting up a business in Abu Dhabi or Dubai, dealing with licensing, start-up and free zone applications, as well as offering ongoing services such as auditing and accounting, HR and recruitment:

Commit *commitbiz.com*
Healy Consultants *healyconsultants.com*
HLB Hamt Chartered Accountants *hlbhamt.com*
Middle East and Africa Monitor *meamonitor.com*
The One Group *theonegroup.co*

Where the World comes to School

Authorised to deliver the **International Baccalaureate Primary Years, Middle Years** and **Diploma Programme** to students of over 75 different nationalities.

Fully accredited by the **NEASC**
(New England Association of Schools and Colleges)
and the **CIS** (Council of International Schools).

Abu Dhabi Education Council (ADEC) rating: high performing school/Band A

Visit **www.ris.ae** to apply online or call **+971 (0)2 556 1567**
Khalifa City 'A', Al Raha Gardens, Abu Dhabi

RAHA
INTERNATIONAL
SCHOOL

táaleem
inspiring young minds

EDUCATION

EDUCATION

Educational standards and the selection of institutions across Abu Dhabi are excellent whether you are enrolling your child into nursery or learning new skills as an adult.

Abu Dhabi is home to various international and government nurseries, schools and universities offering top quality education. There has been a high level of investment and rapid expansion within a relatively short timeframe in the capital – and the educational landscape continues to change and improve. School inspections are now compulsory, and teachers will soon have to be 'licensed' (as is the case in western countries).

Local schools are restricted primarily to Arabic-speaking Emiratis, so you will need to enrol your child into a private school. Although prices can be high, your child will learn Arabic and other languages from a young age, the facilities are world-class, and classes are a melting pot of nationalities. There are currently 185,000 students enrolled in private schools across the capital – and plans to build more new schools by 2020.

There is also a growing number of internationally accredited colleges and universities offering courses in the arts, sciences, business and engineering sectors. Although the majority of places in Abu Dhabi are filled by locals, there are both expat and mature students studying here.

The first thing anyone will tell you about education in the UAE is to get your child's name on several school waiting lists as soon as possible. The demand for school spaces is high, and you can never apply too early. Secondly, try to negotiate school fees in your expat package with your employer. Also, check to see if your company has a corporate debenture with a particular place, as that will quickly move you up the waiting list.

Whether you are a parent or a mature student, this chapter will guide you on the path to education.

NURSERIES & PRE-SCHOOLS

Some nurseries, or kindergartens, accept babies from as young as one month to accommodate mothers who need to return to work after their standard 45 days maternity leave, although most prefer to take on children who have started walking (around 12 months). Fees and timings vary dramatically, so it's best to call around and visit a few nurseries to get an idea of what's available. As a general rule of thumb, most nurseries are open for four or five hours in the morning and charge anything from Dhs.3,000 to Dhs.12,000 per term. In general, classes of between 10 and 20 children are staffed by a nursery teacher and as many as three teaching assistants, though it does vary so do ask what the care ratio of staff to children is.

The more popular nurseries have unbelievably long waiting lists, so, if you're after a particular establishment, it may be necessary to enrol your child before he or she is even born just to make sure they get a spot. Some of the bigger primary schools also have nursery sections or an affiliated nursery – if you've got a primary school in mind for your child, it is worth checking to see if they have a nursery, as this may help you secure a place in the school itself a few years down the line.

Selecting A Nursery

The Ministry of Social Affairs is currently developing a nursery rating system to help you choose a nursery but, for the time being, parents will have to make this decision based on their own research.

Some of the nurseries in Abu Dhabi only operate morning hours which may rule them out if you are working full time. However, for an extra fee many also run late classes until 6pm and have early-bird drop-offs from as early as 7am. Many also organise summer camps and other sessions during the holiday periods.

Most nurseries will follow one particular curriculum – mainly American, English (the Early Years Foundation Stage) or Montessori – so bear that in mind. Another factor worth thinking about when selecting a child's nursery is whether or not they provide meals – having to make a packed lunch every morning when you're trying to get ready for work may not be suitable if time is of the essence.

American Curriculum

If you're planning to send your child to an American curriculum school then finding a nursery that adheres to the American structure may be worthwhile. Based on the kindergarten system, children will progress from their last year at nursery (aged four) into KG1 when they start at primary school.

Bright Beginnings Nursery
Villa 22/2, Al Khaleej Al Arabi St, Al Bateen
02 445 5339
brightbeginnings.ae
Map **2 F11**
This multi-lingual (English, French and Arabic) nursery, which also has a branch in Al Mushrif (02 449 2840), prepares children for both the American and the British curriculums. It has a lovely covered outdoor play area with splash pool, and excellent art facilities. Parents can opt for a two, three, four or five-day week depending on your child's age. Open from 7am to 2pm, with an optional programme until 4pm. **Age:** 4 weeks to 4 years. **Fees:** on request.

Busy Bees Nursery
Sultan Bin Zayed The First St, Al Danah
02 621 9492 busybees-nursery.com
Map **2 N5**
Formerly known as Sesame Street Private Nursery, Busy Bees Nursery follows an American curriculum. Its focus is on learning through social play. English is spoken by all teachers and a 30 minute Arabic lesson is given daily. Busy Bees is open from 8am until 1pm. **Age:** 18 months to 4 years. **Fees:** Dhs.22,230 per child, per year.

Teddy Bear American Nursery
16th St, Nr Geant Easy, Khalifa City
02 556 8566
teddybearnursery.net
Map **1 R9**
An excellently equipped American nursery with a curriculum based on the intellectual, physical, social, moral and emotional development of children. The nursery offers plenty of creative activities and also runs a summer camp. **Age:** 12 months to 4 years. **Fees:** from Dhs.24,000 per year.

Early Years Foundation Stage

In line with the National Curriculum for England, children between the ages of three and five follow the EYFS (Early Years Foundation Stage) curriculum which is specifically designed to meet the needs of this age group and to prepare them for entry to Key Stage 1 (Years 1 & 2) at school. EYFS focuses on: communication and language, physical, and personal, social and emotional development. Assessments are made throughout a child's time at the nursery, creating a profile that can help teachers understand the child and tailor a curriculum to suit their continuing development. Children typically attend nursery until Foundation Stage 1. Once they are aged four, they start Foundation Stage 2 at a primary school.

Blooming Buds Nursery

Nr Indonesian Embassy, Al Bateen **02 491 8068**
bloomingbudsnursery.com
Map **2 F13**
Operating from 7.15am to 3pm Sunday to Thursday, Blooming Buds is based on the British Early Years Foundation Stage curriculum, where there's equal focus on learning through playing, creativity, activities and interacting with learning tools. **Age:** 12 months to 4 years. **Fees:** from Dhs.22,800 per year.

British Orchard Nursery

Nr Spinneys, Sultan Bin Zayed The First St
Al Nahyan **02 443 9892**
britishorchardnursery.com
Map **2 N8**
One of Dubai's most well-known British curriculum nurseries, British Orchard Nursery, brings its highly qualified team and activity-packed programme to the capital. There are also all sorts of extras (holiday camps and kids' parties) available. **Age:** 6 months to 5 years. **Fees:** on request.

Caterpillar Nursery

Shk Zayed Bin Sultan St, Hadabat Al Zaafaran
056 634 4419 caterpillarnursery.com
Map **1 G6**
Newly opened in 2014 and offering the EYFS curriculum. With spacious classrooms and large outdoor areas including sand and climbing areas. They also have an indoor auditorium for performances and events. **Age:** 6 months to 5 years. **Fees:** on request.

First Steps Nursery

Al Karamah St,, Al Karamah **02 446 0960**
firststeps.ae
Map **2 K8**
A popular nursery and pre-school, the atmosphere is extremely friendly and the excellent staff combine fun and creativity with expression. Based on the British curriculum, it also features a basic introduction to Arabic. Both three-day and five-day weeks are offered. **Age:** 18 months to 4 years. **Fees:** on request.

Giggles English Nursery

Al Meena St, Al Meena **02 673 4226**
gigglesenglishnursery.com
Map **2 S2**
Giggles is a well-established nursery and follows the British curriculum. Bus transport is available at an additional cost. Two Giggles nurseries are in operation: one on Al Meena Road and one at Giggles English

School on Airport Road. **Age:** 12 months to 4 years. **Fees:** from Dhs.17,400 per year.

Jigsaw Nursery & Creche

Nr Shk Zayed Academy for Girls, Al Karamah
02 445 5222
jigsawnurseryad.com
Map **2 K9**
Based on the British curriculum for the full age range of pre-schoolers, Jigsaw Nursery & Creche promotes a balanced development. There is a second branch at Mohammed Bin Zayed City. **Age:** 12 months to 4 years. **Fees:** from Dhs.13,915 per year.

Little Smarties Nursery

21st St, Khalifa City **02 556 5500**
littlesmartiesnursery.com
Map **1 R7**
In Khalifa City, Little Smarties prepares students for the British school system. The applied curriculum is based on Letterland and Jolly Phonics and their priority is to create a safe environment where children's confidence, creativity and curiosity can be nurtured. Hours are 8am–2pm daily. **Age:** 2 months to 4 years. **Fees:** on request.

Montessori

Montessori is a popular teaching method that encourages a more flexible approach to learning. Children are encouraged to discover new things through imaginative play, social interaction and physical activity. The method is also used to help children to develop their own instinct to learn and is a good foundation for the International Baccalaureate (IB) curriculum.

Butterfly Montessori Pre-School

Khalifa Bin Shakhbout St, Al Bateen **02 665 8611**
admont.ae
Map **2 H6**
Butterfly Montessori Pre-School follows an American nursery curriculum and uses the Montessori education method, encouraging learning through exploration, expression and play. It is open daily between 7.15am and 1pm. **Age:** 12 months to 4 years. **Fees:** on request.

International Montessori Nursery

Dafeer St, Hadabat Al Zaafaran **02 558 0062**
imn.ae
Map **1 H7**
Classes here are mixed in age with a high teacher to child ratio. It offers flexible drop-off and pick-up times – between 7.30am and 9am and 12pm and 1.45pm – with two, three and five-day weeks available. **Age:** 18 months to 5 years. **Fees:** on request.

Kotwals Nursery

Nr Kotwals Montessori School,
Mohammed Bin Zayed City **02 559 0068**
kotwalsmontessori.net
Map **1 Q11**
This nursery programme uses an innovative approach to learning using linguistics, non-competitive study and encourages children to make their own decisions. It also offers afternoon care and other care programmes. **Age:** 6 weeks to 4 years old. **Fees:** on request.

Radiant Montessori Nursery

Nr Shk Zayed University, Al Wahdah
02 445 5576
rmn4me.com
Map **2 L9**
This school provides a Montessori nursery education to children for three, four or five days per week. It also has optional afternoon sessions and transport is available. There's a variety of facilities to keep little ones educated and entertained, whatever the weather. **Age:** 3 months to 4.5 years. **Fees:** from Dhs.16,000 per year.

Stepping Stones Nursery

King Abdullah Bin Abdulaziz Al Saud St, Al Bateen
02 681 5583
steppingstones.ae
Map **2 D5**
Stepping Stones Nursery encourages children to learn through play, themed activities, crafts, and cooking. The nursery has four branches: Al Rawda and Bain Al Jasrain, Al Bateen and Khalifa City. **Age:** 18 months to 3.5 years. **Fees:** from Dhs.20,400 per year.

SELECTING A SCHOOL

Choosing the right school for younger children is one of the most difficult decisions to make when you arrive in Abu Dhabi. Here are several things to consider when selecting a primary or secondary school:

Curriculum Pick a school that offers the best curriculum for your child, based on your nationality and future plans.
ADEC rankings The government inspects and rates all schools every two years. As the last one was in 2012-2013, results for 2014-2015 are due soon.
School fees These can vary considerably.
The 'school run' Rush-hour traffic can turn a short journey into a tedious trek every day – so you might want to check if school transport is an option.

Curriculum

There is a wide choice of international curriculums at Abu Dhabi's primary and secondary schools. International schools are typically open to all nationalities, and so the choice is yours. To help you get started, this chapter features an overview of schools teaching the English, American and IB curriculums; see also askexplorer.com for a more comprehensive list covering other curriculums.

Other curriculums include the CBSE/ICSE, an ideal option for Indian nationals who want to continue their child's education internationally, but expect to settle back in India. It educates students to CBSE and ICSE level to the end of Year 12. The Canadian International School Abu Dhabi (cisabudhabi.com) offers an Alberta based curriculum; the Australian School of Abu Dhabi (aia.vic.edu.au/abu_dhabi) offers the Diploma (DP), the Middle Years (MYP) and the Primary Years (PYP); and the French School Abu Dhabi, or Lycee Louis Massignon (llm.ae), is one of several to offer the French curriculum.

ADEC Rankings

The Irtiqa'a programme launched by the Abu Dhabi Education Council (ADEC) rates the quality of schools in Abu Dhabi every two years. Eight standards are taken into consideration: students' attainment and progress; students' personal development; the quality of teaching and learning; the meeting of students' needs through the curriculum; the protection, guidance and support of children; the quality of the school's property; their resources; and the effectiveness of leadership and management. All schools fall into one of three bands: A, B and C.
- **Band A** – 1: Outstanding; 2: Very Good; 3: Good
- **Band B** – 4: Satisfactory and Improving;
  5: Satisfactory
- **Band C** – 6: Unsatisfactory; 7: Very Unsatisfactory;
  8: Poor
As stated earlier, with schools being inspected every two years, the next inspection results for 2013 and 2014 are expected in by the end of 2015.

Top Scores

Only 15% of the private schools in Abu Dhabi (23 institutions) are considered to be high-performing by ADEC's Irtiqa'a ranking system. None of the 146 schools inspected in 2012-2013 achieved the top score of outstanding. SInce they were rated, however, the best schools, according to ADEC, are the Yasmina School (Aldar Academies), GEMS American Academy, German International School, Pearl Primary School, The British School – Al Khubairat and The Cambridge High School.

School Fees

School fees are a contentious issue. For a good school, you can expect to pay Dhs.25,000 plus per year for primary years, Dhs.30,000 and up for the middle primary years, and as much as Dhs.80,000 per year for secondary school. Ouch! If you're lucky, your company may include school fees in your package – although this is no longer very common. Additionally, you will usually pay around Dhs.500 to put your child's name on a waiting list, and a registration fee (around Dhs.2,000), which is deducted from your annual costs. Crucially, you must sign your child up for your chosen school as soon as you can (sign-up is usually in February), as competition for places is extremely fierce.

Financial Headache

They say what goes up must come down, but not when it comes to UAE school fees, it seems. A recent survey found fees are causing parents a great deal of stress. WhichSchoolAdvisor.com surveyed 1,072 UAE parents. A high 90% said school fees were a source of financial stress, one in three said they paid fees late, and two out of 10 took personal loans to pay them. A total of 77% said they never send their kids on school trips and 19% never send them to extracurricular activities, due to the cost. UAE schools don't usually offer grants, bursaries and scholarships. Parents struggling with fees are advised to notify the school, which may agree to a payment plan. Banks can advise on a savings scheme or loans; Barclays, for example, offers an education loan.

All Change!

In 2011, the Abu Dhabi Education Council (ADEC) announced a major rehaul of the schooling system. Part of the Abu Dhabi 2030 vision, ADEC said that 40 schools will be merged, 23 new will open, 11 will be renovated and 19 relocated. ADEC also announced the closure of six villa schools and plans to set up affordable private schools. None of the schools listed in this guide are subject to the rehaul, which is predominantly aimed at improving the public schooling sector.

School Transport

If you are not able to do the school run every day, you can make use of the bus services offered by most schools. The advantages are that you avoid having to deal with heavy traffic, and strict regulations mean that bus safety standards are high.

The disadvantages are that it can be very expensive – you pay the same fees regardless of how close you live to the school – and if your child is one of the first to be picked up, it will mean an early start and a long journey while the bus collects the other kids.

The very identifiable bright yellow school buses are heavily regulated: bus drivers must have valid school bus driver permits, a supervisor must accompany pupils below the age of 11, and they are not permitted to exceed a speed of 80kmph.

PRIMARY & SECONDARY SCHOOLS

Having selected a school, you will need to register your child on the waiting list (there's usually a Dhs.500 non-refundable fee). If places are available, your child will be assessed and then either offered a place or placed on a waiting list.

Assessments are usually held at the child's nursery or at the school, and tend to just 'observe' the child at play. It's a stressful time for parents, especially as school's registration procedures happen at different times of the year, but apply to three or four schools and you are more than likely to get a place. Your chances increase with siblings, who get priority, or if your child is in an affiliated nursery.

School Regulators

The Abu Dhabi Education Council, (ADEC) was established in 2005 to monitor standards at Abu Dhabi's schools. Visit ADEC's website (adec.ac.ae) for more information on its criteria and the Irtiqa'a rankings. ADEC also regulates school fees: all annual increases must be pre-approved.

School Uniforms

Most private schools in Abu Dhabi will insist on students wearing the official school uniform. Each school will use a particular uniform supply shop and this will be the only place where you can buy official school items. Before heading out and spending a fortune on uniforms, check with the school and with other parents which items are compulsory and which are not: a sturdy pair of black school shoes and a pair of non-marking trainers are usually essential items, whereas a branded school bag is often not.

Packed Lunches

Many private schools in Abu Dhabi do not offer school meals, so children have to bring a packed lunch and a water bottle (or drink) in with them every day. This is worth bearing in mind, especially if you know you won't have time to prepare packed lunches every morning when you're busy getting your children ready for school and yourselves ready for work.

Holiday Calendar

Be prepared to accept that there are a lot of school holidays here in Abu Dhabi. The summer holidays stretch for 10 long weeks over the hottest months of July and August, when many kids return to their home countries for extended holidays, or attend summer camps. There are also holidays in April and December. Schools close for at least a week (twice a year) for the religious celebrations of Eid Al Fitr and Eid Al Adha, and will most likely also open for reduced hours during the month of Ramadan. If one of you is a stay-at-home parent, then this poses few problems in terms of childcare; however, if both of you work, you will need to make sure that you have alternative arrangements for childcare during school holidays and random days off – many of which are announced at short notice, sometimes as late as the evening prior to the holiday.

Other Options

Boarding Schools

Cranleigh Abu Dhabi represents the first boarding school in Abu Dhabi since its opening on Saadiyat Island in 2014. Cranleigh Abu Dhabi caters for over 1,600 boys and girls aged three to eighteen, on the UAE's biggest school campus. Cranleigh began as a boys' school in Surrey in 1865.

Some parents are opting to send their children abroad – usually back to their home country – for a boarding school education. There are various boarding school agents in the UAE who provide impartial advice and guidance on selecting a school, such as Sue Anderson Consultants (andersoneducation.co.uk).

Homeschooling

One of the main reasons for homeschooling is to avoid the hefty private school fees. K12 (k12.com) in Dubai's Knowledge Village offers some online courses, but schools in your home country will provide you with the curriculum, materials and online testing, for a fee. For excellent additional support and organised group outings, log on to the Abu Dhabi Home Schoolers Association website (abudhabihomeschoolers.org), where you'll find information on membership and homeschooling resources. The Ministry of Education does offer homeschooling for all nationalities but the curriculum is only in Arabic.

Many expats who have a number of children find nurseries tend to be more affordable than in their home countries. However, when it comes to schooling, the fees here (for a private school) are expensive. Although your company may help, some expats return home where education is often offered by the government for free.

American Curriculum

A popular curriculum, the American curriculum is an option which is well suited to those who will be moving Stateside before their children graduate. Students aged four start in KG1 and progress through to Grade 12 when, aged 17, they take their High School Diploma exams. There is some variation in US curriculums and students might be tested in a range of methods from IQ assessments to exams based on understanding and recollection. Usually private schools in Abu Dhabi will choose the curriculum of one of the largest accreditation bodies in the US, such as the New England Association of Schools and Colleges or the Middle States Association of Colleges and Schools. For young children, the focus is very much on play, with a gradual move to more formal education as they get older.

Abu Dhabi International Private School

Al Karamah St, Al Karamah **02 443 4433**
aisuae.com
Map **2 J8**
Abu Dhabi International Private School teaches American, British or International Baccalaureate curricula and it has a set percentage of slots reserved for children with special needs. The school also offers various sports and activities. **Age:** 3.5 to 18 years. **Fees:** Dhs.13,200-28,300 per year. **Transport:** Bus. **ADEC ranking:** Unrated.

Al Ittihad Private School

Nr Geant Easy, Khalifa City **02 556 2666**
ittihadschools.com
Map **1 S9**
Al Ittihad Private School teaches a varied American programme for most subjects, with the UAE national curriculum for certain areas like Islamic Studies and Arabic. **Age:** 4 to 18 years old (KG to Year 12). **Fees:** Dhs.18,100-37,100. **Transport:** Bus. **ADEC ranking:** Satisfactory (improving).

American Community School

Al Bateen St, Al Bateen
02 681 5115
acs.sch.ae
Map **2 E5**
The American Community School serves over 1,000 students of many nationalities. It offers the American curriculum, although it also offers the International Baccalaureate (IB) curriculum as well. Learning is encouraged through a diverse mix of activities, and there is a full extra-curricular programme available. The facilities here are excellent, with a range of sports arenas, science labs and ICT rooms. **Age:** 4 to 18 years (KG to Year 12). **Fees:** Dhs.39,960-73,130. **Transport:** NA. **ADEC ranking:** Good.

American International School
Nr Pepsi Beverages Company, Shk Rashid Bin Saeed St, Hadabat Al Zaafaran 02 444 4333
aisa.sch.ae
Map 1 H7
Founded in 1995, this school is one of the largest in Abu Dhabi, with over 1,200 students. It offers both the American and IB curriculums. **Age:** 4 to 18 years (pre-school to Year 12). **Fees:** Dhs.29,078-52,852. **Transport:** Bus. **ADEC ranking:** Satisfactory (improving).

Emirates National School
Abu Dhabi-Al Ain Rd Mohammed Bin Zayed City 02 559 0000
ens.sch.ae
Map 1 Q11
Emirates National Schools offers American diploma and International Baccalaureate programmes. English is the main language, although Arabic children are offered language and culture lessons and western children have the opportunity to learn Arabic and French. **Age:** 4 to 18 years (KG1 to Grade 12). **Fees:** Dhs.21,340-53,570. **Transport:** NA. **ADEC ranking:** Satisfactory.

GEMS American Academy
3rd St, Khalifa City 02 557 4880
gemsaa-abudhabi.com
Map 1 R7
GEMS American Academy has been operating in a purpose-built facility in Khalifa City since 2011. With its excellent facilities and high standards, the academy has garnered a sound reputation. While fees are on the expensive side, they do include textbooks and supplementary materials for the American curriculum. **Age:** 3 to17 years (KG to Grade 12). **Fees:** Dhs.47,880-66,780. **Transport:** Bus. **ADEC ranking:** Very good.

GEMS World Academy Abu Dhabi
Fatima Bint Mubarak St, Al Dhafrah 02 641 6333
gemsworldacademy-abudhabi.com
Map 2 P6
Part of the GEMS global school network, this school teaches the International Baccalaureate curriculum and has highly qualified western staff and facilities that include playgrounds, artificial fields, music rooms, a climbing wall and a health clinic. **Age:** 3 to 10 years (KG1 to Grade 5). **Fees:** Dhs.38,000-55,650. **Transport:** Bus. **ADEC ranking:** Good.

The Glenelg School of Abu Dhabi
Nr Petroleum Institute, Khalifa City 02 599 2018
gsad.sch.ae
Map 1 M8
Run by the Glenelg School of the US, this branch follows the American school curriculum. **Age:** 3 to 18 years (KG1 to Grade 12). **Fees:** Dhs.19,000-

36,000. **Transport:** Bus. **ADEC ranking:** Secondary – Satisfactory (improving); Primary – Satisfactory.

Horizon Private School
Nr Abu Dhabi Women's College, Khalifa City 02 556 0811 horizonprivateschool.com
Map 1 T8
The school educates around 1280 international students, offering a varied American curriculum. **Age:** 4 to 17 years (KG1 to Grade 11). **Fees:** Dhs.26,300-49,000 (including bus and textbooks). **Transport:** Bus. **ADEC ranking:** Satisfactory.

English National Curriculum

Taught by many private schools in Abu Dhabi, the English National Curriculum (commonly known as the British curriculum) is extensively used by international schools around the world. It's a skill-based curriculum that covers a student's entire education, aged three to 18, and fits into the English public examination system (GCSE and A Level), which is accepted by universities worldwide.

The Early Years Foundation Stage (EYFS, Foundation Stages 1 and 2) for children aged three to five, is focused on developing the social and academic skills of young children through learning and play. Students then move on to the Key Stages 1 to 4, which covers core and foundation subjects; they complete their GCSEs, aged 16 and A Levels, aged 18.

Horizon Private School

WELCOME TO THE FUTURE OF EDUCATION IN ABU DHABI

CRANLEIGH
ABU DHABI

CRANLEIGH SCHOOL
DELIGHTING IN PERSONAL ACHIEVEMENTS

A Cranleigh education stands apart in the values and attitudes of its passionate pupils. We offer an inspiring environment for the education of boys and girls aged 3 to 18, in the firm belief that every one of them has the potential for excellence both in and out of the classroom, along with qualities of perseverance, humility, inquisitiveness, compassion, tolerance, integrity & generosity of spirit; all of which underpin a dedication to academic excellence.

Our passion for bringing out the unique talents in each pupil lies at the heart of our educational philosophy: we recognise and nurture the innate ability in every child - including intellectual, artistic, athletic, spiritual and social development. Through our supportive family atmosphere, the school aims to produce grounded young men and women capable of tackling life's challenges within a global community, taking with them a lasting sense of moral, social and spiritual confidence and responsibility.

Our expansive seven hectare campus - one of the largest in the Emirate of Abu Dhabi - is located on an ideal site in the heart of Saadiyat Island, the cultural showpiece of the United Arab Emirates, within minutes of the New York University Abu Dhabi campus, Louvre Abu Dhabi, Zayed National Museum and Guggenheim Abu Dhabi.

We are open for admissions Years FS1 – Year 10.

Please contact our Admissions Team for further information:

Email **admissions@cranleigh.ae**
Telephone **02 497 0110**

Opening Hours:
Sunday – Thursday 8am – 5pm

www.cranleigh.ae

Ex Cultu Robur
from culture comes strength

Ajyal International School
Nr Shk Fatma Mosque, Mohammed Bin Zayed City
02 409 7100
ajyal.sch.ae
Map **1 Q12**
Newly opened, the breadth of their British curriculum is combined with the strength of a Significant Learning Model in a state-of-the art environment. **Age:** 3 to 14 years (FS11 to Year 9). **Fees:** Dhs.26,500-44,500. **Transport:** Bus. **ADEC ranking:** Unrated.

Al Ain International School
Salam St, Central District Al Ain **03 715 1000**
alaininternational.sch.ae
Another of the six Aldar Academy schools, offering excellent facilities and high standards. Students are taught the English National Curriculum tailored to life in Al Ain alongside the local curriculum of Arabic, Islamic studies and social studies. **Age:** 3 to 18 (FS1 to Year 13). **Fees:** Dhs.53,361- 62,844. **Transport:** NA. **ADEC ranking:** Good.

Al Bateen Secondary School
Khalifa Bin Shakhbout St, Al Rowdah **02 813 2000**
albateen.sch.ae
Map **2 F6**
Al Bateen Secondary School is an Aldar Academy school with excellent facilities and teachers. It provides a high-quality British curriculum and an International Baccaluareate programme was introduced in September 2014 for Year 12s. **Age:** 11 to 18 years (Years 7 to 13). **Fees:** Dhs.53,361- 62,844. **Transport:** NA. **ADEC ranking:** Good.

Al Muna Primary School
Zayed The First St, Al Danah
02 501 4777
almunaprimary.sch.ae
Map **2 M4**
One of six under the successful Aldar Academies umbrella, this high-performing British curriculum school has great facilities. Well-equipped with a large astro-turf field, outdoor swimming pool, well stocked library, a large multi-purpose hall and gym, a number of computer suites and an outdoor play area. **Age:** 3 to 11 years. **Fees:** Dhs.41,580 per year. **Transport:** NA. **ADEC ranking:** Good.

Al Mushrif Primary School
Khalifa Bin Shakhbout St, Al Rowdha **02 813 2200**
almushrif.sch.ae
Map **2 H8**
Al Mushrif School performs very well with a host of extra-curricular activities including Arabic poetry and traditional dance. Entrance exams needed for Grade 1 (sibling priority given). **Age:** 3 to 11 years. **Fees:** Dhs.43,560. **Transport:** NA. **ADEC ranking:** Good.

Al Yasmina School
Al Raha Gardens, Al Raha **02 501 4888**
alyasmina.sch.ae
Map **1 P7**
One of six Aldar Academies, this British school has excellent facilities and a comprehensive extra-curricular programme. **Age:** 3 to 18 years (FS1 to Year 13). **Fees:** Dhs.41,580- 57,330. **Transport:** Bus. **ADEC ranking:** Very good.

Belvedere British School
Nr Al Safeer Mall, 31st St, Mohammed Bin Zayed City
02 509 0000
belvederebritishschool.com
Map **1 N12**
A spin-off from the highly rated independent British school that has been one of the UK's best since 1880. **Age:** 3 to 14 years. **Fees:** Dhs.23,000-27,460. **Transport:** Bus. **ADEC ranking:** Unrated.

Brighton College Abu Dhabi *> p.IBC, 171*
Nr Bloom Gardens Al Matar **02 815 6500**
brightoncollege.ae
Map **1 H6**
An offshoot of the successful Brighton College in the UK, the Brighton College Abu Dhabi offers its 1,300 students a unique learning environment where an independent British school ethos compliments the culture and values of the UAE. Scores highly for facilities, pastoral care, leadership and parental engagement. **Age:** 3 to 16 (FS1 to Year 11). **Fees:** Dhs.47,530-72,680. **Transport:** Bus. **ADEC ranking:** Good.

Cranleigh Abu Dhabi *> p.167*
Nr Manarat Al Saadiyat, Saadiyat Island **02 497 0000**
cranleigh.ae
Map **1 G1**
Established by a group of Old Cranleighans based in Abu Dhabi, the school opened in September 2014 on a seven-acre campus and already has 700 students. Its broad British curriculum is led by teachers who emphasise the individual potential of the child. With excellent facilities for art, music and sport, students can explore their full scope. Email admissions@cranleigh.ae. **Age:** 4 to 18 (FS1 to Year 13). **Fees:** Dhs.65,000-80,000+. **Transport/ ADEC ranking:** NA.

GEMS Winchester School
Sultan Bin Zayed The First St, Al Danah **02 403 5499**
gemswinchesterschool-abudhabi.com
Map **2 N6**
Modelled on the successful GEMS network that is now well-established across the UAE and the countries in the region, this new branch follows GEMS' winning formula. **Age:** 3 to 14 (FS1 to Year 9). **Fees:** Dhs.14,000-22,000. **Transport:** NA. **ADEC ranking:** Unrated.

The British International School
Nr Abu Dhabi University, Zayed City
02 510 0100
bisabudhabi.com
Map **1 Q11**
Offers British curriculum and the IB diploma programme. The impressive purpose-built site, operated by Nord Anglia Education, has state-of-the-art facilities for sport, technology, culture and arts. **Age:** 3 to 19 years (FS1 to Year 13). **Fees:** Dhs.47,900-63,200. **Transport:** Bus. **ADEC ranking:** Satisfactory.

The British School Al Khubairat
Al Karamah St, Al Mushrif **02 446 2280**
britishschool.sch.ae
Map **2 K12**
A non-profit school was established in 1971 and is one of the best-known in Abu Dhabi. It follows the British curriculum, taught by multinational teachers. Facilities include: auditorium, sports pitch, libraries and pool. **Age:** 3 to 18 years (FS1 to Year 13). **Fees:** Dhs.35,800-62,300. **Transport:** NA. **ADEC ranking:** Very good.

The Cambridge High School Abu Dhabi
Nr Safeer, Mohammed Bin Zayed City **02 552 1621**
gemscis-abudhabi.com
Map **1 N12**
A British curriculum school with facilities including a swimming pool, science lab, multimedia labs, music and art studios, a library and sport options. **Age:** 3 to 18 years (FS1 to Year 13). **Fees:** Dhs.13,438-28,380. **Transport:** Bus. **ADEC ranking:** Very good.

Developing The Future
The Pearl, Al Yasmina, Al Muna, Al Ain, Al Mushrif and Al Bateen schools were established, and are run by Aldar Academies, a subsidiary of the government-backed developers behind Yas Island. Aldar Academies teach the British curriculum and IB programmes with an international dimension tailored to their unique UAE learning environment. See aldaracademies.com for more information.

Diyafah International School
Nr Bareen International Hospital
Mohammed Bin Zayed City **02 558 5665**
diyafahinternationalschool.com
Map **1 Q12**
Still expanding from its well-established school in Dubai, this primary school in Abu Dhabi opened in September 2013. Diyafah International School follows the British curriculum and has great facilities, including fully equipped science and computer labs. **Age:** 3 to 11 years (FS1 to Year 7). **Fees:** Dhs.24,200-32,000. **Transport:** Bus. **ADEC ranking:** Unrated.

The Pearl Primary School
Hazaa Bin Zayed The First St, Al Dhafrah
02 641 8887
pearlprimary.sch.ae
Map **2 N7**
The school teaches a UK Curriculum under the Aldar Academies umbrella. It has top-class facilities including an 25 metre swimming pool, astroturf playing fields, a library and a technology lab. **Age:** 3 to 11 years. **Fees:** Dhs.39,600. **ADEC ranking:** Very good.

International Baccalaureate Programme
A third curriculum option is the International Baccalaureate, also known as the IB curriculum, which is compatible internationally and means your children should be able to fit into any school around the world if you decide to move them at any time during their school careers. As there are some differences between the curriculums, do your research first.

Aimed at students aged three to 19, the IB focuses on developing the intellectual, personal, emotional and social skills of children through a range of subjects. The IB Primary Years Programme (PYP) is for up to 12, the IB Middle Years Programme for aged 11 to 16, before final year students sit an IB Diploma.

Al Rabeeh School
Shk Rashid Bin Saeed St, Hadabat Al Zaafaran
02 448 2856
Map **1 F6**
A well-established junior school. The curriculum is a varied and international one, although all classes are given in English. **Age:** 3 to 11 years (KG1 to Year 6). **Fees:** NA. **Transport:** On request. **ADEC ranking:** Good.

The Australian School Of Abu Dhabi
Nr Civil Defense, Shakhbout City
02 586 6980
australianschoolabudhabi.ae
Map **1 V12**
Australian and IB programmes with classes available to Muslim students. Sports and activities are important here. **Age:** 3 to 18 (KG1 to Grade 12). **Fees:** Dhs.14,975-35,534. **Transport:** Bus. **ADEC ranking:** Unrated.

German International School
18 Al Falah St, Al Manhal **02 666 8668**
gisad.ae
Map **2 J7**
Teaching to the German International Arbitur (final exams), lessons from Grade 8 are either in English or bilingual. Arabic lessons are compulsory up to Grade 9. There's also a kindergarten for the young ones. **Age:** 3 to 18 years. **Fees:** Dhs.31,600-40,000. **Transport:** Bus. **ADEC ranking:** Very good.

International Community School
Fatima Bint Mubarak St, Al Danah **02 633 0444**
icschool-uae.com
Map **2 P5**
With campuses at Al Najda (KG to Grade 12) and Al Mushrif (KG to Grade 10), the school fosters high standards of education and follows a well-balanced curriculum that meets international standards **Age:** 3 to18 years. **Fees:** On request. **Transport:** Bus. **ADEC ranking:** Satisfactory (improving).

International School Of Choueifat Abu Dhabi
Mohamed Bin Khalifa St, Al Mushrif **02 446 1444**
iscad-sabis.net
Map **2 L11**
The nine International Schools of Choueifat located throughout the GCC run almost as one school, sharing knowledge, expertise and encouraging interaction. The Choueifat curriculum is an individual one based around learning 'points'. **Age:** 3 to 18 years. **Fees:** On request. **Transport:** NA. **ADEC ranking:** Secondary – Satisfactory (improving).

Raha International School > p.75,158
Al Raha Gardens, Khalifa City **02 556 1567**
ris.ae
Map **1 R7**
The IB's Primary Years and Middle Years Programmes is offered. Facilities include a swimming pool, large sports hall and art studio. **Age:** 4 to 18 years (EY1 to Grade 12). **Fees:** Dhs.36,100-56,900. **Transport:** Bus. **ADEC ranking:** Good.

Canadian Curriculum

Canadian International School
Nr Abu Dhabi Women's College, Khalifa City **02 556 4206**
cisabudhabi.com
Map **1 T8**
This school follows the Alberta programme of study. All teachers are educated and certified to teach in Canada. Excellent facilities include a 25 metre pool. **Age:** 4 to 18 years. **Fees:** Dhs.35,000-50,000. **Transport:** Bus. **ADEC ranking:** Good.

Special Needs Education

The UAE boasts an excellent private school system for expats; however, it is sometimes more difficult to find quality education for children with special needs although with increased awareness, the situation does seem to be improving. If your child has physical or learning difficulties, there are several organisations that can help, while certain other private schools

in Abu Dhabi will offer places to children with mild dyslexia or Down's syndrome.

Unfortunately, the picture is not so bright for children with more severe learning difficulties or special needs. While in an ideal world it may be desirable for these children to attend 'normal' schools, the truth is that the majority of private schools in the UAE do not have sufficient facilities or support to cope with severe disabilities or meet the special needs of some children. While this may result in, for example, a child with a physical disability not being able to attend a mainstream school despite not having any cognitive impairment. The British Institute for Learning Development and Dots & Links (see below) bridge these gaps, offering specialised learning support programmes which address children (and young adults) learning and behavioural problems.

Abu Dhabi Centre For Autism
Nr Al Mafraq Hospital, Mahawi **02 698 5782**
zho.ae
Map **1 T13**
The largest centre of its kind in the UAE, the non-profit organisation helps autistic children and their families. It deals with the medical side of the condition in terms of diagnosis, therapy, psychiatry and neurology, while also working on a holistic approach to increasing children's comfort and social interaction.

British Institute For Learning Development
Nr Horizon Private School Abu Dhabi, Khalifa City **02 556 6078**
british-ild.com
Map **1 S8**
Specialist school run by British experts and supported by St Andrew's College International. Offers speech therapy, educational psychology, reading development, play therapy, therapeutic listening and an 'astronaut programme' that aims to increase learning capacity and intelligence.

Dots & Links
Al Wahda Tower Corniche Road **02 445 9994**
dotsandlinks.ae
Map **2 M6**
A specialist skills development centre focused on improving the underlying learning skills of children and adults. There training falls under two tailored Step Works and BrainRx ('Train Your Brain') programmes, which are delivered by a team of expert and special education specialists. Experienced staff at Dots & Links work with each individual to unlock a learner's core capabilities to learn faster, easier, and better with excellent resources.

Future Centre For Special Needs

Nr Mazyad Mall, Abu Dhabi-Al Ain Rd,
Mohammed Bin Zayed City **02 5533 506**
future-centre.org
Map **1 P11**

A non-profit institution for youths between 3 and 14, catering to those with ADHD and behavioural disorders, Down's syndrome, cerebral palsy and traumatic brain injury; there's also an autism unit. The combination of education, therapy and care enables specialised and holistic services to be offered, while also supporting students' families.

After-School Activities

Most schools pride themselves on offering a broad spectrum of after-school extracurricular activities and often see these as important parts of a child's overall development. Activities can include anything from sports teams, watersports, drama and computer clubs to dance lessons, singing, gardening classes or even kids yoga classes. According to the WhichSchool Advisor.com Fees and Financing Survey 2013, one in 10 respondents claims to be spending more than Dhs.30,000 annually on education.

Local sports clubs in Abu Dhabi also provide a range of children-friendly activities; check Activities for Kids in the Family & Parenting section, or the Clubs & Groups chapter to see which sports are on offer across the capital.

Many schools have also embraced the UK's Duke of Edinburgh Award youth achievement programme. Established in 1956 by Queen Elizabeth's husband, the scheme encourages youngsters to learn skills, build confidence and engage in voluntary work. Meanwhile, Zayed Scout Camp, near Samla, hosts social, scientific, art and cultural clubs for young people in the capital.

Scouts & Guides

Brownies, Guides, Cubs and Scouts Groups are all well established in the region, having been in Abu Dhabi since 1967. All children, from five through to 18 and older, can join the groups, which are based on the UK Guide and Scout movements.

Parents who want to get more involved should feel free to volunteer as they're always looking for adults to help run the units. For more information on either Brownies or the Girl Guides, you can contact abudhabi.dc.bgifc@gmail.com; for more information on Cubs and Scouts, please contact Geir Johnsen, Group Scout Leader (geirkj@broadpark.no, 050 613 3912) or Ade Waite, Group Scout Leader (adewaite@hotmail.com, 050 815 6537). The rules and structure of the groups follow the World Association of Girl Guides and Boy Scouts. For further information, turn to the Things To See & Do chapter in this guide.

Summer Camps

Due to the hot weather, children can find themselves cooped up indoors for much of the long summer holidays – but fortunately Abu Dhabi has a variety of activities to keep kids occupied. Many nurseries offer day care for pre-schoolers, and most of the hotels now run programmes that include swimming lessons, ball games, island trips and more to keep kids busy throughout the summer. Word of mouth is usually the best way to find out about new camps and activities, alongside forums on sites such as expatwoman.com or call the hotels and clubs directly.

There are holiday programmes aimed at children of all ages available across the emirate – perfect for working parents. Zayed Sports City and Al Forsan International Sports Resort are particularly popular. Places for the best summer schemes tend to fill up quickly, so book well in advance.

Family Festival

Abu Dhabi Tourism Authority hosts an annual festival of family activities (summerinabudhabi.ae) at the Abu Dhabi National Exhibition Centre and shopping malls right across the city. Make sure you visit their website to see the 2015 line-up. Shows, sporting events and educational activities are organised to keep both kids and parents entertained.

UNIVERSITIES & COLLEGES

Many expat teenagers still return to their home countries when moving from secondary to tertiary education, though now, a growing number of institutions within Abu Dhabi and the other emirates entice more people into studying in the UAE, with degrees and diplomas offered in the arts, sciences, business, and engineering and technology.

There are public universities open to everyone: Zayed University has been upgraded and relocated, and there will be a new University City constructed in the next couple of years. The Abu Dhabi Vocational Education and Training Institute opened in late 2007, providing vocational training and qualifications in sectors such as health, law and tourism.

The amount of international universities is increasing in Abu Dhabi as the interest in higher education grows, with both New York University and the Paris-Sorbonne University having branches in the emirate. In addition, there are also plenty of college options available. The New York Film Academy Abu Dhabi opened in 2008, offering both two-year and shorter term courses in acting and film making, while the Masdar Institute of Science & Technology provides cutting-edge programmes based around sustainable development.

Education UK Exhibition

Organised annually by the British Council, the Education UK exhibition allows students in Abu Dhabi to attend the event in order to gather information on British universities, whether they have campuses here in the UAE or in the UK. Check britishcouncil.org for details of future events.

Destination Education

With the growing number of leading education providers now based in Abu Dhabi, more and more students will find a suitable degree on offer close to home. Should you wish to broaden your options, Dubai's Knowledge Village (kv.ae) and Academic City (diacedu.ae) both offer a number of other options for further study. Knowledge Village groups a number of leading international universities and colleges together in the same area and encourages students and faculty members to interact. It also provides access to student housing and other useful services.

Academic options in the UAE include the American University in the Emirates (aue.ae), Birla Institute of Technology and Science (bits-pilani.ac.in), Cambridge College International Dubai (cambridgecollegeinternational.nsw.edu.au), Heriot-Watt University Dubai (hw.ac.uk), Manchester Business School (mbs.ac.uk), The British University in Dubai (buid.ac.ae), University of Wollongong in Dubai (uowdubai.ac.ae), European University College Brussels, Royal College of Surgeons in Ireland (rcsileadership.org) and the Canadian University of Dubai (cud.ac.ae). Elsewhere, in Qatar, Carnegie Mellon University is well established in Doha, at the first class learning environment of Education City.

Some universities, including several listed above, offer students the opportunity to study part-time, or in a structured e-learning environment through a range of learning strategies. International correspondence courses and distance learning schemes are other options for learning and gaining new qualifications. The UK-based Open University (open.ac.uk) is a popular choice, as is the South African-based UNISA (University of South Africa). UNISA recently opened an office in Dubai (unisa.ac.za). Gulf News' classifieds section carries adverts for the numerous other study options for short courses. For more detailed advice however, most seconday schools have a dedicated further study and careers advisor to guide your child.

International Universities

Leading international higher educational universities such as Paris-Sorbonne University Abu Dhabi and New York University have an established presence in the emirate and in nearby countries like Qatar. Open to all nationalities, a university in another country might still be nearer than your home country.

Carnegie Mellon University > *p.IFC*

Education City, Doha, Qatar
+974 4454 8400
qatar.cmu.edu

Carnegie Mellon University Qatar's branch is located on a world-class campus at Doha's Education City, but under an hour's flight from Abu Dhabi, this is still nearby. For over a 100 years CMU has been inspiring innovation and is constantly top ranked. Offers undergraduate courses in biological sciences, business, computer biology, computer science and IT. **Best for:** Science and computer studies.

Paris-Sorbonne University Abu Dhabi

Al Reem Island **02 656 9555**
sorbonne.ae
Map **2 V9**

The renowned Paris-Sorbonne arrived in Abu Dhabi in 2006 and now has over 700 students from over 75 countries enrolled there. The university is based in a cutting-edge campus on Al Reem, offering top facilities for undergraduate and masters degrees in the Humanities, Sciences, Arts, Languages, Economy, Law, French Literature, performing arts management, tourism, banking and finance, and multimedia publishing. **Best for:** Humanities and social sciences.

New York University Abu Dhabi > *p.189*

Shk Khalifa Hwy, Saadiyat Island
02 628 4000
nyuad.nyu.edu
Map **1 H2**

The Abu Dhabi branch of this well-regarded American institution is primarily a research university, with a liberal arts and science college. Undergraduate education is based on a varied curriculum that results in full NYU degrees. Appealing to international students, the university is looking to give students the traditional college experience, including an exceptional extra-curricular and sporting programme. **Best for:** Liberal arts.

Public Universities

Public institutions include Khalifa University, Zayed University and Abu Dhabi University. They are funded by the Abu Dhabi government and, although admission to these institutions is traditionally for UAE nationals, international students are now being accepted and scholarships are available.

Abu Dhabi University

Abu Dhabi-Al Ain Rd, Khalifa City **02 800 23968**
adu.ac.ae
Map **1 Q11**
With campuses in both Abu Dhabi and Al Ain, courses include business, computer science, IT and education. Contact the admissions office for more information. **Best for:** Its BSc in Aviation.

Khalifa University

Shakhbout Bin Sultan St, Hadabat Al Zaafaran **02 401 8000**
kustar.ac.ae
Map **2 L13**
Based on the American system, with strategic global partnerships, the focus is on Information and Communication Technology (ICT), Aerospace, Transport & Logistics, Energy & the Environment, Healthcare and Security. These subjects are in line with Abu Dhabi's commitment to furthering the UAE's economy. **Best for:** Aerospace engineering.

Zayed University

Zayed City **02 599 3111**
zu.ac.ae
Map **1 R9**
Located in a massive, brand-new and purpose-built complex with separate colleges offering arts, science, business science, communication and media, education studies, languages and information technology. Also has postgraduate and masters courses, predominantly in business and management. **Best for:** Media and international studies.

Colleges & Institutes

Abu Dhabi Vocational Education & Training Institute

Abu Dhabi - Al Ain Rd, Al Maqta **02 508 2700**
adveti.abudhabi.ae
Map **1 M8**
The institute offers vocational diplomas in IT, fashion, finance, hotel management, property development, paralegal studies and graphic design. **Best for:** Vocational courses.

Alliance Francaise Abu Dhabi > p.177

Al Bateen St, Al Bateen **02 666 6232**
afabudhabi.org
Map **2 F5**
An established institute offering French language and cultural classes in Abu Dhabi, Dubai and Al Ain.

Centre of Excellence For Applied Research & Training

CERT Technology Park, Al Wahdah **02 404 8501**
certonline.com
Map **2 N12**
Offers various courses, including engineering, business and health sciences. Specialised courses such as advanced diplomas in professional training, business, food inspection and highway maintenance, and the University of Strathclyde MBA, are also available. **Best for:** Engineering and sciences.

Emirates College of Technology

Millennium Tower, Al Danah **02 626 6010**
ect.ac.ae
Map **2 N3**
There are two locations in Abu Dhabi, its male-only campus on Hamdan Street and a campus for women on Defence Street. The college offers diplomas in business administration and computer information systems, HR management, e-commerce and marketing, banking and finance, accounting, computer design and animation, mass communication and public relations. **Best for:** Business.

European International College

Dafeer St, Al Matar **02 449 1450**
eic.ac.ae
Map **1 H6**
An institution focused on hotel management and tourism, with several courses on offer including a bachelor's degree in hospitality. The college is affiliated with prestigious western hospitality institutions and offers a full and diverse student experience. **Best for:** Hospitality.

Masdar Institute of Science & Technology

Nr Abu Dhabi International Airport, Khalifa City **02 810 9333**
masdar.ac.ae
Map **1 U7**
Since 2009, this institute has provided cutting-edge education and research into renewable energy, advanced technologies and sustainable development. The intake grew from 88 graduate students in 2009 to reach more than 200 students by September 2014. Seven two-year long, graduate level degrees are currently on offer. **Best for:** Renewable/sustainable energy studies and cutting-edge research.

New York Film Academy Abu Dhabi

Sultan Bin Zayed The First St, Al Wahdah **02 446 6442**
nyfa.edu
Map **2 L11**
This film school offers full-time and part-time courses in everything from on-camera acting to documentary and feature filmmaking. The courses cover a broad

range of necessary disciplines, including writing, directing, editing and cinematography, which should be perfect for any budding Spielbergs.
Best for: Film making.

New York Institute of Technology
CERT Technology Park, Al Wahdah **02 404 8523**
nyit.edu
Map **2 N13**
The Abu Dhabi branch of the well-known higher education institute. Principal academic offerings are in architecture and design, the arts, science, engineering, and computer science. Students also have the chance to spend time studying at its other locations, like Canada, China, Jordan and, of course, Manhattan.
Best for: Business technology.

The Petroleum Institute
Sas Al Nakhl Island **02 607 5800**
pi.ac.ae
Map **1 M8**
This institute is dedicated to education and research in areas significant to the engineering, geoscience and general oil and gas industries. The institute is supported by many of the world's biggest oil-producing companies and there's a wide portfolio of undergraduate and graduate programmes available.
Best for: Engineering and geosciences.

Language Courses

As you would expect from a city with such a diverse range of nationalities, there are plenty of options to learn a different language. While English is widely spoken in the workplace, some people may need to hone their English-speaking skills at a language centre. Living in Abu Dhabi can also be a great reason to give Arabic lessons a go, or to learn the mother tongue spoken in your next port of call. Many institutes cater for adults and children with a range of classroom times for daytime or evening lessons. It is compulsary for children from primary level to learn Arabic. Generally, an adult course will cover between 28-36 hours with varying levels of intensity. Courses run from six to over 12 weeks. Expect to pay anything from Dhs.1,800 per course.

Alliance Francaise Abu Dhabi > *p.177* Choithrams Bldg, Al Manhal, 02 666 6232, afabudhabi.org
American Language Center Al Marjan Plaza, Nr Hamdan Centre, Shk Hamdan Bin Mohd St, Al Danah, 02 626 7577
Berlitz Bin Haiyai Bldg, Nr Khalidiya Park, Zayed The First St, Al Khalidiya, 02 667 2287, berlitz-uae.com
British Council CERT Technology Park, Al Wahdah, 600 529 955, *britishcouncil.ae*
Eton Institute Park Rotana Office Complex, Khalifa Park, 02 449 9649, *eton.ac*
Goethe-Institut Gulf Region Zayed The First St, Al Zahiyah, 02 672 7920, *goethe.de*
The Mother Tongue Arabic Language Center Bin Fardan Tower, Shk Zayed The First St, Al Manhal, 02 639 3838, *mothertongue.ae*

Teaching English
If you're interested in a new career, why not consider a TEFL (Teaching English as a Foreign Language) or a TESOL (Teaching English to Speakers of Other Languages) course. Abu Dhabi Men's College, the British Council and Abu Dhabi Higher Colleges of Technology offer courses; a four-week course costs around Dhs.9,000.

GEMS American Academy

ADULTS COURSES &
CERTIFICATIONS

KIDS AND TEENAGERS COURSES
& CERTIFICATIONS

OFFICIAL CENTER FOR DELF
& TEF & TCF EXAMS

ENJOY OUR CULTURAL
EVENTS

BORROW BOOKS, DVDS,
CDS IN OUR LIBRARY

BECOME A MEMBER WITH
BENEFITS!

TEL: +971 2 666 62 32
INFO@AFABUDHABI.ORG
WWW.AFABUDHABI.ORG

THINGS TO
SEE & DO

THINGS TO SEE & DO

From world-class sports to desert tours – there's no time to be bored when you live in Abu Dhabi.

Sheikh Zayed Grand Mosque

Abu Dhabi has well and truly put itself on the map over the past few years as a top place to visit. Its desire to attract some of the globe's biggest sporting events has captured the world's attention. The city's ever-changing skyline, audacious re-imagining of desert islands, vast hotels and permanently sunny weather have combined with its position as an increasingly important airline hub to transform it into an international tourist destination and the region's sporting capital.

All this is good news for expats lucky enough to have relocated to this headline-grabbing emirate – but there's more to Abu Dhabi than just the high-living holiday highlights.

Scratch beneath the surface and you'll discover plenty of cultural delights, traditional gems, leisure activities and places to keep the kids entertained.

Souks, forts, local restaurants and beautiful mangrove-packed waterways provide a contrast to the mind-boggling modern developments on the island, popping up off the island and in newly created areas. The city's arts scene is also taking off, with galleries attracting major local and international talent. There's a full calendar of international events to keep sports fans happy too.

During the cooler months, there are some excellent outdoor options; Abu Dhabi's parks are superbly maintained, while the beaches draw crowds of sunbathers at the weekends. Beyond the city limits, the desert provides one of the world's biggest adventure playgrounds. Head off road to make the most of the awe-inspiring dunes and wadi beds, hike in the mountains, go camping or take to the sea for some excellent diving, snorkelling and sailing.

PLACES OF INTEREST

Abu Dhabi has an inspiring mix of old and new places to explore, from traditional boatyards and heritage villages to spectacular buildings, high-living hotels, shopping delights and more. Each year, the city welcomes in a host of new attractions which also makes living here interesting.

Al Bateen

The Al Bateen area (not to be confused with Al Bateen Airport) stretches along the coast on the south western side of Abu Dhabi Island, between the InterContinental hotel and 19th Street. A world away from the bustling city centre, it is one of the capital's most affluent areas and has a pleasant, residential neighbourhood feel with plenty of green, open spaces to enjoy.

The Bateen dhow yard is well worth a visit, with its evocative smells of freshly cut African and Indian teak. Craftsmen use traditional skills to build the dhows and racing hulls that can be seen in competitions off the Corniche. If it's not too busy, the craftsmen will happily share the intricacies of their art. The yard is open every day except Friday and the best time to visit is at 5pm.

Al Mushrif

This central area of Abu Dhabi island is perhaps lacking any major attractions, but it's a pleasant part of town consisting of leafy boulevards. Abu Dhabi City Golf Club is here, as is the interesting Women's Handicraft Centre and several good parks.

The main draw of this area is the extensive waterfront area, including the Fishermen's Marina and the Yacht Marina. The area is undergoing development and is changing rapidly, but after strolling around and admiring the yachts you can visit one of the marina's restaurants and cafes which have scenic views across the Arabian Gulf. There are also a number of shops and diving clubs based in the marina. Overlooking the marina is the InterContinental Hotel, one of Abu Dhabi's landmark hotels, with renowned seafood restaurant Fishmarket and the always-popular Chamas Churrascaria and Bar.

Al Bateen has several public gardens and parks, popular for picnics and ball sports when the weather is cooler. There's a special green and pink running/ cycle track along parts of the way. Wedged in between the mangroves surrounding the palace, Al Bateen Beach was upgraded with superb facilities, including children's play areas and toilets, and entrance is free.

Al Meena

The dhow harbour here, off Port Road, is a contrast of past and present with several hundred dhows resting in their berths. It is a fascinating place to explore early in the morning when the fishermen return from sea with their catch. Try out the nearby restaurants, which offer an authentic selection of local cooking – mainly grilled or fried seafood. The harbour is well worth a visit at sunset when the dhows return. A number of dinner cruises also set sail from here.

Between The Bridges

Just off the main island, spanning the land between Mussafah Bridge and Al Maqtaa Bridge, this area is noted for a cluster of grand hotels and nearby Abu Dhabi Golf Club. The Arabic name is Bain Al Jessrain but, to just about everybody now, it's known as 'Between the Bridges'.

The area is defined by the Shangri-La, Traders Hotel and Fairmont Bab Al Bahr, which provide the main entertainment focus. Sharing the same stretch of creek and beachfront, the hotels have top-notch restaurants, plus a wide range of facilities including spas, gymnasiums and swimming pools.

The hotels are adjacent to the Souk at Qaryat Al Beri development, a Disney-esque recreation of a traditional souk in a modern setting. It offers a variety of shops and restaurants under one roof, connected by a waterway on which Arabic gondolas, or abras, slowly meander through the unique architecture, under arches and past restaurant terraces.

The whole complex overlooks Abu Dhabi's architectural piece de resistance, the Sheikh Zayed Grand Mosque, which sits across the creek – a stunning masterpiece reminiscent of a sultan's palace, the mosque is one of the very few in the country that allows tours. For more traditional architecture, look across the road from Qaryat Al Beri to one of the most ornate Persian-influenced mosques in the city. This small turquoise blue gem is not open for tours but you can admire the craftsmanship from outside.

Just across the water, looking back from the island side, is the Ritz-Carlton Grand Canal hotel, which added signature restaurants, a couple of bars and other poolside dining options to the area's attractions. In the evenings, an abra runs between the Ritz to the hotels on the opposite side. Rides are free, although priority is given to hotel guests.

The Entertainment Island

A handy guide to making the most of Yas Island's wet, wild and wonderful attractions.

Stay in style

Yas Island's six hotels are perfect for holidaymakers, event visitors or local residents. Together the Yas Plaza's five hotels and the Yas Viceroy Abu Dhabi account for 22 of the island's restaurants and 12 of its bars – and that's not including lobby lounges.

Whether you're after fantastic value or something more high-end, every taste is catered for and each hotel has its own standout features: stunning views, brilliant pools or incredible design.

Get active

Regarded as one of the best courses in the world, Yas Links Golf course is a beautiful venue that offers serious golfers a real challenge, with a separate course where less confident golfers can hone their skills.

Yas Marina Circuit's driving experiences cater for your inner speed demon with everything from Aston Martin GT4s to Formula Yas 3000 single seaters. If you prefer to shun petrol power, run or cycle around the circuit on Tuesday evenings – for free!

On Yas Beach, Noukhada Adventure Company (noukhada.ae) has your watersports needs covered with windsurfing, sailing and kayaking through the nearby mangroves.

Feel the rush

Ferrari World Abu Dhabi draws crowds from around the world with the lure of the 'world's fastest rollercoaster', the Formula Rossa. Head inside and you'll also have fun driving miniature cars, ogling world famous Ferraris and exploring a mini Italy.

Yas Waterworld makes for a fabulous family day out with kid-focused interactive games and the excellent Marah Fortress splash park. But 'big kids' can have fun too, lounging by the pool, relaxing in a private cabana or enjoying one of the park's adrenaline-pumping slides. Highlights include the heart-thumping Liwa Loop. Wet and wild fun at its best.

Shop 'til you drop

Yas Mall, the city's biggest, will keep hardcore shoppers entertained with its 300 plus stores. IKEA and Ace Hardware are nearby, too. Smaller shopping options include theme park stores, a F1 store at Yas Viceroy and a pro shop at Yas Links.

Party the night away

For the ultimate nightclub experience, head to either the super exclusive O1NE Yas Island – a purpose-built club from the team that created Beirut's world famous Sky Bar – or Rush, the party spot on Yas Viceroy's impressive circuit-crossing bridge.

FLASH Entertainment regularly brings world-famous musical acts to perform at the island's du Arena. Madonna, The Rolling Stones, Jay Z and a host of other pop, rock and dance talent have performed there. The smaller du Forum puts on entertainment throughout the year such as boxing events, Oktoberfest celebrations and science festivals for kids.

Dock, dine and discover

From US-inspired food at Stars 'n' Bars to funky alfresco tapas at Diablito and fine dining at Cipriani and Aquarium, Yas Marina is one of the hottest food spots in town. To work up an appetite, why not charter a boat for a tour of Abu Dhabi's waters from Azure Charters. If you want to dock your own boat, berths can be had from Dhs.16,455 – which includes F1 passes, concert tickets and dining discounts. A great, relaxed place to hang out, eat or party.

Formula 1 weekend

Every November Yas Marina Circuit, and the whole of Yas Island, hosts the Abu Dhabi FIA Formula 1 World Championship. Huge yachts pour into the marina, roads become packed and the atmosphere gets charged with excitement as helicopters buzz overhead. Even if you're not an F1 fan, the concerts, restaurant and bar events, and boat parties make for four days you don't want to miss.

Yas Express

A free bus, the Yas Express covers two circuits of the island. The Blue Route will ferry you between Yas Waterworld, Yas Plaza, Yas Viceroy, central Yas and Ferrari World Abu Dhabi/Yas Mall; the Red Route goes from Yas Plaza, to Yas Viceroy then on to Yas Marina and Yas Beach followed by Yas Links Golf Club. The free Saadiyat route leaves from St. Regis and Park Hyatt hotels on Saadiyat Island three times every morning with drop-offs at Yas Waterworld and Ferrari World. For timetables see yasisland.ae.

Explorer's Top Five

If you're visiting Yas Island, this checklist should help you make the most of your stay.

1. Watch the sun go down over Abu Dhabi at Yas Links Golf Club, either from the course or with a chilled drink on the terrace of Hickory's bar.

2. Be courageous by braving Yas Waterworld's infamous Liwa Loop ride.

3. Be even more courageous by taking the front seat of the Formula Rossa rollercoaster at Ferrari World Abu Dhabi.

4. Take a kayak eco-tour from Yas Beach to learn about Abu Dhabi's mangroves and sealife.

5. Experience the Yas Marina Circuit with one of their driving experiences then head to Skylite at the top of the Yas Viceroy for an evening under the iconic canopy.

Yas Waterworld

Breakwater

This area of reclaimed land is entirely man-made and connected by a causeway to the south western end of the Corniche. The main draw here is Marina Mall, a popular leisure hub with a variety of international brands and a cinema. Poking out from the roof of the mall is the 100m high Sky Tower, where you can have some lunch and enjoy panoramic views of the city. Behind the mall looms a huge new Fairmont Hotel, set to open in 2016.

The beachfront walkways are also great for admiring and photographing the city's superb skyline. Along the waterfront there are a number of popular Arabic restaurants and cafes along with Heritage Village, a quirky place to soak up some history.

Abu Dhabi International Marine Sports Club offers watersports facilities and hosts local and international racing events. The round Abu Dhabi Theater building is also worth a look, although its interior is accessible only during occasional events and concerts. Next to it stands an enormous flagpole which was, for a time at least, the tallest unsupported flagpole in the world at 123.1m.

Al Ras Al Akhdar Peninsula

Connecting Breakwater to the main island is Al Ras Al Akhdar peninsula. This area is dominated by the beautiful, and massive, Emirates Palace. The hotel is one of the city's most iconic landmarks and should be at the top of every visitor's list of 'must sees' in Abu Dhabi. It is a stunning property set in more than 85 hectares of landscaped gardens, surrounded by a pristine stretch of white-sand beach and a new yacht marina. Palatial in every sense, luxury and opulence oozes from every inch of the hotel, from the huge gold domed roof in the reception area to the massive hand-woven carpets displayed on the walls.

The hotel is also home to some exceptional restaurants, a couple of excellent galleries and seasonal exhibitions and a 1,500-seat auditorium that hosts a variety of shows throughout the year, including films during the Abu Dhabi Film Festival and concerts during the Abu Dhabi Classics series. Over the road, Jumeirah At Etihad Towers has views over Emirates Palace, and indeed the entire city. Head to the tallest of the five impressive towers and take a trip up to the Observation Deck at 300 on the 74th floor for afternoon tea.

The Corniche

Seen as the face of the city, the Corniche runs along the western coast of the island and is one of the best places to while away a relaxing day. Home to some of the city's most impressive buildings, Corniche Road is lined with high-rise towers, but there are plenty of opportunities to get out and enjoy the open air. As city beaches go, it's a spectacular location for a day by the sea, and you can rent sun loungers at one of three BAKE beach clubs. The beach side of the road is paved all the way along and is popular with promenaders a casual stroll along the Corniche is a favourite part of many residents' evening routine. It's ideal for rollerblading, jogging and walking, while the special cycle path draws both enthusiastic amateurs and more serious cyclists. At the intersection of Khaleej Al Arabi St there's a range of cafes and restaurants for refreshments and refuelling.

Inland

The inland side of the Corniche Road has been beautifully landscaped with parks, picnic grounds, small gardens, fountains, cafes and covered seating areas lining the pavements. All areas are easily accessible, with parking and safe (and surprisingly attractive) pedestrian underpasses. Al Nahyan Park has some wonderful play areas, including a skateboard park, splash area and pretty fountains. To explore these attractions from a different perspective, visitors can book a dinner cruise along the Corniche on board a traditional wooden dhow or cabin cruiser. Cruises generally last for several hours and can be booked through a tour operator. Yellow Boat tours offer a zippier, less formal alternative or you can take a hop on-hop off Big Bus tour (bigbustours.com) where the Corniche is one of the scheduled stop offs. Several luxury hotels line the Corniche and offer fantastic dining and nightlife, including the Hilton Abu Dhabi, the Sheraton Abu Dhabi and the Sofitel Abu Dhabi Corniche. The skyline is ever-changing and the next few years will see the continued construction of hotels and residential developments.

The New Corniche

The Corniche should not be confused with the New Corniche or Eastern Corniche, which runs along the north eastern side of the island overlooking mangroves. It's a popular place for picnics and fishing, with shaded areas for the joggers and cyclists to rest. The Eastern Mangroves promenade has new cafes and venues, as well as watersports.

Al Khalidiya

Al Khalidiya is one of the most popular areas in the city with leafy green suburban streets leading to high-rise towers. Khalidiya Mall on Mubarak Bin Mohammed Al Nahyan St houses many shops, a number of food outlets, a children's play area, and a well-stocked hypermarket. More traditional food can be found at the multiple shawarma stands and this area has some of the best examples of these tasty, greasy joints: try Seashell Cafeteria behind Khalidiya Mall or Shishwarma behind NBAD Corniche.

After scoffing that down, The Folklore Gallery for culture lovers is a great place to head to for some browsing, with interesting displays of local pottery and art. This area also has the popular Al Khalidiya Park, bustling with families late into the evening during the cooler months.

Saadiyat Island

With its bluer-than-blue sea, soft white sands and laid-back vibe, Saadiyat Island feels a world away from the city. Thanks to the Sheikh Khalifa Highway, though, it's only 10 minutes from Downtown Abu Dhabi. If Yas is all about thrills and spills, Saadiyat is evolving into the cultural, arty capital of the Middle East. Abu Dhabi's very own world-famous Louvre and Guggenheim are expected to open in the next few years, along with the much-anticipated Zayed National Museum and even a Performing Arts Centre.

For your immediate art fix however, head to the impressive NYUAD Art Gallery (nyuad-artgallery. org) on NYU's Saadiyat Island campus. This fantastic addition to the capital's art scene is free to visit and features exciting museum-style exhibitions of art, sculpture and culture, covering both historical and contemporary subjects. Manarat Al Saadiyat is another art space with seasonal exhibitions, talks and workshops. Hotel offerings on Saadiyat Island and at the impressive Saadiyat Beach Club offer sumptuous retreats and amazing dining venues, as do the St Regis and Park Hyatt, all beautiful beachfront properties.

The enticing Saadiyat Beach Club offers a taste of luxury by the sea; there is pool and beach access, a Jacuzzi and spa facilities, private cabanas and bungalows, as well as a handful of restaurants and bars to choose from. For something much more budget-friendly, BAKE beach club runs Saadiyat Public Beach where you can rent sun loungers and try some non-motorised watersports.

Al Zahiyah

This area, formerly known as the Tourist Club, forms the northernmost corner of Abu Dhabi Island. One of the oldest areas of the capital, its narrow streets, quirky restaurants and interesting shops are buzzing with activity and offer visitors and residents alike a true taste of cosmopolitan Abu Dhabi.

Along with neighbouring Al Markaziyah, this is the city centre and, currently at least, the main business district. The area is a real fusion of residential and commercial, with high-rise business towers, embassies and the Al Noor Hospital surrounded by a good range of local and international shops. The older buildings interspersed with shiny new towers offer a glimpse of the city's heritage and history. Two of the busiest roads in the capital, Hamdan Bin Mohammed St and Shk Zayed First St, run through the district. It's a haven for those in need of some retail therapy, as the local, traditional shops share the streets with big name international stores, quirky discount shops and smaller malls (which, 20 years ago, were considered huge!).

Al Zahiyah

Nearby Madinat Zayed Shopping Centre is a great place to go for colourful fabrics, Indian and Arabian gifts and jewellery – there are shops selling all sorts of bizarre items. The backstreets next to the centre have many shops selling traditional abayas and kandooras as well as touristy knick-knacks for a fraction of the prices you'll pay elsewhere. For a more comfortable and comprehensive shopping trip, Abu Dhabi Mall will more than suffice.

There are some interesting ethnic dining options to be found too. India Palace and Beijing Restaurant offer the best of their respective country's cuisines on a stretch of Shk Zayed Bin Sultan St opposite the municipality, and a well-known Ethiopian restaurant is near the National Hospital.

The area also has its share of hotels with the Crowne Plaza, Southern Sun, Grand Millennium and Le Meridien all within walking distance. Then there's the Beach Rotana Abu Dhabi, which has a great members-only beach club and some superb restaurants and bars, including chain favourite Benihana.

Before being renamed Al Zahiyah, the area got its colloquial name from the long-gone Abu Dhabi Tourist Club that used to be in the area between Le Meridien and Abu Dhabi Mall. These days, this whole area is being redeveloped and spruced up.

To escape the mass of buildings, your best bet is to head for Capital Park on Khalifa bin Zayed The First St. You'll pay a dirham entrance fee to find a large pond with fountains, a children's play area, a small amusement arcade and an on-site restaurant – it's a world away from the busy city streets.

Yas Island

A destination in its own right, Yas Island has become one of the UAE's most popular leisure hubs. Luxurious hotels, record-breaking attractions and the Formula 1 Grand Prix define this loud, unparalleled entertainment complex.

Yas Marina Circuit, which hosts the Abu Dhabi Formula 1 Grand Prix every November, has a unique design; the track runs through the island's flagship hotel, the Yas Viceroy Abu Dhabi, giving lucky VIPs enviable views on race weekends. What's more, the dazzling Yas Marina is incorporated into the circuit, so the yachting crowd can not only make grand entrances but also view the race from their boats. Other F1 fans – of more modest means – still enjoy thrilling racing moments, with some 50,000 people attending each year.

And racing is only part of the draw of the F1 weekend: the end of each day brings performances from A-listers at du Forum that have included Pharrell Williams, The Who, Beyoncé, Aerosmith, Jay Z and Prince over the years.

Equally, Yas Marina Circuit is a year-round venue where petrolheads can put their driving skills to the test with karting, drag racing, drifting and supercar driving. In keeping with the theme, Ferrari World – the world's largest indoor theme park – has enough attractions to keep motorsports enthusiasts entertained, including the world's fastest rollercoaster. If all that speed makes you sweat, cool off at nearby Yas Waterworld, and enjoy 40 rides and attractions.

The striking Yas Viceroy and Yas Marina Circuit

ART & CULTURE

The internationally-recognised Louvre and Guggenheim museums in Saadiyat's budding Cultural District are a few years from completion. In the meantime, there's a growing art scene that's attracting local and international talent to the UAE capital. A number of galleries have interesting exhibitions of art and traditional Arabic artefacts; the impressive NYUAD Art Gallery (nyuad-artgallery.org) on NYU's Saadiyat Island campus is a fantastic addition to the capital's art scene with museum-style exhibitions of art, sculpture and culture. Most operate as a combined shop and gallery, or provide studios for artists. Exhibitions are also staged in the city's upscale hotels.

Art Galleries

Abu Dhabi Art Hub
Mussafah Industrial Area **02 551 5005**
adah.ae
Map **1 K12**
The Abu Dhabi Art Hub (ADAH) is a unique offering out in the industrial area of Mussafah. A gallery with regular exhibitions, it also invites resident artists from around the world to stay, work and pass on their knowledge in special classes which are open to anyone. Their visiting artists also create one-off works that visitors can see, some of which are also exhibited in select hotels in the city.

Abu Dhabi Tourism & Culture Authority
Shk Zayed Bin Sulan St, Nr Khalifa Park Al Matar
02 444 0444 tcaabudhabi.ae
Map **1 K7**
The foundation in charge of Abu Dhabi's culture, heritage and leisure offerings is based near Khalifa Park. The ADTCA organises exhibitions, screenings, performances and lectures all over the city.

Barakat Gallery
Emirates Palace Al Ras Al Akhdar **02 690 8950**
barakatgallery.com
Map **2 B2**
Located in the Emirates Palace hotel, this addition to Abu Dhabi's developing art scene also has branches in London and Los Angeles. Barakat specialises in ancient art and has on display a multitude of fascinating antiquities from China, Egypt, the Near East, Africa, Greece and Rome. There's a wide variety of items including statues, jewellery, coins and pottery.

Etihad Galleries
Al Falah St **02 621 0145**
etihadmodernart.com
Map **2 F6**
This new gallery, comprised of two adjacent villas, hosts impressive collections of both global modern and ancient Islamic art and artefacts. Swords, armour, and centuries-old prayerbooks fill the Etihad Antiques gallery, available to see by appointment only. Next door, the Etihad Modern Art Gallery showcases its contemporary pieces, much of which are by local artists, daily from 10am to 10pm (except Fridays). The Art House Cafe is also a unique place to take guests or grab a coffee.

Folklore Gallery
Shk Zayed The First St Al Khalidiya **02 666 0361**
folkloregallery.net
Map **2 H4**
A simple but welcoming art and exhibition space, this gallery focuses on local artistic and craft offerings, with traditional Bedouin ceramics and jewellery available at reasonable prices. Art comes in the form of prints and paintings that have been inspired by the country's landscape.

Gallery One
Souk At Qaryat Al Beri Al Maqtaa **02 558 1822**
g-1.com
Map **1 L8**
Gallery One regularly hosts exhibitions of international note – the most prominent to date being Art of Islam and Picasso Abu Dhabi – and runs a series of lectures alongside each event. Exhibitions also bring together diverse works from across the Middle East and UAE. Entry to all shows and events is free.

Abu Dhabi Art
This annual art fair boasts an impressive programme of exhibitions, lectures, debates and workshops. Based in Manarat Al Saadiyat, the exhibitions focus on museum quality artworks from modern, contemporary and design galleries. Check out abudhabiartfair.ae for more information.

NYUAD Art Gallery > *p.189*
NYU Campus Saadiyat Island
02 628 8000
nyuad-artgallery.org
Map **1 H2**
Located at the entrance to the new NYU campus, the NYUAD Art Gallery displays museum-quality exhibitions covering past and present subjects with a special emphasis on the region. A second gallery, the Project Room in the university's Arts Centre,

highlights community-driven works of art. The gallery also supports academic and experimental installations, and international landmark exhibitions. Free admission.

Manarat Al Saadiyat
Saadiyat Cultural District Saadiyat Island
02 657 5800
saadiyatculturaldistrict.ae
Map **1 G1**
Meaning the 'place of enlightenment', Manarat Al Saadiyat is a bright, modern space with several galleries hosting temporary exhibitions, by masters such as Picasso and Klee. Exhibitions, talks and workshops for all ages are held throughout the year.

Salwa Zeidan Gallery
St Regis Saadiyat Island Resort Saadiyat Island
02 666 9656
salwazeidangallery.com
Map **1 G1**
Showcasing painting, sculpture and photography as well as installations and performance pieces with a local focus. The gallery is also the driving force behind Abu Dhabi's annual sculpture symposium.

Heritage Sites

Abu Dhabi has a handful of interesting places offering a glimpse into a time when the city was little more than a small fishing, pearling and trading port. Many of the pre-oil heritage sites have been or are currently being restored, with special attention being paid to traditional design and the original building materials. The Abu Dhabi Ministry of Current Affairs website (mofa.gov.ae) is a useful source of information for any heritage news on Abu Dhabi and the UAE at large.

Al Maqtaa Fort
Nr Maqtaa Bridge Al Maqtaa **02 444 0444**
visitabudhabi.ae
Map **1 L8**
This renovated fort is one of the few remaining examples of its kind in the city. The 200 year-old fort was built to fend off bandits and provides a wonderful contrast to the modern bridge right next to it. Be careful taking photographs here as it is a sensitive military zone and there are often police patrols.

Bateen Dhow Yard
Nr Al Bateen Wharf Al Bateen
Map **2 B6**
Connected to the island via a short causeway, this shipyard is a charming area where boat builders continue to craft vessels in the way they have done for decades. Visit early in the morning or late afternoon.

Sheikh Zayed Grand Mosque

Heritage Village
Nr Marina Mall Breakwater **02 681 4455**
Map **2 F2**
An oasis village recreation where visitors can get a taste of what Emirati life used to be like. Traditional aspects of Bedouin life, including a camp fire with coffee pots, a goats' hair tent, a well and a falaj irrigation system, are displayed and there are workshops where craftsmen demonstrate traditional skills. There are also camels to ride. Entry is free and views from the beach across to the city are superb.

Qasr Al Hosn
Hamdam Bin Mohammed St Markaziya West
02 666 4442
abudhabi.ae
Map **2 K4**
Also known as the Old Fort or the White Fort, this is the oldest building in Abu Dhabi, dating back to 1793. It was the official residence of the rulers when they moved from the Liwa Oasis to the island. Unfortunately, at the moment Qasr Al Hosn is closed for major renovations, although you can still see parts of the exterior or glimpse inside at special events.

Sheikh Zayed Grand Mosque
Shk Rashid Bin Saeed St Al Maqtaa
02 419 1919
szgmc.ae
Map **1 K8**
This stunning Abu Dhabi icon is a truly remarkable architectural feat, reminiscent of a sultan's palace from the *Arabian Nights*. This architectural marvel

PERFORMANCES
EXHIBITIONS
TALKS

VISIT

NEW YORK
UNIVERSITY
ABU DHABI

NYUAD مركز الفنون
THE ARTS
CENTER

nyuad-artscenter.org

Located on Saadiyat Island, NYU Abu Dhabi's new campus hosts world-class public programs, including scholarly conferences and lectures, museum and gallery exhibitions, performances, and film festivals.

For more information and to join our mailing lists, please check our websites.

جامعة نيويورك ابوظبي
NYU ABU DHABI

INSTITUTE

**nyuad.nyu.edu/
news-events**

NYUAD معرض الفنون
ART GALLERY

nyuad-artgallery.org

has captivated worshippers and visitors alike since it opened in 2007 and never fails to impress. Plus, unlike most mosques in the UAE, it is open to non-Muslims and you can take guided tours throughout the week (except Friday mornings and on the first day of Eid Al Fitr and Eid Al Adha). It is essential that visitors dress respectfully during the tour – you should wear loose-fitting garments that cover your wrists and ankles. Women must wear an abaya, and these are provided free of charge at the mosque.

Grand Mosque Facts

This astonishing building is one of the largest mosques in the world – the main prayer hall alone accommodates up to 7,000 worshippers. Add to that over 80 domes, 1,000 columns, 24 carat gold-plated chandeliers and the world's largest hand-woven Persian carpet, and you have a truly awe-inspiring architectural marvel.

Women's Handicraft Centre

Shakhbout Bin Sultan St Al Mushrif **02 447 6645**
visitabudhabi.ae
Map **1 E7**
A creative initiative run by Abu Dhabi Women's Association to showcase local art and crafts. Examine handiwork by local artists and learn about the work on display, which includes Arabian oils, hand-made souvenirs, local dress, silver thread work and weaving as well as keepsakes from their shop. Ask first before photographing the veiled women in their workshops.

Qasr Al Hosn

Museums

Zayed National Museum promises to be something of an architectural and cultural landmark when it opens on Saadiyat Island, but until then here are a few quirky exhibition spaces worth checking out. The great thing is that most museums are free to enter.

Al Ain Palace Museum

Central District Al Ain **03 751 7755**
visitabudhabi.ae
Map **3 E3**
This museum offers a fascinating insight into the life of Abu Dhabi's revered founder, Sheikh Zayed Bin Sultan Al Nahyan. It's housed in a palace dating from 1937, making it one of the oldest standing buildings in the emirate. Sheikh Zayed and his family lived in this very building and high level meetings were once held in its many majlises and gardens. For an unrivaled view of UAE history, this definitely merits the drive to Al Ain.

Emirates National Auto Museum

Abu Dhabi-Tarif Rd Al Dhafra **050 810 2211**
enam.ae
Map **3 D3**
Located 45 kilometres south of Abfu Dhabi, this impressive pyramid houses a mix of cars from one dedicated collector: Sheikh Hamad bin Hamdan Al Nahyan, aka the 'Rainbow Sheikh'. The museum has recently undergone development and is now home to almost 200 cars, including a vast collection of off-road vehicles, American cars, the Sheikh's rainbow Mercedes collection and the largest truck in the world.

Maritime Museum

Khalifa Park Al Matar
Map **1 K7**
The Maritime Museum in Khalifa Park features a fascinating Time Tunnel; a sit-on ride that takes you on a tour through the history of Abu Dhabi from pre-union times. Not many people seem to know about the museum or the ride, but Khalifa Park is undergoing an update so it may get busier yet. In the same building there's also a decent aquarium, which is free to enter once you're in the park and a great place to spend some time.

Sheikh Zayed Bridge

This 842 metre-long bridge linking the mainland to the city was designed by world famous Iraqi born architect Zaha Hadid – and is another stunning addition to Abu Dhabi's rich architectural offerings. Hadid has also designed the upcoming Performing Arts Centre due to be built on Saadiyat Island.

YAS ISLAND YOUR TICKET TO A WORLD OF MAGIC

FOR MORE INFORMATION VISIT **YASISLAND.AE**
CONTACT US AT **HELLO@YASISLAND.AE**

   You Tube

YAS ISLAND.AE
UNITED ARAB EMIRATES

Abu Dhabi Art Scene

An ever-growing arts scene and the imminent arrival of world-class galleries will make Abu Dhabi a cultural hub for the UAE and beyond.

The art of the city

Saadiyat Island is already a special place; golden beaches stretching into the turquoise sea, top class dining venues, all only minutes from downtown Abu Dhabi. However, it's about to get a stroke of added artistic inspiration as it becomes host to the city's Cultural District. Aside from the Zayed National Museum and the Performing Arts Centre, both to be housed within stunning architecture, the globally recognised institutions of the Louvre and the Guggenheim will be represented, making Abu Dhabi, and the UAE, a focal point for the arts across the world.

Louvre Abu Dhabi
Due to open: in the near future

The Louvre Abu Dhabi will be the first of the new museums to open, and construction is well underway. The building, designed by the legendary Jean Nouvel, will be an impressive landmark; a 180m diameter, 7,000 tonne dome sat atop four pillars on a man-made platform. The area is dammed off, but before its opening in 2015 water will be flooded back to give it the feel of an island. The large dome will also let natural light through, dappling the public areas with sunshine. Inside the galleries, the museum will present major objects from the fields of archaeology, fine arts and decorative arts, plus all regions, periods (including contemporary art) and the narrative of art history.

Guggenheim Abu Dhabi
Due to open: in the near future

The fantastic Frank Gehry-designed architecture for the Guggenheim Abu Dhabi will create one of the most unusual buildings in the country. The 450,000 square foot museum will house a huge collection of modern and contemporary art, as well as special exhibitions from the Guggenheim Foundation's extensive collection. It will be built on the corner of the island stretching out to sea and will incorporate many traditional Arabic design elements.

Manarat Al Saadiyat

Home to a fascinating exhibition showing the future development of the island, Manarat Al Saadiyat is also a functioning gallery in its own right. The high ceilings and light, airy feel of this contemporary space create the perfect place to appreciate the sculptures, paintings and other works displayed in ever-changing exhibitions, including previews of the Louvre and Guggenheim collections. Next to Manarat Al Saadiyat is the Norman Foster designed UAE Pavilion. The striking structure was first exhibited at the Shanghai World Expo 2010 then shipped to Saadiyat Island and re-erected. It's now a regular space for art and other exhibits. The NYUAD Art Gallery (nyuad-artgallery.org), on the university's new Saadiyat Island campus, is also free to visit and has two excellent galleries.

Elsewhere in Abu Dhabi

There are a number of independent galleries around the city including the Salwa Zeidan Gallery (salwazeidangallery.com), that recently moved to Saadiyat Island, and Ghaf Gallery (ghafartgallery. com). The Etihad Modern Art Gallery in Al Bateen is an extension of the Etihad Antique Gallery (etihadgallery. com). For something different, Abu Dhabi Pottery (abudhabipottery.com) showcases some fine ceramics and also holds classes. To find like-minded people to explore the art scene with, try Abu Dhabi Art Squad (abudhabiartsquad.com). Art work can also be found in many of the city's hotels, from classic antiquities at The Barakat Gallery in Emirates Palace, to contemporary work from international artists at places like the Lightbox in the Yas Viceroy. The Souk Qaryat Al Beri also houses Gallery One. Other hotels like the Rosewood, Fairmont Bab Al Bahr and the Jumeirah at Etihad Towers have all hosted one-off exhibitions too, so keep your eyes open for those as they crop up.

Abu Dhabi Art Hub

If you want to get more involved, the Abu Dhabi Art Hub (adah.ae) in Mussafah is the place to go. As well as having a gallery and holding affordable art fairs, it's also a working studio. Most months a small group of invited artists from a specific country is invited to live and work in the specially designed accommodation for residency artists. Not only do they each produce a series of works inspired by the region, but they also give classes and workshops to UAE residents, helping to spread their knowledge and techniques. ADAH also promotes traditional crafts and tries to help artists find new ways of incorporating them in contemporary pieces.

Super Saadiyat

The UAE is on track for a cultural awakening, the heart of which will undoubtedly be Saadiyat Island's Cultural District. With the Louvre Abu Dhabi, designed by Jean Nouvel, due to open in the near future, and the Frank Gehry-designed Guggenheim to follow, there'll be some seriously impressive exhibitions housed in soon-to-be iconic buildings. Zayed National Museum is another eagerly awaited centre that is due to open in 2016. It's a refreshing and admirable investment by the capital, and for cultural splendour, puts Abu Dhabi firmly on the global map.

*Zayed National Museum
(image: Tourism Development
& Investment Company)*

ATTRACTIONS

Abu Dhabi is well geared-up to provide thrills and spills for families, whether high octane or of a more leisurely pace. Yas Island is one of the most lively destinations with Ferrari World Abu Dhabi and Yas Waterworld offering rides galore, and the many malls around the city often have special amusement areas, aimed more exclusively at kids. Alternatively, if bright lights and wild rides are not your thing, places like the Abu Dhabi Falcon Hospital make a fantastic day out, allowing you access to the amazing birds of prey and some insight into the Emirati art of falconry. Or, become a zookeeper for the day at Emirates Park Zoo.

Throughout the year, Abu Dhabi also stages a number of events such as Summer Season (abudhabievents.ae) which create temporary attractions, so it's worth keeping your eyes on local newspapers or askexplorer.com for updates.

Amusement Centres

There are plenty of children's play zones around the city, from parks to soft play areas, and most shopping malls have at least a small kids play area, if not more. The following larger amusement centres offer fun for the whole family.

Action Zone
Meena Centre Al Meena **02 673 4577**
actionzone.ae
Map **1 D2**
Action Zone is big, bright and noisy – a kid's paradise. There are amusement rides, a bungee trampoline, video games and a climbing maze. Food is served and birthday parties hosted. To play, purchase a swipe card and load it with credit. Games are Dhs.4 to Dhs.20. Open weekdays from 10am to 11pm, and until midnight on weekends.

Fun City
Marina Mall Breakwater **02 681 5527**
funcity.ae
Map **2 D1**
Themed as a tropical forest, this high-tech, bright lights amusement outlet has a dramatic entrance built into a rock with the sound of thunder crashing all around. An array of computer and video games, carousels and other funfair facilities await. It's a good option for keeping kids busy while you shop; games and rides cost Dhs.4 to Dhs.15.

Adventure Zone
Dalma Mall Mussafah **02 445 8903**
adventurehq.com
Map **1 N13**
This huge new indoor adventure park, hosted at the outdoorsy Adventure HQ store, offers four distinct zones for older kids and teenagers to explore. A skate park, trampoline area, and climbing walls will keep kids occupied for hours. For the truly brave, there is an elevated rope obstacle course suspended above the 1,860 sq m complex.

Sparky's Family Fun Park
Khalidiya Mall Al Manhal **02 635 4316**
sparkysme.com
Map **2 H5**
A boisterous centre that takes up a large section of Khalidiya Mall's top level, Sparky's has a kids' rollercoaster, bumper cars, a 4D cinema, a bowling alley, a football striker zone and a soft play area, as well as arcade games and even an ice rink. Sparky's can also be found in Mazyad Mall and Mushrif Mall.

Wanasa Land
Al Wahda Mall Al Wahdah **02 443 7654**
wanasalandcom
Map **2 M7**
For younger children, this centre has a large, soft play area and animal themed carousels and amusement rides. Older children have a choice of 45 high-tech computerised games and five hair-raising rides. There is no entrance fee, but rides start from Dhs.4.

Theme Parks

Ferrari World Abu Dhabi
Yas Island West **02 496 8000**
ferrariworldabudhabi.com
Map **1 T4**
The world's largest indoor theme park has enough attractions to keep motorsports enthusiasts of all ages entertained. Kids can learn to drive in a miniature Ferrari, while grown-up fans get to take a glimpse into the F1 paddock or experience race driving in a simulator. For thrillseekers, the main attraction is the world's fastest rollercoaster, Formula Rossa.

Formula Rossa
This theme park highlight is a must-do for adrenaline junkies. The record-breaking ride begins by launching you 52m into the air and reaches Grand Prix-worthy speeds of up to 240kmph, which is why anyone brave enough to tackle it has to wear safety goggles. Not for the faint-hearted.

Don't Leave Abu Dhabi Without…

There are some attractions that you simply must visit during your time in Abu Dhabi to truly experience this incredible city.

Sheikh Zayed Grand Mosque
This iconic architectural masterpiece is a must-see for anybody living in or visiting Abu Dhabi. You'll be welcomed by the mosque's ethereal magnificence each time you cross the bridge onto Abu Dhabi Island, but be sure to head inside for a tour to fully appreciate the intricate detail and sheer size.

Ferrari World Abu Dhabi
Beneath that red roof are a host of rides, attractions and, importantly, Ferraris to explore. But you can't leave Abu Dhabi without hopping on the Formula Rossa rollercoaster – the fastest in the world and possibly the country's biggest adrenaline hit.

Abu Dhabi Corniche
The city's heart resides in this stretch of coastline, with glittering skyscrapers towering to one side and the Arabian Gulf stretching out to the other. It's a bustling hub lined with cafes, parks and gorgeous beaches – for a slice of city action, head here.

Desert safari
Abu Dhabi's biggest playground is waiting to be explored, whether you go bashing through the dunes in a 4WD or rampaging through the sands on a dune buggy. End the day with shisha and Arabic entertainment as the sun sets and the rolling dunes take on a lustrous orange hue.

Yas Marina Circuit
Whether you race around it on one of their driving experiences, run around it with TrainYAS or watch the F1 drivers hammer around it, the circuit is one of the best in the world. The impressive Yas Viceroy hotel and Yas Marina form part of the complex, adding some high life to the unmissable top speed thrills.

Emirates Palace
It may be one of the most expensive hotels in the world – you can even buy gold from their vending machine – but mere mortals can take a peek round this extraordinary building and enjoy the numerous culinary delights on offer, including the renowned afternoon tea. Be sure to check out the art collection at the Barakat Gallery.

Cultural Saadiyat island
The future home of some of the world's most prestigious art establishments, there's already plenty to see, including St Regis or Park Hyatt hotels, the Saadiyat Beach and Golf Clubs, the Manarat Al Saadiyat museum and NYUAD Art Gallery. This is one of the coolest and artistic places to visit in Abu Dhabi.

A round of golf
There's an impressive number of championship golf courses in the UAE, so take your pick – whether you want to watch the pros in action or tee off on a world-class green. The 27 hole Abu Dhabi Golf Course is home to the PGA European Tour Abu Dhabi HSBC Golf Championship and designed by Peter Harrandine.

On the water
Abu Dhabi's unique geography as an archipelago of islands make it a fantastic place to explore by water. Take a boat trip to one of the desert islands and spot some dolphins, kayak through the mangroves or try out some adrenaline-fuelled wakeboarding with a glamorous backdrop. The possibilities are endless.

Abu Dhabi Falcon Hospital
Visit here for an in-depth insight into this fascinating bird of prey and traditional Emirati culture. Get up close to the birds and watch as the specialist vets perform minor surgery on them. If you're good, they might even let you hold one of the prized falcons.

Masdar City
The expanding Masdar City offers a glimpse into the future and Abu Dhabi's admirable efforts towards creating the world's most sustainable city. It's worth a visit to ride one of the driverless electric cars and witness the smart, green thinking that cities across the world will likely adopt one day.

Yas Mall
The country's second-largest shopping destination Yas Mall opened in November 2014. The flash 2.5 million sq ft of retail and entertainment space means you can have your pick of over 400 stores. There's the city's largest Geant hypermarket, a 20-screen cinema, a Fun Works kids' zone and a broad choice of eateries.

Ferrari World Abu Dhabi

Water Parks

Murjan Splash Park
Khalifa Park Al Matar **050 878 1009**
murjansplashpark.weebly.com
Map **1 K7**
This mini water park, aimed at children aged three
to 12, packs a lot of fun into a small space and at an
affordable price. There's an enormous water play
climbing structure with tunnels, waterslides and a
giant tipping bucket, plus games and a lazy river,
while a surf board simulator allows mini surfers to test
their balance and skills.

Yas Waterworld Abu Dhabi
Yas Leisure Drive Yas Island West **02 414 2000**
yaswaterworld.com
Map **1 T4**
The latest water park in a country that has some of the
best record-breaking rides in the world has managed
to raise the bar even higher. For thrill seekers, the Liwa
Loop is a near-vertical drop that shoots you through a
winding loop at an incredible speed, or slither down
the world's first 'rattling' waterslide complete with
special effects. For gentler thrills simply make yourself
comfortable on a tube and float down the lazy river.
A fantastic day out for all of the family.

Wildlife & Sealife

Abu Dhabi Falcon Hospital > *p.vii, 123, 198*
Sweihan Rd Al Shamkha **02 575 5155**
falconhospital.com
Map **3 D3**
The specialists here provide diagnosis, treatment and
disease prevention for falcons and other bird species,
even poultry. Due to keen interest from the general
public, the hospital also offers a fascinating guided
tour on weekdays (these must be booked in advance)
where you can see them at work. Also on the same
site is the Animal Shelter (abudhabianimalshelter.com)
and the Saluki Centre.

Abu Dhabi Wildlife Centre
Abu Dhabi-Al Ain Truck Rd Mafraq Industrial Area
050 721 8169 Map **3 D3**
Abu Dhabi Wildlife Centre was created with a vision
of caring for sick and orphaned animals – specifically
cheetahs. It is now a fully fledged rehabilitation and
breeding centre for endangered species and rare
animals, including many big cats – lions, jaguars,
leopards and tigers, to name a few – as well as
tortoises, crocodiles and llamas. Entrance costs Dhs.65
for adults and Dhs.35 for kids under the age of 12,
and is inclusive of an informative and entertaining 60
minute tour of the facilities.

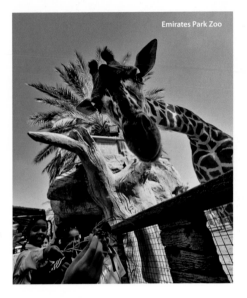
Emirates Park Zoo

Emirates Park Zoo > *p.195*
Abu Dhabi-Shahama Rd Al Rahba **02 501 0000**
emiratesparkzoo.com
Map **3 D2**
Located 45km outside the city on the road to Dubai,
children can get up close to their favourite animals.
There are a number of interactive attractions,
including the Giraffe Cafe, where you can feed the
animals. The five-acre zoo houses peacocks, ostriches,
ibex, camels, horses, raccoons, ferrets, hippos and
exotic fish and birds, and children can even volunteer
to be a 'zoo keeper' for the day.

Khalifa Park Aquarium
Khalifa Park Al Matar
Map **1 K7**
It might not be on the scale of some other aquariums
in the UAE, but this interesting corner of Khalifa Park
is sure to keep kids amused. Free to enter, there are
plenty of different species on display, including one of
the most friendly turtles you'll ever come across.

Sir Bani Yas Island
Sir Bani Yas Island **02 406 1400**
desertislands.com
Map **3 B3**
The island's Arabian Wildlife Park is home to more than
10,000 free roaming animals, including Arabian oryx,
gazelles and giraffes – along with the newest arrivals,
hyenas and cheetahs. Take an organised wildlife walk
or safari drive through the park. For access you must
book a stay at one of three outstanding hotels from
Anantara's Desert Islands Resort & Spa (anantara.com).

Event facilities of
Abu Dhabi Falcon Hospital
the unique event venue in Abu Dhabi

Falcon World Tour
Your Exclusive Tourist Destination
Abu Dhabi Falcon Hospital

To make a booking or for more information call Mr. Amer Abu Aabed, mobile 050-6660739
P.O.Box 45553, Abu Dhabi, United Arab Emirates
Phone: +971-2-5755155, Fax: +971-2-5755001
Email: info@falconhospital.com   Web: www.falconhospital.com

BEACHES & PARKS

Abu Dhabi has some of the best outdoor facilities in the country, with an extensive coastline of natural beaches spread over its 200 islands, plus large, well-maintained parks all geared towards families. What's more, heading for the beach or the park is extremely budget-friendly. As beaches and parks are the pride and joy of the capital they are well managed by the Municipality's Abu Dhabi Ministry of Current Affairs, with sensible restrictions in place to safeguard and keep them clean. For information, visit mofa.gov.ae.

Beaches

Warm turquoise waters, white sandy beaches and lush greenery characterise Abu Dhabi's beaches and will transport you a hundred miles from the stresses of city life. At weekends, beaches are always very popular especially for picnics, for a casual stroll, a healthy jog and an invigorating dip. Swimwear, as westerners may know it, is not the norm on free public beaches so be prepared for a few stares. As well as the free beaches though, check out the many hotels who boast private stretches of beach or BAKE's Beach Clubs on the Corniche and Saadiyat Island. At BAKE you can access all the facilities of a luxury beach club, such as sun loungers and changing facilities, at a nominal price.

Abu Dhabi Corniche
Corniche St Al Khalidiya
visitabudhabi.ae
Map **2 G3**
The golden stretch of Blue Flag beach along Abu Dhabi's Corniche is dotted with kids play areas, cafes, gardens and activities, and is a bustling hub for families and friends – particularly during the cooler months. Some of the beaches are free to visit, while others (by BAKE) charge Dhs.10 admission and Dhs.25 for the comfort of a sun lounger with parasol.

Al Bateen Beach
Khalifa Bin Mubarak St Al Bateen
bakeuae.com
Map **1 E7**
This recently overhauled and popular beach overlooks Hudariyat Island and is known for its great facilities and clean waters. There's a play area for kids and sun loungers available from BAKE. Look out for the unusual Hudariyat Bridge, or 'bridge to nowhere'; it makes for a surreal backdrop.

Saadiyat Public Beach
Saadiyat Island **050 109 9996**
BAKEuae.com
Map **1 H1**
This gorgeous stretch of natural beach feels miles from the city, with pristine white sands and good waves. Dolphins have been known to come quite close to the shore. The beach is run by BAKE beach club, which charges Dhs.25 admission and rents sun loungers, umbrellas and lockers. Stand up paddleboarding and kayaking lessons (including equipment rental) are also available at weekends – ring 02 406 9404 for more details and bookings.

Blue Flag Status
Abu Dhabi's 6km long beach at the Corniche was the first beach in the UAE to be awarded an internationally recognised Blue Flag. The flag highlights cleanliness, safety and environmental management. Al Bateen beach has since been awarded a Blue Flag too. Meanwhile, Yas Marina and Al Bandar both fly a Blue Flag for the marina category.

Western Extension Corniche Beach
Markaziya West
Map **2 K3**
A 1.5km extension of the existing Corniche beach that is free to all, though be prepared to walk a bit to find facilities. The upside is that this beach isn't nearly as crowded as the main one. Beach football, volleyball and marine sports are all set to be catered for, although an area of the sea will be specially reserved for swimmers.

Yas Beach
Yas Leisure Drive Yas Island West **056 242 0435**
yasbeach.ae
Map **1 S5**
Perfect for holidaymakers in nearby hotels who want a break from the pool or for local residents (within 15km) who get discounted entry. Enjoy the licensed beach bar overlooking nearby islands, and either relax on a lounger or cabana, perhaps with some shisha, or utilise the volleyball net and watersports activities at the end of the beach.

Beach Clubs

Visit any of the hotels along the Corniche, on Saadiyat Island, or near Qaryat Al Beri and you'll find a beach club with your name on it. Expect to pay from Dhs.100-300 per day to use the sun loungers and beach facilities (rates vary between weekdays and weekends), and if you want to make it a regular

Abu Dhabi New Unified Addressing and Wayfinding System

Benefits

 Improving emergency response times

 Reducing travel time with more effective signage

 Helping to reduce environmental impact

 Expanding exploration by residents and tourists

 Delivering goods, simpler and quicker

 Tapping into the growth of local and global online commerce

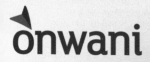

day out, consider splashing out on the annual membership fee (from Dhs.3,000-15,000). Hotels without beaches offer the same service if you'd prefer to lounge around their pools instead. Meanwhile new beach clubs continue to open, such as Nation Riviera on the Corniche Road West.

Beach Rotana
Nr Abu Dhabi Mall Al Zahiyah
02 697 9000
rotana.com
Map **2 S5**
Right in the business district of the city, Beach Rotana's private beach club is one of the most popular in Abu Dhabi. It's massive, with an adult pool, supervised kids' pool, loads of watersports on offer, and a creche. Prices start from Dhs.150 per person on a weekday and Dhs.210 on a weekend.

Fairmont Bab Al Bahr
Nr Maqta & Mussafah Bridges Al Maqtaa
02 654 3333
fairmont.com
Map **1 L8**
One of the smaller beach clubs in Abu Dhabi, the Fairmont has excellent service and a fabulous 50 metre pool to swim in and lounge by. Off the narrow beach, there are plenty of activities available, such as kayaking and even a floating trampoline. Keep in mind that it's more cost-effective to enter as a couple than as an individual, as the weekend price for two is Dhs.350 and for singles it's Dhs.200 – so grab a partner and head down there.

Saadiyat Beach Club

Hiltonia Beach Club
Corniche St Al Khubeirah **02 692 4205**
hilton.com
Map **2 C3**
Next door to the public Corniche beach, the Hiltonia has Abu Dhabi skyline views and pools for all ages, making it a good choice for families. There are activities like snorkelling and swimming lessons for the kids, a swim-up bar, and a poolside bar serving alcoholic beverages. Prices from Dhs.150 for adults.

InterContinental
King Abdullah Bin Abdulaziz Al Saud St Al Bateen
02 666 6888
intercontinental.com
Map **2 C4**
Perfect for relaxing, the InterContinental's recently remodeled beach club is just by the Emirates Palace. The parasols have buzzers that sunbathers can press for service – perfect for lazy afternoons. Although there isn't a kids' club, families are still welcome, and prices start from Dhs.150 on a weekday, making it surprisingly cheap.

Saadiyat Beach Club
Shk Khalifa Hwy Saadiyat Island **02 656 3500**
saadiyatbeachclub.ae
Map **1 H1**
This swanky beach club on the gorgeous beach of Saadiyat Island is basically a five-star hotel without the bedrooms. Sumptuous, sprawling cabana-style day beds surround a large pool, and there's a fully-equipped gym, a coffee lounge, a restaurant and a couple of bars, with swift poolside service, plus a palatial Jacuzzi, sauna, and steam room.

Parks

Abu Dhabi has a number of excellent large parks, most of which have lush green landscaping to create perfect escapes from the construction and concrete jungle of the city. During the winter months, the more popular parks can get very busy at weekends. In the summer they can be somewhat deserted. Most have a kiosk or a cafe selling snacks and drinks, and some even have barbecue pits – just remember to bring your own wood or charcoal.

Neighbourhood parks are springing up all over the city; the government's aim is to provide 25 square metres of open space for every resident of Abu Dhabi, while no resident should live more than 400m from a park or open space. Regulations among the parks vary, with some banning bikes and rollerblades, or limiting ball games to specific areas. Pets are not permitted and some parks have a ladies' day when entry is restricted to women, girls and young boys.

WALL MAPS

Many of our customers love to hang our maps from their walls to serve as a useful tool, interesting art or even unique wallpaper.

All of our maps are available in different sizes, styles, formats and languages to suit your needs. Add a personal touch with your colours, branding, photographs and selection of points of interest.

ask**explorer**.com/corporate/wallmaps

askexplorer

Capital Park
Khalifa Bin Zayed The First St Al Danah
Map **2 N3**
This refurbished park in the middle of the city centre has a selection of climbing frames, swings and slides in every small cove. A large pond in the middle regularly erupts with a fountain, while vending machines and the enclosed cafeteria provide welcome refreshment.

Delma Street Park
Nr One to One Hotel Al Nahyan
Map **3 A2**
This recently opened park has proved to be a big hit with area residents who come to play basketball and tennis or run on the shock-absorbing track. A big central plaza area is a nice spot for a picnic. Its convenient location off Shk Zayed Bin Sultan St close to the One To One hotel also explains its popularity.

Al Khalidiya Kids Park
Zayed The First St Al Khubeirah
Map **2 F4**
This is one of the more popular parks in the city with the area's residents flocking here during the cooler months. Costs of the various rides and play equipment vary, but the standard entry fee remains at Dhs.1.

Al Khalidiya Park
Al Khaleej Al Arabi St Al Manhal
Map **2 G4**
Taking up a whole block, this large city park is a favourite with families. It has a variety of safe play spaces for toddlers and older children. Its lovely grassy areas are great for picnics, with a number of large trees providing excellent shade. Entry is Dhs. 1.

Khalifa Park
Nr Al Bateen Executive Airport Al Matar
adm.gov.ae
Map **1 K7**
One of the best, this is by far the island's largest park and its gardens are inspired by traditional Arabic and Islamic architecture. They're dotted with canals, fountains, waterfalls and lakes – all best explored by foot or on the miniature train ride. There is lots inside, including a library, maritime museum, desert garden centre, the Murjan Splash Park, amphitheatre and barbecue spots. The park even hosts farmers' markets.

Al Nahyan Park
Mubarak Bin Mohamad St Markaziya West
Map **2 J3**
Formerly known as the 'Family Park', this well-maintained amenity is near the Sheraton Khalidiya. There is a playground, a splash park, a skate park as well as walking paths, several fountains and well-maintained gardens.

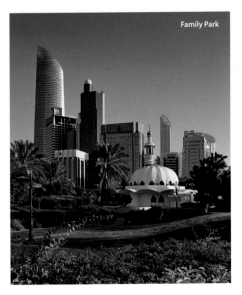
Family Park

Old Airport Park
Nr Zayed Sport City Al Madina Al Riyadiya
Map **1 J7**
One side of this large park has swings, playsets and small tidy gardens, while the other side is more ornamental, with plenty of trees offering shade. Maintenance takes place in the mornings, so be prepared to run from sprinklers. There's a KFC right on the edge of the gardens, which are also referred to as Al Zafaranah Park.

Shk Hassa'a Mosque Park
Zayed The First St Al Zahiyah
adm.gov.ae
Map **2 R4**
Also known as Al Zahiyah Park, this is yet another serene retreat in the heart of the city. Like most other parks, it offers swings and slides for children to play on. It's rarely busy and therefore ideal for families. You'll find the park located opposite the Colours building on Shk Zayed First St just after the intersection with Shk Zayed Bin Sultan St.

Yas Gateway Park
Yas Island
Map **1 U4**
Some days it's open; other days, barricades stretch across the entrance. If you can get in, it's a big, largely deserted but well-maintained space. It has several tennis and basketball courts but unfortunately, they're usually locked. Still, it is a very peaceful place for a stroll or a bike ride and is conveniently located in the northwestern loop of Yas Leisure drive.

SPORTS & LEISURE

There are two key dedicated sports hubs in Abu Dhabi: Zayed Sports City, which is open seven days a week and has an ice rink, bowling alley, tennis courts and gym, and Al Forsan International Sports Resort, boasting go-karts, shooting ranges, archery, paintball, horse riding and watersports. It's also due to have a 400 room hotel, which makes it a great holiday spot for sports fans. Elsewhere, the Armed Forces Officers' Club houses the best swimming pool in Abu Dhabi as well as two Olympic-standard shooting ranges, squash courts and a bowling centre. The Club (the-club.com), has excellent facilities for watersports and racquet sports. There's also a wealth of sporting leisure activities from boating to golf to enjoy.

Archery

Al Forsan International Sports Resort
Nr Abu Dhabi Golf Club Khalifa City **02 556 8555**
alforsan.com
Map **1 P8**
There are 10 archery lanes here offering distances of up to 60 metres. Lessons are on offer from Dhs.100, or you can pay more for private instruction.

Bowling

Bowling City
Al Mariah Mall Al Danah **02 676 0444**
bowling-city.com
Map **2 P3**
With billiards lounges, karaoke booths, internet cafes and gaming zones, there is so much more to Bowling City than just bowling. There are two locations in Abu Dhabi: Khalidiya Mall and Al Mariyah Mall. Parties, corporate events or competitions between groups of friends can all be arranged.

Emirates Bowling Village
Marina Mall Breakwater **02 681 1185**
ebv.ae
Map **2 D1**
With 32 lanes, this is a pretty big bowling centre, and handy for shoppers spending the day at Marina Mall. There are four 'VIP' lanes and a pro shop, plus lots of billiards tables, network gaming and a restaurant.

Khalifa International Bowling Centre
Zayed Sports City Al Madina Al Riyadiya **02 403 4648**
zsc.ae
Map **1 J8**
This state-of-the-art bowling centre, off Rashid Bin Al Maktoum Rd, boasts 40 lanes and is one of the most modern bowling alleys in the world. Prices start from Dhs.13 per game. There are usually instructors on hand to provide help and tips. Billiards is also on offer here, with an hour's play setting you back just Dhs.30.

Khalifa International Bowling Centre

Spectator Sports

From local competitions to world-class headliners, Abu Dhabi's sports calendar draws crowds from across the globe.

The UAE's sunny winter climate, central location, excellent sporting facilities and ability to stump up monstrous sums as prize money mean the country is growing ever more attractive as a venue for international sporting events. From headliners like the Formula 1 and tennis and golf tournaments, to local horse and camel racing meets, there's plenty going on.

Boating

With the Abu Dhabi Grand Prix in November and the Dubai Grand Prix in December, the UAE is the only country with two stops in the Class 1 World Power Boating Championship (class-1.com). In addition to Class 1 events, there's the Wooden Power Boats Championship and the UAE Jet Ski Championships (adimsc.ae), as well as sailing and dhow races held throughout the year at the Abu Dhabi International Marine Sports Club. The fantastic Volvo Ocean Race has also made stopovers in the city and is a huge draw.

Camel racing

This local sport is serious business, with racing camels changing hands for as much as Dhs.10 million each, while up to Dhs.25 million in prizes is won each year. The Al Wathba Camel Race Track is 45km from Abu Dhabi, on the road to Al Ain. Morning races take place throughout the winter on Thursday and Friday from as early as 6.30-8.30am. Periodically, major races are held on public holidays like National Day. Admission is free.

Cricket

Sheikh Zayed Cricket Stadium, near Khalifa City on E22, is host to many international matches of cricket. There's almost always something going on at the stadium, with England training there last year in preparation for their series in India and other teams regularly using it for pre-season preparation. See emiratescricket.com.

Football

Football is as popular in the UAE as it is the world over and, in recent years, there has been plenty of action for fans of the game to watch. There's a strong domestic competition too – the UAE Football League – and attending one of these games makes for a really colourful experience.

Golf

Golf fans have plenty to keep them entertained throughout the year, with major tournaments taking place in the UAE. The Abu Dhabi HSBC Golf Championship (abudhabigolfchampionship.com) is staged each January at the Abu Dhabi Golf Club near Khalifa City. The championship is the opening event on the European PGA Tour's Middle East-based Desert Swing Trio, with over $2 million in prize money given away each year.

Horse racing

Horse racing is extremely popular in the United Arab Emirates and is accessible to everyone through free admission to many race meetings. The season runs from November to early April. Abu Dhabi Equestrian Club (adec-web.com) in Al Mushrif hosts races on Sunday evenings beginning at 6pm during the racing season, with show jumping and endurance events also taking place. Gambling is not allowed in the UAE, but there are competitions to select the winning horses, with the ultimate aim of taking home prizes or cash.

Motorsports

The Yas Marina Circuit has been a boon to motorsports fans in the capital. Ever since the facility opened for the Grand Prix in 2009, announcements of new events just keep pouring in. In addition to the Formula 1 Grand Prix, the circuit has hosted endurance races, drag racing, a GT1 'battle of the brands' and Australian V8 Supercars. See yasmarinacircuit.com for information on upcoming events.

For fans of more rugged terrain, the Abu Dhabi Desert Challenge (abudhabidesertchallenge.com), which has stages right across the emirate, is the opening round of both the FIA and the FIM Cross Country Rally World Cups.

Tennis

The Abu Dhabi Mubadala World Tennis Championships usually kicks off around the New Year's celebrations at the International Tennis Complex at Zayed Sports City. For the past few years, the three-day tournament has attracted six of the top players in the world, including Roger Federer and Rafael Nadal, to the capital.

Abu Dhabi F1 Grand Prix (*image: Infiniti Red Bull Racing*)

Golf

The UAE is quite rightly known as the best golf destination in the Gulf, with excellent facilities and many important tournaments being held here, not to mention the year-round sunshine. Courses are either fully grassed or brown (sand) courses, or a mixture of the two. Be prepared for high-tech golf karts with ice coolers and GPS navigation, and accurate guidance on your distance from the hole.

Abu Dhabi City Golf Club
Khalifa Bin Shakhbout St Al Mushrif **02 445 9600**
adcitygolf.ae
Map **2 J13**
This unusual course is set within a horseracing track and its par 70 course boasts one of the longest par five holes in the Gulf, at 630 yards. Competitions are held each Friday and the Junior Golf Academy offers courses for children aged eight to 14. Although there are only nine holes, there are alternative tees for the back nine.

Abu Dhabi Golf Club
Abu Dhabi-Al Shahama Rd Khalifa City **02 558 8990**
adgolfclub.com
Map **1 N8**
This course hosts the Abu Dhabi Golf HSBC Championship, part of the European PGA Tour. Just 30 minutes from the Abu Dhabi city centre, its excellent facilities include 27 holes, a par 72 world-class 18 hole course, a driving range, putting greens and an academy. The falcon-shaped clubhouse includes bars, restaurants, a pro-shop, gym, pool and spa.

Al Ghazal Golf Club
Intl Airport Rd Abu Dhabi Intl Airport **02 575 8040**
alghazalgolf.ae
Map **1 V8**
This golf course has 'browns' rather than greens – it's a purpose-built 18 hole sand golf course with a driving range, academy and licensed clubhouse just two minutes from the airport. It is home to the World Sand Golf Championship. Anyone can play, and lessons are available. You even get a patch of 'grass' to take with you around the course, from which you can play your shots.

Saadiyat Beach Golf Club
Shk Khalifa Hwy Saadiyat Island **02 557 8000**
sbgolfclub.ae
Map **1 H1**
This par 72, 18 hole links-style championship course was designed by golfing legend Gary Player and is the only local course designed for pay-and-play daily members. The spectacular beach-side location includes three lakes and 60 bunkers. UAE residents can play at a discounted rate, and lessons are available. Early morning golfers often spot dolphins.

Yas Links Abu Dhabi
Yas Leisure Dr Yas Island West **02 810 7710**
yaslinks.com
Map **1 T4**
Yas Links is another of the region's top golf destinations. The 18 hole course was designed by Kyle Phillips as part of the Yas Island development and has gorgeous seashore views that make full use of the enviable location. It's also home to a nine-hole academy course (which is floodlit in the evening), traditional clubhouse, golf academy and floodlit practice facilities. Hickory's bar is incredible at sunset.

Ice Skating

Marina Mall Ice Rink
Marina Mall Breakwater **02 681 8506**
marinamall.ae
Map **2 D1**
This small rink is handy for shoppers looking for a little exercise or a place to keep the kids entertained. A one-hour session costs just Dhs.40. Beginners need to wear safety helmets which are included in the price, and you can pay extra to hire gloves. They also put on exciting ice shows throughout the year.

Zayed Sports City Ice Rink > p.211
Zayed Sports City Al Madina Al Riyadiya
02 403 4333
zsc.ae
Map **1 J8**
This Olympic size rink has great facilities with a separate children's area. It's often used for ice hockey (the national team practises here) and figure skating rehearsals, so call ahead to check the public session hours on the day you'd like to visit. Skating prices start at Dhs.45, and Thursdays are ladies only. For those who need a break from the ice, there's a Figaro's Pizza restaurant onsite.

Motorsports & Karting

Al Forsan International Sports Resort
Nr Abu Dhabi Golf Club Khalifa City **02 556 8555**
alforsan.com
Map **1 P8**
The ultra-modern Motor Sports Centre at Al Forsan boasts a 1.2km track with a Supermoto section built to FIM regulations and three models of karts, the fastest reaching speeds of 110kmph. There is also a karting track available for children aged eight to 11. A 2km off-road circuit provides a fun challenge for the more adventurous. Visitors aged 12 and older can try out the resort's off-road buggies – these fun vehicles provide a heart-thumping way to hit the dunes.

Abu Dhabi Golf Club

Saadiyat Beach Golf Club

Yas Links

THINGS TO SEE & DO

Yas Kartzone
Yas Marina Circuit Yas Island West **02 659 9471**
yasmarinacircuit.com
Map **1 T5**
For some family-friendly auto fun, head to Yas Kartzone. There's no need to book – you can arrive and drive. Prices start at Dhs.55 and there's a junior model for kids between 8 and 12 years. The track is outdoors and open until 10pm, which makes for an atmospheric night drive.

Yas Marina Circuit
Yas Leisure Drive Yas Island West **02 659 9800**
yasmarinacircuit.com
Map **1 T5**
Petrolheads can get behind the wheel of a supercar and race it around the track at the home of the Abu Dhabi F1 Grand Prix. Prices vary according to the experience, and there's a range of high octane vehicles – including the Formula Yas 3000, the closest competitor to an actual F1 car. They even have a dedicated drag strip (with open nights) and drift area.

Multi-Sports

You can try your hand at everything from archery and shooting to motorsports and karting, with the following spots each providing an excellent spread of activities like those to try. These venues crop up time and again throughout this guide as they provide so many sporting experiences; they truly are an asset for residents and visitors alike who want to do more than brunch, shop or lounge by the beach.

Abu Dhabi Country Club
Shakhbout Bin Sultan St Al Mushrif **02 657 7777**
adcountryclub.com
Map **2 J13**
In 2013 ADCC added a new Sports Complex which expanded its offering by two squash courts, three fitness halls and one multi-purpose hall. Coupled with bowling alleys, basketball and padel courts, a swimming pool, football pitches and tennis courts, it makes for a comprehensive offering for those right in the city of Abu Dhabi. It also has a sauna, spa, beauty salon and a range of excellent eateries.

Al Forsan International Sports Resort
Nr Abu Dhabi Golf Club Khalifa City **02 556 8555**
alforsan.com
Map **1 P8**
This popular spot is the ultimate multi-sports hub, with everything from paintballing and horse riding to clay pigeon shooting and archery. The watersports facilities for cable boarding (like wakeboarding but without a boat) are superb and not to be missed.

Armed Forces Officers Club & Hotel
Nr Sheikh Zayed Grand Mosque, Al Khaleej Al Arabi St Officers Club **02 441 5900**
afoc.mil.ae
Map **1 K9**
While primarily a hotel, the Armed Officers Club has enviable sporting facilities that guests and visitors alike can enjoy. The indoor Olympic-sized swimming pool and shooting range (home of Caracal Shooting Club) are the headline-grabbers, but you'll also find a martial arts stadium, bowling centre, outdoor paintball field, and track and field facilities.

Zayed Sports City > p.211
Al Khaleej Al Arabi St Al Madina Al Riyadiya **02 403 4200**
zsc.ae
Map **1 J8**
Zayed Sports City, just on Abu Dhabi island near the Grand Mosque, is a superb complex that caters for your regular sporting needs. A number of local football and rugby clubs call it home, thanks to the excellent grass pitches. It's arguably the top destination for tennis, tenpin bowling and ice skating, with facilities for each of a world-class level. Gyms, sports courts, paintballing and hospitality are all extra reasons to visit.

Paintballing

As well as Zayed Sports City (see above) there some great places for paintballing in Abu Dhabi. If you're struggling to find people to play with, sign up to the forums on Middle East Paintball (mepaintball.com) and you'll soon have pals to splatter with paint.

Al Forsan International Sports Resort
Nr Abu Dhabi Golf Club Khalifa City **02 556 8555**
alforsan.com
Map **1 P8**
Paintballing fans get to choose from three separate, themed indoor spaces: The Wild West, Alien Encounter and Pacific Island Zone. It also contains an international standard tournament field, as well as laser tag modifications for children.

Armed Forces Officers Club & Hotel
Nr Sheikh Zayed Grand Mosque, Al Khaleej Al Arabi St Officers Club **02 441 5900**
afoc.mil.ae
Map **1 K9**
The club boasts two paintball fields complete with cinder block shelters, wrecked cars and other detritus of urban warfare to get you into the spirit of the game. Note that advance bookings are essential, and there must be a minimum of seven players to reserve exclusive use of the field.

9 HARD COURTS

4 SAND COURTS

PRIVATE AND GROUP LESSONS

TENNIS@ZSC.AE

BACK TO BASIC FITNESS

HADDINS.COM

13 BILLIARD TABLES

6 TABLE TENNIS TABLES

40 BOWLING LANES

BOWLING@ZSC.AE

CERTIFIED SPINNING CLASSES

THEROOM.AE

AIKIDO

14 MULTI-PURPOSE PITCHES

PITCHES@ZSC.AE

3 BASKETBALL / NETBALL COURTS

ICE SPORTS

LEARN TO SKATE
FIGURE SKATING
ICE HOCKEY
RINGETTE

ICE@ZSC.AE

3 PAINTBALL ZONES

SPEEDBALL
DESERT SCENARIO
TARGET PRACTICE

PAINTBALL@ZSC.AE

GOLF SIMULATOR

مدينة زايد الرياضية
ZAYED SPORTS CITY

Abu Dhabi is your new home and Zayed Sports City is your home for sports.
We'll help you find ways to keep fit and have fun. Be in touch!

zsc.ae // 🔲 🔲 ✈ ZayedSportsCity

Zayed Sports City

Shooting

Al Forsan International Sports Resort
Nr Abu Dhabi Golf Club Khalifa City **02 556 8555**
alforsan.com
Map **1 P8**
Al Forsan provide dedicated indoor and outdoor
ranges, including the first clay shooting course in
the Gulf region. With simulated game flush shooting,
Olympic trap and skeet fields, rifle ranges and a laser
shooting simulator, the options are plentiful. Opt to
have a go at the indoor shooting range and you'll be
given a range of pistols to fire with expert tuition from
the friendly tutors – most of whom are ex-forces so
know what they're doing. At the end of your session
you'll be able to keep the targets you fired at; proof
to those at home that you're a sharp shooter. You can
also pay for more rounds at the time if you're having
fun. Lane rentals start from Dhs.100 and there are
training sessions available too.

Caracal Shooting Club
Armed Forces Officers Club & Hotel Officers Club
02 441 6404
caracalsc.ae
Map **1 K9**
Caracal has a 25 metre shooting range and a 10 metre
simulator room that involves laser technology. There's
an entry fee that includes a safety briefing and 25
bullets but depends on which firearm you choose. You
can then pay for your bullets as you go. Training courses
are also available, and spectators can watch the action.

Skate Parks

Adventure Zone
Dalma Mall Industrial City of Abu Dhabi 1
02 445 8903
adventurehq.ae
Map **1 N13**
You wouldn't guess it from the Dalma Mall storefront,
but this giant outdoor equipment store is also home
to a skate park. Half pipes, bowls, and a street section
give skaters aged six and over ample opportunities to
develop their skills. Prices start at Dhs.50.

Corniche Skate Park
Nr Al Nahyan Park Markaziyah West
Map **2 K3**
With its picturesque location along Abu Dhabi
Corniche, this popular skate park is a great spot to
spend a sunny afternoon. There are multiple ramps
with varying levels of difficulty where daring skaters
can show off against the backdrop of the city skyline.

Zoo Skate Park
For skateboarding enthusiasts who fancy venturing
to one of the other emirates, Dubai is home to Zoo
Skate Park (igniteextreme.com) – the largest indoor
skatepark in the emirate. Kids can hang out and skate
in a fun and safe environment and there is a great
choice of lessons and party options. Open daily, from
1pm to 7pm.

INTERESTING FACT
ABOUT PENGUINS:
THEY ARE ADORABLE.
For more information visit www.skidxb.com
/SKIDXB /SKIDXB /SKIDUBAI /SKIDXB
SKI DUBAI
سكي دبي
DO SOMETHING DIFFERENT

ACTIVITIES

The UAE's diverse topography lends itself perfectly to a wide range of outdoor pursuits, including mountain biking, dune bashing, wadi driving and camping. Thanks to the endless kilometres of coastline, watersports are particularly popular, with scuba diving, sailing, wakeboarding and kayaking all firmly within the realms of possibility. Whether it's sand or surf you're after, the emirate has it covered.

Biking

Away from the cities, the UAE has a lot to offer outdoor enthusiasts, especially mountain bikers. On a bike it's possible to see the most remote and untouched places that are not even accessible in 4WDs.

Beginner bikers: for the most exotic off-road rides in Abu Dhabi, check out Anantara resorts (anantara.com) which offer adventures across the dunes of the Liwa desert or the terrain of Sir Bani Yas Island. At the latter, you'll come across wildlife as amazing as the island is; in fact, it's a protected wildlife reserve.

For advanced bikers, there is a good range of terrain, from super-technical rocky trails in areas such as Shuwayah and Shawka, to mountain routes such as Wadi Bih, which climb to over a thousand metres

Cycling at Yas Marina Circuit

and can be descended in minutes. The riding is mainly rocky, technical and challenging. Even if you are an experienced biker, always be sensible and go prepared – it's important to remember that the sun can be very strong, you will need far more water than you think, and it's easy to get lost. You'll find wide, knobbly tyres work much better on the loose, sharp rocks. For further information on mountain biking in the UAE, including details of possible routes, refer to the *UAE Off-Road Explorer*.

Noukhada Adventure Company
Abu Dhabi-Al Ain Rd Khalifa City **02 558 1889**
noukhada.ae
Map **1 N8**
There are no mountains nearby so Noukhada will take you out to trails deep in the desert. Expect to run into camels, gazelles and horse riders, and to watch the sun set and the stars come out over the impressive dunes and vast salt flats. Noukhada supplies a helmet, gloves and a bike for Dhs.50 per person per hour.

Boating

With calm waters and year-round sunshine, the UAE offers ideal conditions for those wishing to sample life on the ocean waves. A number of companies provide boat charters, offering everything from sundowner cruises of a couple of hours to scuba diving excursions in remote destinations such as Musandam.

Large sailing yachts and speedboats can be hired for private charter and corporate events; other companies offer outings on dhows and also cater to weddings and birthday parties. Fishing trips and watersports packages are also available. If you're a boating enthusiast, make sure you pick up Explorer's *UAE Boating & Yachting* book.

Abu Dhabi Sailing Club
The Club Al Meena **02 673 1111**
abudhabisailing.com
Map **2 V3**
A sub-section of The Club, Abu Dhabi Sailing Club has a fleet of Kestrels, Lasers and Optimists, with social races held every week; they also participate in several national regattas each year. There are also beginner courses for adults and children from the age of six. Fees are around Dhs.1,600 per four month term.

Arabian Divers & Sportfishing
Charters > *p.219*
Marina Al Bateen Resort Al Bateen **050 614 6931**
fishabudhabi.com
Map **2 C6**
Arabian Divers offer sport fishing and scuba diving, alongside snorkelling and sightseeing boat charters.

Boats come with certified captains and all are coastguard safety approved. Based at Al Bateen Marina Resort, there is also a training pool and classroom on site, and there are PADI courses available for beginners to advanced divers.

Belevari Marine
King Abdul Aziz Saud St Al Bateen **02 643 1494**
belevari.com
Map **2 D6**
Belevari offer catamaran cruises, including a sunset cruise, and boat charters for their catamarans or speed boats – hourly rates start at Dhs.1,500. On the catamaran island cruises you can snorkel, swim, spot dolphins and spend time on an island beach, and there are also beanbags and sun loungers on board. Cruises depart from the Emirates Palace Marina.

Ports Of Call

If you've already established that sailing is your pastime, and either have a boat or are looking to buy one, you're going to need to store it somewhere. There are still waiting lists at a few of the UAE's most established marinas but, by and large, there is availability and rates are competitive. Yas Marina is one of the capital's most popular and has a guide price from Dhs.16,445 a year. Alternatively, some villa owners leave smaller boats parked outside their houses and launch them from sites in Al Bateen or Bain Al Jisreen.

Noukhada Adventure Company
Ali & Sons Bldg Abu Dhabi-Al Ain Rd Khalifa City **02 558 1889** noukhada.ae
Map **1 N8**
For those who want to learn how to sail, Noukhada is a perfect starting point; staff are experienced and their Hobie catamarans are light and easy to manoeuvre. For expats who are already accomplished sailors without access to a boat, Noukhada's sailing club (Dhs.5,000 per year) offers the use of its boats without storage or overheads to consider.

Watercooled
Hiltonia Beach Club Al Khubeirah **02 639 5997**
watercooleduae.com
Map **2 C3**
Operating out of the Hilton hotel, Watercooled runs courses in sailing, powerboating and windsurfing, all accredited by the Royal Yacht Association. There are also loads of other water-based activities on offer, such as stand up paddleboarding, kayaking, wakeboarding, and fishing trips. Hobie catamarans and RS dinghies can be privately rented, for those who already know how to sail or are keen to organise their own fishing trip. Basic kit can be hired onsite.

Camping

To really appreciate the surroundings that Abu Dhabi has to offer, you need to venture out and experience the natural wonders of the Arabian countryside for at least a night or two. While the weather is rarely bad, the ideal time for a camping trip is between October and April. Generally speaking, there are no restrictions on where you can camp, with the exception of some private beaches, but obviously people's privacy and property need to be respected.

Beach Spots

About 140km west of Abu Dhabi, Mirfa is a small, quiet town located on the coast. While there are not a lot of attractions, the long stretch of beach is a kitesurfer's paradise and many choose to pitch tents here. You can also try the gorgeous headland of Ras Khumais. Turning off the main road 15km after Sila, this small road takes you up to a great camping spot just before the military post. You can drive right onto the beach and camp while watching pink flamingos as they bob along the water.

Desert Spots

The consummate desert camping experience is found in the sand dunes at Liwa, where you can sleep beneath a starry sky and wake up surrounded by one of the world's most mesmerising dunescapes. To get to the perfect camping spots, follow the E11 and take the slip road signposted Madinat Zayed and Mezaira'a. Once you reach Mezaira'a, stock up on provisions and fuel then follow signs for Liwa Resthouse and turn left at the roundabout signposted Tal Mireb (Moreeb Hill). With the giant 300m high dune on your left, camp just over one of the smaller dunes and you'll feel secluded but safe in the knowledge that a solid path isn't too far away. Be warned that this isn't the most peaceful camping site, as you'll hear the drone of dune buggies and sandrails climbing the dune well into the night.

Caving

Where there are mountains, there are usually caves and the rocky eastern part of the country boasts plenty of opportunities for intrepid types to discover what lies beneath our feet.

UAE cavers head to the area around Al Ain, where a network weaves under Jebel Hafeet and, just past Buraimi on the Oman side of the border, there are many more underground passages and caves to explore with spectacular displays of stalagmites and stalactites, as well as gypsum flowers. For more caving suggestions, check out Explorer's comprehensive guide, the *UAE & Oman Ultimate Explorer* or visit the website at askexplorer.com.

Climbing

There are a surprising number of climbing walls in the UAE, which are ideal places for getting started, improving your ability or practising techniques. They are also where you'll meet like-minded individuals, learn about excursions, and pick up pointers from experienced climbers.

Once you're ready to take the leap away from walls and try your hand at some real rock climbing, the region has many challenging verticals and overhangs.

Bouldering

Bouldering is a form of 'free' climbing without ropes or harnesses, and there's a spin-off branch of bouldering known as DWS, or 'deep-water soloing'. For those in the know, the coastline near Dibba and up into Musandam is one of the best places in the world to practise DWS. Basically, hire a boat for the day and find a dramatic cliff with overhangs to climb. The idea is that, when you fall, you'll drop into the deep sea below. Of course, it's more dangerous than that and you should always go out with someone who has done some DWS before.

Adventure Zone
Dalma Mall Industrial City of Abu Dhabi **02 445 8903**
adventurehq.ae
Map **1 N13**
This newly opened superstore is a paradise for outdoor enthusiasts, and you can buy basic climbing gear and loads of outdoorsy items here. More importantly, however, you can practise climbing on a 3.5m high wall – there's over 50 routes, so you'll feel well-prepared when you're faced with the real deal.

Where To Climb

Ras Al Khaimah: The local climbing capital and where you'll find the majority of good ascents.
Wadi Bih: A favourite climbing hotspot.
Wadi Madbah (Oman): Offers some reasonable climbing in the form of the aptly-named Wonderwall.

Desert Rangers
Churchill Business Tower Business Bay Dubai
04 357 2200
desertrangers.com
Map **3 E2** Metro **Business Bay**
Desert Rangers offers rock climbing trips to well-established locations, suitable for everyone from the total beginner to more experienced climbers. Trips include instruction, all necessary safety equipment and lunch. All excursions depart from Dubai and a day of scaling the peaks will cost Dhs.400 per person.

UAE & Oman Rock Climbing & Outdoor Adventures
Various locations **055 770 8629**
Providing rock climbing adventures around the UAE, Oman and further afield, UAE & Oman Rock Climbing & Outdoor Adventures welcomes everyone from beginners to experienced climbers. There's a wide variety of activities, including traditional climbing, bouldering, DWS, sport climbing, caving, and aid climbing, and the company aims to build a large community of keen climbers.

Desert Activities

When it comes to the UAE, there's one place that demands our attention more than any other: the desert. It makes up more than 90% of the UAE and it's the biggest outdoor adventure playground ever. If you can't agree on one desert activity, or want to try them all, join up with a desert tour. Alternatively, load up your 4WD and combine a spot of off-roading with some desert fun!

Dune Buggying

Unless you've got Dhs.60,000 to spare for a neat motorised vehicle used solely for the pleasure of revving up and down dunes, chances are you've not got a dune buggy. But ask almost every adventure junkie in the UAE and they'll tell you that getting out to the dunes to shred some sand is top on their list on fun. Dune buggying is a full-on adrenaline bender spent rocketing across the desert plains in custom-made two-seater buggies that resemble something you might see on a lunar landing.

Sandboarding

Sandboarding is a sport of its own and requires balance, strength and no small amount of tenacity. Once you climb your way to the top of the dune, it's best to wax the bottom of the board to reduce friction between the board and the sand. Strap your feet onto the board, bending your back knee slightly and slide on down, using your heels and toes to turn. All major tour operators (see Desert & Mountain Tours) offer sandboarding experiences with instruction.

Quad Biking

More adrenaline-fuelled than a desert hack and closer to the action than a 4WD tour, on a quad you're down at sand level and feeling every dune contour. It is especially exciting as the routes get more challenging. Riding in sand is a lot different to riding on a conventional track so it may take you a while to 'read' the desert – and your first experience may be a little scary. Just remember to listen to the instructions of the professionals accompanying you.

CARRY WHEN CAMPING

- ☐ Tent (to avoid creepy crawlies, heavy dew, wind and goats)
- ☐ Lightweight sleeping bag
- ☐ Air bed
- ☐ Torches and spare batteries
- ☐ Maps or a GPS system
- ☐ Cool box (fully stocked)
- ☐ Water
- ☐ Food and drink
- ☐ Camping stove, firewood or BBQ and charcoal
- ☐ Newspaper to light the fire
- ☐ Matches or lighters
- ☐ Insect repellent and antihistamine cream
- ☐ First aid kit (including any personal medications)
- ☐ Sun protection (hats, sunglasses, sun cream)
- ☐ Warm clothing for cooler evenings
- ☐ Toilet rolls
- ☐ Rubbish bags
- ☐ Mobile phone (fully charged)
- ☐ Explorer's camping shower

Camping in the desert

Abu Dhabi Desert Safari
Sultan Bin Zayed The First St Al Wahdah
02 446 6346
abudhabidesertsafari.ae
Map **2 M8**
Organises tours that range from day tours to overnight trips. Activities include a camel-back safari, belly dancing performances, sun set from the dunes, and a barbecue dinner. Those on an overnight safari can stay in a Bedouin camp, with the option to try on traditional dress and enjoy various flavours of shisha.

Al Badeyah Eyes Tourism
Sultan Bin Zayed The First St Al Nahyan
02 445 2644
abet-uae.com
Map **1 N8**
Al Badeyah Eyes Tourism aims to give tours that focus on the traditional elements of Emirati desert life alongside various activities, with safaris that involve camel rides, sand boarding, horse riding, henna tattooing, quad biking and barbecue dinners. There are half-day safaris and overnight camps from which to choose, as well as quad biking tours.

Emirates Tours & Safari
Nr RAK Bank Al Firdous St Al Zahiyah **02 491 2929**
eatours.ae
Map **2 R5**
Offering half-day desert safaris, dune buggy and quad bike tours, overnight desert safaris and a full-day tour in Liwa, Emirates Tours & Safari have a team of multi-lingual staff and a range of activities. Camel riding, henna tattoos, and sand skiing are just some of the things you can do on safari, and a half-day tour costs Dhs.290 per adult.

Diving

The warm seas and clear, calm waters of the Arabian Gulf on the UAE west coast and the Gulf of Oman on the east are perfect for exploring the region's varied underwater terrain. There are many dive sites on the west coast that are easily accessible from Abu Dhabi.

Cement Barge is one of the more popular dive sites. Having sank in 1971 when it ran into heavy weather en route to Dubai, this cement barge sits more or less intact and upright in 12 metres of water. Today, it is a magnet for a variety of fish. Located within easy reach of most of the capital's harbours, it's well worth a visit.

Breakwater is known as the 'city dive' and it is located just off Abu Dhabi's Al Bateen area. The area is characterised by a combination of sandy seabed and lots of hard coral growing along the side of the Breakwater. There is also a large container box which attracts a plethora of marine life.

Jazirat Sir Bu Na'air is a small island that lies 70km off the emirates' coast. It's a military outpost and coastguard station, but also a protected turtle breeding area – a fact that makes it a delight for divers. Its nature reserve status means that divers also get to admire some fantastic coral formations and a huge variety of fish.

There are plenty of dive companies in the UAE that can help you should you want to try diving for the first time or improve on your existing diving skills. PADI training is available for all levels, from beginner through to instructor qualifications. Most companies offer both tuition and straightforward dive outings, with equipment provided.

Decompression Sickness
While diving is generally a safe sport, there is always a risk of decompression sickness if a diver stays too deep for too long or ascends too rapidly. One of the first symptoms is aches and pains in the joints, and following that there may be a skin rash or dizziness and other neurological symptoms.

If you notice any of these symptoms after diving, consult a doctor as soon as possible – it is likely that you will need oxygen and possibly hyperbaric re-compression. Before you can receive treatment in a re-compression chamber, a qualified diving doctor must sign a consent form – there's no point just turning up at the chamber.

For diving related questions, you can contact Dr Ronald McCulloch at his Al Noor Hospital Office (02 626 2677). He is a Senior Medical Examiner of divers with years of UAE experience in diving-related issues. The UAE only has two hyperbaric re-compression chambers – one at Zayed Military Hospital in Abu Dhabi (02 444 8100) and another at Aqua Marine Diving Services in Al Qouz industrial area (aqua-diving-services.com).

Snorkelling
If you'd like a glimpse of underwater life without making the investment to become a certified diver, snorkelling is the way to go. It's a great hobby regardless of your age or fitness level and you can pretty much snorkel anywhere off a boat – all you need is a mask and fins. The dive sites listed here are perfect for snorkellers and divers alike.

If you want to venture further afield, head to Sandy Beach Hotel in Fujairah to swim and snorkel around Snoopy Island. In winter, the distance you swim decreases but so does the water temperature. Many hotels in the area also run snorkelling trips to Snoopy Island, taking you there on a glass-bottomed boat. You can also drive to Musandam, just across the Omani border, for a dhow cruise and snorkelling trip; make a night of it and stay at the Atana Musandam or the Atana Khasab (atanahotels.com).

Fishing equipment

and videography. Snorkelling sessions near the Breakwater offer a chance to see plenty of marine life and the centre also organises trips to the east coast, Musandam and even overseas.

Arabian Divers & Sportfishing Charters > *p.219*
Marina Al Bateen Resort Al Bateen **050 614 6931**
fishabudhabi.com
Map **2 C6**
With over 20 years of experience, this company has a complete range of onsite facilities based out of the Al Bateen Marina, including a training dive pool. A range of PADI courses are available, including in specialties such as night diving and wreck diving. They also offer dedicated snorkelling charters, with experienced captains who know the best local spots so that you can spot plenty of exotic fish and turtles. Other activities available include sightseeing boat tours and sports fishing trips.

Emirates Diving Association
Heritage & Diving Villages Dubai **04 393 9390**
emiratesdiving.com
Map **3 E2** Metro **Al Ghubaiba**
This non-profit group aims to conserve, protect and restore the UAE's marine resources by promoting the importance of the environment. It has a coral monitoring project, and organises annual Clean-Up Arabia campaigns. A quarterly newsletter details current activities. Diving enthusiasts are encouraged to join, with membership costing Dhs.100 per year.

Freediving UAE
Various locations **050 613 0486**
freedivinguae.com
This group of divers practises the art of freediving – diving without the aid of breathing apparatus. Freediving AIDA-accredited courses are offered for everyone from beginners to qualified freedivers to give all levels of diver the physical skill, mental preparation and theory training required to practise this challenging sport safely and successfully. Training sessions are held every Sunday and Tuesday, and there are monthly courses, with trips to dive sites in Khor Fakkan organised periodically. Participants must be at least 18 years old to take part and prices start at Dhs.800 for an introductory course.

7 Seas Divers
Nr Safeer Centre Khor Fakkan **Fujairah**
09 238 7400
7seasdivers.com
Map **3 F1**
This PADI dive centre is the oldest in the UAE and offers day and night diving trips to sites around Khor Fakkan, Musandam and Lima Rock. Training is provided at all levels in a variety of languages, and the centre's speedboats are fully-equipped with all the necessary safety equipment.

Abu Dhabi Sub Aqua Club
The Club Al Meena **02 673 1111**
the-club.com
Map **2 V3**
This club, operating from Abu Dhabi's The Club, is affiliated with the British Sub Aqua Club (BSAC), so safety standards are high, and training courses are regularly held for all levels, including beginners. Dive trips take place at weekends, and include locations around Abu Dhabi, Musandam, Fujairah and five other sites in the region.

Al Mahara Diving Center
Nr Main Bus Terminal Al Nahyan **02 643 7377**
divemahara.com
Map **2 N7**
This centre organises PADI training, from beginner open water courses to specialist diving. If you're looking for a career change, the centre also offers instructor training. Special training includes children's programmes, underwater photography

Fishing
Apart from open water fishing, there are plenty of places along the Corniche where fishermen tend to congregate, but be aware that you must first obtain a licence. You can apply and pay online for an annual (Dhs.120) or weekly (Dhs.30) fishing licence (abudhabi.

ae). Some of the other popular shore fishing areas are from the breakwater at Mina Port, from the Corniche opposite the Sheraton Hotel and from Reem Island.

For a chance of hooking bigger bites, or to let someone else handle the licence admin, it's best to get out on the water and hire a fishing guide. From September to April is the peak fishing season, although it's still possible to catch queenfish and sailfish during the summer months.

Arabian Divers & Sportfishing Charters >p.219
Marina Al Bateen Resort Al Bateen **050 614 6931**
fishabudhabi.com
Map **2 C6**
This boat charter company has more than 20 years of experience in the region, and offers dolphin watching trips, scuba diving and snorkelling, boat charters and big game sport fishing. An IGFA (International Game Fishing Association) certified captain is on hand to help you reel in your catch.

Beach Rotana
Nr Abu Dhabi Mall Al Zahiyah **02 697 9000**
rotana.com
Map **2 S5**
The hotel's boat is available for hire for fishing or cruising the pristine waters of the Arabian Gulf. The driver will suggest different fishing spots depending on the season, but with hundreds of small islands just off the coast, good fishing and scenery are guaranteed. For details, contact the hotel or call Mr Sunil on 052 801 7372.

Hiltonia Health Club & Spa
Nr Hilton Abu Dhabi Al Khubeirah **02 681 1900**
hilton.com
Map **2 C3**
An experienced guide from the Hiltonia Beach Club can organise fishing trips, an island cruise or a combination of both which includes a barbecue for the catch. Though the best fishing is during the cooler months, under expert guidance there are big fish to be caught even in the height of summer.

Noukhada Adventure Company
Abu Dhabi-Al Ain Rd Khalifa City **02 558 1889**
noukhada.ae
Map **1 N8**
For something a little different, Noukhada brings you closer to the action with kayak fishing. Because the company focuses on eco-tourism, catch and release is promoted, but that only means bigger fish in the stories you tell your friends. Fly fishing options are offered. The company also organises eco-tours, stand up paddleboarding and moonlight kayaking; kayak tours around the mangroves are also popular.

Sheraton Resort Health Club
Sheraton Abu Dhabi Al Zahiyah **02 697 0272**
sheratonabudhabihotel.com
Map **2 Q2**
Expeditions are run from the resort for deep sea fishing, with large catches of barracuda, hammour, kingfish and shari (seasonal) virtually guaranteed. Everything is provided as part of the trip, including refreshments and equipment, plus there are experienced guides on hand to ensure every trip brings in a successful haul.

Hiking

Despite Abu Dhabi's generally flat terrain, spectacular hiking locations can be found just a few hours outside the city limits. In the very north of the UAE, the Ru'us Al Jibal Mountains are home to the highest peaks in the area, standing proud at over 2,000 metres, while the impressive Hajar Mountains stretch from Musandam in the north all the way down to the Empty Quarter desert (also known as Rub al Khali) in the south. Inland, Al Ain provides some excellent hiking routes, with plenty of mountains, including the imposing Jebel Hafeet, teamed with seven lush oases. Hiking routes vary in difficulty, and range from short, easy walks leading to spectacular viewpoints, to all-day treks over challenging terrain, and can include some major mountaineering.

Safety First
As with any trip into the UAE 'outback', take sensible precautions. Tell someone where you are going and when you should be back, and don't forget to take a map, compass, GPS equipment and robust hiking boots. Don't underestimate the strength of the sun – take sunscreen and drink lots of water. Be particularly careful in wadis (dry riverbeds) during the wet season as flash floods can immerse a wadi in seconds. Also note that there are no mountain rescue services in the UAE, so anyone venturing out should be reasonably experienced or accompanied by someone who knows the area.

Some hikes follow centuries-old Bedouin and Shihuh mountain paths, a few of which are still being used. One of the easiest places to reach is the foothills of the Hajar Mountains on the Hatta Road, near the Oman border. After passing through the desert, the flat, stark, rugged outcrops transform the landscape. Explore any turning you like, or take the road to Mahdah, along which you'll find several hiking options. Other great areas for hiking and exploring include the mountains in and around Musandam and the mountains near the east coast.

The mountains in the UAE don't generally disappoint, and the further off the beaten track you venture, the more likely you are to find interesting villages where residents live in much the same way as they did centuries ago.

For somewhere a bit further afield see *Oman Trekking*, a guide book from Explorer with great pull-out maps covering major signed routes in Oman.

UAE Trekkers
055 886 2327
uaetrekkers.com
This hiking club takes small groups on day hikes or overnight trips. There are a variety of treks that cater to most levels of fitness. Jabal Qatar is one of their more popular hikes, and it is also the trek that everyone must first do if they want to take part in more challenging mountain hikes with UAE Trekkers.

Off-Roading

Getting out into the deserts and wadis by 4WD is a must-do while you're an Abu Dhabi resident and, once you're out there, there are some super hiking and camping spots to take advantage of too. If you're desert driving for the first time, go with an experienced person – driving on sand requires very different skills to other surfaces. Always take a mobile phone, a first aid kit, plenty of drinking water and wear your seatbelt. It's also good to travel with friends in a convoy in case you get stuck or break down.

Tour companies offer a range of desert and mountain safaris (see Desert & Mountain Tours). 4WDs can be hired from most car hire companies (see Car Hire Companies).

Al Ain
The oasis town is worthy of a visit in its own right, but nearby the imposing Jebel Hafeet and Hanging Gardens have great driving spots.

Liwa
A trip to Liwa is one you'll never forget – it's one of the few remaining chances to experience unspoiled dunes. As the drive from Abu Dhabi is long, why not camp or book a room at the stunning Tilal Liwa Hotel, and make the most of your trip. Prepare for the most adventurous off-road driving the UAE has to offer alongside some of its most incredible scenery.

Northern Emirates
For a full day out or weekend away – one that takes in some of the best driving in the Emirates – why not combine a trip to the mountains around Wadi Bih, near Ras Al Khaimah, with one of the interesting wadi routes on the east coast.

East Coast
From Abu Dhabi, the east coast can be reached in about three hours. The mountains and beaches are fantastic spots for camping, barbecues and weekend breaks, as well as various other activities. There are some great wadi and mountain routes here, and the area is also renowned for its diving and snorkelling opportunities, particularly around Snoopy Island.

Desert Driving Lessons
If you're really keen to learn, OffRoad-Zone (04 339 2449, offroad-zone.com), located in Jebel Ali on the way to Dubai, runs a driving centre at the JA Shooting Club where you can practise tackling various obstacles that you might find while off-roading, including deep water, loose rocks and steep descents.

Hatta
The Hatta region is home to the popular Big Red sand dune, a huge draw and a must-do challenge for off-roaders and quad bikers, as well as the Hatta Pools, a great swimming spot in the Hajar Mountains. Both are popular with outdoorsy expats.

For more information and tips on driving off-road, check out *UAE Off-Road Explorer* and *Oman Off-Road Explorer*. These books feature detailed routes and give advice on how to stay safe, where to camp and things to do along the way. If you want a wilderness adventure but don't know where to start, contact any tour company offering desert and mountain safaris (see Desert & Mountain Tours).

Dune bashing

Abu Dhabi 4x4 Club
Various locations
ad4x4.com
This off-road club is based in Abu Dhabi and the club tries to include families in its range of activities. Members can meet other off-road enthusiasts and share off-road driving tips and experiences, at regular events and on the website's forum.

Water Activities

Abu Dhabi offers plenty of opportunities for water-based fun, from the latest craze of flyboarding to the more relaxed thrills of stand up paddleboarding or kayaking around the Eastern Mangroves. Before grabbing your kayak or board, make sure the beach is open to the public. Certain stretches of Abu Dhabi coastline are restricted, so check first before hitting the sand. Also remember that beaches in the UAE are not patrolled as diligently as some European beaches.

Canoeing & Kayaking
Whether after a leisurely paddle along the coastline, or wanting to try your hand at competitive sea racing, kayaking is one of the easiest sports to take part in. Many of the beach hotels provide hourly kayak hire (around Dhs.100 per hour) and tour companies, such as Sea Hawk Watersports (sea-hawk.ae) will take you on a kayaking tour of the Eastern Mangroves.

Mangroves: Taking to a kayak is just about the best way to get up close to the region's wildlife and wild coastline. For a paddle through the lush mangrove habitats of Abu Dhabi, head to Qasr Al Bahr – from there, you can launch your kayak off the jetty.

Khor Kalba: Head over the bridge towards the Children's Park and make your way to the conservation reserve. In most areas of the swamp you'll come across curious turtles that like to pop up and say hello.

Al Ain: If you're looking for a more challenging and intensive ride, try the white water rapids at Wadi Adventure (wadiadventure.ae) where both brave beginners and hardcore kayak enthusiasts can test their skills down one of the three man-made routes. Instruction is available.

Kitesurfing
In Abu Dhabi there are two main kitesurfing beaches close to the city, one on Yas Island and another at Al Dabayyah, which is a half-hour drive west towards Mirfa, although it should be pointed out that neither of these locations boast facilities or lifeguards. There are both individuals and companies that offer kitesurfing lessons for private or group sessions.

Stand Up Paddleboarding
For a great workout and a good way to get out on the water when conditions are still, the new craze of paddleboarding is a welcome addition to the watersport scene. Since the length and width of the board is a generous size, balancing on top of one is far easier than a surfboard. Abu Dhabi Stand Up Paddle Club frequently offers trips around the Corniche and the mangroves.

Wakeboarding
Waterskiing has long been a firm favourite with thrillseekers, while wakeboarding is the cool, young upstart that has become the newest, hippest watersport around. If you don't have a boat, you'll find that many of the big hotels' beach clubs offer the sport with a going rate of about Dhs.140 for 15 minutes.

Cable-boarding
A popular sport in the US and Europe, cable-boarding allows you to wakeboard while being pulled along by a zip line. The Al Forsan International Sports Resort has two excellent cable-boarding lakes.

Wake Park World Championships
The premier Wake Park (Cable) Wakeboard and Wakeskate contest in the world touches down at Al Forsan International Sports Resort every year. Professionals and amateurs battle it out over ramps and ollies to win the coveted champion title.

Jet-skiing
There are several places that offer jetski rental and prices vary. Jetski Dubai is actually located on the Abu Dhabi side of the border in Ghantoot. It's a great, safe area to ride, with the man-made channel running from Ghantoot right down to the sea.

Flyboarding
Flyboarding is the new craze in watersports, where you'll be strapped onto a miniature wakeboard that's connected to a giant hose, that in turn is connected to a jetski. As soon as your jet-skier flips the throttle, water is sent through the hose at high pressure into the board giving you powerful propulsion. Harness that power, balance on a cushion of water pressure – and fly. Check out flyboards-uae.com for flyboarding off Yas Island for Dhs.300 per 30 minute session.

Abu Dhabi Stand Up Paddle Club
Various locations **056 319 2642**
abudhabisup.com
Stand up paddleboarding is exactly what it sounds like: participants stand on an oversized surfboard and use a paddle to propel the board. Hour-long group lessons are available for Dhs.200 per person.

Al Forsan International Sports Resort
Nr Abu Dhabi Golf Club Khalifa City **02 556 8555**
alforsan.com
Map **1 P8**
Two freshwater lakes offer the only cable system in the Middle East, where wakeboarders are pulled along at speeds of 29-38kmph, the controlled environment allowing for quick progress.

Beach Rotana
Nr Abu Dhabi Mall Al Zahiyah **02 697 9000**
rotana.com
Map **2 S5**
Beach Rotana offers a range of watersports, including windsurfing, waterskiing, banana boat rides and laser dinghies. Prices vary, with windsurfing at Dhs.90 per hour. Waterskiing costs Dhs.75 for 20 minutes.

Hiltonia Health Club & Spa
Nr Hilton Abu Dhabi Al Khubeirah **02 681 1900**
hilton.com
Map **2 C3**
A day pass to the Hiltonia Health Club will set you back Dhs.250 at weekends and during public holidays. You can try your hand at wakeboarding, with prices starting at Dhs.75 for 20 minutes or take a kitesurfing lesson (two hours costs Dhs.580). Leave enough time to enjoy the club's spa facilities afterwards.

Kitepro Abu Dhabi
Various locations **050 544 1494**
kitepro.ae
This established kitesurfing school takes students to the best spots according to the weather conditions, and they cater to anyone from beginner to expert standard. One-hour tuition for one costs Dhs.350.

Noukhada Adventure Company
Abu Dhabi-Al Ain Rd Khalifa City **02 558 1889**
noukhada.ae
Map **1 N8**
Open every day except Sunday, Noukhada Adventure Company is best known for their kayak tours of Abu Dhabi's rich mangrove habitats, with sailing lessons also on offer. They run kayak fishing tours too, but because the company emphasises eco-tourism, catch and release is encouraged.

Sea Hawk Water Sports
Various locations **02 673 6688**
sea-hawk.ae
Similar to Noukhada, Sea Hawk also runs tours of the eastern mangroves. If you've taken a tour previously, you can rent a kayak and head off on your own – just don't get lost! If you'd prefer a leg workout, they also rent two-person pedal boats for mangrove explorations. The company also runs diving courses.

Wadi Adventure rafting

UAE Kiters
Various locations **055 755 1439**
uaekiters.net
Kitesurfing is growing a good following in the area. UAE Kiters is a group of Abu Dhabi based IKO-certified gurus who will get you up and kiting in no time.

Wadi Adventure
Jebel Hafeet Al Ain **03 781 8422**
wadiadventure.ae
Map **3 E3**
This resort has three world-class white water rafting and kayaking runs. The top-level run is so challenging that Olympic athletes actually come to train on it during the winter. There's also a huge surf pool that generates a dramatic three-metre high wave every 90 seconds. The rugged backdrop of Jebel Hafeet simply adds to the experience. Entrance costs Dhs.100 and activities are extra.

Watercooled
Hiltonia Beach Club Al Khubeirah **02 639 5997**
watercooleduae.com
Map **2 C3**
Watercooled offer loads of watersports and can be found at the attractive Hilton Abu Dhabi. Water-based options include paddleboarding, wakeboarding and topsy-turvy banana boat rides. Their convenient Corniche location means you'll start off in a protected bay, which can be reassuring for beginners. They also offer power boat hire as well as RYA-accredited power boat courses; a Level One course takes 12 hours in total and costs Dhs.2,000.

TOURS

What better way to experience Abu Dhabi than through customised land, sea or sky tours led by experienced guides? Desert safaris or dhow cruises allow you to take in the beauty of the area while also getting a feel for the traditional Emirati culture. Abu Dhabi's spectacular geographic location makes for an ideal touring site and the surrounding desert is a more-than-just-sand area that begs to be explored. Most tour companies offer desert safaris and dhow cruises, but some offer helicopter tours, diving, mangrove kayaking and snorkelling trips. The water surrounding the coast is teeming with marine life, and the year-round warm weather and calm waters make ideal conditions. Tour companies will work with adventurers to customise their experience. When booking, it is often advisable to reserve spaces three or four days in advance.

Aerial Tours

With its towering skyscrapers and shifting sand dunes, rocky peaks and turquoise waters, Abu Dhabi reveals its wonders from the air. Swoop over the cityscape in a helicopter or take in the serenity of the desert from a graceful hot air balloon (see Desert Tours). Either option will make memories to last a lifetime.

Etihad Towers from above

Falcon Aviation Services
Al Bateen Executive Airport Al Matar
02 444 8866
falconaviation.ae
Map **1 J7**
Take off from Marina Mall in a luxurious six-seater Eurocopter EC130 for a bird's eye view over Abu Dhabi, Saadiyat and Yas Islands.

Hala Abu Dhabi
Etihad Towers Corniche St Al Bateen
02 599 0700
etihad.com
Map **2 B3**
Helicopter tours that sweep the Corniche before heading out to Saadiyat and Yas Islands, taking in Raha Beach, the Sheikh Zayed Grand Mosque and Emirates Palace on the way back.

Seawings
JA Jebel Ali Golf Resort Dubai **04 807 0708**
seawings.ae
Offers aerial tours all over the UAE in its fleet of seaplanes. Tours last 35-45 minutes, depending on take-off point, and up to nine people can fly at a time. Keep an eye out for special promotional prices throughout the year.

Boat Tours

The waters around Abu Dhabi's 200 islands are rich in marine life and on a day cruise you may be lucky enough to spot the local population of humpbacked dolphins or the endangered dugongs on your trip. Between March and July, head farther out and there is the possibility of catching a glimpse of the migrating whale species found in the region, including the blue whale. You can even stop off on a deserted island to explore, barbecue or simply relax in absolute peace.

For a romantic evening spent taking in the city's arresting skyline, several companies run dinner dhow cruises with buffet and entertainment.

As an alternative to an organised tour, you can charter a fully staffed boat for a couple of hours and sail around the Arabian Gulf, admiring Abu Dhabi's stunning coastline with its countless islands and beautiful mangroves. And although there are no organised tours around the islands off Abu Dhabi's coastline, Net Tours (nettoursuae.ae) can tailor a trip for you. Choose which island you would like to visit or sail by and enjoy a personalised island hopping programme; hire a speedboat from Dhs.1,800, or a larger boat for up to 19 people from Dhs.2,400.

Arabian Divers & Sports Fishing Charters (fishabudhabi.com) can also organise private charters onboard a speedboat or 23-metre luxury yacht.

Al Dhafra

Nr Meena Fish Market Al Meena **02 673 2266**
aldhafra.net
Map **2 S1**
As well as dinner cruises, Al Dhafra has several traditional Arabic dhows available for charter.

Sea Cruiser

Al Maya Island Halat Al Bahraini
050 800 9495
seacruiser.ae
Map **3 D3**
Tours in large air-conditioned vessels with huge wrap-around windows as well as plenty of space out on deck. Numerous routes available.

The Yellow Boats

Nr Emirates Palace Marina, Corniche St
Al Ras Al Akhdar **800 8044**
theyellowboats.com
Map **2 B1**
These high speed RIBs offer great tours of Abu Dhabi waters, zipping by the Corniche, Meena Port, and Emirates Palace, but they are not for the faint of heart.

Bus Tours

Big Bus Tours

Nr Carrefour Al Madina Al Riyadiyah **800 244 287**
bigbustours.com
The ideal way to see the best of the capital and get your bearings. It covers 14 must-see sights, including Sheikh Zayed Grand Mosque, the Meena souks, the Corniche WTC Mall, the public beach and the Heritage Village. The 24 hour hop on, hop off ticket includes free entry to the Sky Tower at Marina Mall, and combined Abu Dhabi/Dubai is available if you want to see both cities. Commentary is available in eight languages including English, Arabic, German and French, and the buses are air conditioned.

Desert & Mountain Tours

Desert (and mountain) safaris are by far the most popular tours available here, perhaps because a good safari offers many activities in one day. Expert drivers blast 4WD vehicles up, down and around massive dunes (dune bashing) while passing old Bedouin villages and pointing out beautiful natural attractions. Mountain safaris lead passengers through the narrow wadis and steep passes of the Hajar Mountains. Some tours include sand skiing or surfing and end the day at a replica Bedouin camp where you can watch a belly dancer, eat Arabic delicacies and ride camels. Many operators even run overnight safaris to the desert.

Most driving safaris include pick-up from your place of residence and lunch. The approximate cost for a desert safari is Dhs.150 to Dhs.350 (overnight up to Dhs.500). Many companies offer these types of tours.

Abu Dhabi Travel Bureau

Nr Chamber of Commerce, Corniche St
Markaziya West **02 633 8700**
abudhabitravelbureau.com
Map **2 L2**
All manner of travel experiences are available through the bureau, including desert safaris, cruises, cultural trips and educational visits. They even offer lunch visits to the Burj Al Arab.

Al Badeyah Eyes Tourism

Nr Spinneys, Sultan Bin Zayed The First St
Al Nahyan **02 445 2644**
abet-uae.com
Map **1 N8**
This company offers a variety of exciting desert safaris, dhow cruises and city tours. Desert tours can include overnight stays under the stars. Quad biking tours are also available if you're feeling adventurous.

Al Badie Travel Agency

Al Badie Tower, Hamdan Bin Mohammed St
Markaziya West **02 632 2775**
albadietravel.com
Map **2 K3**
Get ready to try everything from golf trips and F1 Grand Prix weekend stays to off-roading in the desert dunes of the Empty Quarter, culinary tours and Bedouin-style desert safaris.

Arabian Adventures

Emirates Travel Shop, Corniche St
Al Khalidiya **02 691 1711**
arabian-adventures.com
Map **2 H4**
This company boasts a number of well-organised adventures, from desert safaris, city tours, sand skiing and dhow cruises to hot air ballooning, camel riding, and wadi and dune bashing.

Arabian Nights

Al Yasat Tower, Fatima Bint Mubarak St
Al Danah **02 677 9988**
arabiannights.ae
Map **2 P4**
This travel company organises its own experiences focusing on the history and culture of the UAE. One option is to spend a night in The Village, an accommodation complex 70 minutes from Abu Dhabi which recreates a traditional desert village. Guests have the option to stay in huts, cabins or tents and eat authentic Emirati dishes at the on-site restaurant.

Life is **a safari,** let's conquer it **together**

nettours
L e a d i n g   t h e   w a y . . .

Big Bus Tour

Desert Adventures
Al Raha Beach Hotel Al Raha **02 556 6155**
desertadventures.com
Map **1 R7**
Offers cultural trips, culinary tours, safari adventures, kayaking and cruises in traditional dhows.

Desert Rangers
Churchill Business Tower, Business Bay Dubai
04 357 2200 desertrangers.com
Map **3 E2** Metro **Business Bay**
Comprehensive range of tours and safaris, including a number of special interest trips such as dune buggy safaris, rock climbing and deep sea fishing.

Emirates Travel Express
Nr Al Ain Central, Central District Al Ain
03 765 0777 eteholidays.ae
Map **3 E3**
This company boasts safaris, dhow cruises and city tours but also offers adventures further afield, with trips to India, Kenya and beyond.

Net Tours > p.227, 229
Nr Sheraton Abu Dhabi Hotel, Khalifa St Al Danah
02 679 4656
nettoursuae.ae
Map **2 Q3**
A leading, award-winning tour operator in Abu Dhabi, Net Tours organsies action-packed safari camps in both Abu Dhabi and Dubai and has its own fleet of luxury cars and coaches with professional drivers.

Omeir Travel Agency
Airlines Tower, Khalifa Bin Zayed The First St
Al Danah **02 612 3456**
omeir.com
Map **2 M3**
Omeir operates all the usual tours – desert, city and cruises – but sets itself apart with some extremely good offers on local accommodation.

Orient Tours
Nr Sheraton Khalidiya Al Manhal **02 667 5609**
orienttours.ae
Map **2 h4**
Orient Tours has an extensive selection of travel experiences. Expect everything from city tours, desert and mountain safaris to 4WD adventures and cruises. You can even visit horse racing events with them.

Salem Travel Agency
Sultan Bin Zayed The First St Al Danah **02 621 8000**
salemtravelagency.com
Map **2 N5**
Experiences on offer through this popular travel company include falconry tours, city tours, cruises, treks, desert safaris and hot air ballooning.

Sunshine Tours
Al Khaleej Al Arabi St Al Madina Al Riyadiyah
02 444 9914 adnh.com
A wide range of tours from heritage site visits to desert safaris, scenic helicopter rides and dhow cruises on Abu Dhabi's turquoise waters.

Life is **a safari,**
let's conquer it **together**

HOTELS

Much of Abu Dhabi's social scene revolves around the city's many hotels, which are where most residents go for a drink, for dinner, to a nightclub and to relax at the weekend. Dozens of the world's leading hotel brands are found here, many of them housed in some of the city's most interesting buildings. Together they offer access to a plethora of restaurants, bars and leisure facilities, including spas, private beaches swimming pools and even golf courses.

Whether you're going out for Friday brunch, after-work drinks or a romantic dinner, the UAE's licensing laws – alcohol can only be served in hotels or sports clubs – mean that it's likely to take place in a hotel. There is a vast array of choice, from one of the most opulent hotels in the world, the Emirates Palace with a rack rate in the region of Dhs.6,000 a night, right down to the cheapest, more basic digs in areas like Shk Zayed Bin Sultan St, costing under Dhs.250 a night.

If it's high-end luxury you're after, note that many hotels also offer seasonal discounts to UAE and GCC residents. In the hot summer months prices can be 50% lower than at peak times, providing a great opportunity for a bargain break.

The Abu Dhabi Tourism & Culture Authority (ADTCA) oversees a hotel classification system that gives an internationally recognised star rating to hotels and hotel apartments so that visitors can judge more easily the standard of accommodation they will receive. See abudhabitourism.ae for more details. Listed here are Explorer's top picks of Abu Dhabi's hotels, whether you fancy some weekend escapism without the travel or have visitors coming to town and want to put them up either somewhere truly memorable.

More To Come

The five-star Royal Rose is one of the newest hotels in the city, remarkably designed with classic Parisian style in mind and offering Mediterranean food with a fittingly French twist at its fine dining Barocco restaurant. Très bien! Novotel Al Bustan, has just opened too, expanding the staying options for ADNEC visitors. In the near future the Four Seasons on Al Maryah Island is set to open its doors, while Saadiyat Island will welcome a host of new resorts from the likes of Rotana, Mandarin Oriental Hotel and Shangri-La in the next few years – all of which should make picking just one hotel to dine in or stay in an even trickier task.

Staycations

With fantastic weather for most of the year, it's possible to have a mini holiday right on your doorstep rather than having to head overseas. Even if it's just a few miles away from where you live, a staycation in one of the city's hotels can make it feel like you're a million miles away. Below is a list of hotels suited to a variety of budgets that will be sure to give you that holiday feeling.

Al Raha Beach Hotel

Nr Al Raha Mall Al Raha **02 508 0555**
alrahabeach.danathotels.com
Map **1 R7**
In a city known for its big, brash, luxurious hotels, Al Raha was Abu Dhabi's first boutique resort and, although it's located just 20 minutes from the airport, is still a popular retreat to escape to. Rooms have sea views and there is a selection of dining outlets, a health club, spa, two pools, squash courts, watersports and a children's playground.

Arabian Nights Village

Abu Dhabi-Al Ain Rd, Al Khazna 02 676 9990
arabiannightsvillage.com
Map **3 E3**
This is a stunning, secluded resort in the desert. Individual detached houses scatter the sand inside the spacious complex where you can stay and relax by the oasis-like pool and soak up the sounds of the desert. Fantastic food and evening entertainment make it a unique and classy way to experience the beauty of the desert while staying true to the Emirati traditions.

Beach Rotana

Nr Abu Dhabi Mall Al Zahiyah **02 697 9000**
rotana.com
Map **2 S5**
An Abu Dhabi landmark, the busy hotel boasts luxury suites with 414 sea-facing rooms. It offers some of the most popular dining options in Abu Dhabi and direct access to the Abu Dhabi Mall. Leisure facilities include a private beach, a covered children's play area, tennis and squash courts, and swimming pools.

Crowne Plaza Abu Dhabi Yas Island

Yas Leisure Drive Yas Island West **02 656 3000**
ichotelsgroup.com
Map **1 S5**
Sitting right next to Yas Links Abu Dhabi golf course, this hotel has four excellent restaurants and two bars to tempt guests and visitors. For sports and leisure fans, it's just a short walk to both the Yas Marina Circuit and Yas Marina, as well as Yas Beach. If there's a du Forum concert that you'd like to see, check if the hotel is offering a night's stay-plus-ticket value package.

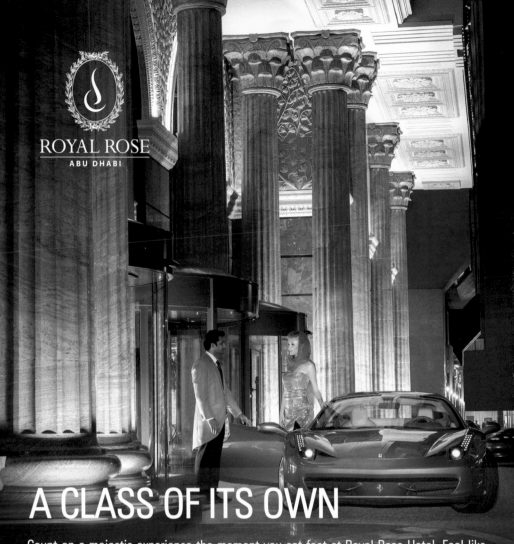

A CLASS OF ITS OWN

Count on a majestic experience the moment you set foot at Royal Rose Hotel. Feel like going back in time with hotel's classy architecture and interior resembling a 17th century French palace. Located at the heart of Abu Dhabi, Royal Rose Hotel offers the best of what the capital has to offer from cultural landmarks to the bustling commercial complex. Check in into a world of luxury along with modern Arabian hospitality at Royal Rose Hotel.

302 Zayed The First (Electra or 7th) Street, P.O. Box 4708, Abu Dhabi, U.A.E
T +971 2 672 4000 | F +971 2 672 0001 | E info@royalrosehotel.com | www.royalrosehotel.com
A member of City Seasons Group of Hotels

Emirates Palace

Corniche St Al Ras Al Akhdar **02 690 9000**
kempinski.com
Map **2 B2**

The lavish, $3bn Emirates Palace – arguably the world's most costly hotel – boasts 392 opulent rooms and suites, all decked out with the latest technology and sumptuous decor. Several outstanding food outlets offer 'seven-star' service and guests can enjoy the private beach, two amazing pools and indulgent treatments at the gorgeous Emirates Palace Spa.

Fairmont Bab Al Bahr

Nr Al Maqtaa Bridge Al Maqtaa **02 654 3333**
fairmont.com
Map **1 L8**

Every bit as luxurious as you'd expect from a Fairmont and part of the Qaryat Al Beri complex, this stylish hotel overlooks the romance of Sheikh Zayed Grand Mosque across the creek. It has two pools and a range of popular bars and restaurants – with Frankie's, Marco Pierre White's Steakhouse and Grill, and The Chocolate Gallery arguably the pick of the bunch.

Hilton Abu Dhabi

Corniche St Al Khubeirah **02 681 1900**
hilton.com
Map **2 C3**

Conveniently located between Abu Dhabi's financial district and Marina Mall, the Hilton is one of the capital's landmark hotels and has 350 beautifully decorated rooms and suites. The Hiltonia Beach Club is one of the city's most popular, with a private beach, swimming pools and a luxurious gym and spa. The restaurants and bars are among Abu Dhabi's most popular.

InterContinental

King Abdul Aziz Al Saud St Al Bateen **02 666 6888**
ichotelsgroup.com
Map **2 C4**

This landmark hotel has 390 modern rooms and suites in a prime location overlooking the Arabian Gulf and a lovely marina. There is a choice of superb eateries, including the always popular Fishmarket and Belgian Beer Cafe, state-of-the-art business facilities, and, for relaxation, a 24 hour gym, beach, outdoor pool, squash court and tennis courts.

Le Royal Meridien

Khalifa Bin Zayed The First St Al Danah **02 674 2020**
leroyalmeridienabudhabi.com
Map **2 P3**

This recently renovated and refurbished hotel has 277 beautiful rooms and suites, most with spectacular views of the Corniche and Arabian Gulf. There are eight restaurants and bars, including the revolving rooftop restaurant, Stratos, and PJ O'Reilly's Irish pub

is packed every night of the week. Leisure facilities include both indoor and outdoor swimming pools and a fitness centre.

Park Hyatt Abu Dhabi Hotel & Villas

Shk Khalifa Bin Zayed Al Nahyan Hwy
Saadiyat Island **02 407 1234**
hyatt.com
Map **1 H1**

Laid-back, elegant and with a sense of effortless luxury, this is a true escape. Looking out over the four swimming pools, landscaped grounds and the private stretch of wild, wave-swept beach, it'd be easy to think that you were in Hawaii or Australia. Despite its 306 rooms, suites and private villas, the sprawling layout makes it feel far smaller and more intimate.

Ritz-Carlton Abu Dhabi Grand Canal

Qaryat Al Beri Complex Nr Maqtaa Bridge
Al Maqtaa **02 818 8888**
ritzcarlton.com
Map **1 L8**

This extensive property has more than 500 guest rooms, suites and private villas, laid out in a Renaissance style around landscaped gardens and large pool and bar areas. Sat beneath the Grand Mosque, it boasts a great location and a huge number of outlets. There's also a cavernous spa and a private stretch of beach.

Shangri-La Qaryat Al Beri

Nr Al Maqtaa Bridge Al Maqtaa **02 509 8888**
shangri-la.com
Map **1 L8**

This luxury resort overlooks the creek and the stunning Sheikh Zayed Grand Mosque – making for a rather romantic poolside vista (of which there are five to choose from). The spa and dining outlets – particularly Bord Eau and Pearls and Caviar – are extremely popular with the city's well-to-do residents looking for an atmospheric night out by the water's edge, and there are more options at the connecting Souk at Qaryat Al Beri.

Sheraton Abu Dhabi Hotel & Resort

Corniche St Al Zahiyah **02 677 3333**
sheratonabudhabihotel.com
Map **2 Q2**

The 272 room Corniche hotel is a long-standing favourite dining venue for expats, with 11 restaurants and bars to choose from; these include a wide range of cuisines to please most culinary tastes. In addition, there's a popular English pub which is good for watching sports. As for leisure activities, the facilities are varied; there are climate controlled outdoor pools, squash and tennis courts, a fitness centre and a private beach offering watersports and volleyball.

St Regis Saadiyat Island Resort
Shk Khalifa Hwy Saadiyat Island **02 498 8888**
stregissaadiyatisland.com
Map **1 G1**

A true beach resort that's quite unlike any other hotel in the UAE, the St. Regis looks more like a California retreat. There are stunning colonial style rooms offering views over the beautiful central pools, restaurants and private sandy beach (and one hole of the neighbouring Saadiyat Beach golf course). The restaurants alone are worth travelling for, and 55 and 5th The Grill is particularly recommended. The perfect place to escape the city, while being just a short drive away.

Yas Island Rotana
Yas Leisure Drive Yas Island West **02 656 4000**
rotana.com
Map **1 T4**

A superb hotel on Yas Island, the Yas Island Rotana has 308 rooms and suites which ooze modern luxury; there are also more sports, fitness and spa facilities than you can shake a tennis racquet at. Another of the city's popular meetings and conferences venues, its food and beverage outlets have also won plenty of fans, particularly Blue Grill, Rangoli and Y-Bar. Yas Island's excellent attractions are all within a short walk or drive.

Yas Viceroy Abu Dhabi
Yas Leisure Drive Yas Island West
02 656 0000
viceroyhotelsandresorts.com
Map **1 T5**

This extraordinary hotel straddles the Formula 1 racetrack at Yas Marina Circuit and became an instant architectural classic and Abu Dhabi icon when it opened in 2009. The property is at once utterly modern but equally tactile, functional, sumptuous and welcoming. Rooms and suites all enjoy incredible views over the racetrack and surrounding Yas Island, and the restaurants are all individually worth a visit. The two rooftop pool bars are otherworldly locations, and the nightlife scene is renowned.

Visitors In Town?

When visitors come to see you there are a few things to consider when recommending where they stay. Do you want them near to where you are, or is having the most suitable hotel more important? Can they afford to splash out, or are they visiting on a budget? This list of hotels covers spots across the city and range from the family (and budget) friendly to the super extravagant. It would be a picky visitor indeed that couldn't find a hotel they love in this lot.

Aloft Abu Dhabi
Abu Dhabi National Exhibition Centre (ADNEC)
Al Safarat **02 654 5000**
aloftabudhabi.com
Map **1 H8**

A true designer offering located at the Abu Dhabi National Exhibition Company (ADNEC), Aloft is a modern, trendy 408 room hotel with a state-of-the-art gym and rooftop splash pool. There's a good range of bars and restaurants, from Dine, the all-day buffet option, to the cool rooftop lounge bar Relax@12 which is a popular hangout for expats.

Dusit Thani Abu Dhabi
Sultan Bin Zayed The First St Al Wahdah **02 698 8888**
dusit.com
Map **2 N12**

The Thai chain's latest UAE offering has an incredibly impressive atrium – it is one of the tallest in the world. Well-equipped for business travellers, it has a huge conference centre, 402 rooms and suites and 131 furnished executive apartments. There's a great rooftop pool and gym, as well as some good dining options including the unmissable signature Thai restaurant, Benjarong. Be sure to factor in a visit to the excellent Namm Spa to sample their extensive menu of indulgent massages and body scrubs.

Eastern Mangroves Hotel & Spa by Anantara
Shk Zayed Bin Sultan St Hadabat Al Zaafaran
02 656 1000
anantara.com
Map **1 H6**

From the elegant but elaborate fixtures and fittings to stunning views out over the mangroves (with not a city skyscraper in sight), Eastern Mangroves is definitely an oasis of calm. Rooms are luxurious but unfussy while, both in terms of service and style, it's 222 rooms offer a delightful mix of the Arabian and the Far Eastern. Steakhouse BOA and Arabic restaurant Flooka, both located in the complex, will have you traveling to your guests' abode for dinner.

Grand Millennium Al Wahda
Al Wahda Complex, Hazaa Bin Zayed St Al Wahda
02 443 9999
millenniumhotels.com
Map **2 M8**

This hotel's convenient location slap bang in the middle of downtown Abu Dhabi, and just a stone's throw from the Al Wahda Mall makes it the ideal choice for visitors intent on sampling the city's many shopping and dining delights. The rooms are bright and modern, the spa and fitness areas are more than adequate and the rooftop pool and relaxation areas are the cherry on the cake.

Hilton Capital Grand Abu Dhabi
Shk Rashid Bin Saeed Al Maktoum St
Al Madina Al Riyadiya **02 617 0000**
hilton.com
Map **1 J8**
Set near to the Grand Mosque and Al Zafranah Park, its location is ideal for ADNEC and for dipping into or out of the city. Inside the stunning curved glass facade are light, modern rooms, a 24 hour fitness centre and some excellent dining options, including the genuinely spectacular Blue, which offers fabulous city views and impressive architecture.

Holiday Inn Abu Dhabi
Shk Rashid Bin Saeed St Hadabat Al Zaafaran
02 657 4888
holidayinn.com
Map **1 H7**
Located between Al Bateen Airport and ADNEC, the 203 room hotel has an excellent, fully staffed business centre and a roof level fitness centre with gym, pool, sauna and steam room. The fitness centre even offers a smattering of reasonably priced spa treatments. Food and drink options are excellent, with a lively pan-Asian restaurant and a fun Thirty 1st bar up near the roof.

Hyatt Capital Gate
Al Khaleej Al Arabi St Nr Abu Dhabi National Exhibition Centre Al Safarat **02 596 1234**
hyatt.com
Map **1 H8**
A business hotel quite unlike any other, Hyatt Capital Gate is located in the world's 'most leaning' building with a mind-bending tilt of 18 degrees. Designed to resemble a tornado, the individuality of the structure is beautifully highlighted throughout the hotel, from the incredible atrium to the overhanging pool. Plus, all the rooms are different shapes and sizes and enjoy breathtaking views. Be sure to dine at 18°, the hotel's signature restaurant, which boasts a great array of Mediterranean-inspired dishes and impressive panoramic vistas over the city.

Jumeirah At Etihad Towers
Nr Emirates Palace, Corniche St
Al Ras Al Akhdar **02 811 5555**
jumeirah.com
Map **2 B3**
Towering above Emirates Palace and offering some of the best views in town, everything here is on a grand and luxurious scale. Finding a balance between business hotel and leisure resort (with a number of residences, a stunning Talise Spa, and stand-alone well-equipped gym), this vast property has something for everyone. The dining options are incredible here too, with many of the tables sharing the same spectacular outlooks as the rooms.

Jumeirah At Etihad Towers

Le Meridien Abu Dhabi > *p.312*
Al Firdous St Nr Old Abu Dhabi Cooperative Society
Al Zahiyah **02 644 6666**
lemeridienabudhabi.com
Map **2 S4**
A recent facelift has rejuvenated this popular hotel's 234 guest rooms and suites. Located in the city's bustling Al Zahiyah area, it's perfect for visitors who want to be at the heart of the action, with plenty of shops, restaurants and bars just a short walk away. Within the hotel, you'll find a good range of top notch leisure facilities, including a private beach, kids' and adults' swimming pools and a health club and spa. The European-style courtyard houses many of the hotel's food and beverage outlets, including a popular traditional pub, The Captain's Arms, and upmarket French, Thai and Italian restaurants.

One To One The Village
Shk Zayed Bin Sultan St Al Nahyan **02 495 2000**
onetoonehotels.com
Map **2 P9**
Resembling a small, European boutique hotel, the One to One group seeks to redefine the region's notion of hospitality, so you can expect a more personalised experience than you might get from the big chains. One To One The Village is within walking distance of Al Wahda Mall (in the winter anyway) but set in a quiet, residential neighbourhood, and the lack of licensed venues will ensure a peaceful night's sleep. For a laid back, alfresco dinner, head to popular The Village Club and choose from a delicious BBQ or treat yourself to something tasty off the a la carte menu.

Park Inn By Radisson, Yas Island

Yas Leisure Drive Yas Island West **02 656 2222**
parkinn.com
Map **1 T5**
A modern and affordable offering on Yas Island, the Park Inn has a particular eye for business travellers and those visiting for Ferrari World, concerts at du Arena and Yas Waterworld. There are 204 rooms (many with fantastic views), two modern meeting rooms, a pool bar and two very good restaurants with the Mexican Amerigos gaining a reputation as a fun venue for groups.

Rosewood Abu Dhabi

Zayed The First St Al Maryah Island **02 813 5550**
rosewoodhotels.com
Map **2 T5**
The 34-floor Rosewood combines modern luxury with Arabic influence perfectly. A host of fine food and drink venues make it a popular spot with residents, especially for the views and proximity to The Galleria. Close to the Central Business District, its ideal for business travellers, with stylish rooms and suites.

Royal Rose Hotel > p.231

Zayed The First St Al Markaziyah **02 672 4000**
royalrosehotel.com
Map **2 Q4**
The new Royal Rose opened in mid 2014 and screams opulence and five-star luxury. Wonderfully central, it is located in the heart of the capital. Its 355 stylish rooms are set on 18 floors and an attractive rooftop boasts two swimming pools, Jacuzzis and city views. The lobby dazzles with a chandelier centrepiece and smiling staff, leading to a galleried first-floor landing and three impressive dining options. The lavish decor, inside and out, is a nod to 17th century France. Meanwhile, a spa and well-equipped gym appeals to tourists and business travellers alike.

Sofitel Abu Dhabi Corniche

Capital Plaza, Corniche Al Danah **02 813 7777**
sofitel.com
Map **2 Q3**
From personal service to exquisite finishing touches, the Sofitel offers a touch of class with modern elegance. Rooms are comfortable and luxurious. The spa is an oasis of calm, or you can relax by the peaceful outdoor pool. Dining options here are top notch.

St Regis Abu Dhabi

Nation Towers Al Khubeirah **02 694 4444**
stregisabudhabi.com
Map **2 D3**
With an enviable location on Abu Dhabi Corniche, this new hotel has over 280 rooms and suites, many of which enjoy gorgeous views over the Gulf.

Along with impeccable service and world-class facilities, the St. Regis is home to the UAE's first Remede Spa – be sure to sample the indulgent treatment menu.

Traders Hotel, Qaryat Al Beri

Abu Dhabi-Al Ain Rd, Nr Al Maqtaa Bridge Al Maqtaa **02 510 8888**
shangri-la.com
Map **1 L8**
This bright, modern hotel is part of the picturesque Qaryat Al Beri Complex that overlooks the creek separating the mainland from Abu Dhabi island. It has a well-appointed gym, relaxed pool area and a private beach. There's only one restaurant in the hotel itself, but plenty to choose from within the complex and in the neighbouring Shangri-La Hotel; try the scrumptious Vietnamese fare at Hoi An or splash out on a lavish meal at the uber chic Pearls & Caviar. Guests also have access to the Shangri-La's facilities.

Westin Abu Dhabi Golf Resort & Spa

Abu Dhabi Golf Club Khalifa City
02 616 9999
westinabudhabigolfresort.com
Map **1 N8**
A smart and peaceful resort located at Abu Dhabi Golf Club, with rooms overlooking the course. Its location on the mainland, away from the city centre, makes it a convenient option from the airport. There are plenty of amenities whether or not you plan to tee off, including two pools and a great spa. It's also home to the outrageous Bubbalicious Brunch at Fairways.

Traders Hotel, Qaryat Al Beri

Thinking hardware? Think again.

There's certainly more to ACE than just a hardware store. From automotive accessories to kitchen appliances, camping gear to barbeques, outdoor furniture to paints and plants, gardening items to pet accessories. There's so much to choose from all under one roof. **ACE. The helpful place.**

SHOPPING

SHOPPING

Spending money is something of a national sport in the UAE; whatever your budget, you'll find no shortage of opportunity when it comes to opening those purse strings.

Shopping plays a big role in everyday life in this part of the world. The malls are gathering places, especially during the hotter summer months when they offer an oasis of cool in the sweltering city – somewhere to walk, shop, eat and be entertained.

But it doesn't end there – the city's shopping highlights include traditional souks and markets, boutiques, a plethora of designer names and a growing number of uniquely original independent stores. One thing that makes shopping here so appealing is the variety; there is very little that is not available and for most items there is enough choice to fit any budget, from the fake designer goods in Markaziya East (between Khalifa Bin Zayed the First Street and Sheikh Zayed the First Street) to the shops in the malls that sell the real thing. You can offload Dhs.30,000 on a state-of-the-art watch, or pick one up for Dhs.10 in a supermarket or souk. You can spend thousands on a designer outfit from one of the top names in fashion, or buy a length of fabric and have a tailor make you up your very own creation for next to nothing. You can buy a treasured Arabian antique from days gone by, or a super-modern home entertainment system.

You will be amazed at how cosmopolitan the goodies are that are loaded in your shopping trolley. If you are an expert bargainer, you can get even better deals at the souks. And for those items with non-negotiable prices, the trick is to wait for the sales – they happen a few times throughout the year and prices are slashed quite significantly.

Ultimately, the UAE is a shopper's heaven, and you won't struggle to part with your money. See the Buyers' Guide to find out where to get hold of what.

NEED TO KNOW

Most shops are open until 10pm every night and even later at the weekends. You can often do your grocery shopping till midnight, and a few of the major supermarkets are open as late as 2am. The malls are particularly busy at the weekend, especially on Friday evenings. Things change slightly during Ramadan, when some shops close from noon until around 7pm.

You may find that imported items and brands, particularly from the international high-street stores, carry an extra few dirhams to compensate for the cost of importing the goods.

to get the best prices. Before you take the plunge, try to get an idea of prices from a few shops, as there can often be a significant difference. Once you've decided how much to spend, offer an initial bid that is roughly around half that price. Stay laidback and vaguely uninterested. When your initial offer is rejected (and it will be), keep going until you reach an agreement or until you have reached your limit. If the price isn't right, say so and walk out – the vendor will often follow and suggest a compromise price. The more you buy, the better the discount. When the price is agreed, it is considered bad form to back out of the sale.

Bargaining isn't commonly accepted in malls and independent shops. However, some shops such as jewellery stores and smaller electronics stores do operate a set discount system so you never know; ask whether there is a discount on the marked price and you may bag a bargain.

How To Pay

You'll have few problems parting with your money. Credit cards (American Express, Diners Club, MasterCard and Visa) and debit cards (Visa Electron) are accepted in shopping malls, supermarkets and many independent shops. Cards mainly use the chip-and-pin system though most shops still require a signature. Aramex also offers a Web Surfer card, a prepaid MasterCard for use online.

Most petrol stations accept cards for fuel payment at the pump though you may prefer to use cash. You are never too far from an ATM in the city and it is preferable to pay with cash in souks and smaller shops – try to have a variety of denominations, because it is better to hand over close to the exact amount. US dollars and other foreign currencies are accepted in some larger shops (and in airport duty free).

Loyalty Cards

Many stores and malls in the UAE participate in nationwide loyalty card schemes. These allow you to earn points while shopping, which can then be redeemed against purchases – so well worth collecting. Shukran, from the region's Landmark Group, has lots of participating shops from fashion to electronics, including Iconic, New Look, Centrepoint and Emax, as well as many restaurants across the capital. Amber, from the Al Tayer Group encompasses Gap, Banana Republic, Areej, Jimmy Choo and Mamas & Papas to name just a few. Several brands have their own loyalty schemes, including Sephora, Virgin Megastore, and Carrefour with its MyClub loyalty card.

Bargaining

Bargaining is still common practice in the souks and shopping areas of the UAE; you'll need to give it a go

Shopping Events

At certain times of the year, Abu Dhabi sees sweeping discounts and promotions. It can be worth holding out for these events to buy certain items, including cars and electronics. While prices are slashed in the shops, many malls hold raffles for big prizes when you spend money – these include cars and large cash prizes. As a result the malls are pretty busy during these periods.

Abu Dhabi Art
UAE Pavilion Saadiyat Island 02 657 5800
abudhabiartfair.ae
This annual art fair takes place in November and is a great place to snap up a bargain or something truly original. Abu Dhabi Art Hub (adah.ae) also holds regular affordable art fairs if you want to start your collection on a smaller budget.

EidFest Abu Dhabi
Various locations 02 444 0444
visitabudhabi.ae
A period during which discounts and prizes are offered in the major malls. You'll also find entertaining performances in those malls throughout EidFest.

SummerFest Abu Dhabi
Various locations 800 555
summerfestabudhabi.ae
This festival runs through the summer months in malls throughout the capital, as well as at ADNEC, the Emirates Palace Hotel and on Yas Island. In addition to prize giveaways and special offers, there are events and attractions to entertain the family. Many of the malls in Abu Dhabi and across the UAE host live music and shows to keep shoppers entertained.

Online Shopping

Knowing where to shop online can be a little trickier than at home. But there's still plenty of choice locally, and delivery is available to your home or office. More online stores are cropping up all the time, and the range is always improving. Souq.com and alshop.com deliver electronics and more in Abu Dhabi at competitive prices. Explorer products are delivered free within the UAE on orders over Dhs.50 – order at askexplorer.com.

International websites are a popular option (such as Amazon UK or US, which both deliver to the UAE), and while not all companies ship to the UAE (and many charge high prices to do so), there are options for getting round this. Aramex (see also Deliveries & Shipping) provides a 'Shop & Ship' service which sets up a mailbox in various global locations including the UK and US and then ships it from there to your UAE address – great for dealing with sites which do not offer international shipping. Borderlinx (borderlinx.com) provides a similar service for stores that will only ship to the USA.

There are sites based in the UAE that will arrange for gifts to be delivered both here and internationally, such as quickdubai.com and papagiftexpress.com, which delivers to India, Sri Lanka, Qatar, Oman and the UAE. International sites are great for sending cards and gifts within the delivery country, such as moonpig.com and Interflora (which operates in more than 150 countries), often with same or next day delivery.

Deliveries & Shipping

The high number of international and local shipping and courier agencies means it is possible to transport just about anything. Both air freight and sea freight are available; air freight is faster and you can track the items, but it's much more expensive. Sea freight takes several weeks to arrive but it is cheaper and you can rent containers for larger items. It is worth getting a few quotes and finding out what will happen when the goods arrive; some offer no services at the destination while others, usually the bigger ones, will clear customs and deliver right to the door.

Aramex

Shk Rashid Bin Saeed St Al Wahdah **02 555 1911**
aramex.com
Map **2 L12**
Offers a great service called 'Shop & Ship' for those wishing to buy online. For a one-off payment of $45, Aramex will set up a mailbox for you in several locations including the UK and the US. The company will then arrange deliveries up to three times a week; packages can be tracked.

Empost

Various locations Abu Dhabi **600 565 555**
empostuae.com
Also known as Emirates Postal Service, Empost offers both local and international courier and air freight services – its prices are competitive and packages can be tracked online. There are branches in Madinat Zayed and Baniyas West.

Refunds, Exchanges & Consumer Rights

Policies on refunds and exchanges vary from shop to shop. It is common to be offered an exchange or credit note rather than a refund. Even with tags attached, many stores will not even consider an exchange unless you have the receipt, and returns must often be made within seven days. For some items, such as those in sealed packages, shops insist that the packaging should be intact so that the item can be resold – a fairly illogical stance if the item proves to be faulty. If you are having no success with customer services, you should ask to speak to the manager, as the person on the shop floor is often not authorised to deviate from the standard policy, whereas managers may be able to offer more flexibility.

The Consumer Protection Department of the UAE Ministry of Economy has been established to safeguard the interests of shoppers. The department tracks and regulates retail prices and has rejected planned price increases for staple goods. It has also mandated that all retail outlets display a notice of their consumer rights policy in the store. Consumers wishing to complain about a retailer can complete a form on the website economy.gov.ae, send an email to consumer@economy.ae, or call the free hotline on 600 522 225.

The Abu Dhabi Food Control Authority (02 818 1111, adfca.ae) primarily deals with unfit food and any cases of reported food poisoning, while the Abu Dhabi Quality and Conformity Council have a website, manaa.ae, where you can report faulty products as well as find out which products have been recalled or don't meet standards.

The Dubai Government's consumer rights website (consumerrights.ae) provides tips and further information on consumer rights which might be useful if you're planning a shopping trip there.

Buyer Beware

Some of the international stores sell items that are far more expensive than in their country of origin (you can often even still see the original price tags). Prices can be as much as 30% higher, so beware.

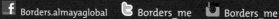

Downtown Abu Dhabi

SHOPPING DISTRICTS

If you're moving to a new area in Abu Dhabi or just planning a shopping trip, it helps to know what your options are across the city. While there is generally a mall within striking distance of anywhere you end up, different areas can also conjure up some different shopping treats. Some places like Mushrif and Muroor are a little more sparse of great shops, aside from Mushrif Mall and a large Carrefour towards the Grand Mosque area; however, as you get closer to the city centre many independent outlets start appearing. Once there, just about anything you need is catered for in Downtown Abu Dhabi or in the numerous smaller shopping centres that follow the Corniche, right down to Emirates Palace. Alternatively, you can try your haggling skills at the souks towards the top of the Corniche near Mina Port. Places like Saadiyat Island can hold a few surprises too, like the growing selection of high-end shops in The Collection precinct at the St. Regis Saadiyat Island Resort.

Corniche & Breakwater

The furthest reaches of Abu Dhabi Island offer contrasting shopping environments. At the southwestern end is the popular Marina Mall on the Breakwater development, where you can browse well-known chains in air-conditioned comfort. Al Meena, at the northeastern end of the Corniche, is Abu Dhabi's main port area and an excellent place for visitors and residents to stroll around and explore. This working port is home to the main fish, fruit and vegetable market, the Carpet Souk, the Iranian Souk and Plant Souk. The Iranian Souk in particular is a treasure trove, selling all sorts of knick-knacks at the best prices. The souks offer an entirely different shopping experience to the malls, and you can utilise your bartering skills.

Dotted along the streets that lead out to the Corniche Road are a number of shopping centres and handy stores, including a good Choithrams.

Al Muhairy Centre

Shk Zayed The First St Al Manhal **02 632 2228**
Map **2 K4**
A nice collection of stores, with a focus on high-end shopping and some of the city's top-end tailors and dressmakers. For kids, there's two play areas.

Avenue At Etihad Towers

Etihad Towers Al Ras Al Akhdar **02 613 3327**
avenueatetihadtowers.ae
Map **2 B3**
A boutique mall containing the most luxurious brands. Spread over two levels you'll find: Cartier, Hermes, Van Cleef & Arpels, Manolo Blahnik, Salvatore Ferragamo, Vertu and a Waitrose for upmarket groceries.

Meena Centre

Nr Toys R Us Al Meena **02 673 4848**
Map **1 D2**
A popular commercial centre with a focus on value, there's an enormous branch of the Abu Dhabi Co-op and a Costless Electronics featuring a vast collection of electronic goods. Costless was gutted by fire in late 2014 with plans to refurbish in 2015. A smaller selection of electronics shops is available in the Co-op.

Nation Towers Galleria

Nation Towers Galleria Al Khubeirah **02 333 8288**
nationtowers.ae
Map **2 D3**
This brand new mall offers a small number of high-end boutique style stores and gourmet outlets including Wafi Gourmet and the Organic Foods & Cafe.

Etihad Towers

Downtown

This buzzing city centre area is the place to go for an eclectic shopping experience. The area is great for finding colourful fabrics and ethnic gifts, while the backstreets between Madinat Zayed and the NMC Speciality Hospital are full of interesting shops selling the things that you can't find in the malls: everything from musical instruments such as ouds, to bizarre electrical appliances and plastic buckets. There are also certain areas that seem to be divided into categories which can be rather handy – one road is lined with opticians, for example.

As well as several shopping centres of varying uses, Abu Dhabi Mall is here and you'll find lots of international fashion brands and an escape from the hubbub of the street. On the edge of this area, right next to the Corniche, you'll also find the new World Trade Center Mall, which houses the first House of Fraser store outside of the UK, as well as the adjacent World Trade Center Souk.

Al Falah Plaza

Nr Jumbo Electronics, Al Falah St Al Dhafrah
02 642 5800
Map **2 M6**
Situated near Habib Bank, this mall is a cheap and cheerful place to stock up on household essentials. Apart from the Lulu Hypermarket on the ground floor, you'll also find a music shop, a pharmacy, a fast food restaurant, a cafe and much more. Stores are open from 9am to 11.30pm, while the supermarket opens at 8am – handy if you need to stock up early in the day.

Al Mariah Mall

Fatima Bint Mubarak St Al Danah
02 671 5577
almariah.com
Map **2 P3**
A range of regional and international shops with a focus on brands that won't break the bank. The shops include Milano and Splash, while eating options range from Chili's to McDonald's. It also houses a FunZone amusement centre with bowling alley and a nine-screen cinema.

Fotouh Al Khair Centre

Shk Rashid Bin Saeed Al Maktoum St Al Danah
02 639 3084
Map **2 L4**
Several of the world's favourite brands are jammed into this spacious mall – Marks & Spencer, Adams, Nine West, and more. Other shops of note include Dune, Monsoon and Accessorize, Areej and Watch House, while Le Atelier Des Artes is great for its quality arts and crafts supplies. Taxi drivers may know it best as the 'Marks & Spencer mall'.

Hamdan Centre
Shk Hamdan Bin Mohammed St Al Danah
02 632 8555
Map **2 N4**

A local shopping institution, this vibrant centre is a good place to buy clothing, leather, shoes, bags, perfumes, sports equipment and touristy knick-knacks, all at reasonable prices. You'll also find a few designer outlets but be careful that you're buying the genuine thing if not from a genuine outlet.

Khalifa Centre
Nr Abu Dhabi Co-operative Society
Al Zahiyah **02 667 9900**
Map **2 R5**

Located behind the Abu Dhabi Co-op building and opposite Abu Dhabi Mall (look for Al Mandoos), this mall is teeming with craft and souvenir shops, as well as shops selling Persian and Baluchi carpets. Be aware that you may find a few controversial items, such as African ivory. If you have strong feelings about this, check before you buy. There's also a Japanese anime fan shop and some interesting tailors.

Liwa Centre
Shk Hamdan Bin Mohd St Al Danah
02 6320 344
Map **2 M4**

This is where to head on Hamdan Street for designer jewellery, clothes, makeup, perfume and more. Be sure to visit the vibrant food court on the second level. If you're not a fan of crowds though, make sure you visit Liwa Centre at quieter times as it does get very busy.

Madinat Zayed Shopping Centre & Gold Centre
Sultan Bin Zayed the First St Al Danah
02 633 3311
madinatzayed-mall.com
Map **2 M5**

Shopaholics will love this mall – it has over 400 outlets selling just about everything from home accessories to clothing. The Madinat Zayed Gold Centre, adjacent to the main mall, glitters with the finest gold, diamond and pearl jewellery. The supervised toddlers' area and a games arcade will keep the kids entertained.

MultiBrand
Fatima Bint Mubarak St Al Danah
02 621 9700
Map **2 P4**

This large, open plan store houses well-known shops such as Mothercare (for baby clothes and essentials) and high-street favourites, Claire's, Next and Oasis. If your taste in fashion is more USA than UK, you'll find the Liz Claiborne outlet a welcome addition. Alternatively, indulge your shoe fetish at Milano.

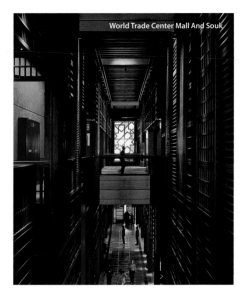
World Trade Center Mall And Souk

World Trade Center Mall And Souk
World Trade Center Al Danah **02 508 2400**
wtcad.com
Map **2 L3**

This brand new mall in the World Trade Center complex is home to the first House of Fraser department store outside of the UK. There's also a good mix of high-street fashion and designer labels, a cinema, a Kool Kidz drop-off 'edutainment' centre for younger children as well as some popular eateries Nando's, Romano's Macaroni Grill and PF Changs.

World Trade Center Souk
World Trade Center Al Danah **02 810 7814**
wtcad.ae
Map **2 L3**

This beautifully themed setting, with traditionally designed wooden panelling, has a growing number of shops and boutiques and attracts faithful regulars, particularly to its many cafes and restaurants. It is part of the wider World Trade Center development, including the World Trade Center Mall that is located right next door.

Business District

The upmarket developments of Reem Island and Al Maryah Island offer something of an exclusive shopping experience. Whilst fairly limited at the moment, future plans should see Paragon Bay Mall open on Reem Island and a host of other outlets to cater for the burgeoning population.

BOUTIK Sun & Sky Towers

Shams Abu Dhabi Al Reem Island **02 674 7850**
facebook.com/boutikmall
Map **2 V8**

A mini mall on Al Reem Island with a large Waitrose. There are also a number of fashion and lifestyle stores spread over two levels, plus a variety of popular food and drink outlets to pick from.

The Galleria

Al Sila Tower Al Maryah Island
02 616 6999
thegalleria.ae
Map **2 T5**

In the swanky Sowwah Square development on Al Maryah Island, the brands here are as exclusive as the address. Luxury fashion brands are plentiful, from Balenciaga and Burberry to Michael Kors and Mulberry, Dolce & Gabbana and Alexander McQueen, and mainstream designer names such as Diesel and Superdry. Fittingly, the mall's restaurants are also top-notch, from Moroccan Al Maz by Momo to Japanese standout Zuma.

Dine With A View

Designer heaven, The Galleria is also a great place for an alfresco supper. You get a different perspective of the city from here, with the Al Zahiyah Area just across the water and the towers of Downtown in the background.

The Galleria

Khalidiya

This is one of the most upmarket areas in the city and its leafy green suburban streets lead to high-rise towers and built-up local shopping areas. Amid wide, open spaces and public parks are bustling, busy streets with traditional shops and eye-catching buildings.

The main shopping draw here is Khalidiyah Mall on 26th (Mubarak Bin Mohamed Al Nahyan) Street, but the area between 7th (Zayed the First) Street and 9th (Al Falah) Street is full of cafes and local shops, offering everything from tailoring to laundry, and chocolate to stationery. It's a great place to get lost and explore on foot at the weekend. For residents, the location near to the Corniche and a short distance away from downtown Abu Dhabi, makes for an ideal shopping launchpad. Anything you want to buy, from cars to pet food, is all within a 10 minute drive from the area.

Dana Plaza

Nr Khalidiya Park, Shk Zayed The First St
Al Khalidiya **02 665 1333**
Map **2 H4**

Packed with outlets selling everything from cosmetics and stationery, to household goods, linen and fashions for the whole family; most of the stores cater largely to local tastes. Abu Dhabi Co-op is open 24 hours a day and bargain hunters should head for the third floor to find a selection of purse-friendly outlets.

Rotana Mall

Sheikh Zayed The First St Al Khalidiya **02 681 4433**
Map **2 G4**

Located between Khaleej Al Arabi Street and Sheikh Zayed The First Street, this mall is best known for a couple of shops selling antiques, carpets, handicrafts, Arabic pottery and wall hangings. Years ago, this was one of the top shopping destinations but bigger and more impressive malls have since taken over.

Grand Mosque Area

The main shopping draw in this area is the Souk at Qaryat Al Beri, but there are several other places worth knowing about, including the many car dealerships that are located on both sides of the Creek. These include a huge BMW showroom close to the Fairmont Bab Al Bahr. There's also a large Carrefour on Airport Road, while Zayed Sports City is home to a Wilson pro-shop for tennis equipment as well as a couple of bowling pro-shops. Head further towards the city and you'll find all sorts of shops tucked in Mushrif and Muroor, from chocolate specialists to small grocery stores, although, aside from Mushrif Mall, it only gets really buzzing as you get closer to the city centre.

Raha Beach & Khalifa City

Several smaller shopping centres in this area provide all the daily necessities and some entertainment options to those living in the new, off-island residential communities nearby. Both Gardens Plaza, home to gourmet groceries favourite Jones the Grocer, and Etihad Plaza are close to the Dubai Road. There's also plenty of shopping opportunities springing up in the area. Nearby Yas Island is home to a huge IKEA, Ace Hardware. More recently, the hotly anticipated Yas Mall opened in November 2014, becoming the UAE's second-largest shopping mall and giving Dubai's shopping clientele a run for their money.

Al Raha Gardens Plaza
Abu Dhabi-Dubai Rd Khalifa City
Map **1 R6**
A smart but small precinct servicing local residents with stores like Boots Pharmacy, Claire's Accessories and Mothercare. There's also a hairdressers, supermarket, Subway and a Jones the Grocer cafe, which all just about cover the necessities. Parking can get tight, but you can park on the development land opposite and cross the normally quiet road.

Al Raha Mall
Abu Dhabi-Dubai Rd Al Raha **02 556 2229**
al-rahamall.com
Map **1 R7**
This reasonable sized shopping centre has a well-stocked LuLu Express supermarket with fresh, appetising produce, along with useful amenities such as a pharmacy, an optician, hair and beauty salons and several bank branches. There's a small cinema playing the latest releases, a foodcourt, and a supervised play centre for younger children.

Deerfields Townsquare
Abu Dhabi-Dubai Rd Al Bahia Old **02 564 5879**
deerfieldstownsquare.com
Drive for five minutes past the airport on the E10 towards Dubai and you'll come across this mall on your left. H&M, BHS, Carrefour, Early Learning Centre, Centrepoint and La Senza are all represented with plenty of space for further stores to come. McDonald's, KFC and Starbucks ensure it has plenty of familiar food options too.

Mohammed Bin Zayed City

This area has several shopping destinations – Dalma Mall just to the west and Bawabat Al Sharq Mall (see Shopping Malls) to the east are both large malls with plenty to keep shoppers satisfied, but there are also some handy smaller shopping centres.

Capital Mall
Mohammed Bin Zayed City **02 419 9000**
capitalmall.ae
Map **1 N10**
Capital Mall only opened in February 2014 and boasts a wide range of stores including a large hypermarket, a few pharmacies, fashion shops along with an indoor garden that also plays host to a range of family events. There is also a large children's entertainment centre.

Mazyad Mall
79th Street Mohammed Bin Zayed City **02 553 2200**
mazyadmall.com
Map **1 P10**
This light, airy mall is not what you'd call a shopping hotspot, but there's a well-stocked LuLu Express supermarket, as well as fashion outlets, cafes and a small foodcourt. The Mall leans more towards family outings than fashionista shopping sprees.

Pink Shops

If you're in Khalifa City then you'll probably find out about the Khalifa City Market shops, known locally as the 'Pink Shops' due to the pink tinge of the buildings. This enclave of independent shops are set on their own and house a kid's hairdressers, fruit and vegetable shops, supermarket, gardening shops and just about everything else you'll ever need. This is a popular market area and makes a great change from visiting the large shopping malls.

Mazyad Mall

PLACES TO SHOP

Depending on what you need to buy, or how you want to spend your day, Abu Dhabi has a place to shop that will match your mood. While the magnificent malls are fantastic places to be entertained, eat and buy from many top international stores, there are also smaller shopping centres, hypermarkets and souks to help you spend your dirhams.

The souks and markets offer a surprisingly authentic Middle Eastern shopping experience – bargaining can be fun and rewarding, and you never know what you might come home with, from fresh fish to Iranian plant pots. The hypermarkets, on the other hand, stock all manner of international brands and you can shop knowing what to expect.

Overall, don't panic that you can't head to your favourite organic grocery store or department store – you're bound to have a new favourite in no time, and many of the chains you are used to are right here.

Department Stores

Department stores are at the heart of some of Abu Dhabi's biggest malls with British stalwarts like Marks & Spencer, Debenhams and most recently, House of Fraser at Yas Mall. Also represented are South Africa's Woolworths, and the regional Jashanmal.

Centrepoint
Marina Mall Breakwater **02 681 5972**
Map **2 D1**
centrepointstores.com
Shopaholics will love this store, a one-stop shopping destination that houses Babyshop, Splash, Lifestyle, Shoe Mart and Beautybay all under one roof. You can dress your family head to toe in one easy shopping trip – and without breaking the bank. Other locations include Deerfields Townsquare and Dalma Mall.

Debenhams

Khalidiyah Mall Manhal **02 635 4994**
debenhams.com
Map **2 H5**
A mainstay of the British high street, it's a go-to for perfumes, cosmetics, homewares and clothing for men, women and children. Brands include Evans, for plus-size clothing, Warehouse and Miss Selfridge, as well as the reasonably priced Designers at Debenhams range that includes John Rocha and Jasper Conran. There are also branches at Dalma Mall and Yas Mall.

House of Fraser

World Trade Center Mall Al Danah **02 627 7558**
wtcad.ae
Map **2 L3**
Brits will be happy with the popular upmarket department store's first outlet outside of the UK. Exclusive brands include Biba, Therapy and Ush, and designer names include Vivienne Westwood. There's a personal shopping service and a Hello Kitty mother and daughter spa.

Jashanmal

Abu Dhabi Mall Al Zahiyah **02 645 6454**
jashanmalgroup.com
Map **2 S5**
A main shopping destination for dinnerware, cookware, bed and bath accessories and home appliances. It also sells a small range of clothing and underwear, perfume and books, and its luggage section is particularly good. It's also located at Marina Mall and Khalidiyah Mall.

Marks & Spencer

Fotouh Al Khair Centre Al Danah **02 621 3646**
marksandspencerme.com
Map **2 L4**
A renowned UK brand, 'M&S' sells clothes and shoes for men, women and children, including a revered underwear range, along with a small, but cultishly popular, selection of food and sweets. The UAE stores carry selected ranges which include Per Una – high-street chic – as well as more classic lines. There's also branches at Marina Mall and Dalma Mall.

Paris Gallery

Abu Dhabi Mall Al Zahiyah **02 645 5004**
parisgallery.com
Map **2 S5**
Set up as a 'luxury retailer', the Paris Gallery stores are home to over 450 international brands covering areas like perfumes, cosmetics, sunglasses and watches. There are other branches in Khalidiyah Mall, Marina Mall and Abu Dhabi Mall which follow the company's ethos of offering true Arabic hospitality, making for a more unique shopping experience for expats.

Salam

Abu Dhabi Mall Al Zahiyah **02 645 6999**
salams.com
Map **2 S5**
This local department store has a good mix of brands and stocks homeware, jewellery and clothing. Designer names on offer include Betsey Johnson, Roberto Cavalli plus LA brand Gypsy 05.

Woolworths

Marina Mall Breakwater **02 681 0881**
woolworths.co.za
Map **2 D1**
A home away from home for South Africans, and renowned as the place to go for high-quality clothes, shoes and home textiles (towels and bedding). The range offers something a little different to standard (UK and US) goods. They also do a great range of accessories and underwear.

Hypermarkets

For a one-stop shop for almost anything you can think of, hypermarkets are the place to go. With a range that goes far beyond food, most sell a range of electronics and home appliances at competitive prices, as well as toys, homewares, luggage, clothes, shoes, music and DVDs and much, much more. Aside from the big names listed below, Abu Dhabi is also home to K.M. Hypermarket in Mussafah.

Carrefour

Nr Zayed Sports City Al Madina Al Riyadiya **800 73232**
carrefouruae.com
Map **1 J8**
Renowned for its competitive pricing and special offers, branches of this French chain can be found throughout the city. As well as a good range of French food products (it's the best place to get crusty, freshly baked French sticks) and a small health food section, there's a fairly comprehensive range of electronics and household goods. Camping gear and car accessories are also on sale here, in addition to garden furniture and hardware. Non-food items can be ordered online.

Emirates General Market

Shk Zayed The First St Al Danah **02 631 6262**
luluhypermarket.com
Map **2 M3**
A destination for the cheap and cheerful rather than designer chic. Known locally as EmGen, you'll find clothes, sportswear, watches, electronics, music and much more. Owned by the same group as the LuLu chain of supermarkets, EmGen stores can also be found in several other locations across the city.

LuLu Hypermarket
Khalidiyah Mall Manhal **02 635 4100**
luluhypermarket.com
Map **2 H5**
Great for those on a budget; LuLu's hot food counters, salad bars and fishmonger are particularly good value, as is the wide-ranging fruit and vegetable section. It stocks a good range of ethnic foods and an ever-increasing amount of western brands and health conscious ranges including gluten free, organic and more. Stores, located across the city, have a range of home appliances and an area selling colourful saris.

Convenience Stores

Aside from the larger supermarkets and hypermarkets, Abu Dhabi has a huge number of smaller convenience stores selling many basic food, drink and essential products, such as toiletries. In 2013, the Abu Dhabi Food Control Authority closed many of these down as they had failed to comply with new food storage and hygiene regulations, with requirements including the fitting of automatic doors, steel roofing, CCTV, a computerised till and lower, more accessible shelves. Those that shut down are gradually being replaced by more branches of good supermarkets, such as Spinneys, to ensure many of the more densely populated areas of the city are serviced for local groceries. If you live close to a convenience store it's quite usual to phone them up and have them deliver small amounts of groceries to you too, with the only extra cost being a tip for the delivery guy.

Supermarkets

Unlike hypermarkets, supermarkets concentrate solely on food and domestic necessities such as cleaning products and toiletries. They all tend to have their own kitchens that cook up freshly baked goods, with some larger stores offering quite an impressive range of pies, samosas and pasties. Some even have fish and meat counters for you to peruse.

You may find that the prices between different brands of supermarket can vary quite dramatically, while the quality of some items like fruit and vegetables can be equally varied; this means it can pay to visit a couple of different supermarkets to get the best balance of quality and price when completing the grocery run.

Abela Supermarket
Al Nahyan St Al Khalidiya **02 667 4675**
Map **2 H4**
Abela is a 'super-store', with a range of shops offering stationery, video rental, books and magazines, dry-cleaning services and jewellery (and much more). In terms of food, Abela has a good selection with a pork section and a good fresh fish counter. There is another popular branch at Etihad Plaza in Khalifa City.

Abu Dhabi Co-Operative Society
Madinat Zayed Shopping Centre & Gold Centre Al Danah **02 632 4500**
abudhabicoop.com
Map **2 M5**
With branches all over the city (some are open 24 hours), this popular store has a good selection of fresh food and vegetables. It sells its own brand of goods as well as international products. Some larger stores have interesting extras like date and spice counters.

Choithrams
Nr Oryx Hotel Al Khalidiya **02 681 6930**
choithram.com
Map **2 F4**
Choithrams is renowned in the UAE for stocking British, American and Asian products. Its stores (there is a second one in Al Khalidiya) have excellent frozen sections and a great range of baby products – particularly food and formula.

Geant Easy
Airport Road Khalifa City **02 556 8836**
geant-uae.com
Map **1 R9**
French chain Geant offers everything you'd expect from a neighbourhood supermarket. Other locations include Marina Square, Reem Island and the largest Geant in Abu Dhabi within Yas Mall.

Abu Dhabi supermarket

Organic Foods & Cafe

Delis, Gourmet & Health Foods

If you have tastebuds that can only be satisfied by the best or healthiest ingredients then you'll soon find yourself in one of Abu Dhabi's gourmet cafes. While you're unlikely to do your weekly shop here, the addition of gourmet or organic stores to some of the city's most popular cafes adds a welcome hit of unusual ingredients, hard-to-find treats or just good, honest, fresh fruit and veg. Places like Jones the Grocer even sell swanky kitchen utensils if you're after some designer touches.

Jones The Grocer

Sultan Bin Zayed The First St Al Nahyan
02 443 8762
jonesthegrocer.com
Map **2 N10**

A gourmet food store that offers deli items and fresh produce. Its international produce is largely free from additives and preservatives and is a particularly good place to fill up your picnic basket. It also has a bakery and cafe, which are very popular with shoppers in the know (particularly for breakfast). Jones the Grocer also hosts many social food related events and workshops, offers a catering service and has popular offers and menus especially designed with kids in mind. If you're a fan of international cheeses, make note not to miss the specialist cheese room in select branches. There six locations in the capital, and the most recent one opened in 2014 in the picturesque Al Muneera area.

Organic Foods & Cafe

Masdar Khalifa City **02 557 1406**
organicfoodsandcafe.com
Map **1 U7**

Long an institution in Dubai, Organic Foods and Cafe now has branches in Abu Dhabi. The store is an organic supermarket, as well as a cafe, and has a good range of products, from fruits and vegetables to skincare and cleaning products. Catering and delivery services are also available. Check the website for details of regular monthly promotions. A second location opened in late 2014 at the popular Nation Towers Galleria.

Spar

Nr Prestige Cars Al Khalidiya **02 679 6491**
spar-international.com
Map **2 G4**

The Dutch retail giant, Spar, is expanding in Abu Dhabi with a supermarket near the Corniche and a hypermarket – with good deli and fresh produce sections – tucked away in Khalifa City. There's also an express store in the Al Zahiyah Area, with more planned throughout the city.

Spinneys > p.v

6th Corniche St Al Khubeirah **02 681 2897**
spinneys-dubai.com
Map **2 E4**

Spinneys, which has seven stores in the city, plus one in Al Ain and another in Ruwais stocks the Waitrose range and other British products, as well as a great range of South African, Australian and US products. The bakery is brimming with freshly baked treats and it is definitely one of the best places to go for pork.

Waitrose

Etihad Towers Al Ras Al Bateen **02 447 1987**
waitrose.com
Map **2 B3**

This upmarket UK chain is well known for its premium range of British produce and gourmet goods, and this is reflected in the prices. It has a well-stocked deli filled with hot and cold selections of pre-made dishes and a great selection of baked goods, meat and cheese. It has other locations at Al Zeina, Reem Island and the Eastern Mangroves Promenade.

Al Rawafed Organic Farm

A little out of town on the Sweihan Road is Al Rawafed Organic Farm, which supplies the likes of Ripe and Etihad Airways with fresh, chemical-free and tasty produce. The farm is currently undergoing expansion, but is hoping to start holding market days and perhaps even some family-friendly attractions. Keep an eye out for more information.

Markets

Several markets more familiar to western expats than the traditionally styled souks now open in the city. You'll find the feel is less rustic and daunting than when visiting the souks for the first time but offer the same great food items, with similar great value.

World Trade Center Mall And Souk
Mushrif Mall Al Mushrif
Map **2 L3**

Formerly known as Central Market as it was built on the site of the city's old souk, the opening of the World Trade Center Souk and the adjacent World Trade Center Mall have revitalised the city center with their eclectic mix of shops, restaurants, and rooftop cafes. The architecture of the Souk is stunning, combining elements of traditional Arabia with something altogether more modern to create a maze of wooden hallways and partitions set over three storeys. The Mall takes the same theme and modernises it further to create a bright shiny mall with a few throwback touches. Don't miss the lovely roof terrace connecting both buildings; the scene is especially beautiful at night. Shops in the Souk are one of the best places to find souvenir gifts and regional artefacts, and the rooftop cafes are popular spots for shisha. Next door at the mall, you'll find a plethora of high end stores – it's anchored by the first Middle East outpost of Fraser – as well as a Spinneys, a bookstore, and a medical clinic.

Ripe
Al Raha Gardens Al Raha 04 380 7602
ripeme.com
Map **1 K7**

Ripe hosts a pop-up farmers' stall every Monday from 1pm to 3pm at Jones The Grocer, Al Raha Gardens, selling fresh local produce. They recently launched their first Ripe Food and Craft Market in Abu Dhabi on Saturdays, at St Regis, which will also include gourmet food stalls and offerings from local artisans. Produce is seasonal and can include anything from leafy, fragrant basil and irregular-sized courgettes, to potatoes with dirt still clinging to them.

Souks

The souks are the traditional trading areas, some more formally demarcated than others. In keeping with tradition, bargaining is expected and cash gives the best leverage. They are worth a visit for their bustling atmosphere, eclectic variety of goods, and the traditional way of doing business. The modern souks tend to be more like malls with high-end shops but with a nod to traditional architecture.

Al Meena Fruit & Vegetable Souk
Nr Iranian Souk Al Meena
Map **2 U1**

Across the road from the Fish Souk, this is a relaxed affair. Cruise around until you spot a shop stocking most of the items you need. The price and quality of the stock is often better than in the supermarkets and you can buy by the kilo or the box, but do arrive early as the best produce exchanges hand in the first hours of trading. There is another fish and vegetable souk in town between Al Istiqlal Street and Al Nasr Street.

Carpet Souk
Al Meena St Al Meena
Map **2 U2**

Also known as the Afghan Souk, Yemeni mattresses and machine-made carpets dominate here, but bargains can be found if you know what you are looking for. Found on the port end of Al Meena Road, some of the vendors will make Arabic 'majlis' cushions to order for a very reasonable price. Don't forget to haggle.

Fish Souk
Nr Al Dhafra Al Meena
Map **2 T1**

Fish doesn't get much fresher than this. The day's catch is loaded onto the quayside and sold wholesale from 4:30am. They move onto smaller quantities after 6:30am and you have to be there early to get the best fish. While the atmosphere is electric, it is not a place for the faint-hearted, as the smell can be pretty strong.

Iranian Souk And Plant Souk
Nr Fish, Fruit & Vegetable Souk Al Meena
02 444 0444
Map **1 D2**

It may not be air-conditioned, but fresh batches of Iranian goods arrive at this authentic souk every three days by dhow or barge. Everything is on sale, from household goods and terracotta urns, to decorative metal, cane or glass items and a great place for plants is nearby at the Plant Souk which lies adjacent and extends from the Iranian Souk along the road in the direction of the Fish Souk.

The Souk At Qaryat Al Beri
Qaryat Al Beri Complex Al Maqtaa 02 558 1670
soukqaryatalberi.com
Map **1 L8**

A contemporary adaptation of a typical souk that forms part of a larger creekside complex with the Shangri-La and Traders hotels. Although over-priced, you can find niche items such as antiques, heritage items, souvenirs and gifts here. There's also an excellent collection of cafes, bars and restaurants with alfresco dining and spectacular views over the water to the Sheikh Zayed Grand Mosque.

Fish Souk

World Trade Center Souk And Mall

Carpet Souk

Souk at Qaryat Al Beri

Getting Started:
10 Shops To Set You Up

IKEA cafe

Whether you're waiting for your freight to arrive from overseas, or are staring at a big empty apartment, you'll need to turn your house into a home. Pretty much anything you'll ever need can be found in these convenient and affordable stores, and at the lowest prices in the city save some serious haggling at the souks. Delivery on larger items is usually free, too.

IKEA
Budget-friendly, well-designed furniture you can take straight home. Also stock up on bits for the house – from towels to tealights, cutlery to curtains.

Carrefour
Stock up on home appliances: toaster, kettle and fridge, and fill your kitchen cupboards with good international branded products as well.

Sharaf DG
Appliances, electronics and related accessories at very welcoming prices.

Ace Hardware
Everything you need for DIY around the house, plus garden furniture and plants, as well as outdoor equipment to get you ready for some exploring in the desert.

Home Centre
Put the finishing touches on your new home with items from this classy but affordable range of essential homeware.

Centrepoint
This is a one-stop shop for several handy and affordable brands – clothe your kids, stock up on baby essentials and decorate the home.

LuLu Hypermarket
Great for all the household essentials – cleaning products and cheap necessities – as well as stocking up on tins and basics. The fruit and veg section is also brilliant.

Emax
A wide range of electronic brands to get your home entertainment sorted, from TVs and games consoles to wireless routers, plus a range of cameras to document your UAE adventures with.

Modell's Sporting Goods > p.178
This popular store is among the city's best for sports gear, clothing and accessories. There are branches in Abu Dhabi Mall and the World Trade Center Mall.

dubizzle.com
Anything you can think of – from cars to furniture, someone will be selling theirs at a pre-owned price on this online expat institution.

Shop Online
Check out these local online stores and you won't even need to leave the house.

carrefouruae.com/webstore
tejuri.com
souq.com
alshop.com
ikea.com
sharafdg.com

Groceries
Chances are high that your local convenience store will deliver to your door, night and day. Pop inside and ask for a phone number, and you'll never need to nip out for milk again.

Shopping Malls

Shopping malls are not just places to shop; a definite mall culture exists here and people come to the malls to meet, eat, play and mingle. Many malls provide entertainment and people of all ages can easily enjoy hours of fun inside them, even without shopping. Smoking is banned in all of Abu Dhabi's malls (and some of the bars attached to them), which makes them clean, pleasant and family friendly.

With so much choice out there, most malls try to offer something unique to draw the crowds, meaning you're likely to end up with a favourite. Some, like Souk Qaryat Al Beri and the World Trade Center Souk And Mall, feature remarkable, modern re-imagining of a traditional Middle Eastern marketplace. Others, such as the newest Yas Mall on Yas Island are huge arenas not only for shopping but for dining out and entertainment too.

Most malls have at least one children's play area, where you can leave your children under supervision while you shop. Many malls will host performances and entertainment for children throughout the year.

At certain periods, however, activities are heightened to draw the crowds. SummerFest Abu Dhabi and EidFest for example, are festivals that run in malls across the capital with giveaways and special offers, and there are plenty of events and attractions aimed at the younger members of the family.

There is another sale period in January and February, when big discounts are offered in stores. In addition, the annual Dubai Shopping Festival, which also runs for a month around this time of the year and features gradually increasing discounts, is an important attraction. Keen shoppers might not want to miss a visit to The Dubai Mall, the largest in the country, or to the popular boutique-style mall, Saga World Mall, which is also in neighbouring Dubai.

Although they're often remarkably quiet and pleasant to stroll through during the day, almost all of Abu Dhabi's malls get extremely busy during these events. This is especially true of evenings during Ramadan. Regular weekends and evenings, particularly weekend evenings, also attract hoards of shoppers; if you're not a fan of crowds, it's probably best to avoid hitting the mall at these times. Most of the malls have plenty of parking and well-served taxi ranks, although both are often stretched to their limits at weekends when everyone turns up to shop.

Abu Dhabi Mall

Nr Beach Rotana Al Zahiyah
02 645 4858
abudhabi-mall.com
Map **2 S5**
One of the main destinations for shopaholics, Abu Dhabi Mall has more than 200 retail outlets covering a broad range, but it's particularly useful if you're looking for jewellery or gifts. There's also a good range of designer clothes shops as well as more mainstream fashion brands, plus a large branch of Abu Dhabi Co-op, a Paris Gallery department store, a Virgin Megastore and a Borders bookshop. There are plenty of restaurants and fast food outlets, as well as a nine-screen Cineplex and a kids' play area. Baby trolleys are available for hire, and the mall provides shop-mobility assistance and rents out electric wheelchairs at the customer service desk on level one. There's also a mother and child room and a feeding area, and a mall-walking club. The mall hosts promotional exhibitions throughout the year, including the popular Christmas Market, which takes over the walkways.

Al Wahda Mall

Nr Al Wahda Sports Club, Hazza Bin Zayed Street Al Wahdah **02 443 7070**
alwahda-mall.com
Map **2 M7**
Located right in the heart of the city, Al Wahda's spacious sun-roofed design is fresh and inviting and, although the layout is open and spacious, it also has a myriad of side passages leading shoppers to hidden delights like Rage skate shop. The mall features a wide range of western brand stores including Gap, Banana Republic and Mamas & Papas, while there's a sizeable branch of Magrudy's that stocks toys and supplies for crafts and hobbies, as well as a wide range of books. More books can be found at the popular British WH Smith store in the fabulous new extension. One of the mall's biggest draws is LuLu Hypermarket, which has a huge choice of products and is particularly popular for its deli counter and pre-prepared meals. For entertainment there's a cinema plus Wanasa Land, with bowling, arcades and pool tables. The mall is home to the usual host of cafes and fast food joints, and there is a sprinkling of higher end restaurants providing more substantial fare too.

Bawabat Al Sharq Mall

Nr GEMS Cambridge Sch Baniyas East **02 503 1400**
bawabatalsharq.ae
Map **3 D3**
This shopper's paradise consists of more than 300 stores, a Carrefour hypermarket, a Grand Cinemas complex, and a Wanasa family entertainment centre. It is also one of the easier malls to find parking at. As well as fashion staples, such as H&M, Springfield and Centrepoint, there's a Victoria's Secret and the city's first branch of Gocco – the kids' fashion brand from Spain. There is also an excellent selection of pharmacies and opticians, and plenty of food and drink outlets scattered throughout the mall. It's a little way out of the city, to the south east, but well worth the trip – there is even a traditional souk area.

Al Wahda Mall

Abu Dhabi Mall

Bawabat Al Sharq Mall

Yas Mall

Dalma Mall

Khalidiyah Mall

Dalma Mall

Nr Mussafah Police Station Industrial City Of
Abu Dhabi 1 **02 550 6111**
dalmamall.ae
Map **1 N13**

Located in Mussafah, this excellent mall has over 300
stores and is now a firm favourite in the city. The mall
is anchored by a large Carrefour, Home Centre, Toys R
Us and one of the country's biggest Marks & Spencer
stores. It is also home to an array of international
brands, like H&M, Warehouse, Miss Selfridge, Topshop,
American Eagle Outfitters, Debenhams and is the
only Abu Dhabi location for Pottery Barn, a popular
purveyor of shabby-chic housewares. There's also a
large foodcourt, a giant 14 screen Cineplex, plus an
indoor skate park, cable climb and trampoline park at
Adventure HQ, as well as a FunCity play zone. There
are over 40 international restaurants to choose from.

Khalidiyah Mall

Mubarak Bin Mohd Al Nahyan St Al Manhal
02 635 4000
khalidiyahmall.com
Map **2 H5**

Not to be confused with the older, smaller Khalidiyah
Centre just up the road, Khalidiyah Mall remains a
popular shopping venue and is often known as the
'British' mall due to the high number of UK high-street
stores. Located on Mubarak Bin Mohamed Al Nahyan
Street in Khalidiya, highlights include a large branch
of LuLu Hypermarket and department stores such as
Debenhams, BHS and Paris Gallery. The usual food and
drink outlets include Bricco Cafe and Cantina Laredo.
Entertainment options include the large Sparky's
Family Fun Centre, which has rides, a bowling alley, an
ice rink and a CineRoyal cinema.

Marina Mall

Breakwater **02 681 2310**
marinamall.ae
Map **2 D1**

Situated in Breakwater, but still within easy reach
of the city's many residential areas, popular outlets
include global favourites, such as Carrefour, Sun &
Sand Sports and Woolworths. Restaurants, fast food
outlets and coffee shops aplenty offer fuel for weary
shoppers, including the restaurant and cafe at the top
of the impressive Sky Tower, which offers panoramic
views over the city to enjoy with your coffee. A nine-
screen Cinestar complex, an indoor entertainment
zone, the Fun City amusement centre and the musical
fountains near the main entrance will keep you and
your little ones busy. There's also a big bowling centre
and a small ice rink. On the same plot but with a
separate entrance is a large Centrepoint department
store and a Home Centre, where you'll find everything
from shoes, fashion and baby items to homeware.

Mushrif Mall

Shk Rashid Bin Saeed Al Maktoum St Al Mushrif
02 690 4422
mushrifmall.com
Map **1 G7**

This mall serves mid-islanders well. Anchored by LuLu
Hypermarket, it is home to a great mix of over 200
shops and an Indoor Market where you can buy fish
from all over the world. There's a large dining court
and Sparky's indoor amusement park. The impressive
aquarium wrapped around the elevator is quirky.

Yas Mall

Nr Ferrari World Yas Island
yasmall.ae
Map **1 T4**

The newest, most exciting addition to the Abu Dhabi
shopping scene, Yas Mall, opened in November 2014
becoming the second largest mall in the UAE after
The Dubai Mall. Take your pick from over 400 stores,
including Zara, Nike, H&M, Virgin, the UAE's first Lego
store and Abu Dhabi's largest Geant hypermarket
and a Debenhams department store. The huge mall
has a 20-screen Vox cinema while the Fun Works
entertainment zone will keep kids amused for hours.
If hunger hits, there are many popular restaurants and
cafes, such as Abu Dhabi's first Cheesecake Factory,
plus Shake Shack, Shakespeare and Co, and Paul Cafe.

Mushrif Mall

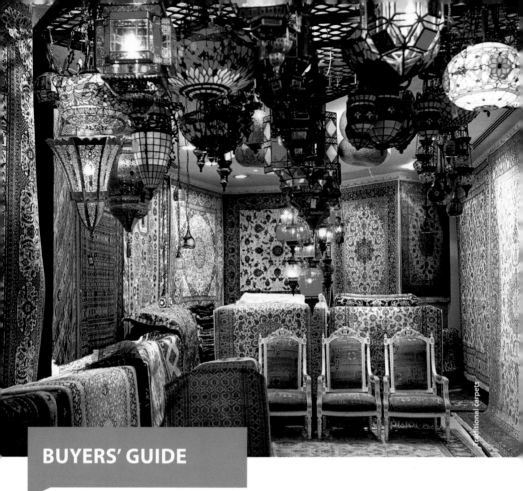
Traditional carpets

BUYERS' GUIDE

From antiques to technology, and from tools to toys, the aim of this section is to let you know what's out there and the best places to buy. It's by no means an exhaustive list, but is designed to help you find those items that, while in your home country you just know how to find, in a new city can be harder to figure out.

Hypermarkets such as Carrefour and LuLu are a good place to start, and Ace Hardware and IKEA are also great for the things you didn't even know you needed. We've referred to the main stores in each category, but many have branches all over the city. See askexplorer.com for a complete list of store locations.

Quick Reference

Alcohol

If you're over the age of 21 you can buy alcohol in Abu Dhabi's restaurants and licensed bars, and some clubs, for consumption on the premises. If you wish to drink at home you will need to apply for a liquor licence (visit auhsl.ae.com for details). How much you are permitted to buy is dependent on your monthly salary and Muslims are not allowed to apply.

Five companies operate liquor stores in Abu Dhabi, with Spinneys Liquor having nine branches in the city centre, Al Ain and Ruwais. Generally speaking, the selection is decent and no tax is added – the price you see on the shelf is exactly what you end up forking out at the till. There is also a good selection of alcohol available at the capital's airport duty free hall. There are a number of 'hole in the wall' stores in the northern emirates that sell duty-free alcohol to members of the public, even if you don't have a licence. Prices are reasonable and there is no tax.

African + Eastern
Zayed The First St Al Khalidiya **02 667 6041**
africaneastern.com
Map **2 H4**
With convenient locations and a wide variety of products, A&E outlets remain a good place to purchase wine, spirits and beer, with typical brands and a few imports of Japanese and German beer.

Al Hamra Cellar
Al Hamra Village Ras Al Khaimah **07 244 7403**
mmidubai.com
Map **3 E1**
Around two hours' drive from Abu Dhabi along Sheikh Mohammed Bin Zayed Road, this licence-free store stocks an amazing selection of beers, spirits and award-winning wines at fantastic tax-free prices – including wine specially selected by guru Oz Clarke.

Barracuda Beach Resort
Nr Dreamland Aqua Park, Khor Al Baida
Umm Al Quwain **06 768 1555**
barracuda.ae
Map **3 E1**
A tax-free, licence-free outlet that is popular with expats across the UAE. There is a superb selection, including the regular brands of beer, wine and spirits. If you need to cater for a party, it worth the drive.

Centaurus International
Ras Al Selaab Ras Al Khaimah **07 228 3117**
centaurusint.info
Map **3 F1**
Another licence-free 'hole in the wall' outlet that offers a good range of products. You can view its range of wine, beer and spirits on its online shop, and it also offers a delivery service.

Cheers
National Corporation For Tourism & Hotels
Al Madina Al Riyadiya **02 409 9703**
Map **1 J8**
With four locations across the city, Cheers stocks plenty of fine grape and premium spirits. A large selection of beers are available too. As with all Abu Dhabi liquor stores, you'll need a licence.

Gray Mackenzie Partners > p.vi
Fatima Bint Muabarak St Al Danah
02 408 1522
graymackenzie.com
Map **2 P6**
With five locations around the city, Gray Mackenzie Partners offers a comprehensive range of branded global beverages in each store. They work with over 500 wineries to ensure a top selection of wines too. They also run a free party service where you can hire glasses and other accessories for when you're entertaining at home.

High Spirits
Nr Carrefour Al Madina Al Riyadiya **02 444 9821**
highspirits-adnh.com
Map **1 J8**
High Spirits has an excellent selection of all types of tipple with friendly staff on hand to help you make your choice. The one at Etihad Plaza in Khalifa City is popular with expats living off the island.

Spinneys Liquor
Centro Capital Centre Al Khaleej Al Arabi St
02 617 2600
spinneysauh.com
Map **1 J8**
This is the largest chain of liquor stores with seven branches across the capital city, and one in Al Ain and another in Ruwais. There's a wide range of premium international brands. If you're a grape fan, Spinneys Liquor also holds wine tasting events. On Fridays, the stores open from 4pm.

Booze Busting

If you're heading to Ajman, Umm Al Quwain or Ras Al Khaimah to buy alcohol, you don't need to worry about being busted buying booze illegally, but you should be careful when driving home; it is the transporting of alcohol that could get you into trouble. This is especially true if you are stopped within the borders of Sharjah, which is a 'dry' emirate, and there have been reports of random police checks on vehicles driving from Ajman into Sharjah. Also, if you have an accident and you're found to have a car boot full of liquor, your day could take a sudden turn for the worse.

Arts & Crafts

A number of shops sell art and craft supplies and you should find there is enough choice, whether you need paints and crayons for children or top quality oils. Check the hypermarkets and larger bookstores for the basics. Magrudy's (magrudy.com) in Al Wahda Mall has a good selection of needles, wool and haberdashery for keen knitters.

All Prints Distributors & Publishers
Hamdan Bin Mohd St Markaziya West 02 633 6999
allprints.ae
Map 2 K3
Stocks an extensive range of stationery, arts and craft supplies for all ages, in addition to related specialist and educational books.

Green Branch
Nr Hamed Center, Shk Zayed The First St
Al Danah 02 621 4507
Map 2 M4
Wools, threads, patterns, paints, beads and other craft essentials can be found at this small shop.

Party Centre > *p.271*
Al Raha Mall Al Raha 02 556 5563
mypartycentre.com
Map 1 R7
Everything you'll need to create a themed party for kids or grown ups, including decorations, plates, helium balloons, party bags and more.

Posters
Nr Al Diar Capital, Al Firdous St Al Zahiyah
02 672 4724
posters.ae
Map 2 R3
Offers a limited range of painting and watercolour supplies, as well as a picture framing service.

United Bookstore
Meena Centre Al Meena 02 673 3999
jarirbookstore.com
Map 1 D2
One of the best arts and crafts selections in town including some professional supplies.

Books, Music & DVDs

You'll find both international bookstores and good local stores in Abu Dhabi. All malls feature at least one bookstore, and if you cannot find a publication, the larger stores let you place an order or enquire whether it is available in another branch. For second-hand books, try St Andrew's Thrift Centre, Book & Bean Cafe

within Ace Hardware on Yas Island or look out for car boot and yard sales advertised on supermarket noticeboards and in online classifieds. A small selection of books, DVDs and games sell in supermarkets and hypermarkets. You can also buy books by Explorer in most bookstores or online at askexplorer.com.

Unless you have particularly obscure taste, you should find a satisfying collection of music in the city's record stores. Music and DVDs are generally more expensive than they are in other countries, but the advantage of Abu Dhabi's multicultural society is that you can open yourself up to new genres – Arabic dance music, for example, is very popular. Everything has to go through the censor, so any music or DVDs deemed offensive will not be sold here, unless it can be edited to make it more acceptable. Retailers will order titles that are on the approved list for the UAE. Bollywood films are extremely popular here and available in most shops.

Online shopping is an alternative if you can't find an item and you'll find more variety on sites like Amazon (amazon.com and amazon.co.uk), which deliver to the UAE. Delivery rates are cheaper from the UK site than the US site, and beware that your package may be inspected by UAE customs. so be extra careful about the material you order. The UAE iTunes store sells a limited selection of music, TV shows, movies and eBooks, but you can log in to the UK or US sites for the extensive library – you'll need a UK or US registered credit card for these.

Book Corner Marina Mall, 02 681 7662, *bookcorner.ae*
Borders Abu Dhabi Mall, Al Zahiyah,
02 671 8980
Isam Bookshop & Stationery Zayed the Second St, Al Danah, 02 634 3557
Jashanmal Bookstore Abu Dhabi Mall, Al Zahiyah, 02 644 3869, *jashanmalgroup.com*
Magrudy's Al Wahda Mall, Al Dhafrah, 02 443 7172, *magrudy.com*
United Bookstore Meena Centre, Al Meena, 02 673 3999, *jarirbookstore.com*
Virgin Megastore Abu Dhabi Mall, Al Zahiyah, 02 644 7882, *virginmegastore.me*
WH Smith > *p.275* Al Wahda Mall, Al Dhafrah, 02 641 7454

Become An Explorer

If you've found this book useful, pick up some of Explorer's other popular titles. Find out more about the region with our Visitors' Guides to Dubai, Muscat and Doha. Get adventurous with off-road guides to the UAE and Oman, *Ultimate UAE & Oman Explorer*, *UAE Boating & Yachting*, or *UAE Diving*. Or, pick up a souvenir photography book from askexplorer.com/shop

Camera Equipment

Photographers can usually find most things in Abu Dhabi, even darkroom equipment and film. Prices of cameras and equipment vary between the larger outlets, where prices are fixed, and the smaller electronics shops. However, while you might be able to bag a bargain from the independent retailers using your powers of negotiation, you will ultimately get more protection buying from the larger outlets. The most important consideration, if you are buying the camera to take abroad, is to ensure your warranty is international; and don't just take the retailer's word for it, ask to read the warranty to make sure.

For second-hand equipment, gulfphotoplus.com (an essential site for all photography enthusiasts) has an equipment noticeboard, as well as being a great source of information. Top of the range cameras, basic SLRs, video cameras and simple home printers, you should also find a decent selection of competitively priced items at electrical stores like Plug-Ins, Jumbo Electronics, and at major hypermarkets like Carrefour.

Emax
Dalma Mall Industrial City Of Abu Dhabi 1
02 557 5400
landmarkgroupme.com
Map **1 N13**
A large electronics chain that carries cameras from main brands such as Olympus, Nikon and Sony. Plenty of choice, especially for compact cameras.

Grand Stores
Abu Dhabi Mall Al Zahiyah **02 645 1115**
grandstores.com
Map **2 S5**
The main retailer for Nikon cameras in Abu Dhabi. The store also stocks Fuji, Canon and Mamiya and you can have your camera cleaned and repaired in its stores.

Salam
Abu Dhabi Mall Al Zahiyah **02 645 6999**
salams.com
Map **2 S5**
Stocks a complete range of professional-grade equipment, including a good selection of filters and tripods. Carries Bronica, Leica, Minolta and Pentax.

Virgin Megastore
Yas Mall Yas Island West
yasmall.ae
Map **1 T4**
Opening soon in the city's newest mall, this British favourite sells all the latest DVDs, films, music memorabilia, headphones, top camera brands and accessories for smart phones. Virgin also sells magazines, books and designer stationary.

Car Accessories

Cars and their accessories are big business in the emirate, so you won't struggle to find what you need. Ace and Carrefour have large departments selling everything from steering wheel covers to fridges that run off the car battery. Near the intersection of Al Salam and Al Falah streets you'll find a number of small workshops where you can buy accessories such as alloys, window tints and custom seat covers and you can get them all fitted there too.

GPS systems are available from major stores such as Plug-Ins, Sharaf DG and Jumbo Electronics. Car stereos are widely available, and are sold by most electronics shops, with some of the car dealerships stocking alternative models for their cars. To have them fitted, head either to a dealer, service centre or to the workshops around Al Salam and Al Falah – it should cost around Dhs.500 if you are providing all the parts.

Many car owners try to beat the heat by having their car windows tinted. The legal limit is 30% tint; if you get your windows tinted any darker you could be fined, and your car won't pass its annual inspection. The options range from the Dhs.75 plastic film from the workshops around Al Salam and Al Falah, up to Dhs.5,000 at V-KOOL which has a clear film that is more heat resistant than the tinted one.

It's worth taking a drive to Yellow Hat in Times Square Center in Dubai for a fantastic range of products from spare parts and in-car technology, to imported, custom-made alloys and under car lighting.

ACE Nr IKEA, Yas Island, 02 565 1945,
aceuae.com
Carrefour Marina Mall, Breakwater, 800 73232,
carrefouruae.com
Harakat Auto Accessories Sultan Bin Zayed The First St, 02 641 0370
V-KOOL 02 443 5333, *vkooluae.com*
Yellow Hat Times Square Center, Dubai, 04 341 8592,
yellowhat.ae

Clothing & Shoes

From BHS to Benetton, and Mango to Marchesa, Abu Dhabi has clothes shopping covered. Upmarket designer stores are found in most shopping malls and many hotels; The Boulevard @ Etihad Towers and The Galleria at Al Maryah Island, are particularly exclusive, but there's no shortage of high-end labels in the city.

All the main malls have a wealth of international high-street labels, including H&M, Topshop, Gap, Mango and so on. Marina Mall, Al Wahda Mall and Dalma Mall are particular favourites for mainstream shoppers. If you're on a really tight budget, you can sometimes find excellent bargains in the souks.

Hypermarkets such as Carrefour stock affordable clothing and shoes too, or head to department stores like Splash and Centrepoint. Shoe Mart does a great range of good, budget-friendly shoes.

For something that stands out of the crowd, boutiques like S*uce, Ounass and Grafika step away from the mainstream selections and offer trendy togs from up-and-coming designers.

If you love designer clothes but not the price tags, browse mapochette.com. The online store stocks designer bags and offers a rental service. For designer fakes head to Markaziya East (between Khalifa Bin Zayed the First Street and Sheikh Zayed the First Street) or better still, to the streets of Karama in Dubai which are crammed with them, ranging from cheap knock-offs to good quality copies.

Mass summer sales take place around August or September, and there are more in January when stores get rid of the old and bring in the new. During the January sales in particular, the offers can be amazing. The Eid sales, around the end of Ramadan, are like January sales in countries such as UK, America and Australia – busy and intense, but well worth it if you're an avid bargain hunter unafraid of equally fervent fellow shoppers.

American Eagle Outfitters Al Wahda Mall, Al Dhafrah, 02 695 8172, *ae.com*
BHS Al Wahda Mall, Hazaa Bin Zayed The First Street, 02 443 7070 *bhs.co.uk*
Desigual Marina Mall, Breakwater, 02 679 6443, *desigual.com*
Gap Marina Mall, Breakwater, 02 681 1255
H&M Abu Dhabi Mall, Al Zahiyah, 02 695 8101, *hm.com*
Mango Abu Dhabi Mall, Al Zahiyah, 02 644 9319, *shop.mango.com*
Monsoon Mushrif Mall, Al Mushrif, 02 491 4689
Next Abu Dhabi Mall, Al Zahiyah, 02 645 4832, *next.co.uk*
New Look Al Wahda Mall, Hazaa Bin Zayed The First Street, 02 443 7070, *alwahda-mall.com*

Electrical Goods & Appliances

Whether you are setting up home or moving house, you'll have to spend time looking for white goods. In Abu Dhabi, unfurnished really means unfurnished and you'll have to fork out for the most standard items, even curtain rails. Unsurprisingly, there are plenty of places where you can buy the necessary appliances and electronics, with most international brands sold here. Competition is high, so prices are reasonable and most dealers will offer warranties. You'll find a similar range of products in all of the electronics stores.

There are several stores dedicated to electronics and appliances in each of the larger malls and you'll find sections in the hypermarkets stocking a superb selection of goods from well-known brands (and some lesser known ones that also do the job). They usually offer a delivery and installation service too. Everything from top-of-the-range televisions, games consoles, fridges, ovens, irons and kettles are covered, although it can be worth waiting for the sales if you can as the price drops are noticeable. Or, if money is not so tight, the likes of Bang & Olufsen and Bose offer a pricey, but undeniably stylish, range of home goods.

You can buy water coolers and water dispensers in all the larger supermarkets, or you can get them directly from the companies that deliver bottled water. These can be a surprisingly crucial first purchase when you move to Abu Dhabi.

On all electronic goods, it's important to check that the warranty is valid internationally, as you may wish to take items back to your home country. Also make sure that the item will work in all parts of the world and find out whether you will have to pay any import duty if you do return home. Find out who will service the items if there are problems too. For second-hand items, check the adverts placed on supermarket noticeboards and online classifieds, like dubizzle.com.

Mobile Phones

Mobiles are big business and you won't need to go too far to find one. Most of the larger supermarkets have areas dedicated to the bigger brands, while smaller shops around the Madinat Zayed and Al Markaziyah areas may offer some bargains on older models. Handsets can also be bought directly from du or Etisalat; it is often cheaper to buy a phone from them as part of a package.

Emax
Dalma Mall Industrial City Of Abu Dhabi 1
02 557 5400
landmarkgroupme.com
Map **1 N13**
Everything from cameras to home appliances and computer consoles are covered by Emax. The stores are large and comprehensive with all the main brands.

Jumbo Electronics
Shk Hamdan Bin Mohammed St Al Danah
02 632 7001
jumbocorp.com
Map **2 P4**
A vast selection of popular brands, with good deals and helpful staff. A good place to head to if you are looking for Sony LCD televisions and home theatre systems.

Plug-Ins

Marina Mall Breakwater **800 758 4467**
pluginselectronix.com
Map **2 D1**

A comprehensive range of electronics, including the latest products from Panasonic, Bose, Sony, LG and lots more big brands.

Sharaf DG

Abu Dhabi Mall 02 650 3570
sharafdg.com
Map **2 S5**

A great first port of call because of its extensive range of appliances and gadgets, from plasma TVs and laptop computers to mobile phones and irons.

Home Audio & Visual

If you are looking for ways to amp up your parties, or you want to set up a home cinema or sound system in your home, AVE (050 676 2864) offer all the advice and assistance you'll need. An independent audiovisual consultant will provide installation services for home audio equipment, projector systems and multi-room audio installation.

Furniture & Homewares

This is one of Abu Dhabi's most buoyant retail sectors; most tastes are catered for, from everyone's favourite Swedish flatpack store to unique ethnic pieces, and the latest designer concepts.

Second-hand bargain hunters can either pay a visit to Nefertiti's warehouse on the Corniche at Khaleej Al Arabi St or peruse the offerings online (useditemsuae.com). There are plenty of deals to be found in the classified sections of newspapers or on supermarket noticeboards. For something completely different, head to the warehouse stores. Try Heritage Touch in the Meena Port area of Abu Dhabi (heritage-touch.com) but you'll find the widest selections are in Sharjah. The hot, dusty warehouses are not the choicest of options, but prices are excellent and after a good polish the furniture looks fabulous. This is a particularly good place to pick up wooden furniture – Pinky Furniture & Novelties in Industrial Area 10 (pinkyfurnitureuae.com) stocks an excellent selection.

ChenOne

Marina Mall Breakwater **02 681 8110**
chenonehome.com
Map **2 D1**

An online store stocked with furniture and goodies for the house – so you can beautify your home without having to leave it!

Grand Royal

Das Tower Al Khubeirah **02 639 5565**
grandroyalarabian.com
Map **2 F3**

The Abu Dhabi stockist of a range of top-notch Italian designer brands, such as Versace Home, Blumarine, Ipe Cavalli, Francesco Molon, Faustig and Mechini.

Home Centre

Liwa Centre Al Danah **02 639 1918**
homecentrestores.com
Map **2 M4**

Inside this store you'll find everything you need for the home from small items including bath towels, kitchenware and accessories, and a wide selection of dining tables, sofas and bedroom furniture. Additional locations can be found at both the Marina Mall and Dalma Mall.

IDdesign

Al Wahda Mall Al Wahdah **02 443 7557**
iddesignuae.com
Map **2 M7**

A selection of modern furniture for the home or office, and a decent range of outdoor furniture. Also offers an interior design service, furniture re-upholstery, and custom-made curtains, pillows and other accessories.

IKEA

Nr Yas Mall Yas Island West
02 493 5888
ikeauae.com
Map **1 T4**

This enormous showroom on Yas Island sells a great range of good value furniture, suitable for most budgets; it stocks everything from Dhs.1 tealight holders to Dhs.20,000 kitchens. Also good for reasonably priced kids' furniture.

Office Furniture

Whether you're looking to set up shop in Abu Dhabi or need to kit out a home office, there are several general furnishers you can turn to; for example, IKEA and Home Centre, while BAFCO (bafco.com) is an office furniture specialist with stores in Abu Dhabi and Dubai.

Interiors

Emirates Tower Bldg, Shk Hamdan Bin Mohammed St Al Danah **02 6797 040**
interiorsfurniture.com
Map **2 Q3**

Offering every style of furniture for the entire house. They offer a home delivery and fitting service and can also be employed for both residential and commercial interior design projects.

Marina Exotic Home Interiors

Abu Dhabi Mall Al Zahiyah **02 645 5488**
marinagulf.com
Map **2 S5**

The items sold here should add an exotic touch to
your home – you can pick up key pieces that reflect
the region, as well as far-flung places from the Orient
to New York. The selection includes large wardrobes,
tables, ornate chests, various styles of comfy sofa and
garden furniture.

THE One

Zayed The First St Al Bateen **02 681 6500**
theone.com
Map **2 F4**

A favourite among the expat crowd because of its
funky, modern style and huge selection of home
accessories in this flag ship Abu Dhabi 'theatre'. The
store also features a well-loved cafe that is popular
with the weekend coffee crowd. A second store
stocking a smaller range of lovely home furnishings
can be found at the Abu Dhabi Mall.

Pan Emirates

Shk Rashid Bin Al Maktoum Rd Al Danah
02 621 1030
panemirates.com
Map **2 L6**

A wide range of furniture and accessories to furnish
your house from top to bottom, from stylish bedroom
suites to themed decor choices. Whether it is an office,
dining area or terrace, Pan Emirates sell neutral and
unique modern styles as well as the more traditional
furniture, mixing up grander and gaudy in equal
measures. There is also a great selection of garden
furniture and it is all quite reasonably priced.

PF Emirates Interiors

Al Sahel Tower, Corniche West St Al Khubeirah
02 635 9393
pfemirates.ae
Map **2 E3**

Part of the Poltrona Frau Group, specialising in leading
brands of high-end furniture including Cassina and
Cappellini. The upmarket store also offers a bespoke
design service if you are after ideas and inspiration to
furnish your new home.

Pottery Barn

Dalma Mall Industrial City Of Abu Dhabi 1
02 612 0658
potterybarn.me
Map **1 N13**

An American giant that sells a good range of quality
household furniture and accessories, and also has an
in-store design studio where customers can get advice
on their home furnishing needs and ideas.

Wooden

Heritage Touch (Dibaj furniture)

Mena Zayed 02 673 2749
heritage-touch.com
Map **3 D2**

This hot, dusty and humid warehouse store is a
popular option with expats seeking well-priced and
solid, wooden furniture. Staff can also paint, varnish or
make alterations. You'll find touristy goods and gifts,
along with carpets and pashminas. Smaller branches
are at the Shangri La, Airport Road's Carrefour and
Spinneys centre in Khalidiya

Lucky's Furnitures & Handicrafts

4th Industrial Street Sharjah
06 534 1937
luckyfurnitureuae.com
Map **3 E2**

This store in Sharjah is popular with expats seeking
well-priced furniture. The range is vast, and staff can
paint, varnish or make alterations.

Marina Exotic Home Interiors

Abu Dhabi Mall Al Zahiyah **02 645 5488**
marinagulf.com
Map **2 S5**

Items here are generally more unique than you'll find
at the usual furniture stores. The selection includes
large wardrobes, tables, ornate chests, beds and
more. The wood is high quality and the designs are so
unique that you will probably want to purchase a few
items to take back home with you.

Unique ethnic furniture

Kids

Pottery Barn Kids

Dalma Mall Industrial City of Abu Dhabi 1 **800 803**
potterybarnkids.me
Map **1 N13**
A slice of the same great furniture design as the full
Pottery Barn stores, but specially modified for kids.
Ideal for nurseries and imaginative bedrooms, it also
sells a selection of toys. Also at Al Wahda Mall.

Art

The capital's art scene is on the verge of new realms
with branches of the Louvre and Guggenheim due
to open in the next few years on Saadiyat Island,
and the industry is enjoying steady growth in
preparation. Most galleries in Abu Dhabi display
traditional and contemporary art by Arabic and
international artists, such as the NYUAD Art Gallery,
also on Saadiyat. Many of the works are for sale so
you can spice up your walls with something unique.
The annual Abu Dhabi Art Fair (abudhabiartfair.ae)
sees top galleries from around the world sell works
from established and emerging artists. Abu Dhabi Art
Hub (adah.ae) also holds affordable art sales.

The Barakat Gallery

Emirates Palace Al Ras Al Akhdar **02 690 8950**
barakatgallery.com
Map **2 B2**
Barakat Gallery was founded in Jerusalem over 100
years ago and specialises brilliantly in ancient art.
On display are antiquities from China, Egypt, Africa,
Greece and Rome. Every item on display in the
cabinets is also for sale.

Folklore Gallery

Shk Zayed The First St Al Khalidiya **02 666 0361**
folkloregallery.net
Map **2 H4**
For more traditional and affordable art, craft and gift
items from the Arab world, selling prints inspired by
the UAE landscape, as well as traditional Bedouin
jewellery, ceramics and a picture framing service.

Gallery One

The Souk At Qaryat Al Beri Al Maqtaa **02 558 1822**
g-1.com
Map **1 L8**
A high-end gallery that sells prints, as well as hosting
art fairs throughout the year that showcase modern
and contemporary art from all over the world. On the
retail side, there is a collection of contemporary art
products and an extensive catalogue of ready-to-hang
fine art paper editions, canvas editions, framed art and
fine art photography, that will enrich both your home
or office environment and make an ideal gift.

Salwa Zeidan Gallery

The St Regis Saadiyat Island Resort Saadiyat Island
02 666 9656
salwazeidangallery.com
Map **1 G1**
Showcases a varied range of art by international
and Middle Eastern contemporary artists, including
paintings, photography and sculpture.

Outdoor

The below stores stock a range of garden furniture.

ACE Nr IKEA, Yas Island, 02 565 1945,
aceuae.com
Bayti Marina Mall, Breakwater, 02 681 8107
Desert Garden Centre Khalifa Park, Al Khalidiya,
02 449 0010, *desertgroup.ae*

Gardens & Pools

Hardware retailers such as Ace also carry a selection
of outdoor furniture and gardening accessories, as do
the major hypermarkets such as LuLu and Carrefour.
IKEA has a good plants section and sells candles,
watering cans and other useful items, and there are
plenty of companies to call on for swimming pool
installation and maintenance.

Absolute Pool 050 559 8807, *absolute-pools.com*
Desert Garden Centre Khalifa Park, Al Khalidiya,
02 449 0010, *desertgroup.ae*
Exotica Emirates Al Zahiyah, 02 644 4416,
exoticagroup.com
Falcon Crest Swimming Pools 4th Street, Dubai,
04 340 5339, *fcstswimming.com*
Pools By Design 050 754 6852, *poolsdesign.net*
Those Pool Guys Nr Berger Paints, Dubai,
04 339 0418, *thosepoolguys.com*

Hardware & DIY

When planning your home improvements it's worth
noting that, with so many companies offering
handyman services, it may be easier and cheaper to
find a 'man who can' rather than invest in the tools
and materials you need for DIY jobs.

However, if you'd rather do it yourself, then the
larger hypermarkets, often have an ample DIY section
to get you started. Furthermore, a basic range of items
can be bought at IKEA. For many expats in the UAE, Ace
Hardware is the go-to shop for tools and other crucial
basics in home maintenance and building. They also
have garden centres and a large selection of garden
furniture, plus a selection of essential car accessories,
emulsion paints, camping accessories and lighting.

Ace Hardware *> p.236*
Nr IKEA Yas Island West **02 565 1945**
aceuae.com
Map **1 T4**
DIY enthusiasts will find all the tools they need to get the job done, especially at the giant superstore on Yas Island. Customised paints, glazes, electronic tools and hardware materials can also be found here.

Jewellery

Whatever your taste in jewellery you'll find an abundant supply here. Gold is available in 18, 21, 22 or 24 carats and is sold according to the international daily gold rate. This means that for an identical piece, whether you buy it in the mall or the Gold Souk, there will be very little difference in the price of the actual gold. Where the price varies is in the workmanship that has gone into a particular piece.

For adventurous jewellery shoppers, there is plenty to choose from, such as silver jewellery from Oman, cultured pearls from Japan, and ethnic creations from India crafted in rich yellow gold. The Gold Souk in Madinat Zayed on Sultan Bin Zayed the First Street has many jewellers including some of the largest jewellery shops in the Gulf and the outlets in this area cater for all tastes. You can browse a host of different outlets and you might be able to haggle down a real bargain.

When it comes to watches, there is also plenty of choice. You'll get plastic cheapies for no more than a few dirhams, diamond-encrusted designer timepieces coming in at over Dhs.100,000 (head to The Galleria at Al Maryah Island, or Avenue @ Etihad Towers for some of the most high-end designer names), and everything in between. Check out the souks – not only will you find all the brands you know, plus some you don't, but you'll have fun haggling with the colourful shop owners – the Hamdan Centre is a good place to start.

Al Futtaim Jewellery Abu Dhabi Mall, Al Zahiyah, 02 645 2001, *watches.ae*
Al Jazira Jewellery Shk Hamdan Bin Mohammed St, Al Danah, 02 634 4141
Al Manara International Jewellery Etihad Towers, Al Bateen, 02 627 2222, *amij.com*
Al Mandoos Jewellery Marina Mall, Breakwater, 02 681 6555, *mandoosjewel.com*
Carcassonne Gold & Diamonds Hamdan Centre, Al Danah, 02 634 7676, *cgdjewellery.com*
Damas Khalidiyah Mall, Al Khalidiya, 02 635 4420, *damasjewel.com*
Le Portique Jewellery Shk Khalifa Bin Zayed St, Markaziya East, 02 626 9133
Tiffany & Co. Abu Dhabi Mall, Al Zahiyah, 02 644 1182, *tiffany.com*

Kids

There is a high concentration of shops selling toys and clothes for children; you'll find an impressive selection of well-known stores as well as smaller outlets. Yas Mall, which opened in November 2014, welcomed the UAE's first Lego Store and a Hamleys is expected soon. Meanwhile, most electronics stores stock a wide range of computer games for 'big kids' to know. Carrefour also has a good selection of toys and is a reliable spot for inexpensive birthday presents and stocking fillers. Remember that not all toys conform to international safety standards so should only be used under supervision, though the launch of a new scheme by the Abu Dhabi Quality and Conformity Council in 2014 aims to ensure toys for children aged up to 14 in the emirate will comply with UAE safety standards. Toys that meet the scheme will be awarded the Abu Dhabi trustmark.

Early Learning Centre
Abu Dhabi Mall Al Zahiyah **02 645 4766**
elc.com
Map **2 S5**
Early Learning Centre stocks a good range of educational products and toys that stimulate play and imagination. Other locations include World Trade Center Mall, Fotouh Al Khair Centre and Marina Mall.

Krash Toys
Abu Dhabi Mall Al Zahiyah **02 644 3223**
krashtoys.com
Map **2 S5**
This smaller toy shop stocks familiar brands like Mattel, Hasbro, Tomy and Leap Frog.

The Lego Store
Yas West Yas Island
yasmall.ae
Map **1 T4**
For budding builders, this is huge news being the country'a first store dedicated to the famous building blocks. Stocking a vast selection of lego kits, young fans and avid collectors will be impressed.

Toys R Us
Nr Royal Furniture, 20th Street Al Meena
02 673 2332
toysrusuae.com
Map **1 D2**
This well-known emporium offers a good selection of products, whether you are looking for small toys to amuse kids or larger gifts like bikes, electronic games and play sets (including Lego). Also at Dalma Mall.

School Supplies
While a lot of schools have book bags as part of their uniform, many kids also take their own school bag

in order to fit in their gym kit and packed lunch. Pull along wheeled bags are popular and can be found in Toys R Us in all manner of characters. If you're looking for pencil cases and the like, then Magrudy's, Toys R Us and Early Learning Centre stock good ranges, as do almost all of the city's biggest hypermarkets.

Mother & Baby

Big business in the UAE, there are a multitude of shops selling baby paraphernalia, and many brands you'll know from your home country. You shouldn't have trouble finding nursery essentials like bottles, buggies, changing bags, clothes, cots, prams, rocking chairs and travel cots, but the choice is more limited than you'll find back home. Surprisingly few places stock much maternity clothing in Abu Dhabi – there's far more choice in Dubai or online. You can shop online at blushandbloom.com and luxelittle.com for fashionable maternity lingerie, nightwear, dresses and 'mama and baby' twinsets.

Supermarkets stock formula, nappies and wipes and many sell a good range of bottles and feeding equipment. Choithrams has the best selection of formulas, stocking popular UK brands SMA and Cow & Gate. Pharmacies sell baby essentials and some also have breast pumps. Safety 1st and Maxi Cosi car seats are widely available and should fit most cars; you can also rent car seats, buggies, strollers and other equipment from Rentacrib (rentacrib.ae) – if you hire a car seat its staff will fit it for you free of charge. IKEA has a very reasonable range of nursery furniture such as cots, changing tables and bathtubs, and a selection of cot sheets and blankets. Boppy breastfeeding pillows are available in Toys R Us, while other essential accessories for pregnancy include a 'Bump Belt', a device that redirects your car seatbelt under your bump for protection, and which can be found in Mothercare and Spinneys.

Babyshop
Marina Mall Breakwater **02 681 8894**
babyshopstores.com
Map **2 D1**
This shop sells low-cost baby clothing and essentials such as feeding items, clothing, toys and baby monitors. Affordable newborn items come in value packs, and sales are held several times a year. Other locations include Dalma Mall and Meena Center.

DbBabies
Al Wahdah Mall Al Wahdah **050 600 3199**
dbbabies.com
Map **3 E2**
You can shop at your leisure at this boutique selling blankets, feeding essentials, slings and skincare

products, among other baby essentials. You can also shop online and they deliver free for orders over Dhs.200.

Happy Baby
Al Jaber Bldg, Shk Zayed The First St Markaziya West **02 632 3266**
happybabyuae.com
Map **2 K4**
Abu Dhabi's answer to the baby boutique. With an extensive range of designer baby gear, including names like Dior, Monalisa Babywear and Lessy, this is the place to go if style is paramount.

Just Kidding
Gold & Diamond Park Dubai **04 341 3922**
justkidding-uae.com
Map 3 **E2** Metro **First Gulf Bank**
Sells a good range of baby items, furniture and clothes from Europe. The stores are located in Dubai, but you can also shop online and have your items delivered.

Mamas & Papas
Marina Mall Breakwater **02 681 6689**
mamasandpapas.com
Map **2 D1**
A household name for well-designed, stylish products for babies and mums-to-be. The store stocks all you need from toys, car seats, pushchairs, cribs, nursery items and decorations to maternity clothes and feeding items. Also available at Al Wahda Mall.

Mothercare
Abu Dhabi Mall Al Zahiyah **02 695 8111**
mothercare.com
Map **2 S5**
A reliable place to shop for baby essentials, with a particularly good selection of clothes. Larger stores stock cots, prams and car seats, and you can order items you've seen on the international website. Other locations include in Dalma Mall.

Musical Instruments

There's a growing number of musical instrument stores dotted around Abu Dhabi, and you'll also find some basic items for kids sold in Carrefour, Toys R Us, and Geant with an excellent range of keyboards, as well as digital music games.

You'll also probably be able to pick up second-hand guitars or pianos from dubizzle.com. If you're looking for sheet music, Magrudy's in Al Wahda Mall has a large range, including exam papers. Meanwhile, Virgin Megastore in Abu Dhabi Mall and now in Yas Mall have an excellent range of musical instruments, DJ equipment and popular music books, too.

AKM Music Centre
Nr Crowne Plaza, Hamdan Bin Mohammed St
Al Danah **02 621 9929**
Map **2 N4**
Has a decent range of musical instruments including pianos and sheet music.

International Music Institute
Nr Grand Stores, Zayed The First St Al Manhal **02 621 1949**
imi-jmc.net
Map **2 K4**
Has a selection of high-quality used Japanese pianos as well as brass and woodwind instruments, drum kits and musical accessories.

House Of Oud
Fancy learning to play a classic Arabic instrument? Abu Dhabi's Bait Al Oud (House of Oud) on the West Corniche Road offers oud (a guitar-like instrument) lessons from Dhs.1,000 per month for three lessons per week.

Thomsun Music
Bin Mohammed St Al Zahiyah **02 672 4703**
thomsunmusiconline.com
Map **2 R3**
Has a decent selection of acoustic and electric guitars as well as some keyboard models.

The Young Musician Music Institute
Al Raha Mall Al Raha **02 556 2080**
tymmi.com
Map **1 R7**
Fender guitars and Yamaha keyboards and pianos are available at this training venue for budding rock stars and concert pianists.

Parties

Accessories
Most major supermarkets and stationery stores sell the basic party paraphernalia, and if you go to the more specialised shops, you'll find an even wider range of goodies to choose from. With everything from cards, balloons, candles, table settings and room decorations to gift wrapping, fancy dress outfits, bouncy castles and entertainers; the choice for both children's and adults' parties is comprehensive. Carrefour, Posters and Toys R Us stock party essentials such as themed plates, cups and hats. If you're after a fancy dress costume, many of the small tailors in Abu Dhabi are able to copy designs from pictures. Birthday cakes are available in the bakery section of all major

supermarkets, although many independent bakeries in the city are capable of stunning creations.

Daiso
Madinat Zayed Centre, Sultan Bin Zayed the First St
Al Danah **02 631 1514**
daisome.com
Map **2 M5**
This Japanese discount store in Madinat Zayed Shopping Centre is good for stocking up on knick-knacks for children's party bags.

Party Centre > *p.271*
Al Raha Mall Al Raha **02 556 5563**
mypartycentre.com
Map **1 R7**
Everything you'll need to host a party for kids or grown ups, including cups, plates, helium balloons, party bags and more. Party Centre's huge selection can cater for just about any celebration. As well as a fab branch in Abu Dhabi's Al Wahda Mall, in Dubai they can be found in Saraya, Garhoud and Media City.

Celebration Cakes
Bakeries are everywhere in Abu Dhabi and you'll find most of them can turn their hands to cake making. Creations range from very simple to mind-blowingly elaborate. If you have an idea for a party cake, someone in Abu Dhabi can make it for you – even if you need it covered in gold.

Baskin Robbins Abu Dhabi Mall, Al Zahiyah, 02 644 0103, *baskinrobbins.com*
Cake Gallery Shk Rashid Bin Saeed Al Maktoum St, Al Mushrif, 02 446 9495, *cakegallery.ae*
Candy Cakes Marina Mall, Breakwater, 02 681 6022, *candycakesme.com*
Khaleej Bakeries & Pastries Salam Tower, Shk Zayed Rd, Al Danah, 02 676 6188, *khaleejbakeries.com*
Mister Baker Shk Hamdan Bin Mohammed St, Al Zahiyah, 02 678 0055

Perfumes & Cosmetics

Perfumes and cosmetics are big business here, from the local scents like frankincense and oud, to the latest designer offerings. Local scents tend to be strong and spicy – you can find the stores by the smell of the incense from their doorways. Oman-based Amouage in Marina Mall sells what they describe as 'the world's most expensive perfumes' if you fancy 'splashing' out. Department stores such as Areej, Sephora, Lifestyle, Debenhams and Paris Gallery (located in most malls) stock a range of international brand perfumes and cosmetics. And, with no taxes, there is little difference between duty free and mall prices.

Larger hypermarkets, supermarkets and pharmacies stock skincare products and some make-up. Anti-allergenic ranges are available at many of the larger pharmacies. Most needs are covered but if yours aren't, specialist retailers often have online shopping facilities or you may find products available at your local beauty clinic. Glambox.me has an online cosmetics store.

Amouage Marina Mall, Breakwater, 02 681 6662, *amouage.com*

Areej Marina Mall, Breakwater, 02 681 5663, *altayer.com*

Bath & Body Works Marina Mall, Breakwater, 02 695 8151, *bathandbodyworks.com*

The Body Shop Abu Dhabi Mall, Al Zahiyah, 02 645 7300, *thebodyshop.com*

Boots Al Wahda Mall, Al Dhafrah, 02 443 7167, *me.boots.com*

L'Occitane Marina Mall, Breakwater, 02 681 6691, *loccitane-me.com*

LUSH Wahda Mall, Al Wahdah, 02 446 9501, *lush.ae*

M.A.C Abu Dhabi Mall, Al Zahiyah, 02 645 4938, *maccosmetics.com*

Paris Gallery Khalidiyah Mall, Al Khalidiya, 02 635 4590, *parisgallery.com*

Red Earth Abu Dhabi Mall, Al Zahiyah, 02 645 6602, *redearth.com*

Sephora The Galleria, Al Maryah Island, 02 644 3984, *sephora-me.com*

Pets

Most supermarkets carry basic ranges of cat, dog, bird and fish food, although the choice is limited. If your pet has specific dietary requirements, many of the veterinary clinics carry specialist foods.

There are pet shops dotted around the city which can supply most items you need for your pet, with Pet Land being well known for aquariums and Tetra products for fish keeping. While there are good pet shops, some can be a little depressing with animals kept in conditions that may make you feel uncomfortable. On principal, it might be better to shop around and spend your money elsewhere. Below is a list of the better ones.

Excellence Pets Shop Nr Abu Dhabi Mall, Al Meena St, Al Zahiyah, 02 644 7670

Pet Land Nr Etisalat, Al Khaleej Al Arabi St, Al Khalidiya, 02 667 2223, *petlanduae.com*

Pet's Delight Gardens Plaza, Al Raha Gardens Village, Al Raha, 02 557 4580, *pets-delight.com*

Quality Pet Shop Cosmos Bldg, Al Danah, 02 627 6200, *qualitypetsonline.com*

Second-Hand Goods

The fairly transitory nature of much of the population results in an active second-hand market. If you are looking to buy or sell second-hand goods, the supermarket noticeboards and the classifieds sections in newspapers are a good place to start. There are also several community websites with classifieds sections – try dubizzle.com, abudhabiwoman.com, expatwoman. com, souq.com and websouq.com.

In most cases you will have to arrange for the items you buy to be transported – head down to the car park next to the Central Post Office in Madinat Zayed, and negotiate with the drivers there for the use of a small truck. The price should include a driver and a few men to help you carry larger items. If you are selling second-hand goods, a number of the local second-hand shops will come to your home and give you a quote (usually way below the purchase price, so be prepared to haggle).

St Andrew's Thrift Shop Nr Shk Mohd Bin Zayed Mosque, Al Mushrif, 02 446 4193

Soft Furnishings

Carpets & Rugs

Carpets are one of the region's signature items. The ones on sale here tend to be imported from Iran, Turkey, Pakistan and Central Asia. The Carpet Souk at the Port end of Meena Road is the most obvious place to start looking for carpets; Meena Souk (also known as Afghan Souk) is similarly well stocked. However, if you prefer a more genteel way of purchasing your carpet, a number of the malls, such as Khalifa Centre, have carpet shops that are less crowded and pushy than the myriad vendors at the Carpet Souk. Ask to see a variety of carpets so that you can get a feel for the differences between hand-made or machine-made, silk, wool or blend carpets. Of course, asking may not be necessary, since vendors will undoubtedly start unrolling samples before you at a furious pace.

Carpets range in price from a few hundred dirhams to tens of thousands, depending on a number of factors such as the origin, the material used, the number of knots, and whether or not they are hand-made. The most expensive carpets are usually those hand-made with silk, in Iran. It is always worth bargaining; make sure the seller knows you are not a tourist, and remain polite at all times to maximise the success of your haggling.

Inspect carpets by turning them over – if the pattern is clear on the back and the knots are all neat, the carpet is of higher quality than those that are indistinct. Do some research, so you have a basic idea of what you are looking for before you go, just in case you happen to meet an unscrupulous carpet dealer who could take advantage of your naivety. Fortunately, crooked carpet conmen are rare, and most will happily explain the differences between the rugs and share their extensive knowledge. If you ask the dealer, you can often garner some interesting information about the carpets and where they were made – for example, some carpets have family names sewn into the designs. The Center of Original Iranian Carpets (coicco.com) near the Corniche may just be the pinnacle of carpets in the region, with some of the highest quality and most fascinating designs. Visitors are welcome to browse and will undoubtedly be given a passionate description of each.

For something practical rather than decorative, IKEA is always a safe bet, or try Carrefour and THE One.

Center of Original Iranian Carpets Nr ADCO, Al Khaleej Al Arabi St, Al Khalidiya, 02 681 1156, *coicco.com*
Gulf Antiques & Carpet Exhibition Khalifa Centre, Al Zahiyah, 02 645 9956
Handmade Carpet House Khalifa Centre, Al Zahiyah, 02 644 0344
Persian Carpet House Abu Dhabi Mall, Al Zahiyah, 02 645 2115

Curtains

Al Hijad Furniture & Curtains Shk Hamdan Bin Mohammed St, Markaziya East, 02 678 0057
Al Khalidiya Curtains Markaziya West, 02 634 3859
Areeca Furniture & Curtains Nr Al Diar Capital Hotel, Mina Rd, Al Zahiyah, 02 679 0010
Bin Husain Curtains & Decor Al Falah St, Al Danah, 02 633 9853, *binhusain.net*

Souvenirs

From typical holiday trinkets to tasteful keepsakes, there is a huge range of souvenirs to be found in Abu Dhabi. Many items are regional rather than local, and several are mass-produced in India, Pakistan and Oman.

The range of ornamental gifts available is endless, with perennial favourites being the Arabic coffee pot and cups (a symbol of Arabic hospitality), metallic decorative plates (traditionally used for serving coffee, and the larger ones for food), framed khanjars (traditional, curved Arabian daggers), wooden trinket boxes and larger handcrafted wooden wedding chests and furniture. For these kinds of traditional or regional items, the souks, particularly the Iranian Souk, and individual gift shops are the best places to look. Prices and quality can vary enormously, and the souks generally offer the best prices – as long as you remember to haggle.

Within the Al Zahiyah area you'll find an array of souk-style shops that sell Persian rugs and other carpets from the Middle East, in addition to trinkets and cultural souvenirs. More expensive souk-style shops can be found in The Souk At Qaryat Al Beri. You'll also find some of these items at the Heritage Village in the workshops where traditional craftsmen ply their trades and produce souvenir replicas, as well as more contemporary keepsakes such as keyrings, t-shirts and bags.

For ladies, pashminas are in abundant supply and make lightweight, handy gifts for family and friends. In some of the souvenir shops, you'll find simple, but extremely heavy, silver wedding jewellery. If the style is not to your liking, these coveted pieces of historical art make excellent displays when mounted in a glass box frame. Alternatively, if gold is more to your taste, the Gold Centre at Madinat Zayed Shopping Centre offers the capital's largest collection of gold vendors and jewellers under one roof.

Once valued more highly than gold, the dried resin from the frankincense tree of southern Oman has been traded for centuries and, nowadays, is often sold in a small wooden chest and with a charcoal burner to give off its evocative scent. Oud is a popular and expensive oil used in many of the perfumes, while myrrh and other sweet smelling mixtures are also sold. Ask for some to be burned, so you can smell it before deciding on your purchase. Arabian Oud has kiosks and shops in most malls.

Shisha or hubbly bubbly pipes are fun souvenirs which, along with flavoured tobacco, make a great gift. The more authentic versions can be picked up in

Souvenirs at Meena Souk

the souks or in the Arabic stores on the top level of Marina Mall but, if your friends and family are unlikely to know any better, good but cheaper shisha pipes and tobacco, in flavours such as apple, strawberry and grape, are sold in Carrefour. Where edible souvenirs are concerned, look out for delicious Lebanese sweets or local dates, both preserved and (in season) fresh, plus date-based products in all supermarkets.

Explorer publishes a number of great, multi-language coffee table books, calendars and postcards with stunning photos depicting the diversity of this vibrant city. Our annual calendars and Visitor Guides also make perfect gifts and souvenirs. Visit askexplorer.com to order copies. In addition, most of Abu Dhabi's tourist attractions also offer their own souvenir shops where you can purchase items to remember your visit.

Gallery One
The Souk At Qaryat Al Beri Al Maqtaa **02 558 1822**
g-1.com
Map **1 L8**
Sells a selection of stylish photographs and canvas prints and is particularly good if you want to take home some images of the region.

Gulf Antiques & Carpet Exhibition
Khalifa Centre Al Zahiyah **02 645 9956**
Map **2 R5**
A chain of stores selling high-end hand-made rugs, furnishings, lamps, jewellery and other traditional souvenir items.

Handmade Carpet House
Khalifa Centre Al Zahiyah **02 644 0344**
Map **2 R5**
Run by the same parent company as Gulf Antiques, this store specialises in hand-made rugs but also carries some antiques.

Marina Exotic Home Interiors
Abu Dhabi Mall Al Zahiyah **02 645 5488**
marinagulf.com
Map **2 S5**
The items sold here should add an exotic touch to your home – you can pick up key pieces that reflect the region as well as the wider Asian influence here. Head here for stunning cushion covers, rugs, wall hangings, boxes, photo frames and ornate chests.

Women's Handicraft Centre
Nr Al Karamah St Al Mushrif **02 447 6645**
visitabudhabi.ae
Map **1 E7**
Showcases and sells local handicrafts from skilled Emirati artisans. The small shop is ideal for picking up authentic jewellery or pashminas. There's an interesting museum onsite.

Sports & Outdoor Equipment

Abu Dhabi is a great place for a variety of sports, from common activities such as tennis, sailing, golf or football to exploring the great outdoors hiking or mountain biking – popular pastimes in the UAE, especially when the weather cools. General sports shops stock a good variety of items including rackets, swimming essentials or sports clothing. You can also find specialist sports shops around the city that offer diving, sailing and desert sport equipment. Many of the major brands have multiple outlets across Abu Dhabi's malls. The new (and huge) Yas Mall boasts an Adidas, Nike, Go Sport and Timberland. You can also pick up a few basic items at Carrefour, especially camping gear and various accessories.

Ace Hardware > p.236
20th Street Al Meena **02 673 1665**
aceuae.com
Map **1 D2**
You can buy all the basic equipment you need for your jaunt in the desert at this store, including tents, sleeping bags and cool boxes. The store also stocks a comprehensive range of hardware and accessories.

Adventure HQ
Dalma Mall Industrial City 1 **02 445 6995**
adventurehq.ae
Map **1 N13**
One of the greatest outdoor stores to reach Abu Dhabi, Adventure HQ is a vast store with everything you could ever need for every outdoor pursuit.

Megasports
Abu Dhabi Mall Al Zahiyah **02 645 6166**
Map **2 S5**
The place to go in downtown Abu Dhabi for sports shoes, exercise bikes and protein shakes. It should cover most of your exercising needs.

Middle East Bicycle Trading
Zayed the First St Al Danah
Map **2 N4**
Fans of something a little different can check out this eccentric vintage bike selection. Some good discounted bikes to be had, some strange novelties.

Modell's Sporting Goods > p.178
Khalidiyah Mall Al Khalidiya **02 635 9888**
modells.com
Map **2 H5**
This popular store is among the city's best for anything from sports gear to clothing and accessories. The sports chain has a number of branches in Abu Dhabi

WHSmith

Oasis Mall • Dubai Mall • Wafi Mall
Al Wahda Mall Abu Dhabi • Yas Mall
Marina Mall • Jw Marriott • Executive Towers
Sharjah University Hospital • Abu Dhabi Airport

Newspapers & Magazines
Books & Stationery
Drinks & Snacks

Mall, the World Trade Center Mall and can also be found in Dubai's Ibn Battuta Mall.

Rage
Al Wahda Mall Al Wahdah **02 443 7617**
rage-shop.com
Map **2 M7**
Urban street sport shop that stocks a range of BMX bikes as well as skateboards and accessories. You can even buy a snowboard.

Stadium
Mushrif Mall Al Mushrif **02 673 7731**
mushrifmall.com
Map **1 G7**
This large store stocks great golf equipment and an excellent range of yoga clothing. You'll also find Quiksilver and Billabong along with all the usual well-known sports brands.

Studio R
Marina Mall Breakwater **02 681 7676**
rshlimited.com
Map **2 D1**
Sells a selection of active wear lifestyle brands such as Quiksilver, Rockport, and sports brands such as Adidas, Reebok and Speedo. Also has a concession for specialised bikes, clothing and accessories.

Sun & Sand Sports
Khalidiyah Mall Al Manhal **02 635 4707**
sunandsandsports.com
Map **2 H5**
Known for selling fitness essentials, they also stock brands like North Face, Timberland and Columbia for outdoor adventures.

Tamreen Sports
Rashid Bin Al Maktoum St Al Danah **02 622 2525**
tamreensports.com
Map **2 L3**
Stocks Cannondale, GT, Mongoose and Schwinn bikes. Also the place to go for flashlights and knives.

Biking/Cycling
For the casual cyclist, various sports shops sell more basic models at reasonable prices. Children's bicycles are widely available in bike and sports shops, while the likes of Babyshop and Toys R Us have a range for tots, as do some supermarkets. Both adults' and children's helmets are available at the main retailers. Supermarket noticeboards and online classifieds, are good places to look for second-hand bikes. For serious bikers, there are several shops selling specialist equipment and accessories. Some even do repairs. Joining a cycling club (see Clubs & Groups) can also help you find the bikes or accessories you need.

Boating
For the fishing fanatic, there is a string of bait and tackle shops along Al Zahiyah Street near Hamdan Street, while the area around the Bateen jetty has a number of marine supply stores; if you need anything for your boat, this is the place to start.

Abu Dhabi Marine Equipment & Industrial Supplies
02 673 2300, *boatadme.com*
Arabian Divers & Sportfishing Charters
Marina Al Bateen Resort, Al Bateen, 050 614 6931, *fishabudhabi.com*
MTM Marine Yas Island Marine Sports Showroom, Yas Island West, 02 565 1110

Diving
Many of the dive centres listed in the Diving & Snorkelling section of the Things To See & Do chapter will also supply equipment. If they can't, they'll be able to advise on where to go to get what you're after. Al Mahara Diving Center (divemahara.com), for example, has everything from underwater watches to scuba equipment, but can also advise on where to get underwater photography equipment to compliment its unique course on the subject.

Gulf Marine Sports Nr Fayrouz Super Market, 10th St, Al Zahiyah, 02 671 0017, *gulfmarinesports.com*

Watersports
If the companies in the previous sections can't supply what you're looking for, then your best bet is to contact one of the companies listed under Activities in the Things to See & Do chapter. Companies involved in watersports will generally have the best access to specialist items, or may even have good second hand items they can sell you.

Textiles, Tailors & Repairs
To buy fabric, head to Madinat Zayed Shopping Centre & Gold Centre, or the streets behind Marks & Spencer in Markaziyah, both of which have a high concentration of textile stores. Compare prices between stores and don't forget to haggle. Look out for sales – the prices are often too low to resist. If you don't fancy pounding the streets, IKEA has a good range of bright, colourful cottons, plus curtain fabrics for kitting out your home.

There are numerous tailors in Abu Dhabi and most operate from small shops tucked away down side streets. The cost of fabric and workmanship is comparatively cheap, and having a shirt, suit, summer dress or even wedding dress custom-made can be a surprisingly affordable option. Tailors can copy a pattern, a garment, or even a photograph, and any good service will include at least one fitting before the garment is finished. Standards of workmanship vary, so ask around to get recommendations of good tailors. In addition, different tailors specialise in different styles of garment, such as saris, abayas, western-style clothes, suits and wedding dresses, so while most tailors will tell you that they can stitch anything you need, you're more likely to be happy with the results if you go to one that can demonstrate their experience in that style.

Agree on the price of the item before the tailor starts work. When the garment is finished, you will be able to try it on and have minor adjustments made if necessary.

Al Omara Textiles Nr Madinat Zayed Shopping Centre & Gold Centre, Al Danah, 02 634 5292
Areeca Furniture & Curtains Nr Al Diar Capital Hotel, Mina Rd, Al Zahiyah, 02 679 0010
Cairo Textiles Nr Al Noor Hospital, Shk Khalifa Bin Zayed St, Al Danah, 02 626 9648
Deluxe Arabian Gents Tailors Nr HSBC, Al Danah, 02 634 8814
Green Branch Nr Hamed Center, Sheikh Zayed the Second St, Al Danah, 02 621 4507
Jeeves of Belgravia Nr Sheraton Residence, Markaziya West, 02 666 3755
Kashmir Traders Fatima Bint Mubarak St, Markaziya West, 02 634 4317
Paris Textiles Nr Habib Bank, Markaziya East, 02 622 5030
Pleats Nr GEMS Academy, Najda St, Al Dhafrah, 02 443 3027, *pleatscouture.com*
The Raymond Shop Mazyad Mall, Mohammed Bin Zayed City, 02 559 2063
Rivoli Textiles Al Mulla Bldg, Al Danah, 02 679 2996, *rivoligroup.com*
Sedar Sheikh Zayed First St, Al Manhal, 02 633 4477, *sedaremirates.com*

Cobblers

There are specialists that can step in to fix a broken heel or where you can go to pick up a pair of new laces.

Clogs Shoe Repair Al Danah, 02 6262 750
The Cobbler The Galleria, Al Maryah Island, 02 621 0109, *cobbler.ae*
Minutes Marina Mall, Breakwater, 02 681 6380

Weddings

Services

Abu Dhabi is a great place to have your wedding, with sunshine pretty much guaranteed for your big day. There's also a whole host of world-class five-star hotel venues to choose from to make sure you have an unforgettable day. Almost all the large hotels offer wedding planning services if you book your wedding and/or reception with them, and can guide you through every little detail to ensure it all comes together perfectly on the day.

Studio Sol (studiosol.me) and Chic Design both make bespoke wedding stationery and gift items for speicla occasions. For anything that you can't find there, confetti.co.uk accepts international orders. Debenhams (Yas Mall) and THE One both offer wedding list services and there are also a couple of local online gift list services like whiteme.net.

As well as offering wedding planning services, several of Abu Dhabi's main hotels can be commissioned to make the wedding cake; alternatively, Le Pont Cafe in Khalidiyah Mall and Tickles Celebration Cakes (ticklscakes.webs.com) create beautiful wedding and party cakes. Most of the capital's florists can turn their hands to wedding bouquets and arrangements too; discuss your requirements with them to find out what will be available. For more information on tying the knot in Abu Dhabi, see Getting Married.

Dresses

Bridal gowns are, however, hard to come by in the capital with most options reflecting the flamboyant Arabic style. The best-known bridal shop in Abu Dhabi is Rahmanian (02 676 7079) at Al Zahiyah end of Hamdan Street. Dubai has a broader range of dresses on offer and has several excellent bridal shops to choose from. Jumeira Beach Road is home to several, including The Bridal Room (04 344 6076) and Frost (frostdubai.com). Pronovias (pronovias.com) has a store in The Dubai Mall. For high-end designer gowns head to Saks Fifth Avenue's (saksfifthavenue.com) bridal department in the BurJuman Centre which stocks the latest off-the-peg designer wedding gowns by Vera Wang and Reem Acra. The store keeps some gowns in stock, but others can be ordered (allow around four months for delivery). The bride will need to attend a number of fittings, but alterations are done in-house and are to couture standards.

There are several specialist bridal gown designers with workshops in Dubai, but Arushi (arushicouture. com) is renowned as one of the best. Gowns take around one month to make, but as Arushi is so popular, there is often a waiting list. Word of mouth for finding out about a great tailor is also a good idea.

Some tailors are also able to work from pictures to create your ideal dress, but proceed with caution as standards vary hugely, so it's best to ask to see some samples of similar work before commissioning an expensive garment like a wedding dress. Bridesmaids and other wedding guests, as well as mothers of the bride and groom, are well catered for at stores such as Coast, Debenhams and Monsoon, among many others.

Enjoy The True Italian Taste

الفـورنـو
الطعم الإيطالي الحقيقي

IL FORNO
the true Italian taste

Enjoy our famous Italian Meals and be mesmerized by the true Italian taste. Dine with a classic Italian ambiance in our restaurants and let your taste buds sing with the love of Pizza and Pasta, along with other Italian specialty dishes crafted by our Italian Master Chefs.

since 2000

GOING OUT

Pearls & Caviar

GOING OUT

Everything you need to know about making the most of Abu Dhabi's great restaurants and nightlife.

Exploring the going out options in Abu Dhabi is one of the best parts of life here. Whether you want to eat, party or stay overnight, this chapter will help guide you on your going out missions.

Hotels

Abu Dhabi's hotels cover the entire spectrum; from celebrity chef restaurants, to cool lounge bars and pumping nightclubs, with the choice expanding all of the time. Whatever your mood, there's probably a hotel in Abu Dhabi to cater for it.

The licensing laws in Abu Dhabi mean that if you like a glass of grape or hoppy brew, you will inevitably seek out a restaurant, bar or nightclub located within a hotel or leisure club – which is why they are the first ports of call for many expats. When eating out in hotels, bear in mind that not only will your bottle

of local water or can of cola cost up to 10 times more than in the supermarket, you will also be stung with a 6% tourism fee, as well as a 10% service charge.

Hotels are also where the most infamous brunches happen. A brunch is a set priced buffet where you can eat and drink as much as you like. They're generally served between noon and 5pm and can be swanky affairs and a real social highlight of a weekend.

The legal drinking age is 21, and it's best to avoid getting staggeringly drunk, as raucous behaviour is not generally tolerated. You may find unusual door policies at clubs, especially when they're busy, with some willing customers getting refused entry for no apparent reason. If you're a single male or a group of males, you're more likely to get in if accompanied by a lady or two. Hotel clubs and bars often close at about 2am, although some go on until 3am.

RESTAURANTS

Abu Dhabi is fast becoming a leading dining destination, and the capital is home to innovative chefs and restaurants that cater to all tastes and budgets. There's an ever-increasing selection of interesting restaurants and while there are five-star eateries aplenty, don't let first impressions deter you from giving some of the cheaper or non-licensed establishments around town a go too.

You will find that restaurants tend to fill up later in the evening, with the hip Lebanese crowd often not eating before 10pm at the weekends. If you're heading to a hotel restaurant or bar, it's best to leave the flip-flops and swimming trunks on the beach and trade up to smart trousers and shiny shoes. Similarly, you may get some funny looks if you turn up to any of the independent restaurants around town looking like you've just rolled off your sun lounger.

Food and drink outlets are subject to regular checks, so basic hygiene requirements are usually met. A good barometer is to choose a busy establishment, that way you know the turnover of ingredients is high. If you suffer from food allergies, don't assume that serving staff have understood your requirements, or that the menu will be suitably labelled. Vegetarians are generally well catered for, as Abu Dhabi is home to a large population from the subcontinent who are vegetarian by religion. It's a good idea to confirm ingredients with staff, as meals which at first appear meat-free, may in fact have been cooked using animal fats. Arabic cuisine, although heavy on meat-based mains, offers a great range of mezze that are mostly vegetarian and certainly worth exploring even if you're a die hard carnivore.

Taxes & Service Charges

Look out for the small print at the bottom of the bill and you may spot the words 'prices are subject to 10% service charge and 6% tourism fee'. The service charge is rather misleading as it isn't passed onto the staff, and there's no choice to opt out if you're not happy with the service. If you do want to tip the waiting staff though, 10% is the norm – and try to give them cash if you can. Tourism tax is only levied in hotels.

Ramadan Rules

During Ramadan, opening hours for restaurants and cafes change considerably. Because eating and drinking in public is forbidden during daylight hours, many places only open after sunset and then keep going well into the early hours. Alcohol is only served after sunset and live entertainment is not allowed during the Holy Month, so many nightclubs remain closed. Ramadan is a great time to sample some Arabic cuisine – iftar buffets are served across the city every evening throughout the month, often accompanied by traditional entertainment and shisha.

Independent Restaurants

While hotel restaurants tend to draw in the crowds, especially at the weekend, Abu Dhabi's independent choices are not to be missed. Areas like Al Markaziyah, the Tourist Club Area, Al Khalidiyah, Saadiyat Island and Yas Island are all home to a plethora of restaurants serving everything from authentic Arabic kebabs (Lebanese Flower) and tempting teppanyaki (Samurai) to Indonesian dishes (Bandung) and fiery Pakistani curry (Karachi City).

Explorer Recommends

Abu Dhabi is bursting with great restaurants, bars and cafes. This chapter picks some of the best, newest or most popular of each, handily categorised into sections according to why you might want to go there. Needless to say, this isn't comprehensive but visit askexplorer. com and you'll find many more, as well as the very latest reviews.

New Openings

The following pages give you an all-round taster of restaurants in Abu Dhabi, whether you want alfresco dining, somewhere to take the kids, a romantic rendezvous, or a cheap and cheerful bite to eat before the cinema or night out on the town. However, more and more places are opening up all of the time which makes the decision of where to dine even trickier. Not only are major international brands increasingly prevalent in the city, with the likes of Applebee's, Nando's, Carluccio's, Papa John's and Olive Garden all in operation, but there are also new and unique venues to try out. This is particularly true when new hotels and malls open up.

In November 2014, Yas Mall opened with exciting new eateries, including Abu Dhabi's first Cheesecake Factory, Shake Shack, Shakespeare and Co and Paul Cafe. Meanwhile, on Al Maryah Island, the glamorous Rosewood Abu Dhabi has top restaurants and bars that serve excellent food. Nearby, the upmarket Galleria Mall's restaurants include top-notch Moroccan Al Maz by Momo and Japanese standout, Zuma. Meanwhile, the Saadiyat Beach Club has excellent restaurants in a shoreline setting. Dine at Safina or De La Costa for a night out with friends. Yas Beach offers a trendy, relaxed beach vibe, while Yas Viceroy has a diverse range, such as Angar, Kazu, and Abu Dhabi's favourite rooftop lounge, Skylite.

CUISINE FINDER

Alfresco

If the weather is cool enough, head outside onto a terrace or balcony for breakfast, lunch or dinner and you'll feel the vacation vibe flow over you – just another reason why life in the desert is good, really good. The outdoor lighting in the evenings can make them atmospheric nighttime dining spots too.

Fanr

Manarat Al Saadiyat Saadiyat Island **02 657 5888**
fanrrestaurant.ae
Map **1 G1**
A hidden gem with a bright European feel and a large outdoor courtyard, Fanr is a bright, arty restaurant in the heart of Manarat Al Saadiyat – the first gallery on Saadiyat Island – where the chalkboard menus are displayed on quaint easels and colourful murals adorn the walls. Head outside and you'll be treated to a gorgeous courtyard area for alfresco dining. Grab some lunch after a wander around the gallery – try the ever-popular fish and chips – and pick up a few gourmet treats from the shop. It's also licensed to serve alcohol.

Hawksbill Restaurant

Saadiyat Beach Golf Club 02 449 8107
sbgolfclub.ae
Map **1 H1**
It may be a golf course restaurant but Hawksbill offers much more than your average clubhouse. Named after Saadiyat's local turtle species, it welcomes non-member diners in search of a modern setting, great views, reasonably priced drinks and a varied menu. It serves up everything from designer burgers to Thai dishes, but the common theme is huge portion sizes. The large terrace is great for a long weekend lunch.

Drinking Water

Bottled water seems to rocket in price in the five-star venues, and if you ask for water you'll often be given an imported brand, costing up to Dhs.40 a bottle. You should specify 'local' water when ordering, but even then you can expect to pay Dhs.10 or Dhs.20 for a bottle of still water that costs less than Dhs.3 in the supermarket.

Imago Restaurant & Bar

Le Royal Meridien Abu Dhabi Al Danah
02 674 1094
leroyalmeridienabudhabi.com
Map **2 P3**
African masks and heavy wicker furniture decorate this excellent restaurant. Seafood dominates the menu of Indian, Thai and Malay dishes but there's also a good selection of meat dishes and a few salads. Low lighting and the spacious setting creates a sense of intimacy, and dining on the terrace when the weather's good.

Safina

Saadiyat Beach Club Saadiyat Island **02 509 8503**
saadiyatbeachclub.ae
Map **1 H1**
Safina lies within the stunning surroundings of the ultra hip, trendy poolside of Saadiyat beach and prides itself on serving top quality and fresh international food. The beautiful location and ambience makes Safina a memorable spot if you want something a little extra special or are looking to impress.

Shang Palace

Shangri-La Hotel Qaryat Al Beri Al Maqtaa
02 509 8503
shangri-la.com
Map **1 L8**
Offers a variety of superb dishes from across China, with seafood featuring prominently. The atmosphere is great and the service faultless, while the large portions are excellent value for money. The breathtaking views from the romantic terrace are more than enough reason to linger for the evening.

Tarbouche Al Basha

World Trade Center Souk Al Danah
02 628 2220
tarbouchealbasha.com
Map **2 L3**
Authentic Lebanese food from this established and remarkably popular restaurant. The ground floor location offers views of the souk, but it's the rooftop terrace that distinguishes Tarbouche; it's a buzzing shisha spot in the evenings and a panoramic place to enjoy the grub. Service is efficient, though expect to pay slightly higher-than-average prices.

Ushna

The Souk At Qaryat Al Beri Al Maqtaa **02 558 1769**
Map **1 L8**
One of the finest Indian restaurants in town, the perfectly prepared north Indian cuisine will have you fighting to finish your meal even when you're full up. There's also an impressive range of premium wines and cocktails served by excellent staff. The interior is sophisticated but book on the terrace and enjoy views across the water to the Grand Mosque.

Vasco's

Hilton Abu Dhabi Al Khubeirah **02 681 1900**
hilton.com
Map **2 C3**
The patio at Vasco's is surrounded by established greenery and delivers views across the water towards

Marina Mall, giving the perfect alfresco venue to sample their fine-dining. Fusing European, Asian and Arabic food in imaginative presentations, it's no wonder this is one of the city's most popular restaurants. Make sure you book your table to avoid disappointment.

Beachfront

Abu Dhabi has plenty of coastline which has spawned a clutch of very special beachfront restaurants. They make for some memorable dining locations, no matter what time of day, but a meal by the beach with a stunning Abu Dhabi sunset is not to be missed.

Beach House
Park Hyatt Abu Dhabi Hotel & Villas Saadiyat Island
02 407 1138
abudhabi.park.hyatt.com
Map **1 H1**
Ordering is a breeze thanks to the large menu full of delectable Mediterranean titbits and a serviceable wine list – not to mention sangrias and cocktails. Cheese platters and innovative desserts round off a meal that will have you returning time and again to relax by the shore in this beautiful and romantic setting, overlooking the waters of Saadiyat Beach. The roof area is a particularly popular spot to dine or enjoy a drink as the sun goes down. If you venture inside there's a distinctively intimate feel with excellent decor reminiscent of a cool Californian beach house.

The Beach Restaurant
Khalidiya Palace Rayhaan By Rotana
Al Ras Al Akhdar **02 657 0000**
rotana.com
Map **2 A3**
A reasonably priced range of international seafood, you can dine alfresco by the pool and beach, or enjoy the cosy indoor setting. The Atlantis platter is worth a special mention, overflowing with aquatic treats and rare-to-find Ceviche. Otherwise, the menu features dishes ranging from Mexican lobster quesadillas to Mediterranean coconut crusted yellow fin tuna.

The Beachcomber
Sheraton Abu Dhabi Hotel & Resort Al Zahiyah
02 677 3333
sheratonabudhabihotel.com
Map **2 Q2**
This chilled-out beach bar feels more Caribbean than UAE. Popular with after-work and weekend crowds, it serves up a tapas menu that, while not truly Spanish, ideally accompanies the cocktails and shisha that are both also must-tries. Beachcomber is closed during the warmest summer months as is the cool B-Lounge outside bar, which puts on regular open mic nights.

Beach House terrace

Escape
Hilton Abu Dhabi Al Khubeirah **02 681 1900**
hilton.com
Map **2 C3**
Swimmers and beach-goers alike can enjoy this casual poolside restaurant with its full canvas canopies and multiple electric fans. Ideal for a casual family dinner or a few lazy sundowners; the hearty sandwiches and healthy, original salads make Escape a great place to recharge after a hard day relaxing on the beach. There's even a special menu for hungry little tummies.

Unique Dining
Saudi Cuisine VIP (02 665 5355) is a real taste of the Middle East; the restaurant has Bedouin influenced design including sheepskins and majlis seating with equally authentic grub. Tori No Su at Jumeirah at Etihad Towers (jumeirah.com) flies in fresh, seasonal ingredients once a month from Japan for a bespoke menu open to just 12 lucky diners.

Samak
Desert Islands Resort & Spa By Anantara
Sir Bani Yas Island
02 801 5400
desertislands.anantara.com
Map **3 B3**
It may take an hour by seaplane to get there, but the long trek to the Desert Islands feels truly worthwhile as you dine on the pristine beach, sampling Samak

restaurant's extensive Asian-inspired seafood menu in flickering candle light. Opt for the dine-by-design concept and you'll be whisked away to a private table set out on the sand – as far as settings go, it doesn't get much more romantic.

Brunch

A Friday ritual, the all you can eat (and drink) brunches are infamous in Abu Dhabi. They're a perfect place to try everything a hotel's restaurants can offer, although you may struggle to find room for a taste of it all.

Choices

Yas Island Rotana Yas Island West **02 656 4000**
rotana.com
Map **1 T5**
While everyday is a buffet day at Choices, Friday sees them pull out all the stops. An excellent pastry and cheese selection, Indian section and plenty of nicely prepared meat and seafood make for good eating. They even have apple crumble. It may not be the most extravagant brunch in the city, but it's friendly, tasty and good value. Outside seating by the pool in the cooler months is a nice option too.

The Garden Restaurant

Crowne Plaza Abu Dhabi Al Danah
02 616 6166
ichotelsgroup.com
Map **2 N4**
This lovely eatery's stylish decor and homely charm make it a thriving favourite. The Mojito Bubbly Brunch (Dhs.250) on Fridays includes, as the name suggests, unlimited mojitos and bubbly, accompanied by live music. You'll need to book in advance and dress on the smart side.

Do You Drunch?

Some venues are even taking the brunch format and moving it to later in the day, effectively a dinner brunch, or 'drunch'. Mai Cafe at Aloft is one of the pioneers; the poolside, rooftop venue offering Thursday evening international BBQs with soft drinks for Dhs.135, or Dhs.199 with free-flowing house beverages. Traders Hotel at Qaryat Al Beri also does a family BBQ on their beach every Friday during the cooler months.

Giornotte

The Ritz-Carlton Abu Dhabi Grand Canal Al Maqtaa
02 818 8888 ritzcarlton.com
Map **1 L8**
The Ritz-Carlton's brunch is an elegant affair with food counters discretely placed to avoid the Friday feeding

frenzy scenes you see elsewhere. Excellent sushi, oysters and caviar are all there to sample as well as fresh noodles, spit-roasted meats and Mexican snacks. The fantastic dessert station's home-made ice cream is a real treat. Dine outside if you want to soak up the sun as well as the occasion.

Jing Asia

Crowne Plaza Abu Dhabi Yas Island Yas Island West
02 656 3000
ichotelsgroup.com
Map **1 S5**
With a colourful, contemporary interior and a rejuvenating sea view, the ambience at Jing Asia is impressive either way. Attentive, friendly staff prepare a range of Asian cuisines from sushi to stir fries, in the open kitchen. Friday brunch broadens its culinary horizons by adding traditional roast meats and expat pleasing Yorkshire puddings.

Origins

Yas Viceroy Abu Dhabi Yas Island West
02 656 0600
viceroyhotelsandresorts.com
Map **1 T5**
The most striking feature of Origins is the amazing view of the Yas Marina Circuit (and some pretty swanky boats). The international buffet is well spread out and presented, with loads of time-honoured favourites from around the world. The salad and dessert bars stand out, offering an excellent selection of fresh, quality produce, and tempting sweet treats. The restaurant also does an excellent breakfast.

Jing Asia

Yas Marina Restaurants

View from Diablito

The delightful Yas Marina is a true dining and nightlife hotspot, boasting some of the coolest bars and licensed restaurants in the UAE.

Diablito
Fancy a casual night out? Head for this Yas Marina favourite for delicious tapas and other Mediterranean bites on a rooftop terrace with brilliant views. The pizzas are an excellent and affordable option. *yasisland.ae*

Cafe D'Alsace
Pick up a home-baked sweet treat at this delightful bakery, inspired by cuisine from France, Germany and Switzerland. Their savoury range includes flammkueche, the French answer to pizza. *cafedalsace.ae*

Rozanah
The UAE's dining scene is blessed with some fantastic Lebanese restaurants and Rozanah is one of the best. Decor is cool and the prices are very reasonable too. *rozanah.ae*

IRIS Abu Dhabi
An ultra-hip bar with a stylish eatery. This chic venue really comes alive during the F1 weekends, and plays host to a variety of cool events and live performances throughout the year. *yasisland.ae*

Aquarium
This aptly named venue is a must-visit for seafood lovers, serving up the fresh catch of the day with a culinary twist. Great for a casual dinner with spectacular views. *yasisland.ae*

Cipriani
This revamped restaurant is already a firm favourite. Enjoy classic Italian fare inspired by Harry's Bar in Venice, with gorgeous panoramic views of the marina. *cipriani.com*

Stars 'n' Bars
A very popular sports bar and restaurant that does an excellent selection of tasty American and western style food. The new shisha terrace is the perfect spot for alfresco sundowners. *starsnbars.ae*

Pearls & Caviar

Shangri-La Hotel Qaryat Al Beri Al Maqtaa
02 509 8777
shangri-la.com
Map **1 L8**

A stylishly modern and sophisticated venue, that offers a cool vibe for the brunching crowd. The food options might not be as vast as other brunches, but the quality is good; the outside grill, in particular, well worth a visit. This perennial favourite amongst those in the know, balances style, flavour, ambience and free-flowing mojitos perfectly.

Sevilla

Al Raha Beach Hotel Al Raha **02 508 0555**
danathotels.com
Map **1 R7**

Sevilla offers a large brunch buffet featuring dishes from Europe, Asia and the Middle East. Inside you can relax to the tinkling sounds of a harpist, or chill on the terrace overlooking the pool and the gardens of the hotel. The brunch at Sevilla is competitively priced, with the kiddie activities making this a great family option. During the week it also serves buffet food.

Sofra Bld

Shangri-La Hotel Qaryat Al Beri Al Maqtaa
02 509 8505
shangri-la.com
Map **1 L8**

Any restaurant that boasts three chocolate fountains is worthy of attention. While an a la carte menu is available, it is Sofra's luxury buffet that is the restaurant's main attraction. The breathtaking selection of cuisine is from all four corners of the globe – from fresh sushi and shawarmas, to kebabs and parrot fish. Brunch also includes a live jazz band.

The Yacht Club

InterContinental Abu Dhabi Al Bateen **02 666 6888**
ichotelsgroup.com
Map **2 C4**

The Yacht Club and Chamas team up at the weekends to offer an excellent fusion brunch, jam-packed with tasty Asian and western dishes. An abundance of barbecued meats and great sushi coupled with harbour views and free flowing mojitos, caipirinhas and bubbly make it a popular Friday destination. Specify in which restaurant you would like to be seated on booking.

Celebrity Chef

Dubai has traditionally had the monopoly on celebrity chefs showcasing their talents in the region. Fortunately, many are now looking to Abu Dhabi too.

Frankie's Italian Restaurant & Bar

Fairmont Bab Al Bahr Al Maqtaa **02 654 3238**
fairmont.com
Map **1 L8**

Famous jockey Frankie Dettori's collaboration with Marco Pierre White offers world-class dining in a chic setting. Diners can feast on the freshest Italian fare, ranging from home-made pastas and wood-fired pizzas to grilled lobster. The gelatos and tiramisu are a must for dessert. Look out for midweek early bird offers on main courses and cocktails.

Marco Pierre White Steakhouse & Grill

Fairmont Bab Al Bahr Al Maqtaa **02 654 3238**
fairmont.com
Map **1 L8**

If a beautifully appointed restaurant with exact yet friendly service delivering classic, hearty British comfort food, elevated to superbly delicious standards, sounds like your idea of heaven, then get yourself to Marco's Abu Dhabi restaurant. He may be a celeb chef but one bite into the foie gras or pepper sauce topped fillet and you'll know this is anything but style over substance.

Mezlai

Emirates Palace Al Ras Al Akhdar **02 690 7999**
kempinski.com
Map **2 B2**

Mezlai at the Emirates Palace is the work of Ali Salem Musbeh Al Badawi, a well-known TV chef in the UAE. It's billed as the city's first purely Emirati restaurant, meaning plenty of perfectly-cooked yet relatively simple food. It's certainly authentic, with warm Arabic hospitality from the staff and its setting in such an opulent hotel makes for a fantastic dining experience.

Mezlai

Publishing

DIGITAL
SOLUTIONS

Our extensive range of content, including maps, points of interest (POI), destination-specific information, photography and more is available through a number of digital platforms.

From websites to mobile apps, eBooks and bespoke solutions, our talented team has the expertise to deliver your digital project, directly to your fingertips.

askexplorer.com/corporate

 askexplorer

Cheap Eats

There's a huge mix of both chain and independent restaurants in the city covering just about every cuisine, that can see two people eat well for under Dhs.100. Perfect for budget nights out or quick lunch.

Caravan Restaurant

Al Hamed Centre Al Danah **02 639 3370**
sterlingcaravan.com
Map **2 M4**

If you're looking for a cheap, 'no frills' Asian meal, Caravan delivers the goods. The menu offers a tasty selection of Chinese, Indian and Thai cuisine, and the evening buffet (incredible value for money) includes soups, salads, a selection of main courses and desserts. The service is remarkably friendly and helpful given that this is a low-cost venue, although you can just use their home delivery service if you prefer.

Evergreen Vegetarian Restaurant

Nr Al Safa Supermarket, Shk Zayed The Second St
Markaziya West **02 676 7361**
Map **2 M4**

This is a traditional vegetarian Indian restaurant where the emphasis is very much on fresh, healthy ingredients. The place is clean but reassuringly basic in the way that only the very best independent restaurants get away with and, true to form, the food is authenticity itself. To the delight of local residents, the restaurant also does takeaways.

Figaro's Pizza

Marina Mall Breakwater **02 681 3300**
figaros.com
Map **2 D1**

More a family or fast food style Italian restaurant than a venue for a romantic evening, Figaro's serves up pizza and pasta which are both more than tasty enough and decent value. It's a good place to stop and carb-up before taking on a second round of shopping. If you're in Dalma Mall, then try Al Forno for a mid-priced slice of yummy Italy.

Kwality

Nr National Bank of Fujairah, Al Salam St
Al Danah **02 672 7337**
Map **2 Q3**

If you like authentic Indian food at extremely reasonable prices, then Kwality is one of the best options in town. From north Indian tandoori dishes to Goan curries, Kwality offers the diner a wonderful culinary tour through India. Watch the chefs in the open kitchen as they prepare succulent kebabs and hot, fluffy naans, while you whet your appetite with peppery poppadoms and spicy chutneys.

Le Shaderwan

Nr Kia Showroom, Al Salam St
Al Zahiyah **02 645 5400**
Map **2 Q4**

Le Shaderwan is one of those rare Arabic restaurants which is neither high-end nor chaotic cafe. The menu has all the traditional Arabic staples covered – complete with photos of each dish so you know what you're ordering. Prices are reasonable, portions generous, and the food served promptly. The restaurant is also a popular indoor shisha spot.

Street Food

Aside from a food van up on the Breakwater in the evenings and some roaming Desert Chill ice cream vans, 'street food' in Abu Dhabi means counter windows selling 'shawarma' (rolled pita bread filled with lamb or chicken as well as chips and a yoghurt sauce). At around Dhs.5 they're a tasty alternative to a burger. These places usually sell dishes like 'foul' (a paste made from fava beans) and 'falafel', or ta'amiya (small savoury balls of deep fried chickpeas). For about Dhs.15 you can even buy a whole grilled chicken, salad and hummus. Pakistani bread, or 'roti', can also be had freshly baked in unusual counters, where bakers crouch on worktops and slap the dough on the side of a buried oven. Abu Dhabi does plan on introducing around 300 street kiosks in the coming years though to help make the city more pedestrian friendly.

Lebanese Flower

Nr ADCB Al Manhal
02 665 8700
Map **2 J4**

The pavement location of this popular joint results in a few parking difficulties, with cars lining up outside to collect takeaway orders. Once inside the brightly lit, comfortable interior, you'll find a range of high-quality grilled meats and fish accompanied by fresh Arabic bread from the nearby bakery. A selection of Middle Eastern curries and meat dishes are available at lunchtime. There's also plenty of outdoor seating.

Rangoli

Yas Island Rotana Yas Island West **02 656 4000**
rotana.com
Map **1 T5**

In the heart of Yas Island, Rangoli is the place for a good-value curry fix and is a firm favourite for spice fanatics. The buffet, with a focus on north and south Indian cuisine, is fresh and attractive. There are also a la carte options. Starters and mains include vegetable samosas or meat, fish or vegetable curries. The friendly staff help create a laid-back atmosphere while inside, the interior is modern yet comfortable.

Marco Pierre White Steakhouse & Grill

Sevilla

Frankie's Italian Restaurant & Bar

Family Friendly

Most places are welcoming, and finding a restaurant with a kids menu or some play facilities can help little ones to enjoy their time out as much as you. Some restaurants in the city have soft play areas for children, or a swimming pool nearby for a splash about.

Assymetri

Radisson Blu Hotel, Abu Dhabi Yas Island
Yas Island West **02 656 2000**
radissonblu.com
Map **1 T5**

Perfect for families with children, this restaurant has its own clown, an assortment of toys and a swimming pool right on the doorstep. The international buffet caters for all, with live cooking stations for freshly prepared grub. Scenic views over the Arabian Gulf makes this Yas Island spot an excellent choice.

Carluccio's

The Galleria Mall Al Maryah Island
02 677 1261
carluccios.com
Map **2 T5**

This Italian gem prepares gorgeous food using the best fresh, natural ingredients, where possible from Italy. It is one, if not the best, Italian in the capital, with delicious signature pasta meals, baked bread and the perfect amount of toppings and sauces. The foodshop features a delicious selection of cheese, olives and baked goods and an unrivalled range of products imported from Italy. Carluccios can also be found on the Eastern Mangroves promenade in Abu Dhabi.

La Mamma

Sheraton Abu Dhabi Hotel & Resort Al Zahiyah
02 697 0224
lamammaabudhabi.com
Map **2 Q2**

This spacious, well-appointed restaurant has a homely atmosphere and offers everything from quick and filling pizza to delicious and generous helpings of pasta and seafood. The staff are attentive and quick to offer extras such as perfumed towels and freshly grated parmesan cheese. An excellent choice for an intimate romantic evening, or a fun family feast.

Nando's

World Trade Center Mall and Souk Al Danah
600 54 2525
nandos.ae
Map **2 L3**

The popular restaurant chain has expanded into the UAE in recent times, with two new outlets now at World Trade Center Mall And Souk, and Al Zeina, Raha Beach. Delivering the same delicious Afro-Portuguese PERi-PERi chicken that is a trademark of Nando's across the world, it's a firm family favourite The good news is they even deliver too.

Prego's

Beach Rotana Abu Dhabi Al Zahiyah
02 697 9011
rotana.com
Map **2 S5**

Prego's boasts an enchanting setting with its large, airy interior and superb terrace overlooking the beach. The food is wonderful – in addition to a varied pizza bar, the menu has a selection of both classic and innovative pasta dishes, main courses and desserts, and an impressive wine selection. Pizzas are prepared in an authentic wood-fired oven. Prego's is family friendly, but it's good for an intimate dinner too.

Shake Shack

Dalma Mall Industrial City Of Abu Dhabi 1
02 612 0750
shakeshack.com
Map **1 N13**

Enjoy an incredibly tasty burger (or two) as the perfect pit stop from shopping. There's an excellent choice of milkshakes, soft drinks or concretes (dense frozen custard blended at high speed with flavoured mixers) to wash them down with. In November 2014, the latest branch of Shake Shack opened in Abu Dhabi's newest and largest mall, Yas Mall on Yas Island.

Spaccanapoli Ristorante

Crowne Plaza Abu Dhabi Al Danah
02 616 6166
ihg.com
Map **2 N4**

This Italian haunt embraces delicious traditional Italian fare from Naples. Baked aubergine with mozzarella, parmesan, tomato and basil is an excellent start and the children love the metre-long pizzas, which are a particular Spaccanapoli trademark. The food is excellent and the prices reasonable.

The Village Club

One To One Hotel The Village, Al Nahyan
onetoonehotels.com
Map **2 P9**

Located in mature landscaped gardens, The Village Club buffet starts with soup, mezze and salads but extends to a whole variety of specialties. From the barbecue, there's a variety of beef, lamb, chicken and fish, along with side dishes. Weekends are great for families, and in the evenings it is a relaxing place to enjoy a calmer meal along with shisha or drinks.

Informal

While it's always worth checking dress codes for evening meal venues (particularly shorts for men), there are still many Abu Dhabi restaurants that ooze the laidback vibe at any time of the day.

India Palace

Nr ADNOC, Shk Zayed Bin Sultan St Al Zahiyah
02 644 8777
indiapalace.ae
Map **2 Q5**

This unassuming restaurant features an extensive menu and is busy at lunchtimes and evenings with a mix of diners. The flavoursome, authentic dishes are generously portioned and offer good value for money. As certain dishes are pretty fiery, those with delicate palates can request milder versions. Quick, courteous waiters will patiently guide you through the menu if you're not an expert on north Indian cuisine.

Jones The Grocer

Various
02 443 8762
jonesthegrocer.com

Stunning open-plan kitchens, unique coffee, gorgeous cafe-style dishes, fine artisanal groceries and European delicacies have made all six outlets incredibly popular. Ingredients are natural, preservative and additive-free to ensure the highest quality food, plus there are great cooking accessories on sale.

Havana Cafe

Nr Marina Mall Breakwater **02 681 0044**
Map 2 D1

Situated in one of the finest locations in the Marine Village area of the capital, Havana Cafe has stunning views that encourage relaxed alfresco dining, although comfortable indoor seating is an option. The menu is international and casual, and while breakfast and lunch are fairly quiet, it transforms into a vibrant dinner venue by night. Due to its delightful setting, this has also become a popular shisha venue too.

The Noodle House

The Souk At Qaryat Al Beri Al Maqtaa **02 558 1699**
thenoodlehouse.com
Map **1 L8**

Views of the Souk Qaryat Al Beri, coupled with delicately prepared oriental dishes, make The Noodle House a popular choice. The service is fast and the food is top notch with lots of vegetarian and diet-friendly options. It's best suited to lunch with friends and family or dinner before a night out. Another branch in Al Wahda Mall is also popular when you need a quick, quality meal between retail therapy sessions or heading to the cinema.

Samurai Restaurant

Nr Al Diar Capital Hotel, Al Meena St Al Zahiyah
02 676 6612
samurai.ae
Map **2 R3**

There aren't too many Japanese restaurants in Abu Dhabi, and some of them can be pricey. If you're a devotee of sushi, maki and yakiniku, then Samurai is a special little find. The food is top draw, while the atmosphere, like the slightly red decor and mismatched plates, is a lot of fun.

Teatro

Park Rotana Abu Dhabi Al Matar **02 657 3333**
rotana.com
Map **1 K7**

An eclectic mix of Venetian masks, thick white candles and modern furniture creates a dramatic, but informal, atmosphere (just don't wear shorts). There's a huge show kitchen knocking out dishes from China, Japan, India and Italy, most of them excellent. You can even book the chef's table for up to eight people if it's a special occasion.

Zest

The Club Al Meena **02 673 1111**
the-club.com
Map **2 V3**

This bistro style eatery offers an array of light and healthy snacks. Delectable soups, salads and sandwiches appeal, with the roasted corn and pumpkin soup and the chicken and mango Thai-style salad recommended. Situated in the fitness centre of The Club, Zest also provides pump for the pros with a range of Myoplex infused smoothies, and low carb and high protein alternatives.

Romantic

Beautiful settings, low lighting and superb food; Abu Dhabi has some truly romantic spots for a dinner date or even a proposal. Just make sure you take your eyes off each other for long enough to read the menus.

BBQ Al Qasr

Emirates Palace Al Ras Al Akhdar **02 690 7999**
kempinski.com
Map **2 B2**

High-quality chargrilled food, served on purpose-built pagoda platforms at Emirates Palace's own beach, this is barbecuing VIP style. The setting is as perfect for a romantic evening as it gets; sedate live musicians play chilled out tunes until late into the night as you sample the excellent Arabic-inspired barbecue menu. Round off the evening with some shisha in this idyllic, luxurious setting.

Benjarong

Dusit Thani Al Wahdah **02 698 8888**

dusit.com

Map **2 N12**

Thai fare from a Thai-owned chain that lives up to expectation. It's particularly recommended for its classic Thai staples; the Pad Thai is perfect and beautifully presented, and the King Prawn Tom Yumis decidedly yummy. You can 'create your own curry' and the staff will try hard to ascertain exactly how spicy you like it. A good venue for a lingering romantic meal.

Cipriani

Yas Marina & Yacht Club Yas Island West **02 657 5400**

yasisland.ae

Map **1 T5**

Dine in style on a very memorable date at Cipriani's. This fine Italian, designed by Florentine architect Michele Bonan, boasts a stunning outdoor terrace overlooking the beautiful marina, Grand Prix Circuit and the magical festivities beyond. The magnificent food and interior design will fool you into thinking you're wining and dining in Florence or Venice.

Finz

Beach Rotana Abu Dhabi Al Zahiyah **02 697 9011**

rotana.com

Map **2 S5**

One of the finer seafood restaurants in the city, the menu at Finz has several pages detailing different preparations and offerings – and none of them, from the lobster to the prawns and sea bass, disappoint. At the Beach Rotana, it is the gorgeous terrace setting which will bring out the romantic in you.

Il Forno > p.278, 295

Al Wahda Mall Al Wahdah
02 443 7344

ilforno-uae.com

Map **2 M7**

For a romantic memory of rural Italy and its cuisine, the fresh, traditional food at any of the 12 branches of Il Forno, are definitely worth a try. A weighty menu offers all the best pasta and pizza choices, all with the inventive Forno family touch and taste. The desserts are tempting too, so if you stumble on an Il Forno anywhere in the city, you won't be sorry.

Silk & Spice

Sofitel Abu Dhabi Corniche Al Danah **02 813 7777**

sofitel.com

Map **2 Q3**

Sofitel's Thai restaurant is a dimly lit and intimate venue, boasting carved wooden ceilings and the option of traditional sunken tables. If your date is a fan of Thai food, the authentic cuisine will have them cooing as you soak up the near magical atmosphere.

Showstopper

In this land of make-believe and headline-grabbing projects it's only fitting that some of Abu Dhabi's restaurants and nightspots put on a show to remember. Whether the decor is themed or the location unique, these venues aim to be number one.

Bord Eau

Shangri-La Hotel Qaryat Al Beri Al Maqtaa
02 509 8888

shangri-la.com

Map **1 L8**

One of the finest dining venues in the city. The wallet-damaging menu takes established luxuries, such as foie gras, scallops, lobster thermidor and Wagyu beef – and adds a subtle but distinctive twist. There's a refined air of fine dining with interesting views of the creek through large picture windows and faultless service. As this is a highly-rated, high-end venue, it is popular for celebrating special occasions.

Burlesque Restaurant & Lounge

Yas Viceroy Abu Dhabi Yas Island West **02 656 0600**

Map **1 T5**

This new restaurant, at the heart of Yas Island, blends entertainment and eating to perfection. Inside, amidst a striking red decor, enjoy tapas at the bar or a full dining experience at the restaurant with mouth-watering Mediterranean dishes. Settle in for dancing, live bands or top DJs any day of the week.

Li Beirut private dining

Enjoy The True Italian Taste

الفورنو
الطعم الإيطالي الحقيقي

IL FORNO
the true Italian taste

Enjoy our famous Italian Meals and be mesmerized by the true Italian taste. Dine with a classic Italian ambiance in our restaurants and let your taste buds sing with the love of Pizza and Pasta, along with other Italian specialty dishes crafted by our Italian Master Chefs.

since 2000

Kazu

Yas Viceroy Abu Dhabi Yas Island West **02 656 0600**
viceroyhotelsandresorts.com
Map **1 T5**

The terrace, overlooking Yas Marina and the race circuit, makes for a unique backdrop to a social restaurant where sharing is the best way to sample as much of the impressive menu as possible. Head chef Yu Cao trained under Nobu Matsuhisa and it shows. The exceptional lightness and clarity of flavours almost defies belief; wash them down with a Japanese beer or some sake.

Li Beirut

Jumeirah At Etihad Towers Al Bateen
02 811 5666
jumeirah.com
Map **2 B3**

Li Beirut is an unexpected delight with plenty of wow factor. While it's officially a Lebanese restaurant, it'd be more accurate to describe it as a European eatery which uses Lebanese flavours. Traditional starters have been reinvented, while pomegranate, pistachio, aubergine and splashes of kebbeh and zaatar add panache to great cuts of meat and fish mains.

Pachaylen

Eastern Mangroves Hotel & Spa By Anantara
Hadabat Al Zaafaran **02 656 1000**
anantara.com
Map **1 H6**

The hotel might be a delicate balance between the Arabian and the Far Eastern, but Pachaylen is all Thai,

from the staff to the menu. You'll be welcomed with a tasty miang kham street snack but after that, it's the best traditional Thai outside Bangkok. The soft shell crab salad is the standout starter, and look no further than the slow-cooked Thai curries for the main.

Quest

Jumeirah At Etihad Towers Al Bateen
02 811 5666
jumeirah.com
Map **2 B3**

Quest stands out as being truly world-class. The 63rd floor restaurant is beautiful and elegant but it's the service and the food that shines. This is the kind of Cantonese or Malaysian food that Heston Blumenthal might serve up – deconstructed and reinterpreted, never pretentious but intriguing, fun and downright tasty. An exciting and innovative culinary experience, with the option of a tasting menu to get your tastebuds as inspired as your eyes.

Rodeo Grill

Beach Rotana Abu Dhabi Al Zahiyah
02 697 9011
rotana.com
Map **2 S5**

Part old English drawing room, part old American shooting lodge, Rodeo Grill is unashamedly geared to carnivores who enjoy full-bodied reds. Salads, seafood and even veggie options are on the menu, but the spotlight is firmly on the steaks. The grade nine marble Wagyu and the bison rib eye are the stars of the show.

Pachaylen

Sardinia

Abu Dhabi Country Club Al Mushrif **02 657 7777**
adcountryclub.com
Map **2 J13**
Sardinia is both an event and a work of art, served
by a white-gloved, highly professional waiting team.
Only the finest ingredients are used and while some
amuse-bouches are off-the-wall, most are sublime
mouthfuls. It's not cheap, it's out of the way and often
it seems like nobody else knows about it, yet it's a real
Michelin-star level experience.

Sontaya

St Regis Saadiyat Island Resort Saadiyat Island
02 498 8888
stregissaadiyatisland.com
Map **1 G1**
Diners on the floating decks or terraces can watch
the sunset dip behind the Arabian Gulf while feasting
on exquisite Thai food. The bewildering setting and
relaxed ambiance make Sontaya a perfect venue to
impress a date or spend a delightful evening with
loved ones. Stylish, fresh and not extortionately
priced, it's yet another reason to visit Saadiyat Island.

Taste Of Home

Variety is the spice of life where Abu Dhabi's
restaurants are concerned, with the many nationalities
that now call this city home bringing their own
flavours to the table. They're great for those days when
you miss home or fancy some familiar flavours too.

Chamas Churrascaria & Bar

InterContinental Abu Dhabi Al Bateen **02 666 6888**
dining-intercontinental-ad.ae
Map **2 C4**
Churrascaria is Brazilian for barbecue and it's a red
meat heaven. Mind you, before you reach meat
nirvana you must wade through salad bar purgatory,
steer through steaming bowls of polenta, hash
browns, black beans, vegetable rice and fried bananas,
and push past a variety of barbecued meats. Only then
will you enter steak paradise.

Cho Gao

Crowne Plaza Abu Dhabi Al Danah
02 616 6166
ihg.com
Map **2 N4**
The menu reads like a food travelogue with an
ingredient from China, a recipe from Thailand and a
technique from Vietnam. The dim sum, steak, duck
and seafood options are recommended – as are the
creative vegetarian options. The ambience is soothing
and the service is attentive without being intrusive.

Hakkasan

Emirates Palace Al Ras Al Akhdar **02 690 7999**
hakkasan.com
Map **2 B2**
This famous establishment is a popular choice for
lovers of Cantonese cooking. Sleek and sophisticated
yet with a real sense of intimacy, the food is excellent
and the service as slick as the decor. It's no wonder
the high-end chain is so popular across the world.
They even do a reasonably priced dim sum brunch on
Fridays if you fancy something a little different.

Kababs & Kurries

World Trade Center Souk Al Danah
02 628 2522
theroyalorchidgroup.com
Map **2 L3**
This upscale restaurant offers, as the name suggests,
both Indian and Arabic food in the World Trade Centre
Mall and Souk. The kababs include chicken tikka to a
more adventurous shikampuri lamb. It may be a pricier
option for this type of food but the quality and dining
experience is good. Another branch can be found at Al
Muneera, Raha Beach.

Le Beaujolais

Mercure Abu Dhabi Centre Hotel Al Danah
02 633 3555
mercure.com
Map **2 M4**
You might be mistaken for thinking you're in a Parisian
bistro when you see the red-chequered tablecloths
and French-speaking clientele at Le Beaujolais. The
menu includes traditional French seafood and meat
dishes, finished perfectly by a dessert selection which
includes creme brulee and French cheeses. A set menu
is also available.

The Meat Co

The Souk At Qaryat Al Beri Al Maqtaa **02 558 1713**
themeatco.com
Map **1 L8**
The Meat Co is a deceptively large restaurant, covering
two floors plus a big outdoor deck. The energy of the
kitchen spills out to the restaurant giving the place a
frenetic atmosphere, but it's the meat that is the best
reason for coming here. Wagyu sirloin, Australian and
South African Grade A, and US Black Angus beef are all
on offer. The burgers are pretty good too.

Scott's

Jumeirah At Etihad Towers Al Bateen
02 811 5666
jumeirah.com
Map **2 B3**
First established in Mayfair, London, this classy British
seafood spot in Jumeirah at Etihad Towers offers a

simple menu, but does everything brilliantly. With indoor and outdoor seating, you can enjoy fare like Scottish smoked salmon of Cornish dressed crab while taking in the sea views and impressive Art Deco interior.

Stars 'n' Bars

Yas Marina Yas Island West **02 565 0101**
starsnbars.ae
Map **1 T5**
Recently renovated, Stars 'n' Bars delivers everything you'd want from an American-themed restaurant. Tex Mex, pizzas and burgers (and even fish and chips) coupled to fun and colourful decor, including a graffiti wall, makes this Yas Marina eatery undeniably family friendly. It also has a shisha terrace and hosts events like quiz nights and ladies' nights.

Taiki

Al Ain Palace Hotel Al Danah **02 679 4777**
alainpalacehotel.com
Map **2 P3**
While the decor is a touch on the drab side and the background music clanging at times, Taiki has a string of satisfied customers which includes Japanese expats. The secret of its success is simple: the food is authentic, fresh and so delicious you won't care about the surroundings so much.

Y Bar

Yas Island Rotana Yas Island West **02 656 4000**
rotana.com
Map **1 T5**
While many go there for the bar and service, the food shouldn't be overlooked at this 'New York urban chic' venue. Not only can you have steak as good as anywhere else in town, there are some homely comfort foods like shepherd's pie too. Needless to say it has quite a regular clientele.

CAFES

Cafes play as important a part in the culinary landscape of Abu Dhabi as the restaurants. While the food on offer may not vary as greatly as in their fine dining siblings, what they do offer is hugely popular for breakfast, lunch and dinner. You'll see many Emirati families enjoying meals in cafes, especially in the evenings when the lack of an alcohol licence is no deterrent, and fellow expats you meet will happily tell you about their favourite spot. The best bet is to try plenty of different ones yourself to find your favourite.

Breakfast

Whether it's grabbing a quick bite before work or indulging in a more leisurely breakfast, the city's cafes are generally geared up to cater for your needs. In fact, many expats find a new love for breakfasts when they move to the city thanks to the options on offer.

Cafe Bateel

The Galleria, Al Maryah Island **02 671 2284**
thegalleria.ae
Map **2 T5**
A local favourite, you'll find all the charms of the Middle East in one cafe, with warm hospitality, amazing coffee and delicious desserts, such as date pudding with caramelised pecans and rhutab dates.

Eric Kayser

Abu Dhabi Mall Al Zahiyah **02 643 4660**
foodhalls.com
Map **2 S5**
This is a great place to grab breakfast before exploring this vibrant area of the city. The French chain can satisfy most breakfast egg cravings, fill you up with a continental platter or labneh and feta bundle.

Godiva Chocolate Cafe

The Galleria, Al Maryah Island
02 667 0717
thegalleria.ae
Map **2 T5**
If gorgeous Belgian chocolate, delicious hot drinks, and sumptious cakes tickle your tastebuds, then a trip to the new Godiva Chocolate Cafe at the upmarket Galleria should be on your wish list.

Jones The Grocer

Al Mamoura Bldg B, Muroor Rd Al Nahyan
02 443 8762
jonesthegrocer.com
Map **2 N10**
This popular Australian chain has six outlets across the capital and offers one of the best breakfasts in town. A favourite for foodies, the chef's special menu changes every two weeks offering high quality dishes with rustic organic ingredients. Plus, they sell delicious gourmet produce and run cooking classes.

La Brioche

Marina Mall Breakwater **02 681 5531**
labriocheuae.com
Map **2 D1**
There are over 10 La Brioche cafes around Abu Dhabi and at each you can be sure of fantastic breads and pastries, with enough choice to satisfy either your sweet or savoury breakfasting tooth. Omelettes are a firm favourite and their baking really stands out.

More food. More fun. More family.

More Café at Marina Mall Abu Dhabi is now open

Saturday to Wednesday 8am-10.30pm • Thursday & Friday 8am-11.30pm

Art Cafes

Coffee houses and the artistic have often gone hand-inhand, and that's a trend evident in Abu Dhabi. From places like Cafe Arabia that hangs local artists' work in regular exhibitions, to the working studio and gallery, Abu Dhabi Art Hub, which flips things around by having its own cafe, it's easy to get your fill of both artistic creations and tasty treats in the city.

Coffee Mornings

Coffee mornings are the perfect way to meet others in the same situation and discover Abu Dhabi. Plus, the fantastic coffee, cakes and sandwiches make for a perfect mid-morning treat.

Cafe Arabia
Nr Mushrif Park, Mohammed Bin Khalifa St
Al Mushrif **02 643 9699**
Map **2 K10**

Spread over three floors, as well as the rooftop terrace, this tastefully decorated and unusual cafe offers light fare based on recipes the owner has collected from family and friends, as well as some inventive hot and cold beverages. Thanks to art shows and coffee mornings, this quirky spot has quickly established a well-deserved following among local expats.

Paul
Yas Mall Yas Island West **02 582 8300**
paul-international.com
Map **1 T4**

Another Paul cafe is welcome news for Abu Dhabi. The French-inspired cafe is a great place to get breakfast, lunch, or even just grab a coffee. The fresh croissants, bread, pain au chocolat and omelettes are all lovely in the morning, and for lunch, there is a healthy selection of sandwiches and salads. The Bawabat Al Sharq Mall and Al Wahda Mall locations are great, but the newest one at Yas Mall is sure to attract coffee lovers and a crowd of Paul fans.

The Club
Al Meena **02 673 1111**
the-club.com
Map **2 V3**

This long-established members' club holds regular coffee mornings in its Main Hall, including a Soft Play Coffee Morning every Thursday. Whilst the kids play on the bouncy castle or delve into their huge toy box, adults can catch up over a selection of teas, coffees, fresh fruits, pastries and biscuits. Waterfront Ladies' Coffee Mornings also take place on a regular basis and are a great way to meet newcomers to the city.

The Living Room Cafe
Nr Khalidiyah Mall Al Khalidiyah **02 639 6654**
Map **2 H5**

Set up in a residential compound behind Khalidiya Mall, this intimate cafe has the ambience of a British sitting room so should make many expats feel at home. It has an enclosed play area for young children, so parents can leave them to it and catch up over sausage rolls, delicious doughnuts and fab coffee.

THE One
Abu Dhabi Mall Al Zahiyah **02 681 6500**
theoneplanet.com
Map **2 S5**

Located inside the eponymous furniture store in Khalidiya, THE One cafe is a great place to relax in the middle of a shopping adventure. Not surprisingly, given the location, the cafe is strikingly decorated, and the menu, though not extensive, offers both traditional and more inventive cuisine, as well as delicious desserts.

Shakespeare and Co
Yas Mall Yas Island West **02 681 6500**
shakespeare-and-co.com
Map **1 T4**

Ever-popular cafe, Shakespeare and Co unveiled their latest cafe at the new Yas Mall in November 2014. With their hallmark Victorian decor and top quality food, the cafe wins again with its superb service and familiar setting. And, as with all their locations, the shining star is the pâtisserie counter, which displays a heavenly selection of French pastries, petit fours, marshmallows and homemade hand-wrapped chocolates.

Working Lunch

Lunch here isn't a meal that gets skipped quite as readily as it might do in your home country. Most workers will take a full hour, or more, and indulge in food from local eateries. But, if you find you're entertaining clients or colleagues through lunch, then these cafes are the business for some lighter food and a conducive atmosphere to clinch the deal.

Emporio Armani Caffe
The Galleria Al Maryah Island **02 676 6995**
altayer.com
Map **2 T5**

You've got the t-shirt, worn the fragrance and now you can eat the food. Ideally situated to capture the masters of finance in Abu Dhabi's new Central Business District, the Emporio Armani Caffe clinches the deal with its gourmet Italian food and legendary pizzas. Modern and sophisticated with great views over the water, it's one cafe whose stock is rising.

The Library

Park Hyatt Abu Dhabi Hotel & Villas Saadiyat Island
02 407 1234
abudhabi.park.hyatt.com
Map **1 H1**
Need a spot for an intimate meeting away from the
bustling metropolis? The hushed atmosphere of the
Park Hyatt's stylish tea lounge, decked with orange
leather and hints of black marble, is the perfect
place to mumble over the finer points of a deal while
gorging on selections of home-made chocolates and
pastries. Follow lunch with a head-clearing walk on
the beach.

Lounge

Hyatt Capital Gate Al Safarat **02 596 1430**
abudhabi.capitalgate.hyatt.com
Map **1 H8**
Set on the 18th floor of the Hyatt Capital Gate it's the
working lunch destination of choice for those visiting
ADNEC. But the elegant yet relaxed lounge-style
cafe attracts people from all over; the views, pastries,
snacks and premium teas are enough to convince
discerning lunchers that it's worth the trip regardless.
A more intimate library area is a useful place to take
tea while talking over a business proposal or deal.

Mirabel

Fotouh Al Khair Centre Al Danah **02 631 5111**
mirabel.ae
Map **2 L4**
Located in the Marks & Spencer building, Mirabel
stands out from the standard shopping mall cafes;
the menu encompasses delicious breakfast, lunch
and dinner options made of fresh ingredients by the
European-led kitchen crew. If you can't leave the office
for lunch, the online automated ordering system will
see a warm delicious meal delivered without the usual
hassle of location explanation.

The Social Hub

Nr Khalifa Park Al Matar **02 447 1010**
Map **1 K7**
A creative environment that's ideal for the media types
of the twofour54 building, the funky decor still doesn't
manage to outshine the menu. Very much the spot for
a casual chat, the Social Hub deals out burgers, pizzas,
salads and light sandwiches. It even does special
breakfast and lunch buffets for very reasonable prices.

Afternoon Tea

A British tradition that's eagerly adopted in the UAE.
While cafes offer afternoon tea in a casual environment,
many of the larger, global hotels in the city will bring
out the silver service – and cucumber sandwiches.

Shakespeare and Co.

The Drawing Room

St Regis Saadiyat Island Resort Saadiyat Island
02 498 8888
stregissaadiyatisland.com
Map **1 G1**
The Drawing Room continues the St Regis tradition
dedicating afternoons to the art of taking tea. 'Time
for Tea' gives sociable takers a selection of finger
sandwiches and baked raisin scones with Devonshire
clotted cream and strawberry jam, along with a
selection of fine French pastries. What could be better?

Le Cafe

Emirates Palace Al Ras Al Akhdar **02 690 9000**
emiratespalace.com
Map **2 B2**
You know you're somewhere special when afternoon
tea offers the option of a signature cappuccino topped
with 24 karat gold flakes. Savoury pies, English tea
sandwiches, fresh scones and a selection of Arabic
pastries, or French pastries and mini cakes make both
afternoon tea options at Emirates Palace a special
occasion. You can even opt for afternoon tea with a
glass of bubbly if you're celebrating.

Library Lounge

Saadiyat Beach Club Saadiyat Island
02 811 5666
saadiyatbeachclub.ae
Map **1 H1**
Settle in for tea and tranquility at the delightful Library
Lounge. This is the place to unwind with friends over
mellow conversation and relax with a cuppa. With

tasty nibbles and such an artistic decor, there is loads to enjoy beyond your pot of tea.

Lobby Lounge

Jumeirah At Etihad Towers Al Bateen **02 811 5666**
jumeirah.com
Map **2 B3**
A stunning piece of architecture will accompany your afternoon tea at Jumeirah at Etihad Towers. Huge angled glass windows give dramatic sea and sky views, as excellent waiting staff bring you a selection of sandwiches, scones, mini pastries (including iced truffles) and freshly baked Madelaines. If you fancy a bigger bite they also do hot mezze, an international cheese board and even fish and chips.

Mirage Marine Cafe

Nr Marina Mall Breakwater **02 635 9957**
Map **2 D2**
A favourite among locals, this large Lebanese restaurant/cafe features a main restaurant, a covered shisha bar and an outdoor garden. Very popular for hookah puffing and coffees, the mezze and mixed grills are also all well above par. No loud music and a chilled out vibe helps it to stand out from other similar cafes.

MORE > p.299

Marina Mall Breakwater **02 447 6325**
morecafe.co
Map **2 D1**
The brainchild of a Dutch collaboration stretching over 60 years, MORE's appeal, identity and reputation extend well beyond Abu Dhabi to its four franchises in Dubai. There is a healthy menu of starters, salads as well as a delicious selection of dishes extending across Europe and Asia. The soups are served in cauldrons, so is filling, and the soup, salad and pie trio is also a

big hit. With fresh, organic ingredients, baked bread and a fantastic choice, the menu has been as expertly crafted as the interior decor.

Shakespeare and Co

World Trade Center Souk Al Danah
02 639 9626
shakespeareandco.ae
Map **2 L3**
Step into the delightful Victorian decor of Shakespeare and Co. and you'll have an instant urge for a cup of tea and some sweets. The menu has an eclectic mix of English, American, Italian and Arab cuisine at moderate prices. The desserts, neatly showcased in a pastry case, are decadent and – almost – too beautiful to eat. A new branch has also opened in the city's newest (and largest) mall, Yas Mall.

Family Friendly

Cafes can be fun places and perfect to keep little minds amused and little bellies well fed. Healthy eating is heavily promoted in Abu Dhabi, and family focused cafes are often the best for organic and nutritious grub.

Cafe D'Alsace

Yas Marina & Yacht Club Yas Island West **02 496 3412**
cafedalsace.ae
Map **1 T5**
Newly opened at the Yas Marina, this kid-friendly cafe blends French, German and Swiss influences to bring some more unusual options to the menu. Riesling sour kraut with pheasant and juniper berry sauce may get adult taste buds tingling, but children might just prefer to try their Flammkuchen – France's answer to pizza; bread and butter pudding is the real winner too.

Sho Cho

The Chocolate Gallery

Fairmont Bab Al Bahr Al Maqtaa **02 654 3333**
fairmont.com
Map **1 L8**
This restaurant-cafe heaven is a chocoholic's paradise. Everything from chocolate crepes and muffins to chocolate martinis and fondue with all the trimmings are there to be savoured. You can even feast your eyes on spectacular chocolate sculptures. They do a mean range of savoury paninis, crepes and salads too if you're experiencing chocolate overdose.

Nolu's

Al Bandar Al Raha **02 557 9500**
noluscafe.com
Map **1 S6**
Inspired by Afghani cuisine and California recipes, this laid back cafe at the Al Bandar complex has a special menu for kids but is definitely a treat for all the family. From chocolate drenched French toast to salmon kebabs and make-your-own salads, it's great for any meal of the day. Home delivery service can be haphazard though, so take advantage of eating in at this funky waterside cafe.

BARS, PUBS & CLUBS

Where there's a hotel, you'll find a bar, pub or club, although a few places outside of hotels now have an alcohol licence making evening options even greater. Most expats will find a favourite, but part of the fun is trying out as many as you can to get to that point.

Alfresco

When the weather cools, the terraces of the city's bars are the places to go. Drink in the sunshine and savour that holiday feeling as you unwind well into the night. Shisha alfresco is also a popular option.

Bravo – Spanish Tapas Bar & Restaurant

Sheraton Abu Dhabi Hotel & Resort Al Zahiyah **02 697 0235**
bravoabudhabi.com
Map **2 Q2**
An intimate setting with lovely decor, Bravo makes for a great place for a date or simply catching up with a friend. While chatting away and sipping on a fruity glass of Iberian tinto or refreshingly cold Estrella beer, you'd do well to dive into the exceptional tapas menu.

De La Costa

Saadiyat Beach Club Saadiyat Island
02 656 3500
saadiyatbeachclub.ae
Map **1 H1**
Enjoy a refreshing beverage with some light snacks and conversation at the classy De La Costa. Relax under a sun-shaded veranda and sip your sundowner. Ideal for a night out with friends or an atmospheric treat for live entertainment. Dance, sing and socialise at one of the city's liveliest venues.

Ess Lounge

Shangri-La Hotel Qaryat Al Beri Al Maqtaa
02 509 8555
shangrila.com
Map **1 L8**
As an extension of Shangri-La's Pool Bar, Ess Lounge is a low key but high fun spot by the beach. Lighting is important – even the drinks menu is illuminated.

Mai Cafe

Aloft Abu Dhabi Al Safarat **02 654 5111**
aloftabudhabi.com
Map **1 H8**
A little out of the way, but Aloft's Mai Cafe can still attract a good crowd once the evening descends. Creative decor around a splash pool; either sit on sofas or find a more romantic spot.

McGettigan's

Al Raha Beach Hotel Al Raha Beach **02 508 0555**
alrahabeach.danathotels.com
Map **1 R7**
The recent opening of McGettigan's brings all the warmth, fun and hospitality of an Irish Pub to the capital. A well known hangout, famous for its great pub grub, ales and entertaining atmosphere.

Sho Cho

The Souk At Qaryat Al Beri Al Maqtaa **02 558 1117**
sho-cho.com
Map **1 L8**
One of Dubai's most achingly hip nightclubs has made it to Abu Dhabi. The outside decking boasts incredible creekside views where you can sip on specially made cocktails and listen to top DJs. If you're peckish, their Japanese-inspired menu is well worth a try.

Safe Driver

If you've gone out and ended up having a drink, don't risk getting back behind the wheel. There is a zero-tolerance approach to drink driving. Instead, you can call Safe Driver (800 831) who will come to where you are and then drive you and your car safely back home.

Cocktails

Cocktails, and their non-alcoholic 'mocktail' cousins, are hugely popular in the UAE. You'll find new and inventive blends by fantastic mixologists in many of Abu Dhabi's cooler bars and restaurants.

Left Bank

The Souk At Qaryat Al Beri Al Maqtaa **02 558 1680**
emiratesleisureretail.com
Map **1 L8**
With views of Sheikh Zayed Grand Mosque and chic contemporary European cuisine, Left Bank has a lot to offer. The terrace bears Arabic influences, while the interior echoes any exclusive international venue, complete with VIP section and inexhaustible cocktail menu. The combination of excellent food, friendly staff and stylish surroundings has earned Left Bank a good reputation among the expat community.

SAX

Le Royal Meridien Abu Dhabi Markaziya East
02 674 2020
leroyalmeridienabudhabi.com
Map **2 P3**
A live jazz band and a well-stocked bar contribute to the vibey atmosphere as you unwind on comfortable sofas in the sunken lounge area, with one of the many exotic cocktails on offer. The decor is clean-cut with avant-garde lighting, which suits the sophisticated young clientele looking for a stylish venue to meet and mingle well into the night.

Stills Bar & Brasserie

Crowne Plaza Abu Dhabi Yas Island Yas Island West
02 656 3000
ichotelsgroup.com
Map **1 S5**
This lively bar serves the cool youth as well as the gracefully aged. There's a nice list of specialty cocktails and whiskeys, as well as several beers on tap and a cigar humidor. There's also a DJ Pool Party night once a month, and Stills serves as a sometime-stopover for touring bands performing at local Yas Island venues.

Trader Vic's

Beach Rotana Abu Dhabi Al Zahiyah
02 697 9011
tradervics.com
Map **2 S5**
The original Trader Vic's in California was where the Mai Tai was invented, and Abu Dhabi's branch doesn't let the side down. If you want fruity cocktails of various strengths, some quirky Hawaii-style decor and a good time, this venue is a good bet. A loyal customer base will testify to its atmosphere and quality beverages.

The Yacht Club

InterContinental Abu Dhabi Al Bateen
02 666 6888
ichotelsgroup.com
Map **2 C4**
If you're a vodka martini fan then, with 52 different kinds of vodka, The Yacht Club should definitely be on your hit list. The terrace benefits from harbour vistas, while, inside, the sparkly decor is one part disco and one part ship's galley. There's a DJ on hand at weekends and an excellent Asian/western fusion menu to dine on.

Ladies' Nights

Lucky ladies in this fair city can go out almost every night of the week and enjoy free drinks. Of course, this isn't a charitable move by Abu Dhabi's bars; where ladies are drinking, the men and their wallets inevitably follow. Wednesday is the biggest ladies' night with many bars and pubs offering at least two free drinks. Skylite at Yas Viceroy even raffles off designer shoes.

Pubs

Wherever expats go, pubs follow. If you miss that slice of home Abu Dhabi has some fantastically authentic venues that are rather good in their own right.

Belgian Beer Cafe

InterContinental Abu Dhabi Al Bateen **02 666 6888**
belgianbeercafe.com
Map **2 C4**
A lively, European-style cafe with lots of noise and hearty laughter coming from the bar. The extensive choice of traditional beers makes this a favourite hangout among expats. The restaurant boasts some of the best fries and the pork is cooked in a number of ways. Their speciality, however, is steamed mussels, all of which makes for a cool escape into Belgian vibes. A new location opened recently on Yas Island.

Brauhaus

Beach Rotana Abu Dhabi Al Zahiyah
02 6979 011
rotana.com
Map **2 S5**
This cosy pub features all things German in a setting almost authentic enough to make you think you're in a remote hunting lodge. European sports are shown on the many TV screens and the menu offers hearty German fare including pretzel dumplings and their signature apple strudel. All their beers are German imports, which includes the Nürburgring fans' favourite and there's a happy hour from 4pm to 7pm.

Captain's Arms
Le Meridien Abu Dhabi Al Zahiyah **02 644 6666**
captainsarms-abudhabi.com
Map **2 S4**
Located in the Village Courtyard and overlooking the gardens, this tavern has a classic British pub interior and upbeat, outdoor terrace; by and large, Abu Dhabi's expat scene soaks it up. The daily happy hour, nightly entertainment and F&B specials bring in those crowds and, although you won't find many culinary surprises, food portions are generous and satisfying.

Hemingway's
Hilton Abu Dhabi Al Khubeirah **02 681 1900**
hilton.com
Map **2 C3**
Tucked away at the back of the Hilton hotel, this lively bar-restaurant offers an unpretentious all-in-one experience. The fun restaurant serves standard Mexican fare and opens out onto a bar with TVs, live music and quiz nights.

PJ O'Reilly's
Le Royal Meridien Abu Dhabi Al Zahiyah
02 674 2020
pjspubabudhabi.com
Map **2 P3**
One of Abu Dhabi's most popular pubs, with a friendly atmosphere. There's a lively bar downstairs, or escape to the quieter upstairs or outdoor. Bright and comfortable, it seldom feels crowded, despite its popularity. Large screen TVs show sport and happy hour lasts from midday to 7pm every day.

Rooftop

Some of the best venues (and views) in Abu Dhabi are up on the rooftops, so make sure you search them out.

Blue Line Bar
Oryx Hotel Al Khalidiyah **02 681 0001**
aldiarhotels.com
Map **2 F4**
Huge white marble columns surround this rooftop pool bar area, adding a grand vibe, even if it might tread the line of kitsch with a distinctively Arabic vibe. Enjoy a light snack and a few drinks as you watch the sun set over Abu Dhabi.

Chill'O Pool Bar
Sofitel Abu Dhabi Corniche Al Danah
02 813 7777
sofitel.com
Map **2 Q3**
An oasis of calm just off the Corniche, where comfy outside lounging and Arabic gazebos go hand in hand

Glo

with Sofitel's signature modern and elegant style. Wind away a day by the pool or escape to the sky for discreet drinks with friends in the evening; either way you're sure to leave nicely chilled.

Glo
Rosewood Abu Dhabi Al Maryah Island
02 813 5550
rosewoodhotels.com
Map **2 T5**
If you want glamour then Glo is the place to be. The Rosewood's newly opened rooftop pool bar is the epitome of cool; incredible lighting, striking umbrella-like structures erupting skywards and drinks under the stars as the lights of the sky-high business towers look on. Grab a cabana and enjoy excellent service, some equally excellent food and a fantastic evening in the open out on Al Maryah Island.

Level Lounge
Crowne Plaza Abu Dhabi Al Danah
02 616 6166
ichotelsgroup.com
Map **2 N4**
A perfect downtown escape for a relaxing drink or two as the sun sets over the urban skyline. Cooling off in, or by, the pool is a great option on Friday afternoons, otherwise the Level Lounge is open nightly from 7pm. The cosy, chilled out rooftop setting serves up some mean tapas and a tasty selection of bitesize snacks. Or, if you're there on a Thursday or Friday night the resident DJ will be on hand to provide a pumping soundtrack to your evening.

Relax@12

Aloft Abu Dhabi Al Safarat **02 6545 138**
relaxat12.com
Map **1 H8**

The name says it all – chill out in the sleek lounge, nibble on some Asian bites and down a cocktail or two as you sink into one of the inviting sofas on the terrace overlooking Abu Dhabi's gorgeous skyline. The decor is modern with glowing bars, dim lighting and angular furniture, and both the terrace and huge-windowed bar attract a refreshingly broad mix of clientele.

Showstopper

There are impressive bars throughout the city, but if you really want to impress visitors or experience something special yourself, then the settings and service of the following might do the job perfectly.

Blue Bar

Hilton Capital Grand Abu Dhabi
Al Madina Al Riyadiya **02 617 0000**
hilton.com
Map **1 J8**

If you want to be wowed by architectural design while supping a drink in sophisticated surroundings, Blue Bar at the Hilton Capital Grand is for you. The signature bar floats inside the hotel's huge 11 storey glass atrium offering great panoramic views of the city to go with the expertly prepared drinks.

BOA Steakhouse

Eastern Mangroves Promenade
Al Matar **02 641 1500**
boaabudhabi.ae
Map **1 H6**

This trendy American steakhouse has already built a stellar reputation. Unique dishes pepper the menu (goat cheese baklava or lobster potatoes, anyone?) and the steak might just be the city's best. The dry aged sirloin and ribeye are packed with flavour and so tender they practically melt in your mouth. A creative cocktail menu and unparalleled views of the Eastern Mangroves complete your experience.

Etoiles

Emirates Palace Al Ras Al Akhdar
02 690 8960
etoilesuae.com
Map **2 B2**

Bar, restaurant or nightclub; the venue brilliantly walks the delicate line between all three. The food is tasty European haute cuisine, while the decor is Paris, New York or Milan chic turned all the way up to 11. As the evening gets later the venue hits full-on club mode, making it an A-listers favourite when they're in town

to party. Etoiles stands out as one of the UAE's very best spots for evening entertainment.

Koi Restaurant & Lounge

The Collection Saadiyat Island **02 678 3334**
thecollection.ae
Map **1 G1**

Step through the doors and there's a cool vibe that mixes dark decor with atmospheric lighting and upbeat music. Upscale yet comfortable, tables on split levels create an intimate dining spot even for larger groups. Koi's Japanese menu is sensational with signature rolls, sushi, soups, sashimi and an exceptional miso bronzed black cod. The kobe style fillet mignon 'toban-yaki' will keep the taste flowing and is especially delightful. Koi is a joy all round.

Ornina Lounge

Nr Spinneys Al Bandar Al Raha
02 556 6090
ornina.ae
Map **1 S6**

A unique proposition, Ornina is a licensed bar-restaurant at the Al Bandar residential complex in Al Raha Beach. The stunning wooden-clad exterior is matched by an equally stylish Scandinavian-inspired interior with impressive views across the water to Yas Island. Food is Mediterranean with a twist, drinks are inventive and the atmosphere buzzing.

Ray's Bar

Jumeirah At Etihad Towers Al Bateen
02 811 5666
jumeirah.com
Map **2 B3**

Up in the clouds on the 62nd floor, Ray's Bar is a refined blend of cocktails and DJs with a chic ambience, cow print cushions and all. The views from high are one reason to go, but you'll want to stay for the service and drink options; expert bar staff will gladly create you a unique mix too.

Skylite

Yas Viceroy Abu Dhabi Yas Island West **02 656 0600**
viceroyhotelsandresorts.com
Map **1 T5**

Possibly the number one night spot in town, you can't help but be blown away by the setting of this rooftop lounge bar under the colour changing canopy of the Yas Viceroy. If you want to go somewhere super stylish that makes a statement, venues don't come much swankier than this. There are light bites and a long wine list, champagne and lush cocktails to choose from and the dress code errs on the smarter and trendier side of casual. The best time to enjoy Skylite is as the sun goes down on the city, but it's easy enough to spend all night here too.

Sports Bars

Some of the liveliest bars in the city are the sports bars. They generally show all the top football and rugby games and tend to be as popular during weekend daytimes as they are in the evenings.

Cooper's Bar & Restaurant
Park Rotana Abu Dhabi Al Matar **02 657 3333**
rotana.com
Map **1 K7**

Not only can you find a friendly pint and some superb pub grub, Cooper's also shows all major football matches (call ahead for details). Convenient for both on and off-island clientele, competitive prices, with 50% off selected beverages during its extended 'happy hour', and plenty of space, including an outside area, makes it a firm expat favourite. Gets louder as the night goes on if you want to keep the party going.

Heroes
Crowne Plaza Abu Dhabi Al Danah
02 616 6166
ichotelsgroup.com
Map **2 N4**

Heroes is your typical sports bar early in the evening and during weekend afternoons. However, once the DJ begins at 9pm, followed by the band at 10pm, don't bother trying to watch TV – it's all about throwing shapes on the dancefloor. Parking around the hotel is nightmarish so use the underground carpark next to the Crowne Plaza or take a cab.

Karaoke King

There are a few places in Abu Dhabi where you can show off your vocal abilities, or even just belt out a comedy version of Ice Ice Baby. Tambayan at Al Ain Palace Hotel (alainpalacehotel.com) is dedicated to karaoke, with King and Queen of Karaoke nights, while there's a karaoke room at PJ O'Reilly's (pjspubabudhabi. com). Bowling City (bowling-city.com) at Abu Dhabi Mall even lets you record your vocal gymnastics on CD for future playback. A number of bars around the city have weekly karaoke nights, or if you're in a band you can hit the open mic sessions at B-Lounge by Beachcomber (sheratonabudhabihotel.com) to show off your vocal chops.

Hickory's Sports Bar
Yas Links Abu Dhabi Yas Island West **02 810 7710**
yaslinks.com
Map **1 T4**

A cosy club-restaurant with sensational views over the water and golf course, Hickory's is a sports bar, but that title doesn't really do it justice. Sure, there are major sporting events and news adorning the large plasma screens on a regular basis, but the feel is that of a private members' club. Visit in the evening for gorgeous sunset views and to sample the robust menu of wood-fired pizzas, huge pies and steaks.

NRG Sports Cafe
Le Meridien Abu Dhabi Al Zahiyah
02 644 6666
nrg-sportscafe.com
Map **2 S4**

Armchair athletes flock to this sports cafe, with its multitude of TV screens, reasonably priced snacks and happy hour that lasts from 7pm to 9pm. Decorated in sporting colours and plenty of paraphernalia, it combines an arena ambience with an open kitchen that pumps out fast and furious fusion food. You can try out your best moves on the dancefloor or, better still, keep your eyes glued to the scoreline.

The Retreat
Westin Abu Dhabi Golf Resort & Spa
Khalifa City **02 616 9999**
westinabudhabigolfresort.com
Map **1 N8**

If you want a more sophisticated spot to watch international sports, the bar at Westin Abu Dhabi Golf Resort & Spa is the place. Combining classic style and contemporary elegance with three large LED TVs and a broad drinks menu, it manages to be both sophisticated and informal. A great place for those living off the island with happy hours from 5pm – 8pm, Sunday to Thursday.

NRG Sports Cafe

Wine Bars & Cigar Lounges

For a more sophisticated evening, Abu Dhabi's wine bars and cigar lounges set the tone perfectly. From high rises to cellars, there's a good varied choice too.

Cristal

Millennium Hotel Abu Dhabi Al Danah
02 614 6000
millenniumhotels.ae
Map **2 P3**

Experience the tranquil but trendy ambience of this bar, where elegantly understated decor is set off perfectly by an excellent range of champagne, sparkling wines and other tipples. Sit back and relax in surroundings of polished wood, leather and subdued lighting – the tinkling tunes played by the in-house classical jazz pianist adding the perfect accompaniment. Happy hour is from 5pm to 7pm.

Havana Club

Emirates Palace Al Ras Al Akhdar **02 690 7999**
kempinski.com
Map **2 B2**

Fine cognacs, Armagnac's and a selection the world's best cigars; if you want to spend a sophisticated and gentlemanly evening with friends, this is the place to do it. Every Thursday the bar has a 'Mojito Extravaganza' too, offering a number of different interpretations of the popular drink. The setting is old school elegance, and while it might not be an obvious choice, the experience is first class.

La Cava

Rosewood Abu Dhabi Al Maryah Island **02 813 5550**
rosewoodhotels.com
Map **2 T5**

A place for dedicated followers of the grape, La Cava is an intimate and live wine cellar. The racks are stacked with over 1,000 premium labels and there's even a secured area with the rarest vintages. If you can't find a good glass here you're beyond help. A cigar room with walk-in humidor and selection of whiskeys makes La Cava a truly exclusive spot for the connoisseur.

Prive

Hyatt Capital Gate Al Safarat **02 596 1234**
abudhabi.capitalgate.hyatt.com
Map **1 H8**

At one point this lounge bar may have been a little reliant on exhibition guests, but it's now becoming more of a destination for residents after an informal hangout spot. Cheese and wine evenings, as well as other themed nights help keep things fresh, or you can simply pick through their excellent drinks menu, including a selection of fine whiskeys, rums and cocktails, while relaxing with a cigar.

Vertical Wine Bar

Cristal Salam Hotel Al Zahiyah **02 659 7712**
cristalhospitality.com
Map **2 Q5**

Claiming to have one of the most extensive wine lists in the city, Vertical's popularity can be put down to the casual ambience, choice of beverages and beautiful

La Cava

decor. It's next to Baroussa Lounge which is good for sports, so you can flit between the two, or simply soak up Vertical's atmosphere. Private dining rooms and great steaks add to the appeal.

Nightclubs

While Abu Dhabi nightlife may not be 'legendary' you might be surprised by what's on offer for nightime revellers. In fact, some of the city's clubs can rival anything that other countries or cities have to offer.

Cinnabar

Hilton Abu Dhabi Al Khubeirah **02 681 1900**
hilton.com
Map **2 C3**
With an eclectic mix of R&B and popular funk, Cinnabar offers a stylish and sophisticated way to round off your night. Guests can either strut their stuff on the dancefloor or simply sit back, relax and let one of the waitresses guide them through the cocktail menu. The champagne and fresh strawberry cocktails slip down easily but, don't fear, the Dhs.100 price tag will keep your excesses in check.

Illusions

Le Royal Meridien Abu Dhabi Al Danah
02 674 2020
leroyalmeridienabudhabi.com
Map **2 P3**
One of Abu Dhabi's best known nightspots, Illusions plays loud, banging dance music in a futuristic venue. The crowd tends to be fairly male dominated and it's not the place to go if you're after a cosy chat with friends, but if you want to dance the night away it's ideal. Head there from about 11pm when it really starts to swing. Saturday and Monday are ladies' nights.

O1NE Yas Island

Nr Flash Forum Yas Island West **052 788 8111**
Map **1 T4**
You can't miss the graffiti covered exterior of the cylindrical O1NE nightclub on Yas Island, and you shouldn't miss what goes on inside either. The DJ booth looks down over the tables and dancefloor filled by the clubbing elite as some of the most impressive lighting displays illuminate the party. They even have limos covered in the same graffiti for VIP guests. Currently opens only every Thursday evening.

People by Crystal

The Collection St Regis Saadiyat Island 02 677 0788
Map **1 G1**
The latest addition to Abu Dhabi's nightlife scene is fast becoming the place to party in the capital. People by Crystal offers a VIP boutique nightclub experience

and plays host to many international acts. A high-end and indulgent experience set amidst a luxurious interior. A real treat any night of the week and you are guaranteed a night to remember. Opens until 4am.

Rush

Yas Viceroy Abu Dhabi Yas Island West **02 656 0600**
viceroyhotelsandresorts.com
Map **1 T5**
The sort of swanky and effortlessly elegant lounge bar you'd expect from the people behind the global Buddha Bar chain. It still hasn't quite hit its stride and is not always as busy as the bar and setting merit, but Rush is still a great place for afterwork tipples, an early stop or a chilled-out but classy night out. The cocktails are excellent, and there's some top quality finger food on the menu too.

ENTERTAINMENT

When you're not eating in fantastic restaurants, enjoying a spa or partaking in the numerous sporting activities around the city, then you may just find time for what else Abu Dhabi has to offer. Every year more events pop up, more venues are built and the decisions become even tougher. From film and music festivals to a comedy or quiz night; if you're bored in Abu Dhabi then you're doing something wrong.

Culture

All of life is a cabaret apparently, which is a good job if you're coming to Abu Dhabi specifically for a show of that ilk as they're in short supply. You won't find drag shows in the city as cross-dressing is illegal in the UAE, although neighbouring Dubai has flirted with the genre. However, many hotels around the city will entertain guests with traditional Arabic belly dancing shows and other cultural displays from the UAE's past. Similarly, if you head out on a desert tour you'll likely be treated to a spinning, skilful display of traditional dancing.

Cinema

There are a number of cinemas around Abu Dhabi – the majority of them situated in shopping malls – which screen largely mainstream Hollywood and Bollywood films. There are also a couple of smaller independent cinemas in Abu Dhabi, which focus mainly on Hindi films. As yet, there are no IMAX screens in Abu Dhabi, so those wanting the full 3D experience will have to head for cinemas in Dubai (Ibn Battuta Mall is the closest). There are local cinema idiosyncrasies – freezing air conditioning, people chatting to each other or on their mobile phones, and the heavy hand of the censor can all affect your experience. Also, sound quality can be a little off and Arabic (and often French) subtitles cover the bottom of the screen. That said, it's a great place to cool off during summer. Vox Cinemas in Dubai rents out screens for private use if you want it all to yourself; you can even play video games on the big screen.

Al Raha Cinemas Al Raha Mall, Al Raha, 02 556 2008
Al Wahda Cinema (Oscar Cinema) Al Wahda Mall, Al Wahdah, 02 443 3244
Cine Royal Khalidiyah Mall, Al Manhal, 02 681 9444, *cineroyal.ae*
Novo Cinema Abu Dhabi Mall, Al Zahiyah, 02 645 8988, *grandcinemas.com*
Vox Cinemas Marina Mall, Breakwater, 02 681 8484, *voxcinemas.com*
Vox Cinemas Yas Mall, Yas Island West, 600 599905, *voxcinemas.com*

Film Festival

Every October the Abu Dhabi Film Festival (ADFF) showcases Arabic and international film-making talent. Films are shown in venues across the city, like Marina Mall or Emirates Palace, and film fans even get the chance to vote for their favourites and take part in question and answer sessions with the directors. Worth checking out if your movie appetite stretches beyond Hollywood blockbusters.

Alternative Screenings

Several of Abu Dhabi's big hotels hold occasional movie nights featuring giant or even poolside screens. The Alliance Française's Cine Club (af-aboudabi.net) has regular screenings of French language films while some of the more progressive art spaces occasionally arrange film nights. New York University Abu Dhabi (nyuad.nyu.edu), in collaboration with the Abu Dhabi Film Festival, runs a series of Cinema Chats during the academic year. Meanwhile, the Space at twofour54 in Khalifa Park screens a cool mix of old international and classical films on Mondays. Shows are free and details can be found at twofour54.com.

Comedy

The Laughter Factory (thelaughterfactory.com) puts on comedy nights in Abu Dhabi and Dubai. Acts are imported straight from the UK and shows are usually held monthly at the Crowne Plaza Yas Island. The Punchline Comedy Club (punchlinecomedy.com) has also brought comedians to Abu Dhabi recently, so it's worth keeping an eye on their website too.

Lights, Camera, Action

Abu Dhabi attracts movie makers by offering 30% discounts on production costs. It has already seen Jerry Bruckheimer film *Beware of the Night* in the Liwa Deser. Initial atmosphere scenes for *Fast and Furious 7* were filmed at Etihad Towers in 2013 and scenes from the new Star Wars film were made at Al Sarab in 2014.

Live Music

Andrea Boccelli, Bon Jovi and Coldplay have all played at the Emirates Palace before, but most acts of this ilk now head to du Forum or du Arena on Yas Island. The Auditorium at Emirates Palace remains active though, but is more likely to host Swan Lake than Eminem, preferring to keep things classical. The du Arena is a large, open-air concert pavilion adjacent to Ferrari World and has seen The Who, Rolling Stones, Linkin Park, Kings of Leon, Beyonce, Kanye West, and Prince play during Formula One weekends, while Stevie Wonder, Eric Clapton, Madonna, Rihanna and Shakira have also performed at other times. If you're after something smaller, Chamas at the InterContinental, Jazz Bar at the Hilton and Sax at Le Royal Meridien all have regular house bands or local bands; the Jazz

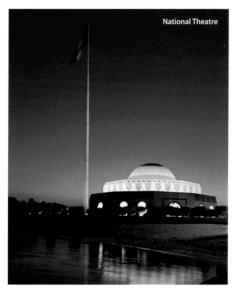

National Theatre

Brunch at St. Regis on Saadiyat Island also has live jazz. Although the classical concerts scene has shrunk somewhat in the last year or two, Abu Dhabi has played host to some big names in the classical music world, including Joshua Bell, Sir Simon Rattle with the Berlin Philharmonic, and Lang Lang, to name a few. The likes of Catherine Jenkins have performed at the du Forum, while Brighton College is also a popular venue for classical acts. The NSO Symphony Orchestra (facebook.com/UAENationalSymphonyOrchestra) aims to regularly put performances together at various locations across the city.

Music Festivals

Abu Dhabi has played host to a number of editions of the WOMAD festivals, and has its own music and arts festival, the Abu Dhabi Festival (abudhabifestival.ae). Abu Dhabi Classics (abudhabiclassics.com) sometimes hold a winter season of classical music in venues across Abu Dhabi and Al Ain. Modern tunes in the form of Creamfields are put on by FLASH Entertainment at du Forum, while every year, Beats on the Beach takes place around the Formula 1 weekend; free concerts on Abu Dhabi's Corniche beach that have seen acts like Ludacris, Missy Elliott and Sean Kingston perform. Free concerts also honoured the recent Volvo Ocean Race. Meanwhile in Dubai, Sandance festivals at Atlantis on the Palm Jumeirah attract big crowds and equally big acts like The Killers. The annual Emirates Airline Jazz Festival (the largest of its kind in the region) has hosted Sting, James Blunt and John Legend among others.

Theatre

The theatre scene in Abu Dhabi remains rather limited, with fans relying chiefly on touring companies and the occasional amateur dramatics performance. Al Raha Theater remains virtually untouched and the National Theater on Breakwater rarely seems to advertise anything itself. Resuscitation Theatre (resuscitationtheatre. com) is an imaginative company that is putting on more shows all of the time and have made use of the impressive venue previously. The Al Jaheli Theatre at the Armed Forces & Officers Club (afoc. mil.ae) is worth keeping an eye on too; acts like the Complete Works of William Shakespeare (abridged) popping up from time to time. Amateur theatre is on the up in the form of Abu Dhabi Dramatic Society and Abu Dhabi Players. They both welcome new members, and organise drama workshops which lead to performance at the end of them. In Dubai the scene is more active, with the First Group Theatre at Madinat Jumeirah (madinattheatre.com), the Palladium and the Centrepoint Theatre at DUCTAC (ductac.org) all having regular shows.

STAYING IN

Fun at home is well catered for in Abu Dhabi. No matter where in the city you are you'll have access to all kinds of delivery services and ways to entertain without having to lift much more than a phone.

Home Delivery

It won't be long before you've assembled an impressive stash of delivery menus in a drawer of your otherwise underutilised kitchen. Assuming you can actually convey your location to the restaurant in question, home delivery is a cheap and cheerful way to enjoy a night at home with friends or in front of the TV. Most places deliver, even the likes of KFC and Burger King, which can open up a whole new world for expats.

Domino's Pizza Various locations, 02 633 0088, *dominosarabia.com*
Hardee's Various locations, 600 569 000, *hardeesarabia.com*
Pizza Hut Various locations, 600 569 999, *pizzahut-me.com*
Soulfull Green Emirates Bldg
Al Wahdah, 02 643 3669, *soulfull.ae*
Sushi Central Various locations, 600 520 007, *sushicentral.ae*

Parties

There are several companies in Abu Dhabi that can do all the cooking, decorating and cleaning up for you, leaving you with more time for your witty after-dinner anecdotes. Many restaurants, hotels, and clubs, including the Beach Rotana, Hilton Abu Dhabi and The Club, have catering departments, so pick your favourite and ask if they can help out. For a novel outdoor party idea, you can get your own shawarma stand set up in the garden, complete with staff or hire an ice cream van from Desert Chill (desertchill.ae).

The D Club Nr Baynuna Flowershop, Al Dhafrah, 02 644 6461, *thedclub.com*
Events R' Us Green Bird Bldg, Al Zahiyah, 02 645 6605
Flying Elephant Shk Zayed Bin Sultan St, Dubai, 04 347 9170, *flyingelephantuae.com*
PartiPerfect Nr Marina Mall, Marina Office Park Villa A, Breakwater, 02 681 0090, *partiperfect.ae*

Le **MERIDIEN**

IGNITE
INSPIRATION

Explore the endless opportunities to unwind and relax in style at
Le Méridien Al Aqah Beach Resort. Fujairah offers rich cultural traditions
and contemporary luxury. Just 90 minutes from Dubai, you enjoy all of the
seclusion and privacy your heart desires. The resort is only 50 kilometers from
Fujairah City and within easy reach of the area's unique attractions, including
ancient fjords, palm groves, hot springs, and historical landmarks.

For more information or to make a reservation,
visit lemeridien.com/fujairah or call +971 9 244 9000

N 25° 30' E 56° 21'
DESTINATION UNLOCKED

OUT OF
THE CITY

Al Ain wildlife

OUT OF THE CITY

Discover the desert dunes, resorts, mountains and oases of Abu Dhabi emirate – and beyond.

Abu Dhabi may have everything from mangroves and marinas to boutiques and beaches, but there are six other emirates in the UAE and five other countries in the GCC, all of which warrant exploration.

Dubai, Sharjah, Ras Al Khaimah, Umm Al Quwain, Fujairah and Ajman are all within a few hours' drive of the capital. From the rugged mountains of Ras Al Khaimah to the cultural grandeur of Sharjah, each emirate has something different to offer, and each can be explored, at least in part, over a weekend.

Outside the UAE, Oman, Saudi Arabia, Qatar, Bahrain and Kuwait are all less than an hour and a half flight away. Oman is considered by many to be one of the most beautiful and culturally interesting countries in the region, and it can easily be reached and explored by car – Muscat is only a five-hour drive from Abu Dhabi.

Outside of Abu Dhabi city is the whole, vast expanse of the emirate to discover. From the verdant palm groves of the emirate's second city, Al Ain, in the east to the stunning deserts of the Rub Al Khali in Al Gharbia, and small pearl villages to the east, this is Abu Dhabi at its most traditional.

Door To Door

Driving is often the easiest way to get around within the UAE. Driving from Abu Dhabi to Dubai or Al Ain takes an hour and a half; it's two and a half hours to Ras Al Khaimah; just under two hours to Ajman; two hours to Umm Al Quwain; three and a half hours to get to Fujairah; and two hours to Sharjah.

To fly out of the UAE, cheap flights with flydubai leave from Dubai Airport to destinations like Oman, while Etihad and Oman Air fly from Abu Dhabi Airport.

AL AIN

Al Ain is Abu Dhabi emirate's second city and of great historical significance in the UAE. Its location on ancient trading routes between Oman and the Arabian Gulf rendered the oasis strategically important. Commonly known as 'The Garden City', Al Ain features many oases and lovely patches of greenery for the public to enjoy. After a greening programme instigated by the late Sheikh Zayed, the seven natural oases are now set amid tree-lined streets and beautiful urban parks. Its unique history means that Al Ain is home to interesting sights and attractions, including the Hili Archaeological Garden and the Al Ain Palace Museum, although there are modern amusements too like Hili Fun City.

Just outside the city sits one of the largest mountains in the UAE, Jebel Hafeet. The rolling, grass-covered hills of Green Mubazzarah Park at the bottom of the mountain are great for picnics and mid afternoon naps. Al Ain's archaeological and historical legacy is of such significance that the city was recently placed on the list of World Heritage Sites by UNESCO.

Attractions

Al Ain Camel Market
Nr Bawadi Mall, Zayed Bin Sultan St Al Ain
adach.ae
Map **4 E3**
Conditions at the souk have improved dramatically with spacious pens for the animals and ample parking for visitors. A visit to the market is a fantastic way to mingle with locals and witness camel and goat trading taking place in the same way it has for centuries. Arrive early, preferably before 9am, to soak up the buzzing atmosphere.

Al Ain National Museum
Zayed Bin Sultan St Al Ain **03 764 1595**
abudhabi.ae
Map **4 E2**
The oldest museum in the UAE is divided into three main sections. The ethnography section focuses on traditional life, culture and pastimes and the archaeology section has examples of Stone Age, Bronze Age and Iron Age objects excavated from sites around Al Ain. The 'gifts' section hosts some weird and wonderful items that were presented to Sheikh Zayed by visiting dignitaries, including golden palm trees, ornamental camels and jewel-encrusted daggers.

Al Ain Oasis
Nr Al Ain Museum Al Ain
visitabudhabi.ae
Map **4 E2**
This impressive oasis in the heart of the city is filled with palm plantations, many of which are still working farms. You are welcome to wander through the plantations, but it's best to stick to the paved areas. The farms have plenty of working examples of falaj, the traditional irrigation system which has been used for centuries to tap into underground wells. There are eight different entrances, some of which have arched gates, and there is no entry fee.

Al Ain Palace Museum
Central District Al Ain **03 751 7755**
abudhabi.ae
Map **4 D2**
The museum was originally a palace belonging to Sheikh Zayed bin Sultan Al Nahyan, dating back to 1937. Now, it tells the story of its previous owner and his remarkable achievements turning the desert state into a wealthy, popular and thriving country. Guided tours are free and highly recommended, and the Emirati guides are proud and knowledgeable. You'll learn about Emirati traditions and culture in general, and gain a real sense of time and place. The museum is a lovely, quiet place to stroll and explore.

Al Ain Zoo
Nahyan The First St Al Ain **03 799 2000**
alainzoo.ae
Map **4 D3**
This zoo is not characterised by small cages and meagre wildlife displays. Instead, it feels much more like a safari park, with spacious enclosures spread across its 900 acres interspersed with smaller exhibitions. Highlights include watching the hippos splash around in their 10m long ravine, catching a glimpse of the rare white lions in their enclosure, and getting up close to the giraffes at their feeding station. It's also an important conservation centre, with nearly 30% of the 180 species being on the endangered list.

Al Jahili Fort
Nr Central Public Gardens Al Ain **03 784 3996**
abudhabi.ae
Map **4 D2**
The impressive Al Jahili Fort is over 100 years old and one of the UAE's largest forts. Celebrated as the birthplace of the late Sheikh Zayed bin Sultan Al Nahyan, it is set in beautifully landscaped gardens and has been the stunning venue for a number of concerts during the Abu Dhabi Classics series (abudhabiclassics.com). If Al Jahili's distinctive three-tiered fort seems familiar, it could well be due to its appearance on the UAE's Dhs.50 note.

Hili Archaeological Park

Mohammed Bin Khalifa St Al Ain
abudhabi.ae
Map **4 E1**

These landscaped gardens are home to a Bronze Age settlement (2,500-2,000BC), which was excavated and restored in 1995. Many of the artefacts found are displayed in Al Ain National Museum. Entry is Dhs.1.

Hili Fun City

Mohammed Bin Khalifa St Al Ain **03 784 4481**
hilifuncity.ae
Map **4 E1**

This recently renovated, 22 hectare theme park offers you the best of both worlds: a theme park packed with rides and activities, and a scenic picnic spot for more relaxed get-togethers with friends. It's best to arrive early and make a day of it. There are more than 30 attractions, ranging from gentle rides for the little ones, such as the zebra-striped safari jeeps, to nail-biting, highflying rides for teens and adults, like the terrifying Sky Flyer, which spins you 360 degrees.

Camel Safaris

Al Ain Golden Sands Camel Safaris offers a selection of tours that include a camel ride over the dunes of Bida Bint Saud. The rides usually last one to two and a half hours and include transfers from Al Ain. Call 050 447 7268 for the details.

Jebel Hafeet

South of Al Ain
Map **4 D4**

Among the highest peaks in the UAE, Jebel Hafeet towers over the border between Al Ain and Oman at an imposing 1,240 metres. It's an impressive backdrop to the city, and the winding road to the top is considered to be one of the world's best driving roads; head to the summit to be rewarded with fantastic views over Al Ain. Alternatively, if you're feeling active, the road is also a challenging cycle route.

Wadi Adventure

Jebel Hafeet Al Ain **03 781 8422**
wadiadventure.ae
Map **4 D4**

A must for adrenaline junkies, this water park with a difference has white water rafting and kayaking runs, of more than a kilometre in length. A huge wave pool generates three-metre high breaks for surfing, or if water isn't your thing, the air park, zip line, climbing wall and canyon swing should keep your excitement levels high. There's a family swimming pool, man-made beach and a splash pool for little ones, making it a fantastic option for a family outing.

Hotels

Al Ain Rotana

Shk Zayed Rd Al Ain **03 754 5111**
rotana.com
Map **4 D2**

This city centre spot is a nightlife hub, thanks to six popular dining spots which include the lively Trader Vic's and the excellent Lebanese restaurant Min Zamaan. The rooms are attractive and spacious, and the pool and gardens are great for sunbathing.

Danat Al Ain Resort

Al Salam St Al Ain
03 704 6000
alain.danathotels.com
Map **4 E2**

Well-known for being one of the UAE's best inland resorts, with its luxurious guestrooms and deluxe villas, the landscaped gardens and swimming pools are the perfect places for enjoying the sun. There are plenty of family-friendly facilities, while adults are sure to enjoy the luxury spa and the swim-up pool bar, as well as the Horse and Jockey Pub.

Green Mubazzarah Chalets

Nr Green Mubazzarah Park Al Ain **03 783 9555**
Mubazzarah.150m.com
Map **4 D4**

Situated among the lush and picturesque foothills of Jebel Hafeet, accommodation consists of fully-furnished two and three-bedroom chalets, ideal for enjoying the Green Mubazzarah natural springs and parkland.

Hilton Al Ain

Khatm Al Shikle St Al Ain
03 768 6666
hilton.com
Map **4 E2**

Located near the heart of Al Ain, this ageing hotel is a key landmark and sits in lush, landscaped gardens that contain a nine-hole golf course, tennis and squash courts, a health club and a nice pool area. It is particularly convenient for visiting Al Ain Zoo. The Hiltonia Sports Bar and Paco's Bar are popular haunts.

Mercure Grand Jebel Hafeet Al Ain

Al Ain 03 783 8888
mercure.com
Map **4 D4**

This hotel's impressive location near the summit of Jebel Hafeet means that visitors can enjoy spectacular views of Al Ain. The rooms here are simple and comfortable, although you may not be spending much of your time indoors with three swimming pools to choose from, a waterslide and a mini-golf course.

AL GHARBIA

Al Gharbia is Abu Dhabi's Western Region – a vast 60,000 square kilometres or 60% of the total area of Abu Dhabi emirate and 51% of the UAE. Al Gharbia's natural resources such as palm trees, pearls, oil, gas and solar energy contribute 45% to the UAE's GDP. The region boasts the highest sand dunes in the world and 350km of coastline with beaches, rare wildlife, and beautiful desert islands such as Delma and Sir Bani Yas fast becoming popular tourist destinations.

Liwa

For most visitors to Al Gharbia, all roads lead to Liwa. On the way, you pass through tumbleweed towns such as Ghayathi (good for stocking up on authentic Bedouin souvenirs) and the regional capital Madinat Zayed. The land in this region holds evidence of life from ancient times; eight-million-year-old fossils have been found at Bu Ghar, while oases and the occasional farmstead are dotted throughout the region. Modern Bedouin criss-cross the interior with entire bungalows on the back of big-wheeled trucks.

Liwa Oasis is one of the largest oases on the Arabian Peninsula. This fertile crescent stretches for more than 150km and is home to the Bani Yas tribe, ancestors of the ruling family of Abu Dhabi. It's a quiet area, dotted with date plantations and small towns. Visitors go to see its ancient forts, traditional falconry, camel racing and trading, and because Liwa is the northern gate to the great desert. It's at Liwa that you'll find the legendary sand dune known as 'Tel Moreeb', or the Hill of Terror, a 300m high slope which attracts only the most confident off-roaders. Prepare for the most adventurous desert driving and incredible scenery and stay in luxury at the Tiwal Liwa Hotel. For detailed routes and practical information, get a copy of Explorer's *UAE Off-Road*.

The Empty Quarter

The Rub Al Khali – also known as the Empty Quarter – spreads south from Liwa and is the biggest sand desert on the planet. It measures a mind-boggling 650,000 square kilometres and spreads over parts of Oman, Yemen, southern UAE and almost all of southern Saudi Arabia. Its dunes rise as high as 250 metres. The Rub Al Khali is one of the world's greatest attractions on an unsurpassed scale of majesty. It was historically regarded as the edge of civilisation by people living in the region. But there is an extraordinary beauty to this landscape, despite it being so harsh and inhospitable. Even today man has been able to make little mark on it. Desert driving in this area is more of an expedition than just a spot of dune bashing, so go prepared for the adventure of a lifetime. The opportunities for camping in the region are endless, and sleeping under the stars is a great way to experience the peace and tranquillity of the desert. Unless of course there's a sand storm.

Al Gharbia's dunes

The Pearl Coast

Drive west from Abu Dhabi and the first stop will be Mirfa, set up in the 1970s as a fishing port and pearling centre. Mirfa is quiet but may change once the Mirfa Corniche is developed under Abu Dhabi's 2030 regional plan. In the meantime the refurbished, 114 room Mirfa Hotel has breathed new life into the area. For now, the biggest draw to Mirfa remains the annual Al Gharbia Watersports Festival (algharbiafestivals.com), opposite the hotel. Crowds flock for a weekend of fireworks, competitive kitesurfing, wakeboarding and kayaking.

A hundred kilometres along the 'pearl coast' is Jebel Dhanna, another historic pearl diving destination. There are two hotels here on a great beach with clear, shallow sea and fantastic facilities that make for a great weekend getaway from Abu Dhabi. Nearby, Ruwais is a town built for ADNOC employees which holds little interest for visitors.

The last stop before the Saudi Arabia border is Sila, a true frontier town. There isn't much happening in Sila today but that may change when it's one of the regular stops of the proposed GCC railway network. Until then, if you're in Sila head down to the harbour for fresh fish from the Abu Dhabi Fishermen's Co-operative Society (02 673 0888). If a beach barbecue is on the menu, pick up extra provisions at Al Rahi Home Grocery next to the co-operative. Drive north, with the quarry-scarred embankment on your left, along the beach track, and find a spot away from the beach houses. This is one of the few spots along the coast where you can camp. Two headlands further west, you'll find an even more pristine spot with white sand, turquoise sea and bobbing pink flamingos.

Kitesurfing Mania

Every year, the world's best kitesurfers gather for the 10-day Al Gharbia Watersports Festival (algharbiafestivals.com) in Mirfa, which takes place in March.

Desert Islands

This eight-island, eco-tourism project involves the larger Sir Bani Yas and Delma islands, and the six uninhabited Discovery Islands.

Sir Bani Yas Island was once Sheikh Zayed's personal retreat and is becoming a noted wildlife reserve. The Desert Islands Resort & Spa By Anantara has received numerous accolades for eco-sensitive luxury, and its even more luxurious sister properties on the island – Al Yamm Villa Resort and Al Sahel Villa Resort – have beautiful self-contained units. Sir Bani Yas Island is 9km off the coast from Jebel Dhanna and offers safaris where you'll see a multitude of animals including giraffes, oryx and maybe even a hyena. There are also a few routes for mountain biking and the clear blue waters and creeks offer peaceful snorkelling and kayaking. Catch the ferry to the island or fly from Al Bateen Executive Airport.

Beyond Sir Bani Yas and 42km off the coast lies Delma Island, a two-hour ferry ride from Jebel Dhanna or a 45 minute flight from Abu Dhabi International Airport. Delma Island is only nine by six kilometres but until recently it was the most important island in the Gulf. With fertile land and more than 200 wells of fresh water it was a favourite stopping point for traders, fishermen and pearlers for thousands of years. Evidence of human habitation on the island dates back more than 7,000 years and even today it supports more than 4,000 locals whose livelihood is fishing and farming. The island's rich earth supports the cultivation of more than 20 varieties of African, Asian and European fruits.

The volcanic landscape literally sparkles and ospreys watch over the fields of ostrich, but even with car ferries plying the route from the mainland, the island's attractions are works in progress. The only accommodation is the Delma Motel (02 878 1222), or you can camp.

Hotels

Anantara Sir Bani Yas Island
Al Yamm Villa Resort
Sir Bani Yas Island Ruwais **02 801 4200**
anantara.com

This special resort offers 30 five-star units in a serene location on the eastern shore of Sir Bani Yas Island, half of which is located on the beach and the other half in the tranquil mangroves. All the rooms have beautiful views of the water, either the turquoise sea or the bird-filled lagoon. Two more properties owned by Anantara – Sir Bani Yas Island Al Sahel Villa Resort and Desert Islands Resort & Spa – also offer impeccable luxury and access to the island's wildlife reserve.

Arabian Nights Under The Stars

An essential part of any Liwa adventure, camping in the desert is a truly unforgettable experience. The expanses of sand rolling into the distance at early dawn and the snaking silvery dunes in the moonlight are quite magical. You can camp just about anywhere, so take any of the roads and tracks into the desert off the main road, but make sure that you drive far enough to find a peaceful spot. Try to get settled long before the sun goes down, for safety reasons and to allow you to enjoy the sunset. One particularly good area is on the road to Moreeb Hill passing the Liwa Resthouse. This minor, paved road heads into the desert for 11.5km, leading you into some of the best dunes, and crossing plenty of sabkha flats.

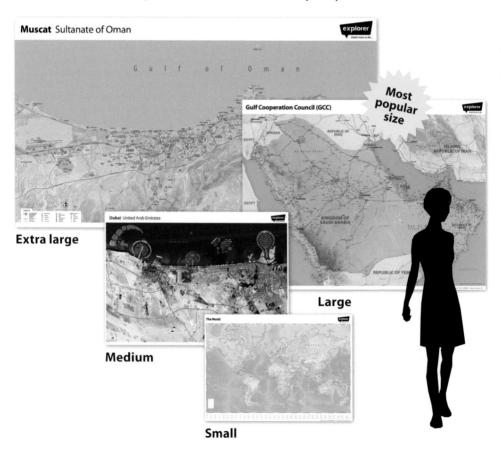

Danat Jebel Dhanna Resort
Jebel Dhanna Ruwais **02 801 2222**
jebeldhanna.danathotels.com
Map **3 B3**

Sitting on 800 metres of private, picturesque beach, this undiscovered treat of a hotel offers 109 luxurious rooms and suites including six waterfront villas. It has a health club and a spa that includes beach massage huts and a nice pool area with swim-up bar. The five dining venues at the hotel include an Italian restaurant, an all-day buffet, cafe and a shisha bar.

Dhafra Beach Hotel
Jebel Dhanna Ruwais **02 801 2000**
dhafrabeach.danathotels.com
Map **3 B3**

A very pleasant and reasonably priced hotel with a variety of rooms and suites to choose from, as well as a handful of dining options, a fitness centre with a sauna, and two swimming pools. A good option if heading west – you can even hire the late Sheikh Zayed's presidential suite for Dhs.3,000 per night.

Liwa Hotel
Mezaira Liwa **02 882 2000**
almarfapearlhotels.com
Map **3 C4**

With its raised location giving spectacular views of the Rub Al Khali (or Empty Quarter) desert, the green oasis and the neighbouring palace on the hilltop opposite, Liwa Hotel is a good option if you're not keen on camping but still want to enjoy the scenery. The hotel has spacious rooms and green, landscaped grounds with an attractive pool. There's also a choice of good dining options and evening venues.

Liwa Resthouse
Mezaira Liwa
Map **3 C4**

A little past its prime, this guesthouse has been eclipsed by the nearby Liwa Hotel and its (mainly Arab) clientele includes visiting business travellers, government officials and families on holiday. Although pretty basic compared to local hotels, it is clean and functional, and the cheapest alternative to camping.

Mirfa Hotel
Sila Highway, Mirfa **02 883 3030**
almarfapearlhotels.com
Map **3 C3**

Located in the quiet town of Mirfa, 160 kilometres from Abu Dhabi, this hotel is perfect for a weekend break or as a stopover if you're driving to Saudi Arabia. The hotel has been renovated and now features 114 comfortable rooms and suites, and lush gardens as well as leisure facilities including two pools, floodlit tennis courts and a kids' playground.

AJMAN

The smallest of the emirates, Ajman still has lots to offer travellers, including fine dining, a growing number of luxury hotels and pristine beaches, with a few heritage attractions thrown in for good measure. It's a more relaxed emirate in all senses of the word; life has a slower pace, while dress codes are a bit more lenient and alcohol can be bought without a licence.

The emirate's star attraction, Ajman Museum, houses a variety of interesting displays in a restored fort that is well worth visiting, as much for the building as for its contents. The emirate's main souks are a reminder of days gone by, while the modern Ajman City Centre is home to shops, foodcourts and a cinema. The tiny emirate is known for being one of the largest boat building centres in the region; while mainly modern boats emerge from the yards these days, you may still catch a glimpse of a traditionally built wooden dhow sailing out to sea.

Attractions

Ajman Corniche
Corniche Road Ajman

Life in Ajman revolves around its pleasant seafront Corniche, especially during the milder months. It is lined with cafes, shops, stalls, and there's a tidal pool for safe swimming. There are some excellent traditional restaurants, too. Try the seafood at Themar Al Bahar or the Middle Eastern cuisine at Attibrah.

Ajman Museum
Ioarh 1 Ajman **06 711 6642**

No trip to Ajman would be complete without a visit to the Ajman Museum. This attractive building is based inside a fort, thought to have originally been built during the late 18th century. The popular cultural attraction houses an astounding collection of artefacts and archaeological finds, including centuries-old manuscripts, weaponry and pottery.

Al Zorah Nature Reserve

This serene mangrove creek is teeming with wildlife, including a huge flock of flamingos. The area is currently under development but you can get a peek from the viewing deck on Al Zorah Street. The development will add more luxury resorts to the city, a golf course and a marina.

Attibrah

Corniche Road Ajman **06 744 8363**

A good option for sampling some authentic Emirati dishes with decor is drawn from local tastes. Go for the gideesha (a fragrant spiced fish dish) and some harris biliyan (a rich eggplant side dish), along with the usual Middle Eastern mezze spread.

Fish Market

Al Rashidiya 1 Ajman

One of the best local fish markets in the country, head here early to see the day's catch being offloaded from fishing dhows and choose something fresh to have prepared and cooked onsite.

Hotels

The Ajman Palace

Al Nakheel 2 Ajman **06 701 8888**
theajmanpalace.com

This gorgeous hotel may not serve alcohol (unusually for Ajman) but it's a relaxing place to spend time. Leisure facilities include an infinity pool and spa.

Ajman Saray

Al Nakheel 2 Ajman **06 714 2222**
starwoodhotels.com

This brand new hotel from the Luxury Collection has its own private beach and brings a splash of glamour to Ajman. There are several restaurants, including a beach bar and grill.

Kempinski Hotel Ajman

Al Nakheel 2 Ajman **06 714 5555**
kempinski.com

This beautiful five-star hotel offers the ultimate in luxury and hospitality. There's a stunning stretch of white sand beach overlooking the Arabian Gulf that's perfect for trying out watersports or simply soaking up the sun. You can even request to have a table set up in the surf for a romantic dinner for two. Be sure to sample the renowned Indian cuisine at the excellent Bukhara, where guests are encouraged to eschew cutlery and dig right in, or the Italian fare at Sabella's.

Ramada Beach Hotel Ajman

Al Nakheel 1 Ajman **06 714 5555**
ramada.com

For a cheap and cheerful stay right on the beach, this four-star hotel has a lot to offer. It has its own private beach where you can get spa treatments, and an enormous five-bedroom penthouse with its own Jacuzzi that can be rented at a very reasonable rate.

Lap Of Luxury

Little Ajman is making big strides in the luxury travel stakes. While the Kempinski remains a hugely popular option for a weekend of pampering, the newly-opened Ajman Saray brings more choice for a deluxe break, and a new offering from the Fairmont will open on the beachfront in 2014. Further luxury resorts are in development at the Al Zorah Nature Reserve.

Ajman Museum

DUBAI

As one of the most sought-after holiday hotspots in the world, Dubai may be the ultimate staycation destination: why would you go anywhere else with so many riches right on your doorstep? With its luxury hotels, gourmet restaurants, pristine beaches, gargantuan malls and record-breaking attractions, this larger-than-life emirate has everything you need for a non-stop short break to really brag about to your colleagues on a Sunday morning.

However, while the emirate boasts an incredible number of attractions claiming to be the tallest, biggest or longest, it's not all bright lights – the atmospheric old town around the Creek and the restored Al Fahidi Historical Neighbourhood are musts for any visitor wanting to scratch Dubai's cultural surface, and the beautiful Jumeirah Mosque is one of the few mosques in the region open to non-Muslims, offering a rare chance to learn about the influence of Islam on the local people.

For more help on planning a trip to Dubai, log on to askexplorer.com where you can find listings of forthcoming events and further information about Dubai hotels and attractions. You can also order a copy of *Dubai Visitors' Guide* or *Dubai Tourists' Map* – the essential guides for your weekend break.

Attractions

Al Fahidi Historical Neighbourhood
Nr Al Seef Rd Dubai 04 353 9090
dubaiculture.ae
Map 3 E2 Metro Al Fahidi

This atmospheric area is one of the oldest heritage sites in the city and offers a beguiling glimpse into the Dubai of a bygone era, with its traditional windtowers, bustling courtyards and maze of winding alleyways.

There are some great cultural attractions to visit in the area, including the Dubai Museum which showcases all aspects of traditional Emirati life. Stroll along the creek towards the Textile Souk and take an abra across to the Gold and Spice Souks in Deira.

Aquaventure
Atlantis The Palm Dubai 04 426 0000
atlantisthepalm.com
Map 3 E2 Metro Nakheel

This 42 acre waterpark is the ultimate destination for family-friendly fun, with beach, loungers and tonnes of rides linked to a 2.3 kilometre river journey on inflatables. To get the adrenaline pumping, there's the new Tower of Poseidon, a heart-thumping slide that boasts the longest zip line in the Middle East. Aquaventure is well-equipped to accommodate mini-adventurers too, with Splashers, a giant water playground specifically for little ones.

At The Top, Burj Khalifa
Burj Khalifa Dubai 04 888 8124
atthetop.ae
Map 3 E2 Metro Burj Khalifa/The Dubai Mall

In less than 60 seconds, a high-speed lift whisks visitors up to the 124th floor of the world's tallest tower. From the Burj Khalifa observation deck, you can survey a 360° view of the city through floor to ceiling windows or outside on the patio. Advance bookings are Dhs.125 for adults and Dhs.95 for children; tickets bought on the day, if available, cost Dhs.400, although children under four enter for free in both cases.

Dubai Dolphinarium > p.323
Creek Park Dubai 04 336 9773
dubaidolphinarium.ae
Map 3 E2 Metro Dubai Healthcare City

An indoor attraction that offers the chance to swim with dolphins, and daily shows where these fascinating creatures show off their aquatic acrobatics. There's also an exotic bird show, a 5D cinema and the UAE's only mirror maze – a dizzying labyrinth.

The Dubai Mall
Financial Centre Rd Dubai 04 362 7500
thedubaimall.com
Map 3 E2 Metro Burj Khalifa/Dubai Mall

The largest mall in the world by floor space, The Dubai Mall offers a huge array of indoor entertainment including an ice rink, SEGA World indoor theme park and the Dubai Aquarium and Underwater Zoo. It is a shopper's paradise housing some 1,200 stores, including New York's iconic department store, Bloomingdales. There are also some great alfresco dining venues overlooking the spectacular musical displays of the Dubai Fountain.

iFLY Dubai
Mirdif City Centre Dubai 04 231 6292
theplaymania.com
Map 3 E2 Metro Rashidiya

Experience the thrill of skydiving without the terror of leaping from a plane. Giant vertical wind tunnels simulate the freefall sensation as you hover over powerful fans while being blasted up to 10 metres in the air by winds of up to 200kph. The facility is located at Playnation, an entertainment complex that is home to Magic Planet, with rides and amusements, a bowling centre and the fantastic educational play zone for kids, Little Explorers.

Ski Dubai > p.213
Mall of the Emirates Dubai 04 409 4090
skidxb.skischoolshop.com
Map 3 E2 Metro Mall of the Emirates
Located in the Mall of the Emirates, the first indoor ski resort in the Middle East boasts more than 22,500 sq m of real snow over five runs and a freestyle area, as well as a snow park for the kids. With temperatures at around -3°C, this is a great place to cool off. It's also home to a colony of snow penguins that perform a show, and visitors can meet them through specially organised 'Peng Friend' encounters. Slope pass and lesson prices include clothing and equipment.

Wild Wadi Water Park
Nr Burj Al Arab Dubai 04 348 4444
wildwadi.com
Map 3 E2 Metro Mall of the Emirates
Wild Wadi Water Park is the perfect place to spend a sunny afternoon, whether you want to brave the white water rapids river or simply bob about in the wave pool. The highlight is the Jumeirah Sceirah, the tallest and fastest freefall slide outside of the United States: you climb up a 32 metre high tower, step into a capsule and then a trapdoor floor opens to shoot you down a 120m long slide at speeds of up to 80kmph.

Hotels

The Address Downtown
Shk Mohd Bin Rashid Blvd, Downtown Dubai
04 436 8888
theaddress.com
Map 3 E2 Metro Burj Khalifa/Dubai Mall
Even at over 300 metres in height, The Address is dwarfed by its neighbour, the Burj Khalifa – but breathtaking views, beautiful interiors and eight dining outlets (including Neos, the panoramic bar on the 63rd floor) make this one of the most popular spots in town. It is perfectly positioned for exploring The Dubai Mall, and centrally located in the city.

Atlantis, The Palm
Crescent Rd Dubai 04 426 0000
atlantisthepalm.com
Map 3 E2 Metro Nakheel
With a staggering 1,539 rooms and suites, all with views of the sea or the Palm Jumeirah, Atlantis is one of Dubai's most famous hotels. It has no less than four fancy restaurants featuring the cuisine of Michelin-starred chefs, including a branch of world-famous chain Nobu. It is also home to Aquaventure and the Lost Chambers Aquarium. Special promotions include tickets to Sandance, a music festival that takes place on Atlantis beach and has drawn such talented acts as Florence & the Machine and The Killers.

Burj Al Arab
Jumeira Rd Dubai 04 301 7777
jumeirah.com
Map 3 E2 Metro Mall of the Emirates
Standing on its own man-made island, this dramatic Dubai icon's unique architecture is recognised around the world. Suites have two floors and are serviced by a team of butlers. To get into the hotel as a non-guest, you will need a restaurant reservation.

Jumeirah Beach Hotel
Jumeira Rd Dubai 04 348 0000
jumeirah.com
Map 3 E2 Metro First Gulf Bank
Shaped like an ocean wave, with a fun and colourful interior, the hotel has 598 rooms and suites and 19 private villas, all with a sea view. It is also home to some excellent food and beverage outlets, including Uptown for happy hour cocktails and a great view of the Burj Al Arab.

Jumeirah Zabeel Saray
Crescent West St Dubai 04 453 0000
jumeirahzabeelsaray.com
Map 3 E2 Metro Nakheel
For an unforgettable pampering experience, there's nowhere better than this structural wonder that can lay claim to being the home of Talise Ottoman Spa, the biggest spa in the Middle East. It also boasts beautiful interiors combining Arabian and Turkish design influences, its own private stretch of beach and several top-quality restaurants.

Madinat Jumeirah
Jumeira Rd Dubai 04 366 8888
jumeirah.com
Map 3 E2 Metro Mall of the Emirates
This extravagant resort has two hotels, Al Qasr and Mina A'Salam, with no fewer than 940 luxurious rooms and suites, and the exclusive Dar Al Masyaf summer houses, all linked by man-made waterways navigated by wooden abra boats which whisk guests around the resort. Nestled between the two hotels is Souk Madinat, opulently drawn from traditional styles and with a plethora of popular shops, bars and restaurants.

XVA Art Hotel
Al Souk Al Kabeer Dubai 04 353 5383
xvahotel.com
Map 3 E2 Metro Al Fahidi
With just nine rooms and a location in Al Fahidi Historical Neighbourhood, this boutique hotel is the closest you'll get to staying in the 'real' Dubai. The rooms have been individually and lovingly decorated and ooze old-world, traditional Arabia. Each has a terrace and en suite, and it makes for a evocative base from which to explore the oldest part of town.

Ski Dubai

Burj Khalifa

Burj Al Arab and Madinat Jumeirah

FUJAIRAH

Fujairah may be less than a three-hour drive when travelling from Abu Dhabi, but the dramatic landscape of the east coast makes it feel like a different world. The journey itself takes you through the spectacular Hajar Mountains before arriving at this picturesque location along the Gulf of Oman.

Fujairah city has seen little development compared to cities on the west coast, but the real draw here is the landscape. The mountains and wadis that stretch west of the coast contain some of the country's best and most accessible camping spots, and the beaches, reefs and villages that line the coast attract visitors from Abu Dhabi throughout the year.

Dibba

Located at the northern-most point of the east coast, on the border with Musandam, Dibba is made up of three fishing villages. Unusually, each part comes under a different jurisdiction: Dibba Al Hisn is part of Sharjah, Dibba Al Fujairah is Fujairah and Dibba Bayah is Oman. The three Dibbas share an attractive bay, fishing communities, and excellent diving locations – from here you can arrange dhow trips to take you to unspoilt dive locations in Musandam. The Hajar Mountains, which run parallel to the east coast,

provide a wonderful and dramatic backdrop, rising in places to over 1,800 metres. There are some good public beaches too, where your only company will be crabs and seagulls, and where seashell collectors may find a few treasures.

East Coast Made Easy

Once you've reached Dubai, getting to the UAE's east coast takes anything from 30-90 minutes. For speed alone, take the Sharjah-Kalba highway and then hit the smart Sheikh Khalifa Highway. For a more scenic route through the mountains, take the E88 from Sharjah to Masafi, passing fruit sellers and local landmark the Friday Market, then turn left to Dibba or right to Fujairah. If you're heading to Dibba outside of rush hour, it's usually quicker to head north on Sheikh Mohammed Bin Zayed Road and take the truck road (exit 119) across the country to the E87, which brings you to Dibba.

Fujairah City

A mix of old and new, its hillsides are dotted with ancient forts and watchtowers, which add an air of mystery and charm; most are undergoing restoration work. Fujairah is also a busy trading centre, with its modern container port and a thriving free zone attracting major companies from around the world. Off the coast, the seas and coral reefs are great for fishing, diving and watersports. It is a good place for birdwatching during the spring and autumn migrations as it is on the route from Africa to Central Asia. Since

Snoopy Island, Dibba

Fujairah is close to the mountains and many areas of natural beauty, it makes an excellent base from which to explore the countryside and discover stunning wadis, forts, waterfalls and even natural hot springs.

Kalba

Just to the south of Fujairah you'll find Kalba, which is renowned for its mangrove forest and golden beaches. Technically the town belongs to Sharjah, but it's a pretty fishing village that still manages to retain much of its historical charm. You can visit Bait Sheikh Saeed Bin Hamed Al Qasimi, an old house dating back over 100 years that's home to fascinating heritage displays and historical artefacts.

South of the town is the beautiful tidal estuary of Khor Kalba (khor is Arabic for creek), one of the oldest mangrove forests in Arabia. It is home to a variety of wildlife not found anywhere else in the UAE. The mangroves in the estuary flourish thanks to a mix of seawater and freshwater from the mountains, but are now receding due to the excessive use of water from inland wells. For birdwatchers, the area is especially good during the spring and autumn migrations when rare species of bird can be spotted, including Sykes's warbler. It is also home to a rare subspecies of white collared kingfisher, which breeds here and in Oman, and nowhere else in the world. Kayak tours through tour operators are possible if you want a close up visit to this unique location. For more information, check with Net Tours on 04 376 2333.

The road through the mountains linking Kalba to Hatta makes for an interesting alternative for returning towards Dubai or Abu Dhabi.

Attractions

Al Badiyah Mosque

Badiyah Fujairah
Map **3 F1**
The site of the oldest mosque in the UAE, Bidiyah is one of the oldest settlements on the east coast and is believed to have been inhabited since 3,000BC. The mosque is made from gypsum, stone and mud bricks finished off with plaster, and is believed to date back to the middle of the 15th century. It is still used by worshippers for daily prayer, so non-Muslim visitors can't enter. Built next to a low hillside with several watchtowers on the ridge behind, the area is colourfully lit up at night.

Dibba Castle

Dibba Fujairah **09 243 1402**
dibbacityguide.com
Map **3 F1**
Hidden away in the Omani part of Dibba (aka Daba), next to vast farms and plantations, Dibba Castle is an interesting place to have a walk around. Built over 180 years ago, it has been restored and, while there aren't a lot of artefacts on show, you can access all the rooms and climb up the towers, where you'll get views over the castle and its surroundings. It is signposted off the road past the UAE border check post.

Fujairah Fort

Nr Fujairah Heritage Village Fujairah
fujairahtourism.ae
Map **3 F2**
The majestic Fujairah Fort is one of the oldest and most important in the emirate, as well as being among the most photographed. It's an impressive building located on a raised hilltop overlooking the city and just a few kilometres from the sea. Explore Fujairah Fort, and stroll around the surrounding heritage buildings, which are open to the public, and the nearby remains of traditional houses are easily viewed.

Bull Butting

On Friday afternoons at around 4.30pm during winter, crowds gather close to the corniche to watch 'bull butting'. This ancient Portuguese sport consists of two huge bulls going head to head for several rounds, until after a few nudges and a bit of hoof bashing, a winner is determined. It's not as cruel or barbaric as other forms of bullfighting, but animal lovers may still want to avoid.

Fujairah Heritage Village

Nr Fujairah Fort Fujairah **09 223 1554**
fujairahtourism.ae
Map **3 F2**
Situated just outside of Fujairah city, this purpose-built village takes you back in time to experience traditional life in the emirate. Walk around the village and see the realities of what traditional Bedouin life was like in the unforgiving desert climate. After a morning of cultural immersion, you can stay and relax in the sun, as there are two spring-fed swimming pools for men and women, and chalets that can be hired for the day.

Snoopy Island

Khorfakkan
Map **3 F1**
Snoopy Island, so named because of its resemblance to the beloved comic book dog, is a popular snorkelling spot in Fujairah. The Sandy Beach Hotel & Resort's beach is a great launch pad (there's a nominal fee for non-guests to enter) as it's just a short swim away. Or you can rent a kayak to get there, as well as snorkelling equipment. For the best visibility, aim for an early morning snorkel. You can expect to be rewarded by an abundance of stunning marine life including turtles and rays.

Fujairah Fort

Hotels

Fujairah Rotana Resort & Spa – Al Aqah Beach

Al Aqah Beach, Dibba Rd Fujairah **09 244 9888**
rotana.com
Map **3 F1**

This resort puts its beachside location to good use, with each of the 250 guest rooms and suites boasting its own balcony with views over the sea. Some of the highlights of the hotel include its private beach, the swimming pool with pool bar and the indulgent spa offering plenty of pampering treatments. You can even opt to have a massage in a hut on the beach with an ocean view.

Radisson Blu Resort, Fujairah

Al Faqeet, Dibba Fujairah **09 244 9700**
radissonblu.com
Map **3 F1**

Its pastel exterior might be an acquired taste, but the modern, corporate interior and wonderful restaurants

that lie within make this hotel a bit of a treat for the senses. The whole place is reminiscent of a spa, with clean lines and wholesome colours – in fact, there actually is a wonderful Japanese spa, as well as a spacious private beach and great pools. The rooms are also extremely spacious.

Sandy Beach Hotel & Resort

Al Aqah Fujairah **09 244 5555**
sandybm.com
Map **3 F1**

Snoopy Island has long been recognised as one of the best diving spots in the United Arab Emirates and the island (shaped like this famous cartoon dog) is right off the coast from the Sandy Beach Hotel. A visit here is a firm favourite with UAE residents for a host of reasons. Day trippers can purchase a pass to the hotel to access the temperature-controlled pool, watersports and beach bar services. There is also a five-star PADI Dive Centre within the hotel that rents diving and snorkelling gear for exploring the reefs around Snoopy Island.

RAS AL KHAIMAH

Nature lovers, take note: Ras Al Khaimah boasts the best natural scenery in the UAE. With the stunning Hajar Mountains as its backdrop and the sparkling waters of the Arabian Gulf on its shore, the northernmost emirate is the perfect destination for an outdoor break with plenty of opportunities for camping, hiking and soaking up the sun. Several five-star hotels offer more for your dirham than you could expect to get in the bigger cities.

Ras Al Khaimah contains several archaeological sites, some dating back all the way to 3,000BC. Take the Al Ram road out of the Al Nakheel district and towards the Hajar Mountains to discover some of the area's history, including Dhayah Fort, Shimal Archaeological Site and Sheba's Palace.

The town is quiet, relaxing and a good starting point for exploring the surrounding mountains, visiting the ancient sites of Ghalilah and Shimal, the hot springs at Khatt, and the quirky local camel race track at Diggagga.

Attractions

Al Qawasim Corniche
Ras Al Khaimah
Map 3 F1
Ras Al Khaimah's Al Qawasim Corniche is a social hub that's lined with a range of cafes. Enjoy the natural beauty of the mangroves and visit the Pearl Museum to learn about the emirate's pearling traditions, followed by a bit of local knowledge at the National Museum of Ras Al Khaimah. You can hire bikes for exploring the area. Round off your evening at Italian restaurant Pesto, followed by shisha on the rooftop terrace overlooking the mangroves.

Ice Land Water Park
Al Jazeera Al Hamra Ras Al Khaimah 07 206 7888
icelandwaterpark.com
Map 3 E1
With its ice-capped mountains and plastic penguins set in the middle of a surreal desert landscape, this gargantuan polar-themed water park is certainly a sight to behold. Ice Land Water Park is a magnet for tots and toddlers, who can't help but love the quirkiness of it all. There's Penguin Bay, an interactive play area that's home to the UAE's biggest rain dance pool and also Penguin Falls, the tallest man-made waterfall in the UAE.

Prince of Sea
Al Hamra Marina Ras Al Khaimah 050 372 1772
facebook.com/princeofseaemirates
Map 3 E1
This luxury two-masted sailing vessel is decked out for optimum fun. Accommodating up to 75 people, the energetic, fun-loving crew will treat you to some traditional performances as well as some more unusual entertainment. Day cruises provide a relaxing opportunity for swimming and snorkelling, with drinks and a barbecue, while after dark the party starts.

Stellar Cellar
Al Hamra Cellar, although owned by MMI (mmidubai. com), is a tax-free liquor store that is well worth the trip. You can take advantage of RAK's relaxed alcohol laws and browse a wide range of fine wines, spirits and beers in a pleasant environment at extremely competitive prices. Call 07 244 7403 for more info.

Ras Al Khaimah Country Club
Al Mazraa Ras Al Khaimah 056 706 4774
Map 3 F1
This new equestrian club is already proving popular with local horse riding enthusiasts and visitors from the UAE and abroad. As well as boasting superb equestrian facilities and expertly trained staff, there's also a restaurant and bar for lingering over a meal or relaxing drink, and a large, scenic swimming pool for cooling off while you soak up some sun. Riding lessons and excursions are available to visitors.

Ras Al Khaimah beach

Hotels

Banyan Tree

Al Jazirah Al Hamra Ras Al Khaimah **07 206 7777**
banyantree.com
Map **3 E1**

The sister property of the gorgeous Banyan Tree Al Wadi, this stunning resort offers 32 beachfront villas built in the style of the Bedouin's tents – but far more luxurious. A lovely hideaway, or great for thrill seekers, with snorkelling, sailing and watersports all on offer.

The Haunted Village

Rumour has it that the residents of Jazirat Al Hamra saw spirits, or djinn, coming out of the sea and evacuated overnight in fear. This huge area of houses has been deserted for more than 40 years, although it has been used as a film set in the past. With hints of a bygone era, it is a fascinating, and somewhat creepy, place to explore. Head north from Al Hamra Marina, take a u-turn at the pink pet shop, and turn right at the signpost to the archaeological park. Follow this road to the end.

The Cove Rotana

Shk Mohd Bin Salem Rd, Ras Al Khaimah
07 206 6000
rotana.com
Map **3 F1**

This sprawling resort, comprising more than 200 rooms and 72 villas, has the feel of an old

The Cove Rotana

Mediterranean hill town, thanks to its location built into the hillsides overlooking the Arabian Gulf. The centrepiece is undoubtedly the lagoon that it is built around, which is protected from the sea by 600 metres of pristine beach. A Bodylines spa and several impressive restaurants round out the package.

Hilton Resort & Spa

Al Maareedh St Ras Al Khaimah
07 228 8844
hilton.com
Map **3 F1**

With 1.5km of private, white sandy beach, six swimming pools, five-star service, loads of watersports on offer and some super fine dining options, you won't really need to leave. As well as rooms in the main building, there are 151 quaint villas with direct beach access, and for all that's on offer, it's actually rather good value. There's even an all-day kid's club to keep the little ones happy.

Waldorf Astoria

Vienna St, Al Hamra Ras Al Khaimah **07 203 5555**
waldorfastoria.com
Map **3 E1**

An enormous hotel styled on an Arabian palace, the Waldorf Astoria is set on 350m of private beach and has various dining options, including the excellent Lexington Grill, as well as a cigar bar, spa, gym, and gorgeous pools. Following in the traditions of Waldorf Astoria hotels around the world, every inch of the place is beautifully designed but favouring elegance over ostentation, and each venue with its own style and story to tell.

New Hotels

Ras Al Khaimah's distinguished list of hotels expanded in 2014, with the opening of the Rixos Bab Al Bahr, the DoubleTree by Hilton Resort and the Marjan Island Resort & Spa on man-made Marjan Island – RAK's answer to the Palm Jumeirah.

Golden Tulip Khatt Springs Resort & Spa

Khatt Ras Al Khaimah **07 244 8777**
goldentulipkhattsprings.com
Map **3 F1**

Simple and subdued, Golden Tulip Khatt Springs Resort & Spa instead relies on stunning mountain views, uninterrupted tranquillity and incredible spa packages to attract weekend visitors. Next to the hotel, you can take a dip in the public Khatt Hot Springs – piping hot water which, it is claimed, has curative powers. Men and women enjoy separate pools and a variety of massages are also available. Avoid the hot springs on Fridays when it is very busy.

SHARJAH

Al Noor Mosque by Khalid Lagoon
(image: Sharjah Commerce & Tourism Development Authority)

Dubai's neighbouring emirate was named the cultural capital of the Arab world by UNESCO in 1998 and the Capital of Islamic Culture for 2014 by the Organisation of Islamic Conference, due to its well-preserved heritage area, an ever-evolving arts scene, some wonderful museums and a thriving cafe culture. Regular events such as the Sharjah Light Festival and Sharjah Biennial draw visitors from all over the UAE and beyond, and that's just the city – the emirate is home to some fantastic desert, including popular spots Big Red and Fossil Rock, and a few enclaves over on the east coast.

For a sense of what the city is all about, head to Khalid Lagoon. At Al Majaz Waterfront you can choose from a cluster of restaurants to watch the nightly fountain show on the lagoon, take an abra ride, or check out the kids' play areas.

A wander further north brings you to the city's heritage and arts areas, currently being restored and developed under the Heart of Sharjah project, with one of the most impressive collections of museums and heritage sites in the region. Shoppers will have a blast too, searching for gifts in Sharjah's souks – Souk Al Arsah is a more authentic experience than those in the rest of the country, and with some canny bartering you could bag a bargain.

Attractions

Al Qasba
Nr Al Khan Lagoon Sharjah 06 556 0777
alqasba.ae
Map 3 E1
Canalside hub Al Qasba is packed with popular cafes and restaurants, and has some interesting attractions to explore. Check out the Maraya Art Centre and the Eye of the Emirates Ferris wheel.

Heart of Sharjah
Al Mareija St Sharjah 06 544 8847
Map 3 E1
The region's largest heritage project encompasses the heritage and arts areas and is dedicated to restoration and renovation; some of the traditional coral stone buildings date back more than 200 years. The narrow alleys and shady cobbled courtyards transport you to another era, and there are several fascinating museums. Check out Majlis Al Midfaa, an iconic round wind tower, as well as Sharjah Heritage Museum and

Sharjah Art Museum, both of which use the unique and beautiful spaces of the area's traditional buildings. The 150 year-old Souk Al Arsah is located here too.

Sharjah Classic Car Museum
Al Dhaid Road Sharjah 06 558 0222
sharjahmuseums.ae
This fantastic museum is definitely worth a visit, whether or not you are 'into' cars. There's a large number of vehicles on display, dating from as far back as 1915. Many of the cars are from His Highness Sheikh Dr Sultan bin Mohammad Al Qasimi's personal collection, including a 1934 Rolls Royce. Displays are quirky and fun – it's a great place to soak up some history and to impress any auto-enthusiasts.

Sharjah Desert Park
Interchange 9, Al Dhaid Rd Sharjah 06 531 1501
epaashj.com
Map 3 E1
Located just off the E611, this complex is worth heading to for its three animal-themed attractions. Arabia's Wildlife Centre is one of the UAE's best in terms of animal care and presentation, and home to a host of fascinating wildlife indigenous to the Arabian region, including the rare Arabian leopard. The Natural History & Botanical Museum features interactive displays on the relationships between man and the natural world in the UAE and beyond, while over at the Children's Farm petting zoo, you can feed some friendly camels, goats and more. The entrance fee, Dhs.15 for adults and Dhs.5 for children, covers all three attractions.

Sharjah Museum Of Islamic Civilisation

Sharjah Museum Of Islamic Civilisation

Nr Sharjah Creek Sharjah 06 565 5455
sharjahmuseums.ae

With more than 5,000 artefacts from across the Arab world, all informatively displayed and housed in a beautiful building that was once a souk, this is one of the best places in the country to learn about Islam.

Hotels

Coral Beach Resort

Al Muntazah St Sharjah
06 522 9999
coral-beachresortsharjah.com
Map 3 E1

With its own pristine sandy beach and a swimming pool with a waterslide, this is one hotel that's bound to keep the kids (and adults) happy. There's also a host of activities and sports facilities on offer, as well as a spa and hammam where you can wind down after a long day exploring the city. Be sure to try the excellent seafood at the restaurant Casa Samak during your stay or visit Al Bahar for their Sunday roast.

Hilton Sharjah

Al Majaz 3 Sharjah 06 519 2222
hilton.com
Map 3 E1

A beautiful art deco styled resort which is located right on Khalid Lagoon and boasting some of the best facilities in the emirate. Enjoy succulent kebabs at the authentic Shiraz restaurant or indulge in a chilled mocktail on the pool terrace.

Radisson Blu Resort

Corniche Rd Sharjah 06 565 7777
radissonblu.com
Map 3 E1

This smart hotel chain has a five-star offering close to the city's historic centre and with its own beach. Dining options are great and prices are reasonable.

UMM AL QUWAIN

A visit to Umm Al Quwain is a great way to see traditional Emirati life; fishing and date farming are still the main industries, as they have been for centuries. It has plenty of modern attractions too – its beach resorts are popular hangout spots among UAE expats, and you can even go skydiving (visit emiratesdropzone.webs.com for details).

The emirate has six forts, and a few old watchtowers surrounding the town. With plenty of mangroves and birdlife, the emirate's lagoon is a popular weekend spot for boat trips, windsurfing and other watersports. Another popular family activity is crab hunting at Flamingo Beach Resort. At nightfall, groups of hunters set off by boat into the shallow mangrove waters with a guide, where they spear crabs which are then barbecued and served up for dinner back at the hotel.

Emirates Motorplex (motorplex.ae) hosts various motorsport events, including the Emirates Motocross Championship, and Dreamland Aqua Park is one of the most popular attractions. Barracuda Beach Resort is a favoured destination for Abu Dhabi residents, thanks to its well-stocked, duty-free liquor store.

Attractions

Dreamland Aqua Park
Nr Barracuda Beach Resort, RAK Highway,
Al Rafaah Umm Al Quwain **06 768 1888**
dreamlanduae.com
Map **3 E1**

This impressive water park is both huge and hugely popular. Perfect for a family day out, there are more than 30 rides, including four 'twisting dragons' that promise white knuckle thrills. There's also a lazy river and a play area if you're looking for something a little more relaxing, as well as a high-salinity floating pool. You can camp overnight, staying in one of the tents or huts provided. However, note that Fridays and public holidays are for families only.

Umm Al Quwain Marine Club
Al Khour 1 Umm Al Quwain **06 766 6644**
uaqmarineclub.com
Map **3 E1**

This watersports centre takes advantage of the calm waters of the placid lagoon, which provides the perfect conditions for wakeboarding, kayaking and stand up paddleboarding through the mangoves. All these and more are offered at competitive prices.

Hotels

Barracuda Beach Resort
Nr Dreamland Aqua Park, Khor Al Baida
Umm Al Quwain **06 768 1555**
barracuda.ae
Map **3 E1**

This comfortable, laidback resort is perfect for a short break or even a quick weekend getaway. There's a variety of rooms, but you might prefer one of the lagoon-side one-bedroom chalets, each of which accommodates up to five people. These are fitted out with kitchenettes and barbecues, which make them ideal for private overnight parties, and the hotel boasts a large pool and Jacuzzi too. You can also take advantage of the tax-free booze emporium while you're there.

Flamingo Beach Resort
Nr Horsehead R/A Old Umm Al Quwain **06 765 0000**
flamingoresort.ae
Map **3 E1**

This cheap and cheerful hotel is perfect for nature lovers as it's surrounded by a shallow lagoon and green islands that attract a variety of fauna, including visiting flamingos. The standard hotel organises a variety of excursions to keep guests entertained, including flamingo tours and deep sea fishing trips. Guests can also go on a night-time crab hunt – not an activity for the faint-hearted, you head out to the shallows with a guide (and a spear), and the crabs you catch will be cooked for dinner. There's a pool, beach bar, cafe and dhow restaurant at the hotel too.

Dreamland Aqua Park

Short Breaks From The UAE

As much as we love living in the UAE, there are so many fantastic places to visit just a few hours away by plane. Here's our top picks.

Abu Dhabi is an ideal base to explore the region. Fly in style with Etihad or Emirates out of Abu Dhabi or Dubai, or check the low-cost carriers for more budget-friendly travel. Air Arabia flies from Sharjah Airport and flydubai from Dubai Airport or Al Ain.

Cyprus
Flight time: *Four hours, five minutes (from Dubai) or four hours 20 minutes (from Abu Dhabi)*
The three main towns, Larnaca, Limassol and Paphos, offer unique accommodation and leisure options, and capital city Nicosia is great for shopping and nightlife. Drive up the mountains for crisp, cool air and awesome views, and explore the local villages.

India
Flight time: *Three to four hours*
Cruise the serene backwaters of Kerala and witness timeless rural life, or party on the beautiful beaches of Goa. Explore the vibrant city of New Delhi before catching the train around the Golden Triangle, taking in architectural marvel, the Taj Mahal, and the majestic palaces and forts of Rajasthan. And that's barely scratching the surface of this enormously diverse and colourful subcontinent.

Jordan
Flight time: *Three hours, 10 minutes*
Jordan's capital, Amman, will keep you busy for a few days, but heading south to Petra, the ancient city carved into solid rock canyons, is a must. Stop at the Dead Sea to bathe in the mineral-rich black mud and test the buoyant waters. Be sure to head to Jerash, which has been continuously inhabited for 6,500 years, and visit holy sites, such as the brook where the baptism of Jesus Christ is said to have taken place.

Lebanon
Flight time: *Four hours, five minutes*
With its unique combination of snow and sun, Lebanon manages to be all things to all travellers. The mountains are ripe for outdoor adventure, the ancient ruins are fun to explore, the food is sublime – and then there's the nightlife. Dubbed the 'Paris of the Middle East', Beirut is considered by many to have the best clubs and bars in the region.

Sri Lanka
Flight time: *Four hours, 40 minutes*
Rainforests, unspoilt beaches, well-populated game parks, great surf, stacks of history, tea plantations, gorgeous hotels offering exceptional rates. Have we got your attention yet? Add into the mix a charming blend of Buddhist, Hindu, Muslim, Christian and indigenous cultures, along with spicy, traditional curries, rotis and egg hoppers – and you have the ideal Sri Lankan holiday.

Seychelles
Flight time: *Four hours, 40 minutes*
Few travel destinations that evoke the image of an island paradise as much as the Seychelles, and with good reason. Lush unexplored jungles, powdery white-sand beaches and an azure ocean teeming with marine life create the overall impression of a modern-day Eden. You can stay on 15 of the 115 islands scattered through the Indian Ocean, 1,000 miles east of Africa. The largest is Mahe, but the smaller Praslin and La Digue have much to offer too.

Maldives
Flight time: *Four hours, five minutes*
As one of the world's top destinations, if not the best for diving and snorkelling, there are few places on earth where you can walk from a stunning beach into the ocean and see a lively coral reef a few feet below you. Time seems to slow down in the Maldives and spending a few days in awe of the ocean, relaxing in a hammock over impossibly pristine beaches, or sipping cocktails and dining on all-inclusive seafood buffets can certainly make for a dream holiday.

Kenya
Flight time: *Five hours, five minutes*
Here you'll find one of the highest concentrations of wild animals on the planet, including, of course, the Big Five. Witness an alpha lion stalk across the dusty plains in the dawn light, or a herd of elephants cross a crocodile-infested river under the hot African sun, or simply sip sundowners while the animal kingdom gathers at the watering hole below – head to Masai Mara National Reserve and you can experience all of that in just a few days.

Book It Online

Don't waste hours scouring the internet for your perfect getaway; whether you want to book an extravagant honeymoon to the Seychelles or a shoestring weekend break to Europe, dnata (dnatatravel.com) is a one-stop shop for hotels, flights and holiday packages. Book online or call 02 674 4488 – and sign up on dnata.com for all the latest travel deals.

Short Breaks From The UAE

For more information on these and many more short-haul destinations out of Abu Dhabi, pick up a copy of Explorer's *Short Breaks From And Within The UAE.*

Maldives getaway

OMAN

The most accessible country in the Gulf for Abu Dhabi residents, Oman is a peaceful and breathtaking place, with history, culture and spectacular scenery, from the southernmost city of Salalah to quaint capital Muscat, and up to the Musandam Peninsula, which is separated from the main body of Oman by the UAE.

A flight from Abu Dhabi to Muscat takes just one hour but, when you factor in check-in times and clearing customs, it's not much quicker than driving – and you miss out on some stunning views en route.

Like the UAE, summers in Oman are incredibly hot and winters much milder, although southern Salalah is actually rather cool and wet during the summer.

Buraimi

This historical town nudges Al Ain from just over the Oman border; although the only problem getting from Al Ain to Buraimi is finding it, as there are almost no signs. If you're heading there in a UAE taxi agree a price, as once they've crossed the border their meters may magically stop working. You don't need a visa but you will need your passport.

Musandam

The UAE's northern neighbour, Musandam is an isolated enclave belonging to Oman. The region is dominated by the same Hajar Mountains that run through the eastern UAE. As the peninsula juts into the Strait of Hormuz, it splits into a myriad of jagged, picturesque fjords. Spending a day exploring the fjords on a wooden dhow is a must for any Abu Dhabi resident. Most trips originate from the region's capital, Khasab, a great base for exploring the inlets and unspoilt waters of Musandam. Stay at Atana Musandam or Atana Khasab (atanahotels.com), both of which are recommended, and book a dhow cruise for dolphin watching and snorkelling. The marine life here is some of the best in region; set off from Dibba with your mask and snorkel and explore the reef of corals around Dibba Island, where you are virtually guaranteed to spot a turtle, or take a dive trip to one of the many dive sites – at the Landing Craft you can explore a shipwreck; check out our *UAE Diving* book.

Alternatively, you can access the famous Wadi Bih off-road route from Dibba and spend a weekend camping atop magnificent mountains. See Explorer's *UAE Off-Road* for more information about the route.

Antana Khasab

Khasab, Oman 968 267 30777
atanahotels.com
In its elevated position, this hotel is all about location, with stunning views out to sea and a gorgeous mountain backdrop. Formerly the Golden Tulip, the hotel has recently undergone refurbishment with impressive results – comfortable rooms and a decor which showcases the rich culture of Oman. Once you've settled in, book a dhow cruise to marvel at the scenery, spot dolphins and snorkel off Telegraph Island.

Six Senses Zighy Bay

Zighy Bay, Musandam Daba 968 267 355 55
sixsenses.com
Located in a secluded cove in Musandam, the resort has been designed in a rustic style and is made up of individual pool villas. Like all Six Senses resorts, the focus here is on relaxation. The spa treatments available are of the highest quality, and expertly prepared dinners can be enjoyed from either the comfort of your own villa or from the mountainside restaurant with breathtaking views of the bay.

Muscat

One of the most charismatic and visually striking capitals in the Middle East, once you've visited, you'll understand why many count Muscat as their favourite regional city. With beautiful beaches, lots of green spaces, a collection of great restaurants and cafes, and some fascinating museums, you'll need at least a few days to fully discover this clean and friendly city.

Rather than a bustling CBD characterised by countless skyscrapers, gridlocked traffic and smog, Muscat has many separate areas nestling between the low craggy mountains and the Indian Ocean. Visit the old town of Muscat or Mutrah, charming clusters of pretty whitewashed buildings sandwiched between rocky hills, for an idea of what life has been like for decades. The warren-like Mutrah Souk is one of the best markets in the region and a hotspot for tourists that's jam-packed with Omani silver, pots, shisha pipes, frankincense, perfume oils and spices. Equally impressive is the Sultan Qaboos Grand Mosque held the record for the world's largest carpet and the world's largest chandelier, until Abu Dhabi's very own Sheikh Zayed Grand Mosque raised the bar.

Exploring the city's majestic coast and charming fishing villages is a must. There are also plenty of rocky coves for snorkelling and dive sites nearby. At Ras Al Jinz Turtle Reserve in Sur, south of Muscat, you can camp overnight and watch nesting turtles lumber up the beach to lay their eggs. After a few hours, watch in awe as the mass of tiny hatchlings struggle out of their eggs and make their journey into the sea.

The Chedi Muscat

The Chedi Muscat
18th November St Muscat **968 24 524 400**
chedimuscat.com

This beautiful boutique hotel on the shore is famed for its clean lines, five-star luxury and an impressive sense of tranquillity – the stunning spa and outstanding restaurant don't hurt either. With an infinity pool, private beach and library, this is the perfect destination for a break from the city hustle and bustle, but perhaps isn't an ideal choice for families.

Crowne Plaza Muscat
Al Qurm St Muscat **968 24 660 660**
crowneplaza.com

This hotel boasts cliff top views over Al Qurum and the beach below. Many of the 200 guest rooms benefit from the striking vistas and several of the restaurants boast outdoor terraces. There's a large swimming pool, gym, spa and dolphin watching trips available, making it a great choice for those looking for relaxation and for visitors who want an action-packed break.

Oman Dive Center
Nr Qantab & Barr Al Jissah Resort Muscat
968 24 824 240
omandivecentre.com

Just south of Muscat, a stay here is an amazing and sociable experience whether you're a diver or not. You can book a barasti hut (they are actually made of stone, with barasti covering) for an average of RO.66 (around Dhs.600) for two people, including breakfast and dinner. For keen divers, the centre offers training, excursions and boat tours.

Shangri-La's Barr Al Jissah Resort & Spa
Al Jissah St Muscat **968 24 776 666**
shangri-la.com

With three hotels catering for families and luxury seekers, this is one of the most gorgeous resorts in the region. The hotels have several swimming pools and enough play areas to keep children occupied for days. The exclusive, six-star Al Husn is incredibly luxurious and perfect for a weekend of out-of-town pampering.

Salalah

Home to several museums and souks, Salalah – in the south of Oman on the Arabian Sea coast – is best known for its lush landscape and is especially attractive over the summer when it is cooled by the monsoon rains sweeping across the Indian Ocean. From June to September, when Abu Dhabi is hitting 50°C, Salalah is enjoying temperatures in the 20s. It is one of the few places in the world that grows frankincense, and has been exporting it to kings and pharaohs for millennia.

It's a fascinating, not to mention fragrant, place to visit – head to the Museum of the Frankincense Land to learn more, and then to Souk Al Hafah to pick up some quality samples. The climate also enables banana plantations and coconut groves to thrive, and fruit stalls line the roadsides giving the place a tropical feel far removed from the desert landscape of the UAE.

Salalah's wild and truly magnificent coastline ranges from wide, untouched beaches to towering jagged cliffs, and is home to the famous blowholes at Al Mughsayl. Thundering waves have eroded caverns underfoot and explode through openings in the rock, drenching the more adventurous visitors.

Taking an impossibly windy road that zigzags its way up a mountain ascent, while minding out for charging camels and wandering donkeys, brings you to the incredible picnic spot of Shaat. At 1,000m above sea level, it's a stomach-turning cliff top that drops straight down to the ocean. Salalah is a 1.5 hour flight from Abu Dhabi.

Hilton Salalah Resort

Sultan Qaboos St Salalah 968 23 211 234
salalah.hilton.com
This attractive resort is set on the beach by the Arabian Sea, and has beachfront pools (with a waterslide and kids' area), a sea-view restaurant, a lively bar, tennis courts and a gym, and a dive centre. The rooms have balconies overlooking the water or the gardens. The Hilton is about 12 kilometres from the city centre, so it's as easy to explore Salalah as it is to escape the crowds.

Juweira Boutique Hotel

Salalah Beach Marina, Sultanate of Oman Salalah
968 23 239 600
juweirahotel.com
This relatively new hotel is on an inlet used by local fishermen. Each room has a terrace and overlooks the waterfront promenade, the mountains, the sea or the plentiful coconut trees that Salalah is famous for. Suites are spacious and light, a heavenly pool area has a bar and comfy sun loungers, and the seafood restaurant serves deliciously fresh Omani lobster.

Western Hajar

The Hajar Mountains stretch all the way down the east coast of Oman, right from the Musandam Peninsula. The most spectacular section is that of the Western Hajar, southwest and inland from Muscat, and is a must for outdoorsy weekend breakers.

Jebel Shams, the 'Mountain of the Sun' has a rugged terrain that is actually a fairly easy trek with several good camping locations. Below the summit, Wadi An Nakhur has some of the most stupendous views in the country as you drive through the 'Grand Canyon of Oman'. Sayq Plateau on top of Jebel Akdhar has beautiful mountain villages.

More popular spots for hiking include the amazing rock formations of Al Hoota Cave, the challenging but spectacular Snake Canyon (which involves some daring jumps into rock pools and a fair bit of swimming through ravines) and the pools of Wadi Al Abyad, just over an hour west of Muscat.

Nizwa

After driving deep into the Hajar Mountains, you'll find Nizwa, the largest city in Oman's interior. This oasis city offers fascinating sights and heritage, including the impressive 17th century Nizwa Fort, set amid a verdant spread of date palms. This fine citadel features a maze of rooms, doorways, terraces, narrow stairways and corridors; its most striking feature is its colossal central tower, soaring 35 metres above the fort. Nearby Jabrin Fort, notable for its ceiling decorations and secret passageways, is also worth a visit. Be sure to pick up some freshly made local halwa at Nizwa Souk, and it's also a hotspot for souvenir shopping. From Nizwa you can also explore the mountains and hill towns that surround the city.

Sahab Hotel

Jabal Al Akhdar Nizwa 968 25 429 288
sahab-hotel.com
On the Sayq Plateau, 2,004 metres above sea level, this boutique hotel overlooks an incredible canyon and a village perched precariously on a cliff face. The surrounding gardens contain marine fossils dating back 270 million years. There are stunning sunrise and sunset views from the infinity pool, and from the hotel you can trek the mountains, have a go at goat herding with the locals, or stay up late to watch the stars.

Visas

Most travellers to Oman will be issued a single entry visa on arrival for Dhs.50. Single women may require a letter of no objection from their employer, while visitors to Dibba must pre-arrange a visa with their accommodation. See askexplorer.com for more.

Lush Salalah

Ruwi neighbourhood of Muscat

Dhow boat at Bandar Al Rowhda

QATAR

Qatar once had a sleepy reputation, but things are changing fast. Development and investment in the country means it is becoming increasingly popular with visitors, especially UAE residents, as it is less than an hour's flight from Abu Dhabi.

With an attractive Corniche, world-class museums, leading hotels and bustling cultural centres, the capital Doha makes an ideal weekend retreat, where dhow cruises mix with modern luxury. Away from the city, the Inland Sea (Khor Al Adaid) in the south of the country makes for a great day trip.

Qatar has a very hot summer and the best time to go is usually over the winter, between October and April. Explorer's *Qatar Visitors' Guide* has more details and includes a pull-out map of the capital.

FIFA 2022 World Cup

The choice of Qatar to host the FIFA 2022 World Cup has been a controversial one, largely due to the intense heat of the Qatari summer and, some reported fatalities of migrant workers who died whilst constructing the various stadiums around the country. However, FIFA still intend to go ahead with 2022 plans in Qatar, although the debate continues about moving the World Cup to winter or adapting stadiums to beat the heat.

Attractions

The Inland Sea (Khor Al Adaid)
80km south of Doha

Known as the Inland Sea, Khor Al Udeid is a natural marvel; the wide inlet narrows in the centre and widens out into a large, seawater lake. It's surrounded by crescent-shaped dunes, and the border between Qatar and Saudi Arabia runs down the middle. Although strong currents make the narrows too dangerous for swimming, taking a dip around the shore is popular and safe. Many tour companies organise trips to this spectacular landscape, either for a few hours or a full overnight camping stay. Dune bashing and sand skiing are also popular here.

Katara Cultural Village
Al Gassar Doha 974 4409 1077
katara.net

This is a unique development, bringing together all the artistic elements in Qatar including music, dance, theatre, photography, painting and sculpture. The site, which looks like a large village, allows artists to meet and collaborate on different projects. It is also open to the public with two concert halls designed for opera, ballet and large theatrical productions, an outdoor amphitheatre, as well as galleries, workshops, cafes, restaurants, souks and a entry-paying beach.

Museum Of Islamic Art
Doha Port Doha Port 974 4422 4444
mia.org.qa

Culture vultures should not miss a trip to this iconic attraction on an island of reclaimed land just off the Corniche. The masterful Islamic-influenced architecture is the work of IM Pei, the legendary architect responsible for the iconic pyramid of the Louvre in Paris. The building itself is simple yet beautiful, with stunning details drawn from Islamic influences. Outside the building are calming pools of water and the MIA Park is popular. The museum houses a marvellous collection of temporary and permanent exhibitions showcased as a journey through time, countries and cultures; the oldest pieces date from the ninth century.

The Pearl Qatar
Al Gassar Doha
thepearlqatar.com

Doha's beloved Pearl (aptly nicknamed the Arabian Riviera) is a stunning series of interconnected man-made islands that are perfect for a leisurely stroll. The most popular areas is the island's Porto Arabia Marina, which boasts everything from high-end shopping to fine dining and cosmopolitan cafes serving up international cuisine. Indeed, the Pearl Qatar is the perfect destination for foodies, who can indulge in everything from nouveau Mexican at Pampano and Lebanese at Al Mayass to modern Japanese dishes at Megu. Perhaps best of all are the decadent treats at Alison Nelson's Chocolate Bar.

Souk Waqif
Abdullah Bin Jassim St Doha

The city's oldest market, Souk Waqif was renovated in 2004 using traditional building methods and materials. The maze-like complex is one of the most beautiful and authentic modern souks in the Gulf. The most refreshing aspect of the souk area is its dual purpose – tourists can easily stroll the narrow alleys in search of exotic wares while locals can purchase everything from fishing nets to pots and pans. Aside from the shops, the Waqif Art Centre, which houses several small galleries and craft shops, an animal souq and the nearby falcon hospital and equestrian centre. Alternatively, order a sweet mint tea and some apple-scented shisha at one of the new restaurants or boutique hotels, and watch the world go by.

Museum Of Islamic Art

Hotels

La Cigale Hotel

60 Suhaim Bin Hamad St Doha 974 4428 8888
lacigalehotel.com

A short drive from the airport, the world-leading La Cigale has a reputation for first-class hospitality and is an exclusive nightlife destination. It has exquisite restaurants ranging from sushi to Mediterranean, a sleek gym and spa, city views from the Sky View Lounge on the 15th floor, and 225 rooms and suites.

Ritz-Carlton Doha

Al Gassar Doha 974 4484 8000
ritzcarlton.com

The opulent Ritz-Carlton is a perfect stop-off if you're sailing in the region, with its 235 berth marina and clubhouse. All of the 374 rooms and suites have breathtaking views over the sea or marina. The beach club has a great selection of watersports and there's a lavish spa, plus nine restaurants.

St Regis Doha

Omar Al Mukhtar St Al Gassar 974 4446 0000
stregisdoha.com

Located equidistant to The Pearl and Doha's diplomatic district, the popular St Regis is a new luxury option right on the beach. The 336 rooms and suites offer stunning views; some with private terraces to boot. Choose from a variety of restaurants including Gordon Ramsay's Opal, Hakkasan, the Astor Grill, Al Sultan Brahim and the lovely Oyster Bay and Vine. Or, to truly relax, allow time for a treat at the Remede Spa.

W Doha Hotel & Residences

Diplomatic St, Al Dafna Doha 974 4453 5000
whoteldoha.com

Adding a touch of fun to Doha's rather conservative luxury hotel scene, the W Hotel chain is known for its funky design and fabulous level and quality of individualised service. Every inch of the hotel is an exercise in architectural minimalism, and its central location makes exploring Doha easy.

Desert Resorts

Within a two-hour drive of Abu Dhabi, the UAE's vast deserts can be easily accessed, should you need to escape for a while. A range of options exist, from five-star luxury resorts, such as Al Maha Desert Resort & Spa or the Banyan Tree Al Wadi, to less expensive hotels for those on a tighter budget.

Out in the desert, you can ride camels, dune buggies and horses, and often watch traditional Emirati pastimes such as falconry. Many resorts have excellent swimming pools and spas, which are perfect for unwinding in their exotic, tranquil surroundings; some also have kids' clubs to keep little ones happy and entertained.

Arabian Nights

For a more authentic experience, check out Arabian Nights Village. They run all sorts of unique desert activities for intrepid explorers, from camping under the stars to dune bashing. Plus, the delicious food, awesome entertainment and pristine pools provide plenty of luxury in the midst of your adventure.

Al Maha Desert Resort & Spa

Al Ain Rd Dubai **04 832 9900**
al-maha.com
Map **3 E2**

Set within the 225 sq km Dubai Desert Conservation Reserve, with breathtaking views of picturesque dunes and rare wildlife, this luxury getaway was named as one of the best eco-tourism models by National Geographic in 2008. Al Maha is designed to resemble a typical Bedouin camp where native Oryx roam freely. Each villa boasts its own pool and butler service. Activities include horse riding, sunset camel trekking, falconry and a ghaff tree tour. There is also a superb spa.

Bab Al Shams Desert Resort & Spa

Nr Endurance Village Dubai
04 809 6100
meydanhotels.com
Map **3 E2**

Bab Al Shams (which translates as 'The Gateway to the Sun') is a beautiful desert resort built in the style of a traditional Arabic fort. Each of its 115 rooms is decorated with subtle yet stunning Arabian touches, and pristine desert dunes form the backdrop. The authentic, open-air, Arabic desert restaurant Al Hadheerah is highly recommended; during dinner guests are treated to an incredible heritage show. There is also a kids' club, two large swimming pools (complete with swim-up bar), desert activities and falconry shows on offer, as well as the luxurious Satori Spa.

Banyan Tree Al Wadi

Al Mazraa Ras Al Khaimah
07 206 7777
banyantree.com
Map **3 E1**

Built in traditional Arabian style and set within a wildlife conservation area in the desert landscape of Wadi Khadeja, this stunning resort combines the wild beauty of its surroundings with exclusive luxury. Villas and luxury 'tents' each have a private pool and sundeck, and views of the desert where oryx trip skittishly by.

Qasr Al Sarab Desert Resort By Anantara

Al Wathba South **02 886 2088**
qasralsarab.anantara.com
Map **3 D4**

This hotel has a stunning location amid the giant dunes outside Liwa. Designed as an Arabic fort, there are enormous villas, each with its own private pool. Guests can enjoy a wide range of desert activities before relaxing in oversized bathtubs, dining on gourmet dishes and being pampered in the spa.

Tilal Liwa

Nr Mezzaira VIllage Liwa
02 894 6111
tilalliwa.danathotels.com
Map **3 C3**

This four-star desert hideaway has a charming pool area and a range of rooms and suites which blend old and new design elements, and provide gorgeous views over the endless sands. Desert safaris in the dunes should be at the top of every visitor's itinerary.

Bab Al Shams Desert Resort & Spa

Al Maha Desert Resort & Spa

Qasr Al Sarab Desert Resort by Anantara

INDEX

INDEX

INDEX

INDEX

INDEX

Explorer Products

Residents' Guides

Visitors' Guides

Photography Books & Calendars

Maps & Street Atlases

Adventure & Lifestyle Guides

Apps & eBooks

+ Also available as applications. Visit askexplorer.com/apps.

* Now available in eBook format.

Visit askexplorer.com/shop

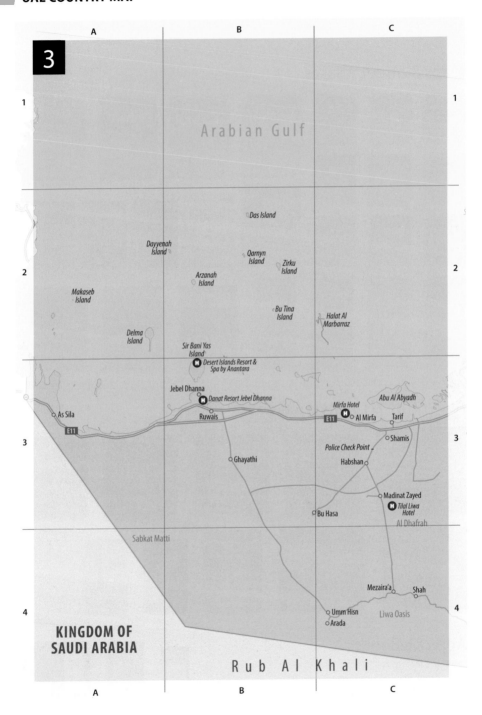

3

Arabian Gulf

Das Island

Dayyenah
Island

Qarnyn
Island

Zirku
Island

Arzanah
Island

Makaseb
Island

Bu Tina
Island

Halat Al
Marbarraz

Delma
Island

Sir Bani Yas
Island

Desert Islands Resort &
Spa by Anantara

Jebel Dhanna

Danat Resort Jebel Dhanna

Abu Al Abyadh

Mirfa Hotel

As Sila

Al Mirfa

Tarif

E11

Ruwais

E11

Shamis

Police Check Point

Ghayathi

Habshan

Madinat Zayed

Tilal Liwa
Hotel

Bu Hasa

Al Dhafrah

Sabkat Matti

Mezaira'a

Shah

KINGDOM OF
SAUDI ARABIA

Umm Hisn

Liwa Oasis

Arada

Rub Al Khali

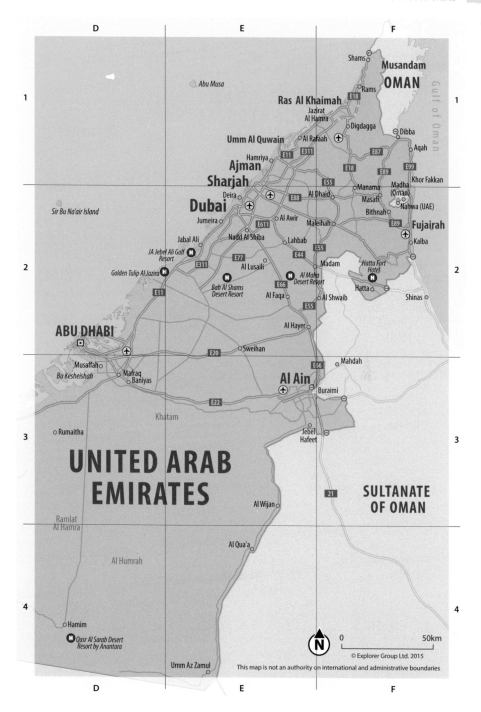

Shams

Musandam

OMAN

Abu Musa

Rams

E18

Ras Al Khaimah

Jazirat
Al Hamra

Digdagga

Dibba

Umm Al Quwain

Al Rafaah

E87

Aqah

E11

E311

Hamriya

E18

E89

E99

Ajman

Sharjah

E55

Manama

Madha
(Oman)

Khor Fakkan

Deira

Al Dhaid

Masafi

Dubai

E88

Bithnah

Nahwa (UAE)

Sir Bu Na'air Island

Jumeira

E611

Al Awir

Maleihah

E89

Fujairah

Jabal Ali

Nadd Al Shiba

Lahbab

Kalba

JA Jebel Ali Golf
Resort

E77

E44

E55

Madam

Hatta Fort
Hotel

Golden Tulip Al Jazira

E311

Al Lusaili

Al Maha
Desert Resort

E11

E66

Hatta

Bab Al Shams
Desert Resort

Al Faqa

Al Shwaib

Shinas

E55

ABU DHABI

Al Hayer

E20

Sweihan

Mahdah

Musaffah

E56

Bu Kesheishah

Mafraq

Baniyas

Al Ain

E22

Buraimi

Khatam

Rumaitha

Jebel
Hafeet

UNITED ARAB
EMIRATES

SULTANATE
OF OMAN

Ramlat
Al Hamra

Al Wijan

21

Al Humrah

Al Qua'a

Hamim

Qasr Al Sarab Desert
Resort by Anantara

N

0   50km

© Explorer Group Ltd. 2015

Umm Az Zamul

This map is not an authority on international and administrative boundaries

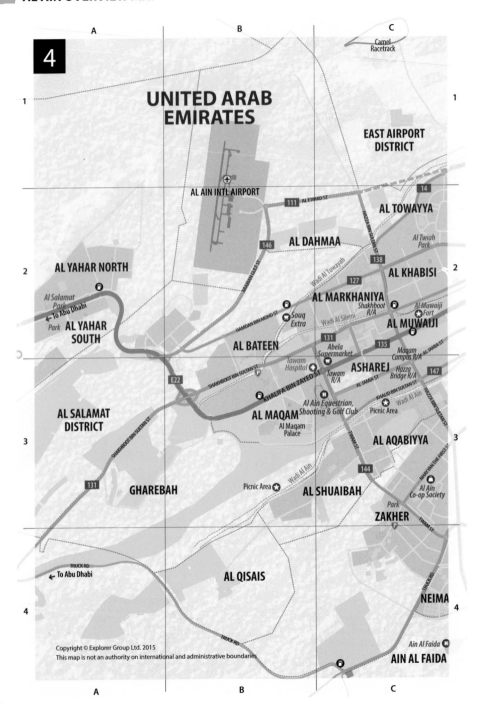

4

UNITED ARAB
EMIRATES

Camel
Racetrack

EAST AIRPORT
DISTRICT

AL AIN INTL AIRPORT

111 AL ETIHAD ST

14

AL TOWAYYA

146

AL DAHMAA

Al Twiah
Park

AL YAHAR NORTH

138

Wadi Al Tuwayah

127

AL KHABISI

AL MARKHANIYA

Al Salamat
Park

Al-Muwaiji
Fort

To Abu Dhabi

Shakhboot
R/A

Park

AL YAHAR
SOUTH

Souq
Extra

Wadi Al Silemi

AL MUWAIJI

HAMDAN BIN MOHD ST

131

AL BATEEN

Abela
Supermarket

135

Maqam
Campus R/A

E22

Tawam
Hospital

AL JAMIA ST

SHAKHBOOT BIN SULTAN ST

Tawam
R/A

ASHAREJ

Hazza
Bridge R/A

147

AL JAMIA ST

KHALIFA BIN ZAYED ST

KHALID BIN SULTAN ST

Wadi Al Ain

AL SALAMAT
DISTRICT

Al Ain Equestrian,
Shooting & Golf Club

Picnic Area

SHAKHBOOT BIN SULTAN ST

AL MAQAM

Al Maqam
Palace

AL AQABIYYA

131

GHAREBAH

Picnic Area

Wadi Al Ain

144

AL SHUAIBAH

Al Ain
Co-op Society

Park

ZAKHER

NEIMA

To Abu Dhabi

TRUCK RD

AL QISAIS

TRUCK RD

Ain Al Faida

AIN AL FAIDA

Copyright © Explorer Group Ltd. 2015
This map is not an authority on international and administrative boundaries

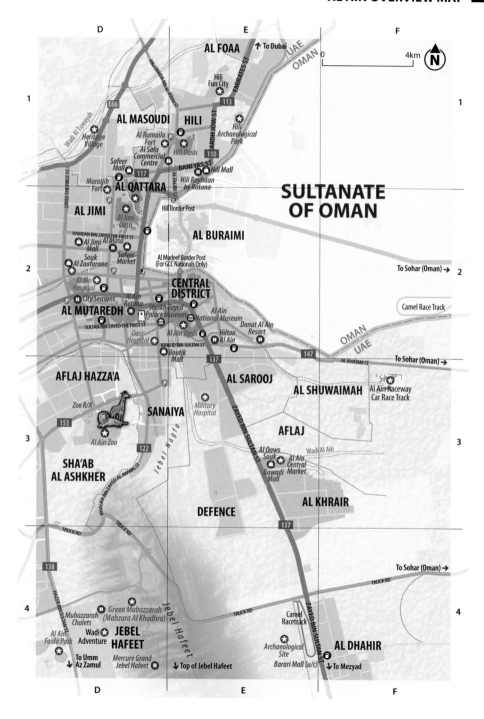

↑ To Dubai

UAE
OMAN

0   4km

N

AL FOAA

Hili Fun City

AL MASOUDI

HILI

Al Rumaila Fort
Al Sofa Commercial Centre

Hili Oasis

Hili Archaeological Park

Heritage Village

Safeer Mall

BANI YAS ST

Hili Mall

Maraijib Fort

AL QATTARA

Hili Rayhaan by Rotana

SULTANATE OF OMAN

Al Jimi Oasis

AL JIMI

Hili Border Post

Al Jimi Mall

Al Masa

AL BURAIMI

Souk Al Zaafarana

Safeer Market

Al Mudeef Border Post
(For GCC Nationals Only)

To Sohar (Oman) →

Al Ain Hospital

City Seasons

Al Ain Rotana

CENTRAL DISTRICT

Camel Race Track

AL MUTAREDH

Sheikh Zayed Palace Museum

Al Ain National Museum

Oasis Hospital

Al Ain Oasis

Hilton Al Ain

Danat Al Ain Resort

OMAN
UAE

Boutik Mall

To Sohar (Oman) →

AFLAJ HAZZA'A

AL KHATAM ST

AL SAROOJ

AL SHUWAIMAH

Al Ain Raceway Car Race Track

Zoo R/A

Military Hospital

SANAIYA

AFLAJ

Al Ain Zoo

Al Qaws Souk

Wadi Al Ain

SHA'AB AL ASHKHER

Al Ain Central Market

Bawadi Mall

AL KHRAIR

DEFENCE

To Sohar (Oman) →

TRUCK RD

Green Mubazzarah (Mabzara Al Khadhra)

Mubazzarah Chalets

Wadi Adventure

JEBEL HAFEET

Camel Racetrack

Al Ain Faida Park

Mercure Grand Jebel Hafeet

↓ To Umm Az Zamul

↓ Top of Jebel Hafeet

Archaeological Site

Barari Mall (u/c)

AL DHAHIR

↓ To Mezyad

Useful Numbers

Embassies & Consulates

Australia	02 401 7500
Bahrain	02 665 7500
Canada	02 694 0300
Czech Republic (Embassy)	02 678 2800
China	02 443 4276
Egypt	02 444 5566
Finland	02 632 8927
France	02 443 5100
Germany	02 644 6693
India	02 449 2700
Iran	02 444 7618
Ireland	02 495 8200
Italy	02 443 5622
Japan	02 443 5696
Jordan	02 444 7100
Kuwait	02 447 7146
Lebanon	02 449 2100
Malaysia	02 448 2775
New Zealand	02 441 1222
The Netherlands	02 632 1920
Oman	02 446 3333
Pakistan	02 444 7800
Philippines	02 639 0006
Poland	02 446 5200
Qatar	02 449 3300
Russia	02 672 1797
Saudi Arabia	02 444 5700
South Africa	02 447 3446
Spain	02 626 9544
Sri Lanka	02 631 6444
Sweden	02 417 8800
Switzerland	02 627 4636
Syria	02 444 8768
Thailand	02 642 1772
UK	02 610 1100
USA	02 414 2200
Yemen	02 444 8457

A&E Departments

Al Ain Hospital	03 763 5888
Al Mafraq Hospital	02 582 3100
Al Noor Hospital	02 626 5265
Al Rahba Hospital	02 506 4101
Al Salama Hospital	02 671 1220
Corniche Hospital	02 672 4900
Emirates International Hospital	03 763 7777
Hospital Franco-Emirien	02 626 5722
Madinat Zayed Hospital	02 884 4444
National Hospital	02 671 1000
NMC Speciality Hospital	02 633 2255
Oasis Hospital	03 722 1251
Sheikh Khalifa Medical City	02 610 2000
Tawam Hospital	03 767 7444

Emergency Services

Abu Dhabi Police	999
Ambulance	998/999
Fire Department	997
AAA (Roadside Assistance)	800 8181

24 Hour Pharmacy

Sheikh Khalifa Medical City ER Pharmacy	02 819 2188
Lifeline Hospital Pharmacy	02 633 3340
Al Noor Hospital Pharmacy	02 613 9100
Al Ain Hospital Pharmacy	03 763 5888
Liwa Hospital Pharmacy	02 882 2204

Useful Numbers

Abu Dhabi Municipality	800 555
Directory Enquiries	181/199
ADWEC (Emergency)	991/992
UAE Country Code	+971
Abu Dhabi Area Code	02
Abu Dhabi Airport Flight Enquiries	02 575 7500
Weather	02 666 7776

NOTES

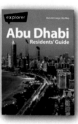

Abu Dhabi Residents' Guide – 12th Edition

Lead Editor Lisa Crowther
Section Editors Kirsty Tuxford
Proofread by Kara Martin
Data managed by Amapola Castillo, Suzzette S.Privado, Maria Luisa Reyes
Data managed by Mimi Stankova
Sales by Bryan Aynes
Designed by Ieyad Charaf, Jayde Fernandes, M. Shakkeer, Niyasuthin Batcha
Maps by Noushad Madathil, Zainudheen Madathil
Photographs by Henry Hilos, Hardy Mendrofa, Pete Maloney, Andy Mills, Victor Romero, Bart Wojcinski, Gary McGovern

Publishing
Chief Content Officer & Founder Alistair MacKenzie

Editorial
Managing Editor Carli Allan
Sr. Corporate Editor Julie Hayes
Editors Lisa Crowther, Kirsty Tuxford
Research Manager Mimi Stankova
Researchers Amrit Raj, Roja P, Praseena, Shalu Sukumar, Maria Luisa Reyes, Lara Santizo, Jacqueline Reyes
Production Coordinator Joy Viernes

Design & Photography
Art Director Ieyad Charaf
Layout Manager Jayde Fernandes
Designer M. Shakkeer, Mohamed Abdo
Junior Designer Niyasuthin Batcha
Cartography Manager Zain Madathil
Cartographers Noushad Madathil, Ramla Kambravan, Jithesh Kalathingal
GIS Analyst Aslam Jobydas KD
Photographer & Image Editor Hardy Mendrofa

Sales
Director of Sales Peter Saxby
Media Sales Area Managers Laura Zuffa, Sabrina Ahmed, Bryan Anes, Simon Reddy, Sean Rutherford
Digital Sales Manager Rola Touffaha
Business Development Manager Pouneh Hafizi
Director of Retail Ivan Rodrigues
Retail Sales Coordinator Michelle Mascarenhas
Retail Sales Area Supervisors Ahmed Mainodin, Firos Khan
Retail Sales Merchandisers Johny Mathew, Shan Kumar, Mehmood Ullah
Retail Sales Drivers Shabsir Madathil, Nimicias Arachchige
Warehouse Assistant Mohamed Haji, Jithinraj M

Finance, HR & Administration
Accountant Cherry Enriquez
Accounts Assistants Sunil Suvarna, Jayleen Aguinaldo
Administrative Assistant Joy H. San Buenaventura
Reception Jayfee Manseguiao
Public Relations Officer Imran Mhalunkar
Office Assistant Shafeer Ahamed
Office Manager – India Jithesh Kalathingal

IT & Digital Solutions
Web Developers Mirza Ali Nasrullah, Waqas Razzaq
HTML / UI Developers Naveed Ahmed
IT Manager R. Ajay
Database Programmer Pradeep T.P.

How Can We Help You?

Ask Explorer
ask**explorer**.com

Log onto our new website for information, event listings and competitions in your city and other places across the Middle East.

Media Sales
sales@ask**explorer**.com

Contact us for details of our advertising rates, corporate bulk sales, online marketing packages, content licensing and customised wall maps.

Corporate Sales
corporate@ask**explorer**.com

For all your corporate needs, Explorer services include bulk sales orders, mapping solutions, corporate gifts, bespoke publications, customised dust jackets and a wide range of digital options.

Retail Sales
retail@ask**explorer**.com

Check out Explorer retail sales options, distribution services and E-shop orders.

General Enquiries
info@ask**explorer**.com

Call us on +971 (0)4 340 8805 as we'd love to hear your thoughts and answer any questions you might have about this book or any Explorer products.

Careers
jobs@ask**explorer**.com

Send us your CV if you are talented, adventurous, knowledgeable, curious, passionate, creative and above all fun.

Explorer Publishing & Distribution
PO Box 34275, Dubai, United Arab Emirates
askexplorer.com

Phone: +971 (0)4 340 8805
Fax: +971 (0)4 340 8806